D0849280

MEDICAL SOCIOLOGY

Second Edition

DAVID MECHANIC

THE FREE PRESS
A Division of Macmillan Publishing Co., Inc.
NEW YORK

Collier Macmillan Publishers
LONDON

FOR MIKE

The Free Press
A Division of Macmillan Publishing Co., Inc.
866 Third Avenue, New York, N. Y. 10022

Collier Macmillan Canada, Ltd.

Library of Congress Catalog Card Number: 77-3850

Printed in the United States of America

printing number

3 4 5 6 7 8 9 10

Library of Congress Cataloging in Publication Data

Mechanic, David, 1936-
  Medical sociology.

  Bibliography: p.
  Includes indexes.
  1. Social medicine. 2. Medical care. I. Title.
[DNLM: 1. Social medicine. WA30 M486m]
RA418.M34 1978   362.1   77-3850
ISBN 0-02-920720-7

CONTENTS

5 THE MACRO SYSTEM OF HEALTH CARE

6 THE MICRO SYSTEM OF HEALTH CARE

7 MENTAL DISORDER AND MENTAL HEALTH

PREFACE

In the decade since the first edition of this book was written, the specialty of medical sociology has grown and matured as an important area of inquiry in the behavioral sciences. Medical sociology is still characterized, however, by a wide range of concerns, approaches, and perspectives. If anything, the field has become even more diverse in the past ten years under the stimulus of the increased interest of society at large in problems of health-care delivery and health policy. As medical technology and knowledge have proliferated—accompanied by growing expectations, increasing governmental responsibility for health care, and rising costs—all developed nations have been grappling with the issue of how best to organize manpower and other limited resources to achieve optimal health outcomes. As these problems have grown, medical sociologists have had greater opportunities for research and training, and there are few areas in the health-services field in which medical sociologists have not made at least some contributions.

Medical sociology, as I deal with it here, is an interdisciplinary field that benefits richly not only from the work of sociologists and social psychologists but also from that of researchers in medicine and public health, epidemiologists, health economists, and physicians involved in researching their own practices. Although it would be possible to present a book on medical sociology that is strictly "sociological" in a disciplinary sense, the presentation would suffer from its failure to capitalize on the excellent work of many others who do research on the interdisciplinary frontiers of medicine, health services, and health. Sociology and social psychology offer unique perspectives on the practice of medicine, and, in part because of my background and interests, these are emphasized here. In my view, work on health-services delivery has been very much handicapped by the absence of adequate theoretical conceptions, and thus much of it has been trivial or of only passing interest. If the field is to flourish, we must develop theoretical perspectives that allow more effective cumulation of knowledge and a sharper focus on the priorities of future research.

In this edition of *Medical Sociology,* I have striven to retain the theoretical coherence of the first. Thus I have necessarily been selective in deciding which among the many threads of research characterizing medical sociology and related research areas should be emphasized. Although I believe that it is now possible to deal with a wider range of material within a coherent framework than was true when I wrote the earlier edition, this edition still focuses on a limited number of general perspectives that have relevance for future research and for the formulation of national health policy. Although much of the book deals with materials that inform the perspective of health policy makers and planners, I have purposely avoided the issues of the moment that concern them, such as the likely effects of professional standards review organizations or detailed comparisons of various proposals for national health insurance. Many of the policy issues we face are phrased in political or social terms. For the purpose of this book I feel it is more valuable to define the generic issues underlying the formation of health and the delivery of health services than to engage in debate on current issues. Those readers who are interested in my views on such topics will find them readily available. Those who wish to fill in substantive gaps in my treatment of the field should refer to pertinent works cited in the bibliography (34; 124; 236; 293; 388; 680).*

Since the first edition, many things have happened in the larger society, as in medicine. Among them is a greater consciousness about the use of personal pronouns—perhaps a trifle, but symbolic of larger and more important issues. Unfortunately we lack an appropriate neuter pronoun, and it is awkward to adopt "he/she" whenever a personal pronoun is necessary. Nor is it particularly stylistic to alternate in a random fashion. Throughout the text I sometimes use "he," "she," and "layman," and in each case it should be understood that these terms refer to all human beings.

This revision reflects my work in medical sociology during the past ten years as teacher, researcher, and consultant. During this period much of my thinking and the research that underlies it have been supported by grants from the Robert Wood Johnson Foundation, the National Institute of Mental Health, the National Center for Health Services Research and Development, and the Milbank Memorial Fund. I was also fortunate in being a fellow at the Center for Advanced Study in

*As in the first edition, I have here used a style of citation that directs the reader to a numbered reference list at the back of the book. Commonly used in the "hard" sciences, this method has much to recommend it: it frees the text of the clutter of bibliographic details, obviates the need for many footnotes, and yet provides the reader with an extensive bibliography.

the Behavioral Sciences at Stanford in 1974–1975. There I was able to develop some of my work on health-care delivery systems, which in consequence is discussed in much greater detail in this edition than in the first. Financial support was provided both by the center and by the Research Committee of the Graduate School of the University of Wisconsin. During 1977–1978 I was fortunate to be a recipient of a John Simon Guggenheim fellowship concentrating on health-care policy studies. The fellowship facilitated the completion of some final details on this book in addition to other projects.

Over these years I have learned a great deal from many of my students, colleagues, and friends—a group far too numerous to name individually. A few have been particularly helpful in relation to the work discussed in this new edition and deserve special mention: Linda Aiken, George Brown, Burton Fisher, Lawrence Friedman, James Greenley, and John Wing. The broadening of my perspective from that in the earlier edition has been influenced by my associations with Charles Lewis, Eliot Freidson, Robert Haggerty, and Victor Fuchs.

Revising a book is in some ways a tedious job. I am not sure that I could have faced it without the very competent and enthusiastic assistance of Lorraine Borsuk and Ann Wallace, to whom I am indebted.

Various proprietors of copyright have granted permission to reprint material in this book. Thanks are due to authors, editors, and publishers of the following works for their permission to quote from the pages cited: Kenneth J. Arrow, "Uncertainty and the Welfare Economics of Medical Care," *American Economic Review* 53 (1963), pp. 945, 946, 949, 951, 956, copyright 1963, American Economic Association; Henry K. Beecher, "Surgery as a Placebo," *Journal of the American Medical Association* 176 (1961), p. 1106; Paul B. Beeson, "Some Good Features of the British National Health Service," *Journal of Medical Education* 49 (1974), p. 48; Richard H. Blum, "Case Identification in Psychiatric Epidemiology," *Milbank Memorial Fund Quarterly* 40 (1962), pp. 254–56; Jacob J. Feldman, "The Household Interview Survey as a Technique for the Collection of Morbidity Data," *Journal of Chronic Disease* 11 (1960), p. 550; Eliot Freidson, "Client Control and Medical Practice," *American Journal of Sociology* 65 (1960), pp. 377–78; David T. Graham et al., "Physiological Response to the Suggestion of Attitudes Specific for Hives and Hypertension," *Psychosomatic Medicine* 24 (1962), pp. 159, 169; Charles Kadushin, "Social Class and the Experience of Ill Health," *Sociological Inquiry* 34 (1964), pp. 75, 78; Evelyn M. Kitagawa and Philip M. Hauser, *Differential Mortality in the United States* (Cambridge, Mass.: Harvard University Press, 1973), table 8.1, p. 167, copyright 1972 by the president and fellows of Harvard College; A. Lewis, "Health as a Social Concept," *British Journal of Sociology* 4

(1953), pp. 112–14; Thomas McKeown, *Medicine in Modern Society* (London: George Allen & Unwin, 1965), pp. 57–58, 180–81, 182; M. Mendelson et al., "A Critical Examination of Some Recent Theoretical Models in Psychosomatic Medicine," *Psychosomatic Medicine* 18 (1956), pp. 363, 368; Elliot G. Mishler and Norman A. Scotch, "Sociocultural Factors in the Epidemiology of Schizophrenia," *Psychiatry* 26 (1963), pp. 326, 342–43, copyright © 1963 by The William Alanson White Psychiatric Foundation, Inc.; J. N. Morris, *Uses of Epidemiology*, 2d ed. (Edinburgh: E. & S. Livingstone, 1964), pp. 274–75; J. N. Morris and J. A. Heady, "Social and Biological Factors in Infant Mortality," *Lancet* 1 (1955), p. 344; Ø. Ødegård, "Discussion of 'Sociocultural Factors in the Epidemiology of Schizophrenia,'" *International Journal of Psychiatry* 1 (1965), pp. 296, 301; Arie Querido, "An Investigation into the Clinical, Social, and Mental Factors Determining the Results of Hospital Treatment," *British Journal of Preventive and Social Medicine* 13 (1959), p. 46; Thomas J. Scheff, "Decision Rules, Types of Error, and Their Consequences in Medical Diagnosis," *Behavioral Science* 8 (1963), p. 101; Thomas J. Scheff, "Users and Non-Users of a Student Psychiatric Clinic," *Journal of Health and Human Behavior* 7 (1966), p. 120; Robert L. Spitzer, "More on Pseudoscience in Science and the Case for Psychiatric Diagnosis," *Archives of General Psychiatry* 33 (1976), p. 462, copyright 1976, American Medical Association; and Marion Radke Yarrow et al., "The Psychological Meaning of Mental Illness in the Family," *Journal of Social Issues* 11 (1955), pp. 22–23.

Some of my own works discussed and quoted in the text appear in part in other forms. For permission to use previously published material, I am grateful to the *American Journal of Orthopsychiatry, Duke Law Journal, Journal of Chronic Disease, Journal of Health and Social Behavior, Mental Hygiene, Pacific Sociological Review,* and *Social Psychiatry* as well as to the publishers of the following books: Leonard I. Stein and Mary Ann Test, eds., *Alternatives to Mental Hospital Treatment* (New York: Plenum Publishing Corporation, 1978), and Burton A. Weisbrod et al., *Public Interest Law: An Economic and Institutional Analysis* (Berkeley: University of California Press, 1978), copyright © 1978 by the Regents of the University of California.

Small sections of the text also appear in modified form in the *Hastings Center Studies, Journal of Human Stress, Health and Society (Milbank Memorial Fund Quarterly)* and in the following books: Barbara Snell Dohrenwend and Bruce P. Dohrenwend, eds., *Stressful Life Events* (New York: Wiley-Interscience, 1974); Howard E. Freeman, Sol Levine, and Leo G. Reeder, eds., *Handbook of Medical Sociology*, 3d ed. (Englewood Cliffs, N. J.: Prentice-Hall, 1978); and *1977 Medical and Health Annual* (Chicago: Encyclopaedia Britannica, 1977).

INTRODUCTION

The basic orientation presented here views much of human activity, particularly the activity surrounding illness, within an adaptive framework; such behaviors are seen as aspects of and reactions to situations in which persons are actively struggling to control their environment and life situation. The behavior of those who deal with and care for the ill must similarly be viewed as taking place within the context of their own adaptive needs and the constraints impinging on their work. This perspective is very different from the prevailing view of medicine; I view the functions of medicine not only as curing illness and alleviating distress and disability, but also as assisting in social control in society. Medicine frequently helps to sustain individuals in their social roles and thus contributes to the reduction of social tensions. Medicine also is often a context in which important and difficult decisions are made about special privileges or social constraints to be applied to individuals in the population, as in determinations of legal responsibility, disability compensation, justified sick leave, and many others.

Illness, illness behavior, and reactions to the ill are aspects of an adaptive social process in which participants are often actively striving to meet their social roles and responsibilities, to control their environment, and to make their everyday circumstances less uncertain and, therefore, more tolerable and predictable. It is these active strivings—the stuff of human behavior—that are often neglected or ignored in many behavioral-science theories that view human behavior as fixed and inflexible rather than as continually changing in response to environmental demands and challenges. The ways in which patients and health organizations define and respond to illness can often be understood as a result of the problems they face in defining the nature of the problem and in mobilizing resources in the social environment to deal with it. Similarly, the reactions of community agencies to the ill can frequently be illuminated through an investigation of the changing po-

1

litical and social environment of the organization and the available resources and skills for dealing with these changes. In short, health and health care can be understood within the larger context of human strivings and adjustments to life situations, and organizational adaptations must be seen in their larger political and social context.

This book has relevance to medicine as an applied field as well as to medicine as a social science. Medicine has three principal tasks: to understand how particular symptoms, syndromes, or diseases occur either in individuals or among groups of individuals; to recognize and cure these or to shorten their course and minimize any residual impairment; and to promote in human populations living conditions that eliminate hazards to health and thus prevent disease. Each of these tasks can be pursued with maximal effectiveness only if the importance of social and psychological, as well as biological, factors is appreciated. Much of medical activity—whether in research, clinical practice, or preventive work—requires an understanding of the cultural and social pressures that influence an individual's recognition that he needs help, his decision to seek it, and his response to it. At the community level, modifying social and environmental conditions to make them more conducive to health, or altering sociocultural patterns and the behavior of individual patients in the direction of greater health maintenance, requires the development of behavioral technologies that still have not become central in medical investigation or medical practice. Unless greater awareness of social and behavioral processes is part of the training of health workers, the delivery of care to patients, and the design of medical and sociomedical services, we shall continue to do less than is possible to enhance health and alleviate disease.

Basic to both medicine and behavioral science is the statistical model, and the weighing of probabilities is inherent in every treatment situation and in every social intervention at the group or community level. Behavioral science enters the picture of disease and its treatment in that social, cultural, and psychological factors affect the probability of certain medical occurrences. Failure to obtain or to utilize such information can result, therefore, in significant biases in the predictions made in treatment situations that have important effects on the patient's welfare. Behavioral science is important to the health-care practitioner because consideration of behavioral factors helps reduce bias or errors in predicting the consequences of actions. If medical decisions are to be fully rational, they must take into consideration not only the salient medical facts but also the manner in which social and organizational factors have molded the patient's motivation and responses.

The practice of medicine, or the practice of the helping professions generally, constitutes a mini social system with its own political processes, values, roles, and social norms. Whether the provider is an individual, a group, a clinic, or a hospital, each has a particular form of social organization that affects how both client and practitioner respond. Both clients and personnel found in any context have arrived there as a consequence of various selective processes in which their own backgrounds, interests, values, and aspirations have played no small role. These actors have their own motives and special interests. The full understanding of clinical contexts and of the patterns of behavior observed requires an understanding not only of the structure and norms of the social organization but also of the selective processes that have brought together the particular assortment of practitioners and clients.

The field of medical sociology—because it must concern itself in part with basic social processes—cuts across many traditional areas of sociological inquiry, and sociologists who work in this field have differing interests and motivations. Many are interested in particular health problems for their own sake, whereas others enter the field because it is an appropriate and convenient context for testing hypotheses and exploring issues relevant to some larger sociological or behavioral question. Although this volume will touch upon almost every major point of view within medical sociology, it emphasizes some more than others. In my view it is more important to maintain conceptual coherence than to touch every base that might have some relevance to the issues at hand. Thus, I have selected what I believe to be the 22 most important and vigorous areas of activity in medical sociology. After presenting a brief description of each, I shall then describe some major perspectives that are repeated throughout the book as I examine various topics.

Topical Description of Medical Sociology

Distribution and Etiology of Disease

Sociologists have long been interested in the distribution of illness in the population and the factors leading to its selective occurrence. Prominent in the literature is a concern with the various chronic diseases, particularly psychiatric disorders, coronary heart disease, and cancer. Although traditionally the sociological literature on disease distribution dealt most frequently with such variables as age, sex, and social class (occupation and income), increasing attention is now given to attitudes, behavioral patterns, and more complex social processes. In the mental-health field, for example, such non-demographic variables as social mobility, social isolation, and social stress play a prominent role in epidemiological investigation. Sociologists are more receptive than before to investigation of interactions among biological, genetic, and social influences, and work on disease distribution is increasingly complex and analytic.

Cultural and Social Responses to Health and Illness

Work in this area is characterized by concern with people's conceptions of their own health and necessary preventive action to conserve or enhance it, their definitions and responses to symptoms or illness, and the effects of varying attitudes and behavior on the course of illness and the success of rehabilitation. Sociological work generally focuses on social and cultural differences as they affect orientations toward health and illness and on processes of social interaction that affect patients' perceptions, understandings, and responses. The work in this area covers a wide scope including such diverse concerns as cultural differences in response to pain, interactional effects on the perceived magnitude of disability, attitudes toward death and dying, and willingness to take actions conducive to health, such as exercising.

Sociocultural Aspects of Medical Care

Although this area first developed around the study of practitioner-patient relationships and how they are influenced by the characteristics of each, work has expanded to consider how culture and social history have molded the organization of health-care systems and the characteristic forms of practice of varying practitioners. While such older concerns as communication, influence, and social roles are still prominent, in recent years growing attention has been devoted to practitioner professionalism, historical patterns and dysfunctions of medical organization, and the intraorganizational complexity characteristic of the health system. While the earlier literature assumed the correctness of the medical model, more recent literature attempts to examine cultural alternatives to medical care for dealing with many of the quasi-medical problems that doctors typically handle. Thus, while the older literature gives prominence to the physician's authority, more recent literature is likely to give more attention to patient responsibility, self-help groups such as Weight Watchers or Alcoholics Anonymous, new types of team practice, and consumer participation. While some of these new concerns are transient, others represent new ways of looking at man's adaptive ingenuity in coping with life problems.

Mortality

The study of mortality has been of greatest interest to sociologists who have had training in demography. Within the larger context of the study of mortality, medical sociologists have been primarily interested in changing patterns of death, social influences on mortality, and the accommodation of medical institutions to changing patterns of disease and death. Work in the area has been limited by the types of aggregate data available; the variables studied most frequently include sex, age, race, socioeconomic status, and region. These studies are often atheoretical in nature and have a disturbingly repetitive quality that leaves one with the impression that the data available, more than a sense of problem, have generated much of the activity. Fortunately, more recently there have been some ambitious studies that add to our understanding of mortality and the methodological problems inherent in much of the aggregate data we deal with. There is also growing interest in attempting to develop a more explicit conceptual approach to mortality that examines the wide range of genetic and social living conditions conducive to health and longevity. One interesting example of such studies is examination of the bases of the growing differential in mortality between men and women and how social and cultural events contribute to this differential.

Social Epidemiology

In part, social epidemiology has already been covered in earlier references to the distribution and etiology of disease. Epidemiology (the study of the occurrence of disease, defects, and disabilities in populations), however, is more than a specific methodology; it constitutes a distinctive way of thinking about problems and investigating questions. As the most important logical perspective and methodological approach in the field of medical sociology, it deserves special emphasis since it provides a framework that usefully integrates a description of disease distribution with a social science perspective on the process of disease occurrence and persistence. Many medical sociologists identify themselves as social epidemiologists, and often their identification is more with the method of study than with a particular theoretical approach or substantive area of concern.

Epidemiology is used to study both the distribution of disease and health services and the social etiology of various disease conditions such as mental disorders, cancer, and heart disease. A similar approach can also be applied to the occurrence of any of a great variety of behaviors in populations, examining their distribution among the population, their determinants, and their consequences for the future health, vitality, and functioning of the person. The basic methodology of epidemiology is a social-science methodology, making use of population surveys and experiments. Epidemiology is distinct from other types of population research in that the dependent variable of concern is usually a symptom, disease, or impairment.

Organization of Medical Practice

This area is concerned with the unique organization of medical practice and the way it differs in varying medical systems or under different community circumstances. Such study usually involves comparisons of medical-care relationships as they emerge in varying organizational contexts with different manpower combinations, different types of remuneration, technology, and intraorganizational arrangements. Examples of such work include Freidson's classic comparison of the pressures on solo community practitioners with those occurring within group practice settings (234; 235; 237; 243), and my own studies of the effects of capitation and fee-for-service payment on physicians' management of their patient loads (497; 500), the consequences of using nurse practitioners as compared with physicians for providing certain defined services (436), and the influence of differing forms of financial and group organization on variations in hospital and surgical utilization, as in comparisons of prepaid group practice with fee-for-service practice (343).

Sociology of the Healing Occupations

This area falls within the larger sociological area of the "occupations and professions" and deals with the social organization and relations among different occupational and professional groups. Studies of the nursing profession and various paraprofessionals are most numerous, but increasing attention is being given to the study of physicians, administrators, and policy makers, who present more difficult problems of access. Although earlier studies tended to emphasize problems of adjustment of paraprofessionals to medical expectations, more attention is now devoted to examining the sociopolitical context of medical work and the manner in which physicians exercise dominance over health work. Freidson (240) and Stevens (670), for example, have studied the sociopolitical divisions among varying specialties and have directed attention to the character of the division of labor in medicine and its ties to a larger sociopolitical culture. Moreover, with the developing emphasis on regulation, attention is now being devoted to the manner in which physicians exercise influence over one another and the work of other health personnel, and to both the prospects and the inherent difficulties of achieving viable peer regulation.

Sociology of the Hospital

This area, central to "organizational sociology," concerns a wide range of independent and dependent variables. Most common in such studies, however, is a concern with growing technology, increasing bureaucracy, intraprofessional rivalry, power relationships, decision making, and the division of labor and centralization. Recently, organizational sociologists have become more cognizant of the complex interrelations between organizations and the environments in which they must function, and attention is now being devoted to the networks of organizations, coordination among agencies with categorical missions, and adaptation of organizations to their changing social and political environments. The importance of this new thrust should be obvious in the medical sector, where the role of the hospital depends largely on the capacity of ambulatory-care institutions to deal with varying problems and on the norms that define which problems should be treated on an inpatient and outpatient basis. The hospital, of course, is often part of a more complex medical center with multiple goals and capacities, offering not only inpatient and outpatient care but also community and home-care services, patient education, and professional training and research.

Community Health Organization

Here study is directed to the developing relationships among various health agencies in the community, both public and private. In the United States in particular, with its mix of private and public involvements in medical-care and public-health functions, there is a bewildering array of agencies and authorities that have some role in community health. The problems of cooperation, coordination, and even information are staggering. Research in this area is concerned with understanding the interpenetration of the goals and community programs of various agencies, the agreements or rivalries concerning the distribution of activities, and the ways in which such organizations develop, expand, and change. Similarly, from a political-science perspective, there are efforts to understand the overlapping authorities, the means through which attempts at coherent policies are brought about, and the ingredients of success. As Pressman and Wildavsky (569) illustrate so vividly, implementation of policy involves complex chains of decision with innumerable possibilities for delay, obstruction, and defeat of effective results.

Social Change and Health Care

This area, by nature historical, crosscuts many of the others. Medicine is a social institution as well as a technical activity, and is shaped by the economic and sociocultural context in which it is embedded. Changes in medical care accompany modifications and advances in technology, development of new scientific knowledge, and new public expectations and social ideologies. Whether medicine has a strong preventive or curative orientation, the extent to which it serves individuals in contrast to bureaucratic needs, the degree to which it is governed by public policy or special interests—these issues all depend on other currents in the society to which health care is closely linked. Studies in this area include the development of the health professions and medical care, modifications in health values and orientations (as exemplified by such current trends as the emergence of self-help groups, the emphasis on patient education, and consumer representation), and the priorities concerning medical organization and the distribution of health resources.

Comparative Health-Care Organization

The difficulties of comparative analysis have limited attempts by social scientists to compare national health systems, but several recent studies have attempted to examine national differences in organization of medical care and in performance of components of the health sector. Much of the work in this area has been devoted to case studies of medicine in one or another nation and their implications for the United States, but there have also been some systematic somparisons, as in the International Utilization Study (396). Although relatively little research has been done at the macro level of analysis, we have gathered considerable comparative information on the use of health manpower, utilization of medical services, hospital use, investments in the health sector, and so on. Health-services research within the United States is increasingly carried out from a comparative perspective, as in comparisons of performance in varying types of institutional settings and among different types of health insurance programs.

Medical Education

Sociologists have given more attention to the sociology of medical education than they have given to the sociology of sociological education. Work in this area falls within the traditional concerns in sociology with continuing socialization and professional training. Important early works in the field were *The Student Physician* (511), by Merton and his colleagues, and *Boys in White* (52), by Becker and his colleagues. Recently sociologists have given more attention to the work of house officers, as exemplified by the books by Miller (518) and Mumford (529) on the internship experience and studies by Kendall (381) and Stevens (670) on trends in medical and surgical specialization. Work is continuing on selection into medical school and into various specialties and types of health-care work. Attention is also being focused on the characteristics of physicians and their training conducive to entering family practice and primary medical care.

From a sociological perspective, emphasis has been placed on the manner in which the character of medical training, particularly clinical responsibility and the hospital teaching experience, encourage a pattern of restricted medical work. Most of the studies give at least some attention to the way in which the adaptive needs of the student or the house officer affect the manner in which he deals with learning tasks and various professional choices. Other areas of interest include the changing social values of the medical student, his coping processes with various personal and professional threats inherent in the process of medical education, and factors affecting choice of medical work and practice location. At the larger societal level some attention has been given to the manner in which medical education has been affected by such environmental factors as federal support for biomedical research, the changing roles and responsibilities of university health sciences centers, and changing student expectations.

Utilization of Health-Care Services

With growing emphasis on medical-care costs, much recent research has stressed factors affecting the use of medical-care and hospital-care services and inequalities in the distribution of and access to medical care. A variety of models and regression approaches have been developed for the purpose of predicting physician and hospital utilization, and there has been some attention as well to the use of drugs, dental and optometry services, and psychiatric resources. From a sociological perspective, various efforts have been made to develop models of help seeking that describe and attempt to predict the conditions under which people come to perceive a problem, the determinants of the definition of the problem, the decision to seek help, and the type of assistance sought. It is clear that the process of help seeking results from a relatively complex sorting process that is dependent on a variety of factors other than the amount or severity of illness.

Public Health

This area is an old and traditional field in medicine that developed from the reform movements of the nineteenth century. Early emphasis in public health was devoted to immunization, improvement of sanitary conditions, and control of the communicable diseases. In recent years public health has become much more concerned with the various chronic diseases, environmental threats and pollution, preventive health practice, and health education. These concerns make the work of social scientists indispensable, since public health practice is largely concerned with producing change in the social environment and in people's behavior. As a result, such traditional areas within sociology as social influence, organizational change, and the community play an increasingly prominent role in public-health work (680).

At the present time the field of public health is in a state of flux, for the concerns of such practitioners have changed enormously in recent years. The traditional concerns have receded in importance while new challenges in such fields as industrial health, nutrition, environmental pollution, accidents, health education and behavior change, health-services research, social epidemiology, and health-care administration loom very large. The separation of schools of public health from medical schools and their lack of ties with ongoing service programs are increasingly a liability as medical schools themselves slowly shift their priorities to engage some of these areas. Schools of public health are now undergoing a reevaluation of their role and responsibilities (514), and it is likely that in the future there will be much closer ties among traditional curative medicine, preventive medicine, and public-health functions. The existing separation reflects the highly curative emphasis of the medical-care system which provided little opportunity to develop public-health concerns except in a fashion parallel to medical education.

Stress, Disease, and Coping

Sociologists and social psychologists have become increasingly interested in the sources of social stress in social organization and social life and in the relationship between social stress and illness. There is now considerable collaboration between sociologists and medical researchers studying the role of social stress in a wide variety of diseases, including such conditions as coronary heart disease and schizophrenia. Stress is being conceptualized in a variety of ways. One approach emphasizes life changes, the extent to which they are trying for the person, and the manner in which they call forth adaptive responses. A second approach attempts to evaluate the impact of life stresses and their cumulation on the occurrence of disease. Still other approaches, more social-psychological in character, attempt to study more specifically those types of life event that are usually associated with a sense of loss or a threat to self-esteem. While some researchers emphasize the events themselves, others are more concerned with persons' perceptions of these events and the manner in which they cope with adversity. With the decline of the psychoanalytic dominance over American psychology and psychiatry, much more work is being pursued on the ways in which people actually cope with problems and difficulties and the role of preparation, experience, and social supports in overcoming difficult life situations.

New Technologies for Changing Social Behavior

One of the most promising currents in the behavioral sciences relevant to medicine is the development of new technologies for modifying behavior based on operant and other conditioning techniques. These techniques have proved quite valuable in modifying a variety of individual behaviors that were troubling to individuals. Developments in biofeedback also suggest some promising possibilities for teaching individuals to control certain physiological responses, and such technologies may be useful in helping people deal with such varied problems as hypertension and migraine headaches. Similarly, the ability to use group supports to assist and succor people trying to overcome some problem has expanded, and in all likelihood our ability to use these supports in a more focused way will develop further in the future. There is also a growing interest in medicine, particularly in psychiatry, in making use of educational models as one of several approaches to rehabilitation (665). Here the concern is to teach people simple skills that facilitate their social and personal adaptation or that allow them to live more comfortably and effectively with their disabilities.

Social and Community Psychiatry

There is a growing realization that social and community factors affect both the development and the course of particular illnesses. Moreover, regardless of the etiology of illness, it is recognized that it may be possible to limit the magnitude of incapacity and disability through manipulation of the social environment. Community psychiatry is a relatively new field, and the designation is applied to a wide variety of efforts—some of a research and planning nature, others more propagandistic and ideological. In any case, sociological analysis is necessary not only to understand how social contexts affect illness but also to describe the sociology of community psychiatry as a social and political movement in the care of the mentally ill.

The field of community psychiatry is, of course, very broad, encompassing such concerns as the social etiology of mental disorders, factors conducive to effective community functioning, the organization of community ambulatory services, and the legal and social problems surrounding the definition and response to mental illness.

Legal and Ethical Issues

As medical science and technology have developed, the possibilities and related ethical dilemmas have become much more profound. Medical science has developed an enormous capacity to prolong life for the hopelessly ill as well as to provide new possibilities for some who were once regarded as hopeless. The implications of the technology for costs, distribution of resources, quality of life of the patients concerned, and human values are no small issues (227; 650). The emergence and development of transplantation have required new medical and legal concepts of death to enhance the acquisition of transplantable organs and to protect those working in the area from legal action. Such issues as informed consent, human experimentation, abortion, and fetal research have stirred controversies suggesting the degree of value conflict and ambiguity surrounding much medical activity. Developments in biology and such current possibilities as the use of amniocentesis to identify fetal conditions raise a variety of questions that we have yet to confront effectively.

The delivery of medical services, similarly, has become more complex and incorporates varying and often conflicting goals. The growth of malpractice litigation reflects changing attitudes and changing doctor-patient relationships. The legal structure is slow in adapting to changes in the development of technologies, manpower, organizational innovations in medical practice, and new social expectations. The legal structure thus is the rope in the tug-of-war between new possibilities and those pushing innovation and more traditional interests concerned with protecting current practices from erosion or change. The issues are hardly clear-cut, and their intelligent resolution depends on empirical study of the true consequences of varying decisions.

Social Aspects of Medical Economics

The field of medical economics has been developing rapidly, and a large number of publications have appeared in recent years defining issues and approaches in this field as well as providing empirical analyses. Although medical sociology does not encompass medical economics, it has particular relevance to the kinds of models and conceptions that medical economists tend to develop. Economists, in dealing with health-care problems, often assume rationality on the part of the consumer and fail to take into account the various social-psychological influences that affect patient and physician behavior and response. Frequently their models are limited and reflect a lack of understanding of the social and psychological aspects of patient perceptions and responses to illness or of clinical practice. Since economists often work on policy issues, it is particularly important that sociologists examine economic assumptions empirically, so that policy implications of economic research are seen in the proper context.

Much patient care takes place under circumstances in which patients are anxious and need to trust their physicians; medical markets often deviate so extensively from economic assumptions of a marketplace as to make analyses based on marketplace models highly unrealistic; and both physicians and patients respond to many factors other than economic incentives and disincentives that need to be taken into account in policy formulation. Moreover, with the tendency to use secondary data in economics and sociology, studies are often based on measures that are only very crude representations of the concepts of major concern, adding further distortions that have to be taken into account. Sociologists can contribute importantly to policy issues by examining how the variables of concern to them interact with economic variables, and through such analysis they enhance efforts in both medical sociology and medical economics.

Behavior Problems and Medical Care

In examining the epidemiology of problems brought to medical-care facilities, it becomes apparent that much of medical care deals not only with disease but with psychosocial problems and psychological difficulties that manifest themselves in physiological symptoms. Understanding how these problems come to be brought to physicians as compared with other resources in the community, how patients present their problems to doctors, and how physicians manage these within the context of a busy medical practice is a major concern of the field of medical sociology. In addition, a great deal of work is necessary to understand how such problems can be better managed from both a medical and social standpoint, since it is inevitable that, whether physicians regard these problems as appropriate or inappropriate for medical care, they will continue to constitute an important segment of medical demand.

The Semiprofessions

Physicians constitute only a small minority of health manpower. An important and perhaps increasing professional role will be played by such persons as nurse-practitioners and nurse-specialists, pharmacists, and social workers. These workers, unlike physicians, do not completely control their own work in medical settings, and thus lack the autonomy usually associated with the professions. With the growing emphasis on teams, with new organizational arrangements in delivering care, and with the political development of these occupational groups, they are likely to have a more central role and possibly greater autonomy in the future. Many factors will contribute to these trends: a new emphasis on women's rights; growing unionization and group militancy; the changing character of medical-care tasks; and more aggressive role making among these new professionals who feel greater confidence in challenging the traditional dominance of medicine. Thus, from the point of view of occupational politics, medicine offers a fertile area for considerable political activity in the definition of new roles, responsibilities, and rights.

Health Policy and Politics

Health-care patterns are the result of joint action among governmental units, voluntary organizations, health-care professionals, and private individuals. Medical politics are highly complex, involving legislative and administrative decisions made at the national and local level, within hospitals and medical associations, and at the level of service delivery. For issues of great visibility, health matters may be resolved within the context of community politics, and compromises are frequently evident. It is only quite recently that political sociologists and political scientists have been studying medical politics as a topic in its own right, examining the coalitions and alliances that become necessary either to develop new programs or to thwart what are perceived as threatening changes.

A number of younger medical sociologists are making efforts to focus on medical care as a political system, attempting to examine who controls the instruments of medical work and in whose interests they are manipulated (see, for example, 12 and 754). This perspective gives much less emphasis to social expectations, norms, values, and consensus, and relatively more to power, control, and special interests. Among the issues of concern to this group are the extent to which special interests—whether medical specialists or medical industrial firms—attempt to define the nature of medical priorities, obtain preferential and protective legislation, and distort the delivery of health services consistent with their own needs and orientations. There is also great interest in the political uses of illness and labeling for purposes of social control. While all of these concerns have long been part of analysis in medical sociology, new efforts are being made to use these ideas as a central perspective for examining the priorities of the medical-care system and medical work.

Some Analytic Perspectives

In part 1 of this book I shall develop in some detail a substantive sociological orientation to the field of medical sociology. However, in order to give the reader a more general perspective, I shall introduce here three analytic points of view that run through much of the data and analyses that follow. These analytic perspectives are not uniquely sociological but tend to characterize a great deal of effort in social epidemiology, public-health, and health-services research as well.

Although the observation is increasingly commonplace, it is important to appreciate that major achievements in the reduction of mortality and morbidity result not from the curative application of medical practice—no matter how sophisticated—but from changes in sanitation, water supply, food production, and environmental conditions, and improvements in standards of living and education. Curative medicine makes some contribution to health, but marginal investments in curative health services, in contrast to alternative investments in environmental and social conditions, have diminishing returns. The epidemiological model is appropriate for viewing disease in its larger social, environmental, and ecological perspective. I shall have a great deal to say about social epidemiology later, relating to both its methodologies and its substantive findings; however, some discussion of the general perspective is appropriate here.

Social Epidemiology

The epidemiological perspective views disease in its larger socioecological context in which disease agents (such as viral or bacterial agents, noxious environmental substances, and dangerous technologies) have differential effects depending on the characteristics of the host (biological, genetic, psychological, and social capacities and characteristics) and on the larger sociocultural and physical environment. The scope of this perspective can be illustrated by choosing two different types of threat to health: tuberculosis and automobile accidents.

The occurrence of tuberculosis is dependent upon a disease agent (a bacillus), but its manifestation as a disease depends on various social conditions as well as on the conditions of the host organism. While persons may have been infected by the disease agent, a given individual's susceptibility to disease is likely to depend on his prior social experience and exposure to the agent, his nutrition and general health status, and possibly his psychological state. The rise of tuberculosis as a major killer followed the social organization of urban areas with the development of industry. The industrial revolution brought large population movements from rural to urban areas and radical shifts in living standards, including more crowded dwellings, closer physical contact, and poor hygiene and sanitation. Industrialization was also accompanied by major changes in living patterns, nutrition, and dependence on traditional support systems. The movement of populations to industrial areas was followed by vast increases in the rates of tuberculosis and associated mortality (188).

At the level of host characteristics, it is apparent that populations that are inadequately nourished are far more susceptible to disease and suffer higher mortality. This remains a major problem in underdeveloped areas in the world, where populations are malnourished and are prey not only to the tuberculosis bacillus but also to several other infections that we find relatively benign. For example, measles epidemics in underdeveloped countries are major killers of children, largely attributable to their poor state of nutrition and general health status. Although individuals may be equally exposed to tuberculosis, the extent of proliferation of the bacillus in the human host is dependent on a variety of host characteristics. A great deal has been written about the role of stress in tuberculosis, and mechanisms have been suggested that attempt to explain how stress results in the multiplication and spread of the bacillus within the organism. While the research is not definitive, it is highly provocative and consistent with a growing literature on the role of noxious life events in the occurrence of a variety of diseases and health problems. This literature will be reviewed in chapter 8.

A somewhat different example, but also illustrative of the usefulness of the social epidemiological approach, is automobile accidents, incidents that are not "accidental" at all. Although it has been typical to think of this major societal problem (the fourth leading cause of death and the major cause of death among the young) as a result of individual carelessness and recklessness, such interpretations provide only a very limited understanding of what is really a far more complex process involving the interaction among a technology, the people who drive, and the physical and social context of driving behavior.

The agent in automobile accidents is the technology of the automobile. It is increasingly appreciated that the structure of the car and its built-in safety features have important effects on both the susceptibility to accidents and the probability of suffering injury or death when a crash occurs. Such features of the automobile as its steering, braking, and maneuverability affect the incidence of accidents; the construction of the car affects the consequences for the occupant in what is known as the "second collision," the forward acceleration of the occupants following impact. While various restraint systems, such as seat belts, harnesses, and air bags, are the most obvious safety features affecting injury and death, there are numerous other construction features that have significant influence on safety (see 306; 533; 634).

The environment of the automobile includes the highway systems, markings, traffic-control patterns, and related factors affecting the probability of accidents. Such factors as the presence of divided highways, open or closed access roads, and appropriate speed limits significantly affect the accident rate. Other environmental factors include anticipatory warnings to the driver, effective markings, adequate lighting, weather conditions, and road maintenance. A dramatic drop in highway mortality followed the reduction of speed limits on major highway systems to 55 miles per hour. Although some of the reduction might be attributed to the reduction of miles driven due to higher fuel costs and to other improvements in the driving environment, it seems likely that this simple legal measure had an effect far more profound than years of effort in the area of driver education.

Although most effort in automobile accident prevention has been devoted to changing host characteristics, this has perhaps been the least successful approach. Yet it is apparent that host characteristics are important in the accident rate. A major factor accounting for fatalities is the use of alcohol; a significant proportion of drivers killed in accidents have blood alcohol content beyond the safe limit. Similarly, the high rate of accidents among young males suggests that patterns of aggressive driving and risk taking are associated with larger sociocultural and socialization patterns in the society. There is also accumulating evidence that both stress and anger may contribute to patterns of driving that are risky or inattentive and that result in a higher probability of injury and death.

Although there have been concerted efforts to change driving patterns to promote greater safety, such efforts have faced considerable difficulties. Level of seat-belt utilization tends to be low despite the recognition by most people that seat belts are efficacious in promoting safety (585; 586). Similarly, while the correlation between drinking and accidents is well known, the pattern persists and appears to be a mounting problem. Increasingly, public-health practitioners have been urging technological approaches to accidents that bypass individual behavior because of their pessimism concerning mass cooperation with safety measures (586). Thus they urge use of restraint systems such as inflatable air bags that, unlike seat belts, do not require individual decision making. Some of these measures, such as lights and buzzers reminding drivers of the need to buckle up, have been less than fully popular; people go so far as to break or dismantle them. And the newly devised interlock system was so unpopular that it led Congress to discontinue this requirement in new automobile production.

In short, driving behavior is part of a larger sociocultural context and is conditioned by values, attitudes, and patterns of age and sex socialization. In a larger sense, it includes not only issues of economics and politics, such as those involving the regulation of the automobile and related industries, but also philosophical values about individual responsibility, government controls, and intrusions in the life of the ordinary citizen. Problems of reducing risks are thus often as much social and political problems as they are issues of changing personal behavior. Often the technology exists, and it may even be inexpensive, as in the case of fluoridation of water supply, but implementation depends on overcoming a variety of economic, political, and philosophical barriers.

Patient Flow

Although from a rational point of view it would seem reasonable that the flow of patients from a community into various types of medical facilities would be closely related to their need for service, the severity of their conditions, and the complexity of care required, such factors account for only part of the variation observable in reality. The decision to seek medical care and the referral of patients by physicians to more specialized services are dependent on a variety of sociocultural characteristics of both patients and doctors, on the availability and accessibility of various types of service and on situational factors. Each stage of patient flow from ambulatory facility to hospital, from one doctor to another, or from one type of facility to another is conditioned by social networks and relationships that go well beyond the obvious medical needs of the patient.

In any given month approximately three-fourths of the population will have some symptom of sufficient concern to them that they take some action, for example, bed rest, restricted activity, medication, or a visit to a doctor (765). Only approximately one-fourth of the population will actually consult a physician. There is considerable overlap between those symptoms persons report as leading to a physician consultation and those that do not. A variety of models have been developed by sociologists and social psychologists to explain such differential response, and these will be reviewed later in the book (see chapter 9). It is sufficient to note here that such help-seeking processes are part of a social process that transcends any medical understanding of the situation.

Similarly, the decision to hospitalize a patient, to refer the patient to another doctor or facility, or to send the patient to a major referral center depends not only on the medical facts of the situation but on the physician's attitudes and professional socialization, the availability of facilities, patient pressures, and a variety of other contingencies. For example, in their exploration of the ecology of medical care, White, Greenberg, and Williams (765) estimated that in any given month approximately nine in a thousand persons will be hospitalized. This statistic, of course, is not fixed; it is dependent on professional norms existing in any community, the extent of insurance coverage, availability of hospital beds, integrity of utilization review, and a variety of other factors. Rates of variation in use of hospital beds among localities with comparable levels of morbidity defy any medical interpretation. It is apparent, thus, that the organization of medical resources in the community and social norms of practice are major determinants of medical practice. Studying such variations and understanding their causes are major aspects of medical sociology. Indeed, any aspect of the referral process can be studied from this perspective. While sociologists have given most effort to developing models of patient behavior in visiting physicians, they have neglected other parts of the flow process from primary to more complicated patterns of care and from one type of agency to another.

Although understanding the selective flow of patients is interesting in itself, it constitutes an important aspect of both sociological investigation and medical-care research. It also has implications for clinical care, medical education, and medical research Let us briefly examine each of these contributions.

Social selection is one of the most pervasive processes characteristic of human communities, and its study concerns the identification of underlying principles of the sorting and re-sorting that go on continuously among social groups. Although it constitutes one of the central processes of social activity, many sociologists view social selection more as an irritation than as an object of inquiry. Since selection is such a powerful force in social life, sociologists must successfully discount it to make other hypotheses credible. For example, the student of social organization, comparing varying types of organizational climates or management styles, must make a credible case for these factors being important in relation to some outcome being studied, and not the types of personalities drawn to different organizations. Similarly, the investigator of any social program must be convincing in stating that the effects he observes are related to a specific intervention, in contrast to the types of client or personnel drawn to varying kinds of program. Indeed, some social scientists, recognizing the power of selection effects, are pessimistic that any reliable study is possible without randomization. Other sociologists devote great effort to understanding selection effects as part of major social processes, as in assortative mating, geographic mobility, social achievement, and patterns of help seeking.

The foregoing similarly has implications for medical research and medical education. Many medical investigations depend on populations of individuals who have sought assistance from a particular clinic or hospital. These patients may be more or less representative of all persons with a given clinical picture or disease pattern. Many such samples are hopelessly biased, possibly leading to erroneous conclusions. By gaining a better understanding of the selection process, we can better assess when it is inappropriate to rely on patient populations for clinical investigation. Similarly, the populations of teaching hospitals are highly selected samples, having been exposed to a variety of decision points in the pathway to such hospitals. White, Williams, and Greenberg (765) estimated that in any given month only one in every thousand people would find himself in such a hospital, and that only one in nine who were hospitalized would be treated in a teaching facility. The patients of such facilities are a highly selected sample reflecting the special research and teaching interests of the institution, the processes of referral from secondary to tertiary care facilities, the characteristics of the areas where such hospitals are located, and the types of patient using their outpatient clinics and emergency rooms. Yet these are the institutions where students are primarily trained and where most research is carried out. The appropriateness of almost exclusive reliance on such facilities for the training of primary-care physicians, who work largely with populations selected out prior to entry to such a hospital, is increasingly questioned. Although the issues are complex, for our purposes here it suffices to note that a better understanding of how such populations are constructed and how they relate to other populations of sick people allows us to plan teaching and research efforts more intelligently.

Finally, understanding the selective flow of patients, particularly the factors that cause it, sensitizes the practitioner to distinctions between factors associated with a particular disease condition and factors that lead persons with given symptoms to seek care or to be referred to a particular facility. In chapter 9 a variety of studies will be reviewed that illustrate how clinicians may come to confuse symptoms with sociocultural patterns of behavior associated with help seeking. Such confusions may lead to incorrect assessments of the patient and misguided treatments that could be avoided with a better understanding of the distinctions between illness and help-seeking patterns.

Social Context of Practice

The third major perspective used in this book is one that seeks to understand the behavior of professionals and client-centered organizations in a social context. The behavior of both clients and health professionals is molded in part by their particular culture and prior training and by the climate of the helping situation. In the analyses that follow, however, I shall emphasize the extent to which the behavior of patients, doctors, other health professionals, and helping organizations is influenced by adaptive needs. I shall focus on the social demands and situational pressures on each of the various participants and how such demands and pressures come to shape their behavior. I view the participants as active parties—each with his own prior values, orientations, and personal agendas—who are not simply reactors to social and situational demands, but who make efforts to shape their settings and work to reduce uncertainty and increase their personal rewards. A few brief examples will illustrate this perspective.

Consider the case of a student. His or her performance is likely to depend on personal characteristics (such as motivation, intelligence, and work habits), on the character of the learning environment (the nature of the demands made, the quality of instruction, and the extent to which it is interesting and motivates effort), and on various personal and social contingencies, such as peer-group influences and family expectations. Frequently the ideal expectations of the student are unrealistic in terms of such real constraints as the breadth of knowledge to be mastered, time available, and competing expectations in various courses. The student thus must develop some strategy of negotiating among these various expectations (see 53). Often he or she may attempt to assess the real as compared with the ideal expectations, such as what material is likely to appear on examinations or how much work is really expected in a particular course to achieve a defined grade. Also, the student must balance efforts in various courses and may relieve the pressure by taking some courses on a pass-fail basis or by choosing some less demanding courses to maintain an appropriate grade point average. These types of strategy and many more subtle ones are not unique to students but rather characterize much social behavior.

The extent to which students in different learning situations use similar strategies to cope with educational demands has been documented in the case of college students, graduate students, professional business students, and medical students. For example, Becker and his colleagues (52), studying students at the University of Kansas Medical School, found major differences between faculty expectations concerning the way medical students should approach their academic tasks and the way they actually behave. Students faced with what they perceived as overwhelming demands sought strategies that would assist in their "getting through the program" rather than those most consistent with ideal academic values. Similarly, Miller (518), in studying the internship at a major teaching hospital associated with the Harvard Medical School, described the strategies interns had to develop to achieve cooperation from hospital staff and to obtain instruction from their teachers, who were heavily involved in biomedical research. Interns would seek cases of particular research interest to their mentors in order to obtain an enthusiastic response from the attending doctor. As another example, it has been commonly observed that first-year medical students frequently report that their goal is to become general practitioners. By their senior year, however, the vast majority decide to pursue a specialty. Although this change is in part a response to the growth of the student's appreciation of the complexity of medicine along with more intensive experience, it also is a product of the medical-school learning environment, the attitudes of medical-school faculty, and social pressures from peers. These changes in choice reflect a coping process in which students bring their expectations into closer conformity with the real demands of different types of work, with the existing reward and prestige system, and with the attitudes and values of those around them.

A more complex example, illustrating how personal adaptations are influenced by social and economic conditions, comes from a study of doctor and patient in the Soviet Union following World War II. Field (217) describes how the shortage of manpower following the war led officials to become concerned with work absenteeism. Patients, however, feeling stressed by the heavy work demands made on them, came to physicians seeking certification of illness so as to miss work legitimately. Physicians were caught between the demands of the government to limit work absenteeism and the individual plight of patients seeking certification of illness. Thus both government and patients were attempting to use the physician as a means for manipulating the definition of illness. The Soviet government, as a means of limiting absenteeism, restricted the number of illness certifications the physician could issue.

In the chapters that follow these three perspectives—social epidemiology, selective patient flow, and study of behavior contingencies—will reappear in many forms and in varying contexts. These general perspectives will prove to be powerful tools to the reader in obtaining an overall grasp of a great many topics involving occurrence of disease and disability, use of medical and other health services, functioning of personal services organizations, and outcomes of health care.

Part 1

MAN, HEALTH, AND THE
ENVIRONMENT

Chapter 1

HEALTH, DISEASE, AND DEVIANT BEHAVIOR

The concept of disease usually refers to some deviation from normal functioning that has undesirable consequences because it produces personal discomfort or adversely affects the individual's future health status. On a practical everyday basis it is possible to identify and deal with disease processes, as persons often complain of pain and discomfort, and these complaints can then be investigated as to whether they fit a recognizable clinical pattern of disease. Assessment of the underlying condition producing the patient's subjective distress usually leads to some attempt to manage the case—i.e., to relieve pain and suffering and if possible to retard the disease process itself, if one can be identified.

When we apply the concept of disease to such conditions as pernicious anemia, syphilis, tuberculosis, and cancer, the underlying condition producing personal discomfort is relatively easily identified in terms of known clinical entities. However, when this concept is similarly applied to such conditions as neuroses, alcoholism, schizophrenia, and obesity, the basic roots of the problem may be much more ambiguous. When it is applied to such social problems as crime, suicide, political deviation, and illegitimacy, it becomes apparent that the concept of disease is widely applied but not always clearly formulated.

It is clear that the concept of disease is used in many different ways. In its most narrow meaning it refers to a medical hypothesis that implies particular pathological processes underlying a specific clinical syndrome. More generally, the concept is used to refer to physical or behavioral deviations that pose social problems for individuals or the community. Finally, there are occasions in which particular personal problems may be defined as diseases although they neither imply underlying pathology nor pose serious problems for the community.

Disease designations are sometimes applied, for example, to such groups of people as religious and political extremists.

Social Context of Definitions

Implicit in all ideas of health and disease—whether specific or more general—is some concept of normal fitness and behavior, but concepts of health fitness and acceptable behavior, as well as those of disease and disability, depend on the state of health institutions and health science and on the social and cultural context within which human problems are defined. A wide variety of diseases are not defined by particular groups as illness conditions because they occur frequently and are regarded as the common state of man. In some tropical countries, yaws, an infectious disease characterized by skin eruptions with a raspberry-like appearance, was so pervasive that individuals did not regard it as deviant. Dyschromic spirochetosis, a disease characterized by spots of various colors that appear on the skin, was so common in a particular South American tribe that Indians who did not have it were regarded as abnormal (187). In short, health and disease, as well as their definitions, are often molded by the social context within which they occur. René Dubos, an eminent microbiologist and medical historian, has made this point most elegantly:

> [Man's] self-imposed striving for ever-new distant goals makes his fate even more unpredictable than that of other living things. For this reason health and happiness cannot be absolute and permanent values, however careful the social and medical planning. Biological success in all its manifestations is a measure of fitness, and fitness requires never-ending efforts of adaptation to the total environment, which is ever changing [186, p. 25].

Although on a practical basis we often have no difficulty in recognizing serious illness, usually implicit in illness definitions are assumptions about what states of physical being are desirable and undesirable, damaging and benign. Thus in some cultures the obese woman is an object of envy and desire; other groups define obesity as a physical and emotional disease. In some societies supernatural powers are attributed to the epileptic, while in others epileptics are regarded not only as ill but also as objects of scorn and social prejudice. Most societies become concerned about the health of members who threaten harm for no apparent reason; although certain benevolent deeds such as heroic rescues and wartime bravery may also stem from pathological motivation or personal confusion, such behavior is more likely to be credited than treated. The extent to which "mental subnormality" is a condition eliciting medical concern will depend on the emphasis a social group places on the acquisition of a high level of conceptual and technical skills. There is no scarcity of examples that can be cited to illustrate how health-illness evaluations implicitly depend on the value orientations and life situations of the people concerned. As Dubos has noted, health and disease are not entities. These concepts are used to characterize a process of adaptation to the changing demands of life and the changing meanings we give to living.

The Healing Arts

Wherever man has existed, he has sought help and relief for pain and discomfort. At times he looked toward the gods and on other occasions toward the assistance of other men. In the beginning of every civilization, medicine, in the words of a famous medical historian, consisted of "a mishmash of religion, magic, and empirically acquired ideas and practices" (646). It is still so today. Empirically acquired information on health and disease constitutes an increasingly large proportion of medical lore, but magic and religion continue to influence the definition of and response to disease.

Throughout the history of medicine, health has been seen as a condition of equilibrium and illness as the disruption of a balanced state. The idea of balance dominated Hippocratic medicine in the fifth and fourth centuries B.C. and persists today in may forms, varying in their scientific authenticity. Ayurvedic medicine, which endures in India, is based on the Hippocratic idea that health results from the proper balance of hot and cold forces and that disease is the consequence of a breakdown in this balance. Similar ideas exist today in Latin America and among Spanish Americans. Throughout early medicine there was considerable discussion about the factors that determined equilibrium. It was argued that since man developed from the seminal fluid, the body humors (or juices) were the prime determinants (646). Some declared that there were only two or three significant humors, while others argued that there were many. A popular view was that there were four humors, making up two pairs with opposed qualities: blood and black bile, yellow bile and mucous. The theory of the four humors, systematized in the writings of Galen (a physician living in the second century A.D.), dominated medical ideas of balance for many centuries.

Although the theory of the humors may seem ludicrous to us today, it was an attempt to build a general theory of bodily functioning that was consistent to some extent with observations made concerning the functioning of the sick. The tremendous number of diverse observations required some conceptual frame of reference to pull them together. As Sigerist has noted:

Medicine must be guided by a theory, for otherwise medical doctrine could not be handed on from teacher to pupil. So long as theory and practice, science and practice, harmonize, so long as theory derives from practice and, in its turn, guides practice, medical science and practice will be fruitful. Every theory is philosophical in its nature. It works with the thoughts, with the concepts, available at any particular epoch, thus molding the culture of the time. Thus, in the Hippocratic theories, there recur all the elements of the natural philosophy of pre-Socratic days. An attempt is made to solve the problem of health and disease conceptually and speculatively, setting out from observation [646, p. 15].

Although Hippocratic conceptions of balance no longer have any relevance to modern medicine, the concept of bodily balance—in modern physiological terms, the concept of homeostasis—has great relevance for understanding the complicated interplay of biological and physiological mechanisms. Much of scientific medical practice involves treatment of the patient's difficulty through attempts to restore the body's balanced state, a concept especially important in such areas as metabolism and endocrinology.

When we attempt to evaluate the ways in which the doctor defines disease, it is obvious that he does not depend on an assessment of social values in order to make his diagnosis of the patient's difficulty. Instead, he has many techniques for assessment. He usually begins by taking a history of the patient's complaints and their development, gathering a variety of information that may bear on the case. Through a physical diagnostic examination and various clinical investigations he adds to the information he has already obtained from the patient or informants. Thus the specification of disease—as it takes place in the medical context—involves a determination of the state of a particular individual. Implicit in the practitioner's frame of reference is an elaborate set of norms of human functioning, developed through a long history of clinical observation and scientific inquiry, and a variety of medical theories concerning the relationships among symptoms and their implications for understanding pathological processes.

In different countries and in different historical periods the implicit frames of reference used by the doctor in evaluating patients are established scientifically to a greater or lesser degree. In the present climate of scientific medicine there still is a great deal that is not known, and many of the standards by which the patient is evaluated are held on only a very tentative basis. The actual practice of medicine, even within the most scientific contexts, continues to be largely a social art rather than a rigorous science. Even knowledge about such conditions as heart disease, malignant neoplasms (cancer), and cerebrovascular disease (stroke) is characterized by great uncertainty and incomplete information; yet these three categories alone account for more than two-thirds of all deaths in the United States (736; 740). Physicians frequently have dramatically opposing views on the management of common diseases; for example, a review on this subject indicates that over 300 methods of treatment for peptic ulcer were recommended between 1946 and 1956 (337). Such variability is inevitable when scientific facts are inadequately specified. In short, the standards used in evaluating the existence and course of disease are to some extent uncertain and in a state of flux.

The Doctor's Role

One of the most important forces affecting the doctor's evaluation of and response to the patient is the social definition of the physician's role in society. What the doctor does or does not do depends not only on his scientific orientation and professional ethics but also on the expectations of the community and the responsibilities assigned to him. Thus doctors are called upon to deal with many forms of distress that may require skills and orientations unrelated to their scientific expertise. The basis of medicine as an art lies essentially in the fact that the doctor's role in society is socially defined, and he is expected to render help and advice irrespective of the state of medical science in the area of concern. It is only through a full appreciation of the social components of the physician's role that the true meaning of the physician's place in society becomes clear and the wide range of his activities becomes intelligible.

Social values play an essential part in medical determinations and in the provision of medical care. Much of medical practice involves attempts at helping people to conform more adequately to social rather than physical standards. The plastic surgeon, for example, may help people to approximate ideals of physical attractiveness and youthfulness more closely through techniques to straighten noses or remove wrinkles from the face. Pediatricians spend a good part of their time dealing with problems of social development in children. Physicians working with the aged may feel it more important to give attention to their patients' social integration in the community and their need for a sympathetic ear than to their various physical complaints. Social judgments also are implied in the definition and care of the mentally retarded, in much of psychiatric practice, in family planning and birth control, in attitudes toward abortion and sterilization, in the prescription of pep pills and tranquilizers, and in the provision of contraceptives for teenagers.

The Patient's Role

Patients come to doctors for many reasons. A visit is always characerized by some need or problem for which assistance is desired, but these needs and problems may vary considerably. There is no single definition of the doctor's role, and there is great variability in the situations people perceive as appropriate reasons for seeking medical attention. Individuals cope with their problems and difficulties in many ways; seeking medical assistance is only one of innumerable possibilities. Whether a person views the doctor as a relevant helper will depend on such factors as his cultural background and information, his personal characteristics, the way he perceives and defines particular indications of illness, the social and physical accessibility of the doctor, and the personal and monetary costs of seeking medical help compared with alternative approaches to the problem. In chapter 9 we shall review these factors in some detail. For the present it is necessary only to note that differences exist in orientations to medical care and that these can be traced to varied influences.

The ability to cope with one's problems—whether physical, mental, or social—depends on the way one defines the problem, the causes one identifies as having brought the problem about, the alternatives one sees for reversing the problem, and one's resources for making use of various alternatives. Whether the patient recognizes or identifies a problem in the first place depends on whether he experiences some change from expectations that he regards as undesirable or troublesome. Thus the recognition of deviations from personal standards of functioning or the experience of unfavorable changes in one's life situation alerts the person to a problem. Frequently it is the person himself who makes this evaluation. He has some implicit ideas as to what physical, mental, and social states are "normal" and what indications are unusual. These ideas are based on personal experience, past cultural conditioning, and knowledge about health and disease acquired in the course of one's life. Such conceptions and knowledge may vary from person to person and group to group. The definition of such deviations is usually a prerequisite for a definition of illness, but is generally not sufficient in itself for such a definition.

Once some deviant signs have been recognized, social and cultural ideas about the cause of particular problems become relevant. The person may believe that he feels the way he does because he is tired and overworked, or because he has committed some wrong; he may see his condition as a result of having been possessed by evil spirits, of someone's having cast a spell over him, or of having been infected by a particular virus. The cultural context not only may affect the interpretation of the symptom but also conditions the alternative responses that are identified to deal with the problem and the remedies defined as most appropriate. Thus, in our own culture, although nondisease interpretations may play a part in the way members of particular subgroups define particular symptoms, many problems are socially defined as relevant to an illness model, and the physician is defined as an appropriate person to assess and treat such conditions. In nonliterate cultures the same symptoms may be dealt with very differently because they are defined in other ways or because there are limited cultural alternatives for dealing with such problems. Finally, whether a person seeks one solution or another for dealing with his problem depends on whether he can cope with the problem on his own and whether outside assistance is available.

When Doctor and Patient Meet

Doctors and patients may come together holding somewhat different conceptions of illness. The doctor's views are largely molded by his professional training and clinical experience. The patient's views are influenced by the need to cope with a particular problem and his cultural and social understanding of the nature of the problem. Thus it is in the doctor-patient relationship that lay and professional cultures most intimately meet and sometimes clash. The definitions of illness or the norms of functioning held by physicians vary in the extent to which they conform to lay conceptions. In some situations the views of particular groups of patients and doctors are closely congruent; in other circumstances they differ widely and clash not only in respect to whether illness exists but also on a cultural level. The definition of illness thus may take place in a context in which there are competing views of the patient's condition, and resolution of the patient's problem may depend on how these different definitions come to be applied in a specific instance. This is not to imply that the doctor is unable to maintain his unique perspective in the situation. However, whether the patient responds to the doctor's expectations and cooperates in treatment, as well as many other facets of care, is intimately linked to the perspective of the patient and his associates.

In recognizing the variability of patient behavior, we should note that physicians also vary widely in their responses. They differ in their views of medicine and its relevance to a variety of problems, in their medical knowledge, their understanding of particular subareas of illness, their training, experience, and philosophical perspectives. Moreover, as we noted earlier, medical knowledge is a mixture of scientifically precise facts and clinical impressions, leaving much room for medical uncertainty and individual variation to manifest itself in regard to many problems that patients present to doctors. The ways in which the doctor deals with such situations of uncertainty and ambiguity are influenced by his views, his personal and social characteristics, and situational circumstances.

Definitions of illness are grist for the sociological mill largely because the standards of normality and dysfunctioning held by lay persons in diverse social groups vary widely, as they may also differ between physicians and patients and even among physicians. Moreover, different personal and social standards for defining illness influence what illnesses are recognized, who seeks care, and whether there is delay in seeking treatment for serious conditions. Both the patient defining his own problem and the doctor evaluating the patient's complaint attempt in one way or another to compare the problem with some *standard of normality*. Patient and doctor will frequently differ in their standards for evaluating symptoms and the manner in which they have been arrived at although both are susceptible to the same type of sociological scrutiny. In general, patients' evaluations of normality are based on their own experience and some synthesis of medical information and "naive" theories of bodily functioning. Medical norms, in contrast, are frequently based on the results of clinical observation, field studies, and experimental investigation. Nevertheless, there are sufficient areas of uncertainty and lack of knowledge within medicine to make many medical norms less than clear-cut. The development and application of medical norms to particular patients are further complicated by great variations in physiological, biological, and social functioning among persons who vary in their age, sex, and way of life.

The foregoing discussion suggests that the concepts of *normality* and *deviation from normality* are implicit in both lay and medical evaluations of disease. These concepts are also central to sociological analysis because the sociologist is vitally concerned with the development of standards of normality and the factors influencing deviation from these standards. Although the content of the standards and evaluations of deviation differs widely depending on who is making the evaluation, the logical processes by which these evaluations are made are strikingly similar. The analysis that follows will explore various approaches to studying "standards of normality" and the use of each of these approaches by the sociologist, the physician, and the patient.

One final caution: As noted in the beginning of the chapter, the doctor may evaluate the patient from a narrow medical standard or from a social standard more akin to that used by the sociologist. He may even, in some circumstances, respond to the patient from a layman's perspective. Thus the fact that it is a physician who is making the definition does not necessarily mean that the standard of normality being applied has a true medical basis.

Norms and Deviant Response

Deviant response is a general designation given to attributes that are thought to digress from a generally accepted range of responses that

define normality. These attributes may include behavior, verbalizations, thought processes, or physiological measurements. As long as the
attribute is measurable, it can be evaluated in terms of how closely it
fits concepts of normality. In an abstract sense, the concept of *deviation
from normal* is very simple. In its more specific application, however,
even scholars become entangled in disagreements and confusion, as it
is no easy matter to define the range of normality in unambiguous terms
and at the same time retain whatever agreement was attained at a general level. The discussion will begin by considering definitions of deviant
behavior from the perspective of social behavior, and will then examine the development of medical norms.

Behavioral Deviation

Behavior that may be regarded as deviant may be the product of different social processes. Sometimes deviant response may be the product of incapacities to behave within the "normal range" because of
bizarre psychological orientations, physiological defects, intrapsychic
abnormalities, or other personal handicaps. Other behavior that appears deviant may have been acquired and expressed in a perfectly normal fashion, but the behavior is inappropriate for the social context and
inconsistent with the values and standards held by the population who
identify the act as deviant. Not only do behavioral patterns develop differently, but the same behavior in different contexts may evoke varying
responses. Understanding how an act comes to be defined as deviant
requires consideration of the actor (the motivations or intentions imputed to him), the particular group context within which the behavior
took place, and varying definitions of the actor and situation which
take into account the consequences of the behavioral sequence for the
various people involved and for the community generally. Such evaluations are more complex than we usually realize, and it is necessary to
note that people who evaluate each other's behavior do not necessarily
share the same standards of normality and acceptability. Understanding deviant behavior, therefore, involves consideration of various perspectives of social life that may be relevant to the same situation. To
make this view plain, it is useful to review briefly the concepts of culture and norms and of socialization, and to make a few remarks about
law and public opinion.

Culture and Norms

The concept of culture refers in a general sense to the designs for
adapting to the social and physical environments that characterize the
life of a particular population. The concept is extremely global and
inclusive; social groups, in contrast, are complex, varied and changing,

and thus the concept of culture is at best a sensitizing one that gives us a way of viewing the social world. It is important to realize that the concept of culture is a scientific abstraction through which the investigator attempts to characterize the consistencies in behavior that he observes as he studies the ways in which people deal with tasks and with other people. Although students of culture seek to find regularities and consistencies in patterns of behavior from which they infer "cultural patterns," there is frequently great variation in behavior among people in a particular community, and thus so-called cultural patterns are only rough approximations of the way people behave in a particular context.

The concept of culture is used in many different ways, and descriptions of cultural values, attitudes, and orientations vary greatly in their degree of abstraction. For example, it is commonly noted that health is an important American cultural value. Talcott Parsons, in an analysis of health values (550), has argued that the emphasis given to health in American society is linked with other cultural values such as "activism" (orientations to mastery over the environment), "worldliness" (an emphasis on practical secular pursuits), and "instrumentalism" (an indefinite progress perspective). In his view, not only does each of these values lead to an elaboration of the health sciences, but also the development of these sciences promotes man's opportunities to live in accord with such values; the maintenance of good health enhances mastery and "progress." In a very different kind of analysis of cultural values relating to health, Zborowski (793) has attempted to specify varying cultural orientations to pain among persons in different ethnic groups. Zborowski notes that Italians have a present-oriented apprehension with regard to the actual experience of pain, while Jews show a future-oriented anxiety as to the meaning of the pain experienced. Further, he notes that Jewish and Italian cultures allow for free expression of feelings and emotions, while "Old American" patients try to take a detached and unemotional view of their symptoms.

Both Parsons's and Zborowski's descriptions can be taken as cultural values or orientations, but these portrayals differ in their level of generality and the manner in which they have been developed. When various investigators describe cultural patterns, the source of data for the generalizations and the kind of inferential process on which they are based are frequently unclear. One can attribute several different meanings to the assertion, "Americans value their health," and these meanings need not necessarily coincide. This assertion can mean that Americans verbalize health values and, when asked about the relative value of health compared with other life dimensions, give health high priority, or it can mean that it is the investigator's view that the population behaves as if health has high priority, irrespective of whether they verbalize health values. Indeed, persons need not necessarily recognize their own values or the cultural factors that influence them. The investigator may infer health values from a variety of possible indicators: the amount of their resources people spend on medicines and health remedies, the propensity to use medical facilities, the amount of time and space they devote to health problems and concerns in their mass media, and so on. In short, the inference that a cultural value or orientation exists may be arrived at by using different data-gathering and analytic techniques.

The statement of cultural values and orientations characteristic of a particular group is an attempt to specify dominant themes in the group's adaptive responses, and it may not apply to all people or even to all situations where the values may be relevant. Although it is possible for us to agree that Americans place great value on health, as evidenced by their concern with sickness, provision of medical care, development of medical science, and so on, it is equally evident that health values often do not dominate people's behavior. Individuals frequently take unnecessary risks detrimental to their health (such as smoking), and elimination of environmental risks is not given first priority. General statements of cultural values are based on a summary of observations that may conflict to a greater or lesser degree. Thus, although statements about culture serve to sensitize us to important uniformities in a society, they do not constitute precise descriptions of the way a particular group of people behaves or thinks.

For our purposes, the concept of culture will be used in a general way to designate a totality of interrelated—but often *disjointed* and *contradictory*—ideas and activities that characterize the way of life of a particular social group. I emphasize the words "disjointed" and "contradictory" because as soon as one looks closely at the behavior of a particular group, the variations in commitments and response are vast and impressive. The concept of culture, however, is valuable in allowing us to see clearly the great differences in behavioral trends as one compares one group with another. Because ideas and activities are to a large extent communicated from generation to generation, an individual's development, thought pattern, and behavior are conditioned substantially by the cultural and social milieu within which he develops. The existence of vast differences among societies needs no elaboration. However, we frequently fail to appreciate the diversity of thought and action in communities that we regard as constituting part of the same culture. The myth of homogeneity is often maintained through a loose cultural consensus that most people may accept in a very general way, and this myth helps people to live together more harmoniously. An investigation of a typical community will show vast differences, however, in ideals and conceptions of morality, patterns of work and leisure, child rearing and caring, and aspirations and values. Our large cities are, of course, more varied in the religious, class, and ethnic origins of their participants, and in such areas it is even more difficult to define the prevailing mode of living. Within the typical community one finds basic and important cultural differences, for example, between men and women, professional and worker, and Catholic and Jew. Similarly, there are substantial regional differences, despite the homogenizing effects of an increasingly standardized industrial complex and far-reaching national mass media. Although we think of ourselves as one people, our culture has many faces; understanding such subcultural differences is essential if one is to make any sense of social processes.

In attempting to define cultural background, the major unit of analysis that sociologists have used is the concept of norms. Like the concept of culture, the concept of norms means many things. Most frequently norms are designated as the expectations, standards, and rules that regulate and mold behavior. It is not always clear, however, when the norm concept refers to standards that are explicitly recognized by the people being described, as compared with instances in which the concept is an analytic convenience used by the sociologist to describe his observations of behavior. The norm that doctors are not to reveal confidential information concerning their patients predicts the physician's unwillingness to discuss the names and attributes of his patients in social situations. This expectation is one that the doctor explicitly recognizes; he has no difficulty describing the expectation to us, and few doctors would deny that the rule affected their behavior to some degree. Consider, in contrast, Parsons's suggestion that the following expectations apply to the sick person to a greater or lesser degree depending on the severity of his illness: (1) that he avoid obligations that may exacerbate his condition; (2) that he accept the idea that he needs help; (3) that he desire to get "well"; and (4) that he seek technically competent help in getting well. Parsons's analysis does not depend on whether or not people recognize these expectations. Rather, he uses these abstractions (the positing of norms) to account for certain uniformities in the behavior of persons who are ill. Normative concepts can be used in analyzing social situations regardless of whether the actors concerned recognize the norm as affecting their behavior. It is important, however, that we understand clearly how we are using the concept of norms.

Even norms that are "real," in the sense that they are recognized by the people whose behavior we are trying to understand, may vary greatly in their degree of explicitness. Many norms are formally and explicitly stated, as in our legal statutes; thus the physician knows that medical procedures such as euthanasia violate the law. Other norms are less explicit and less salient, and thus more difficult to describe. It is a widely cited expectation that the doctor should put the patient's interests and welfare before his own. Although, in its extreme form, physicians would agree that it would be improper to use the doctor's privileged situation to exploit the patient, the bounds of this norm are poorly specified and not really discussed very much. As one moves away from extreme types of exploitation, such as taking sexual liberties with a patient, the degree of diversity in the behavior of doctors toward their patients increases. Most social norms are of this kind; they may apply across the board in extreme instances, but for the most part they are informal, fluid, and loosely applied. Since these norms are not verbalized explicitly, in contrast to many codified rules and regulations, it is possible for great social differences to exist in a community with only limited conflict and social disruption. If social norms were all explicit and inflexible, social life would be unbearable, if not totally impossible.

The lack of explicitness of informal norms makes it possible for many competing standards and ways of life to be tied together by a tacit acceptance of general values such as honesty, integrity, and responsibility. The beauty of these values, sociologically speaking, is that they mean different things to different people and therefore allow diverse patterns of behavior to persist while people verbally agree that they believe in the same things. Such words as "honesty" or "integrity" have no meaning apart from a particular situation; although most people will agree that honesty and integrity are good, they do not necessarily behave similarly in situations involving honesty or integrity. People are much more similar in their verbal statements than in their behavior, and such verbal agreement does much to keep the community functioning.

Formal norms as incorporated into the law are sometimes in opposition to informal ones. These contradictions result because formal rules do not equally represent the viewpoints of different social groups and because laws often change slowly in adjusting to changes in social life. Such rules are applied through legislative action and judicial decision, and although they may be relevant to everyone, all persons and groups do not have equal opportunity to affect equal knowledge of the legal norms. Thus the clash of norms, standards, and frames of reference is pervasive in social life, and such confrontations constitute an essential component in the analysis of social situations.

Socialization

The most important feature of culture is that it can be transmitted, and thus the young can acquire adaptive repertories through the learning process or, in sociological terms, the socialization process. Although the most marked experience of cultural learning occurs during the child's development, persons continue to learn and to change, and in this sense socialization is a continuing process throughout life.

The subculture within which the child is socialized affects not only his thoughts and values in a general sense but also his life chances and personality. The accident of birth in a particular social class or ethnic or religious group, or being of a particular color, or from a particular region, all have a profound significance in social development. On a simple statistical basis, the subculture within which a child develops is related to the probability that he will survive following birth, average expected life span, health and disease patterns, educational aspirations and achievement, future occupational status, pattern of work, and leisure (see, for example, 375; 465; 635). Study of the social forces operative in different subcultural environments reflects vastly different opportunities and potentialities for the development of particular attitudes, aspirations, and effective behavior (582). One's sex and origins in a racial, ethnic, religious, and economic sense all play an important role in restricting particular opportunities and opening others, but in addition there are many other important factors operative in defining subcultural differences in respect to socialization. To take one important example, in a society like our own in which educational achievement is given such great emphasis, many families in particular groups fail to stimulate, interest, and prepare the child adequately. Or to state the idea somewhat differently, there are considerable subcultural differences in the extent to which intellectual tasks and competence are valued and the extent of preparation of children to acquire and value these skills. Yet we know that particular kinds of cultural enrichment stimulate interest and striving for competence. In short, differences in subcultural values and preparation may serve to accelerate or retard particular kinds of motivation, skills, and achievement.

Thus far emphasis has been given to the *content* of learning, but the *process* of socialization is also important. The manner in which ideas and ideals are communicated and enforced, the ways in which rewards and punishments are allocated, and the fashion in which annoyance and support are expressed, all play an important part in the development of personal traits. Responses characterized as deviant and different patterns of reactions to bodily indications and to life difficulties may be acquired in a variety of ways. Persons may behave in a way that is regarded as deviant because their subcultural values and behavior are very different from others in the community, and thus their behavior may be considered inappropriate in contexts outside their own community. In this case the deviant pattern of response may be culturally conditioned through a "normal" learning process. However, deviant behavior may also occur because the learning process itself became disrupted in some fashion. Such failures may stem from a variety of causes: The person may have minimal innate ability or physiological defects that make the necessary level of learning impossible; the parents may have been haphazard and inconsistent in responding to the child, and therefore the child may become confused with subsequent disruptions in the learning process; or the parents may expect too much of the child, forcing him to withdraw from learning situations, with subsequent disruptions in learning. These and many other aspects of the learning process may have some relationship to deviant response, but it is essential to separate such factors from those associated with differences in what people learn.

Law and Public Opinion

To the extent that a community is characterized by groups that differ in values and behavior, it is likely that many of the prevailing community norms will characterize the accepted morality of some segments of the community more than others. Legislators are not usually a random sample of the population, and the laws they establish tend to represent their own moral values as well as the various pressures brought to bear upon them by organized segments of the community—churches, social agencies, unions, businessmen's groups, newspapers, and so on. All groups do not share equal influence in making their wishes felt, and thus the law may not necessarily portray the sentiments of the entire community. Similarly, the law may often give little consideration to the sentiments of small minority groups and unorganized majorities that have not been able to mobilize their strength.

The processes through which laws are made are not fully rational. The passions of men and the pressures of organizations are involved, and sudden events that capture newspaper headlines and the interest of people may have consequences far out of proportion to their true meaningfulness. Thus a violent crime committed by a mental patient released from the hospital may stimulate demands and even legislation affecting procedures for dealing with the mentally ill. A violent sexual crime may lead to harsh legislation affecting all sexual deviants. In short, a highly advertised case may greatly prejudice the gist of human experience, and the atypical event may become the basis for legislation when passions become aroused.

Approaches to Studying Deviant Response

Having briefly examined the social context within which definitions of deviant behavior are made, let us now consider various ways in which deviant response can be viewed. We have already seen that the commonsense notions of deviation as a digression or departure from normality are difficult to apply, because the multiplicity of conflicting norms and values in any complex society makes it difficult to define the range of normality. Therefore, it is not clear from which set of standards one should judge deviant response.

Sociologists have been unable to arrive at a simple and clear definition of deviant behavior that is applicable and useful in all situations where analysis is necessary. However, they have utilized three general approaches to the problem. These approaches used singly and in combination provide a meaningful basis for analysis. None of them stands adequately by itself in defining deviant behavior, but when they are combined they provide the analyst with a useful perspective that suggests various problems and concerns relevant to understanding deviant response. For simplicity, we shall refer to these approaches as the positivistic, the statistical, and the societal reaction approaches.

The Positivistic Approach

The most obvious approach to deviant response is to *adopt some ideal* as a *point of reference* and then attempt to describe and account for divergence from this ideal. For convenience, this type of analysis shall be designated as the positivistic approach. Students of deviant behavior frequently take the law as their point of reference and attempt to account for deviations from the legal statutes (632). Earl Quinney, for example, in a study of deviation among retail pharmacists, selected prescription violators as his deviant group. These pharmacists "had been officially detected by state and federal investigators as violating a prescription law or regulation" (573). He was able to demonstrate that violators were less professionally oriented than nonviolators. In another study concerning legal stigma, Richard Schwartz and Jerome Skolnick (624) investigated the consequences for doctors resulting from legal suits against them for malpractice. They obtained their sample of accused doctors (the alleged "deviant" group) from the records of Connecticut's leading carriers of malpractice insurance. Their findings supported the idea that doctors (even those found guilty) suffer little economic loss from malpractice suits, because other doctors are sympathetic toward them and may send patients to them to offset losses resulting from litigation.

Epidemiologists (investigators of the occurrence of disease in human populations) also sometimes use a positivistic approach. For example, they may arbitrarily define certain symptoms and clusters of symptoms as evidence of handicap, and then describe human populations in terms of how they distribute in reference to these definitions. In a study of the mental health of residents of midtown Manhattan (662), the investigators developed various criteria defining mental impairment. They then attempted to assess the proportion of the population that was impaired in reference to these arbitrary criteria. As we shall see later, the doctor in general practice frequently functions with an implicit idea of the normal range of response. In decisions as to whether his patient is obese, physically inactive, or neurotic, for example, he must have some implicit concept of what is normal, and this is arbitrary to some extent. Obesity is usually thought of as a marked deviation from statistical values of average height-weight dimensions in the population for persons of varying body builds. Obesity is often arbitrarily defined as a deviation of 20 percent or more from average values. Obviously, being fat is a continuum, but doctors must work with some implicit impressions of when people are beginning to get too fat, for at this point they must encourage the patient to give more attention to controlling or reducing his weight.

Positivistic definitions are frequently used in attempts to define mental health as compared with mental illness. Since definitions of positive mental health must be arbitrary to a large extent, there is considerable disagreement as to the criteria that allow experts to differentiate reliably among persons who are not clearly suffering from particular diseases. Marie Jahoda (360) has investigated in detail the many professional views of positive mental health, and she has attempted to locate recurring themes in such views. Although the themes were numerous and often contradictory, it was her conclusion that six primary themes recurred throughout the writings on this topic: (1) attitudes toward the self, including its accessibility to consciousness, correctness of self-concept, self-acceptance, and sense of identity; (2) growth, development, and self-actualization; (3) integration, including the balance of psychic forces, a unifying outlook on life, and resistance to stress; (4) autonomy; (5) perception of reality, including freedom from need distortion, and empathy or social sensitivity; and (6) environmental mastery (including ability to love and experience orgasm; adequacy in love, work, and play; adequacy in interpersonal relationships; efficiency in meeting situations; capacity for adaptation and adjustment; and efficiency in problem solving). One need be no expert to recognize the difficulty in defining these themes in specific behavioral terms and the extent of their implication with social values and social judgments which vary widely in differing social contexts. It is not surprising therefore, that Jahoda, who is sympathetic toward developing concepts of positive mental health, should comment that "there is hardly a term in current psychological thought as vague, elusive, and ambiguous as the term 'mental health' " (360, p. 3) and that, "apart from extremes, there is no agreement on the types of behavior which it is reasonable to call 'sick' " (360, p. 13).

Use of the positivistic approach involves an important assumption:

the supposition that the defining criteria in identifying deviation are meaningful. For the investigator studying response to legal norms (as in the case of prescription violators), the assumption that the legal rules constitute reasonable criteria for measuring deviance is a fair one, in that the law is binding on all people, regardless of whether they approve of such laws or whether such laws are consistent with their subcultural values. Thus it is theoretically reasonable to assume that the legal statutes define expected behavior for all classes of persons to which these laws apply, and it makes sense to attempt to explain deviation from these rules. In the case of prescription violators, for example, conflicting orientations may be one of the influences explaining deviant behavior in that those pharmacists with a business orientation are more motivated to violate prescription laws than pharmacists with solely a professional orientation.

The positivistic approach has associated problems, as our discussion of positive mental health already suggests. Often it is extremely difficult to arrive at a reasonable and analytically valuable definition of normality. Thus in studies such as that of midtown Manhattan (662), the amount of impairment (or deviation) that one observes in the population is largely an artifact of one's definition of impairment. If stringent criteria are used, then the number of deviants will be rather small; if a lenient definition is used, then the number of impaired persons will be very large (173; 174; 456). One analysis of prevalence studies in psychiatry found rates of mental disorder to vary from under 1 percent to 64 percent (176). These variations were a result of the different definitions of illness used from one study to another. Although such studies may provide valuable information, often the social relevance of the definitions used is unclear. Such definitions are most useful when we have some independent way to assess their predictive value. We may, for example, be concerned with particular irregularities in heart functioning; if we know through independent studies that those irregularities we have defined and measured are related to future illness and to mortality experience, then we have independent proof of the usefulness and relevance of the definition.

High blood pressure is an important and interesting example of this principle. Such arterial hypertension is extremely common in modern developed nations and is associated with a variety of medical complications and early mortality. Moreover, controlled studies have demonstrated that drug treatment of hypertension results in lowered blood pressure and increased longevity for persons with the condition. However, because there are wide variations in the occurrence of blood-pressure values, it is difficult to define the condition by any single value, although such a point is usually adopted arbitrarily. In most populations studied, arterial blood pressure increases with age and is higher among men than among women. It is also higher among some ethnic and racial groups than others; for example, blacks in the United States have higher blood pressure than whites. These differences are not well understood (212), and thus it is extremely difficult to establish normal values. There is some indication that persons with blood-pressure values in the "high normal" range may benefit from drug treatment to lower their pressure, but there is uncertainty as to the value of treating such persons (9). Part of the difficulty is in the definition of the population used to describe the distribution of blood-pressure values. For example, there is evidence from some nonliterate societies that blood pressure does not necessarily increase with age, and the elevations observed in modern societies may be linked with the demands of competitive industrialized societies (567). Thus, what may be within the normal range for such societies may be high from an evolutionary biological view and may be conducive to sickness and death.

Another difficulty with the positivistic approach is the frequent inability of the investigator to record all or even a significant proportion of the deviations from the defined norm. State and federal investigators discover only a tiny proportion of prescription violators; those who are discovered may be very different from typical violators, and they may have been discovered primarily because of the factors that distinguish them. Similarly, doctors who are sued for medical malpractice constitute only a tiny proportion of those who commit medical malpractice. Independent studies suggest that malpractice suits against doctors are more likely to occur when the doctor-patient relationship has deteriorated. If the doctor-patient relationship is a good one, patients are often willing to forgive even serious errors on the part of the doctor (74). Thus it is evident that although we may be able to state what a deviation is, we may not have the means for recording a representative sample of all such deviations. Only a small fraction of people who violate legal norms are ever identified; even a smaller number are arrested, and of these only very few ultimately are defined as deviants. Thus, studying known violators of particular laws does not necessarily give us a good understanding of typical violators (392). Such studies, therefore, are not concerned with deviation in its original form, but rather characterize a combination of events surrounding deviation, such as the recognition and punishment of the deviant.

The Statistical Approach

Another typical way of approaching the problem of describing norms involves an analysis of observations of what people actually do. A number of years ago Floyd Allport (13) demonstrated what he called the J-curve hypothesis of conforming behavior. His notion was that when a rule is in effect the statistical distribution of behavior relevant to that rule could be described as a J curve in reverse (without the tail of the J being turned up). Allport's data in support of his hypothesis suggested that statistical distributions of behavior may prove useful in attempting to understand the structure of rules underlying behavior. For example, Allport presented observations of motorists' behavior in two situations: the first at stop signs, at cross traffic corners, the second at similar cross traffic corners that have no traffic signals. In the first situation these observations show that 75.5 percent of the drivers stopped, 22 percent proceeded at a very slow speed, 2 percent went through with some slowing of speed, and less than 1 percent retained their original speed. If one plots these percentages, the curve resembles the letter J in reverse. In the second situation, without traffic signals, 17 percent of the drivers stopped, 37 percent went through at a very slow speed, 34 percent diminished their speed slightly, and 12 percent of the drivers retained their original speed. This distribution tends to approximate a normal one. Allport argues that the former type of distribution suggests the presence of a rule, while the latter does not.

Allport presented various other data describing the times people appear at work in the morning, religious attitudes and behavior, and so on. He found support for his idea that statistical distributions can be utilized to describe rules. Obviously the statistical approach by itself is not sufficient to define deviant behavior, but it constitutes a useful aid in analysis.

The statistical approach has been fiercely attacked from time to time. Those who criticize it argue that what people ought to do and what they actually do should not be confused. Many of these criticisms are based on moralistic grounds and have little relevance to the question of the usefulness of the statistical approach. Frequently such criticisms are responses to advocates who argue that community conceptions and law should be made to conform to what people actually do.

The statistical approach is one of the major techniques for arriving at medical norms. Doctors frequently can recognize disease because it becomes apparent that in various ways the patient deviates from "normal values." In many cases the range of normal values has been established through observations of community populations over a period of time and thus marked deviations can easily be determined. Consider, for example, the area of growth and development. Various genetic, congenital, endocrine, and nutritional disorders may become visible through distortions in normal growth and development. It is important for the physician to recognize such deviations as early in life as possible, because through early recognition corrective measures can be taken (453). A physical examination provides the doctor with information about the patient's growth and development along many dimensions: his general appearance, his stature and proportions, size and shape of head, curvature of spine, development of the hair and teeth, and so on. In each case he must compare his observations with values for a normal population of the same age and sex. For example, he will evalute the patient relative to a normal population in terms of height, weight, and body proportions; objective normal values are available in prepared charts for all of these characteristics. Such body dimensions and proportions normally change as growth progresses, and this is why divisions by age are essential. Proportionality of the body, for example, is conveniently measured by developing a ratio of the upper development (trunk) to the lower development (lower extremities). This changes in different periods of the growth cycle; at birth the ratio is approximately 1.7 : 1. The legs grow more rapidly than the trunk, however, and by the time the child reaches the age of 10 or 11 the size of the upper and lower segments are approximately equal (453). Deviations in proportionality may be indicative of a variety of diseases. For example, in hypothyroidism there is a delay in the growth and maturation of skeletal proportions, so that the upper to lower ratio stays high, reflecting a relative immaturity of proportions in relation to the patient's age (453). In contrast, in some conditions the spine may become shortened, and thus the upper to lower ratio may be less than normal in a similar age group. The utility of laboratory tests in medical practice similarly depends upon an accurate knowledge of normal range and average values.

The difficulty with the statistical approach is that, without other information, it fails to provide an appreciation of the significance of deviation from average or normal values. The doctor is not interested in deviations from normal growth for their own sake. Such deviations concern him only when they imply basic disease processes or negative social consequences for the patient. Similarly, sociologists do not give equal attention to all varieties of deviation; rather, they tend to concentrate their efforts in studying deviations that are of consequence for individuals and the society. Thus it should be clear that all deviant values are not similarly defined; such attributes as very high intelligence, excellent physical fitness, and exceptionally honest and moral behavior may be statistically deviant, but they are defined as assets and cause little societal concern. In short, the statistical approach by itself gives us little indication as to the meaning of deviations, their triviality or importance, or whether such traits are assets or liabilities.

If we consider the distribution of human attributes, we can see that doctors and sociologists sometimes concern themselves with deviations at both extremes of the distribution, whereas on other occasions only one extreme is defined as relevant to their concerns. Although there is some attention given to the education and problems of youngsters with particularly high intelligence, doctors, behavioral scientists, and the society at large give more attention to the problems of intellectual subnormality. It is really only the subnormal population that is viewed as a medical and social problem. On other occasions, both ends of the distribution are important. In the example cited earlier on growth, doctors must concern themselves not only with stunted growth, but also with excessive growth. Both dwarfism and gigantism may result from pituitary dysfunctions, and thus both stimulate medical concern.

In short, the statistical approach to deviation is extremely valuable and important to medical and sociological efforts. Unless it is allied with other types of information, however, the approach can be very misleading.

The Social-Reaction Approach

The third approach is an attempt to understand social norms and deviant behavior in terms of the ways people react to deviant signs in other people or in themselves. The basic assumption underlying this approach is that a person's belief that he has a problem, or the belief of others that his behavior constitutes a problem, defines deviation. This view is in line with a long tradition in social analysis exemplified by the observation of W. I. Thomas that when men define situations as real, they are real in their consequences (701; 751). Thus a person who convinces himself that he is sick is a problem to himself and others despite the doctor's assessment that he suffers from no disease. Indeed, the patient's inability or refusal to accept the medical opinion concerning his condition marks him as different from the average. The social response approach emphasizes the manner in which particular attributes become identified as different, the ways they are reacted to and defined, and the ultimate condemnation or approval that may follow.

Social reactions to deviation include two components: self-definitions and social responses. Self-definition refers to the way in which the person comes to regard himself, the values to which he becomes committed, and the investments he makes in other people and activities; in other words, it defines the individual's self-identity. Social reactions refer, in contrast, to the identities that other people attribute to the individual. When we consider social reactions, we may concern ourselves only with the identity attributed to a person by some of his significant relations: his spouse, parents, or friends. On other occasions it becomes important also to study the reactions of others: workmates, employers, and various social and official agencies. In rarer circumstances it becomes necessary to consider the reactions of the mass media and even general public opinion if we are to obtain a relevant view of a person's social identity. It should be clear that because there are many groups that can assign social identities to others, a person may have many different social identities assigned to him at the same time.

This third approach usually involves the assumption that social reactions follow behavior that is regarded by the defining group as deviant. Consider again the earlier example of doctors sued for medical malpractice. The social response—a legal suit against the doctor—implies that the doctor has deviated from the defining group's expectations of him. However, the doctor may not have committed medical malpractice in the opinion of his colleagues; indeed, the social response may be as much a product of those who define the act as it is of those acts being defined. There is some reason to believe that not only do certain types of doctor get sued, but also certain kinds of patient tend to sue them.

An important limitation of the social-reaction approach in assessing amounts of deviant behavior is that only a very small proportion of deviant behavior calls forth visible or significant social reactions. As we have already noted, a tiny proportion of all cases of medical malpractice lead to a legal suit (708). The patient may have no desire to sue or, more likely, may not be aware that medical malpractice has taken place. Moreover, the ability to initiate litigation depends on finding a lawyer willing to take the case and on obtaining medical testimony supporting the claim. Although more apparent responses are likely to follow visible and serious deviations, there is no simple one-to-one relationship between degree of deviation and social response. Also, errors or distortions in social reactions may be motivated and planned by particular groups in the community. Indeed, much of social and political activity involves attempts by specific groups to influence and mold the types of social reactions made by others in the community to particular forms of behavior. Thus social reactions and social notions of deviant behavior are always to some extent in a state of flux.

Analysis of social responses to alleged deviation is important not only for studying deviant behavior but also in that they reveal the adaptive needs and responses of individuals, groups, and organizations that attempt to influence social definitions. Social agencies may wage campaigns against alleged deviants for political and organizational reasons unrelated to the seriousness of the problem (427). Police harassment of known deviants may reflect political pressures and changes in public opinion. Vociferous complaints by doctors in prepaid practice about patients who present trivial and inappropriate complaints reflect in part the doctors' heavy workload, the organization of medical practice, and the climate of medical politics (500). If the doctor received a fee for each such consultation, it is unlikely that he would feel so strongly about such "deviants." Hospitals, private organizations, and government agencies frequently have a stake in promoting attention to particular problems, even when these problems have diminished greatly in importance, as administrators are usually loath to have their agencies or institutions closed or phased out. Similarly, medical organizations have developed particular identities that are no longer fully appropriate but they are very slow in shifting their efforts to new problems, although they must eventually do so if they are to survive.

The social-reaction approach to deviation is an important tool in sociological analysis, and some students of deviance have even used it for the development of a sequential model of deviant behavior (50; 616). However, the social approach is not very important or useful in the development of medical norms, although social reactions indirectly influence the doctor's work. The doctor's social role involves much more than is encompassed in the application of statistical norms concerning physiological and psychological functioning. He is expected to provide help and assistance to persons who are distressed for a variety of reasons not specifically related to disease. To say that someone is physically ugly or too hairy is a social definition, but the doctor may do what he can in improving the person's appearance even though no disease is involved. Much of the average doctor's time is spent in managing situations, many of which are the product of social reactions in the wider community.

I have tried to show how various approaches to deviant behavior are useful in social analysis and in understanding how medical norms are developed. Medical norms are both positivistic and statistical, and the work of the doctor may be molded by the social context in which problems are defined. We will see more clearly later, when we consider the doctor's approach to the patient in more detail, how these approaches merge in medical contexts. From the perspective of behavioral analysis, we can see that no single approach covers the full scope of deviant behavior and reactions to deviant behavior. However, by linking these approaches we can generate several interesting questions that give us a useful frame of reference for analyzing deviant response. We all can agree that social life and social interaction are governed by norms and standards; we can similarly agree that deviations from these standards occur; finally, there is no doubt that reactions of varying intensity develop in response to deviation, and efforts of differing magnitudes are made to intervene in various situations and remedy deviations. Given the acceptance of these principles, several research questions become evident: Under what conditions does deviant response arise? When deviation occurs, what factors determine the definition of the deviation and the intensity of the social reaction to it? What factors lead to the repetition and continuation of deviant response? We shall develop these questions in later chapters. Before leaving the present topic, however, we must deal with one question thus far neglected: In what ways is illness a deviant response?

Illness as Deviant Behavior

Deviant behavior can be viewed from many different perspectives. The two most influential of those used in evaluations of deviation are the "health-illness" perspective and "goodness-badness" perspective. Whether one or the other of these perspectives is more likely to be adopted depends on the form that deviant behavior takes, the characteristics of the actor, and the social climate within which the social dialogue develops.

It is important to note that views of deviation are conditioned by two conflicting philosophical conceptions that most of us accept concurrently. On the one hand, our legal system and much of social life are based on the assumption that man is able to control his actions and must be held accountable for his behavior. Scientific efforts, however, are based on the differing conception that nature and the behavior of people rest upon some underlying order. A science of behavior would not be possible if we assumed that the ways people behave are largely a product of the exercise of man's will and reason. Such a science is viable only if we assume that human development is a consequence of a particular developmental and evolutionary history. There is no scientific way of resolving this philosophical dilemma, although much has been written on the topic. In social life, however, both views are important, and on the whole we tend to tread a middle path, often accepting the assumption of man's accountability for his behavior, but at the same time arbitrarily recognizing certain exceptions to this assumption. From the behavioral scientist's point of view, it is illuminating to study which exclusions to accountability are accepted and which are considered doubtful, and to understand the ways these definitions vary in different social contexts and in changing circumstances.

The debate as to the extent of man's accountability is ongoing, and the definitions of appropriate exclusions are always in flux. Many "exclusions" are issues of active debate, such as whether and to what extent particular kinds of violator should be excluded from criminal responsibility because of mental illness (see, for example, 87; 180; 267; 309; 544; 695; 785). Rehabilitation and therapeutic personnel tend to attack the legalistic concept of *mens rea* (guilty mind) and seek what they believe is a more humanitarian and intelligent view of the violator. In contrast, many of those who defend the basic assumptions of our legal system emphasize that it is important to our system of social order to view man as a responsible agent. We will reserve discussion of these issues until a later chapter; at this point it is essential to recognize that the philosophical concepts of will and determinism have an important bearing on definitions of deviation and ways of dealing with the deviant.

If for the moment we exclude self-definitions of deviation (such as in the case of the person who feels ill and seeks the help of a doctor), we might note that deviation becomes visible to people in the community when they recognize a person's inability or reluctance to respond in a particular expected way (in terms of normative expectations) (477). The view taken of the deviant depends in large part on the frame of reference of the observer and the extent to which the deviant appears to be able or willing to control his responses. The evaluator views the act within the context of what he believes the actor's motivation to be. If the behavior appears reasonable in terms of the assumed motivation of the actor, there is a good chance that deviant behavior will be defined in terms of the goodness-badness dimension. If the behavior appears to be peculiar and at odds with expectations of the motivations of a reasonable person, such behavior is more likely to be characterized in terms of the sickness dimension. In those cases where the evaluator feels unable to empathize with the actor and finds it difficult to understand what motives may have led to the response, he is likely to characterize the behavior as "strange" or "sick." For example, most people would find it difficult to understand why a rich woman should be found stealing food from the local grocery, and such a person is likely to be viewed within the context of "sickness" rather than "badness." The same act committed by a less wealthy person would more likely be seen within the "badness" perspective. The difference in definition lies not only in the act but also in the motivation imputed to the actor.

Most physical illnesses (deviations from medically derived standards of normal functioning) fall within definitions of "sickness" rather than "badness." We rarely hold people responsible or accountable for their physical ills, and although persons might not always take necessary precautions to avoid risks of illness, we assume that illness is an event that happens to people and that it is not motivated. There are, of course, occasions on which physical illness may be viewed as "badness" if there is reason to believe that the patient's condition was self-inflicted for special advantages, as may happen, for example, among soldiers who wish to avoid combat and obtain release from the armed services. And there are other situations in which patients are considered "malingerers" because no clear evidence of illness can be found, and others become suspicious of the patient's motivation (621). In such cases doctors and other evaluators may be dubious as to whether the patient's condition is really an *event* (something that happens to a person involuntarily) or a motivated reaction. Most often, clear physical complaints and difficulties in functioning are viewed as sickness.

Some conditions raise doubts as to the appropriate perspective to be used in evaluating a patient's complaint. When the patient complains frequently, and when it may be difficult to find tangible evidence either to substantiate or to account for the complaint, questions may be raised concerning the patient's desire to avoid obligations and use illness as an excuse. Similarly, the person's significant others (dependents and intimates) are less likely to accept such complaints, as compared with more clear-cut physical signs, unless they are diagnosed as "true illness" by a doctor. The visibility of illness plays some part in others' accepting a definition of "sickness," especially in circumstances in which there is some reason for doubting the patient's motives. Even when there is no visible symptomatology, deviation is usually accepted as a true "sickness" unless the doctor himself raises doubts because an individual's significant others and those who may have direct authority over him (such as an employer) will frequently accept the professional medical assessment without serious question (474).

Problems related to visibility arise particularly in the case of patients who are at risk, such as those with high blood pressure but who may neither feel sick nor appear ill to others. Under conditions of low visibility it not only is more difficult to get others to recognize one's limitations and needs, but also one's own motivation to adhere to a continuing medical regimen may be more difficult to sustain (45).

Difficulties of definition arise most frequently in psychiatric and behavioral disorders, and in such circumstances the community is uncertain as to whether a definition of "sickness" or of "badness" is more appropriate. From a social-development point of view, which regards deviance as an adaptation to a particular history of biological, environmental, and sociocultural events, any behavior can be subsumed under the "sickness" perspective. The decision to call certain patterns, such as alcoholism, homosexuality, or criminality, "sickness" is arbitrary, and such decisions tend to have a higher political than scientific content. As attitudes and values of the larger society change, definitions of "sickness" and "badness" are also in flux, and concepts may be refined in terms of a new social consensus. The process can lead to redefinitions in either direction, as in the current tendency to view alcoholism more as an illness and homosexuality more as an alternative life style. While it is possible to demonstrate emotional difficulties among most deviants, it is difficult to establish that such difficulties have any direct relationship to the particular deviance involved. Moreover, most people who have emotional problems do not engage in any obvious deviant pattern. The ambiguity of the relationship between emotional problems

and patterns of deviance allows for considerable discretion in definition, and thus the way a particular deviant is handled may reflect situational contingencies and administrative needs more than the specific
behavior involved or the person's needs, to the extent that these can be
ascertained. There is considerable overlap in behavioral manifestations,
for example, between violators who are sent to psychiatric institutions
and those found in prisons; the variation in disposition may reflect the
manner in which the person came to the attention of the authorities, the
availability of certain facilities, or disagreements among psychiatric experts and judges as to the proper distinctions between sickness and
badness. Some psychiatric disturbances are more easily and reliably
recognized than others. But psychiatric diagnostic systems often
include ambiguously defined residual categories, such as "the inadequate personality" or "the disordered personality," that clearly overlap
with public and community conceptions of "badness."

Having placed the concept of illness within the general context of
the sociology of deviant behavior, we will now move on to consider
various behavioral-science perspectives in medical sociology.

Chapter 2

BEHAVIORAL-SCIENCE PERSPECTIVES

If the concept of health is defined in a negative fashion—that is, as the absence of apparent disease and infirmity—then it is possible arbitrarily to regard all persons who do not feel ill, and who show no evident signs of illness on careful examination, as healthy. This concept seems very restricted when compared with the definition offered by the World Health Organization, which describes health as a state of "complete physical, mental, and social well-being, and not merely the absence of disease and infirmity" (473, p. 28). The broadness of this definition makes it inapplicable for differentiating the healthy from the sick in an operational sense, and thus it is not very useful except as a guide to the broad dimensions of health and a reminder that even physical well-being is dependent on the contexts in which we live, our associations with others, and the physical and social assaults to which our living situation exposes us. Understanding the implications of the concepts of health and disease is essential, even if they are difficult to define and measure precisely. Moreover, even from a practical standpoint, we must come to appreciate that in the long run our well-being is less dependent on the elegance and sophistication of medical practice than on how we choose to live and what is done to the environment in which we live. Moreover, much of our physical vitality comes from active involvement and a sense of meaning in daily activities and relationships with others. To deny this is to see man as nothing more than a machine and the members of the health professions as mere tinkerers, maintenance men, and engineers. In the sections that follow I consider the major behavioral dimensions of the health-illness continuum and begin to illustrate the inadequacy of the man-machine analogy. Before discussing these, however, it is necessary to consider briefly some aspects of biological adaptation.

The Biological Perspective

The biological perspective has traditionally been the most important aspect of medical science, and the major part of a physician's training is devoted to biological theories of bodily functioning and disease. But even biological factors must be understood in light of the environments in which they operate. The external environment makes particular demands upon bodily functioning, and the body adapts to these demands in both a physiological and evolutionary sense. It is fairly obvious that man's physical development and physical adaptations depend in part on the demands his environments make of him. His muscles and physical fortitude are in part the result of the efforts his environment demands, and of the physical skills necessary for survival. Biological adaptations to environment, weather, altitude, and so on, may vary from one physical context to another. For example, the Aymara Indians of the Lake Titicaca region in the Peruvian Andes adapt to life at an extremely high altitude. The Indians have developed large chests, great depths of respiration, and blood rich in hemoglobin. These physical adaptations permit them to engage in vigorous physical effort in areas above 12,500 feet, where we would tire rapidly because of the low oxygen supply (186). Similarly, anthropologists have described various primitive groups that can sleep in the open in extremely cold weather quite comfortably without clothes or blankets. The tremendous ability of biological systems to adapt in a functional way to external conditions is indeed remarkable, and René Dubos offers a fascinating discussion of some of these biological adaptations in his interesting books, *Mirage of Health* (186) and *Man Adapting* (187)

Environments are continuously changing, and man adapts to these changes not only in a social and psychological sense, but also, as noted, in a biological sense. His body accommodates to new threats and challenges, and through such accommodations biological homeostasis is maintained. But these biological accommodations to changing environments also may be disruptive in that they cause personal discomfort and strain to the biological organism. Similarly, social adaptation to new patterns of culture and new ways of living may pose serious threats to the body's integrity. Thus, although the body may accommodate to environmental changes, these adaptations also cause problems of health and disease.

In one sense disease is a biological adaption. It is an outgrowth of the body's accommodation to internal stresses and noxious external conditions. Since particular biological adjustments result in personal pain and discomfort and threaten longevity and capacity for activity, societies have always had a place for practitioners who attempt to influence the course of biological adaptation in a more benevolent direction.

Aubrey Lewis (435) has noted three traditional medical criteria in identifying disease: (1) the patient's experience of subjective feelings of
sickness; (2) the finding that he has some disordered function of some
part; and (3) symptoms that conform to a recognizable clinical pattern
(that is, they fit a typological theory of disease held by the diagnos-
tician). In short, a person is found to be diseased when his symptoms
and complaints, or the indications from physical and laboratory investigation, fit a model of disease assumed by the doctor.

Although the specific details of the biological approach are outside
the sphere of this book, it will be necessary to consider diagnostic medical models if we are to gain some perspective on the way the doctor as-
sesses the patient. The details of the medical model of disease are discussed more appropriately within the context of chapter 3, which considers the doctor's approach to the patient. We now turn more directly
to a discussion of behavioral perspectives in medical sociology.

The Cultural Perspective

The cultural approach to health involves study of the relationships between cultural content and cultural life styles, and between definitions
of health and responses to illness. Cultural patterns and typical ways of
life give substance to the manner in which illness is perceived,
expressed, and reacted to. To some extent the cultural context defines
the conditions that are recognized, the causes to be attributed to them,
and the persons who have legitimate authority to assess and define
such conditions. Similarly, cultural definitions influence the consequences of being defined as having a particular condition. Many
traditional Mexican Americans, for example, recognize several "illnesses" that occur within their group which they believe do not occur
among Anglo-Americans. These conditions include *caida de la mollera*
(fallen fontanel), *mal ojo* (evil eye), *susto* (shock), and *mal puesto* (sorcery). It is believed that "Anglo" doctors do not understand these conditions, and help for them is sought from local folk practitioners. Although these conditions are seen as superstitions by Anglo-Americans,
it is clear that they are seen as important life crises by some Mexican
Americans, and such conditions are treated as meaningful within the
cultural group context (602).

Similarly, as Linton noted, the manifest forms taken by many illness
conditions (particularly hysteria) are culturally patterned (449). He
believed further that if one knew the content of the culture, one could
predict in a fairly reliable fashion the form this condition would take.
Although Linton's optimistic contention remains to be demonstrated,
it is fairly clear that the social course of many illnesses is largely

influenced by the cultural content of a society and is well integrated with the patterns of life as they exist in that culture. This is illustrated nicely in Linton's discussion of *tromba*, a form of violent possession (or what we might regard as a form of psychosis), which is defined as a state of being possessed by an ancestral spirit:

> This seizure usually followed a period of frustration and of conflict. Eventually the increasingly disturbed individual would be conscious of a mounting tension. Suddenly everything would waver in front of his eyes. Then the individual becomes unconscious for a brief period, falls down and then picks himself up again and begins to dance. Sometimes he goes directly into a dance without this momentary unconsciousness. . . . The most important thing is that, as long as the person is possessed, all his orders have to be fulfilled under pain of incurring the hostility of the spirit. . . . I know that an old woman, who seems to be rheumatic and decrepit, will dance sometimes for forty-eight hours at a stretch, and dance down one partner after another, so shifts of dancers and of drummers have to be provided. . . . Individuals who have this form of possession are regarded as a nuisance, because one can't really get anything out of the spirits. Therefore, their demands are a sort of supernatural blackmail. Yet, one can readily see that such seizures work to the advantage of the possessed, since the family is rather reluctant to cause them to have a *tromba* seizure by frustrating them [449, pp. 128–29].

Perhaps the most impressive phenomenon that anthropologists have observed regarding health is the apparent effect of sorcery performed on persons who believe in the effectiveness of this phenomenon. Several cases of death following sorcery involving young healthy persons have been witnessed by different observers. Walter Cannon (103), who attempted to analyze this phenomenon from the physiological point of view, came to the following conclusion:

> A persistent and profound emotional state may induce a disastrous fall of blood pressure, ending in death. Lack of food and drink would collaborate with the damaging emotional effects, to induce the fatal outcome. These are the conditions which, as we have seen, are prevalent in persons who have been reported as dying as a consequence of sorcery. They go without food or water as they, in their isolation, wait in fear for their impending death. In these circumstances they might well die from a state of shock, in the surgical sense—a shock induced by prolonged and tense emotion [103, p. 179].

The culture of a group affects every aspect of growth and development, the acquisition of goals and aspirations, the risk factors to which one is exposed and modes of response and adaptation. From conception to death, almost every major life experience is conditioned to some extent by cultural beliefs and orientations. Who is eligible to mate, forms of contraception, family size and spacing, feeding and weaning—these and many more depend on social customs and taboos. The mother's acquisition of health values and mothering skills affects the development of the young and may explain in part why mothers in the more advantaged classes and those who are better educated experience lower infant mortality. Similarly, nutrition is a key factor in health, but food preparation and eating behavior are influenced by cultural norms. Culture determines modes of agriculture, production, food processing, and promotion. While in much of the world persons consume diets often deficient in protein, calories, and vitamins, in developed nations diets rich in fats, sugars, calories, and additives are implicated in various diseases, including diabetes, cancer, and coronary heart disease.

Despite the subsistence economies of traditional societies, most mothers who followed traditional cultural patterns of breast feeding could provide their infants with adequate nutrition, at least prior to weaning. With the diffusion of modern infant-feeding practices in which formulas replace breast feeding, new problems arise in the nutrition of the young. In many underdeveloped countries, there is a marked departure from breast feeding, yet families cannot afford sufficient quantities of commercially available formulas and lack the knowledge and sanitary conditions necessary to prepare them adequately (787). With the abundance of commercially available fast foods and highly promoted foods of low nutritional quality, there is increasing evidence of malnutrition among middle-class youngsters in contemporary American society as well.

It is a truism that the health of a people reflects the way it chooses to live, but it remains a point of great significance. Patterns of illness and death in society are very much influenced by values affecting organization of the family, work, and recreation. Behaviors surrounding smoking, the use of alcohol and other drugs, diet, exercise, and driving constitute major risk factors in heart disease, cancer, accidents, and cirrhosis of the liver (223; 407). Man's constructed environment is a major cause of most cancers and accidents. Cultural patterns affecting child rearing, the family, social aspirations and competition, and decreasing social solidarity probably also contribute to the high rates of psychological distress, suicide, and violence characteristic of many modern technological nations. Moreover, there is growing indication that the so-called Type-A personality pattern, typical of many people in Western societies and characterized by a driving competitiveness, concern with time, and generalized hostility, is an important risk factor in coronary heart disease and perhaps in other illnesses as well (248).

Subcultures within American society are associated with substantially different risks of poor health and death. While such differences cannot be entirely separated from biological and genetic factors as-

sociated with population selection and assortative mating, even biological processes are influenced by sociocultural processes. Group norms
concerning smoking, drinking, sexual practices, and standards of living
either predispose or protect adherents from risks of disease. A study in
the Los Angeles area found that Seventh-Day Adventists—a sect that
disapproves of smoking—had an incidence of lung cancer that was one-
eighth the incidence found in the control group (750). Comparisons of
Utah and Nevada—states very similar in income, education, and medical facilities—show vast differences in mortality; the much lower rates
of death in Utah are probably attributable to the Mormon population,
which disapproves of the use of alcohol and tobacco and encourages a
quiet, regularized, and spiritual life [257, pp. 52-54]. Perhaps the largest influence in the prevalence of obesity is social class. While obesity
affects social class to some degree because of social discrimination of
the obese, the factors encompassed by social class have a clear
etiological impact. Similarly, obesity varies substantially among ethnic
groups (678, pp. 144–49).

As the child develops in any culture, he learns the acceptable
modes of coping with the usual tasks relating to subsistence, social
relations, and community obligations. He acquires a conception of himself and others, instrumental and expressive skills, and psychological
defenses through which he protects his place in his group and his self-
image. Such conditioning may be more or less consonant with the
challenges of daily living; when groups are subjected to rapid social
change, long-accepted patterns of cultural adaptation break down, subjecting individuals and groups to higher risks of social disruption,
disease, and death. Communities undergoing rapid transition are characterized by high rates of social pathology and disease, in part a product of the inadequacy of old solutions, in part the result of the breakdown of traditional supports before they have been replaced by new
sociocultural patterns.

Cultural conditioning may contribute to or insulate individuals
from serious health problems. Controlled drinking associated with
religious Jewish culture and the condemnation of drunkenness characteristic of Jewish values result in low rates of alcoholism in this group,
although with increasing secularization Jewish alcoholism is becoming
more common (656). High rates of alcoholism among the Irish are attributable to a learned permissive drinking pattern that tends to be exacerbated under stress. Thus Irish immigrants to the United States,
faced with the harsh conditions of a new and unfamiliar environment,
adapted with very high rates of alcoholism (41). Mormons, by contrast,
who forbid drinking, have low rates. Unlike Jews, however, Mormons
who use alcohol have been found to have a higher risk of developing

problems associated with its use (676). Traditional sex roles in Western societies that discouraged women from smoking and drinking insulated them from risks of lung cancer, alcoholism, and other diseases. With the movement toward equality in sex roles and changes in the limits of acceptable behavior for men and women, women's rates of lung cancer and alcoholism have been increasing.

Even on the grossest level of cultural generalization, cultural beliefs have a profound influence on the health of people. Indians may starve but they are reluctant to kill their cattle and will even share their homes and scarce food with them. They will often allow monkeys to plunder their crops because they similarly define the monkey as sacred. Faced by a growing population, food shortages, and competition with animals whom they will not harm, they have responded by attempting to control the cattle population through contraceptive devices. Health experts who work in cultures other than our own have frequently found it difficult to convince people of the protective value of immunization, decontaminated water supplies, and other health measures, without reinterpreting these measures so that they fit common cultural conceptions (473). Some problems in public health work not only illustrate the importance of culture, but also show why public health programs must take such factors into consideration:

1. Health officials attempt to persuade villagers in underdeveloped countries to build latrines. Even when built, they are often not used because they are inconsistent with traditional forms of behavior, or because their location interferes with cultural concepts of modesty or typical patterns of interaction. Going out "into the fields" to relieve oneself can be both a biological and social event.

2. For people to whom family and companionship is a central value (e.g., Burmese, American Navaho, Spanish Americans), the hospital is perceived as a threatening place. Rules of isolation for infectious diseases, visiting regulations, and other restrictions produce a feeling of "aloneness" when people in these cultures may feel the greatest need for companionship and expect a large amount of familial attention.

3. People in many cultures are oriented to the present rather than the future. Thus they are reluctant to undergo pain and discomfort to achieve some future protection against disease, unless these protections are offered in a fashion consistent with other cultural beliefs, values, and goals.

4. Consider the example of the Tiv, an African tribe in southern Nigeria. Apparently the principle of inoculation was consistent with Tiv cultural ideas, since inoculation against smallpox was

known and practiced before the arrival of the Europeans. However, attempts in some regions to vaccinate the population during a smallpox epidemic caused the Tiv to flee in terror. One explanation is that they viewed the conditions and procedures involving vaccination as magically septic and feared exposing themselves to magical death.

5. Public health personnel frequently find it difficult to change people's diets because social and religious ideas as well as nutritional ones, are associated with food. Certain foods are religiously unacceptable; other foods must be prepared in particular ways if group taboos are not to be violated. In other cases the introduction of new foods disrupts the pattern of family and group associations. Therefore, any attempt to introduce changes must consider making these new patterns consistent with dominant-group conceptions and behavior.

Existing cultural values in our own society promote a wide range of threats to health that are so familiar that they hardly need recitation. At the level of personal health behavior, advertising and peer culture promote smoking, consumption of alcoholic beverages and junk food, and the use of unnecessary drugs. Production processes increasingly pollute the environment, not only with foul-smelling and unesthetic wastes but also with large numbers of substances that are carcinogenic or conducive to other health problems. Our media, particularly television, promote violence and passive learning, and our automobile culture is not only a major factor in the occurrence of death and disability but also contributes indirectly to sedentary living, disruption of community, and pollution.

Yet we know that most people are resistant to giving up the benefits associated with these health hazards. The automobile provides personal mobility and convenience that are not easily replicated by public transportation systems. Junk foods are readily accessible with minimal or no preparation. The same processes that produce environmental pollution also produce jobs and incomes for many people. In short, conflicting interests are at stake, and those who gain the advantages are not necessarily those who most bear the costs. The environmental movement has contributed importantly in making clear the costs as well as the benefits of industrial and commercial development. When there are conflicts at issue, health factors may not always be very high in the priorities of those who make decisions, but the new consciousness of risks to health and the environment is to some extent affecting the calculus of decision. Even if it seems compelling to move ahead in certain areas despite health risks, careful consideration of both risks and benefits, as well as of those who are advantaged or disadvantaged by any decision, increases the possibility of minimizing threats to health and of allocating the costs of such preventive measures more fairly among the parties involved. For example, industry must assume more of the costs related to the adverse consequences of production processes by developing means to minimize pollution and other health risks. We are moving away from the concept that the adverse effects of production must be borne by the community rather than by those who produce these effects. Such costs, of course, are usually passed on to consumers in the form of higher prices. When prices reflect the true costs of producing a product, those who consume that particular product pay the costs as compared with others who do not. For example, if the costs of a product do not reflect the cost of cleaning up the pollution resulting from its production or use, then all people in the community share that cost, whether or not they use the product. However, when the price of the product also reflects pollution control, the costs of such control are placed more directly on those who use the product.

There is little question that the cultural patterns of modern developed nations that put great emphasis on materialism and competition create much personal distress and vulnerability to a variety of chronic illnesses. Many of these patterns are beyond the capacities of individuals to affect, such as the levels of dangerous pollutants in the air, risks to life and health in the work place, and fluctuations in the business cycle and employment opportunities. Only by collective action is it possible to have an impact on such risks, which inevitably involve a clash of varying interests in society. Many risks, however, also result from more mundane patterns of recreation, life style, and social and moral predispositions. Our moral codes continue to give great emphasis to policing crimes without victims, to denying contraceptive advice to people who need it, to making it difficult for persons of limited means to obtain abortions, and so on. Reluctance to provide particular kinds of help may reflect the political balance of the community and the cultural beliefs and values of those groups that are most dominant. In short, much of what we are willing and unwilling to undertake in the area of public health reflects dominant cultural beliefs and the balance among different subgroups having somewhat different subcultures. Such situations in a dynamic society such as our own are always in flux, and an area that is taboo in one period may become the cause of community action at some other time. One need look no further than the past decade to see some dramatic changes in governmental activity that would have been inconceivable a decade earlier: community birth-control clinics, community-organization programs to develop power blocs among deprived groups, increasing participation of government in the health-care field, and so on. It is inevitable that government efforts in many areas of health concern will be accelerated significantly in coming years.

The Social Perspective

The social perspective, although it overlaps the cultural one to some extent, directs attention specifically to the requirements of family life, work, and social activities generally. Here we are concerned with the manner in which human qualities and responses fit social demands and the physical and economic environments. In any system of communal activity there is a wide array of possibilities for fitting particular people into varied social niches. Failure in biological adaptation may depend not only upon the personal characteristics of people, but also upon the degree of fit between the person and the social positions he assumes or which are thrust upon him. There are some situations that most people would find difficult; other situations are more trying to some than to others. Social adaptation is a complex process involving a person's psychological and instrumental capacities, his skills and training, the extent of social support and assistance, the magnitude and nature of the demands his physical and social environments make upon him, and the fit between the person's qualities and these demands. Although there are some rare individuals who deal brilliantly with almost any situation, most of us perform better in some spheres than in others, and frequently the difference between success and failure is a consequence of the manner in which we are called upon to participate. Studies of the performance of soldiers show, for example, that some who made a poor social adaptation to army conditions were able to make a satisfactory adjustment when removed from these conditions, while others who performed well in the armed forces had difficulties in meeting social demands in other life contexts (263). In short, persons with similar capacities, skills, and training may make a more or less adequate adjustment to their circumstances, depending on the rigor of the demands they must face and the peculiar form these demands may take. Particular personality traits that are useful in one context may constitute distinct liabilities in other situations.

The social perspective also takes into account the norms involving sickness and response to sickness. The social context determines the conditions under which one can claim illness and be released from usual obligations and responsibilities without stigma. Sociologists have treated the social definition of illness in terms of the concept of the sick role, which has been conceptualized as an ideal type for the purpose of attempting to define the social properties of sickness definitions, the conditions under which persons can legitimately claim illness, and their responsibilities in responding to their illness (549). Although attempts have been made to state theoretically the specific norms applying to sickness situations, it is clear that the sick role is not a single concept that applies equally to all people who claim illness, but varies considerably with the person, the conditions involved, and the social context within which illness is claimed. I shall have more to say about this later in the volume.

I have already referred to the social aspects of problems in discrimination between badness and sickness. A related problem concerns the issue of threat or danger and its relevance in evaluating ill people. In general, we tend to regard illness as an individual concern, and what people do to care for themselves is for the most part dependent on their own judgment. There are, however, circumstances in which illness is of sufficient threat to the community to lead to some form of community action. Obviously, if too many people in a society are sick or disabled and if there is a shortage of manpower, sickness will have serious implications for productivity, the family, and the community. On other occasions illnesses are seen as endangering others as well as the person directly involved, and thus governments assume the right to intervene in illness and to instate measures to protect the health and welfare of the community. Governments not only assume the power to remove and isolate certain contagious persons, but also the right to license public facilities and personnel who may pose particular threats to the health of the population, such as those who handle and serve food in restaurants. On the whole there is nothing very complex about the use of such government powers, since we start with the basic assumption that government can intervene in situations wherein persons pose threats for the community. Careful study of intervention in health affairs, however, will show that the decisions to regulate some things and not others are not always fully rational or consistent with the degree of threat posed, but are very much influenced by public passions, social frames of reference, and the power of the various participants.

The approach to health dominant in modern nations has been called the engineering perspective (350; 567). While medicine is oriented to modifying individual biological processes, most major health risks transcend the individual, and their elimination may require collective action. Governments for the most part have skirted the issue of collective interventions since they raise so many issues of a social, political, and economic character. By treating medical care as a simple transaction between patient and doctor, it has been possible to neutralize what is substantially a political matter. As the industrial and community environments of modern societies have become more complex and pose more obvious threats, not only of increased disease but also of major disasters, governments can no longer maintain the illusion that health is a concern divorced from larger social processes and social conditions.

One area in which government was willing to impose itself through the legal process was in dealing with bizarre and disruptive individuals who could not accommodate themselves to a complex, industrialized society and could not easily be contained within the increasingly mobile nuclear family. With industrialization and urbanization came the growth of the large custodial mental hospital and use of the legal process to keep individuals in these institutions against their will (488). The irony was that while mental patients were incarcerated ostensibly to be treated for their own good, very little actual care was provided, and these hospitals often had devastating effects on the patient's ability to sustain any coping skills for dealing with the outside world. In recent years there has been a major shift in the use of the legal process to contain deviance related to mental illness, and involuntary commitment processes for the mentally ill have become much more rigorous. Moreover, courts increasingly insist on the "least restrictive alternative" and the "right to treatment," vastly changing the manner in which mental patients are dealt with (497, pp. 227–48). The shift in processes for dealing with the mentally ill was related to many factors, including appreciation of the detrimental effects of large custodial institutions, development of new drug technologies, growth of confidence about the ability to treat most patients in community settings, growing costs of keeping large numbers of persons in custodial institutions (often for life), growth of a vigorous civil-liberties movement and legal efforts on behalf of the mentally ill, and increased tolerance for deviance within the society in general. The role of government thus reflects a wide variety of social conditions and ideological orientations and has only limited relationship to the magnitude of threat posed in any particular area.

Social analysis of the factors leading to differential treatment of persons with various illnesses and behavior problems not only helps us to understand the social context of illness but also illuminates social processes and social points of view generally. Relevant to an analogous issue in the field of criminology, Sutherland (689) has pointed to a large variety of offenses involving social harm that are not usually treated as crimes; when action is taken in these cases it is typically within the confines of the civil rather than the criminal courts. Because this category of "crimes" involves those most usually committed by businessmen and persons with upper-class status in the course of their occupations, Sutherland called them "white-collar crimes" and believed that these differing social and legal definitions were a result of the high status typical of such violators. Mental patients, in contrast, were frequently detained involuntarily, not usually because of their particular social status, but because it was commonly assumed that persons exhibiting bizarre symptoms are not in a position to appraise their situation rationally and thus to ascertain what is best for them. Although several analysts challenged the presumption that the mental patient could not make rational decisions about his own welfare (see 695; 696), this view was commonly held by laymen and professionals who worked with the mentally ill, and frequently was cited as justification for taking action against the person's stated wish.

Still another factor influencing differential response is the symbolic character of particular kinds of deviant behavior. Although we may feel threatened by drunken drivers, the concept itself is not unfamiliar to us. Most people drink at one time or another and most people drive. Given the nature of social life it is not puzzling that the two activities frequently merge, and when we think of the drunken driver we tend frequently to think of people like us who perhaps made a mistake in judgment in combining these two activities. In contrast, the image of the drug addict or the child molester is less familiar. We find it more difficult to perceive ourselves, our friends, or our neighbors in this position, and thus we feel more threatened and alarmed about such deviation. The image of the molester is reinforced by our awareness of the friendliness and vulnerability of children and by the high value we place upon them. Thus, although the molester may be for the most part a fairly harmless person who seeks undue familiarity with children and who may obtain sexual satisfaction from fondling them, the defining picture of this kind of deviant in the layman's mind is the rather rare and unusual case in which the deviant commits a brutal and violent crime. In general, we are much less threatened by behavior that we understand than by patterns that are unfamiliar and that puzzle us, and often such stereotypes are given priority, as opposed to the actual amount of harm resulting from a particular category of offenders.

Illness and Disability

In using the social perspective, one of the most important distinctions is that between illness and disability. Illnesses vary widely in the degree of disability they necessitate, and the same illness may produce considerable variation in disability among persons so afflicted. Although the "illness condition" itself may be an important contributor to disability, many other factors not associated with the illness may influence the extent to which the person feels unable to undertake a variety of activities. Illness is frequently regarded as disabling when the person's physical or physiological condition makes it impossible for him to perform his usual role obligations. But it is important to note that this is as dependent on the nature of his role obligations and his attitude toward them as it is on his physical condition. It is also dependent on the attitudes and reactions of family members, employers, and physicians (8). A permanent leg injury may lead to complete disability for a stevedore, but the same injury suffered by a college professor would hardly interfere with his activities at all. Similarly, the length of disability following illness or injury will depend on the physical and mental requirements particular occupations demand.

As soon as one begins to consider disability as a phenomenon separate from illness, it becomes apparent how complex and multidimensional it is. Because disability is usually a temporary condition, persons are encouraged to take whatever measures possible to overcome it. There are, however, some chronic and serious conditions that disable the person more or less permanently. Such is the situation when a person becomes blind, or develops paraplegia, deafness, or some other condition that renders his ability to occupy normal social roles either limited or doubtful. In such cases, family members have to change their expectations of the individual and tolerate his inability to do many of the things he previously did. In the past persons who became so handicapped were almost always denied admission to any kind of occupational role. Today, of course, the handicapped are frequently trained, or retrained, either for full-time activity in an occupation better fitted to their disabilities or for a more limited involvement in their previous occupations. In a complex and specialized society like our own, there are many limited and specialized activities that can be performed satisfactorily by handicapped persons. Moreover, much of the disability associated with chronic illness and impairment is a result of social definitions in contrast to physical incapacities (580).

In considering the social aspects of disability, we must note that the individual's willingness or motivation for retraining plays a crucial role. Individuals who have a keen attitude toward rehabilitation appear to overcome vast difficulties, while others who seem handicapped by medical criteria only to a minimal extent are greatly hampered in their rehabilitation by attitudes that encourage their disability. The attitude of family and colleagues can have a similarly substantial impact on the course a pattern of disability takes. To the extent that the family and others value the person, they are more likely to try to impose their own definition of the situation on him (474). From the viewpoint of medical rehabilitation, it is important that the perspective they encourage be consistent with the potentialities of the case.

It is important to investigate the nature of and relationships among the various dimensions of disability. To what extent, for example, does an illness have equal impact on a man's family life and his occupation? Does disability generalize to all activities, or is selective disability more common? A venereal disease, for example, may prevent adequate performance as a sexual partner, but this condition has no necessary relationship to the person's occupation or other spheres of life. In some situations, problems that arise in one sphere of life generalize to others, and it is important to try to understand the social contexts in which such generalized responses are most likely to occur. In a study of nonmedical disability by Komarovsky (398), for example, it was found that in some families unemployment of the main wage earner led to improved family relationships, rather than deteriorating ones. In attempting to differentiate those families in which relationships deteriorated from those that improved when unemployment occurred, the investigator suggested that the state of family life prior to unemployment could be used to predict the future course of events. If the relationship between husband and wife was good, the families pulled together under stressful circumstances; if the relationship was strained, external crisis led to difficulties well beyond the area of crisis.

A question often overlooked in the study of illness and disability is the extent to which a particular aspect of an entire constellation of activities is actually enhanced as a result of illness. It is possible for a person disabled by illness not only to achieve secondary gains for himself but also to behave in a manner leading to increased gain for others. For example, a husband who has spent most of his time in occupational activities may improve the quality and frequency of interaction with his wife and children as a result of occupational disability through illness. The disability prevents his participation in occupational roles, but is functional in terms of his family roles. In the study of unemployment mentioned above, it was found that when some husbands lost their capacity to earn a livelihood they attempted to compensate for this inadequacy by becoming more considerate of their wives, helping more around the house, and, in general, changing their usual role behaviors in relation to their family. It may be that the value the person places on various aspects of his life activities will play some part in determining the way disability in one or more roles will affect his performance in others. If the disability occurs in a role viewed as a means toward satisfying another more important role (for example, being a good wage earner may be instrumental in being a better husband), disability in that role will be less destructive to a person's identity than if the role is viewed as an end in itself.

The Value of Health

Finally, in our social analysis, we must not fail to recognize that health is a social value and is often judged relative to other social values. Because we place such emphasis on the individual and his uniqueness, in a popular way we tend to assume that health and the preservation of life are not negotiable. In a symbolic way we pay great homage to the preservation of life and health as exemplified in efforts, no matter how expensive, to save persons trapped in a mine or lost at sea. This attests to the extent we hold such values high within our hierarchy of ideals. However, it is one thing to place great importance on a particular value, and quite another to implement it when it comes into sharp conflict with other values and needs. We all recognize that individual life is regarded as secondary when our nation's security or interests are attacked. So there are obviously circumstances when a person is expected to sacrifice his life and health for what are regarded as greater goals.

But in noting such an exceptional situation as war, it is possible to draw attention away from everyday situations in which health values are subsidiary. To take a less extreme example, the costs of health care are usually weighed against other societal and personal needs. Every doctor, either consciously or unconsciously, must take economic factors into account in rendering care and in making medical decisions. Moreover, we all know that persons in our society receive varying amounts and quality of medical care, and many receive inadequate health care. In an absolute sense, resources are limited and health must be weighed relative to other social needs, thus limiting public expenditures in any single area. But even within the range of possible and tolerable expenditure, particular groups often oppose the provision of better care to disadvantaged groups because they place greater emphasis on other values such as lower taxation or more abstract values such as "local responsibility," "free enterprise," or "individual initiative." Thus, in an indirect sense, all societies forego providing opportunities for health in that they fail to do what is possible to enhance the health of people and provide better facilities for the sick. Ideally it would be a violation of our cultural views to ask explicitly: "How much is a person's life worth?" In practice such decisions are made in the aggregate every day in a wide variety of ways.

To restate a question that the noted philosopher Morris Cohen used to ask, "If a man came from another world offering you a fine system of transportation in return for sacrificing several thousand of your countrymen, would you agree to the bargain?" Given our social values, we obviously would not consider such a barbarous trade. Yet each year we sacrifice almost 50,000 lives and sustain personal injuries many times this figure as a cost we assume in adopting the automobile as a cultural artifact. Many persons who would react to Cohen's question with emotion and regard the proposal as an inconceivable transaction are scarcely moved by the knowledge that the number of deaths and injuries could be significantly reduced by the design and production of safer automobiles and improvements in various facets of road systems. Obviously, the difference in reactions involves in part the question of choice. One cannot specify beforehand the particular people who will be killed or injured in car accidents, and thus the loss is viewed as more tolerable. In the bargain that Cohen suggests, someone has to choose who will be sacrificed, and this seems to make the offer more odious in terms of our ideals concerning freedom. But let us suppose that the offer included the stipulation that we did not have to choose who would be sacrificed; rather they would be plucked away from us by some mysterious random process. Would this make the offer acceptable? This is only one of many dilemmas that could be suggested that characterize our lives; in almost every other aspect of our economic and social lives the costs of health and safety are considered not as absolutes but in reference to other needs, desires, and social, economic, and personal goals.

It is reasonable to ask why our state and national governments are willing to engage in vast heroic and tremendously expensive rescue efforts but take no action in other areas where need is so evident. As we have already noted, the failure to take action may result from conflicts of interests and resulting cross-pressures from various segments of the society. But even when other value conflicts are not apparent, cost considerations are relevant. Rescues are single discrete events that imply no responsibility for future action. Thus the government commits itself to no large-scale continuing program. Moreover, the expense of such operations is usually overestimated, because manpower and equipment are readily available and thus overhead cost would exist whether or not such equipment and men were utilized. In contrast, programs affecting health are undertaken cautiously when they involve commitments to an ongoing and growing problem. Given our value system, once a state, a locality, or the federal government commits itself to keeping patients alive through some apparatus, for example the artificial kidney, it morally commits itself to continue to do so as long as the patient lives; to reverse such a program would involve a direct decision to allow people to die. Although we are often willing to allow people to die by the failure to do what is possible to preserve life, we find it much more difficult to make decisions that lead directly to the elimination of life. This, as well as many other issues, has considerable influence on the way health values are defined and acted upon in relation to other aspects of living.

The Social-Psychological Perspective

The social-psychological perspective draws on both sociology and psychology in that its central concern is with the ways in which individuals interact, communicate, and influence one another. Thus this field illuminates the question of how individuals affect the social process and, in turn, how their intrapsychic states and personality are influenced and developed in the context of social processes. Social psychologists, depending on their orientation, look at the processes of influence in different ways. Some investigators view influence in terms of its sources and strategies, others see influence as an ongoing dynamic interactive process, and others concern themselves with studying the recipients of influence either in specific terms (such as in the study of susceptibility to influence) or in developmental terms (such as in the study of the development of particular personality traits as a consequence of a long-term influence process). Much that we have already said about definitional processes in illness is of a social-psychological nature.

Each of the approaches to influence described above has direct relevance to the health field. Understanding the strategies of influence is not only relevant to the work of the doctor in getting his patient to conform to his instructions and advice but is also central in presenting public-health programs to the public and encouraging people to use them. Similarly, the doctor-patient interaction is a dynamic influence process subject to some of the same forces and tendencies as any other interaction situation (see 336; 700). It is also of great relevance for health personnel to understand the kinds of person who are susceptible or immune to different kinds of influence processes and the basic factors underlying such differences in receptivity (249).

Social psychology also has some very special implications for medical sociology:

1. Many of the disorders that medical sociologists study are believed to be in part or in whole products of the interaction of intrapsychic and social forces, and later we will devote chapter 8 to this important area.
2. Although psychosocial influences may not be directly relevant to the occurrence of many conditions (such as heart disease, tuberculosis, or schizophrenia), they may influence the course of these conditions and resulting disability.
3. The occurrence of illness frequently has important consequences for people's psychosocial states and for family life.

Social psychology is itself a vast field bordering on many different substantive areas and crosscutting sociology, psychology, anthropology, psychoanalysis, and even to some extent psychophysiology, biology, and linguistics. It therefore encompasses a wide variety of views, orientations, and methodological approaches. Different orientations and perspectives may have important consequences for the way phenomena are viewed and studied. And when such approaches are used for generating ideas for treatment and control—as they frequently are in such fields as medical sociology and mental health—these different perspectives may encourage the adoption of contrasting alternatives for therapeutic programs. The consequences of using alternative social-psychological models within the field of medical sociology are of sufficient importance to merit a detailed discussion here. Although there are many ways of looking at the implications of such models, primary emphasis will be given to the extent that various perspectives embody a view of man as capable of influencing his surroundings and life alternatives. In short, the concern here is with varying concepts of behavioral effectiveness.

All social-psychological theories, implicitly if not explicitly, make assumptions about the adaptive potentialities of man's behavior: the balance between those elements of his behavior that are fixed and unchangeable and those that are flexible and adaptive. All social psychologists are, of course, determinists in that they believe that there is an underlying pattern to behavior explainable on the basis of biological, psychological, and social principles. But even within this context it is possible to place more or less emphasis on the "willfulness" of man and the role of "behavioral effectiveness" in the course of human events. Because men are symbolic animals and have a highly developed language encompassing a complex vocabulary of motives, man can conceptualize goals, work out paths to their achievement, and behave as if he has control over the course of his life.

In recent years a great deal of experimental research has involved the concept of helplessness, a psychological state that may result when events are uncontrollable. Seligman (631) has brought together a great deal of evidence showing the similarity of response in experiments producing helplessness to depression. Moreover, helplessness has been linked experimentally to ulceration and other bodily damage in animals, and even death. Although the question of whether people control their environment may be philosophical, beliefs about such control may have a pervasive effect on their health and welfare.

In the final analysis man's goals and thinking processes are determined by the culture within which he develops, the structure of his language, and the course of his learning and experiences, as well as by his biological capacities. However, the complexity of human experience and the cultural assumption of human responsibility make it important to study behavior not only as the consequence of events that happen to people, but also in terms of the ways persons organize and structure their environment. In this view, man's intentions and choices must become important variables in understanding human behavior and social processes.

In order to illustrate how varying theoretical systems deal with the problem of adaptive capacity, I shall briefly compare Freudian thinking, symbolic-interaction views, and learning approaches. I choose these frames of reference because they have had an important influence on medical sociologists and other workers in the health field, although each has very different implications for developing rehabilitation programs. I shall also comment on a perspective that is more vague—the collective-mobilization approach—but has tremendous potential for improving health practices.

The Freudian View

In Freud's view man was a product largely of his early psychological environment, which was mostly influenced by inevitable conflict resulting from the clash of psychobiological needs and the demands of living to which the child is forced to accommodate. The inevitability of man's fate—and later psychological difficulties—was implicit in the fact that biological development must occur within a social context, and society must control and modify man's development. Thus man's personality was visualized as resulting from an inevitable and natural antagonism between an innate unfolding biological pattern and a repressive and demanding environment. Man's inabilities and difficulties were thus understandable by an exploration of the past history of the person's development.

The view of adaptation that Freud provided depicted man as a rather feeble force in controlling his environment or personal history. Later psychodynamic theorists have argued that personality is not determined by innate biological needs to the extent that Freud believed (252; 253; 340; 685), and it is generally conceded that many societies are not as repressive as the one within which Freud lived and worked, and upon which the structure of his argument was largely based. In any case, Freud's importance and influence lie not so much in his specific theories as in his clinical observations and the techniques he developed that made such observations possible.

Perhaps Freud's most important contribution was his clinical description of the techniques people used to defend themselves from painful thoughts and ideas (245; 246). His emphasis on the fact that persons often could not remember threatening experiences and his concern with defense processes (such as denial, projection, repression, and reaction formation) gave social scientists an entirely new way of looking at psychological functioning. Although Freud described the way people dealt with painful thoughts and feelings, he gave little attention to the potentialities for behavioral effectiveness (see 411). To Freud, the defense mechanisms were unintentional and pathological. They were unconscious attempts to deny and falsify reality, not attempts at healthy psychological adaptation (308). Indeed, Freud's thinking leaves little room for healthy adaptation; neurosis in Freud's view was inevitable in the contest between man's needs and the repressive demands of society.

Freud discusses one psychobiological technique that might be viewed as a quasi-healthy attempt to come to terms with one's life situation—the process of sublimation, through which libidinal energy could be attached to activities that were creative and socially constructive. But while Freud gave analytic attention to a variety of pathological defenses, he encompassed all of "healthy adaptation" into a single concept. In sum, Freud tells us very little about the way men manage to come to terms with their environment and social situation on a behavioral level. Nor do modern adherents of Freudian theory provide a much clearer view of man's possibilities for effectiveness. They have moved Freud's descriptions of intrapsychic defense from the realm of the pathological to the larger arena of human activity in general. Such theories, however, continue to focus almost exclusively on intrapsychic techniques for managing anxiety and painful feeling states, and treatment is seen largely in terms of making unconscious thoughts and wishes conscious. In this view man deals with problems by intrapsychic analysis rather than through sustained efforts to come to terms with his environment and other people. Analysis of one's inner feelings and needs may affect behavior indirectly, of course. But the basic thrust of the psychoanalytic view serves to portray men as usually weak and ineffectual reactors to the biological and social forces that play upon them. Perhaps most ominous is the realization that the psychological conception of man embodied in such theories plays a part in influencing man's conception of himself and the efforts he exerts to influence his environment. Thus when psychoanalytic techniques and views are applied to the rehabilitation of the mentally ill, they carry with them basic assumptions about the nature of failures in functioning and the limits of man's adaptive capacities to reverse environmental problems. These views thus influence in a substantial way the manner in which care for the sick and disabled is organized. Psychoanalysis has perpetuated an extremely deterministic and pessimistic view of behavioral effectiveness, and the possible means through which persons can come to terms with their environment in an active striving sense are largely ignored and often deemed irrelevant. As we shall later see, the psychological and social conceptions used in treating the sick influence their motivation to regard themselves as accountable and affect their efforts to cope with their environment.

The Symbolic-Interaction View

During the period when Freud was developing his psychoanalytic theories, Charles Horton Cooley at the University of Michigan was developing a competing point of view that, together with the later work of

Mead, provides the groundwork for symbolic-interaction theory. To Cooley, man's development and social demands were not inevitably competing; rather, they were two aspects of the same process. In Cooley's view (144; 145) man's nature and his social needs were molded and nurtured through psychological development and contacts with other people. It was only through other people that children developed investments in living and a view of themselves. Cooley, unlike Freud, depicted socialization primarily as a constructive process through which people became human, not as a thwarting influence that frustrated the child and set the stage for future psychological difficulties. In sum, to Cooley the concepts of development and "human nature" were meaningful only within the context of social life, and man's needs—emotional as well as social—were seen as developing only through interaction with other people.

In a similar vein, George H. Mead (472) at the University of Chicago was developing a picture of man whose personality was derived through the interaction of symbolic communications. Although Cooley and Mead took account of the fact that man's opportunities could vary as a result of group and class membership, they left considerable room to regard man as an active participant in social processes and to consider the social dialogue among men. Thus man was at the center of his stage; his intentions and behavior were seen in the light of his views of other people's reactions to him. In this sense man was viewed as having active control over his environment.

W. I. Thomas also contributed to a sociological view of man as an effective agent in his environment (442). He believed that control of and adjustment to the environment resulted from the active manipulation of knowledge. Man, of course, must be socialized; he must acquire skills and techniques to mold the environment. It is the culture of the group, he wrote, that limits the power of the mind to adjust to adversity and changing circumstances. If knowledge is insufficient and material resources are scanty, an individual will find no way out of an emergency that under different circumstances would be only the occasion for further progress. In collaboration with Znaniecki in the epic work *The Polish Peasant in Europe and America* (701), Thomas illustrated in a detailed way how people's definitions of their life circumstances influenced the alternatives they recognized and the means they used in dealing with their environment.

Basic to the symbolic-interaction position was the idea that social action was constructed through the manipulation and negotiation of symbolic values, and thus life was limited only by the scope of the symbolic environments to which man was exposed. But the symbolic environment in a complex and dynamic society as our own is so vast in scope and so rich in complexity that man has considerable opportunity to affect the direction of his life. In short, within the symbolic-interaction view man has unlimited opportunities to develop new institutions and alternatives for dealing with his problems and changing the course of his life. Although this view has few specific suggestions for the rehabilitation of patients suffering from various disabilities, it is optimistic in its implication that man can create and develop new symbolic environments and communities that nurture the sick, develop their skills, and motivate their increased participation in the social scene.

The Learning Approach

The psychological study of learning processes has a long history, and a variety of models have been developed based on detailed experimental evidence. Although these competing models need not concern us here, they all share a common view that much of human behavior is a consequence of past schedules of conditioning and reinforcement. Learning principles have recently been extended to the autonomic system, serving as the basis for a growing interest in using learning therapies in the treatment of a variety of diseases, from hypertension to migraine headache, and in the development of biofeedback, through which persons learn to monitor their own internal processes and to control them in a healthful fashion (64; 517). Although this movement is still characterized more by potentiality than by realization, it constitutes an exciting new area in the application of psychological principles to medicine.

The man most closely associated with the application of learning to behavior change is B. F. Skinner, whose views of operant conditioning have had great influence in many areas outside academic psychology. Skinner has been audacious in explaining individual and social behavior as almost exclusively a product of learning schedules as they are incorporated into education, social life, and the larger social structure (651). Learning principles are used increasingly, and with some success, in dealing with a wide variety of behavioral disorders, such as phobias, discipline problems in children, and inappropriate behavior of psychotic patients (43). While there is still considerable dispute concerning the scope of useful application of learning principles to behavior change and the value of dealing with discrete behavioral dysfunctions in contrast to more complex behavior patterns, the application of these notions is one of the more promising recent advances in the behavior-change field.

There is considerable philosophical objection to the application of learning theories because of what they appear to imply about the nature of man and his malleability. To some—particularly those in the humanities—the notion that man is primarily a product of the conditioning factors to which he has been exposed is an odious concept that violates cherished notions about the essential nature of man; to those with a more biological bent, learning notions give too little emphasis to the extent to which man has been preprogrammed through biological and evolutionary processes. Still others react most violently to what they perceive as the passive attributions to man that learning approaches seem to imply. Yet the implementation of these principles depends on man's ability to select desired goals, to develop intermediate objectives, and to design programs of rewards and punishments that motivate behavior in terms of larger aims. The fact that man can design his own reinforcements to achieve desired ends implies possibilities for man and society that are less passive than the usual stereotype held by many critics of behavior control.

Collective Mobilization

A final perspective, referred to here as collective mobilization, arises more from practice than from theory. Collective mobilization involves the use of social and political control to achieve health and other social goals through the creation of highly valued shared commitments, service to others, and high levels of integration and social cohesion. The People's Republic of China offers an impressive example of great advances in public health through the social mobilization of the population, a strong commitment to public health and preventive medicine, and widespread use of paraprofessionals in the delivery of preventive and curative services (339; 644). Observers of varying persuasions familiar with pre- and postrevolutionary China have been impressed by the enormous changes in the health and well-being of the Chinese population brought about largely through social measures and a widely shared equalitarianism and group commitment. The Chinese have made advances in such areas as birth control, control of venereal disease, and nutrition. Although the full implications of the Chinese experiment for modern industrial nations remain unclear, it is testimony once again to the close interrelationship between the culture and social structure of a country and its health situation.

Although much of the demand for medical services in modern nations arises as much from a general malaise and loss of community as from other causes, health care is largely reactive, because health workers feel they have little capacity to deal with the fundamental causes of ill health in society. Yet it is apparent that pouring additional billions of dollars each year into an already overextended curative health industry yields less and less for the increased investments. What is needed—but difficult to implement—is a means of motivating individuals, neighborhoods, and communities to develop the types of community patterns and social relationships that are supportive of more healthful patterns of living. Although many health problems are beyond the scope of individual communities—because they are tied to modern living and industrial development, or to cultural patterns defining what is valuable and successful (208)—effective community organization can be a useful approach in dealing with many health-care problems with which the existing health-care system is relatively ineffective in coping. These include health education and self-care; social care for the aged, persons with chronic disease, and those with impairments and handicaps; and improved health socialization of children. The effects of such measures, however, will remain relatively modest unless these group efforts can begin effectively to challenge the larger social assumptions and cultural forces conducive to ill health in modern societies.

A useful development in recent years is the growth of a great variety of self-help groups in which persons of common persuasion, or those facing similar problems, come together to support and assist each other in both tangible and intangible ways. Self-help groups serve as a useful antidote to the growing medicalization of social problems, in which professionals widen their domain to include areas where they have little special knowlege or competence. The growing medicalization is as much a product of the breakdown of social supports in ordinary social life as of professional imperialism, but strong self-help movements serve as a useful check on what could be a dangerous trend. Many self-help groups reject professional hegemony and share the ideology that only those affected by a problem can really understand it. Although the self-help movement has many constructive aspects, it is frequently subject to fads and exploitation that can damage vulnerable persons seeking help or meaning (38). The most successful self-help groups are those that provide tangible help as well as group support, that are organized to resist bureaucratic organization and individual profiteering, and that are operated exclusively by their own members (for example, Alcoholics Anonymous and Parents Without Partners).

Summary of Influences

Freud's view of man as passive was intrinsic to his whole scheme of thought, and it is basically a philosophical view. In contrast, many other social psychologists with a stronger experimental-scientific orientation than characterized the Freudians adopted a similar view of man as passive because such a view was convenient in their work. As social psychology has developed as an experimental discipline, it has been convenient for experimenters to control the stimuli affecting behavior, making appropriate measurements of changes in response.

Indeed, this is the beauty of the experiment; the researcher controls the input, attempting to vary only one influence at a time. Because he randomizes his subjects into experimental and control groups, he can then infer that any change in response in the experimental group as compared with the control group is attributable to the variation of the stimulus. Such an approach leaves little desire for assuming that man's symbolic processes must be studied to understand reactions to experimental stimuli.

The psychoanalytic perspective characteristic of Freud and his followers depicted little potentiality for controlling deviance by manipulating the social structure or environmental contexts. Nor did this conception see man as developing the facility to overcome his disabilities through his own efforts and development. Therapy was seen as a remedial procedure in that it facilitated man's appreciation of his unconscious wishes, with resulting "maturity" and "psychological freedom." But the structural contexts producing or exacerbating personal conflict and distress were seen largely as fixed and unalterable.

Although symbolic-interaction theory provided a view of man as having an active capacity to structure his environment and relations with others, it lacked a clear and easily implemented method of treatment. Thus, while symbolic interactionists could illustrate the complexity of contacts and the value of interactional analysis for understanding problems and deviance, they did not develop a simple technology for translating the perspective into action. In contrast, Freud had developed a useful tool for both research and treatment; the therapist could listen to the patient's free associations, dreams, and fantasies and try to analyze his unconscious fears and motivations. Freud's techniques could easily be generalized to a wide variety of problems and contexts, and this greatly facilitated the diffusion and adoption of the underlying philosophy and view of man. Later therapies—such as interpersonal therapy, developed by Sullivan (685), and more recent types of transactional analysis—combined psychoanalytic and symbolic-interactional conceptions, but continued to be based on the premise that talking about problems was an effective means of achieving behavior change. Although these therapies sometimes encouraged changes in the way people dealt with problems, they viewed the external social environment for the most part as relatively fixed and unalterable. More recently there have been a great many types of therapy that attempt to change social units in contrast to individuals—such as couple, family, and social-network therapies—but even they tend to be weighed down by a vague concept of their goals and a continuing emphasis on psychological change.

Learning theory has provided the most important contrast to other individual therapies concerned with behavior change. Using the principles of operant conditioning and desensitization, it strives to teach patients new repertoires in relation to specified social and environmental stimuli (43). This is achieved by rewarding types of behavior that allow a person to make a better adjustment to his environment and by exposing persons slowly and in a graduated fashion to painful stimuli they find threatening, thus helping them achieve gradual mastery of their fears and avoidance tendencies. What makes learning therapies distinctive is that they require clear specification of the goals of the therapy so that appropriate schedules of reinforcement can be developed. Thus learning therapies, whatever their limitations, require a clarity and planning that are commonly absent from many other types of therapeutic encounters. They have been incorporated into many of the existing therapeutic approaches and in the construction of treatment and rehabilitation milieus and are beginning to seep into the everyday practice of medicine. These approaches are used to train teachers to modify the behavior of their pupils and to train parents to change the behavior of their children. Behavior modification, unlike traditional psychotherapy, is not dependent on the voluntary participation of the patient because reinforcement schedules are under the control of the trainer. (This evokes in many people the image of thought and behavior control and accounts for the highly emotional antagonism characteristic of some reactions to these new developments.) However, because people understand that others may be manipulating the social situation to control them and because individuals have the capacity to reward themselves for certain types of behavior, learning approaches are unlikely to be effective in involuntary situations unless there is almost total coercive control. Thus, while such techniques suggest no major dangers for society at large, their use in coercive organizations such as prisons, mental hospitals, and institutions for the retarded requires careful monitoring and supervision.

It is ironic that we live in an age in which human instrumentality and efficacy are highly valued and are often evident, yet many of the more influential social-psychological models see man as a captive of his development, social position, and life situation. We are not denying what every sociology student knows: that social background, group values, and developmental factors have profound influences on people's capacities and behaviors. However, in a complex dynamic society like our own, individuals are presented with numerous and diverse opportunities to develop psychological and social skills that are effective in influencing the social scene.

In a changing world, man must develop the capacity to plan the course life will take, and much of what in the past has appeared to be a matter of fate or chance is now under man's control. However, there is great variability among people in the extent to which they experience

life as a combination of inevitable and accidental events and the extent
to which they actively seek out alternatives, make choices, and facilitate their own welfare by anticipatory planning. Even within our own
Western culture there are great differences in the extent to which people
view illness as controllable or a matter of fate. Only in recent years has
there been widespread acceptance of the importance of family planning, but even today in some parts of the world the size of family is
viewed as beyond the scope of the individual's control. Obviously, cultural values and norms restrict the means people can use to control
their lives, but even within the range of normative acceptability there is
great variability among people in the extent to which they view themselves as active forces in their environment and as capable of controlling their alternatives and choices.

Self-help groups at the individual level and collective mobilization
at the social level are renewed expressions of people's capacity to
reconstruct society in terms of their own images and needs. Both movements depict people as active agents in their own environments, with
the ability to meet their problems by collective action rather than by
continued passivity and dependence on the further elaboration of
health-care bureaucracies and professionalization. Although the long-
range potential of these movements in modern industrial societies
remains unclear, they offer an optimistic and spirited reaction to the
growing specialization, segmentation, and depersonalization of modern life. Whereas Freud saw man as captive of an inevitable neurosis
and learning theory depicts man as the product of the history of his
conditioning, the new movements are based on the premise that people
have a great capacity to control their own fate.

The Societal Perspective

The fourth perspective—the general societal perspective—concerns
the relationship between health and other social institutions. Basically, this perspective involves analysis of the ways in which health is used
to deal with problems in other spheres of social activity. The societal
approach is more abstract than the others we have described. Implicit
in this approach is the assumption that it is possible to separate different components of social life analytically, and to investigate the relationship between these components. Here we are interested in such
issues as the relationships between health institutions and industrial
organizations, law, family life, and so on. We are concerned with ascertaining the extent to which health institutions and practitioners play a
role beyond their more limited medical functions, and what pressures
are placed on them to do so.

Role Concepts

The sociologist's most important tool within the context of the societal approach is the concept of roles. Role theorists seek to understand the interrelations between different spheres of social activity by studying the behavioral regularities that result from established identities within specific social contexts like families, hospitals, and communities. The underlying premise of most role theorists is that a large proportion of all behavior is brought about through socialization within specific contexts, and much behavior is routine and established through learning the traditional modes of adaptation in dealing with specific tasks. Thus the positions persons occupy in organizations and the community account for much of their behavior.

Although role theorists have argued much about vocabulary, the premises underlying their thought have been rather consistent. Their argument is essentially that knowledge of one's identity or social position is a powerful index of the expectations a person is likely to face in social situations. Because behavior tends to be highly correlated with expectation, prediction of behavior is therefore possible. The approach of role theorists to the study of behavior within organizations is of particular merit in that it provides a consistent set of concepts that are useful analytically in describing recruitment (that is, how people come to occupy particular social positions), socialization, interaction, and personality, as well as the formal structure of organizations. Thus the concept of role is one of the few concepts that effectively links social structure, social process, and social character.

Because role theory is a major conceptual tool in medical sociology, and because it encompasses several problems and difficulties in relation to materials we will discuss later in this book, it is necessary to review briefly its development and some of its major shortcomings. In the first few decades of this century much of sociological knowledge was based on community studies and observations of different cultural groups. During this period sociologists and anthropologists were struggling with the need for a conceptual system to integrate and organize the observations of various cultural communities. The concept of culture, however useful, was much too global for general analytic use. Thus Ralph Linton's concepts of status and role quickly became popular in sociological analysis and constituted the beginning of "role theory." To Linton (448) "status" was a position in a particular structural pattern. Clusters of potential behaviors could be learned as repertories by persons who held certain statuses, and Linton maintained that human beings were sufficiently mutable that almost any normal person could be trained so that he could adequately occupy almost any status. "Role," to Linton, was the enactment of particular social statuses; it was the process of putting the rights and duties of the position into effect. Sociologists were very much taken with these distinctions because they tied together some of the most important areas of sociological study: the training of the child, social structure, the division of labor, interaction, and so on. In short, role was seen as a valuable concept in that it tied together the static and dynamic components of social life; the concept could be used to describe formal organizations and at the same time to explain behavioral enactments on the individual and interaction levels. It thus linked sociological concerns into a theoretical fabric and served as grist for the beginnings of a theory of social systems (see 549).

The concept of role served as both a unifying and a simplifying concept. And in recent years we have frequently heard that persons occupying particular social positions learn particular bundles of activities associated with these positions; that these bundles of behavior are enacted by persons holding the relevant positions at the appropriate time; that new roles are communicated to and learned by people as they assume new social positions; and that roles are reciprocally related to other roles and thus these links serve as the backbone of social organization. Some even went so far as to assert that people (or personalities, if you like) were different only in that the social positions they held were different or differently organized within their hierarchy of role bundles (85; 536).

There are many ways in which role theory can be used, and it is not our purpose here to review the varied opinions about the nature of role theory (69; 301; 788). For our purposes, the important thing to recognize is that role theory, as compared with symbolic-interaction analysis, had put man into such a tight structural cast that he resembled a "social robot." This problem has been recognized by several analysts, and in recent years many modifications within role theory have attempted to rebuild to some extent an image of role actors capable of manipulating and restructuring their symbolic environments. It was clear that early conceptions of the theory of roles were too deterministic. To deal with this problem it was necessary to revive motivational ideas (224), and thus we had the introduction of such concepts as involvement, role distance, and role embracement (270). These concepts attempted to deal with the fact that people were more or less emotionally committed to their roles and performed them with more or less seriousness, effort, and enthusiasm. To deal with the confusing fact that persons occupying the same role behaved differently in reference to a variety of other categories of people required the introduction of the concept of role-set (508). In this way it was possible, for example, to account for the fact that doctors enacted different behavioral patterns in reference to colleagues, patients, and nurses. Similarly, a rather large vocabulary of additional concepts was introduced—role-presentation

(268), role-conception (705), role strain (277), role-standpoint (705), role-taking (150)—to account for the continuing feeling that an unelaborated theory of roles did not adequately portray the richness and complexity of the intercourse among men.

It is important that I state my own view of the role concept here so that it is clear as to what I see as its advantages, and also why I view some extensions of role ideas with a lack of enthusiasm. Role is an important analytic tool because frequently we can predict a great deal about a person's behavior just by knowing his social position. Although doctors and bricklayers may vary greatly among themselves, knowing that a person is a doctor or a bricklayer tells us a great deal about the way he lives his life and spends his time. In my conception, roles are functional-adaptive units. All social positions have associated with them particular tasks that require specific patterns of behavioral enactment (doctors must know how to examine patients; bricklayers must know how to lay bricks). Thus certain task skills and associated attitudes and values become patterned. The organization of such repertories allows the task skills to be taught more easily to new occupants of the position, and thus their patterning is functional. Moreover, since we participate in social life in terms of our anticipations of others' social positions and expectations, "role stereotypes" are required if social life is to flow smoothly, in that we must be able to anticipate what to expect from others who have particular social identities.

The idea that roles have an important adaptive significance is stated effectively by Thibaut and Kelley (700), who define roles as clusters of norms:

> At the most general level, norms are viewed as being functionally valuable to social relationships by reducing the necessity for the exercise of direct, informal personal influence. Norms provide a means of controlling behavior without entailing the costs, uncertainties, resistances, conflicts, and power losses involved in the unrestrained, *ad hoc* use of interpersonal power. As substitutes for informal influence, norms have specific functions in providing solutions to problems about which members of a dyad otherwise find it necessary to influence each other directly. Thus norms deal with such problems as trading, synchronization, eliminating unsatisfactory behaviors, reducing differences of opinion, and communicating effectively. In all of the ways mentioned above, norms, if they are effective, can reduce the costs of interaction and eliminate the less rewarding activities from a relationship. They can act to improve the outcomes attained by the members of a dyad and to increase their interdependence [700, p. 147].

Norms and roles, of course, are not always adaptive. In fact, frequently they detract from the task and the individual's ability to meet his responsibilities. However, when formal definitions of roles become dysfunctional and maladaptive, we often see role occupants violating the norms, cutting corners, building new and more functional repertories, and generally adjusting their behavior to the changing demands of their situation and environment. This is why analysts of particular role occupants observe such diversity in behavior within the same role (see, for example, 301). Roles are the shells within which adaptive struggles take place; they condition the way adaptive attempts are made and set limits on such attempts. But within each of these contexts there is considerable variability in adaptive response conditioned by the demands of the situation, the needs and inclinations of the actor, and the alternatives available to him.

The Sick Role

Thus far I have made reference to the sick role as a limited personal role, but analysis of the sick role is also possible on an institutional or societal level. Parsons, in his well-known analysis, has pointed out that adequate health on the part of most group members, much of the time, is a functional requirement of any social system (549). A definition of disability that is too lenient would impose severe strains on the workings of a society, and therefore it is necessary for definitions of disability to be controlled socially to some extent so as to insure that not too large a proportion of the population is released from its usual social responsibilities. Parsons argues that this control is applied through the manner in which sickness is defined and dealt with—the sick-role mechanism.

Having a legitimate procedure for the definition and sanctioning of the adoption of the sick role is functional for both the social system and the sick individual. Because illness is widely regarded by us as a natural event, the ill person is usually not blamed for causing his own illness. Also, because some relief from the usual demands on and obligations of the individual is presumed to contribute to his recovery, both the individual and the community gain from such a sick-role mechanism in that the long-range well-being of the individual is protected, and also in that the individual, if he receives appropriate care, may be more rapidly restored to his usual responsibilities in the community. Finally, the existence of such a mechanism enables persons other than the patient himself and medical practitioners to adjust the meaning of illness and disability according to different situations and the changing needs of the community itself.

Our statement thus far appears largely academic because our own society, and indeed any modern automated industrial society, can absorb a large amount of illness and disability without too great a difficulty. The issue becomes a more practical concern if one shifts to societal contexts in which labor is severely limited and needs are great.

These conditions were fulfilled in the Soviet Union in the past few decades, where production and labor needs were enormous and work demands on the population were severe (216; 217). In this context, many persons who had difficulty meeting the strenuous industrial demands or who were unmotivated toward work came to doctors seeking help and a legitimate excuse for failing to appear at work. Some of these people used various techniques of malingering, such as artificially elevating their temperature before seeing the doctor. To protect economic production the government restricted the number of sick-role clearances that physicians could grant during a particular period of time. An official medical clearance was necessary for the individual to be exempted from his usual occupational role, yet by fiat the number of clearances was rationed to insure that the needs of the factories would be met. It is clear from Field's description of the situation in the Soviet Union that the sick role was being manipulated from the standpoint of both workers and the government. Patients who were not really sick were attempting to get sick-role clearances to excuse them from the arduous demands of work. Thus the doctor was being used by these people as a means for escaping societal demands not directly relevant to health. By regulating the doctor's behavior in this matter, the government was able to counteract this trend and insure a sufficient manpower pool. Even in this example it is important to note that the government did not dispense with sick-role clearances; its intent was to maintain a more rigorous standard of the degree of illness that justified work disability. We should note that similar phenomena appear on the American scene. Some informal observers of our military organizations have noted that legitimate occupancy of the sick role by military personnel can be defined and redefined by medical officers in accordance with external situation requirements. Under combat conditions, when manpower is at a premium, it becomes increasingly difficult for an individual to have his claims for disability accepted and legitimized. To move into our own backyard, the university, it is evident that students frequently attempt to use the excuse of illness to justify failure to meet their academic responsibilities. Many physician visits within this context are not for medical advice but rather to seek medical justification for missing an examination or failing to meet some other academic responsibility. Moreover, illness is a common and acceptable explanation for social failure and ameliorates a sense of stigma (137).

In our own society and most Western societies, the doctor's primary responsibility rests in his allegiance to the patient. The patient, except in unusual circumstances, seeks the physician's assistance voluntarily, and the physician by law and medical ethics is required to serve the patient's interest. Thus Western doctors are placed under great pressure by patients to help them in various situations by certifying illness to justify or explain the patient's failures in areas that may be unrelated to health. Many such requests are honest ones, but situations in which false excuses are desired or the nature of the patient's disability is ambiguous are frequent. It is particularly in the area of providing such medical justifications for social disability that the social and medical aspects of medical practice become intermixed, and it is frequently unclear as to whether the judgment being made is of a medical or a social nature. As noted in chapter 1, the ways in which deviant behavior is defined have an obvious bearing on the social fate of the patient. To the extent that his behavior is seen as sick rather than as bad, certain advantages result. Thus, in the social dialogue concerning public decisions regarding deviant behavior, one frequently finds that persons who encourage more humanitarian treatment of particular kinds of offenders usually describe the offensive behavior as a consequence of "sickness." It is thus implied that treatment in contrast to punishment is the more appropriate community response.

The dilemmas involving health and other social institutions become particularly difficult within the context of psychiatric practice. Particular violators may gain considerable advantage if their violations are seen as products of sickness rather than badness. Frequently the definition of the act controls whether the person is released under condition that he seek proper treatment for his "illness" or whether he is fined and sent to jail. Within the area of psychiatry and the law there has been considerable controversy concerning the proper definition of legal responsibility (as in the concept of legal insanity: 180; 267; 309; 544; 695; 785). Although our legal system is based on the idea that the person has control over his actions and is therefore responsible for them, certain exceptions must be made when it is obvious that it is not reasonable to regard particular individuals as responsible agents, at least in the sense of being criminals. Children who commit acts viewed as punishable are absolved of criminal intent in that we assume that children cannot have a "guilty mind." Similarly, the criminal law makes exceptions to criminal responsibility in situations involving accidents, duress and compulsion, self-defense and so on.

One of the major exceptions to criminal responsibility within our legal system refers to acts resulting from a form of insanity that makes it impossible to presuppose that the violator had a criminal intent. The nature of the controversy among psychiatrists, lawyers, and others involves the way such a concept of insanity is to be defined. The M'Naghten rule (which requires judgments of whether the person knew "right from wrong" and whether he was driven by an "irresistible impulse") has been bitterly attacked by many psychiatrists as too harsh in that it fails to take account of serious mental disorders that involve neither failure to appreciate the nature of right or wrong, nor an irresistible impulse. They argue that a definition based on current psychiatric understanding that takes into account whether the person was suffering from a mental disorder and whether the disorder had any relationship to the act in violation of the law, would be a more appropriate basis for determining criminal responsibility in such cases. Thus they supported the Durham rule applied by Judge Bazelon of the United States Circuit Court in Washington, D.C.: "that an accused is not criminally responsible if his unlawful act was the product of mental disease or mental defect." Somewhere between the M'Naghten and Durham rulings stand the recommendations of a distinguished group of experts (the American Institute's Model Penal Code) who advocated the following rule:

1. A person is not responsible for criminal conduct if at the time of such conduct as a result of mental disease or defect he lacks substantial capacity either to appreciate the criminality of his conduct or to conform his conduct to the requirements of law.
2. The terms "mental disease or defect" do not include an abnormality manifested only by repeated criminal or otherwise antisocial conduct.

Those who oppose modifications of the criminal responsibility rules as they pertain to mental disorder point to the vagueness of the term "mental disorder" and indicate the great difficulty in specifying after the fact that a particular act is a result of a "mental disorder" rather than a result of some other aspect of the personality of the violator. They argue further that changing the rule will have little effect on the scientific nature of psychiatric testimony in the courts because the problems of delimiting the nature of mental disorders continue to persist within all of the definitions, as well as the difficulty of linking the act with the person's psychological state. In the next chapter, when the question as to whether and in what ways mental disorders may be regarded as disease states is considered, some of the problems surrounding such assessments will become clear. However, one need not go into the details of either law or psychiatry to realize that the debate has little to do with the scientific validity or invalidity of psychiatric knowledge, although this is the rhetoric within which the dialogue is maintained. The issue most fundamentally involves the attitude the law will take concerning personal responsibility and the extent to which the law will be humanistically oriented. The jockeying among advocates and opponents is primarily geared to defining just how rigid or lenient the legal attitude will be toward violators whose acts are surrounded by extenuating circumstances of a psychiatric nature. Thus much more than definitions is involved; even if the definition is more lenient, the existing resources may be insufficient for implementing serious changes, and old practices will continue under a new label (35; 87).

Just as the label "mental illness" may be useful under some circumstances, there are other situations in which such a designation may do harm to a person's reputation and standing. In the minds of many people "mental illness" implies the inability to act rationally and responsibly, and thus such labels are frequently discrediting. Under some circumstances the label "mental illness" can be used to discredit the integrity of a person and his views (695). There are occasions when a prominent person holding unpopular views may be labeled mentally ill because the community has no other adequate way of coping with him. This phenomenon is extremely difficult to document because such persons often hold views or behave in a manner that is sufficiently deviant to substantiate in the minds of many the claim that they are mentally ill. However, there is a considerable danger in equating deviant views with mental disorder, and there are occasions when the mental illness label is used for political or social purposes unrelated to illness. For example, a black civil-rights leader was sent involuntarily to one of New York's psychiatric observation wards after he attempted a citizen's arrest on the mayor for failing to enforce the law regarding discrimination. This was clearly a political gesture meant to embarrass the mayor; the use of psychiatry in this situation was also politically motivated. Although in this case the attempt to discredit the person concerned was too obvious to be effective, there is no doubt that this technique is sometimes successful. Although it is important to recognize this phenomenon, we should perhaps be careful not to exaggerate its importance. But even in ordinary normal conversation among people it is interesting to note the frequency with which concept of sickness is used to discredit behavior and opinions we dislike.

When we consider the use of sickness labels for purposes that are clearly not medical, we find ourselves once again considering the social role of medicine and psychiatry. This role is only very generally defined, giving the doctor considerable flexibility in dealing with problems that arise in society for which there are no clear and obvious solutions. In criticizing this ambiguity and lack of definition, we must not be oblivious to the important social functions that such practitioners take on because they have such flexibility. Social concepts of disease frequently are used to facilitate action in situations for which there are no socially constructive alternatives. Perhaps an example will make this clear. Within the law it is not difficult to take action against a person who attacks another person or does him bodily harm in some fashion. It is much more difficult—and in many cases impossible—to take action against a person who engages in various types of psychological harassment of others. Members of families may go to fantastic lengths in threatening and harassing others in the family psychologically without any legal or other social recourse available to the victims. It is not unusual, when such circumstances reach the breaking point, for psychiatrists to be engaged in order to separate the offending person from others in his family under the aegis of the illness concept. Thus in such situations psychiatry may serve as a "safety valve" which meets problems for which there are no ready solutions. The law is not always sufficiently flexible to deal with many human conflicts and problems that occur and require some mode of assistance.

Such uses of medicine are intimately tied to the values and goals of a society. The increasing movement of decisions from the court to medical and other social and regulatory agencies in many situations provides a more humane atmosphere for dealing with various social problems; such powers, if they are abused, may also produce conflicts in relationship to the values of freedom. Although the necessity for such flexibility in dealing with problems is fairly obvious, it is equally important that these decisions receive proper review and that appropriate safeguards be instituted to insure the rights of persons who feel injured by such decisions.

Integration of Perspectives

Although an attempt has been made to separate different perspectives for didactic purposes, frequently these constitute varying ways of looking at the same behavioral and social processes. In subsequent analyses we shall not be concerned with maintaining these artificial divisions, but will merge them in a fashion that will help explain the occurrence of disease, the reactions of the ill, and the mobilization of help resources. Implicit in the orientation presented is the assumption that man can control events and that his ability to do this depends on his motivation and biological capacities (his strength, energy, and intelligence), the symbolic environments available to him, the manner in which he organizes his efforts and knowledge, and access to the instruments of influence. Development of influence over social affairs as well as over nature depends on gaining access to instrumentalities, skills and knowledge, information, and people. Instrumentalities include all material things that allow people to affect their environment: money, machines, equipment. Skills and knowledge refer to available technologies for changing objects, people, or interpersonal relations. Information includes awareness of actions and reactions in the environment, and patterns of feelings and motivations that govern these. And access to people refers not only to numbers of people but also their "importance," as measured by their access to instrumentalities, information, knowledge and skills, and other people.

The underlying assumption of this book is that much of human activity and the activity surrounding illness can be accounted for within a framework that views such behavior as aspects of and reactions to situations in which persons are actively struggling to control their environment and life situation. Much of the behavior of the patient in defining illness and responding to it can be explained in terms of his adaptive needs. Similarly, the behavior of those who deal with and care for the ill must be viewed as taking place within the contexts of their own everyday needs and routines. Dealing with the sick is for them an everyday task; in contrast to the perspective of the patient and his family, health personnel must routinize and organize procedures in dealing with the sick. In Roth's terms (599), they must develop "timetables" to structure the passage of time and avoid living in a state of perpetual emergency. In short, illness behavior and reactions to the ill are aspects of a coping dialogue in which the various participants are often actively striving to meet their responsibilities, to control their environment, and to make their everyday circumstances more tolerable and less uncertain. The ways in which patients and health organizations define and respond to illness can often be understood as a product of the problems they face in dealing with the social environment. Often the failure of patients, doctors, nurses, and other health workers to conform to usual concepts of health practice and health care is explainable in part in terms of the pressures and conflicts they face as they go about dealing with their daily routines. Reactions to the ill can often be illuminated through an investigation of the changing situations to which a community is exposed and the available resources for dealing with the problems accompanying change.

Two short examples will illustrate this phenomenon. Lewis and Lopreato (439) interviewed 104 mothers (primarily lower class) in order to study the conditions under which arational means were used in dealing with their children's illnesses. They found that arational techniques were more likely to be used among those with little medical information, when respondents believed an illness was dangerous, and when they thought that medical treatment could not effect an improvement of the illness. Moreover, arationality was significantly associated with uncertain situations and with illnesses of long duration. The use of magical, religious, and other nonmedically relevant techniques of dealing with illness thus serve as adaptive techniques among certain subgroups in coping with the uncertainty and anxiety of their situation. The use of arational techniques is not a fixed pattern that manifests itself in all illness situations to the same degree; such techniques reflect the needs of the person to cope with his limited understanding and other uncertainties in the illness situation.

In another study, David Sudnow (684) observed the ways hospital personnel dealt with the dying and dead patient in two hospitals. During the study he had the opportunity personally to observe approximately 200 to 250 deaths. He illustrates in various ways how the handling of the dying patient may reflect the needs of the staff to cope with their work, even at the cost of committing significant improprieties. Sudnow, for example, observed a nurse trying to force a woman's eyelids closed before she died because it would be more difficult to do so after she died because of a tightening of body muscles. He also describes the detailed wrapping procedure necessary when a person has died. On a busy ward, where death is a frequent occurrence, the wrapping for the morgue may be started while the patient is still alive:

> What occasionally occurs here is that portions of the wrapping are done before death, leaving only a few moments of final touch-up work with the dead body . . . they will occasionally go into the room of such a patient (one they believe will die shortly), change the bedsheets, insert dentures, and, in several cases I know of, diaper a patient who is still "alive." Such predeath treatment is likely to occur only during the night shift, when aids are assured that relatives will not visit and discover their work [684, p. 82].

Similarly, hospital procedures require that when a person dies the bedding must be stripped, the room cleaned and disinfected, and so on. This requires considerable staff work. Sudnow observed that when patients were brought to the hospital in a near-death state, they were frequently left on the stretcher on which they came in and put in the supply room or in a laboratory room. A nurse explained to him that this was done in order to avoid messing up a room which would have to be recleaned. If the patients were still alive in the morning, nurses would quickly assign them to beds before the arrival of physicians and relatives.

Admittedly, I have chosen extreme examples to make my point. But the processes that I have described are always going on in a variety of more subtle forms as well as in some extreme ones. People have a great need to control their environment and their activities. The patient uses whatever means are available to him to control the uncertainties that illness poses. Similarly, health workers cannot live in a constant state of crisis, emergency, or disruption; they need to be able to control their work and the demands their work makes on them. The attendant who has dying patients partly prepared for the morgue controls to some extent the disruption of his work pace and schedule resulting from a death. The physician who refuses to make a house call except for a very serious cause controls the extent that his office routines and efficient distribution of his time will be infringed upon. The shortcuts the doctor frequently takes in establishing a diagnosis may constitute poor medical practice, but they are often a result of the pressure of work, the flow of patients, and economic aspirations. In short, the health worker is no less concerned with adapting his situation to his needs and orientations than is the patient.

In the coming chapters we shall consider in some detail the perspectives of both the doctor and the patient. We shall seek to discover how the patient comes to regard himself as sick and as needing medical attention and what factors influence his responses to illness and his relationships with the doctor and other health workers. Similarly, we shall attempt to assess how the doctor comes to view the patient, and how he influences him. Before involving ourselves in a discussion of the social transactions between patient and doctor, however, we must first consider in more technical detail the concept of disease held by the doctor, the underlying logic of medical diagnosis, and the distribution of illness and health problems in the population.

Part 2

**IDENTIFICATION OF DISEASE
IN POPULATIONS**

Chapter 3

THE DOCTOR'S VIEWS OF DISEASE AND THE PATIENT

It is the role of the doctor to evaluate the complaints presented to him, to interpret the patient's symptoms, to assess what effects these symptoms have on the patient and may have in the future, and to manage the case in some fashion for the patient's benefit. The nature of the role demands that the doctor not only attune himself to the patient's condition in a physical sense but that he direct himself to the whole man. It is a fact, however unfortunate, that the more scientific and technically developed aspects of medicine are concentrated on evaluation of the patient's symptoms as compared with his overall needs. Thus, both in the training of doctors and in daily medical activity, the major emphasis tends to be given to the medical diagnosis and treatment of acute illness. Because the diagnostic approach is central to the practice of medicine, it is essential to consider its logical structure.

Medical Diagnosis and the Disease Model

Models of disease may vary widely in their character, but in one sense all diagnoses are hypotheses based on some underlying theory. In modern medical practice many such theories are biological, but they need not necessarily be biological or even scientific. Folk and spiritual healers may use diagnostic models that logically may not be too different from diagnostic models used by doctors. The patient complains of subjective feelings of distress, and the healer observes evidences of dysfunctioning (i.e., deviation from implicit norms of functioning). His underlying theory may be that such manifest symptoms are a consequence of spiritual failings on the part of the patient or a result of possession by evil spirits, and he may thus attempt to treat the patient by helping to adjust his spiritual state or by exorcising the spirits.

The usefulness of one theory in comparison with another depends on its ability to predict outcomes. Thus the value of medical biological theories over primitive religious theories is that they locate the nature of the condition more effectively and suggest more viable remedial measures. The adequacy of a healing theory depends on the advancement of scientific knowledge concerning a particular aspect of bodily functioning. The utility of the diagnostic hypothesis is in turn dependent on the ability of the practitioner correctly to discern symptom complexes which may differ greatly in their degree of definiteness. Scientific theories of disease may vary substantially in the degree to which they are confirmed, and diagnostic judgments may vary substantially in their reliability.

If the theory underlying a diagnosis is sound and scientifically confirmed, it implies the course the doctor is to follow. If a scientific theory of disease is fully confirmed, the diagnosis will provide a sound prediction of the course the disease will take, it will imply its etiology, and, perhaps most important of all, it will suggest the course of treatment that will later alter its progression. The value of making a diagnosis increases with the definiteness with which such predictions are possible once the diagnosis is made.

If one takes into account the function of a diagnosis, the importance of diagnostic reliability becomes apparent. If a diagnosis is incorrect, predictions of the course of the disease, its etiology, and its treatment are also likely to be incorrect. Thus correct and reliable diagnosis is the basis of the sound pactice of scientific medicine.

At any point in time the degree of confirmation of scientific theories of disease varies from one area of functioning to another. If we consider the entire spectrum of medical knowledge, it becomes obvious that a physician, having made a diagnosis, may have at his disposal information varying in quality as to the course of the condition, its causes, and the proper mode of treatment and care. It is possible that the theory underlying the diagnosis of some conditions answers all of these questions effectively. In other conditions, even after the diagnosis is made, definite knowledge on all of the components we have described is lacking. Most diseases fall somewhere between the two extremes: after the diagnosis has been made, some facts are reliably implied, other predictions are questionable, and still others are impossible to make. I shall cite some examples to make this issue as clear as possible.

Consider the case of the disease pernicious anemia, a condition in which the concentration of hemoglobin in the peripheral blood falls below the normal range. The patient may come to the doctor complaining of fatigue, weakness, difficulties in balance and coordination, or some other symptoms. On observing the characteristic physical signs of what he hypothesizes to be pernicious anemia, and on finding a macrocytic anemia through a blood count, the doctor is in a position to confirm the diagnosis of pernicious anemia through a series of further clinical tests. First he may examine a sample of bone-marrow cells for the presence of megaloblastic anemia; then he may test for a histamine-fast achlorhydria. Given positive confirmation through these procedures, he can then reliably clinch the diagnosis by the Schilling test.* The untreated course of the disease is predictable; the patient will show progressive and severe symptoms of anemia, increasing weakness of the legs, and loss of balance and coordination. Once having made the diagnosis, the physician is in a position to feel certain of the etiology and effective treatment. He knows that in this disease the body cannot absorb vitamin B_{12} because of the lack of the intrinsic factor in the stomach, and that injections of this vitamin cure the anemia.

In contrast, consider a disease called Boeck's sarcoidosis. This disease may first become apparent through a TB-screening X-ray that shows enlarged lymph nodes within the chest. The diagnosis is usually established by a positive lymph-node biopsy (although other tissues may have to be examined), by a skin test that is helpful if positive, and by excluding the presence of tuberculosis, with which it can be confused. In this disease, however, the course is unpredictable, the etiology unknown, and the treatment ineffective. The patient may have no evident symptoms for a number of years, or he may have a relatively rapid acceleration of symptoms and die within a few years. Although it is helpful to make the diagnosis, it does not lead to a clear course of action.

As noted earlier, most disease conditions conform to what might be regarded as partially confirmed or incompletely confirmed theories. Let us consider two further conditions. The disease rabies results from one's being bitten by an animal carrying the rabies virus. The diagnosis can be confirmed by a pathological study of the animal in question. Although symptoms may develop slowly after one has been bitten by a rabid animal, once they begin to develop the disease is rapidly fatal because of the effect of the virus on the central nervous system. Once symptoms begin there is no effective treatment for rabies, although antirabies serum may prevent the disease prior to onset of symptoms. Thus here is a case in which the diagnosis, course, and etiology are fairly certain, although treatment following the onset of symptoms is ineffective. In Graves's disease (overactive thyroid), in contrast, although an effective treatment is available, the etiology is unknown. In this condition the patient may present a variety of symptoms such as palpitations, nervousness, loss of weight accompanied by a hearty appetite, or an

---

*The medical details pertaining to the technical aspects of these tests are complicated and irrelevant to my point. All the reader need recognize here is that there are objective procedures for determining the diagnosis.

enlarged thyroid. Once having observed a characteristic clinical picture, the physician can make a reliable diagnosis through one or more laboratory tests, depending on the situation. The course of hyperthyroidism resulting from a generalized overactivity of the thyroid gland takes on one of several characteristic pictures. The disease may progress rapidly and the patient die, or the condition may be cyclic over many years. Permanent remission without treatment is rare. Although the etiology of this condition is unknown, it may be treated effectively through antithyroid drugs, thyroid surgery, or therapeutic doses of radioactive iodine to the thyroid gland.

In making a diagnosis the physician compares observations of the patient and the symptoms he reports with various medical norms based in part on scientific observations and research, and in part on clinical experience. In some cases normal values are specified with considerable validity, as in various clinical tests such as blood-sugar determinations or blood counts. A diagnostic investigation can be said to have validity when a person's result can be used to predict other aspects of his health situation. But as we noted in chapter 1, medical norms may vary in their degree of definiteness and in their usefulness for predicting important aspects of a person's health status. As Lewis has noted:

> The physician is of course trained to relate signs of disturbed function and structure to the norm. His personal experience and the accumulated experience of others are at his disposal. For some organs he has much fuller and more exact information at his disposal than for others: he can, for example, with much more confidence judge the state of the heart than that of the liver. But for each organ and system he has a body of knowledge about the range of normal function and the evidences of normal structure, so that equally well-trained physicians would agree about whether a particular system is working normally (which, in this context, is the same as being healthy). I do not want to overstate this: there can be much difference of opinion in difficult cases or regarding organs difficult to assess as to their functional and structural integrity: but on the whole the criteria are well known and become sharper with every advance in physiology, biochemistry, pathology, and anthropometry [435, p. 112].

The norms used are usually based on a particular population. But there are many instances in which average values in one population are not representative of others. For example, in the United States and in most other developed countries the criterion for hypertension based on population values is 140/95. Prospective studies, however, indicate that persons who maintain a blood pressure below this level, and as low as 100/60, have lower risks of death (208). Although such a lowered criterion might be more consistent with scientific knowledge, too few people in the developed countries have blood pressures this low to make it useful.

Frequently physicians must make evaluations when the norms denoting the presence of dysfunction are unclear, or the normal range varies widely among persons suffering no dysfunction:

> The adequate performance of the body working as a whole is highly individual; the range of variability in the human species is wide: performance is not the same in different races, in different climates, at different ages, in the two sexes, under innumerable conditions of past and present environment. And no instruments of precision, no application of recent discoveries in chemistry or physics can remove the difficulty. In short, for the most important of bodily functions, that which regulates the working of the whole, norms are so wide in range, or need to be so extensively hedged around with qualifying conditions that in clinical practice the physician must take the patient pretty much as supplying his own norm of total performance or behavior, and proceed by rough and ready appraisal of whether there has been any departure from this, when due allowance has been made for the environment in which the patient has been living [435, p. 113].

The Disease Concept in Psychiatry

Because I shall deal with mental disorders in some detail throughout this book, it is necessary to review the controversy as to whether these are diseases. The term "mental illness" is very general; its limits are ambiguous and arbitrary, and the rubric is presumed to contain a wide variety of conditions having little in common. Although this term is frequently used by psychiatrists as well as laymen, it is basically a social label describing deviation of specified types rather than a clear medical phenomenon. In practice, the term "mental illness" is used widely by experts, and thus it is not surprising that considerable confusion exists. In part this confusion is the result of the wide-reaching and somewhat ambiguous scope of psychiatric practice.

In recent years the most vociferous critic of the concept of mental illness has been Thomas Szasz (693; 695), a professor of psychiatry and a psychoanalyst. It is his contention that the notion of mental illness is derived from such phenomena as syphilis of the brain or similar conditions, in which it is apparent that peculiarities of behavior and thought are a direct result of the condition. He observes, however, that most of the symptoms called "mental illness" are observable not through brain lesions or similar physical indications but rather through deviation in behavior and thinking. It is Szasz's belief that the metaphor of illness is used to characterize problems in living that have no biological basis and that such judgments are based on ethical and psychosocial criteria. Szasz admits that particular disorders in behavior and thinking result from brain dysfunctions, but he contends that it would be more appropriate to say that some people labeled as mentally ill suffer from

diseases of the brain than to assert that all of those called mentally ill
are sick in a medical way. In his opinion, using the concept of mental
illness to characterize both disorders of the brain and deviation in behavior, thinking, and affect arising from other causes results in confused thinking and misuses of psychiatry. Szasz's argument proceeds
in the following way:

> The concept of illness, whether bodily or mental, implies *deviation from
> some clearly defined norm*. In the case of physical illness, the norm is the
> structural and functional integrity of the human body. Thus, although the
> desirability of physical health, as such, is an ethical value, what health *is*
> can be stated in anatomical and physiological terms. What is the norm
> deviation from which is regarded as mental illness? This question cannot be
> easily answered. But whatever this norm might be, we can be certain of only
> one thing: namely, that it is a norm that must be stated in terms of
> *psychosocial, ethical*, and *legal* concepts. For example, notions such as
> "excessive repression" or "acting out an unconscious impulse" illustrate
> the use of psychological concepts for judging (so-called) mental health and
> illness. The idea that chronic hostility, vengefulness, or divorce are indica-
> tive of mental illness would be illustrations of the use of ethical norms (that
> is, the desirability of love, kindness, and a stable marriage relationship). Fi-
> nally, the widespread psychiatric opinion that only a mentally ill person
> would commit homicide illustrates the use of a legal concept as a norm of
> mental health. The norm from which deviation is measured whenever one
> speaks of a mental illness is a *psychosocial and ethical one*. Yet, the
> remedy is sought in terms of *medical* measures which—it is hoped and as-
> sumed—are free from wide differences of ethical value. The definition of
> the disorder and the terms in which its remedy are sought are therefore at
> serious odds with one another. The practical significance of this covert
> conflict between the alleged nature of the defect and the remedy can
> hardly be exaggerated [693, p. 114].

One cannot help feeling some sympathy for Szasz's criticisms, as it
is apparent that many of the faults he points to are common in the practice of psychiatry. Yet it is not fully clear whether Szasz's criticism is
appropriate to a consideration of the viability of the disease concept
in psychiatry, or whether it is basically directed at the "uses" and
"abuses" of psychiatry for social purposes. It is true that many psychiatrists and others believe that anyone who commits homicide is mentally ill. But there are many psychiatrists who would not agree with
this judgment, which, in any case, is a social judgment and not a medical one. As we noted earlier, physicians—and particularly psychiatrists—often use a social concept of disease in evaluating their patients and in rendering judgments in various aspects of their participation as advisors in social matters. It is one thing to argue that many
psychiatrists use a social concept under the guise of a medical concept; it is quite another matter to argue that the medical disease concept has no place in the practice of psychiatry. Although many of

Szasz's specific criticisms of psychiatry have more or less justification, his contention that "mental illness" is a myth requires further scrutiny.

One of the most articulate spokesmen for the relevance of the disease concept in psychiatry has been Sir Aubrey Lewis, the late professor of psychiatry at the University of London. It therefore seems of some value to examine his viewpoint in depth in relation to the issues raised by Szasz. In essence, Lewis's position is that inappropriate and deviant behavior (although labeled as mental illness from a social point of view) is not sufficient to be labeled as a psychiatric condition. He believed that maladaptive and nonconforming behavior is pathological only when it is accompanied by a manifest disturbance of some function such as is evidenced by disturbed thinking as in delusions, or disturbed perceptions, hallucinations, and disturbed emotional states as shown by excessive anxiety or depression:

> What then is mental illness? Can it be recognized, as physical disease often is, by the qualitatively altered function of some part of the total, by disturbance of thinking, for example, or disturbance of perception? This is possible: we very frequently recognize a man to be mentally ill because he has delusions or hallucinations. But not always, for if the disturbance of part-functions is without influence on his conduct, or falls within certain categories which we regard as "normal," we do not infer "mental illness" from their presence. Thus in their *Phantasms of the Living* Myers, Podmore and Gurney devoted a chapter to the hallucinations of the sane. The procedure is then semantically confused: we have a class of perceptions judged abnormal on statistical grounds, which can be assessed as normal by certain value-judgments. The confusion is manifest in the discriminatory use made of certain signs of disturbed thinking: if a man expresses an irrational belief, e.g., that he has been bewitched, we do not call it a delusion, a sign of disease, unless we are satisfied that the manner in which he came by it is morbid. This would not necessarily be the case if he had been brought up among people who believed in witchcraft, whereas if he is an ordinary twentieth-century Londoner who has arrived at such a conviction through highly individual, devious, suspicion-laden mental processes, we call the belief abnormal and the man who holds it unhealthy.
>
> Two criteria have apparently been applied, then, to changes in function: a psychopathological one paying regard to the process, and a statistical one paying regard to the frequency of its occurrence.
>
> When the psychopathological criterion is looked at, it shows its kinship with the pathological criterion applied in evaluating physical diseases. Unless the phenomenon to which it is applied is gross, it can be used only by experts: just as the decision whether a tumour is malignant requires a highly trained judge, so does the decision whether a queer belief or a turn of mood is due to a pathological process. "Pathological," however, often has elusively vague referents. Most commonly the highly trained judge equates it with "unbalanced," i.e., lacking in stable internal and external adjustment [435, pp. 113-14].

It is clear from Lewis's statement that his concept of mental disease is more limited than those that Szasz describes as typical of psychiatry. This difference is explained in part by the fact that Szasz is directing his attention primarily to the work of American psychiatrists, while Lewis represents a rather different psychiatric tradition more characteristic of European psychiatry. American psychiatry has been more influenced by psychoanalysis and a variety of neo-Freudian views. In contrast, the basic orientation of most European psychiatrists is more strongly organic, and thus European psychiatrists are more apt to use limited disease concepts in describing psychiatric disorders. When American psychiatrists talk about disease they use this concept in a much wider sense than their European counterparts, including a variety of problems in living that many European psychiatrists would not regard as disease.

But even within the more limited European psychiatric context, Lewis's position has one basic weakness which he himself recognizes—the vagueness of the concept of psychiatric pathology. In the absence of clear physical and laboratory tests, the psychiatrist is dependent on his experience, judgment, and training in assessing which mental processes are normal and which ones are morbid, and the reliability and validity of such judgments must be demonstrated. In short, although the disease concept in psychiatry is not logically fallacious, as Lewis so aptly shows, the usefulness of adopting a medical disease concept in psychiatry remains to be demonstrated. As noted earlier, the medical disease concept is useful when a reliable diagnosis is possible and when the diagnosis implies the course of the disease, its etiology, and treatment procedures. Depending on the psychiatric dysfunction we discuss, these conditions are met to a greater or lesser degree. But, on the whole, the value of psychiatric disease models in terms of prediction largely remains to be demonstrated.

Lewis's position on the disease concept in psychiatry is further complicated by the social role and social position of psychiatry. While he himself argues for a limited role for psychiatry and cautions against expanding psychiatric concepts to all forms of deviation, psychiatry has concerned itself increasingly with problems many of which are related to morbidity and pathology only tangentially if at all: poverty, education, delinquency, marital unhappiness, political deviations (105). To the extent that these problems are characterized in the medical disease framework without a clear demonstration of "psychological pathology," the language of psychiatry becomes increasingly confused.

A paper by Rosenhan (596) has aroused considerable controversy concerning the diagnostic issue. He reports on eight "pseudopatients," researchers with no psychiatric histories or obvious psychiatric problems who gained admission to twelve different hospitals by complaining that they "heard voices." Once admitted to the psychiatric ward, the pseudopatients ceased simulating symptoms of abnormality. With the exception of one case, all patients were admitted with a diagnosis of schizophrenia and, when released, were discharged with a diagnosis of schizophrenia in remission. These pseudopatients were given more than 2,000 pills, including Elavil, Stelazine, Compazine, and Thorazine. Rosenhan describes many instances of powerlessness and depersonalization experienced by patients in these psychiatric units and, more to the point, argues that we cannot distinguish the sane from the insane, and therefore psychiatric diagnoses are neither reliable nor useful. He notes:

> It is clear that we cannot distinguish the sane from the insane in psychiatric hospitals. The hospital itself imposes a special environment in which the meanings of behavior can easily be misunderstood. The consequences to patients hospitalized in such an environment—the powerlessness, depersonalization, segregation, mortification, and self-labeling—seem undoubtedly countertherapeutic [596, p. 257].

Rosenhan's description has been given much uncritical attention in the social-science literature, yet the implications of his demonstration are not so clear as they might appear. What he actually shows is that patients requesting admission and reporting unusual symptoms frequently associated with a serious psychiatric ailment are suspected of having that ailment. This inference has been strongly defended by Robert Spitzer (661) as justifiable:

> Auditory hallucinations can occur in several kinds of mental disorders. The absence of a history of alcohol, drug abuse, or some other toxin, the absence of any signs of physical illness (such as high fever), the absence of evidence of distractibility, impairment in concentration, memory or orientation, and negative results from a neurological examination all make an organic psychosis extremely unlikely. The absence of a recent precipitating stress rules out a transient situational disturbance of psychotic intensity or (to use a nonofficial category) hysterical psychosis. The absence of a profound disturbance in mood rules out an affective psychosis....
>
> What about simulating mental illness? Psychiatrists know that occasionally an individual who has something to gain from being admitted to a psychiatric hospital will exaggerate or even feign psychiatric symptoms. This is a genuine diagnostic problem that psychiatrists and other physicians occasionally confront and is called "malingering." However, there was certainly no reason to believe that any of the pseudopatients had anything to gain from being admitted to a psychiatric hospital except relief from their alleged complaint, and therefore there was no reason to suspect that the illness was feigned. What possible diagnoses are left in the classification of mental disorders now used in this country for a patient with a presenting symptom of hallucinations, with the previously considered con-

ditions having been ruled out? There is only one—schizophrenia! [661, p. 462].

Furthermore, Spitzer maintains that the discharge diagnosis of the pseudopatients (schizophrenia in remission) is atypical, reflecting the fact that these patients were puzzling to the physicians who evaluated them. Quoting Kety, he makes the point that if a patient drank a quart of blood and came to a hospital emergency room vomiting blood, the hospital staff would predictably suspect that he had a bleeding peptic ulcer. Kety then asks whether such a demonstration would argue convincingly that medicine does not know how to diagnose peptic ulcers.

A careful reading of Rosenhan's paper would indicate that there is nothing in his study that speaks in any definitive way to the usefulness or validity of psychiatric diagnosis. What Rosenhan has shown is that hospital staff can be fooled by a patient who reports a serious symptom that cannot be independently validated, a situation characteristic of many areas of medical practice. In much of medical practice problems are identified by the fact that patients experience pain and discomfort and come seeking help; the patient's history and reports of symptoms are important aspects of the assessment. Rosenhan, however, like many others before him, does raise important issues concerning typical psychiatric practice. His study suggests the bias of physicians toward active treatment in situations of uncertainty, when the treatment may potentially do more harm than the symptoms disturbing the patient. Further, he shows how readily psychiatric hospitalization can be achieved, particularly if the patient is receptive to a hospital admission. Such practices have implications not only for the patient and the way he conceives of himself but also for the medical-care system, because hospitalization is an expensive endeavor. In short, Rosenhan, like Szasz, raises more issues about the manner in which psychiatrists perform than about the usefulness of a medical disease model for psychiatry.

Both Szasz and Rosenhan make useful and valid points about assumptions and practices in everyday psychiatry, but their criticisms do not negate the usefulness of the disease model in psychiatry. The further development of such a model must, however, be pursued with circumspection and awareness of the dangers involved. The study of psychiatric phenomena requires more refined classification that effectively distinguishes among varying symptom clusters. The specifications for making varying diagnoses must be clear and understood. As I indicated earlier, if the diagnosis is wrong, the predictions resulting from this assessment are also likely to be faulty. Although the disease model is still very poorly developed in psychiatry, there are important diagnostic distinctions that are increasingly related to the treatments used. Drugs for the treatment of schizophrenia and depression are quite different, and the manic and depressive phases of bipolar depressive conditions require management different from other types of affective disorders.

A major problem in expanding the disease approach is that the domain of psychiatry has become very large, and a great deal of psychiatric practice has little to do with anything remotely resembling psychiatric disease. As Szasz has noted so well, much of psychiatry deals with ordinary problems of living and existential crises, and pseudomedical approaches that label these problems as illnesses but provide no useful information or improved management may do considerable damage. Some psychiatrists interested in a disease model feel that psychiatric efforts should be more restricted and that much of the counseling typical of everyday psychiatry should be left to other professions. The fact is, however, that many psychiatrists deal with these problems, which are a lucrative aspect of their practices; it seems unlikely that they will soon abandon these areas. Present-day psychiatry is once again moving closer to a biological disease perspective, but it is important that in doing so practitioners do not confuse the usefulness of this model for investigation and improved understanding with its usefulness for dealing with many of the problems that psychiatrists are now called upon to manage. Much of the progress in the care of the mentally ill has developed from an optimism about the coping resilience of patients— positive expectations increase patients' levels of performance. Too great a focus on a disease model—and an assumption of biological or biochemical determinism—may not provide a great deal of added information and at the same time may be a disincentive to do the things we know how to do (488, pp. 53–54).

Diagnostic Reliability

I have already noted that general assessments of psychiatric health are less than adequate. Marie Jahoda, a psychologist sympathetic to psychiatric efforts in this sphere, has observed that "apart from extremes, there is no agreement on the types of behavior which is reasonable to call 'sick'" (360; p. 13). Similarly, Redlich (577; 578), a psychiatrist and former dean of the medical school at Yale University, has come to the conclusion that the practical criteria used by psychiatrists in assessing mental health and illness are similar to those criteria used by other definers in the community. Although Redlich overstates his view, his comments and the views of many others who have studied the problem of definition suggest that the criteria used in the general assessment of mental health vary considerably from one psychiatrist to another.

Although it is fairly obvious that it is extremely difficult, if not impossible, to define in concrete terms differing degrees of "mental health" (for a sympathetic view toward this effort see 654; 655), there is reason to believe that it is possible to identify at least some psychiatric conditions in a reasonably reliable fashion. Various techniques have been used in attempting to define cases of psychiatric disturbance: clinical interviews, structured and guided interviews, psychological tests and scales, symptom reporting, and measures of social adjustment. Psychiatrists tend to regard the clinical interview as the most valid mode of assessment, and we shall therefore devote our primary attention to this technique.

In evaluating the adequacy of the clinical interview for the purpose of psychiatric assessment, it is essential that we be sensitive to the characteristics being assessed, the conditions under which assessment was being made, and the function of the assessment (461). Psychiatrists make diagnostic assessments for many purposes, and the level of diagnostic reliability may be considerably higher in some spheres of assessment than in others. For example, diagnostic classifications may be used for clinical psychiatry, for psychiatric research and epidemiological investigations, for social purposes as when the psychiatrist participates in legal and organizational proceedings, and for various other reasons. The levels of reliability obtained in one type of situation may be very different from those obtained under different circumstances, because in each case the psychiatrist may be directing himself to different questions.

If we attempt to make an overall judgment of psychiatric assessment, we must conclude that the level of agreement among different psychiatrists is extremely variable. Blum (75), for example, who has reviewed numerous studies on psychiatric assessment, concludes that there are many sources of interview error, and unless they can be controlled the psychiatric assessment can be inadequate and unreliable. The studies Blum reviews reflect concurrence among persons who have studied the issue that levels of agreement in everyday practice are low. In order to give the reader some feeling for these findings, a short excerpt from the Blum review is reproduced below:

> Ash reports that three psychiatrists working in a clinic could agree on the major diagnostic category on only 45 percent of the patients who were seen by each. . . . Clausen and Kohn, studying diagnostic consistency among patients with two or more hospital admissions, found that there was consistency on the major syndrome diagnosis in only 28 percent of the patients who were diagnosed in first one and then another hospital. Lilienfeld, reporting on field interviews, found only a 55 percent agreement between two interviewers. . . .
>
> Using military data Terris, in reviewing selective service statistics

presented by Stouffer, points out that the range of neuropsychiatric rejections varied from .05 per hundred to 51 per hundred, depending on the induction station. Stouffer also reported a wide variation in specific diagnosis given to rejected selectees, for example the proportions diagnosed as psychoneurotic varied among stations from 2.7 percent to 90.2 percent. . . .

Mehlman distributed one group of 597 patients for diagnosis among nine psychiatrists and another group of 1,358 patients among sixteen psychiatrists. He tested for significant differences in diagnostic tendencies among the psychiatrists, and found differences significant at the .001 level between the proportions of patients different diagnosticians assigned to the organic versus the psychogenic categories. There were differences significant at the .01 level between the proportions various psychiatrists diagnosed as manic-depressive versus schizophrenic [75; pp. 254–56].

There are many studies and reports consistent with the studies reported by Blum, which reflect the low level of reliability in diagnosis in the everyday practice of psychiatry. However, it is essential that these results be viewed in proper perspective if we are to understand both the difficulties and potentialities of psychiatric assessment. In reviewing such studies, it is important to consider: (1) what was being assessed; (2) the population being evaluated (Are they a group of patients complaining of suffering, or are they a "normal" population such as army recruits or students?); (3) the circumstances under which the assessments were made (Were they hurried judgments without careful examination, as with selective service, or were they judgments based on a careful history and examination?); (4) the competence of the assessors (Who were the assessors and what kinds of training had they received?); (5) what kinds of effort were made to reach agreement (Were the interview and the various criteria standardized, and were the assessors trained to use the same system of assessment?) (401).

It is fairly obvious that the issues mentioned above are likely to have a substantial influence on the degree of agreement reached by psychiatrists judging the same patients independently. Doctors trained in a standardized and rigorous fashion can probably rate many specific symptoms with high reliability. The fact, therefore, that psychiatric screening in selective service is unreliable cannot be taken as support for the conclusion that reliability of psychiatric diagnosis cannot be achieved. In the selective service situation, for example, the assessor attempts to select unstable persons from a flow of young men who are not presenting particular symptoms to him. Moreover, these judgments are often made in a minute or two on the basis of a few general questions. Such data reflect little more than the abysmal quality of psychiatric assessment within this context.

Having determined some of the criteria for evaluating psychiatric diagnosis, we must consider what evidence there is to support the idea that a high level of agreement among psychiatrists is possible under more rigorous and standardized conditions. Is it possible, for example, to eliminate the chaotic quality of psychiatric assessment in research endeavors aimed at studying particular problems of mental disorder? Research directed toward this issue presents a more hopeful picture than the Blum statement suggests, although the results are far from ideal.

Vera Norris (539), in a statistical study of patients in London, investigated 2,804 men and 3,459 women who were transferred from observation units to mental hospitals. The transfer provided the opportunity to compare the provisional diagnosis made at the observation unit with the final diagnosis made at the mental hospital. Norris found the following levels of agreement for various diagnoses: schizophrenia (68 percent), manic-depressive psychosis (69 percent), mental deficiency (70 percent), and psychoses resulting from specified organic causes excluding cerebrovascular psychosis (80 percent). In contrast, she found rather poor levels of agreement for such diagnoses as paranoid psychosis (29 percent), senile dementia (53 percent), and cerebrovascular psychosis (29 percent). A similarly low level of agreement was found in the diagnosis of the psychoneuroses. Although Norris's results are less than fully heartening, her levels of agreement are further complicated by the fact that the psychiatrist in the mental hospital was aware of the diagnosis made at the observation unit; in short, the two judgments were contaminated. The author's conclusion that this awareness was likely to have little influence on the second diagnosis is curious, and the lack of independence in the two diagnoses raises questions about the levels of agreement reached. On the positive side, Norris's findings suggest that even within a nonstandardized diagnostic situation a reasonable level of agreement could be reached in several areas.

Another study in England by Kreitman and his colleagues (402) compared the evaluations of patients referred to the Chichester Mental Health Service who were independently examined by two psychiatrists at approximately three-day intervals. The evaluators used an agreed-upon list of 11 possible diagnoses and agreed in their diagnoses in approximately 65 percent of the cases. Agreement was particularly high in the affective psychoses, organic conditions, and psychoses of old age. Agreement on schizophrenia, anxiety states, neurotic depression, and other conditions was low. In the same study the evaluators had a checklist of 28 common symptoms, and were asked to mark for each patient the symptoms they considered important in deciding diagnosis and disposition. The overall level of agreement about symptoms was 46 percent, and the rate of agreement varied considerably with different symptoms. The highest level of agreement was reached in the case of depression (85 percent), but levels of less than 50 percent agreement were found in such symptoms as loss of concentration, hallucinations, loss of memory, and anxiety. The levels of agreement described by Norris and by Kreitman and his colleagues are considerably higher than those in several other comparable studies, but even these levels are not particularly high.

From the point of view of psychiatric research, psychiatric records are frequently used for the purpose of selecting a diagnostic group for study. The reliability of such assessments made from records constitutes an important issue in epidemiological and psychiatric research. Such investigations are frequently undertaken without making serious attempts to assess the reliability of the selection of patients for study. In one study of the reliability of such selection, two psychiatrists independently rated records of mental patients as to whether the patient was probably schizophrenic, a doubtful schizophrenic, or whether the diagnosis could not be confirmed as indicating schizophrenia. If such estimates were made completely on the basis of random guessing we would expect agreement in assessment in approximately one-third of the estimates. The evaluators were able to agree in 68 percent of the cases, a level of agreement considerably better than chance, although not ideal (547). In another study a similar method was used to select patients from three hospitals for inclusion. The casenotes were read independently by two psychiatrists, who classified each case as "probably schizophrenia," "possibly schizophrenia," or "probably not schizophrenia." On the basis of chance we would expect the two psychiatrists to agree in about one-third of the cases. The levels of agreement reached in the three hospitals were 71 percent, 79 percent, and 80 percent (95).

The levels of agreement cited above typify what can be achieved when psychiatric evaluators use similar criteria and definitions in their assessments. In the general practice of psychiatry, however, psychiatrists work with very different concepts, ideas, and criteria, and thus it is unlikely that levels of agreement of similar magnitude can be achieved in general clinical practice. The variability of such criteria is suggested by the tremendous differences in the diagnostic classification of patients from one hospital to another. Similarly, the substantial differences in reported rates of varying diagnoses in the United States and England suggest that psychiatrists in the two countries have different diagnostic conceptions. For example, in 1956 first-admission rates for schizophrenia were 56 percent greater in American public and private mental hospitals than in England and Wales (40 percent more men and 73 percent more women). Conversely, there was a relative scarcity of patients diagnosed as "manic depressive" in the United States (400).

In order to understand these variabilities better, the National Institute of Mental Health initiated a collaborative study of schizophrenia in England and the United States. By using a standardized instrument, similarly administered to comparable hospital populations in the two countries, it was demonstrated that the reported variation in the prevalence of schizophrenia in the two countries was a product not of real differences but of variabilities in diagnostic criteria used by American and British psychiatrists. When the same criteria were applied in the two countries, the proportion of schizophrenics was similar (146).

Because the content of psychosis varies in different cultural groups, there has been disagreement as to whether these different manifestations represent a single illness expressed differently in different countries. Using standardized diagnostic criteria (775), as in the collaborative study in England and the United States, the World Health Organization sponsored a collaborative study in nine countries in such varied contexts as Agra, Cali, Ibadan, Moscow, and Washington. Although these data are not completely analyzed, they suggest that schizophrenia, when defined comparably in varying areas, is very much the same in its basic symptoms despite different modes of expressing disorder (786).

The possibilities for reliable psychiatric diagnosis under carefully constructed interview procedures are suggested by the work of the British Medical Research Council's Social Psychiatry Research Unit. An elaborate semistructured diagnostic interview, involving more than 400 items, was developed for the purpose of assessing the patient's present psychiatric state (772; 775). In order to evaluate the reliability of this interview, 172 patients were evaluated independently by two psychiatrists using the same interview and trained to use the same diagnostic criteria and definitions. The two psychiatrists independently agreed on the diagnostic category in 83.7 percent of the cases, and they partially agreed in a further 7 percent of the cases. They disagreed in approximately 10 percent of the cases. Agreement was highest for schizophrenia (92 percent) and the other psychoses (87 percent), but agreement on psychoneurotic categories was considerably higher than in previous studies: neurotic depression (80 percent agreement), anxiety state (76.5 percent agreement), and others (64.6 percent agreement). It is important to note, however, that these levels of agreement were reached by an extremely talented group of professionals, and only with substantial effort. These methods are now used widely in diagnostic investigation, but diagnosis in everyday psychiatric practice tends to be sloppy and unreliable.

In taking a critical view of psychiatric assessment, it is important to recognize that many medical assessments also have very low reliability, particularly when criteria are not explicit, when evaluators are not trained in a standardized way, and when assessments are made in a hurried and careless fashion (132, 221, 260). Similarly, there are wide differences among the diagnostic skills and abilities of doctors, so that levels of reliability achieved among particular specialists are considerably higher than those achieved in everyday general medical practice. In the field of roentgenology, for example, we know that reading of X rays can achieve very high levels of reliability among skilled and experienced radiologists, especially when particular kinds of readings are required. However, under hurried conditions of medical practice even a well-trained person reading hundreds of X rays at a time may miss as many as 20 to 25 percent of the films showing abnormalities, some of which are apparently very large and easily discerned (387). In a similar vein, Fletcher (221) had eight experienced physicians interested in respiratory disease examine 20 patients indicating the presence and absence of signs of emphysema, such as impaired chest expansion, impaired breath sounds, and absent cardiac impulse. Clinical assessments varied substantially among these physicians. Bakwin (40) reported on physicians who judged the advisability of tonsillectomy for 1,000 school children. Of these children, 611 had their tonsils removed. Those remaining were examined by another physician, and 174 were selected for tonsillectomy. Another group of doctors examined the final 205 children, 99 of whom were adjudged as requiring tonsillectomy. In short, each group of doctors established a different frame of reference for judging deviation from the norm.

Although it is fairly clear that psychiatrists cannot agree on such global concepts as the presence of health and illness, given the lack of specificity in these concepts, we have shown that it is possible to achieve improvements in the reliability of diagnosis in particular conditions if careful modes of assessment are developed, standardized norms arrived at, and assessors trained in a rigorous and standardized fashion. In noting the possibilities for improving reliability, we have not demonstrated the usefulness of such definitions, which depend on their adequacy in predicting the course the disease is likely to take, for implying etiology and for optimally suggesting treatment plans to control or remedy these conditions. We now turn to a brief consideration of the validity of psychiatric diagnoses.

Usefulness of the Disease Model in Psychiatry

Once a diagnosis is established as reasonably reliable, we then must consider what we have achieved. It is apparent that modest and limited concepts of psychiatric disease have some value. Psychotic and confused behavior can often be traced to disorders caused by or associated with damage to brain-tissue function. Such disorders may be a consequence of infection, trauma, and nutritional, metabolic, and circulatory disorders. A disease model is useful and informative in such conditions as an intracranial tumor or paresis due to syphilis. Of course, debate does not focus on such conditions, which account for a minority of the mentally ill. The area of controversy centers primarily around the majority of mental disorders that have no clearly defined tangible cause and involve no definable structural changes; it is such conditions that make up the bulk of the psychiatrist's work.

In a diagnosis of schizophrenia (the most important group of psychotic conditions), a reasonable degree of reliability is possible under careful investigatory conditions. Although the course of these conditions is difficult to predict, once he has made a diagnosis the psychiatrist has a reasonable concept of the prognosis, given some information on the premorbid personality of the patient. Diagnosis, however, provides no information about etiology, because this issue is uncertain and hotly debated and treatment techniques have not yet proved successful. Thus establishing a diagnosis of schizophrenia in a medical sense does not determine to any great extent how the doctor will manage the case. As Professor Ødegaard, a prominent European psychiatrist, has noted:

> Confusion may arise if one does not keep in mind the nature of the concept of schizophrenia. It is not, and should not be treated as, a disease entity of a biochemical or genetical nature, but merely a reaction type which has been selected more or less arbitrarily because of its operational usefulness (Adolf Meyer). It does not, therefore, serve any useful purpose to let "ideological" considerations influence our diagnostic practice: we do not reduce the chances of recovery of our patient by calling him, or not calling him, a schizophrenic, and the choice of therapy (psychotherapy versus ECT or drugs) is quite independent of our diagnostic label [541, p. 296].

If Ødegaard's statement is to be taken as correct, the diagnosis of schizophrenia constitutes, for the most part, an unconfirmed medical theory.

In contrast, the diagnosis of depressive conditions leads to a more hopeful prognosis and better alternatives for managing the case. The recognition of depression as a symptom is quite reliable, although the reliability problems increase substantially when psychiatrists attempt to differentiate among varying types of depressive conditions. Indeed, major psychiatric authorities on depressive illness are divided as to whether subdivisions of depressive conditions can reasonably be differentiated. Sir Aubrey Lewis (434), an eminent lifetime student of this condition, took the view that the symptoms of depression occur in a wide variety of combinations and that significant subtypes cannot be abstracted from these variations. Others believe that there are at least two distinct subtypes: endogenous (having no clear relationship to environmental stimulation) and reactive. The observation that a patient has a depressive condition, however, often leads to a reasonable prediction of its course and particular remedial measures, although etiology is still uncertain. Available means for managing depression through drugs and electric convulsive therapy appear to relate to improvement in the patient's condition, and lithium seems successfully to contain the manic phase of bipolar affective disorders (745), even though the specific effects of treatment in depression are not well understood. In recent years considerable progress has been made in tracing the effects of drugs on norepinephrine and dopamine in the brain, and these effects are believed to be relevant to both mania and psychotic symptoms (102, p. 8; 386, p. 5).

There have been a variety of other exciting leads in biological psychiatry as well. Research is proceeding, for example, on the endorphins, brain peptides that act like opiates. It has been suggested that these substances may be involved in maintaining "normal behavior," and one group has reported dramatic improvement in schizophrenic patients given a particular opiate antagonist (303a). While similar enthusiasms in the past have turned out to be unjustified, there seems little question but that better understanding of brain processes will contribute importantly to understanding and treating mental illness more effectively.

In the area of the psychoneuroses diagnosis is difficult and frequently unreliable, although some diagnoses of particular neuroses, such as some of the phobias and obsessive-compulsive conditions, tend to be reasonably adequate. In general, information on the course, etiology, and treatment of the psychoneuroses does not follow from the diagnosis. The course tends to be uncertain, the etiology disputed, and the usefulness of available treatments questionable. Some specific conditions within this larger group, however, do conform to scientific diagnostic models. Certain phobias, for example, can be explained in terms of learning, and they tend to respond to desensitization therapy based on learning theory (457). The extent to which behavioral conditioning theories and associated treatments will be useful in a variety of psychoneurotic conditions is still, however, a matter requiring continued study.

Social Concept of Disease

The disease model and its application are an indispensable aspect of the doctor's orientation and role. Learning to use a disease-diagnostic model is adaptive in that it provides the doctor with a helpful orientation to the patient's problem and facilitates his ability to do his job. The actual practice of medicine, however, is more complicated than the disease model suggests because the role of physician is a social role as well as a highly technical medical role, and much that comes to the doctor's attention involves conditions that are not diseases in any sense. Much of medical practice involves the care of nondiseased persons, as in preventive medicine: immunization, pre- and postnatal care, and well-baby care. Another large proportion of practice is involved with difficulties of a social and familial nature and in rendering social judgments concerning health fitness, as in employment and insurance examinations. Still another large part of practice involves persons who are clearly deviant in their behavior and feelings but who are frequently not sick according to a medical theory of disease: the behavior problem, the person seeking certification of disability, the person who wishes to improve his appearance by losing weight or through some form of surgical correction, and so on. Because doctors themselves are frequently unclear about the logical structure of the theories they use, disease metaphors are often adopted to describe from the medical-scientific perspective problems that are clearly not diseases. Many laymen, and some doctors as well, will use the concept of disease to discuss aspects of people and situations they find repulsive, threatening, or in need of remedy; these, however, are social judgments and not medical ones. Similarly, doctors often use such metaphors when they are really rendering social judgments; because doctors are experts in disease, we often assume the correctness of such labels without careful scrutiny. For our purposes it is essential that we recognize that physicians use the disease concept both as a medical hypothesis and as a social concept, and it is this double use of the term that creates dangerous misunderstandings. Ambiguous use of the concept of sickness may, however, facilitate meeting particular social needs and dealing with particular social problems.

In their social capacity, doctors are called upon to manage people and situations. Frequently, in dealing with the chronically ill or with known patients, the diagnostic assessment has already been made; the patient's physical condition is no longer problematic. Treatment, however, may have to continue over a long period of time and the doctor, if he is to meet his responsibilities as a physician, must attune himself to the social situation of the patient. He must understand what consequences the illness has for the patient, his family, and his work, and he must also appreciate that the environment in which the patient lives can have a profound influence on the course his condition takes. Whether it be a problem of adjusting the diabetic's use of insulin or dealing with the heart patient's work situation, failure to consider the social context of disease may affect not only the patient's health condition but, perhaps even more important, his social welfare.

Throughout history the social aspects of medical practice have been part of the doctor's responsibility. It is primarily in recent years, with the proliferation of technical medical knowledge, that many doctors, in concentrating on what they know how to do well, are failing to give attention to the "whole man." And it is increasingly recognized that the modern doctor does not perform very well in this sphere. There are those in our age of technical specialization who would like to divorce the doctor's technical medical role from his social role and assign the latter to a new specialist. It is not my intention to get involved in these polemical arguments, although later we shall consider some of the problems that have accompanied the technical development of medicine.

In commenting on the social role of the doctor, it should be noted that the psychiatrist—perhaps more than any other doctor—occupies a social as well as a scientific role, and his judgments have social influence well beyond the medical context. In turn, the views of health and disease held by the psychiatrist reflect social philosophies to a very large extent. The psychiatrist's view of disease, more than that of his nonpsychiatric colleagues, will reflect the particular center where he has been trained, the theoretical orientations he holds, his psychiatric interests, and even his values. Raines and Rohrer (575), in an investigation of psychiatric assessments, found that two psychiatrists, each interviewing the same man, not only observed different personality traits but also reported different dominant defense mechanisms used by him in everyday behavior. Raines and Rohrer also found that particular psychiatrists had a preferred personality-type classification that they used more frequently than other psychiatrists. In attempting to account for their results, these investigators suggest that each psychiatrist's life experiences make him more sensitive to certain aspects of the patient, resulting in particular distortions of his perception of the patient's personality structure that may be projected in the diagnosis.

Structural Features of the Physician's Role

As Talcott Parsons (549) has pointed out in his classic analysis of medical practice, there are several features of the physician's role that must be explicitly recognized because of their great importance. First, he notes that caring for the sick is a functionally specialized full-time professional activity. This position is *achieved* through the development of a minimum standard of technical proficiency. The high technical competence required of the doctor also implies a *specificity of function*. Moreover, the doctor is expected to maintain a stance of *affective neutrality*, i.e., whether he dislikes or likes a patient should have no bearing on the way he deals with the case. He is expected to approach the patient in objective and scientifically justified terms. Finally, the ideology of the profession emphasizes the welfare of the patient, which the doctor is expected to put above his personal interests.

This system of expectations defining the doctor's role, of course, does not guarantee that the physician will live up fully to these standards nor that doctors will be selected only on achievement criteria. Although professional medical status involves the achievement of technical skills, the sons of fathers of varying social status have very different opportunities to acquire these technical skills. Because medical schools drop very few students, getting into a medical school constitutes one of the major barriers in achieving medical status. Although the doctor's competence in human affairs is relatively specific, there is no question that doctors are called on to deal with many problems outside the scope of their technical competence, and some doctors come to regard themselves as experts in areas in which they have little technical competence. Although we expect the doctor to treat all people equally regardless of his likes and dislikes, doctors, like most mortals, show preferences that affect the way in which they orient themselves to their patients. Although this is a matter that has not been intensively studied, and although doctors do not consider this a polite area of conversation, there is no question that preferental behavior is common in medical practice, and the doctor's social values affect not only the way he deals with particular patients but also decisions about such vital matters as the maintenance of life. Sudnow (684), in his study of dying, provides several examples of the way the doctor's social definition of the patient affected the measures he would take to keep the patient alive. In a similar vein, it has been found that Catholic doctors are not as liberal in providing birth-control information to their patients as are their non-Catholic counterparts, even when the patient was non-Catholic (149). Finally, although doctors are expected to be sacrificing and to place the patient's needs above their own, doctors as a group seem to distribute along the entire spectrum of this dimension. Many doctors refuse to make night calls and home calls even in emergencies; some doctors give great emphasis to maximizing their profits even if this involves great financial hardship on the part of the patient; and some doctors frequently behave in a selfish manner in many other spheres. The medical profession has, of course, many dedicated people who give of themselves and literally sacrifice their own interests for the sake of their patients. The point is that medicine has its share of both angels and scoundrels.

If all I have said is correct, then it is reasonable to inquire as to the value of such representations of the structural characteristics of the physician's role, because it is clear that Parsons's observations are not accurate descriptions of the physician's behavior. They do, however, have some utility for predicting those elements of the physician's behavior that the public will criticize and those the doctor will be defensive about. Thus, although the doctor may show preferential behavior toward particular patients or behave in a selfish and unsympathetic manner, the visibility of such behavior will lead to public criticism. The doctor will feel a need at that point to justify or excuse his behavior. We do not become angry when we become aware that the businessman is motivated primarily toward making a profit in his transactions with us; but should the doctor-patient relationship have too great a profit taint, the patient will see this as cause to criticize the doctor. Thus it becomes clear that the expectations of the physician's role are different from those of many other roles in the community.

It is important that we do not overestimate the utility of such structural characterizations. The behavior of doctors, like the behavior of most other people, varies widely in response to their learning and experience and the community contexts to which they are exposed. Because doctors are the products of different experiences and life contexts and because the environments in which they work vary widely, it is reasonable to expect to find large differences in their behavior. It is our basic contention that the orientations of doctors are as much molded by their environmental context and their adaptive needs as are those of patients. Having considered the ways the physician views disease and the patient, we now turn to a consideration of what we know about the occurrence of health and disease in human populations. We begin with a discussion of the major techniques for studying such issues: epidemiological investigation and controlled clinical trials.

Chapter 4

METHODOLOGICAL PERSPECTIVES

Our understanding of health and disease is based on countless observations, a wealth of clinical experience, study of disease occurrence in various populations, natural and laboratory experiments, and masses of statistical data gathered in surveys and from the records of hospitals and health agencies. The techniques and problems underlying each of these methodological approaches have sufficient substance for many volumes. Thus all I can do in this chapter is suggest some of the more important approaches, methodological issues, and problems characteristic of the study of health and disease. I shall emphasize those issues that are of most importance for studying social factors as they affect health and disease.

Clinical Approach

Until recently, most of our knowledge of disease factors and the effects of mental states on bodily ones came through the study of clinical material that reached the physician's attention through his own practice, clinics, and hospitals. Over the years such clinical material has provided much knowledge and insight into disease processes. The clinician usually approaches his material by collecting a series of cases of specified kind. His procedure is to study them carefully, making detailed observations on the manifestations and course of the condition. By observing a number of cases he develops insights into those aspects of the disease that are common to the group and those that are more idiosyncratic. He may also observe the factors and agents that seem to be associated with changes in the course of the condition. In short, the clinician is concerned with why people get ill and how ill people get better; he seeks clues to the possible etiology (or cause) of various conditions, as well as to those methods of intervention that seem to relieve the patient or his condition.

Much of our knowledge concerning the effectiveness of various drugs and other therapeutic agents came in the past largely from the cumulation of the experiences of various doctors. Drug firms would distribute new medications for particular conditions to a variety of general practitioners, asking them to report on the efficacy of the agent in contrast to alternatives already on the market. Much of medical opinion concerning the effectiveness of various drugs was based on such clinical experiences rather than on careful experimentation. Often these clinical impressions were correct, but errors were also frequent. As medical practice and investigation became more complicated and scientific in character and as the number of therapeutic agents and new techniques used by physicians multiplied, it became apparent that medical knowledge and the imputed effectiveness of medical techniques and therapeutic agents must depend on more rigorous evaluations and more adequate samples than the clinical context makes available. Higher standards of evaluation are also encouraged by new developments in methodology and statistics and increasing expectations and demands for medical effectiveness, not only from the consumer but also from a variety of government agencies such as the Food and Drug Administration. It is therefore not surprising that growing attention has been devoted to controlled clinical trials and population studies.

From the point of view of the methodologist, the clinical perspective has three major shortcomings: (1) it often fails to provide an adequate or *representative sample* of the entity being studied; (2) the techniques for *evaluating change* are often faulty or biased; and (3) it often fails to provide appropriate *comparison groups* for proper evaluations of effectiveness. Because these issues are central to all investigation in medicine and medical sociology, we shall briefly discuss each of them in turn.

Adequate Sampling

As evaluation moves from clinical to more sophisticated techniques of evaluation, it is increasingly recognized that an adequate sample is an important prerequisite for competent studies of disease processes. The meaning of the term "adequacy" depends, of course, on the aim of the investigation, but usually it refers to the degree to which the sample is representative of the population to which the investigator wishes to generalize. Medical studies, however, have depended too often on populations of persons who came to clinics, hospitals, and other medical facilities for diagnosis and treatment, but who were not necessarily representative of the populations with which the investigator was concerned. Such populations are accessible and convenient, and research based on such captive groups is relatively economical. Moreover, the assumption is often made that sampling problems are less important when basic human processes are being studied. However, to the extent that known clinic and hospital populations are not representative of those having a particular disorder, and to the extent that selection of these persons as patients occurs on some systematic basis, biases that may lead to incorrect and unwarranted conclusions are often introduced into studies of disease and disability (482).

Various factors other than severity of illness bring people to medical facilities. These selective influences may so bias the arrival of diseased persons that samples drawn from such contexts are *unrepresentative* of the population of ill people. For example, Miller, Court, Walton, and Knox (515), in their study of 847 children during their first five years in Newcastle-upon-Tyne, recorded 8,467 significant incidents of illness of which 42 percent were untreated. They reported that untreated illness was not insignificant in that it included one in five attacks of bronchitis and pneumonia during the first year, and two of every three attacks of vomiting and diarrhea during the five-year period. Similarly, Mechanic and Volkart, analyzing data relative to a college-student population, demonstrated that patients in various diagnostic groups constituted persons who were overrepresented in respect to particular social variables. This suggests that there were biases in the way patients with certain diseases became subjects for treatment, as compared with those who had similar difficulties but did not become patients (503). These and several other studies demonstrate that there are various selective forces that influence the way clinical populations arrive from a population at risk. Populations characterized by such factors may give clinicians a view of disease that is not representative of the diseased population.

In many situations clinical observations have been adequate for providing a rather good view of the natural unfolding of disease. There have been occasions, however, on which field studies have revealed the erroneous nature of clinical observations of the natural history of a particular disease. Until the late 1940s, for example, histoplasmosis was thought to be a rare tropical disease with an expected fatal outcome. Subsequently it was discovered that the disease is widely prevalent, with fatal outcome or impairment rather rare (614). At one time it was believed that Buerger's disease afflicted primarily Russian Jews. It was later found that this erroneous notion arose from the fact that work on the disease was done at Mount Sinai Hospital in New York City, which had a large population of Russian-born Jews (524). Professor Morris recalls searching the pathology archives of the London Hospital in a study of coronary disease and being puzzled by the rarity of reports on ruptured ventricles, although there were many examples of other manifestations of the disease. He later discovered that almost all such cases were sent to the district medical examiner because he had a special interest in such cases; thus they became part of some other set of records (524). Patients with similar types of problems may go to varying types of therapists, including physicians, psychologists, and social workers. To the extent that such a process is selective, no single type of therapist will provide a representative sample of patients with a particular kind of problem(296; 501).

Various field studies in recent years have supported the observation that samples drawn from medical and hospital contexts do not provide a representative clinical or social picture. As Scheff comments:

> In recent years physicians and social scientists have reported finding disease signs and deviant behavior prevalent in normal, non-institutionalized populations. It has been shown, for instance, that deviant acts, some of a serious nature, are widely admitted by persons in random samples of normal populations. There is some evidence which suggests that grossly deviant, "psychotic" behavior has at least temporarily existed in relatively large proportions of a normal population. Finally, there is a growing body of evidence that many signs of physical disease are distributed quite widely in normal populations. A recent survey of simple high blood pressure indicated that the prevalence ranged from 11.4 to 37.2 percent in the various subgroups studied [614, p. 101].

Frequent occurrence of particular symptoms or groups of symptoms in untreated populations may imply diverse interpretations. If the symptom is one that when observed in clinical settings is believed to have medical significance, then the observation that it is common in the general population may mean either that the assumption of "significance" may be incorrect or, in contrast, that there are many persons in the population who require medical attention but have not received it.

The significance of any symptom or sign is frequently dependent on its adequacy for predicting future morbid signs. Determination of the importance of a symptom or sign is thus a matter that can be settled by the collection of facts that allow for evaluating the hypothesis of "significance." In short, understanding the course of disease in untreated populations helps clarify the meaning of particular symptoms and signs, and at times such information may even lead to the revision of medical norms.

Evaluating Change

The clinician must be his own tool for evaluating change. His observations of change will be impressionistic, and his gradations of severity of illness and amount of change are likely to be imprecise. Even such standard techniques as taking blood pressure, reading X rays, and listening to the heart and lungs are subject to considerable unreliability (i.e., low correspondence between test and retest) unless the procedure is standardized and checked. Among the many factors, for example, that may affect blood pressure readings are variations in the size, rigidity, and proper application of the cuff, dirtiness or deviation from verticality of the manometer, variations resulting from various aspects of the patient (changes in posture, physical repose, mental state, and so on), and errors in reading the scale (222). When the clinician moves to a level of general assessment of change, the situation becomes much more precarious.

Several difficulties in assessing change result directly from the clinician's position in the medical-care sequence. Patients often enter treatment during periods of severe distress; in the case of mental disorders and many other conditions they frequently enter at a point of very high intrapsychic pain and disorganization of behavior. Because many conditions are self-limited and others recurrent, the natural course of most complaints is improvement and alleviation of symptoms. Thus physicians tend to see patients improve, and it is not unnatural that they often attribute such changes that occur after entering treatment to therapeutic intervention and not to the natural course of the complaint. It is particularly interesting to note that patients with incurable diseases often improve dramatically before beginning on a long downward course. It is difficult to explain these dramatic improvements except to note either that they result from placebo effect or that the base from which such improvements are noticed is the point at which the patient entered treatment; frequently the degree of distress felt at this point is higher than an average level for the condition, because increased distress is one factor bringing people into medical care.

The clinician's assessment of patient improvement frequently depends on what patients tell him. But there are subtle psychological pressures on the patient that encourage him to report improvement even when no real improvement is taking place. The patient very much wants to feel that he is getting better, and he may present a picture of improvement motivated by a desire for rewarding the doctor for his efforts on the patient's behalf. Also, because doctors like to believe— like most of us—that their efforts make a difference, subtle psychological forces are operating that encourage the doctor to see improvement in his patients. The amount of research in recent years illustrating these subtle judgmental influences forces us to take them into account. We must be on guard so as not to make the error of the fictitious doctor who concluded that he could cure colds because all of his patients with colds got better, and none of them died. All therapeutic effects must be weighed against improvements in patients' conditions that would follow in any event.

Perhaps most central to evaluation of the efficacy of therapeutic agents is assessment of the degree to which improvement is the effect of a curative agent and the extent to which it is a result of suggestion, encouragement, and support offered by the physician, or the influence of other factors. Until very recently in medical history the efficacy of clinical medicine has depended mostly on the suggestive power of the physician; even today placebo effect accounts for much of the improvement experienced by patients treated by physicians (337; 338; 441; 638). In clinical evaluations it is not difficult to confuse improvement in the patient resulting from suggestion with the change that can be attributed to the effective specific action of the therapeutic agent.

Proper Comparison Groups

Much of what has been said concerning the difficulty of evaluating change in a clinical context suggests the importance of having an appropriate comparison or control group to use as a basis for measuring change resulting from a specific factor. In theory, the specific influence of a variable must be evaluated in relation to what would have occurred in the absence of this variable had all other factors remained the same. Because favorable change commonly occurs in the absence of treatment and because suggestion may be a powerful influence on the patient's state of mind, if not on body processes, it is necessary to evaluate change using a variety of experimental devices. One of the most important methods in recent years involves the use of "control groups" who receive dummy drugs. A dummy drug may be an inert substance such as a sugar tablet, an injection of distilled water or saline solution which is physiologically inactive, or some active ingredient (one known to have a clear physiological effect) known to have no direct physical effect on the patient's specific condition. It is presumed that the group receiving dummy drugs serves as a comparison to a parallel experimental group, thereby excluding the possibility that the result could be accounted for by suggestion, encouragement, or support provided by the physician or by some other factor in the therapeutic situation.

The development of control groups receiving dummy drugs did not solve the problem of providing a proper comparison group in many situations because it was observed that various other biases could creep into evaluations as a consequence of the fact that the doctor, the patient, or both might know when a dummy drug was being administered. It was still possible, therefore, for the doctor or patient subtly to bias the results as a consequence of their knowledge of those who received active drugs and those who received dummy drugs. Various observations led to the belief that even if the patient did not know what was being administered, the doctor might behave differently toward those receiving active and dummy drugs and influence their response. These considerations led to the development of the double-blind methodology —a set of techniques in which an outside person prepares the drugs in such a way that neither doctor nor patient is aware whether a dummy or an active drug is being administered.

Double-blind techniques attempt to control four components of the test situation: (1) different amounts of self-suggestion by patients who are aware of whether they receive active or dummy substances; (2) different tendencies to report improvement to the doctor due to an awareness of whether a dummy or active drug was taken; (3) different attitudes or information communicated consciously or unconsciously to the patient by therapeutic personnel who are aware of which patients received different treatments; and (4) biases in evaluations of patient improvement by therapeutic personnel due to their awareness of those who received different treatments. It is hoped that the double-blind methodology will provide a safeguard against these common biases, making it possible to separate the degree of observed change resulting from the specific action of an active treatment from the observed change that is a product of suggestion, personal biases, and a variety of other variables.

In theory, a double-blind clinical trial should eliminate the differential impact of suggestion in the use of inert and real drugs. This outcome is not always so easy to achieve. Often the patient and doctor are able to discriminate when the real drug is being used and when the placebo is being used, and thus once again suggestive forces become uncontrolled. Because the drug may have a greater power than the placebo to arouse a person's physiological state, the patient may define his feelings and situation differently in these two circumstances. Let us take a simple example. Suppose we wished to test the effectiveness of 100-proof Scotch whiskey in improving some particular medical condition. Assume we develop our study using a double-blind technique, with some patients receiving Scotch whiskey and others an equal amount of water, or with patients receiving Scotch during one week and water during the next. We, of course, would insure that both substances have the same form, taste, and coloring, so that they could not be readily distinguished. However, we know that drinking a glass of Scotch produces different diffuse bodily feelings than drinking a glass of water; persons drinking the Scotch are more likely to feel aroused and to experience a feeling that the remedy they are taking is having an effect on them. In short, it is very difficult in practice to match a placebo with a real drug.

Investigators usually attempt to overcome this problem by comparing several therapeutic agents that are believed to have some effect on the relevant condition. Thus it is possible to conclude that some therapeutic agents are more effective than others in dealing with the same condition. Although such investigations often also utilize a placebo group, it is not always clear that all of the suggestive influences are eliminated as factors affecting the experiment. This, of course, is only one of several methodological problems in double-blind clinical investigations. Among the other important problems are those concerned with isolating cases for study, proper allocation of patients to experimental and control groups, grading severity in the cases used, measuring improvement, and finally, but not least important, the serious ethical problems involved in the allocation of subjects in such investigations, especially where there are therapeutic agents that are known or believed to have some usefulness in alleviating the condition. Stringent requirements for informed consent in human experimentation also complicate such controlled trials. Federal regulations require institutions receiving funds for biomedical research to establish institutional review boards that review research using human subjects and that insure the adequacy of procedures to achieve informed consent (44).

Although it has been asserted that individuals under drug arousal are more likely to be affected by suggestive influences than those receiving placebos, it has not really been explained why this should be so. In this regard, an experiment by Stanley Schachter and Jerome Singer (611) is particularly illuminating. Schachter and Singer had subjects report to the laboratory for what was described to them as various tests of vision. They told their subjects that they were particularly interested in the effects of a vitamin compound called Suproxin (a nonexistent substance) on their vision and asked for permission to give the subject an injection; all but one of 185 subjects agreed. Each subject was then asked to wait while the drug took effect in a room with another person who appeared to have received the same injection for the same experiment. (The other person was actually a confederate working with the experimenters.)

The injection that the subjects really received was epinephrine bitartrate (adrenaline), while subjects in control groups received an injection of saline solution (the placebo). Some of the subjects who received epinephrine were told what reactions to expect from the drug—heart pounding, hand tremor, and a warm and flushed face; this group was correctly informed. A second group receiving epinephrine was given no information about what to expect; this was called the ignorant group. A third group receiving epinephrine was misinformed about what to expect—they were told that their feet would feel numb, they would have itching sensations, and they might get a slight headache; this was called the misinformed group. While the subject was waiting for the "experiment" to begin, the confederate of the experimenter went into a scheduled act in which he slowly worked himself up into a euphoric state, playing imaginary basketball, flying paper airplanes, hula hooping, and so on. During this period the subject was observed behind a one-way window, and his behavior rated in terms of relevant categories. Later he was asked to report, as well, his subjective feelings in regard to the relevant dimensions of the study. Three additional groups were studied in a variation of the same situation—another epinephrine informed group, an epinephrine ignorant group, and a placebo group. In this new situation, however, the confederate of the experimenter worked himself up into a state of anger instead of a state of euphoria. Thus it is possible in this experiment to assess the influence of epinephrine, the influence of the various explanations of side effects (i.e., the varying explanations subjects have for their feeling states), and the influence of different environmental cues (i.e., an angry or euphoric stooge.)

To summarize briefly a complicated picture, subjects who received an injection of epinephrine and who had no correct or appropriate explanation of the side effects they experienced (particularly the epinephrine misinformed group) were most influenced in their behavior and feeling states by the cues provided by the confederate. In the euphoria situation they tended to become happy; in the anger situation they tended to become angry. Schachter and Singer summarize their results with the three theoretical statements which follow:

1. Given a state of physiological arousal for which an individual has no immediate explanation, he will label this state and describe his feelings in terms of the cognitions available to him. To the extent that cognitive factors are potent determiners of emotional states, it should be anticipated that precisely the same state of physiological arousal could be labeled "joy" or "fury" or "jealousy" or any of a great diversity of emotional labels depending on the cognitive aspects of the situation.
2. Given a state of physiological arousal for which an individual has a completely appropriate explanation, no evaluative needs will arise and the individual is unlikely to label his feelings in terms of the alternative cognitions available.
3. Given the same cognitive circumstances, the individual will react emotionally or describe his feelings as emotions only to the extent that he experiences a state of physiological arousal [611, p. 398].

Let us now apply Schachter and Singer's findings to the clinical situation. Assume that a patient with a bad cold is treated with Scotch whiskey. Although the whiskey may not affect his cold symptoms, it

will produce a general feeling of arousal that the patient may find difficult to explain in relation to his major symptoms. The knowledge that
he was given the "mixture" for his cold symptoms and the favorable attitude toward the treatment expressed or implied by the doctor may
thus lead the patient to define his arousal as an aspect of a process of
improvement in his symptoms, and he may actually feel better. If the
patient was given water as a placebo in a comparable situation, he
would feel less aroused, and thus the water would have less effect in
producing a state of susceptibility to suggestive cues. (For a discussion
of the specific effects of epinephrine, see 612).

Placebos

Although the theory of placebos has never been worked out in detail, medical history suggests that the concept of arousal played an important part in the development of medical remedies. Doctors—and
primitive healers—have frequently suggested treatment remedies that
were repulsive and disgusting—leeching, crocodile dung, putrid
meat. Although we cannot assume the correctness of the folklore concerning medications, doctors have believed that medicine is more effective if it has a bitter or strong taste, and there are many folk notions
about the advantages of colored or large pills (337). What little
research there is on this topic is not definitive, and the ideas that
guided such research have not been clearly formulated. The general
idea that many doctors hold—that discomfort in treatment is associated with therapeutic success—seems to have considerable support on an anecdotal level, and appears to be related to the arousal hypotheses already discussed.

Although the evidence is not clear-cut, it does appear that injections are more effective placebos than orally administered dummies
(337). In psychiatry, most therapists believe that working with patients
who are not willing to make an emotional investment in their treatment
is difficult. Similarly, it has been noted that surgery may evoke a
placebo effect of great magnitude, although the specific surgical intervention is of dubious value or worthless (56). This, too, is consistent
with the idea of discomfort or arousal influencing the magnitude of response to treatment. Beecher makes the case for placebo studies in
surgical work:

> The circumstances surrounding surgery are fraught with anxiety and stress.
> It is, therefore, essential for the surgeon to be on his guard, lest he deceive
> himself, and others, in perpetrating costly, dangerous, even fatal operations
> whose effectiveness is only that of a placebo.
> Today, no one would defend as anything more than placebo action any
> benefit arising in colectomy for epilepsy or laparotomy alone for tubercu-

lous peritonitis or pelvic inflammatory disease. Few would defend posteri-
or gastroenterostomy alone as acceptable treatment for duodenal ulcer, and
probably no one would now support the ligation of the internal mammary
arteries for the relief of angina pectoris. Incidentally, it is interesting to observe that the life cycle of this placebo operation was 2 years in this
country, a remarkably short time for the introduction and discrediting of a
surgical procedure. Significantly, it was destroyed by 2 or 3 well-planned,
double-blind studies.

Difficult as it is to carry out controlled study of extensive surgical
procedures, the truth often cannot be arrived at acceptably without it, that
is, without undue cost in money, time, suffering, and life itself. The 2 rather
well-controlled studies referred to prove that well-controlled surgical
procedures are possible. Scores of practitioners treating hundreds of cases
over years of time may eventually prove a given procedure valuable or
worthless. But why perform scores or hundreds of such operations with a
definite death rate when, say, a comparison of 25 exposures of the suspected area, with nothing else done, and 25 exposures plus the new surgical
procedure, would make clear the desirability or the uselessness of proceeding [56, p. 1106]?

However logical Beecher's argument may be in favor of comparisons
involving exposures with no other action taken, such procedures
would clearly be unacceptable to patients if they understood what was
to be done. Although many patients willingly accept participation in
drug trials in which they may receive a placebo, subjecting oneself to
an operation and a risk of death with the understanding that there is a
possibility that no procedure at all will be performed is more than most
people would accept. Procedures affecting human experimentation are
becoming more strict, and as noted earlier all such studies must be
reviewed by an institutional review board before the investigator is
allowed to use human subjects (44). These peer committees are expected to make judgments concerning the adequacy of the consent
procedures used and whether the benefits of the investigation outweigh
the risks. The area of experimentation with human subjects involves
many complexities that are increasingly being subjected to sociological
scrutiny (291; 500, pp. 255–79). For our purposes here, all that has to be
understood is that such studies place a considerable ethical burden on
the investigator, which he must seriously consider, and also vastly
complicate the methodological problems in carrying out such investigations successfully.

Controlled Trials and Health-Services Research

Many other elements of controlled trials must be considered in addition to the use of dummy drugs and double-blinds (412). Such studies must be competently designed and based on adequate techniques of

statistical analysis. Similarly, the diagnostic categories being evaluated must be based on criteria that are reliable and valid, for, as we noted earlier, observer error can be very large in some situations. Assignment to experimental and control groups should be on a random basis in order to insure against systematic differences among those assigned. But when this is impossible for practical reasons, every effort must be made to insure that the mode of assignment of patients to various treatment groups introduces no systematic bias into the analysis. For example, if all of the schizophrenic patients on one ward are assigned to the treatment group and all of the patients on a second ward assigned to the control group, it becomes extremely difficult to distinguish the effects of the differential treatment from differences in the administration, personnel, and life regimen on the two wards. If this is the only way a study can be done, the investigation may still be valuable if careful measures describing relevant dimensions of the different administrative units are developed. It may be demonstrated that the actual differences between these administrative units are very small and not plausibly related to the changes taking place among patients in the different treatment groups. But in general, as one deviates from the principle of random assignment, the results of clinical trials become more difficult to assess. The reader who would like to pursue these problems in greater detail may wish to consult *Medical Surveys and Clinical Trials*, edited by Professor L. J. Witts (776), or some other standard reference.

Although the controlled clinical trial has been viewed primarily as a technique for evaluating the effectiveness of drugs, surgical interventions, and other medical and surgical modalities, it is an equally elegant technique for evaluating the effectiveness of procedures in the delivery of health care, including varying types of insurance arrangements, health-care programs, and particular patterns of treatment. A. L. Cochrane, in *Effectiveness and Efficiency*, argues strongly for more common use of randomized controlled trials in health-services evaluation (130). Although it is often difficult to achieve randomization, opportunities do present themselves for ingenious investigators who value such experimental investigation. Such techniques, for example, have been used in studies of the negative income tax, in a national study by the Rand Corporation of the effects of varying schedules of coinsurance and deductibles on medical-care utilization and costs, and in studies of particular types of care patterns, as described by Cochrane.

One example with profound implications is a randomized controlled trial carried out in England on the relative value of home and hospital treatment for patients with acute myocardial infarction (heart attack) (462). Four hundred and fifty-eight general practitioners in four cities agreed to participate in the study. These doctors carried a sealed envelope that indicated whether the patient was to be hospitalized in intensive care or treated at home. Because of both ethical and strategic considerations, physicians were allowed to exclude patients they felt were inappropriate for the study prior to consulting the instructions, but when patients were included in the trial the treatment they received was determined on a random basis. The fact that more than 10 percent of patients in each group died, as well as other data, indicates that the doctors were not just choosing the less serious cases for the controlled study. The randomized groups were not significantly different in respect to past history of chest pain, infarction, or hypertension, or in respect to age. For the most part there were no differences in outcomes between the home and hospital groups. Indeed, the hypotensive patients did somewhat better at home. This study has been replicated in England with comparable results. The findings are particularly important in light of the enormously expensive development of coronary intensive-care units, which are increasingly accepted as the customary treatment of myocardial infarction. If the contribution of such expensive units to improved outcomes cannot be demonstrated, then the wisdom of such investments is brought into serious question (460). These data are consistent with other controlled trials on lengths of hospital care following myocardial infarction, which show that short periods of hospitalization result in no poorer outcomes than more lengthy and expensive periods of care.

Epidemiology and Disease Study

Often clinical investigations can be stimulated, illuminated, and supplemented through a wider population perspective. Epidemiology is one of the most important investigative perspectives in the study of health and disease (444; 766). As Hollingshead has written, "The triumph . . . has been its utility in helping researchers trace out, step by step, interdependencies between the life ways of individuals and the appearance and nonappearance of disease in a population" (329, p. 6). The epidemiologist attempts to determine who in a particular population develops a disease, on what occasions, and under what influences. Typically, the epidemiological approach is used in attempting to gain increased understanding of a disease whose causes are unknown. By learning something about whom the disease strikes in the population—whether young or old, male or female, Catholic or Jew, rich or poor—various ideas are suggested that lead to more focused investigation. The epidemiological method can be used for other purposes as well, such as to explore specific hypotheses involving not only gross social characteristics like race, sex, and social class, but also those involving expectation systems, social attitudes, and other characteristics of persons and groups. In short, the epidemiologist concerns himself not with clinical samples but with populations and samples of populations. He directs his attention to the "healthy" as well as to the "sick," attempting to differentiate these groups in terms of factors that might help explain or at least suggest some clues as to the forces in populations that affect the onset and progression of disease and those that influence the help-seeking process.

A definitive statement, *Uses of Epidemiology* by J. N. Morris (524), notes seven major areas of use for epidemiological methods; all achieve their main importance from the fact that epidemiology is based on a *population* or *group* perspective rather than a clinical one. The seven major areas he describes are as follows:

1. To study the history of the health of populations, and of the rise and fall of diseases and changes in their character. Useful projections into the future may be possible.
2. To *diagnose the health of the community*, and the condition of the people, to measure the present dimensions and distribution of ill-health in terms of incidence, prevalence, and mortality; to define health problems for community action, and their relative importance and priority; to identify vulnerable groups needing special protection. Ways of life change, and with them community health and health problems; new indices of health and disease must therefore always be sought.
3. To study the *working of health services* with a view to their improvement. Operational research translates knowledge of community health in terms of needs and demand. The supply of services is described and how they are utilized; their success in reaching standards and in improving health ought to be appraised. All this has to be related to other social policies and to resources. Knowledge thus won may be applied in experiment, and in drawing up plans for the future .... The regular supply of information on health and health services is itself a key service needing as much scrutiny as any.
4. To estimate from the group experience what are the *individual risks* and chances, on average, of disease, accident and defect.
5. To *complete the clinical picture* of chronic disease, and describe its *natural history*: by including in proportion all kinds of patients wherever they present, and by following the course of remission and relapse, adjustment and disability; by detecting early subclinical disease and relating this to the clinical; by discovering precursor abnormalities during the pathogenesis. Longitudinal studies are necessary to learn about the mechanisms of progression through these various stages, each of which may offer opportunities for research into causes and preventive action.
6. To *identify syndromes* by describing the distribution, association and dissociation of clinical phenomena in the population.
7. To *search for causes* of health and disease by studying the incidence in different groups, defined in terms of their composition, their inheri-

tance and experience, their behavior and environment. To distinguish causes, describe their patterns, and estimate the relative importance of different causes in multiple aetiology; to investigate the mode of operation of the various causes. With knowledge of causes comes the possibility of preventing the incidence of disease. Postulated causes will often be tested in naturally occurring *experiments of opportunity*, and sometimes by *planned experiments* in removing them [524, pp. 274–75].

Some examples of historical contributions of an epidemiological kind communicate the significance of this approach. In 1854 John Snow, by observing the pattern of occurrence of cholera in several areas in London, was able to trace the outbreak of an epidemic to a contaminated water source. Thus it was possible in this instance to control the outbreak of cholera well before bacteria were discovered. Equally striking is the case of Hungarian obstetrician Ignaz Semmelweis. He observed that the death rate among women in hospitals was considerably higher in units where doctors came directly to the wards from the morgue, and he hypothesized that puerperal fever (childbed fever), a major source of mortality, was transmitted by the physician from corpses to the patients. Semmelweis insisted that every doctor and student in his clinic wash his hands with chlorine water before making an examination; this led to a substantial decline in mortality (646).

Consider the situation when Semmelweis made his discovery. At the major lying-in hospital, where students received their medical training in obstetrics, mortality in childbirth averaged 10 percent, and at times went up to 30 percent; in a second hospital where midwives delivered the babies mortality was only 3 percent. The prevailing atmospheric and cosmic explanations for this disease could not account for this difference, and one hypothesis asserted that the excess mortality was due to the emotional strain suffered at the teaching hospital by women who had to be examined by male students. This led to the exclusion of foreign students (646). When Semmelweis developed his hypothesis of the transmission of childbed fever, it explained the differences in mortality in the two hospitals, as midwives had little opportunity for postmortem dissection. It also explained why women who were delivered rapidly before there was a chance for an examination had low mortality and why those who had prolonged labor and many examinations had very high mortality (646).

Semmelweis was largely ignored by his colleagues, despite his discovery that puerperal fever was a kind of wound infection, his demonstration that mortality could be substantially diminished, and his early awareness of the notion of antisepsis. He fought bitterly with his colleagues, affronting them by calling those who ignored his findings murderers and assassins. Writing to a famous colleague, he said; "If, Sir, without having refuted my doctrine, you continue to teach the students and the midwives you train that puerperal fever is an ordinary epidemic disease, I proclaim you before God and the world to be an assassin..." (646, p. 341). Semmelweis died bitter, unhappy, and somewhat deranged, his teachings largely ignored. It was under the influence of Joseph Lister and others, at least two decades later, that the discoveries of Semmelweis became widely acceptable to physicians. It is not irrelevant to our purposes to note that the social factors leading to the acceptance or rejection of innovations may be as important as the innovations themselves (138).

Although many historical examples of the usefulness of epidemiology are worthy of citation, the value and logic of the approach can best be illustrated by choosing one example and describing the progression of analysis in more detail; we shall, therefore, devote the remainder of our attention from a historical perspective to the work of Joseph Goldberger on pellagra. In a letter to the journal *Public Health Reports*, dated September 4, 1914, Goldberger, then Surgeon in Charge of Pellagra Investigations, elaborated on his belief that many current notions of pellagra were erroneous. He wrote:

> Although pellagra has been known and studied abroad for nearly two centuries, not only is its essential cause not known, but the broad question of whether it is to be classed either as dietary or as a communicable (contagious or infectious) disease has never been satisfactorily determined. . . .
>
> In the United States, with the progressive and alarming increase in the prevalence of the disease, there has developed both in the lay and the medical mind the opinion that pellagra is an infectious disease. This opinion has received support, first, from the Illinois Pellagra Commission and, second, from the Thompson-McFadden Commission . . . [272, p. 2345].

Goldberger then pointed out that his investigations were giving consideration to both the dietary and communicable disease hypotheses. Discussing studies of the hypotheses that pellagra is an infectious disease, he notes that evidence thus far has been negative. He then goes on to describe epidemiological studies of pellagra:

> In a paper published in the Public Health Reports of June 26, 1914, I called attention to certain observations which appear inexplicable on any theory of communicability. These observations show that although in many asylums new cases of pellagra develop in inmates even after 10, 15, and 20 years' residence, clearly indicating thereby that the cause of the disease exists and is operative in such asylums, yet at none has any one of the employees contracted the disease though living under identical environmental conditions as the inmates, and many in most intimate association with them [272, p.2355].

After describing the results of study of records of the Georgia State Sanitarium, Goldberger notes that these confirm that cases of pellagra develop among inmates, but that there was not a single case among the staff. He then goes on to describe studies of cases of pellagra at the orphanage at Jackson:

> The distribution of these cases with respect to age developed the remarkable fact that practically all of the cases were in children between the ages of 6 and 12 years, of whom in consequence over 52 percent were afflicted. In the group of 25 children under 6 years of age there were 2 cases and in the group of 66 children over 12 years of age there was but 1 case. In as much as all live under identical environmental conditions, the remarkable exemption of the group of younger and that of the older children is no more comprehensible on the basis of an infection than is the absolute immunity of the asylum employees [272, pp. 2355–56].

> A minute investigation has been made at both institutions of all conceivable factors that might possibly explain the striking exemption of the groups indicated. The only constant difference discovered relates exclusively to the dietary. At both institutions those of the exempt group or groups were found to subsist on a better diet than those of the affected groups. In the diet of those developing pellagra there was noted a disproportionately small amout of meat or other animal protein foods, and consequently the vegetable food component, in which corn and sirup were prominent and legumes relatively inconspicuous elements, forms a disproportionately large part of the ration... the evidence clearly incriminates it [diet] as the cause of pellagra at these institutions. The inference may therefore be safely drawn that pellagra is not an infection, but that it is a disease essentially of dietary origin; that is, that it is caused in some way such as, for example, by the absence from the [diet] of essential vitamins... [272, p. 2356].

Goldberger then goes on to comment on the observation made by previous investigators that at insane asylums the "untidy" (the group in which Goldberger found the highest rates of scurvy and beriberi) were the most afflicted with pellagra. He particularly directed himself to what he believed was the incorrect conclusion, the notion that the relationship between "untidiness" and pellagra could be explained by filth infection:

> The true explanation, however, is that both the untidiness and the supposed excessive susceptibility of these inmates are primarily dependent on the apathy and indifference typical of most of this group. The deteriorated mental condition causing apathy and indifference results not only in untidiness of person, but passively or actively in an eccentricity of the diet [272, p. 2357].

In short, Goldberger argues that the association between untidiness and pellagra is not a causal relationship but rather that the observed relationship results, in some fashion, from the fact that both are related to apathy.

Goldberger's work thus far would appear as a monumental accomplishment; this letter was written less than six months after Goldberger began his research on pellagra. (He continued to work on this topic until his death, his last paper of a long series on the topic being published after his death in December 1930.) Goldberger and his colleagues demonstrated in 1915 that pellagra could be prevented in institutional patients by a diet that included generous amounts of milk, eggs, meat, beans, and peas. Almost at the same time they were successful in producing pellagra by means of a deficient diet in healthy convicts at the Mississippi State Penitentiary who volunteered for the study. The following year, in experiments on 16 volunteers—including himself and his wife—Goldberger showed that they could not demonstrate any transmissibility of pellagra via the blood, nasopharyngeal secretions, and epidermal scales from pellagrous lesions, urine, and feces. This was followed by several economic and dietary studies that confirmed among other things that pellagrous households had much more restricted supplies of animal protein foods—lean meats, milk, butter, cheese, and eggs—than nonpellagrous homes. After much further experimentation and research, Goldberger and his colleagues came to the conclusion that "water-soluble B" vitamins included a pellagra-preventive factor. In 1937 C. A. Elvehjem—later to become president of the University of Wisconsin—demonstrated that nicotinic acid cured blacktongue in dogs and that it was the pellagra preventive factor. For the reader who wishes to follow the progression of Goldberger's work in greater detail, much benefit can be gleaned from the edited collection of Goldberger's writings and the fine introduction to this volume by Professor Milton Terris, on which much of the preceding discussion is based (698).

The epidemiological description of disease in human populations has two major aspects—the study of incidence and the study of prevalence. A measure of incidence refers to the number of new cases of disease that occur within a specified period of time among a specified population. Prevalence, on the other hand, refers to all known cases of a disease in a specified population during a particular period of time irrespective of when they first began. Each of these measures provides important but different information. Prevalence measures reflect the amount of disease present in a particular population; incidence measures provide a picture of the way new cases are distributed in the population.

Measures of prevalence of disease are most useful in estimating the magnitude of various health problems; such data are often helpful in planning the provision of necessary health facilities for those who are in need of care. Knowing how much disease there is in the population, and how disease spreads itself regionally, in different social segments, and among the various age groups, we are better prepared to plan our resources intelligently and efficiently. Measures of incidence, in contrast, provide a basis for studying the etiology of disease, because, as a result of knowing how a disease first occurs in a population and whom it strikes, we are likely to obtain some clues as to factors that are favorable to the occurrence of disease. Prevalence data are not adequate for studying etiology because they bind together the results of factors that produce the disease and many different factors that may affect the course of disease: its severity, access to treatment, adequacy of treatment, health habits and practices, and illness behavior generally.

An example or two will help make clear the important distinction between a measure of incidence and a measure of prevalence. Let us assume we were interested in the amount of irreversible functional impairment resulting from polio. If we concerned ourselves with the incidence of such impairment, our figure would be rather low because of the widespread protection of the population resulting from the use of the Salk and Sabin vaccines. An incidence measure may reflect the degree of success of vaccination in a protected population, or it may be used as a rough index of failure in preventive medicine. A measure of prevalence of such impairment would yield a larger figure because many people were affected by polio prior to the introduction of the vaccines. A prevalence measure broken down by various age groups would give us considerable information for estimating the future need of medical resources among the population disabled in this way. In most circumstances it is also important for public-health purposes to know the incidence figure—the number of new cases occurring each year—as this is helpful in making future projections.

As a second example, let us look briefly at depressive illnesses. If we were interested in studying etiological factors in depression, we would require an incidence measure; if we were interested in planning facilities for depressed persons requiring help, we would be concerned with the prevalence rate (and its various components), as this would indicate the magnitude of the problem and the future resources required. The incidence and prevalence figures of depression would not be comparable for several reasons. Depressive illness may persist for a long time, so that the prevalence rate at any point in time will be considerably higher than the incidence rate. Moreover, it is unlikely that the prevalence figure will be merely a summation of various incidence figures. Some depressed patients recover quickly and suffer no further relapses of a significant nature; others have long, drawn-out depressive illnesses, and still others have regular cycles of occurrence of symptoms separating intervals of good health. In short, persistent cases that began at some point before the study and become part of the prevalence rate are very different in character from those that have a short and limited course. Finally, the course of depression is dependent in part on what is done for a person with such a condition. Because treatment offered to depressed patients may differ under varying social, geographic, and historical circumstances and may be utilized differently among various social strata, these factors, too, may lead to variations in the longevity of the condition. It would be extremely difficult, therefore, to estimate the need for help facilities solely from a measure of the number of new cases that develop within a specified period of time. Also, because so many factors other than the nature of the illness— treatment received, willingness to seek treatment, social and environmental supports, and so on—affect the longevity of the condition, prevalence data merge attributes of the illness with those of the social environment affecting the illness. If one attempted to use prevalence data to study etiology, one might easily confuse factors producing the illness with those that affect its persistence and recurrence.

It is frequently difficult to ascertain when a disease begins. Most diseases are the culmination of long-term biological adaptations to the internal and external environment. Although symptoms may not appear until much later in life, biological study will demonstrate deterioration of body organs over many years. Although coronary heart disease does not usually occur until we reach the 50s and 60s, autopsy studies of children and young soldiers who die of causes other than heart disease indicate that many of them already have considerable evidence of atherosclerosis (arterial deposits of cholesterol, fats, and other substances). Thus, although an infarction is a discrete and easily identifiable event, the underlying process contributing to it begins at an early age. In the cases of many chronic diseases such as rheumatoid arthritis, renal failure, and diabetes, symptoms progress over a period of years, and it is even more difficult to identify the occurrence of a new case, although the first diagnosis is usually used as the appropriate criterion. The problem is even more pronounced in the study of many mental disorders, where it is difficult to specify when a case exists and even more difficult to define when it is new, because sufferers do not usually come to the attention of evaluators until the disorder has become acute (662). Moreover, if the assumptions of some psychiatric theories are accepted—that all functional disorders have their roots in early childhood and develop slowly over a number of years—it is extremely difficult and, from a purist's point of view, not really possible to specify when a case is new.

We must be especially cautious before we assume that problems of etiology can be attacked through prevalence data. Such data usually cannot do the job because they confuse the factors producing the disorder with those that exacerbate it, and with those that influence care seeking, treatment received, and so on. There are, however, some occasions on which prevalence data serve as a substitute for incidence data in studying problems relating to etiology. This situation will apply depending on the degree to which the following conditions are fulfilled.

1. The disease is irreversible, i.e., once it occurs it will persist throughout the person's life and will not be affected by differential treatment.

2. The disease is sufficiently severe or visible so that case finding is unlikely to be biased by variations in case-finding techniques or differences in the availability of medical facilities. (If case finding techniques improve and medical facilities are more available at some later point in time, the proportion of cases observed in cohorts of similar age in the past will be lower than the proportion of cases found at that same age among present cohorts, even if the rate of occurrence of the condition is exactly the same.)

3. There is no reason to believe that the incidence of new cases is variable during different periods within the total time period studied. Such conditions as lung cancer, stroke, and some congenital defects fit these criteria somewhat better than most psychiatric conditions, common respiratory complaints, and accidents.

The practical problems typical in research require that compromises be made, and frequently the best data available are less than ideal. But we have to be continuously on guard that the compromises we make do not obviate the utility of our data and retard further understanding of our problem. In the area of psychiatric epidemiology, for example, where it is frequently difficult to specify exact case-finding criteria and where such case finding may be vastly expensive and fraught with difficulties, investigators attempt to develop heuristic criteria that best approximate the phenomena that concern them. Thus, in the study of serious disturbance, measures of treated incidence and prevalence are most frequently used. The assumption is made that if a condition is sufficiently serious, treated rates of illness closely approximate total rates and thus such data do not involve a very large error. On the other hand, treated incidence and prevalence rates can be very poor approximations of total rates, and decisions to use treated rates must be based on some firm knowledge that they are good approximations, or on a clear understanding of the consequences resulting from errors of approximation. Good research, like most other human activities, benefits from judgment and good sense in making important decisions.

For example, first admission to a hospital may approximate incidence quite closely. If we were interested in fractured legs, it is unlikely that treated incidence would depart very greatly, if at all, from "true incidence." Even in such difficult areas as the psychoses, measures of treated incidence may be sufficiently close to true "incidence" under some circumstances to make such estimates useful. Ødegård (541) has been one of the major proponents of the usefulness of "treated incidence" of the psychoses for estimating true incidence:

> The problem of hospital admission data as indicators of "true morbidity" is a real one, but even here the difficulties are often overstressed. Even moderately serious cases of schizophrenia will *ultimately* reach some hospital as in- or outpatients, and so a system of continuous registration will come to include them. A short-time study, on the other hand, will naturally lose many. Our Norwegian material has shown that morbidity from schizophrenia as measured by first admissions to psychiatric hospitals is the same as that found, for instance, in Denmark and Sweden by means of the census method: 0.9–1.3 per 100 [541, p. 296].

In short, blanket generalizations as to what data are useful for what purpose are not very helpful. The approximation an investigator chooses will have to be worked out on the basis of the questions he is trying to answer, the disease categories he is working with, and the practical alternatives available to him.

Frequently, epidemiological studies are carried out using groups rather than individuals as the significant unit. In such studies one set of characteristics of a population is correlated with another set of characteristics in order to account for variations among populations. The use of such correlation—usually referred to as ecological correlations—is common in public-health work because official data are frequently available on important social and health characteristics of particular populations. For example, there are abundant data available on population units established by the census, which can then be examined in relation to the amount of mortality and illness that occurs within these units. The investigator may develop various social indices that he regards as important (such as the proportion of nonwhites, average educational or income status, proportion unemployed) and investigate these in relation to such dependent variables as rate of infant and adult mortality and tuberculosis morbidity.

Although the ecological method is very useful, it is important to recognize that it cannot be used to impute individual causation. Thus the finding that population areas characterized by low socioeconomic status are also characterized by high rates of mortality does not insure that persons who have low socioeconomic status have a higher risk of mortality than those with higher status. The ecological fallacy (that is, the imputation of an individual correlation on the basis of a group correlation) is a common error. Group correlations, however, are often stimulants for further investigation on an individual level, and from the point of view of public policy they may have considerable significance in their own right.

In summary, epidemiology is a useful descriptive and analytical discipline. Most frequently it is used for the purpose of generating clues for better-controlled clinical and experimental investigation, for estimating the need for health services, and for describing the workings of health-care systems. Diseases also have psychological and social components of importance, and epidemiology can be used fruitfully for the purpose of testing hypotheses about the influence of social, cultural, and psychological factors in disease. In later chapters when we discuss sickness and death, it will become evident that the epidemiological approach has borne much fruit.

Methodology in Mortality Study

There is no issue more fundamental to medical sociology than differential mortality and the biological, environmental, and sociocultural factors contributing to such differences. Evaluations of medical needs as well as public-health planning are frequently based on interpretations of mortality experiences. Too frequently, however, analyses of such statistics by public-health workers are superficial, often reflecting a lack of awareness of the substantial methodological difficulties in the data, which may lead them to erroneous conclusions. Although I cannot provide a detailed discussion of methods and problems in mortality analysis here, it is intended that the discussion should alert the reader to difficulties in analysis and the need for a cautious approach. It would be desirable to examine these issues further by studying Dorn (181), Dublin, Lotka, and Spiegelman (184), and Kitagawa and Hauser (391).

Correct assessments of mortality and longevity are the products of joining two sources of data: the *census of the population* at a specified point in time and a *complete registration of deaths* occurring in that population during the same period of time. Each of these two sources of data is characterized by a variety of problems that detract from their reliability, and the synthesis of these two bodies of data may involve further problems of *comparability*. Mortality is usually expressed as a rate, i.e., the number of occurrences during a particular period of time for a specified unit in the population. Thus the rate is constructed on the basis of knowledge of the number of deaths occurring in a subgroup of the population as well as information concerning the number of people in that subgroup. In short, the comparability of *death registration systems* and the *population census* determines the validity of mortality analysis.

In general, methodological difficulties in mortality analysis increase as the scope of analysis increases in time. The quality of collection systems and the data collected at different periods in history vary substantially, as do medical diagnosis and record maintenance. Thus, studies of trends over time are subject to greater distortions than studies at a particular point in time when the statistics are subject to less uncertainty. Moreover, as understanding of the problems in mortality analysis increases, changes in definitions are instituted in the collection of data, resulting in some lack of comparability among sets of data collected during different periods of time. The administrative organization of data-collection systems is also crucial in comparisons involving data collected by various state, national, and international agencies, because the definitions and assumptions used by different agencies may vary, resulting in a low level of comparability. For convenience, this discussion will concentrate on problems in studying mortality in a particular period of time and when problems of comparability of data-collection systems are limited.

Depending on the country involved, the richness of data for mortality analysis varies. Sociologists, of course, are interested in variations in mortality by age, sex, residence, occupation, and other important variables. Sometimes these data are not available or are too unreliable to be very useful. For example, very few areas in the world provide adequate data for studying the relationship between socioeconomic factors and mortality; as a consequence, knowledge in this area is not very well developed. Even in such countries as Great Britain and the United States, where such data are available, they are inadequately specified and subject to considerable unreliability.

Registration of deaths in the United States is subject to little unreliability except in respect to fetal deaths. A fairly large number of embryos are delivered dead, and the criteria for classifying such deaths as stillbirths rather than as fetal deaths are not consistent from one area to another or even from one hospital to another. Because the causes of death of fetuses during the last two weeks of pregnancy are similar to those among live-born infants who die early in life, it has been suggested that the term "perinatal mortality" be used to include stillbirths and all deaths occurring in the first month of life (neonatal deaths) (also see 719). This helps resolve to some extent the problem of when a birth is a stillbirth. The complexity of this problem of definition is suggested by Sudnow's (684) study of death in two hospitals. He notes that a fetus that makes any kind of sound might be classified as a neonatal death, although it is below the period of gestation required for differentiating a stillbirth from a fetal death. In contrast, he notes that other fetuses characterized by a longer period of gestation who make no sounds might be classified as fetal deaths. Definitions may vary from place to place depending on the legal requirements for burial for different kinds of fetal and infant deaths, the religious inclinations of the medical staff, and other variables. A neonatal death might be classified as a fetal death because it occurred before baptism; such factors are important when many births occur outside of a hospital with a midwife in attendance. Fetal deaths are the most unreliable of all death statistics, as many such deaths do not come to the attention of medical or hospital personnel, and thus official reports of such deaths encompass a large degree of error.

From the sociologist's point of view there are two major difficulties with mortality statistics. First, death-registration and population-enumeration methods may yield incorrect information on such important variables as age, residence, and occupation. Second, and most important, is the fact that the kinds of error typical of information entered on death certificates may be very different in character from those typical of population enumeration. Thus it is possible for the error resulting from using data from both systems to be greater than that of either information source. The opposite possibility also exists; the two sources of error may cancel each other out. As far as death registration is concerned, mortality is certified by a wide variety of people with varying knowledge concerning the dead person and varying abilities and inclinations to assess the facts properly. The most relevant person who can provide the information is probably the deceased, but even the most enthusiastic researcher cannot rouse him from his dormant state. Thus there are many errors in reporting the deceased's age and occupation, and assessment of the cause of death is frequently incorrect; these errors are probably much more serious when the death occurs outside a hospital. Even with the best of intentions and sustained interest, occupation would be difficult to specify. Does one indicate the occupation at the time of death, which may be related to retirement or previous morbidity, or the most common occupation during a person's active working period? Frequently, the occupation is not specified in enough detail to be coded accurately, and problems exist even under ideal conditions. It is essential to recognize, however, that death certificates are not completed under ideal conditions! These judgments are usually hurried, and those who provide the information have little appreciation of mortality analysis or the needs for accuracy.

The other source of error in mortality analysis involves inadequacies in the census of the population. Although the census is organized and planned by methodologically sophisticated people, a certain degree of error must be expected in enumeration of the population. Some people are extremely difficult to find; census enumerators may vary widely in their quality, interest, and motivation in doing a good job, and even in their honesty. It is reasonable to assume that the national census may involve an error of 3 or 2 percent in enumeration of the population.* Considering the problems of the census, this is really a

* Errors in enumeration involve both the failure to count some people and the counting of some people more than once.

low degree of error; however, from the point of view of sociological analysis the *degree of error may be prohibitive for particular subgroups* in the population. Although it is difficult to know for sure, one may suspect that underenumeration of black males aged 15 to 35 may be substantially larger than 5 percent, and possibly as high as 15 or 20 percent (576, p. 89). To the extent that a subgroup in the population is underenumerated, the computed rates of mortality for that group will be inflated because the registration of adult deaths is almost complete. It should be pointed out that census data are also subject to biases in the reporting of age, occupation, and other information. Middle-aged men and women may report their age somewhat lower than it really is; old people may exaggerate their age; and many people tend to report their age in round numbers. Similarly, it is likely that many people distort, consciously and unconsciously, reports of their occupations.

Harold Dorn (181), in his excellent discussion of deficiencies in mortality data, points out some other difficulties as well: There may be serious lacks of comparability in definitions from area to area, as in the registration of fetal deaths; with the growth of political boundaries and legal administrative units, increasing errors in classification of residence are possible; the definitions for classification used in the census are not always comparable to those used in the enumeration of deaths; changing procedures in processing and tabulating deaths by type change the mortality picture presented; and death-registration systems are highly inflexible, and it is difficult to bring about standardized procedures in reporting important information.

Specific and Standardized Rates and Ratios

The crude death rate that describes the number of deaths per year per standard unit of population is too gross for most sociological purposes. Since death may vary so greatly at different ages, by sex, and in terms of other variables as well, it is necessary to take such factors into account in discussing mortality. Thus it is common to compute age-specific death rates or age-sex-specific death rates that will indicate rate of death per 1,000 persons for particular age-sex categories. It is common to divide the age structure in terms of five-year groups and to develop an age-specific rate for each such group. Specific death rates may be computed for any significant social variable depending on the purpose of the investigation. Thus it is possible to generate occupation-specific rates, race-specific rates, and so on.

In comparing one social unit to another in terms of rate of death it is frequently necessary to take into account that the populations being compared have different proportions of persons of different age and sex status. Thus the data may be computed so as to specify overall rate of death, if the actual specific death rates are applied in a situation in which the population structure is of some standard form. One can compute such hypothetical (standard) rates in terms of any number of hypothetical standard populations; the standardized rate is a kind of weighted average.

For comparison purposes it is convenient to compute standardized mortality ratios that depict the standardized mortality experience of a subgroup of the population relative to the total population. In using this kind of statistic, the population under study is divided into a number of subgroups, and the mortality in each subgroup is calculated as a proportion of the mortality in the total group under study. Because the base of 100 represents the total population, a standardized mortality ratio lower than 100 reflects a situation in which the particular subgroup concerned contributes less mortality to the population than would be expected had the age-specific death rates in the total population applied to this subgroup. Similarly, standard mortality ratios above 100 would reflect a situation in which the subgroup contributed more mortality than would be expected on the basis of the age-specific death rates in the total population.

Life Tables

One of the most useful instruments in the study of mortality is the life table, a construction of the mortality experience of a hypothetical group exposed to a particular history of age-specific death rates. Thus it is possible to develop a mortality biography of any group, imagined or real, exposed to any possible set of mortality conditions. The basic principle of the life table is nicely stated by Dublin, Lotka, and Spiegelman:

> Since both deaths and population are commonly classified according to age, it is possible to compute mortality rates specific for age. From these rates, a life table is then constructed to show what would be the number of survivors from birth to successive ages, and what the average length of life would be *on the basis of the mortality at each age in the calendar year or period for which it was constructed.* For want of a better name, such a table might be termed an "instantaneous" or "snapshot" life table, inasmuch as it reflects the longevity experience of a group of people on the supposition that their mortality at each age corresponds to a snapshot observation of mortality in a certain year or period [184, p. 11].

The life table is a hypothetical model in that the cohort that the life table describes will not in actuality be exposed to the same age-specific mortality experience of the population when the life table is constructed. The various factors affecting mortality at different ages change over time, but in the typical life table it is assumed that the mortality rates remain stationary. From the point of view of medical sociology, life tables are useful because they yield the expectation of life at any age. It is also this fact that makes life tables such useful devices for insurance companies in calculating expectancies for persons of different ages. For predictive purposes one can build a life table reflecting any hypothetical set of age-specific death rates.

One common error in the interpretation of life tables concerns the mean expectation of life at birth. It is commonplace to observe the substantial increase in expectation of life since the beginning of the twentieth century, and the favorable American expectation of life in comparison to various nonindustrialized nations. The usual implication is that the average person today lives much longer than the average born in 1900, or that the average American lives much longer than the average non-Westerner. Although there has been considerable improvement in mortality at all ages since 1900, by far the greatest decline has occurred at the infant level. Much of the increase in average expectation of life at birth is a consequence of a substantial decline in mortality among infants. Similarly, the major difference among countries in expectation of life is often a product of widely discrepant rates of infant mortality and much smaller differences in mortality in other age categories.

Methodology in Morbidity Study

The relationship between social factors and morbidity can be studied in one of three general ways: (1) through study of doctor, clinic, and hospital records summarizing a large variety of data on persons who came to these various places seeking help for their problems; (2) through systematic and standardized clinical evaluations of a particular population; and (3) through an interview that attempts to obtain reports of illnesses, symptoms, and use of various forms of care. Although these three sources provide most of the information we have about general rates of morbidity, each suffers from a variety of difficulties. Most disturbing to the social analyst is the fact that these sources of data provide very different estimates of the degree of morbidity present in the populations.

Medical Records

Many morbidity studies are based on analyses of medical records or summary statistics gathered from various institutions describing the populations who received care for a variety of conditions. Because people with a variety of conditions are selected into care on the basis of various personal and social factors, estimates based on such selected populations are frequently biased. The utility of institutional records for morbidity estimates depends on the condition being considered. To the extent that there is a close correspondence between occurrence of a condition and help seeking, record data will be more adequate. However, for many illness conditions the degree of correspondence is poor or unknown, and thus record systems cannot provide adequate estimates. Moreover, record systems are frequently unstandardized; they tend to merge information obtained from many different practitioners and institutions characterized by varying diagnostic standards and different criteria for establishing illness. Such information is often transcribed under the pressure of a busy work schedule and frequently is incomplete, carelessly recorded, and unreliable.

Clinical Assessments

The most valuable mode of assessing morbidity is through field studies of representative samples of the population using standardized techniques of clinical assessment. This means that physicians undertaking the clinical assessments are trained in utilizing identical techniques and criteria for assessment and that efforts are made to eliminate the various sources of bias that may be introduced into such investigations. Such studies depend on the cooperation of the population; if too many people refuse to participate, the sample studied may be too biased to allow an adequate estimate for the population as a whole. Various techniques are used to make participation in such studies convenient for the respondents. But such studies have been infrequent because they are very expensive; even when they are undertaken, it is often extremely difficult to insure the reliability of many diagnoses unless case-finding procedures are clear and intensive evaluation techniques are used. Most examination studies involving psychiatric disorders, therefore, have been superficial.

The most ambitious plan for carrying out standardized clinical assessments on a representative basis has been initiated through the federal government's Health Examination Survey. Its purpose is to provide statistics on the medically defined prevalence of a variety of diseases in the United States population on the basis of standardized diagnostic criteria, and to obtain norms for the general population for certain physical and physiological traits:

A key characteristic of the plan of the Health Examination Survey is to make actual physical examinations of, and tests upon, the individuals selected in the sample. Such examinations and tests can yield morbidity information unobtainable through the other mechanisms of the National

Health Survey. They can provide information not only about diagnosed conditions which persons fail to report or are incapable of reporting in a survey based upon individual interviews, but they can also reveal previously undiagnosed, unattended, and nonmanifest chronic diseases. In addition to serving this primary purpose, the first-cycle examinations are intended to obtain baseline data on certain physical and physiological measurements . . . . Data such as these on a defined population have been either nonexistent or inadequate. They are needed to understand departures from normal as well as to carry out certain specific programs dependent upon human engineering information [718, p. 2].

The greatest uncertainty in health examination surveys involves the degree of cooperation obtained from the sample population. Various examination surveys on a smaller scale than the National Survey suggested that the rate of refusal to cooperate might be as high as a quarter or a third of those in the sample. However, approximately 85 percent of the sampled population responded to the first phase of the National Examination Survey, and cooperation has continued to be very satisfactory in subsequent efforts; this is a credit to the ingenuity and technical competence of those connected with this survey. Particular groups in the population are overrepresented in the sample: more younger people than older people cooperated; more blacks than whites participated; and there are differential rates of participation for various other social categories as well (715). On the whole, however, the examination sample is a remarkably close approximation to the American population.

Household Interviews

The most abundant source of data is the household morbidity interview, in which representative samples of the population are questioned in a detailed fashion about the symptoms, illnesses, and disabilities they experienced, and what they did about them (see 713; 730). However, even in the most carefully formulated household interview studies underreporting of illness is a significant problem, and the information obtained from respondents tends to be highly discrepant from information obtained from clinical evaluations of the same population. These discrepancies are not unexpected, as it should be obvious that clinical assessments and household interviews provide different kinds of data. Illness conditions reported in a household interview depend on the individual's awareness of morbidity. Thus people may report illnesses and symptoms under detailed questioning that they would not report to a doctor in another context. Moreover, what patients know about their illnesses depends to some extent on what doctors tell them, and the physician's assessment need not necessarily be communicated to the patient. If the doctor fails to communicate such information, the patient may be unaware of his condition. On the other hand, patients may be willing to report some information to physicians that they are unwilling to report to a household interviewer, thus further increasing the discrepancies between household reports and clinical assessments. In short, although household morbidity data are not difficult to obtain, their meaning and usefulness for research purposes are not unambiguous (129; 213; 509; 704). As Feldman has concluded, the bulk of research evidence can be interpreted as indicating that a clinical assessment of general health and the responses to survey questions about health are only slightly correlated.

Although various methodological studies concerned with the adequacy of reporting in morbidity interview studies have not yielded fully consistent results, they all tend to support the general principle that accurate reporting occurs when the symptom or illness in question is salient to the person, and social and psychological barriers to reporting are absent (509). Barriers to reporting include feelings of stigma, threat, or embarrassment that may become relevant in reporting particular conditions such as mental disorders or venereal diseases; reports for such conditions are particularly unreliable and discrepant from clinical estimates. The idea that salience of symptoms or experiences affects the reporting process can be inferred from a variety of findings: self-reports tend to be more complete than those by proxy (when a person reports the symptoms of another household member); conditions requiring a single consultation with a physician are reported much more poorly than those requiring many consultations; conditions requiring a short stay in a hospital are reported much more poorly than those requiring a longer stay; episodes involving surgery are reported more adequately than those not involving surgery.

The period of recall required by the interview affects substantially the amount of illness reported. The National Health Survey for most purposes uses a recall period of two weeks, i.e., the person is questioned about the two weeks prior to the date of the interview. Such a recall period will yield results different from one based on a month, or a week, or a day. Mooney (521), for example, using data from the San Jose Health Survey, found that estimates of the occurrence of illness based on a one-day recall period were substantially greater than those based on a calendar-month recall period. The one-day recall period provided monthly incidence rates that were more than four times the comparable rates for a calendar-month recall period. This was true for both acute and chronic illnesses. When illness within the restricted activity category was viewed, the prevalence rates derived, using the shorter recall period, were 40 percent higher. In this case, reports of restriction of activities because of acute illness account for most of the difference.

There are many other problems in using morbidity data from health interviews. It is well known that more symptoms of illness will be reported if various checklists are utilized (784), and the more elaborate the questioning, the more illness appears to be elicited from the respondent. Under some circumstances such continued questioning can elicit the report of symptoms that may not have been recognized or regarded as significant by the person had the questions not focused awareness on them. We know enough about response tendencies to realize that they, also, may vastly influence the results elicited by morbidity interviews (155; 197; 198; 458), but our information is not sufficient to evaluate or control these biases very effectively.

Although the inadequacy of prevalence estimates based on morbidity interviews is widely recognized, such data are often used to analyze differences by such variables as age, sex, region of residence, and socioeconomic factors. Here it is generally assumed that the biases in reporting are distributed in similar ways among the various social categories, and thus that morbidity data elicited from interviews can be used to estimate the kinds of illness trends that exist among the various segments of the population. Feldman, in his excellent review on the topic, has even questioned this assumption:

> Actually, the absolute level of an incidence or prevalence rate is rarely important from the strictly medical point of view. What is usually desired from surveys for epidemiologic purposes are estimates of the differences in the incidence rates of particular conditions among various classes of individuals or over time. It has been suggested that the derivation of estimates of such differences from household survey data will generally result merely in attenuation, i.e., the expected value of the difference between two population subgroups in the incidence of a given disease will be diminished by using survey data rather than clinical data. If this were generally true, survey data could be viewed as a rather inefficient but nevertheless permissible substitute for clinical data, particularly when one is only interested in discovering quite large differences between subgroups and when a much larger and more complete survey than clinical sample is feasible. A positive association between the survey responses and the clinical diagnoses would of course, be necessary, but this condition would certainly almost always be met. But, in addition, a considerably more dubious assumption underlies the biomedical use of survey data. The rates of false negatives within the various population subgroups being compared must be identical. The condition of equality must also hold among the rates of false positives. In other words, if one were interested in comparing the incidence of a given disease among individuals exhibiting considerable anxiety, the rate of false positives in the two groups would have to be approximately equal, and the rate of false negatives in the two groups would also have to be approximately equal [213, p. 550].

The conditions and assumptions discussed by Feldman are never completely guaranteed when health-interview data are used for intergroup comparisons, for we rarely have sufficient information to feel confident that false positives and false negatives are equally distributed among the subgroups we are studying. In a general way, we might feel that this assumption is plausible since studies have not been able to isolate subgroups that are consistently different in their reporting tendencies, even though individual studies have noted such effects. For example, Shapiro, Balamuth, and Densen (742), observing low correspondence between health-interview responses and medical records from the Health Insurance Plan of Greater New York, attempted to analyze the factors that contributed to poor reporting. They found little difference in adequacy of reporting of chronic conditions by sex or race, nor did they find any consistent difference by education or income. They conclude that:

> The results of the current study illustrate the complex problem posed by attempts to interpret data on chronic diseases collected through the household interview process. They suggest strongly that the survey information does not conform even moderately well to the universe of conditions inferred from physician reporting. It would appear that this lack of conformity cannot be explained by simple population attributes and characteristics of the interview situation. Age, sex, socioeconomic status, respondent status, ethnic background, and other conventional demographic attributes exert suprisingly little influence on the degree to which the knowledge that a physician has about the existence of illness is reflected in a household interview. . . .Until now the emphasis in methodological study has been on determining how well the household interview reports mirror the reports of physicians. But if this relationship should, on repeated study, prove to be a poor one, the need to know what it is that survey information does in fact reflect will still remain. Through follow-back studies to physicians and patients some understanding could be obtained regarding the influence on respondent reporting of doctor-patient communication, the assessment and interpretation the patient made of his illness, and the circumstances that make the respondent aware of and ready to report a given condition in an interview situation [742, pp. 29–30].

Although consistent differences in adequacy of reporting have not been found for various demographic subgroups, it is still necessary to make the assumption of equal distribution of false positives and false negatives with hesitation and care. Although such studies do not show consistent trends, they do show differences between subgroups that often exceed chance expectations. Also, the definitions used in recording the results of health interviews may bring about different kinds of biases among groups that are being compared. The National Health Survey, for example, defines morbidity as including only conditions "as a result of which the person has taken one or more of various actions" such as restriction of usual activities, bed disability, work loss, the

seeking of medical advice, or the taking of medicines (716). Their rationale is that:

> If the condition is of so little importance to the individual that, although
> aware of it, he takes no action of any sort, in the majority of instances it is of
> little health significance. Furthermore, the experience of earlier surveys
> reveals that there is a considerable degree of response error in the reporting
> of illness which has involved no disability or medical consultation. These
> minor illnesses seem to be subject to a good deal more memory bias and
> reporting variability than those which have affected the life of the individ-
> ual to the extent that specific forms of action have been taken [716, p. 4].

This assumption can be erroneous. Action is frequently taken for
trivial symptoms, while very serious ones may be ignored. Moreover,
the inclination to take some action may vary among cultural and other
subgroups, and therefore it is incorrect to assume that taking action is
similarly defined and distributed among various population groups.
For example, if lower-class persons are likely to have many symptoms
that are left untreated, and upper-class persons are likely to have fewer
symptoms that more frequently lead to action, morbidity figures based
on an action criterion may overrepresent upper-class morbidity and
underrepresent lower-class morbidity. Mechanic and Newton have
found that different attitudes toward the sick role lead to different rates
of inaccurate reporting (584), and attitudes toward the sick role are differentially distributed in various social groups. In consequence, morbidity interview data may involve reporting errors that mask important
trends in the distribution of illness.

It would be incorrect to leave the reader with the impression that
those who design and execute such surveys do so without an awareness
of the problems and difficulties such data encompass. These investigators have undertaken much of the work that has exposed such difficulties; the National Health Survey, for example, has been characterized
by an active orientation toward improving the quality of data collected
and the methodological techniques used. The development of the National Examination Survey is an attempt to obtain data that cannot be
adequately elicited through a household interview.

Medical-Resources Measurement and
Health-Services Utilization

As the health-care industry has grown and as the federal government
has assumed larger responsibilities for planning, financing, and
regulating the health sector, the need for information on resources and
health-care utilization has become more pressing. In 1971 the President's Commission on Federal Statistics (747) made many recommen-

dations for improving the acquisition of information for policy purposes, and the Panel on Health Services Research and Development of the President's Science Advisory Committee (748) also addressed this problem. These groups recommended the acquisition of data better fitted to the needs of policy formulation and encouraged support for data development that would produce with greater rapidity information pertinent to examining the performance of the health-services sector. Such efforts were already under way in the National Center for Health Statistics, but in recent years surveys on resources and utilization of facilities and care have been greatly expanded. Although we cannot discuss all of these surveys here, this section provides some flavor of the major sources of data and the types of data gathering characteristic of these new efforts.

In 1967 the National Center for Health Statistics established a master facility inventory for institutions in the United States providing medical, nursing, personal, or custodial care to unrelated persons on an overnight basis, as well as certain residential training facilities and correctional institutions (722). Included in this inventory were hospitals with six or more beds, nursing homes, homes for unwed mothers, and many other facilities; thus it serves as a useful sampling frame for many special surveys. Such inventories of facilities are extremely useful and have expanded over the years, as in the recent development of a National Inventory of Family Planning Services (738). One of the more important continuing efforts on the performance of facilities is the Hospital Discharge Survey (732), which samples hospitals with six or more beds from the National Inventory Survey and obtains a sample of discharges from these institutions. Data are obtained on the age, sex, race, and marital status of each patient discharged, and on discharge status, length of hospitalization, final diagnoses, and operations performed. For example, in 1974 some 225,000 discharge records were abstracted, and these provided useful data on the diagnoses of hospitalized patients, lengths of stay, rates of varying types of surgery, and so on. Such data are important for understanding what is happening in the hospital sector, and many health-care researchers have urged the development of a uniform hospital abstract for all hospitals (724).

In order to obtain information on care provided to hospital inpatients that is comparable across hospitals and regions, a uniform abstract is extremely useful. A summary of about 15 items of information for each hospital patient, or for a sample, would provide data useful for planning, evaluation, documentation for reimbursement, and health-care research. Such data would facilitate the identification of problem areas and the vast variations among hospitals in comparable situations, thus providing feedback for improved performance as well as for evaluation of performance.

In the past 15 years there has been an extraordinary expansion in nursing-home beds in the United States. The number of nursing-home beds now exceeds the number of hospital beds, and the nursing home has become an important component of the overall health-care sector. We know remarkably little about nursing homes, and few sociologists have done any work in this area despite its vast size and significance. The National Facility Inventory is a useful sampling frame for nursing homes and was used in the special 1973–1974 National Nursing Home Survey carried out by the National Center for Health Statistics (733). This survey provides some basic information on the operations of these institutions, but it is to be hoped that more sociologists will concern themselves with this sector in greater depth.

In most developed nations there is a renewed interest in ambulatory medical care, an issue discussed in greater detail in chapter 13. As physicians became more specialized in their work, fewer were interested in first-contact care. As this problem reached crisis proportions, renewed efforts were made to train physicians, nurse practitioners, and others for primary-care roles. Successful planning and training depend on a good understanding of the content of primary care and how it may be changing, but existing data were inadequate except for indications from special studies of relatively small groups of primary-care physicians (254; 348). Moreover, existing data tended to classify ambulatory-care consultations using the International Classification of Diseases, which was developed for hospital use and was inadequate and inappropriate for categorizing a significant proportion of problems presented to primary-care physicians by patients (763, p. 247). Even more important is the fact that most ambulatory care is provided in physicians' offices yet we know very little about the content of the work of such physicians. In 1973 the National Center for Health Statistics initiated the National Ambulatory Medical Care Survey (729), a study of physicians in office-based practice responsible for ambulatory patient care. In the first such survey a sample of more than 1,700 office-based physicians was selected and assigned randomly to each of the weeks of the year, so as to eliminate seasonal variations in the data collected. Each physician completes data-collection forms relevant to patient visits during a single week. The physician provides a list of all patient visits during the week and, for each patient or a sample of patients, depending on the circumstances, a patient-encounter form about the visit is completed, including birth date, sex, seriousness of the problem, and diagnoses. These data are collected so that they can be coded in terms of both presenting complaints or problems and more traditional diagnoses.

While the National Ambulatory Medical Care Survey is an important addition to our sources of data, it would be useful if the survey were expanded to non-office-based contexts providing ambulatory medical care, such as clinics and emergency rooms. The survey tells us a great deal about the work of the office-based physicians, but supplemental data are needed for care provided in other contexts. Blacks, other minorities, and persons of lower socioeconomic status are much more likely to receive their care from clinics and outpatient departments than is the population as a whole, and many types of policy questions require more comprehensive comparisons than can be provided simply by a survey of office-based practitioners.

It should be remembered, however, that the data system developed by the National Center for Health Statistics is not intended to answer all the important questions that can be formulated. Many additional surveys are necessary to understand the dynamics of selection into medical care and the types of care provided in varying contexts and to different types of patient. For example, it would be valuable to have sound data that allowed us to estimate the consequences of having primary care delivered by physicians or by other practitioners trained in varying ways. How do a family physician, an internist, and a cardiologist differentially evaluate a patient who complains of chest pain? What consequences flow for cost and quality of care from different types of physician assessment and evaluation? Such questions are beyond the scope of these larger national surveys and require much more subtle investigation through a variety of special studies, surveys, and controlled experiments.

In this chapter an attempt has been made to familiarize the reader with some of the sources of data and some of the difficulties involved in various approaches to studying social factors as they relate to health. It is assumed that awareness of some of the methodological issues in studying health and illness allows one to approach research findings in a more critical fashion. Having reviewed the approaches, let us now turn to the findings.

Part 3

DISTRIBUTION OF DISEASE IN POPULATIONS

Chapter 5

DEMOGRAPHIC STUDIES OF MORTALITY

Since 1700 the average expectation of life in North America and Europe has increased by approximately 100 percent (184). Dorn (181) attributes this remarkable advance to four developments characterizing man's increasing control over his environment: (1) increased food sources and raw materials with the expansion of population into new continents; (2) the development of commerce and the transportation of food and other commodities over long distances; (3) changes in agricultural technology and the development of modern industry; and (4) increased control over disease resulting from better housing, food and water supplies, adoption of sanitary measures, developing knowledge in preventive medicine, and new discoveries in pharmacology and chemotherapy. The three factors usually cited to explain improved health and increased longevity of the population in more recent times are rises in the standard of living, the introduction of better sanitary conditions, and the growth of health sciences. McKeown has attempted to trace the specific factors contributing to declining mortality and an increased lifespan in England and Wales in the nineteenth and twentieth centuries:

> Five diseases or groups of diseases accounted for the decline of mortality in the nineteenth century (after 1838): tuberculosis, for a little less than a half; typhus, typhoid and continued fever for about a fifth; scarlet fever for a fifth; cholera, dysentery and diarrhoea for nearly a tenth; and smallpox for a twentieth. Consideration of possible reasons for the trend of deaths in each of these disease groups suggests that in order of relative importance the main influences were: (a) a rising standard of living, of which the most significant feature was possibly an improved diet (responsible mainly for the decline of tuberculosis and less certainly, and to a lesser extent, of typhus); (b) the hygienic measures—control of water, sewage disposal, etc.—in-

troduced by the sanitary reformers (responsible for the decline of the typhus-typhoid and cholera groups of diseases); and (c) a favourable trend in the relationship between infectious agent and human host (which accounted for the decline of mortality from scarlet fever and may have contributed to that from tuberculosis, typhus and cholera). The effect of therapy was restricted to smallpox and made only a trivial contribution.

In the twentieth century the outstanding feature has been the reduction of infant mortality (deaths in the first year of life). Because of the introduction of more effective forms of therapy, and of the personal health and social services, the task of interpretation is more complex. But there have been further advances in the standard of living and in the control of the physical environment by hygienic measures and, particularly in view of the proportion of the improvement which occurred in the nineteenth century, there can be little doubt that these have been the two most significant influences on mortality since 1838 [468, pp. 57–58].

The contribution of an increased standard of living to declining mortality in recent decades has been questioned by George Stolnitz, who has studied a century of available life tables from various countries. It is his hypothesis that rising standards of living have had only a secondary role in prolonging life since 1875. From that time, he argues, increases in life chances developed in various countries in the face of substantial variations in Western economic levels and trends. He sees this later improvement in longevity as attributable to the spread of environmental sanitation and the development of effective public-health programs (61).

In the present century average length of life at all ages increased in the United States until approximately the middle 1950s, when it stabilized. More recently it has been increasing slightly, and there are no indications that we can anticipate any dramatic improvements in the foreseeable future. From 1950 to 1969 in the United States there were decreases in mortality resulting from diseases of the heart, cerebrovascular diseases, accidents, influenza and pneumonia, certain causes of infant death, arteriosclerosis, congenital anomalies, nephritis and nephrosis, and peptic ulcers. In contrast, mortality increased for malignant neoplasms, diabetes mellitus, bronchitis, emphysema and asthma, cirrhosis of the liver, and suicide and homicide (728). These increases seem closely linked to social and environmental patterns, including increased carcinogens in the environment, smoking, excessive drinking, and the breakdown of social cohesion. In 1975, the latest period for which data are available, the age-adjusted death rate dropped to 6.4 per 1,000, the lowest in U.S. recorded history (740). The reduction in recent years reflects the drop in deaths due to diseases of the heart, cerebrovascular diseases, and accidents (737; 740).

Mortality and Related Social Factors

The most significant twentieth-century influence on the death rate until recently has been the substantial decline in infant deaths. Much of the advance in the early part of this century is attributable to the prevention of deaths from infectious disease; although there are many areas in which progress may still be possible, such developments are unlikely to have a marked effect on overall longevity. Levels of mortality tend to be higher in the United States than in some other Western countries, and it does not appear that we shall improve our position greatly in the near future (714). If one compares the United States with Sweden, which has a more favorable mortality experience, it becomes apparent that the differences at younger ages are largely attributable to variations in rates of accidents and violence, and at older ages to deaths from heart disease (257). Significant improvements in American mortality experience are unlikely without major inroads in environmental and behavioral change related to the exposure to risks of chronic disease, accidents, and violence. A similar situation applies in most other developed nations, but perhaps not to the same extent. As we proceed in our discussion of factors affecting mortality and morbidity, some of the special difficulties in reducing mortality in the United States will become clearer.

Age

Death rates are clearly associated with age. The period following birth involves a fairly high risk of death, with the most dangerous period the first hour after birth. The viability of the infant increases with each subsequent hour, and after the first day the risks of mortality are markedly reduced. While the first week is still a period of relatively high risk, deaths decrease substantially after that. In the first year approximately 16 children of every 1,000 born will die; in the next five years perhaps another three to four will die. In the next ten years, however, the safest period in the total lifespan, only about four more children of the original cohort of 1,000 will die (735, pp. 5–8).

Death during the first week of life is most frequently attributable to a variety of poorly defined conditions of early infancy. A large number of these deaths do not result from a clear or specific disease process, and about two-fifths fall into such general categories as ill-defined diseases peculiar to early infancy, unqualified immaturity, and unqualified and postnatal asphyxia and atelectasis. About another one-tenth of the deaths are due to birth injuries, which describe a wide variety of circumstances, and congenital defects are also an important cause of death during this stage of life (639, pp. 25–30; 734). During the first year of life, the three most important causes of death are influenza and pneumonia, congenital malformations, and accidents. Accidents are the major cause of deaths between the ages of one and four, followed by influenza and pneumonia, congenital malformations, and malignant neoplasms. Deaths during the next ten years of life are rare, and of these approximately 40 percent are attributable to accidents (adapted from 639 and 720).

The death rate begins to increase in the age period 15–19 years and continues to grow with increasing age. Up to approximately age 35, accidents are the most important cause of death. In the age group 35–44 years, however, major cardiovascular-renal disease and malignant neoplasms become the most important causes of death and remain so throughout the remainder of the lifespan. Accidents, particularly those involving motor vehicles, continue to be extremely important causes of death. As people reach their 50s, heart disease, cancers, and strokes account for most deaths, but cirrhosis of the liver, influenza and pneumonia, and suicide also have considerable importance. In 1975 heart disease accounted for approximately 38 percent of all deaths, followed by malignant neoplasms (accounting for 19 percent of all deaths) and vascular lesions affecting the central nervous system (accounting for 10 percent of all deaths). Thus these three groups of conditions accounted for approximately two-thirds of all deaths in 1975. Other major causes of death in 1975, and the percent of deaths accounted for, were as follows: accidents (5 percent), influenza and pneumonia (3 percent), diabetes mellitus (2 percent), cirrhosis of the liver (2 percent), and arteriosclerosis (2 percent) (740).

Sex

The life expectancy at birth in the United States was 76.5 years for women, based on death rates during 1975; the comparable life expectancy for men was 68.7 years (740). The age-adjusted death rates in recent years indicate a male excess in mortality of 78 percent in comparison to women. This male-female excess has increased from an excess of 65 percent in 1964 (720), continuing a long-term trend favoring female longevity. In the United States, in the period 1900–1902, average expectation of life at birth among women was a little less than three years longer than men; the differential grew to only three and one-half years by 1929–1931, and by 1975 it was approaching eight years.

A variety of factors help account for the more favorable mortality experience among females. Certainly part of this difference is biological.

The female advantage exists in most animal species that have been studied (142a), although there is evidence of higher female mortality in birds and mammals (755). The fact that many more females than males survive in utero and in the first year of life suggests some biological selective factor. In 1974 and 1975, for example, male mortality in the first year of life was almost 30 percent higher than female mortality (737; 740). Many attempts have been made to explain the male-female mortality differential in terms of differential environmental risks for males and females. Although such differential risks explain at least some of this variation, they are not sufficient in themselves to account for the substantial difference noted. In an intriguing study by Madigan, mortality in Catholic nuns and monks was compared (454). Since both the nuns and monks were engaged primarily in teaching and lived a similar kind of life (without the confounding influences of marital status and childbearing), this situation provides a good context for studying biological differences. The investigator found that the male-female differential was as large as in the general population, and that the increasing difference between the sexes found in the general population was characteristic of this group as well.

Although biological factors account for part of the male-female differential, they do not explain why this difference has increased so substantially in recent years. A variety of factors explain this trend. First, the risk of childbearing has substantially decreased. In the period 1930–1934 there were approximately 669 deaths for every 100,000 live births. In 1975 the comparable rate was 12.8 deaths per 100,000 live births. Most important, however, has been the general shift in causes of death that affect men and women differentially. With the exception of cancer of the breast and cancer of the genital organs, which occur most frequently among women and which are amenable to early detection and treatment, in contrast to cancers more common among men (primarily lung cancer), male mortality exceeds mortality among women for every cause of death except diabetes mellitus. The excess of death among men for many of these causes is very high and is related to behavioral patterns that differ between the sexes. In 1967 the ratio of male to female deaths was 5.9 for cancer of the respiratory system and 4.9 for emphysema and other bronchopulmonic diseases (these diseases being closely linked to smoking); 2.8 for motor vehicle accidents, 2.7 for suicide, and 2.4 for other accidents; 2.0 for cirrhosis of the liver (often believed to be a result of alcoholism); and 2.0 for coronary and arteriosclerotic heart disease (755). Differences in the ratio of coronary and arteriosclerotic heart disease are less apparent in the postmenopausal age groups, and it is believed that female hormones may play some part in the greater invulnerability experienced by premenopausal women (143). Similarly, women have benefited more from advances in cancer therapy.

Marital Status

Married people have lower mortality than those who have never married. In part, this relationship is the product of selection into marriage. Persons with obvious physical defects are less likely to marry. But this relationship is also probably due in part to the care and help marital partners give to one another, and the regularity of diet and patterns of life that marriage implies. In England during the 1930s the mortality rate among Protestant clergy who married was less than three-quarters of the national average, while the celibate Roman Catholic clergy had higher mortality than the national average (142a). Benjamin (61; 62) points out that in most age categories the mortality of married people in England of both sexes is lower than the mortality of single people. Also, with the exception of particular age groups, mortality of the widowed and divorced is higher than among both married persons and those who have never married.

In the Matched Records Study of deaths for the period 1959–1961 (391), it was found that single, widowed, and divorced men (among both whites and nonwhites) had a higher excess mortality relative to the married than did comparable women. Women may not only have more coping skills in taking care of themselves because of prior socialization, but also may experience more restraints in following behavioral patterns conducive to high risks of illness and death. The highest ratios of death for divorced, widowed, and single men relative to those who are married include such causes as homicide, suicide, motor vehicle accidents, cirrhosis of the liver, and tuberculosis (543, pp. 165–166). White divorced men of ages 35–64 had a mortality rate 130 percent higher than comparable married men; single and widowed men had an excess mortality of 75 percent. The rates of excess death among equivalent groups of women were 37 percent for the divorced, 30 percent for the widowed, and 34 percent for the single. Among nonwhites the widows had the highest excess risk.

The differences in rates of mortality by marital status have been relatively consistent across a wide range of studies. Many of these effects among the single and the divorced are probably due to selection and to the physical and psychological dispositions of these persons. Differences among widows cannot be explained so easily. There is growing evidence that extreme grief and life disruption contribute both to behavioral change and to physiological change (548). These influences will be discussed in chapter 8.

Socioeconomic Status

Data on socioeconomic status and mortality are not available for most countries, and even the data available from the United States and England are less than ideal. Yet socioeconomic status has for many years been one of the central variables in the study of social patterns and human behavior. It has long been recognized that socioeconomic indicators provide clues revealing the risks and opportunities characteristic of the lives of persons who come from a variety of social settings, and such indicators have been fruitful in accounting for differences in such varied phenomena as crime and delinquency, suicide, political behavior, economic values, and child-rearing orientations.

Use of the concept of social class, and various socioeconomic indicators, is often based on the assumption that the sociocultural environment within which persons develop adaptive life patterns has a far-reaching influence on life experience. Thus socioeconomic indices are rather gross ways of denoting the style of life—describing contexts within which persons are reared and within which they develop, their likely access to opportunities and experiences, and the kinds of life demands with which they must cope. Behavioral scientists often deal with data which do not measure these factors directly, and thus they must depend on gross indicators.

For the most part, analysts studying mortality do not have data that measure directly the socioeconomic status of the deceased. When official statistics are used, one must work with the data available, and therefore analysts usually have two kinds of data that suggest socioeconomic differences—occupation and race. Since occupation is highly correlated with education, income, and residence, it serves as a very good indicator of socioeconomic status. The racial variable combines several other factors in addition to socioeconomic ones, i.e., possible biological differences, consequences of differential treatment due to racial status, and so on. However, the nonwhite group in the United States is composed of many individuals of low socioeconomic status, and white-nonwhite distinctions are, at least in part, a result of living under different socioeconomic circumstances. Thus, in the absence of better indicators, we shall consider, but with caution, the racial distinction as a distinction in socioeconomic level. Throughout the discussion we must recognize that the indicators map social patterns very roughly, and that the differences noted among the various socioeconomic and color groups may result from any combination of a large variety of possible variables linked with socioeconomic status.

The life styles that characterize various social groups may expose them to different environmental risks that have an important bearing on health status. Although such risks may occur with greater frequency and intensity in some social strata as compared with others, they are not distributed throughout the class structure in any fully consistent way. Even the clearest cases of differential risk—let us use nutrition as an example—may reveal some inconsistencies in grouping families. We might assume, for example, that the adequacy of nutrition is likely to be better in higher as compared with lower socioeconomic groups. Although the assumption is reasonable, if we actually studied individual families we might find that many lower-income families had an adequate diet, while some higher-income families do not because of carelessness or some other factor. Although it is sometimes useful to oversimplify matters, we must recognize that life styles are varied and complicated, and while some components of a particular style of living may be conducive to health and longevity, related components may increase the risks of particular diseases and conditions.

Although some discussions have assumed that magnitude of risk is inversely related to social status, it is increasingly clear that affluent styles of life as well as poverty increase vulnerabilities to particular diseases and disorders. Thus the rich diets of higher-status groups and the occupational demands that involve considerable social stress but little physical exercise have been linked by some investigators with a high prevalence of coronary heart disease (524). Similarly, the failure to develop immunities to particular viruses in early life has been cited as an important factor in explaining higher rates of certain diseases among the relatively affluent as compared with those less so (688). In short, although it is reasonable to assume that lower social status and poverty may produce greater disease risks and vulnerabilities than does the style of life characteristic of the affluent classes, we must not fail to note the extent to which variability is apparent within particular socioeconomic categories. Moreover, as an increasing proportion of the population reaches a level of satisfactory subsistence, linked with a continuing decline in the importance of the infectious diseases affecting health and longevity, it will be difficult to characterize life styles and health risks through gross socioeconomic indicators.

The concept of life style itself is global. As it is usually used, it encompasses a large variety of interacting variables: nutrition and housing; infant rearing and caring; habits, attitudes, and values; life aspirations and goals; willingness to take risks; self-care and concern with health; and so on. It is already clear that investigations relating social status to health status require careful consideration of specific components of the more complex lifestyles.

In every age group except among the very old, where mortality data are particularly unreliable, nonwhite age-specific death rates are higher than white rates. Although the gap between whites and nonwhites has

**Table 1. Life Table: Average Life Remaining
—United States 1973**

	MALE		FEMALE	
At Age	White	Nonwhite	White	Nonwhite
0	68.4	61.9	76.1	70.1
5	64.9	59.1	72.3	67.1
20	50.5	44.9	57.7	52.6
30	41.4	36.7	48.0	43.3
40	32.2	28.7	38.5	34.4
50	23.6	21.5	29.5	26.4
60	16.2	15.6	21.1	19.3
70	10.4	10.7	13.7	13.2

Source: Adapted from U.S. National Center for Health Statistics, Health Resources Administration. *Vital Statistics of the United States,* 1973, *Life Tables,* vol. 2, sec. 5 (Washington: Government Printing Office, 1975).

been closing, the differences continue to be substantial (112). Table 1 shows a portion of the life table for whites and nonwhites, revealing the average expected life remaining at various ages. As an examination of the table will show, nonwhites have a less favorable mortality experience than whites among both males and females.

Until recently, the only U.S. data available for analysis of occupational and socioeconomic differences in mortality came from the merging of mortality and census statistics (749). These data showed very large differences between the laboring class and all other occupational groups among both whites and nonwhites.

They were especially large in the nonwhite group, in which the standardized mortality ratio for laborers was almost three-fifths greater than for all nonwhite occupational groups. The comparable figure for white laborers as compared with all white men with work experience was 38 percent higher. There were also very substantial differences between whites and nonwhites. We have already discussed some of the problems of census enumeration, and it is not inconceivable that some of the large differences noted between the laboring class and other occupational groupings, particularly among nonwhites, are inflated by errors in enumeration of the population, which provides the base figures for computation of death ratios. Moreover, errors in the reporting of age and in the occupational data obtained from death certificates as compared with census reports are substantial. Thus, such data must be viewed with some care (181) as the basis for more detailed study rather than the substance on which to base definitive conclusions.

Fortunately, the 1960 Matched Records Study by Kitagawa and Hauser (391) helps a great deal to clarify issues concerning socioeconomic and occupational differences in mortality. In this study 340,000 of the deaths during May to August 1960 were matched individually with the 1960 census records in order to obtain information on the social and economic characteristics of those who died. Since analyses can be undertaken on characteristics that are not included on death certificates, these data offer a richer source of analysis than is conventionally available. In earlier studies by Kitagawa and Hauser (390) in the city of Chicago they found that differences in socioeconomic level between whites and nonwhites explained most mortality differences. Although this had not been the case in 1930 and 1940, there was little difference in 1950 that could not be attributed to socioeconomic variations resulting largely from the lowest social stratum in the occupational structure.

Table 2 provides results from the 1960 Matched Records Study (391) showing excess deaths (the proportion of deaths for various categories above what the expected mortality would be if "the mortality level of white men [or women] of high socioeconomic status had prevailed among all men [or women]"). Socioeconomic status is measured here by years of schooling and represents not only economic factors but probably attitudes and knowledge as well. Both education and income have important independent effects on mortality when controlling for the other. As can be seen from the table, some of these excess levels are very high, particularly among the nonwhite group. Nonwhite women aged 25–64 with four or fewer years of education had an excess mortality of 70 percent, and comparable nonwhite men had a 51 percent excess; the equivalent figures for whites are 53 and 30 percent. For the total population there was an excess of 26 percent in mortality relative to what might have been anticipated if everyone had the socioeconomic characteristics of the highest group.

Kitagawa and Hauser also examine differences by occupation, an issue that has received a good deal of attention in the literature and is of renewed interest with increased emphasis on occupational health. Time series studies of occupational mortality go back to a study initiated by William Farr in England and Wales in 1851, and these series have continued to the present. Farr found in 1851, for example, that farmers had low death rates while miners, bakers, and innkeepers had relatively high death rates (391, p. 37). Some of the influence of occupations can be attributed to general socioeconomic factors while others are a consequence of the specific effects of the conditions of the occupation on the health of the worker. The relevance of socioeconomic factors in mortality is supported by studies in England and Wales, and France. In an English investigation by the General Register Office of Mortality during the period 1949–1953, unskilled workers had approximately 20 percent more mortality than other occupational groups. In general, the wives of these men had higher mortality as well, suggesting

Table 2. Index on Excess Mortality by Color, Sex, Age, and Years of School Completed—United States 1960

SEX, COLOR, AND YEARS OF SCHOOL COMPLETED	25 YEARS & OVER	25–64 YEARS	65 YEARS & OVER
Number of Excess Deaths			
Total population	291,838	139,528	152,310
All males	92,049	84,139	7,910
All females	199,789	55,389	144,400
All whites	231,695	92,984	138,711
All nonwhites	60,143	46,544	13,599
Index of Excess Mortality (Percent)			
Total population	19	26	15
All males	11	25	1
All females	30	29	30
All whites	17	21	15
All nonwhites	36	52	18
White males	10	21	2
0–4 years	9	30	3
5–7 years	12	29	2
8 years	10	25	1
High school, 1–3 years ⎱ High school, 4 years ⎰	11	24 ⎱ 16 ⎰	0.1
College, 1 year or more	0	0	0
Nonwhite males	25	45	0.5
0–4 years	25	51	5
5–8 years	23	43	−8
High school or college	28	39	−3
White females	27	21	30
0–4 years	42	53	40
5–7 years	33	36	32
8 years	31	30	31
High school, 1–3 years ⎱ High school, 4 years ⎰	18	12 ⎱ 4 ⎰	26
College, 1 year or more	0	0	0
Nonwhite females	49	60	39
0–4 years	51	70	41
5–8 years	50	63	34
High school or college	44	42	41

Source: Evelyn M. Kitagawa and Philip M. Hauser. *Differential Mortality in the United States: A Study in Socioeconomic Epidemiology* (Cambridge: Harvard University Press, 1973), p. 167.

that the mortality differences could be attributed in large part to patterns of living characterized by socioeconomic status (61). Similarly, a French study of men aged 25–54 in 1955 found that the rate of death among unskilled nonagricultural workers was 76 per 10,000 males as compared with much lower rates of death among other occupational groups (intermediate personnel [31 per 10,000], liberal professions and senior personnel [32 per 10,000], employers in industry and commerce [51 per 10,000], nonmanual workers [52 per 10,000], and so on) (61).

The socioeconomic differences in mortality observed in the United States for the year 1950 appear to be significantly more pronounced than those observed in England and Wales in the same year. Although such comparisons are always fraught with difficulties and uncertainties, in an intriguing analysis Moriyama and Guralnick (522) compared at various ages the ratio of death rates by occupational level to total death rates in the two countries. They found that in every age group the range of ratios for the United States was greater. The highest occupational level in the United States was below the mean mortality in every age group, while the lowest occupational category was above the mean mortality in every age group. In England and Wales, however, the differences from the average were smaller and not always in a consistent direction. They conclude that "relatively, the professional workers of the United States have a more favorable mortality than their peers in England, while the laborers are at a relative disadvantage" (522, p. 69).

In a study of time series data from England and Wales, Antonovsky (31) found that mortality differences between the highest social classes and the middle classes have decreased or disappeared over time, but the lowest social class still remains at a considerable disadvantage. This is consistent with a great deal of other data on both mortality and morbidity, indicating particularly high risk in the very lowest social strata. Similarly, Kitagawa and Hauser found that the mortality ratios among white men aged 25–64 were 1.37 for service workers, 1.19 for laborers (except farm and mine), and 1.25 for those for whom no occupation was reported (391, p. 40). Lowest mortality ratios, as in most other analyses, were found for agricultural workers (.76) and for professional, technical, and kindred workers (.80). For those who did not work after 1950 the mortality ratio was 2.04, but this is probably due mainly to social selection because of illness and disability. Sample sizes for nonwhites are too small to calculate reliable mortality ratios.

At a more aggregate level, Harvey Brenner (83) has carried out extensive time series analyses for various countries, relating economic recession to mortality patterns following these difficult economic periods. He finds a substantial relationship between economic changes and health status, with unemployment rates representing a powerful predictor of increased mortality. Suicide, cirrhosis mortality, homicide, automobile deaths, and infant and maternal mortality all increased within two years of adverse economic swings. Somewhat longer periods were required for increases in cardiovascular death to become evident, but such increases did appear. These analyses, supported by many other studies, attest to a close link between social and economic conditions and the health of the people.

Mortality by Cause

It is important to inquire as to the kinds of disease conditions that account for the large differential in mortality among various socioeconomic status groups and between whites and nonwhites. As we have already noted, there is a strong tendency for those with the lowest occupational positions, or the least education, to have particularly high risks of mortality. In general, the differences among other occupational levels are smaller and not fully consistent. In interpreting these indications it is important to keep in mind the possibility that sicker workers tend to drift into laboring or service occupations. Selection may be important in that a healthy, vigorous, and ambitious worker may move upward in the occupational structure, while a sickly one tends to stay in lower occupations or be downwardly mobile. The data from the English mortality study that shows frequent correspondence between the mortality experience of husbands and wives in various occupational categories argues to some extent against this interpretation. But even the English study was not fully consistent on this point; in several occupations the husbands' mortality was considerably higher than wives' mortality (61). These differences may be due to the dangerous character of particular occupations, or to selective factors.

An examination of causes of death among white males aged 25–64 for 1960 reveals that those with fewer than eight years of schooling have high excess deaths in the following categories: hypertensive disease (mortality ratio 1.27), accidents other than motor-vehicle incidents (1.55), cancer of the stomach (1.25), of the intestine and rectum (1.19), and of the lung, bronchus, and trachea (1.18), suicide (1.25), and other causes of death (1.44). They also seem to have excess tuberculosis, influenza, and pneumonia, but the numbers are too small to be reliable. Among women aged 25–64 with comparable education, the categories of high excess death include cancer of the intestine and rectum (1.23), of the uterus, ovary, fallopian tube, and broad ligament (1.42), major cardiovascular-renal disease (1.38), stroke (1.44), arteriosclerotic and degenerative heart disease (1.52), other cardiovascular-renal disease (1.27), accidents (1.19), and other causes (1.38). Death from diabetes mellitus and cancer of the lung, bronchus, and trachea are also high among the group with lowest education, but these statistics are unreliable because of small numbers (391, pp. 76–78).

Kitagawa and Hauser do not provide data for the nonwhite group by cause of death in relation to education because of the small sample sizes. Data are available, however, for nonwhite men aged 20–64 by occupation for the year 1950 (749). Among nonwhite laborers, large excesses in mortality occur in comparison with whites in every category shown with the exception of suicide. Also, nonwhite mortality from most diseases appears to be substantially higher than white mortality from the same diseases when whites and nonwhites at the same occupational level are compared, and often when higher-status nonwhites are compared with lower-status whites. The great difficulty with comparisons across occupational levels is that the occupational categories are large, and the occupations within each group vary considerably. It is thus possible that nonwhites tend to occupy much lower positions than whites within the same occupational levels. However, when higher-status nonwhites are compared with lower-status whites and the differences in favor of whites persist, this suggests that factors other than socioeconomic differences associated with color account for these gaps.

What are the indications that suggest that these differences include factors other than more limited socioeconomic standards of living? All white occupational groups, for example, have lower mortality from tuberculosis than any nonwhite occupational group. A similar observation holds for diabetes mellitus, major cardiovascular-renal disease, vascular lesions affecting the central nervous system, chronic and unspecified nephritis and other renal sclerosis, and death by homicide. With one slight exception, each of the nonwhite occupational groups faced greater risks of mortality from influenza and pneumonia than any nonwhite occupational group. Obviously there are many deficiencies in the reporting of occupation and causes of death, and since data are limited, caution in interpretation is required. However, it is difficult, at least from these data, to conclude that socioeconomic factors narrowly conceived can explain all of the observed differences.

Table 3 presents ratios of nonwhite to white mortality for selected causes of death among men aged 25–59. Excess nonwhite mortality as compared with white mortality is greatest for homicide, syphilis and its sequelae, ill-defined symptoms, tuberculosis, influenza and pneumonia, vascular lesions of the central nervous system, and chronic and unspecified nephritis and other renal sclerosis. Some of the smaller differences noted in the table cannot be taken too seriously, since the data have many defects. Kitagawa and Hauser (391) have found, for example, that nonwhite-white comparisons using uncorrected census and death registration data exaggerate the excess mortality among nonwhites. Correcting for the census undercount of nonwhites, they estimate that for the year 1960 age-adjusted death rates for nonwhite women were 34 percent greater and for nonwhite men 20 percent

Table 3. Comparison of Nonwhite to White Standardized Mortality Ratios among Men 25–59 Years, by Selected Causes of Death—United States 1950

CAUSE OF DEATH	WHITE	NONWHITE	RATIO: NONWHITE TO WHITE
Tuberculosis	78	316	4.05
Syphilis and its sequelae	60	500	8.04
Malignant neoplasms	97	126	1.23
Diabetes mellitus	94	158	1.68
Alcoholism	92	182	1.98
Major cardiovascular-renal disease	93	169	1.45
Vascular lesions CNS	81	294	3.63
Diseases of heart and rheumatic fever	96	140	1.46
Chronic unspecified nephritis and other renal sclerosis	85	250	2.94
Diseases of respiratory system	85	249	2.93
Influenza and pneumonia	80	298	3.73
Ulcer of stomach	93	170	1.83
Ulcer of duodenum	101	91	0.90
Cirrhosis of liver	102	83	0.81
Symptoms ill-defined	69	405	5.87
Accidents	94	153	1.63
Suicide	106	47	0.44
Homicide	45	607	13.49

Source: Adapted from U.S. Public Health Service, National Vital Statistics Division, *Mortality by Occupational Level and Cause of Death Among Men 20 to 64 Years of Age, U. S., 1950*, Special Reports, vol. 53, no. 5 (Washington: Government Printing Office, 1963).

greater. This is in contrast to the uncorrected rates of 48 percent and 25 percent. In any case, blacks have the highest mortality of any racial group. Age-adjusted mortality rates for Japanese were about one-third lower than those of whites, in part a result of their more favorable socioeconomic status. American Indians also had very high mortality; corrected mortality was 37 percent higher than whites among women and 24 percent higher among men.

Table 3 suggests that disorders associated with social deprivation and cultural disorganization are more prominent in white-nonwhite differences than the chronic disorders. To take perhaps the most blatant example, the fact that a large number of nonwhite laborers die by homicide can hardly be seen as a direct manifestation of socioeconomic factors. Such differences must be understood within the context of the life nonwhite laborers live. Henry and Short (318) have addressed themselves to this problem, observing that there is a tendency for rates of suicide and death by homicide to be inversely related. Their theory is based on the psychological idea that both suicide and homicide reflect aggression; in one situation the aggression is expressed outwardly, and in the other inwardly. Henry and Short suggest that when individuals are free of external restraint they are more likely to blame themselves for their life situation and to express aggression inwardly; in contrast, those whose lives are characterized by considerable external restraint (which would certainly describe the black in America) are more likely to express aggression outwardly, and most frequently within their own group—thus the high rate of homicide among nonwhites. Henry and Short further believe that low social status reflects external restraint. Following this assumption, lower-class persons are exposed to more restraints than those who have higher social status; this would explain the concentration of homicide among the lowest nonwhite occupational groups.

In sum, it seems clear from various studies that there are major socioeconomic and racial differences in mortality. The socioeconomic factors have varying effects on men and women. Educational differences appear to have a more considerable effect on the mortality of women, while income differences are greater for men. Most important, however, is the fact that each of these factors has an independent effect on mortality. Comparing those with fewer than eight years of schooling and those with at least one year of college, differences in mortality controlling for income are 21 percent for men and 36 percent for women. Controlling for education, the income difference is 56 percent for men and 19 percent for women (391). These differences in mortality by socioeconomic status reflect a wide variety of factors: nutrition and exposure to disease, access to preventive medicine and medical care, protective health behavior, sanitary practices, and attitudes and ways of life. Above and beyond these factors, the data reflect further differences in mortality (especially between whites and nonwhites) that appear to be related to a deprived way of life, apathy and neglect, and a disorganized cultural pattern.

Infant Mortality

In the middle 1970s the infant mortality rate in the United States dropped to approximately 16 deaths per 1,000 live births (737; 740). This shows a substantial decline since 1915, when the rate was approximately 100 deaths per 1,000 live births (639). Although all segments of the population have experienced a substantial decrease in the rate of infant mortality, socioeconomic differences persist. In 1975 the nonwhite infant mortality rate was still two-thirds higher than the white rate, and this difference can be attributed largely to socioeconomic factors. The gap between whites and nonwhites has narrowed in the past 15 years from an excess of infant deaths among nonwhites of 80 to 90 percent (716a; 718a; 718b; 737). There are still large variations in infant deaths in the United States, from a low in 1975 of 12.9 deaths in Hawaii per 1,000 live births to a high of 29 deaths in the District of Columbia (740). In 1973 the United States ranked fifteenth in favorable infant mortality among nations in the world; in Sweden infant mortality dipped below 10 deaths per 1,000 live births (739, p. 349).

Figure 1 provides the essential definitions of fetal and infant death. Infant mortality is divided into two periods: The first, from birth through the twenty-eighth day, refers to the neonatal mortality rate; the second, from the twenty-ninth day to one year, refers to the postneonatal mortality period. The infant mortality rate reflects both neonatal and postneonatal mortality. About three-quarters of infant deaths occur during the neonatal period. Deaths shortly following birth arise mostly from conditions existing prior to birth or reflective of the birth process and appear to have a relatively high biological component. After the first 28 days the causes of death are more clearly specifiable and seem to be more reflective of social and environmental conditions affecting the infant; for example, infectious diseases (particularly influenza and pneumonia) and accidents become major factors affecting mortality (639). In short, the distinction between neonatal and postneonatal death provides a crude but useful way of distinguishing between deaths that are more heavily affected by biological factors and those more influenced by social and environmental conditions. Obviously, all deaths are influenced by both biological and environmental factors, but this distinction is a valuable one. This is illustrated by the fact that in 1968 the ratio of the black infant mortality rate to the white rate was 1.82 to 1; for neonatal deaths the ratio was 1.59 to 1, but after the first month of life it increased to more than 2.5 to 1 (355, p. 103).

Figure 1.   Definitions of Fetal and Infant Death

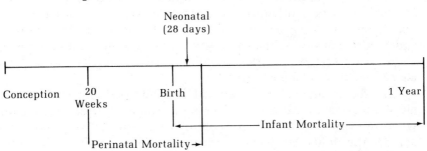

Since the causes of neonatal death seem to be much the same as those occurring prior to birth, it has been suggested that fetal deaths and neonatal deaths be combined for analytic purposes. Unfortunately, fetal deaths occurring prior to 20 weeks are very unreliably reported, and even those in the later period involve much higher risks of unreliability than those characteristic of neonatal death. It has been argued, however, that combining fetal deaths following 20 weeks of gestation (in some definitions 28 weeks) alleviates certain other methodological problems. The concept of perinatal mortality refers to those deaths occurring from the twentieth week of gestation through the first 28 days following birth. This definition overcomes variations in how doctors and hospitals report deaths occurring immediately after birth (stillbirths). Also, with more sophisticated medical care, pregnancies that would have resulted in fetal deaths in the past now sometimes result in babies who die shortly after birth (639). Although use of the perinatal rate solves some problems, the added and unknown degree of reliability introduced makes it a statistic that should be interpreted very cautiously. (For an excellent discussion of fetal and perinatal mortality, see Shapiro and colleagues, 639, especially pp. 41–46.)

Infant mortality is associated with a number of interrelated factors, and thus it is difficult to explain with precision existing differences among social groups. Survival of the infant depends on such factors as weight at birth, which in turn is related to the size and health condition of the mother, her age, number of previous pregnancies, her smoking behavior, and so on. Infants weighing five and one-half pounds or less at birth have a neonatal death rate that is fifteen to twenty times higher than infants of greater weight, and nonwhite infants have twice the probability than white infants of being born at low birth weights (355; 717). Moreover, an unfavorable environment for nonwhites appears to persist after the initial period following birth, since the differential white-nonwhite infant mortality rate increases in the postneonatal period. Such factors as adequacy of postnatal medical care, apathy and neglect of the child's health, and nutrition probably play some part. In short, the differential mortality between whites and nonwhites is related to a complex of factors including the health and pregnancy experience of the mother, the higher rate of venereal disease among nonwhites, the adequacy of medical care, the deprivation syndrome and apathy concerning the care of the child, and cultural patterns of child caring. Precise specification of the relative contribution of these factors remains to be determined.

Low socioeconomic status in itself does not lead to high infant mortality, since there are many lower socioeconomic areas and groups where rates are low. And several countries that are relatively poor compared to the United States have a lower rate of infant mortality than we do. At least two studies of infant mortality in America—in Syracuse, New York, and in Providence, Rhode Island—provide some support for the contention that socioeconomic status in itself is not a particularly good predictor of infant mortality (671; 768). In both studies infant mortality rates for areas are correlated with socioeconomic ratings for each area based on census characteristics. The Syracuse study showed little association between infant mortality rates and the socioeconomic status level of census areas. However, family income was significantly associated with neonatal and postneonatal mortality rates, while the socioeconomic status index based on education and occupation was only associated with postneonatal mortality. The study of rates in Providence showed that socioeconomic status was only associated with postneonatal mortality, and even this relationship was not very large.

On first appearance it is difficult to equate the continuing gap between white and nonwhite infant mortality rates with such studies showing little relationship between socioeconomic status and the infant mortality rate. This problem is alleviated to some extent if we conceptualize the relationship between socioeconomic status and infant mortality in some fashion other than as linear. Thus the relationship may hold only when deprived social and cultural groups are involved, so that we might expect the curve characterizing the relationship to reach a plateau at a level of income that might ordinarily be thought of as relatively low. In Willie's study of Syracuse, for example, although there is no clear linear trend, the lowest socioeconomic areas had a rate of infant mortality almost 50 percent higher than the highest socioeconomic areas, which had the lowest rates. The data from Providence, however, do not support this observation.

These studies tend to suggest that low socioeconomic status is not a sufficient condition for a high rate of infant mortality. The data on infant mortality reveal considerable variability among low-income areas. A high rate of infant mortality is probably associated with factors that occur more frequently in circumstances of impoverishment (789), but high rates of infant mortality do not characterize all impoverished communities. Odin Anderson (22) has reviewed a wide variety of studies of infant mortality, and he has suggested that patterns of infant care probably play an important role in explaining differences among various lower socioeconomic groups.

In a study of tuberculosis morbidity that shows a white-nonwhite pattern similar to infant mortality, Guerrin and Borgatta (303) conclude that the major concomitant is *cultural deprivation*, and that this factor can be identified most clearly with literacy level. They further note that almost all of the variance explainable by socioeconomic factors is accounted for when literacy level is controlled, but the reverse does not occur. In short, they see tuberculosis as part of a deprivation syndrome.

If we entertain the hypothesis that infant mortality is similarly part of a deprivation syndrome, we would expect to find such mortality correlated with patterns of living of a deprived type (576). A study in the northern regions of France supports this idea (61). This study found that, discounting socioeconomic differences, infant mortality was higher in families that did not take summer holidays, had poorer parental care, where there was not a habitual daily bath, infants were not taken out daily, babies were weighed irregularly, diets were poor, and there was little regard for the importance of sanitation. There is no question that similar factors characterize the nonwhite ghettos where infant mortality is extremely high.

Some of the most comprehensive studies of infant mortality have been undertaken in England and Wales by the Social Medicine Unit of the British Medical Research Council. Morris and Heady (526) observed that the gap between social class one and social class five shows no signs of narrowing despite improvement in social conditions and the increased quality of health services. In reviewing such trends they write:

> It is a commonplace of the study of infant mortality that social influences are at their strongest in the post-neonatal period, related as they are to infection; but it does not follow that their effect on the *still-birth and neonatal death-rates* is negligible. There is a step-by-step increase in both these rates from social class I to social class V in the scale, based on the occupation of the father, which is used by the General Register Office. The rates of death attributed to prematurity—one of the most important considerations in perinatal mortality—are similarly affected. The incidence of premature birth, defined by weight, in a national sample was higher (6.6%) in the children of manual workers than in those of professional workers (4.3%). In Aberdeen in 1949–51, premature births were twice as common in social classes IV and V as in classes I and II. The babies of parents living in the poorer districts of Birmingham are not so heavy, on the average, as the babies of parents living in the more prosperous districts. Moreover, there are marked and consistent differences between different towns and regions of England and Wales in their still-birth rates, and in their neonatal mortality-rates, also. These differences are of the familiar kind, with high rates in Wales and the industrial North of England [526, p. 344].

In England, as in the United States, infant mortality increases in large families, in those characterized by illegitimate births, and in those in which the mothers are old. In sum, infant mortality is related to a complex pattern of deprived living conditions, poor health, an unsatisfactory level of infant care, and a high birth rate. These conditions are further complicated—at least in the United States—by inadequate pre- and postnatal care among nonwhites and a variety of disease conditions present in these high infant-mortality areas.

In recent years there has been considerable interest in the role of varying types of medical care in accounting for the reduced rates of infant mortality. Generally, three types of care have received discussion: conventional prenatal and postnatal care, neonatal intensive-care units, and increased abortions. It has been argued that all three of these types of care that became more prevalent in the last 10 to 15 years were important factors in preventing infant death. New primary medical-care programs, such as maternal- and child-health programs and neighborhood health centers, provided access to care that was not previously available, particularly in the case of lower-income groups (438). Similarly, a number of reports from demonstration projects on neonatal intensive care suggested lower neonatal mortality rates and better long-term outcomes among surviving infants (355, pp. 139–43). With the legalization of abortion there was a clear drop in maternal mortality and some evidence that abortion contributed to a lowered rate of infant death as well.

The role of adequate prenatal and postnatal care in infant survival has been examined in depth in a study based on infant deaths in New York City in 1968 (355). This study used linked birth and death records, thus providing more detailed information on the characteristics of infants that died as compared with those who survived. The study utilized a three-factor measure to represent the quality of maternal health services, including the time of the first prenatal visit, the number of prenatal visits, and whether the mother was delivered on a private service (taken care of by her personal physician) or on a public service (taken care of by the house staff). The third item was included in the index because it was believed that the continuity of care characteristic of having one's personal physician throughout the pregnancy was an important feature of the quality of care. Data available from the records also allowed classification of the mothers into obstetric and social risk groups, into a variety of ethnic groups, and by education.

The study found that all of the above factors were important in accounting for infant survival. Quality of maternal health services was strongly correlated with birth weight of the infant and with survival. In this population the death rate for infants whose mothers had inadequate care was two and one-half times that of those whose mothers had adequate care, and the investigators estimated that if all the mothers had adequate care the 1968 infant mortality rate in New York City could have been reduced by a third. The importance of the quality-of-care variable was generally consistent within each of the ethnic groups and each of the social and obstetric risk groups. Regardless of the level of care, however, mothers with low education and those who were black or Puerto Rican were more likely to lose their infants or have infants of low birth weight. For example, the infant mortality rates were twice as high among mothers who did not complete high school as compared with those who had a year or more of college, and the infant mortality rate among black women was almost two and one-half times the rate among whites. However, when risk level and level of care are controlled, the black excess in mortality is reduced to 50 percent.

As with any other study without random allocation, there are alternative explanations for the results concerning the effects of adequacy of care. The design of the study leaves open the possibility that the relationship between good care and infant mortality is in part or in whole a product of social selection and not the direct result of the care received. Certainly it would be possible that a black woman with low education, or a member of any other subgroup with social risk and low education, who obtains adequate prenatal care may be different in attitudes or behavior from others in the subgroup who do not receive comparable care. Unless one believes that the type of care received by women with comparable social characteristics is purely an accident, then it is necessary to ask whether those who found better care had better health-care attitudes, had more initiative, or were different in some other important way. At least two types of information support this alternative interpretation. First, we would anticipate that the quality of prenatal and delivery care should have its impact primarily on the period during birth and in the period just following birth (the neonatal period); we would anticipate that the influence on the postneonatal experience (the next 11 months) would be considerably less. In fact, no such differential effect was found, suggesting either that the women receiving varying types of care were different in other ways or that receipt of good maternal care was closely linked with good child care. It is possible that when mothers received good care, provision was made for their babies to receive good care as well.

The second type of information comes from a study by Slesinger (653), who analyzed data from a survey of black women and their children in Washington D.C., concerning utilization of prenatal and child care. She found that a significant amount of the variance in explaining the adequacy of care received, controlling for socioeconomic levels, was attributable to household composition and various attitudes toward health. Mother who were more isolated from informal relationships with associates or formal community groups had lower utilization rates for preventive medical care. Such data, if applied to the mothers in the 1968 New York City study, would suggest that mothers with similar social demographic characteristics who received different levels of care were probably different in a variety of ways. A sophisticated reanalysis of the New York City data, using more powerful methodological techniques, suggests that the effects observed are probably a combination of receiving both good prenatal and delivery care and of social selection (279).

Toward a Social Theory of Mortality

Although death is a biological process, how and when it occurs are conditioned by sociocultural and psychological factors. While existing studies show the variety of social factors that have an important impact on the differential occurrence of death between men and women and among varying age groups, socioeconomic strata, and types of household units, little attempt has been made consciously to construct a social theory of mortality. With the growth of evidence that behavior types, personality patterns, types of social supports, and cultural incentives toward risk taking also have a large differential impact on death, it would be useful to tie more closely the gross sociodemographic findings to the intervening variables related to differential mortality. Such an attempt requires integration between variables on the social-structural level and those on the social-psychological level. The examples below illustrate this approach.

Beginning with the work of Emile Durkheim (192), sociologists have devoted a great deal of attention to the relationships between social structure and the occurrence of suicide. This tradition of work has emphasized the role of social cohesion and social restraints in the production of varying rates of suicide in different social contexts (see 182; 318). These social-structural variables, however, affect the suicide rate only through their effects on the individual behavior of persons living in particular contexts and through their influence on individual affect, interpersonal relations, sense of alienation, and so on. Thus the social structural interpretation is not inconsistent with the frequent psychiatric observation that patients attempting suicide are often depressed, because lack of social cohesion and a loosening of social constraints are probably conducive to a higher rate of depression in the population. What is needed is a serious effort to bring together different levels of analysis within a single theoretical conception (354, pp. 321–32).

Consider the more difficult case of the relationship between marital status and mortality. Marriage is an important factor that gives stability to the individual's life and a sense of commitment to persons other than oneself. Marriage is also one of the major supportive forces in social life, and the family context allows for a sharing of assistance, the scheduling of meals and other important events, mutual care when ill, and so on. Marriage, in a sense, tends to regularize life routines; family life involves certain compelling demands and requirements for stability that are less apparent among the single, the divorced, or the widowed. While the family may be its own source of stress, most studies find that married persons are happier (79) and less likely to engage in behavior destructive to health. The excess of death among the unmarried, particularly the divorced, separated, or widowed, is especially large in such categories as suicide, homicide, accidents, and cirrhosis of the liver (283; 535). Selection factors may be operative here, of course, because the divorced, among whom these rates are highest, may be different types of people from those who stay married. A similar case, but with less persuasiveness, can be made for the other categories. The advantages of marriage also seem to be greater for men than for women, suggesting that women may have better coping skills for living by themselves.

There are considerable changes in family structures in modern society, and data based on earlier living patterns may not be representative of a future in which other types of living structures are more acceptable and less socially stigmatized. It is not my purpose here to come to any conclusions about family structure per se but rather to suggest the value of considering such factors as concerns to be taken into account in understanding the production of differential mortality in society. In doing so we will not only integrate existing data on mortality that tend to be highly fragmented, but we also will generate new and interesting hypotheses and more focused investigations that will allow us to understand better those aspects of family life that are both protective and possibly also damaging to health.

Chapter 6

DEMOGRAPHIC STUDIES OF MORBIDITY

Death is a clear and easily measurable event. In contrast, sickness is in part a subjective experience, and the extent to which people recognize symptoms as worthy of attention and define them as requiring care may vary widely from one group to another and from one medical condition to another. Similarly, the influence of social variables on disease processes may vary greatly from one disease condition to another. Since the range of disease is so wide and complicated, any short discussion of morbidity trends can only be illustrative. Thus the major intent of the discussion that follows is to illustrate the various ways social and demographic factors influence the occurrence and course of morbidity and to explore some of the problems in studying such issues.

Measures of Morbidity

Physicians think of morbidity in terms of specific clinical entities or diagnoses, such as those specified by the International Classification of Diseases. The various data in the previous chapter relating to mortality were based on such categories. In contrast, much of the illness for which patients seek help is difficult to classify in these terms, and interview data on sickness tend to represent the patients' subjective appraisals of feelings both of a bodily and psychological nature and of the impact they have on their functioning. Patients do not clearly differentiate psychological and physical feelings, and studies of determinants of physical health status indicate that psychological distress plays an important role in one's evaluation of his health and in the use of medical-care facilities (699).

Measures of illness thus tend to cover a wide range of territory from a sense of well-being to a sense of distress, from acute to chronic illness, and from disability to impairment. Since in this chapter and

181

elsewhere in the book we will be drawing on various data from health interview surveys, it is useful to specify some of the definitions used by the National Center for Health Statistics as well as some other frequently used concepts of morbidity (730). Conditions reported by those interviewed are classified as acute or chronic. An acute condition is one that involved either medical attention or restricted activity and that had its onset during the two weeks prior to the interview. (Remember that a two-week recall period is used to minimize memory error in the case of such illnesses.) Chronic conditions, in contrast, refer to one having first been noticed more than three months before the week of the interview or one of 30 conditions so classified (for example, cancer, diabetes, epilepsy, heart trouble, hernia, high blood pressure). Impairments are chronic or permanent defects, usually unchanging in their nature, resulting from a disease, injury, or congenital malformation—for example, blindness and deafness. In addition, the center has a variety of measures of disability of which the following are most important for our purposes: restricted-activity days (in which a person cuts down on his usual activities for the whole of that day because of illness or injury); bed-disability days (in which the person stays in bed for all or most of the day because of a specific illness or injury); and work-loss days (in which a person did not work at his job or business for at least half of his normal workday because of a specific illness or injury). The center also classifies data in terms of chronic activity limitation and chronic mobility limitation. The former refers to the person's inability to carry on his major activity, whether work or keeping house. The latter refers to the extent to which people cannot get around freely—for example, being restricted to bed most of the time, being restricted to the home, and needing the help of another person or of a special aid such as a cane or wheelchair to get around.

A variety of other measures are used in studies of illness to assess levels of disability and functional physical capacity (201). One such ambitious example is the "sickness impact profile," which describes behavior in terms of 14 categories including social interaction, sleep and rest, and ambulation (61; 566). Patrick, Bush, and Chen (552) have made a related attempt to measure health status through classification of 29 function levels from optimum functioning to death. These function levels are based on three scales of social activity, mobility, and physical activity. Ratings within each scale are based on the degree of impairment of the activity. For example, the mobility scale varies from traveling freely to traveling with difficulty, to being restricted to home, hospital, or other institutional care, and finally to being restricted to a special unit of a hospital such as intensive care. The difficulty with the classification of function levels is that they are heavily weighted toward impaired function and cannot differentiate effectively within the normal range of health-status variations. Thus while these are useful scales for some purposes, they are not sufficiently sensitive for assessing variations in community-health status. (For a review of various efforts to develop health-status indicators, see 65 and 202.)

It is much easier to develop measures of physical incapacity for specified population groups than it is to devise reliable and valid measures of overall health status. For example, a major comparative study of old people in three countries developed a simple but revealing index of physical incapacity: the ability to go out-of-doors; the ability to walk up and down stairs; the ability to wash and bathe oneself; the ability to dress oneself and put on shoes; the ability to get around the house; and the ability to cut one's own toenails (636). But overall health status is so involved with subjective perceptions, social expectations and role demands, and value judgments that it is extraordinarily difficult to translate it into any set of empirical measures. A variety of proxy measures are frequently used to measure health status, such as subjective appraisals of one's health and the absence of chronic conditions, but these are only poor approximations of the concepts investigators really wish to study.

Still another level of health-status measurement further from the concept of illness includes attempts to evaluate distress, self-esteem, and happiness. Most of the frequently used measures of distress were originally intended to serve as case-finding items for identifying the mentally ill in the community. Such measures as the Langner 22-item scale and the Health Opinion Survey were based on items from the Army Neuropsychiatry Inventory that were used for screening recruits who might be mentally ill. Such measures of psychological disturbance have been used in major psychiatric epidemiological investigations (174; 425; 662). These items were seen as effective screening criteria because they differentiated successfully between known mental patients and normal populations in validity studies (409). However, these items tend to confound physical and psychiatric symptoms (therefore creating biases in comparisons among age groups having varying degrees of physical illness) and are biased by problems of social desirability response (151; 455; 564; 630; 703). In populations of considerable ethnic and cultural heterogeneity there are major differences in the perceived social undesirability of some of the items (175). Perhaps the most revealing inadequacy of these items is that psychiatric outpatients tend to score higher than hospitalized mental patients, suggesting that the items are more indicative of distress than of frank mental illness (172). Finally, when such items are administered to mental patients at different points in time there is high test-retest stability in scores, while in normal populations the test-retest correlations are much lower (172, pp. 485–86). This suggests that the items probably have different meaning to mental patients and patients in the "normal population," and that among normals they tend to depict transient stresses. The fairest conclusion is that these screening tests identify large numbers of false positives (people who are not mentally ill in any conventional sense) and perhaps measure levels of distress at the point of measurement more than they accomplish any other purpose.

Self-concept and self-esteem are not only important for positive feelings, but also have considerable significance for health and response to illness. Various studies suggest that self-esteem may play an important role in the manner in which persons deal with health threats and illness (429; 495). Rosenberg (594), for example, developed a measure of adolescent self-esteem and validated it on a group of volunteers hospitalized at the National Institute of Health's Clinical Center. Nurses' ratings of these volunteers were compared with subjects' scores on Rosenberg's self-esteem measure. Those with lower self-esteem were more often seen as gloomy, frequently disappointed, and depressed, and they reported many more psychosomatic symptoms. In short, self-esteem can serve as an important dimension of positive health status.

The most global indicator of well-being—and perhaps most removed from health status as it is conceived of conventionally—is happiness. Happiness appears to be a product of two types of factors that are relatively independent of one another: positive feelings and experiences and the absence of psychophysiological types of distress (79). Studies of happiness draw attention to the fact that well-being must be viewed not only in terms of the absence of symptoms but also in terms of the presence of supporting experiences and positive involvement with others. It has been found, for example, that community leaders in New York City may have more psychophysiological distress and more symptoms than the public at large, but they also have more experiences supportive of their status and self-esteem (175). Happiness indicators, of course, are highly susceptible to environmental fluctuation and may be fundamentally different from other types of symptom indicators that are less responsive to environmental change. However, happiness and satisfaction tend to be associated with a variety of bodily feelings and over the long range may have important effects on people's health and welfare even when measured in terms of traditional concepts of disease.

Social Demography of Illness

Patterns of illness vary in relation to a variety of sociodemographic indicators including age, sex, socioeconomic factors, and residential and geographic conditions (205). While such data on illness are the most abundant, they have some major limitations. First, broad social designations such as age, socioeconomic status, and residence are representative of many biological, environmental, sociocultural, and social-psychological factors. Although such general relationships provide important clues to basic processes, detailed analytic epidemiology is essential to narrow down the analysis to the more specific conditions that explain these variations. Second, much of the data are based on techniques of reporting that introduce systematic biases in the relationships noted between sociodemographic factors and illness. Thus superficial analysis of findings can be misleading. Third, while it is convenient to make general statements about sociodemographic factors and disease occurrence in general, processes of disease are not uniform and summary measures often hide great variability and inconsistency in sociodemographic patterns from one disease to another. In the following sections I emphasize two examples of such relationships and their complexities: the relationship between sex and illness and the association between socioeconomic status and the occurrence of the chronic diseases. Chapter 7 provides more detailed examples of analytic epidemiology in the attempt to understand the cause of more specific disease conditions.

Much of the total illness in the population consists of acute, self-limited conditions that have little effect on longevity and mortality. Mild upper-respiratory conditions are the most frequent type of illness and contribute significantly to work and school absenteeism, although for the most part they are not disabling. With increased age the incidence of acute conditions decreases, a change particularly striking for upper-respiratory conditions (136). In contrast, chronic illness increases substantially with age, and in the older age groups it is common for people to have multiple chronic conditions. While many of these conditions are associated with mortality, as described in chapter 5, others are primarily debilitating, resulting in limited activity, pain and distress, and reduced social functioning. Persons over 65 have nearly two and one-half times as many restricted activity days as the general population, and over twice as many bed and hospital days as well, resulting from the fact that older people are more likely to have conditions involving significant periods of disability. Thus analysis of illness patterns requires control for age variations.

Sex and Illness

A large body of research based mostly on household interview surveys indicates a higher prevalence of a wide variety of illnesses for women as compared with men. This relationship, which is receiving increasing attention, is of particular interest because of the much greater longevity among women. As Nathanson notes:

> One of the most consistent observations in health survey research is that women report symptoms of both physical and mental illness and utilize physician and hospital services for these conditions at higher rates than men. At the same time, in Western Europe and North America, women's expectation of life at birth has exceeded men's since the 18th century or before, and the gap between the sexes both in expectation of life at birth and in age-adjusted death rates has continued to increase . . . . The apparent contradiction between women's biological advantage and their unfavorable morbidity experience has received surprisingly little attention from sociologists. Explanations have been offered for specific findings, but there has been no systematic attempt to account for the range of differences between the sexes in reported illness and in the utilization of health services [534, p. 57].

A major issue in interpreting reports of sex differences concerns the relative role of psychological aspects of expressing distress as compared with more objective features of illness. Much of the data based on perceptions and reports and on the use of medical services fail to differentiate adequately between illness and illness behavior.

It is difficult to locate aggregate data on illness rates by sex that are measured independently of patient perceptions. Although there are data available from standardized multiphasic screening procedures, they have not been used for studying sex differences. In the 1950s various studies were carried out under the sponsorship of the Commission on Chronic Illness, including surveys in Hunterdon County in New Jersey (704) and in Baltimore (131). In Hunterdon County a sample of 846 patients was clinically evaluated by three physicians. Males were found to have 2.7 chronic conditions compared with 2.5 for females. The slight male excess was inconsistent by age group, however. Diseases found to be more prevalent among males included tuberculosis, other infective and parasitic disease, arteriosclerotic heart disease, hemorrhoids, respiratory diseases, stomach ulcers, and abdominal hernias. Conditions more common among women included neoplasms, asthma, thyroid disease, diabetes mellitus, obesity, varicose veins of the lower extremities, and gall-bladder diseases (704, p. 156). In this study a large number of screening tests were also administered to the sample. Eighty percent of the men, but only two-thirds of the women, had some abnormal finding (704, p. 274). The examinations carried out in Baltimore found women to have more chronic disease. The age-adjusted number of complaints was 1.4 for men and 1.7 for women (131, p. 50).

In a study carried out by the National Center for Health Statistics, diagnoses of hypertension and heart disease were compared for 6,672 adults as obtained through the health-examination survey and through a self-administered medical history (721). When the medical history was used, diagnoses among women far outnumbered those among men: 441 to 355 for heart disease and 709 to 431 for hypertension. With examinations, however, the comparable numbers were 794 and 806 for heart disease and 977 and 966 for hypertension. These and other data make measures of chronic disease by sex based on a self-reported medical history appear highly suspect.

There are serious problems in using reported symptoms to diagnose hypertension and many other disorders (for a discussion of this problem see 151). On the basis of expert judgments, the symptoms used to diagnose hypertension were headaches, nosebleeds, tinnitus, dizziness, and fainting. Women were substantially more likely to report headaches, dizziness, and fainting, but these symptoms may be indicative of problems other than hypertension (721, p. 65). Women were not very different from men in reports of nosebleeds. Although women reported tinnitus more frequently, excess in reported prevalence was not as large as the symptoms referred to earlier. It is worthy of emphasis that sex differences in reporting are *smallest or nonexistent in regard to the most tangible and observable of the symptom items* (563).

Reported rates of chronic disease, when compared with medical-record information, are not substantially influenced by sex, although both sources of information may be biased in the same way. In a methodological study designed to examine such differences in chronic-disease reporting, men and women were not found to be very different in rates of underreporting. Women, however, reported more conditions in interviews that were not verified by the medical records (45 percent as compared with 37 percent) (725, p. 7).

Women may perceive and report more symptoms because they actually have more or because of social, cultural, and situational factors. Women may perceive more symptoms than men because they have more interest in and knowledge of health, and thus health is probably more salient for them (214, pp. 112-13). Knowing more about the specific indications of various diseases and giving more thought to health issues, they may be more likely to notice changes and appreciate their possible significance. Alternatively, women may not perceive any more symptoms than men but may be more willing to report symptoms to an interviewer. This is consistent with socialization patterns that allow women to complain more readily and to appear less stoical. These sex differences in response to symptoms are apparent in young children and increase as they become older (483).

A more subtle interpretation to explain sex differences is the argument that the perception of symptoms is dependent in part on what people do about them. Bem (60) has presented a theoretical social-psychological analysis based on the idea that external circumstances and behavior help people interpret their internal feelings. Because of their social roles, women may be able to accept and accommodate illness with less social cost than men. Thus women may be more ready to respond to unorganized symptoms and distress by limiting their activities, having some bed rest, or taking some other measures. Men, in turn, may be more likely to deny vague, unorganized symptoms. If women are more likely to take some action, it is probable that they are also more likely to organize a perception of the incident as an illness and to report it. There is good evidence that persons are more likely to report symptoms if they did something about them; the more salient the action, the greater the recall (504). To the extent that women take more actions or use more medications, they should be more likely to conceptualize the situation as one involving illness. There is substantial evidence that women use much more medication than men, particularly psychoactive drugs (148; 191; 447).

In sum, existing data from health-examination surveys in contrast to interview surveys suggest that much of the excess chronic illness reported by women as compared with men probably reflects, at least in part, differences in how they define and respond to illness and to their life situations. Differences between men and women either disappear or become much smaller when objective measures are used, when the symptoms of the illness are more tangible and visible, or when a greater degree of incapacity or impairment is evident. However, women seem to report many more subjective symptoms than men, particularly those symptoms that may be indicative of either physical disease or psychological distress.

While it is difficult to support the argument that women have more illness than men, apparently they feel or express more subjective distress of all kinds. Although cultural learning, dependency patterns, life situations, and modes of expressing distress may all be relevant to understanding different behaviors in regard to health among men and women, simplistic interpretations based on these ideas do not account adequately for the known facts. If women express illness differently or report symptoms more readily, it is not uniformly in response to all types of symptoms. If women are more inclined to seek help because they are more dependent or affiliative, such patterns are to some extent selective and do not generalize to all sources of assistance. Clarification of sex differences in the distribution of illness requires detailed study in specific instances that test alternative hypotheses. Greater emphasis should also be given to examining the sex differences issue with more objective indicators than those characteristic of perceptions and reports in household interviews.

Socioeconomic Status and Chronic Disease

We have already noted how changing conditions of living and of sanitary and preventive health measures greatly affected mortality and morbidity among the poor. In recent years, however, the simple traditional relationship between socioeconomic indicators and health has been challenged as either no longer correct or inadequately sophisticated to account for differences in an increasingly affluent society. Charles Kadushin (373) has questioned the assumption that socioeconomic indicators are associated with the occurrence of disease:

> All of the pertinent studies have not been reviewed here but there is every indication that in modern Western countries, the relationship between social class and the prevalence of illness is certainly decreasing and most probably no longer even exists.
>
> Not even Malthus attributed the greater rate of diseases among the lower classes to something inherent in class itself. Rather, he called attention to some specific intervening variables such as malnutrition and lack of proper attention. As countries advance in their standard of living, as public sanitation improves, as mass immunization proceeds and as Dr. Spock becomes even more widely read, the gross factors which intervene between social class and the exposure to disease will become more and more equal for all social classes [373; p. 75].

The degree to which Kadushin's conclusion fits the facts is an important issue. There is no doubt that with increasing affluence there has been a homogenization of illness rates in the various social classes. But the substantial mortality differences noted earlier would suggest that there are many categories of conditions that have different rates of incidence among various status groups. There is no question, for example, that such conditions as the venereal diseases and tuberculosis have a higher degree of occurrence in deprived as compared with more affluent socioeconomic circumstances. On the other hand, we also recognize that some diseases are associated with affluence. In short, when we are dealing with gross combinations of morbidity we must recognize that such statistics are tricky and that gross comparisons can be misleading. With these cautions and considerations, let us consider more closely the evidence in support of Kadushin's thesis. In evaluating the evidence concerning the occurrence of the chronic diseases, we must recognize that there are several features of morbidity studies that would lead to no observable differences even when such relationships did, in fact, exist:

1. Many studies of chronic disease are limited to very select populations. Often these studies exclude nonwhites, and as a matter of course persons in the hospital or receiving specialized care also

usually are excluded. Moreover, such studies are often restricted not only to a particular region but to a small community within the region, which is hardly representative of the entire population trend. In short, investigators often work with a highly truncated socioeconomic distribution, which hardly reflects the range in socioeconomic status in other communities.

2. Often the categories used to denote socioeconomic status are very crude. Such crude distinctions may mask differences such as those between the lowest social segment and the rest of the population. As we noted in our discussion of mortality trends, major differences exist between the laboring group and other groups, and a simple dichotomous distinction may hide such differences. Moreover, as mortality data show, there are considerable differences between laborers and agricultural workers (749). Although the bulk of agricultural workers might be classified as members of the lowest status group in chronic-disease studies, they *would be expected* to have different disease experiences from other laborers. Thus the population from which the sample is drawn must be sufficiently extensive and the classifications used must have some refinements.

3. In many kinds of survey, persons of the lowest socioeconomic groups are frequently the most difficult to find and to interview. Although the data are inconsistent, they tend to suggest that low-income persons and nonwhites report less completely than higher-status persons. In contrast, Kadushin's argument is based on the assumption that lower-class persons are more likely to be concerned about illness than those of higher status, and thus are more likely to report conditions they do not have. The confusion as to the relative adequacy of reporting among the different social strata is not surprising as a large variety of factors are relevant to reporting, and it is difficult to control these factors in viewing the relationship between socioeconomic status and reporting adequacy. Cannell and Fowler (743), in comparing three procedures for hospital reporting, found that in all procedures the underreporting rate was higher for nonwhite than for white persons, and in two of the procedures reporting was significantly poorer for low-income and low-education persons than for high-income and high-education persons. In reference to income and education, there were some inconsistencies in the data. An earlier study by Cannell (741) similarly showed that low-income persons and nonwhites underreported to a greater extent than high-income persons and whites. There were inconsistencies in the data relevant to education. In another study comparing health-in-

terview responses with medical records (742), color and socio-economic variables do not show a clear or consistent trend. However, this study was based on health-plan enrollees, and thus the population studied was not representative and probably excluded the lowest social group in the population. It is difficult to understand how Kadushin could argue so unequivocably that "respondents of lower income or education in various studies are either *more* likely or hardly less likely than higher class persons to match a physician's report of conditions" (373, p. 78). It is true that lower-class persons are more likely to agree that they have symptoms of a psychiatric or psychosomatic sort (presented on a checklist basis) when such symptoms reflect general feelings of misery rather than specific physical indications. It is essential to differentiate between these general symptom items and more specific reports of illness and health experience.

4. Still another difficulty that occurs in chronic-disease studies is the refusal of persons to cooperate. Often the same social factors that lead to poor preventive practices (such as failure to obtain immunizations) can also contribute to unwillingness to participate in health programs and health surveys. Thus the persons of the highest and lowest social segments who select themselves as participants may do so for different reasons and bias the results in different ways.

We must also consider the factors that would lead us to observe a relationship between socioeconomic circumstances and the occurrence of illness when no such relationship existed. One cannot justifiably argue for a difference in occurrence of disease from the study of prevalence data or mortality data, as such data may be biased by the fact that members of the various socioeconomic groups live under different cultural and nutritional conditions, have varying access to medical care, and so on, and these factors may produce differential illness outcomes even when the incidence rate of disease is the same in all groups. Too few studies allow us to separate the occurrence of illness from the course illness takes under particular environmental circumstances.

In assessing the relationship between socioeconomic factors and chronic disease we must also attempt to evaluate the extent to which disease affects earnings and work status and the extent to which low socioeconomic status leads to serious health problems. In an interesting study, Lawrence (415) analyzed data obtained in a household interview of 1,310 families in 1923 and 1,010 families resurveyed in 1943. The sample allowed Lawrence to compare the extent to which rates of occurrence of chronic disease were higher in lower socioeconomic groups with the extent to which chronic diseases affected socioeconomic status between the two periods. Although Lawrence observed a clear trend for the prevalence of the chronic disorders to increase as one moved from the "well-to-do" to the "very poor" during the two periods studied, his data revealed that during the period 1923–1943 chronic disease affected socioeconomic status to a greater extent than socioeconomic status affected chronic disease. Although there is no question that chronic disease may affect the ability to earn an adequate livelihood, it seems unlikely that the trend observed by Lawrence could account for most of the differences in mortality from chronic disorders by occupational level, especially among nonwhites. It is unlikely that chronic illness is a major reason in explaining the low occupational status of nonwhites; educational and occupational discrimination against nonwhites in our society is a major factor in explaining the social position of this group (692).

A source cited by Kadushin (373) to support the argument of little relationship between socioeconomic status and chronic disease is a study by Saxon Graham (290) of 3,403 white persons living in Butler County, Pennsylvania, in 1954. A careful reading of this study reveals that the findings are not very clear. Although Graham did not find a statistically significant relationship between socioeconomic status (using Edward's occupational categories) and chronic disorders, he did find a linear trend, with the age-adjusted percentages of persons reporting chronic disorders increasing from 12.7 in the highest social stratum to 19.0 in the lowest social stratum. It is important to note that Graham found that the *percentage of persons with chronic illness was 50 percent higher in the lowest social group as compared with the highest social stratum;* it is essential not to confuse statistical significance with the magnitude of differences. There are other difficulties in interpreting Graham's results. As compared with other studies, Graham's respondents report rather little chronic disease, and it is difficult to assess what effect the probable high rate of underreporting had in this investigation.

Data best suited for analyzing the relationship between socioeconomic factors and the prevalence of chronic disease comes from standardized health-examination procedures used to study large representative samples of the general population. There are few such studies. One of the best-planned efforts to obtain data on this topic comes from a large investigation of chronic disease in Baltimore (131). Using clinical evaluation techniques, the investigators found an age-adjusted rate of 1,807 chronic disorders per 1,000 persons in the income group under $2,000. In the other income groups the rates varied in a consistent way from 1,592 to 1,419 per 1,000 persons. Thus there was substantially more illness in the lowest social segment than in other income groups. Clinical evaluations revealed a lesser difference between whites and nonwhites, with the nonwhite excess only 55 conditions per 1,000 persons.

Even the data from this relatively careful study must be viewed with some suspicion. The response rate for the clinical evaluation was only 63 percent, with substantial differences in response rate by age, color, and sex. Nonwhites, for example, participated in much larger proportions than whites, and it is difficult to infer what implications this might have for the differential rates for whites and nonwhites. Furthermore, some patients who were not examined were included in the sample because good medical records were available for them. Similarly, past medical records were used in making evaluations, and one would expect that the relative accuracy of this information might vary systematically in some fashion. Physicians are more likely to identify conditions if there is a past history of them, and it is probable that more adequate medical records were available for whites and higher-status persons. Finally, a large variety of physicians participated in the clinical evaluations; they were not trained in a standardized fashion, nor did they receive centralized supervision. The degree of unreliability, therefore, is probably substantial, although it is difficult to evaluate in precisely what directions biases would be introduced.

Much of the other data on chronic disease come from household interview studies. We have already noted many of the difficulties involved in such surveys. An examination of the National Health Survey data from July 1962 to June 1963 reveals that 57.6 percent of all persons with a family income of under $2,000 reported one or more chronic conditions as compared with 44.5 percent of all persons (744). While there were no appreciable differences reported in the age groups under 15 and 15 to 44 years, there was a sizable difference (12.5 percentage points) in the age group 45 to 64 and a somewhat smaller difference in the age group over 65. When only chronic conditions involving limitation of activity are considered, socioeconomic conditions are more pronounced. Persons with higher incomes tend to report more chronic illnesses that do not involve activity limitation than do lower-income persons, but when such limitations are considered the situation is quite different. For example, in 1972, after correcting for age, more than a fifth of those with less than $3,000 income reported limitation of activity, while less than a tenth of those with $15,000 or more had a similar limitation. Although the largest difference exists between the lowest income group and all others, the relationship with income is linear. A similar trend exists for limitation of mobility and for white-nonwhite variations, correcting for age (727).

It appears likely that the data involving activity limitation provide a reasonable estimate of the degree of relationship between income and chronic disease. We know that more salient and serious conditions are more accurately reported than lesser conditions. The effects of differential reporting tendencies by income are therefore likely to be more substantial in the area of chronic disease without activity limitation. And indeed it is here that we find higher rates of chronic disease among persons from high-income families as compared with those from low-income families. In the area where the data are likely to be more reliable—and not subject to such large reporting tendency effects—the relationship is in the opposite direction. The fact that greatest differences occur between the lowest income group and all others suggests that much of the difference is due to the extent to which limitation of activity affects earning capacity.

Many epidemiological studies of the more serious chronic diseases suggest that they have higher prevalence in the lowest socioeconomic groups. For example, although coronary heart disease has increased in modern affluent countries, the prevalence is greater in lower as compared with higher socioeconomic groups. Moreover, it is difficult to explain the striking differences in mortality rates by cause in relationship to socioeconomic status without assuming differential vulnerability to major chronic diseases. While some of the differences are accounted for by social selection and by differences in medical care, lower socioeconomic status appears to be related to the risk of disease occurrence as well.

In summary, the relationship between socioeconomic status and the occurrence of chronic disease is less than clear-cut. However, the data certainly do not appear to support Kadushin's conclusion that a relationship "most probably no longer even exists." Indeed, the most careful investigations point in the opposite direction! The excess of chronic disease in the lowest income group can be attributed in part to a process whereby illness and disability reduce income, but it is likely that some of the variance is attributable to increased vulnerability that results from less favorable living conditions. The process is in all probability a complex one in which illness occurs more often in more vulnerable groups, resulting in disability and income reduction. Lowered socioeconomic status probably affects access to medical care and other favorable environmental factors, and limitations of access may further result in unnecessary disability and an earlier death.

In future studies of chronic disease in relation to socioeconomic factors it would be important to distinguish more adequately among the various chronic diseases. Since some diseases are associated with affluent life patterns, while others are associated with poverty, the combination of such conditions leads to a process in which each cancels out the effects of the other. It will also be necessary to distinguish more adequately the forces producing diseases from those that affect their course. Finally, it is important that we move away from dependence on interview surveys and give greater emphasis to results from standardized examinations.

Use of Health Services

Since I have suggested that the reported prevalence of chronic disease may have some relationship to access to medical and hospital care, it is important to discuss briefly some trends in the utilization of medical care in the United States. The utilization of medical and hospital care is a complex topic, and the data available (primarily from household interview surveys) have many shortcomings. The data obtained from such surveys are of a summary nature and usually fail to separate the occurrence and prevalence of illness from factors affecting utilization. It would be desirable to have data comparing utilization among groups with comparable degrees of illness, but for the most part such data are unavailable. Even the utilization component of health care is a complex phenomenon; its components are worthy of analytic separation because the utilization of care depends on both external and individual factors.

Utilization of health services implies both the availability of care facilities and the willingness of persons to use such care as is available. The first component—availability—depends on such factors as financing of care, accessibility of medical resources, availability of medical manpower, and the energy, enthusiasm, and planning efforts of health administrators. The second component—willingness to use facilities —depends not only on economic factors but also on various aspects of illness attitudes and behavior including health knowledge, attitudes toward illness and health agencies, ability to recognize symptoms, and cultural and social definitions that give more or less meaning to particular symptoms. Although most of the data we shall discuss use statistics that combine all these dimensions, keeping these factors in mind helps us see alternative explanations more clearly.

Most available data support the conclusion that in the United States the patient's decision whether or not to use care is related to both sex and socioeconomic status as well as to a variety of other factors. Men and persons in lower socioeconomic status groups are less likely to utilize medical facilities. A brief review of these data as well as some of the multivariate models used to predict utilization is provided below.

Sex and Utilization

Most studies show that women are more likely than men to use ambulatory medical-care facilities as well as such specialized services as psychiatry. In the United States, for example, women have consistently reported more physician visits per year than men. In 1973 women had a yearly average of 5.6 visits as compared with 4.3 for men (731). This difference exists for all age groups except for the earliest years when the mother usually makes the decision to seek care for her children, and the differences are largest between ages 20 and 40. More important, a variety of studies show that sex differences persist even when many other variables are controlled. For example, Tessler, Mechanic, and Dimond (699), in a prospective study of enrollees in a prepaid group practice, examined the role of sex in utilization, controlling for a variety of sociodemographic, attitudinal, health-status, and distress variables. Sex continued to have a significant direct effect on utilization despite the control of these other factors. Similarly, Greenley and Mechanic (296) examined the use of psychiatric and counseling services among students in a university population. Sex was one of the most influential variables affecting use of these services, regardless of the controls utilized.

The World Health Organization International Collaborative Study of Medical Care Utilization is a rich source of data for further analysis of sex differences. A comparable utilization survey was carried out in 12 population areas in 7 countries (764). Although reports from this survey have not addressed the theoretical issues concerning sex, the data are amenable to instructive secondary analysis. In each of the 12 study areas women were more likely than men to report contact with a physician during the prior two weeks. This finding was consistent for the vast majority of comparisons by age, although there were some exceptions (396, p. 145). As part of their analysis the investigators report beta coefficients for sex in each of the study areas for both adults and children, based on a model with a large number of variables, including severity, chronicity, 15 predisposing factors, and 4 enabling factors. The resulting 24 beta coefficients are all positive, but only 2 are statistically significant, and these are small as well (396). Thus the investigators have succeeded in virtually eliminating the sex effect by controlling for 20 other variables. Unfortunately, this type of analysis results in small and nonsignificant results for all the variables other than severity. These data should be used for further analysis that specifies varying theoretical models that take into account the relationships between sex and the other variables considered.

The results of the International Collaborative Study suggest that sex has its influence on utilization through its association with other predictors of utilization such as tendency to use services, anxiety, and skepticism. For example, in our prepaid practice study we found that women were less likely than men to feel they had control over illness; while only 27 percent of men had a low efficacy score on our scale, two-fifths of women had a low score. However, in our analysis the sex variable was more powerful than the efficacy scale; when sex, distress, and health status were taken into account, efficacy added nothing more to the coefficient of determination (699). We do find, however, that levels of personal distress are an important trigger in the use of medical services. Since women have higher levels of distress, they are more likely to use medical services, but distress itself cannot explain the total sex effect.

Another possible explanation for the higher rate among women is that they are more dependent and affiliative and thus more likely to seek interpersonal solutions to feelings of distress. As boys get older they learn to be stoical and uncomplaining, while girls have been in the past taught to seek solace from others. In my study of children's responses to illness (483), I found that among fourth-grade children there were no sex differences in the willingness to tell others when they did not feel well; about three-quarters of both boys and girls were willing to relate their feelings. Among eighth-graders, however, while three-quarters of the girls were still ready to confide, less than three-fifths of the boys had similar inclinations.

Most data on health-services utilization for children indicate few sex differences, probably because the mother usually makes decisions about utilization for both boys and girls. Lewis and his colleagues (437), however, established a child-initiated health-care service in an experimental school in Los Angeles and monitored utilization over two academic years. They found that girls aged 5-12 used these health services much more frequently than boys: Girls used a mean of 4.1 services as compared with 2.5 among boys during the first year; comparable figures for the second year were 4.8 and 3.3 (437). Fifteen percent of the children accounted for use of approximately half of the services, and girls were much more likely to be high users.

Data from the National Ambulatory Medical Care Survey indicate that physicians are less likely to regard the principal problems reported by women as serious as compared with the problems of men; while 22 percent of men's problems were seen as serious or very serious, the comparable percentage for women was 17 percent. These data are consistent with the hypothesis of greater readiness among women to use services (739, p. 299).

While there are large sex differences in rates of utilization of hospitals, they are substantially reduced when corrections are made for obstetrical admissions (5). The remaining difference is difficult to interpret for a variety of reasons. First, in the process of seeking prenatal and obstetrical care, women are likely to become aware of other problems requiring medical care. Second, since women seek more ambulatory care than men and since the patient's appearance at an ambulatory-care facility is a prerequisite for evaluation and subsequent hospitalization, remaining differences in hospital admissions may be a product of initial rates of contact. To understand these differences effectively requires comparison of utilization rates among men and women known to have comparable morbidity of specific types.

Socioeconomic Status and Utilization

Innumerable studies indicate that while the poor have a greater prevalence of illness, disability, and restriction of activity because of health problems than do those of higher status, they have less accessibility to many types of health services and receive lower-quality care in many respects. Following the implementation of Medicare and Medicaid there has been a reversal in the traditional direct relationship between socioeconomic status and use of physician services. Prior to these programs the lowest socioeconomic groups had fewer physician visits than those with more income, but these differences are no longer evident. In 1971 persons with family income of less than $3,000 had the highest visit rate per year (6.2). This is due mostly to the fact that the lowest income group has a disproportionately large number of persons aged 65 or more. When physician use by income is examined in relation to age, a somewhat different pattern is evident. Children to age 14 in families with more than $10,000 income have more physician visits than those of comparable age in low-income families; differences in utilization are small in the middle years; in most age groups beyond 35, the lowest income group uses more services (731). These data are limited, however, because they tell us nothing about the need for services in various income groups. Aday (6) has developed an index of use of services that takes into account need for care as measured by disability data. She finds—contrary to much of the current existing data—that the poor continue to use fewer services relative to medical need than do those in higher socioeconomic circumstances.

Physician visits also vary by color and education. In 1973 whites reported 5.1 physician visits per year in contrast to 4.5 among nonwhites; this gap has decreased substantially from 1963–1964, when whites had an average of 4.7 visits in contrast to 3.3 visits among nonwhites. Persons with more education also report more visits; in 1973 those whose heads of family had 13 years or more of education had 5.5 visits in contrast to 4.8 visits among those in families whose heads had less education. Controlling for income, those with more education tend to use more services. Similarly, controlling for income, whites use more physician services than nonwhites, although these differences are not consistent for all age groups (731).

Another way to examine socioeconomic differences is to investigate the relative burden of medical expenditures that the patient must assume on his own relative to total income. In 1974 only 35 percent of personal health-care expenditures were paid directly by the patient in contrast to public expenditures, private health insurance, and so on (739, p. 41). In 1970, according to a study by the Center for Health Administration Studies of the University of Chicago, those with family incomes of less than $2,000 paid 12.6 percent of their total family income for health care, and those with family incomes between $2,000–4,000 gave 9 percent of their total income for this purpose. The comparable proportion of income paid for health services by those with family incomes of more than $7,500 was 3.5 percent (21). Thus, despite large federal programs such as Medicaid, the costs of medical care are a disproportionate burden on the poor.

Data on trends in the utilization of health-care services are generally consistent with trends in the occurrence of illness. Although the poor are now using more ambulatory services, the evidence indicates that they require more services than they are receiving; paying for them— despite existing federal programs—continues to be a heavy financial burden. When such areas as preventive services, dental services, and more specialized medical services are examined, the gap between those with more and less income and education, and between whites and nonwhites, remains very large. Although the United States has made some progress in equalizing services, we still have a long way to go. The use of services, of course, depends on more than income, education, and color. In recent years various efforts have been made to develop models describing the factors affecting the use of services, and it is appropriate here to describe them briefly.

Andersen and his colleagues (18; 19; 20) have developed a descriptive multivariate model that they use to account for differences in medical-care utilization. They view utilization as a consequence of predisposing, enabling, and illness variables. Predisposing variables include demographic indicators (such as age, sex, and marital status), social-structural variables (such as race, education, religion, and ethnicity), and beliefs and knowledge about health and medical care. Enabling factors include family income, availability of health insurance, source of care, and access to a regular source of care, as well as the availability of health services and other community characteristics. Illness variables include disability, symptoms, and diagnoses.

Andersen's model, although it accounts descriptively for a certain amount of variation in use of services, lacks a theoretical basis. A more theoretical approach is suggested by Antonovsky (32), who has put forth a model attempting to explain variations in physician utilization among populations comparable in morbidity. For example, why should countries such as the Soviet Union and Israel have a per capita utilization of 9–12 visits, the United States and England average 4–6 visits, and countries such as Sweden fall within the 2–3 visits a year range? These differences obviously reflect cultural variations, availability and accessibility of services, and social ideologies, as well as other factors. Antonovsky classifies predictor variables into three general classes: host characteristics, characteristics describing medical institutions, and those describing the larger sociocultural environment. Host characteristics include latent need, intolerance of ambiguity of symptoms, and an orientation toward the use of professionals. The class of medical institution characteristics includes availability of facilities, ability to be responsive to various hidden functions of medical practice such as legitimation of illness, and the degree of receptivity of physicians to patients. Variables describing the larger sociocultural environment include organizational facilitation in using medical services, absence of stigma for such use, cultural pressures to have problems diagnosed, and degree of availability of functional alternatives.

The only empirical study with comparative data on physician utilization in varying countries is the International Collaborative Study (396; 764). Bice and associates (68) have examined various predicted relationships in each of 12 study areas in seven countries, using a path model including age, education, income, skepticism of medical care, and the reported tendency to use services. Sociodemographic variables such as age, education, and income yielded inconsistent relationships or patterns contrary to those predicted.

There are a variety of social psychological models that describe how people come to perceive and react to illness or how they decide to engage in preventive health behavior. These will be discussed in the context of my review of illness-behavior research in chapter 9. I shall also wish to examine to what extent the types of social variables reviewed by Andersen and Antonovsky influence the occurrence of symptoms as well as illness behavior. Social and social-psychological factors can affect utilization directly or indirectly through the modification of illness occurrence or perceptions of it.

Hospital Utilization

Factors affecting hospitalization are complex, and a hospital admission is largely a medical decision rather than a choice of the consumer.

Available statistics on hospital utilization thus tell us more about decisions by physicians and the availability of hospital beds and related personnel than they do about consumer response. Use of hospitals is substantially affected by the availability of insurance for hospital costs and of payment for the poor and the aged through federal health programs. Since most available data on hospital use do not control for need or severity of condition, they are often difficult to interpret.

Data on discharge from short-term hospitals in 1973 indicate an inverse relationship between income and hospital use. Those with family incomes of less than $5,000 who were discharged from hospitals had a rate of 236 discharges per 1,000 and an average length of stay of 9.6 days in contrast to those with incomes over $15,000, who had a rate of discharge of 126 and an average stay of 6.4 days (739; p. 309). These rates are affected by the fact that those with lowest incomes have a high representation of persons over 65 years of age. The discharge rate for those over 65 was 350 per 1,000 population in contrast to a rate of 186 among those aged 45–64. The income effect is clear within the age group 15–44, where those with less than $5,000 income had a discharge rate of 204 and 5.8 days length of stay on the average in contrast to a rate of 136 among those with incomes in excess of $15,000, who had an average length of stay of 5.4 days (739, p. 513). Similar income differences are found for those under 15 years of age and those in the age group 45–64. In the past ten years rates of discharge from short-stay hospitals have increased among the poor and decreased among the nonpoor, providing a more adequate distribution of hospital services relative to need. A similar reversal has taken place in respect to whites and nonwhites. In the past decade, with the growth of federal subsidy, there has been a significant redistribution of hospital care to the nonwhite population.

Length of hospital stay is a difficult index to evaluate. It depends on such varied factors as the seriousness of morbidity for which hospitalization occurs, the relative priorities given to patients of different social status within the hospital in terms of diagnostic evaluation and scheduling procedures, the rate status of the patient and the extent to which he may be used in medical-education programs, or even the medical staff's anticipation of the patient's home environment and the adequacy of convalescent care the patient is likely to receive at home. Length of hospital stay is clearly related to both color and income of the patient, although the exact reasons for longer lengths of stays among lower-status persons are not clearly understood.

One plausible interpretation of length of stay is that it is a proxy for severity of the problem. For example, in the last decade average length of stay among the nonpoor in short-stay hospitals has remained the same, while among the poor, and particularly among minority groups, length of stay has decreased significantly from an average of 22.6 days in 1964 among persons aged 45–64 to 15.3 days. Thus as access and use of services increased, length of stay decreased, suggesting that now the range of problems being treated among the poor in hospitals is broader and less serious on the average than in the past (739, pp. 518–19).

We have now reviewed some of the evidence pertaining to the degree of relationship between socioeconomic factors (especially income) and health status and health care. As we have noted throughout the discussion, the relationships among these variables are complex and are not easily abstracted from official statistics and surveys, which often fail to separate theoretical dimensions of considerable importance. Similarly, the methodological problems faced in morbidity studies are very difficult. In summary, it is the author's opinion that one of the major problems in such studies has been the tendency to collect data without giving sufficient attention to the theoretical issues that are important to the student of illness. Granted that the collection of these data may be useful for government and other nonacademic purposes. But if we are to understand illness phenomena and resolve some of the questions we have raised concerning the effects of environmental conditions on health, we must strive to collect data that separate incidence from prevalence, being sick from "feeling sick," and disease from utilization of facilities.

Chapter 7

EPIDEMIOLOGY AND MORBIDITY

The concept of etiology with which one approaches the study of disease is often formed for the convenience of investigation. Under varying investigative conditions, different ways of conceptualizing cause may promote research and understanding. Today, for example, it is frequently useful to seek a preventable or treatable "essential" cause in disease processes, although researchers may well understand that disease is a consequence of no single agent by itself, but results from the complicated interplay among aspects of the person and agents in his environment.

One of the major difficulties in the study of disease involves the fact that many categories of disease are not single entities but constellations of similar entities. Thus such categories as schizophrenia, cancer, and heart disease are groups of diseases that may have manifest similarities that lead them to be grouped with other similar conditions. Often it is impossible to study disease at such a level of specificity that all the component conditions can be clearly differentiated, and thus many "causes" will be found relevant to these conditions.

Another aspect of the concept of etiology involves the fact that disease is a consequence of the interaction among environmental conditions, specific agents, and a wide variety of aspects of the host. A known agent may or may not produce disease, depending on the condition of the environment and the host. In past years it has often been convenient for the researcher—especially in the study of infectious diseases—to conceptualize all of the factors characterizing the environment and host under a single rubric such as "immunity," "tolerance," "susceptibility," or "resistance." Thus genetic factors, nutrition, immune mechanisms, social roles, stress, personality, and climatic and atmospheric conditions are all made part of a single concept. But if we are really to understand what the concept of resistance refers to, it is necessary that we apply ourselves to understanding scientifically its various components. A number of examples will illustrate this point.

Tuberculosis is a disease resulting from an attack of the tubercle bacillus on the host; that is, without the bacillus we would not find tuberculosis. Given an attack of approximately the same virulence, however, it appears that different hosts have differential ability to withstand attack (188). Thus the bacillus serves as a *necessary* but not a *sufficient* cause for the disease we call tuberculosis. Although the differences in response from different hosts are not well understood, it appears that social and psychological conditions may play some part in affecting a person's resistance. While it is obvious that crowded conditions and lack of cleanliness lead to the transmission of disease, and that poverty may affect nutrition and the probability of receiving treatment when afflicted, it is not as well recognized that the attitudes of men may affect their abilities to withstand physical attack.

It is frequently asked why the researcher should trouble himself with the study of such social, psychological, and environmental factors since the ability to deal with the tubercle bacillus provides control of the disease without concerning oneself with such factors as overcrowding and attitudes. We have already noted that many investigators choose to work on isolating a specific cause, and frequently this provides control over disease without concern for the other complicating factors. There are at least four reasons why these larger issues remain important:

1. Many disease conditions do not easily yield to the assumption of a single necessary cause that can be controlled.
2. Often when the major cause is isolated, it is extremely difficult to control. Thus control must be sought elsewhere. For example, we know that various substances in the cigarette increase the risks of lung cancer. We do not as yet know how to remove these harmful substances. Thus the risks of lung cancer are contingent on smoking habits, and preventive work at this point must focus on discouraging smoking among young people. Similarly, it would be desirable to get smokers to give up the habit, but methods for achieving this goal have thus far been disappointing.
3. Understanding social factors in disease frequently provides the basis for reform important to health. Although we may not understand the cause of a particular disease, changing conditions associated with disease help to control it indirectly. In 1854, when Snow discovered that a contaminated water source was responsible for the outbreak of cholera in London, it was possible to control the spread of the disease, although the particular microorganism contributing to it was undiscovered. Similarly, ob-

servation of the association between doctors washing their hands and complying with antiseptic conditions generally and the spread of disease led to important controls over the spread of disease well before the method of transmission and agents involved were understood. Thus changing social conditions and practices may lead to control over disease in the absence of more direct data.

4. Detailed knowledge of disease processes in general provides a more sophisticated perspective on disease problems and increases our understanding of both disease and behavior. In addition to the practical significance of being aware of various indirect and contributing factors in disease, we should not forget that understanding has value for its own sake.

To return to our example of tuberculosis, epidemiologists have given considerable attention to this disease, and there is some evidence to suggest an association between a high mortality from tuberculosis and migration from rural to urban life and from one country to another (186; 188; 780). Unfortunately, many of the studies on social aspects of tuberculosis have various methodological deficiences, and thus these results must be regarded as tentative suggestions rather than definite proof. For example, one study reports that the transportation of Bantu-speaking Africans from the vicinity of Johannesburg into the outskirts of the city itself and their employment in industry were associated with a high tuberculosis mortality rate. While TB was also widespread in the tribal villages, mortality appeared to be considerably lower. Similarly, it has been found in the United States that during relocations of Navaho and Sioux Indians within the same climate and geographic area, the TB mortality rate greatly increased. Some reviewers have postulated that the resentments experienced by the Indians were an important factor in the TB mortality rate. In still another report data are presented for a large rural population, largely farm laborers, who left Ireland because of severe economic stresses and settled mostly in U.S. cities between 1840 and the early 1900s. Economic conditions here were probably better and more food was available. The TB mortality rate among American Irish, however, was twice as high as among those who stayed in Ireland. Obviously these results are based on crude comparisons, with few controls for selective influences and changes in working and living conditions that may play some part in the transmission of infectious disease. Nor can we dismiss the idea that these results are due to different opportunities for primary infection and the buildup of biological resistance. Yet the accumulating evidence, with all its deficiencies, makes a strong case for important environmental and social influences in the process of this disease. René Dubos has argued that the peak incidence of TB mortality occurs in a society within ten to twenty years after industrialization has been established; thereafter, he observes, it declines sharply (186; 188).

In more recent years there has been accumulating evidence that tuberculosis patients are characterized by extremely high stress during the two-year period preceding the onset or relapse in tuberculosis: "The nature of their attitudes and life experiences made it unusually difficult for them to decide what was expected of them or what they expected of themselves. As a consequence their attempts at adjustment were characterized by unrealistic striving which was not only unrewarding but also productive of cumulative conflict, anxiety, and depression" (331, p. 252). Moreover, it has been found that the onset of tuberculosis is preceded by a high prevalence of broken marriages, change in residential and occupational status, alcoholism, frequent and persistent psychosomatic disorders, and mental illness. Although the mechanisms through which stress relates to the occurrence of disease are not fully clear, Holmes (331) believes that adrenocortical activity plays a role in resistance to tuberculosis, and that adrenal changes are clearly related to stress. On the other hand, it is plausible that highly disruptive life patterns affect exposure to infection, health habits, nutrition, and various other circumstances favorable to disease processes.

To take another example, various observers have argued that peptic ulcers seem to be influenced by psychological and social factors, although the importance of such factors is far from clearly proven. The data are not really comparable and involve many methodological problems, but it appears that in Western Europe, Scandinavia, and the English-speaking countries an extensive change has occurred in the incidence of peptic ulcers. In the late nineteenth century this disorder afflicted more females than males, yet today peptic ulcers apparently occur several times as often among males as among females (780). As Edmund Volkart has noted, there is no evidence that physiological mechanisms of males and females have altered substantially during this period, but extensive changes in the roles of men and women are apparent, as well as changes in the structure of the family (753). What is even more difficult to understand is the large increase in duodenal ulcers among men in the earlier half of the twentieth century, changing in recent years to a significant rate of decline (524). Similarly, the social-class distribution of ulcers is puzzling. While mortality from gastric ulcer has been highest in the lowest social classes, mortality from duodenal ulcer has been highest in the highest social class (524). Although more adequate data than are presently available are needed to assess the role of social and psychological factors in the distribution of ulcers, it may turn out that exploration of social factors may contribute to our understanding of this set of diseases.

Another illness receiving increasing attention from the sociological point of view is ischemic (coronary) heart disease. Various epidemio-logical studies suggest that style of life has considerable bearing on the impact of this disease, although no single factor or combination of fac-tors studied seems to provide a satisfactory explanation of the condi-tion. The dynamics of the disease remain indefinite, and it is evident that ischemic heart conditions are the products of many causes. Many researchers continue to seek a necessary cause for the occurrence of such conditions; it is conceivable that some answer may lie in the rela-tionship between fat metabolism and arterial thrombosis (524). At this point there is considerable uncertainty about the relative influence of a wide variety of particular factors correlated with the occurrence of these conditions: diet, exercise, heredity, and stress. Smoking and hypertension are clear risk factors, however, and the evidence indicates that cessation of smoking and control of blood pressure increase lon-gevity. Interest in the social aspects of coronary heart disease followed the observation that rates of these conditions were rising in West-ern countries, and that they appeared to be much higher in highly industrialized countries than in less developed ones. Because the populations of developed countries were believed to have diets with high saturated-fat content, it was argued that patterns of life as they af-fect diet were important factors in explaining the occurrence of this disease. The matter now appears more complicated. For example, Japan, a highly industrialized modern nation, has an extremely low mortality rate from coronary heart disease relative to the United States. A major reason given to account for this difference was the low sat-urated-fat content of the Japanese diet. A major study of Japanese in Japan has recently found no relationship between saturated-fat intake and incidence of coronary heart disease (459). Also, while coronary heart disease occurs more frequently in affluent societies, it does not necessarily occur with greater incidence among more affluent individ-uals in these societies.

An increasing body of work suggests that patterns of physical activi-ty may be important in ischemic heart disease (99), although the protec-tive effect of exercise may be primarily among those who do heavy ex-ercise (545). A study in England of bus drivers and conductors showed that the less active of the two, the bus drivers, had higher rates of ischemic heart disease. Other studies in several countries have con-firmed the relevance of physical activity in understanding this disease (84; 99; 524; 525; 641). Further studies in England show high rates of coronary disorder among government clerks, executive officers, and male post-office telephonists, as compared with postmen of the same age. Such data support the contention that physical activity rather than the stress of the job contributes most to the occurrence of this disease. Despite the growing evidence supporting the activity hypothesis, various complications arise. Morris, in an ingenious analysis using waistband measurements of busmen's uniforms, found that those selected as drivers, as compared with conductors, are different types of men. His data suggest that the drivers have higher inclinations toward obesity that are brought with them into their jobs (524). Thus it is difficult to ascertain to what extent the differences noted in the bus driver-conductor study are due to selective influences or to activity on the job.

Smoking has been found to increase significantly the risk of coronary heart disease, and it is one of the few risk factors about which there is good evidence that modification of the habit results in reduced risk. The effects of cigarette smoking act independently on the cardiovascular system as well as together with other factors to cause serious damage. While the risk is lower among cigar and pipe smokers as compared with those who smoke cigarettes, smokers of whatever kind have higher risk than nonsmokers. As the Public Health Service has noted:

> Autopsy studies have demonstrated that aortic and coronary athero-sclerosis are more common and severe, and myocardial arteriole wall thickness is greater, in cigarette smokers than in nonsmokers....Experimental studies in humans and animals suggest that cigarette smoking may contribute to the development of CHD through the action of several independent or complementary mechanisms: The formation of significant levels of carboxyhemoglobin, the release of catecholamines, inadequate myocardial oxygenation which may result from a number of mechanisms, and an increase in platelet adhesiveness which may contribute to acute thrombus formation. There is evidence that cigarette smoking may accelerate the pathophysiological changes of preexisting coronary heart disease and therefore contributes to sudden death from CHD [709, p. 3].

Stress and personality variables have been found to be of importance in explaining rates of coronary heart disease. There is some confusion in the literature, however, as to what types of stress and personality trait contribute to risk. Since stress variables will be discussed in detail in chapter 8, where we will review both the strengths and weaknesses of the evidence, suffice it to say here that social and psychological variables have an important impact on this disease.

The fact that social factors are relevant to the occurrence of disease processes does not exclude the possibility of finding a "necessary condition." Even in the area of clearly infectious disease there has been mounting evidence, with more sophisticated study, that social factors are important to some extent. In a study by Meyer and Haggerty (512), for example, susceptibility to streptococcal infections in families was investigated. Sixteen lower-middle-class families, including 100 people, were intensively studied for one year with systematic throat cultures and clinical evaluations of all illnesses. Family stress was one of the factors the investigators found to be important in determining whether a person acquired a streptococcus, became ill with it, or developed a subsequent increase in antistreptolysin O. Although the study is impressive in various ways, it does not show clearly how family stress influenced the development of disease. The study did not attempt to take into account factors that may mediate family stress and the development of illness. Did the family stress increase susceptibility in some direct way by making individuals more vulnerable to attack, or did stress lead to various forms of neglect of health or to increased exposure? Further work in this area would be very fruitful.

The history of fluctuations in etiological concepts is quite illuminating. Early concepts of etiology emphasized the multiplicity of factors responsible for disease, and early writings often pointed to the great variety of factors—both atmospheric and social—that played an important role in the disease process. Yet the concepts of multiple etiology that prevailed were unenlightened in that they were not based on specific knowledge of disease processes (593).

The attack on infectious diseases and concentration on the concept of specific etiology brought in a new era in the study of disease processes. Although the germ theory was philosophically too simple, it was tremendously useful in that it focused attention and study on specific agents of disease, which could then be attacked. The model of specific etiology was thus methodologically useful, playing an important part in the advancement of medicine and the more specific understanding of disease. It was through the use of this model that the infectious diseases—the most important cause of mortality and illness in 1900—were controlled to the point where they now play a relatively insignificant role in limiting health and life.

We are now perhaps in a new stage of thinking about disease processes. Having had considerable success in the attack upon the deadliest of infectious agents, we must now demonstrate our ability to deal with a new constellation of conditions that have come to the forefront among contributors to morbidity: heart disease, cancer, the mental disorders, accidents, diabetes, and so on. Although medical scientists vary in their approaches to etiology, it is evident that many chronic conditions and accidents are not so amenable to understanding in terms of specific concepts of etiology as were the infectious diseases (679). A considerable amount of work is proceeding relevant to the search for specific agents, but it is generally recognized that a more expansive etiological approach that takes into account the wider context of illness is also necessary, and probably crucial. But it is important to recognize that more modern use of the concept of multiple etiology strives for some utility, and this new concept is motivated by the need to make specific contributions to the study of disease processes. The concept of multiple etiology must be more than a catchphrase citing numerous causative factors that is used to shield our ignorance and lack of sophistication in understanding particular disease areas. If the concept of multiple etiology is to be fruitful, it must stimulate particular kinds of research that capture the interplay between environmental and internal factors and add to the study of basic processes.

As the preceding disussion implies, the findings of epidemiological investigation are often complex and not infrequently inconsistent. Moreover, such investigations involve difficult theoretical and methodological issues. There is, therefore, limited benefit in attempting to catalog the diverse and frequently contradictory findings in the epidemiological field. Investigators have developed a vast array of information relevant to a wide variety of disease, and the reader who wishes to get some further feeling for the scope of epidemiological work could benefit by referring either to Morris's book (524) or to one of the other works on this topic (143; 378; 554; 558; 687).

As our main concern here is with the logic and approach of the epidemiologist in his search for causes, more can be gained by directing ourselves to a more intensive view of particular issues. In the sections that follow I shall examine the evidence concerning two causative questions that have interested health workers to a considerable extent in recent years. In our first example some of the evidence pertaining to the relationship between smoking and lung cancer will be examined; in this situation the imputation of a causal role to smoking appears to be substantially supported. In the second example the imputed relationship between social class and the occurrence of schizophrenia will be explored. Here we shall find that the evidence is contradictory, and the imputed causal role of social background is not effectively demonstrated.

Case One: Smoking and Lung Cancer

Clinical observations of the possibilities of a relationship between smoking and lung cancer go back at least five decades. Sustained interest in the problem was activated more recently, as lung cancer changed from an infrequent to a major cause of death in many countries. It became apparent that although death rates from other forms of cancer and other respiratory diseases were declining, deaths from lung cancer were rising, and this appeared to be linked with the growing habit of smoking. Many groups have now looked into the evidence linking smoking and lung cancer; our short summary is based on the work of two such distinguished committees—one appointed by the Royal College of Physicians in England (601), the other the Advisory Committee of the Surgeon General of the American Public Health Service (750)—and on subsequent reports issued by the Public Health Service (see, for example, 709; 710; 711). The reader is urged to consult these reports in their original, since our discussion is fragmentary and cannot really convey the care and thought that went into these excellent summaries of the evidence. Each year the evidence linking smoking to a substantially increased risk of lung cancer and many other diseases strengthens and extends the earler findings. Smoking is clearly dangerous to one's health!

Three kinds of information are relevant to ascertaining the relationship between smoking and lung cancer: (1) animal studies; (2) clinical and autopsy studies; and (3) population (epidemiological) studies. In animal studies several chemical compounds in tobacco smoke and tars have been established as cancer producing. Moreover, other non-cancer-producing substances in tobacco and smoke experimentally produce noncancerous damage often seen in the tissues and cells of heavy smokers, which lowers the threshold to known carcinogens.

Population studies of cancer have been of two kinds: retrospective and prospective. In retrospective studies persons with lung cancer are matched with control groups not having lung cancer, and the smoking habits of the two groups are compared. In prospective studies large groups are followed over time in order to discover which persons develop lung cancer. Although prospective studies provide more impressive evidence less subject to various biases, they require considerably more cost and effort than retrospective studies. At the time of the American report, data were available from 29 retrospective studies carried out in many different countries and using a large variety of methods and survey designs. Many other studies have been carried out since then. All of these studies show a consistent link between smoking and lung cancer, which is remarkable, given the varying situations studied and the differing methods used. In addition to the retrospective studies there have been a number of prospective studies, all of which support a relationship between smoking and lung cancer. Smokers have approximately 10 times the risk of developing lung cancer than nonsmokers; heavy smokers have approximately 20 times the risk of developing lung cancer than a comparable nonsmoking group.

The strong case for a relationship between smoking and lung cancer is supported not only by the great consistency of results among studies, but also by the internal consistency characteristic of such studies. The risks of lung cancer are higher the longer a person has smoked; they are lower among persons who give up the smoking habit than among those who continue smoking; and the risks increase with heavy smoking. Some of the puzzling features of these studies have been cleared up by further investigation; for example, the higher mortality from lung cancer found in the British studies as compared with the American ones may be explained partly by the finding that the British smoke more of each cigarette than do the Americans, thus receiving a larger dose of smoke from each cigarette. Further, this finding can perhaps be explained in part by the greater degree of air pollution from chimney smoke in Great Britain. Few critics have challenged the belief that a relationship between smoking and lung cancer has been demonstrated.

Those critics who have challenged the link between smoking and lung cancer generally accept the demonstration of an association between these two factors, but suggest that the relationship may be spurious and that both smoking and lung cancer are the product of some unknown third factor. The only tenable hypothesis offered is that some hereditary factor produces both the smoking habit and a susceptibility to lung cancer; the fact that the smoking habits of identical twins are more alike than those of fraternal twins offers slight support for this contention. While a direct causal link between smoking and lung cancer remains to be completely proven, the evidence is sufficiently impressive that it is impossible to discount. There are persons who, because of genetic factors, may be more susceptible to the effects of smoking (711, p. 72), and smoking combined with exposure to other carcinogens may vastly increase risk. For example, asbestos workers who smoke have been found to have 90 times the risk of developing lung cancer than persons who are exposed to neither asbestos nor smoking (711, p. 49).

There are many reasons for rejecting the hereditary hypothesis as an alternative explanation of the link between smoking and cancer. In a California study of Seventh-Day Adventists—a sect disapproving of smoking—it was found that the incidence of lung cancer was one-eighth of the incidence found in the control group. The only two male Adventists with lung cancer were converts who had been cigarette smokers until middle age. In order to explain these results from a hereditary standpoint, it would be necessary to posit a gene factor underlying not only smoking and lung cancer, but also membership in the Adventists. Similarly, the lower incidence of lung cancer among persons who discontinue smoking or who began smoking at a later age would require greater specificity in the hereditary hypothesis. Moreover, the large increase in both smoking and lung cancer when other types of cancer have been decreasing in incidence would be difficult to explain on a hereditary basis, because such a sharp change in the gene pool would be highly unlikely. As the American report comments:

In assessing the importance of a possible genetic influence in the etiology of lung cancer, it should be recalled that the great rise in lung cancer incidence in both men and women has occurred in recent decades. This points either to a change in the genic pool, or to the introduction of an agent into the environment, or a quantitative increase of an agent or agents capable of inducing this type of cancer. The genetic factors in man were evidently not strong enough to cause the development of many cases of lung cancer under environmental conditions which existed half a century ago. In terms of what is known about rates, pressures, and equilibria of human mutations the assumption that the genome of man could have changed gradually, simultaneously and identically in many countries during this century is almost inconceivable [750, p. 191].

The wide differences in lung cancer between males and females, attributable to the different prevalence of the smoking habit among the two sexes, would pose equal problems for a hereditary interpretation. The facts that are available, and they are abundant, are much more consistent with the assumption of a causal link between smoking and lung cancer than they are with the hereditary view.

Many hypotheses alternative to the hereditary view have been suggested, but they are too easily disputed to make it worthwhile to discuss them in detail. For example, since heavy drinking and heavy smoking appear to be correlated, it has been suggested that alcohol is the common factor associated with both lung cancer and smoking. The relationship between smoking and lung cancer has been demonstrated to be independent of the alcohol factor, however. Of the other factors suggested as important, only air pollution appears to be of large import, and the data support the contention that air pollution is a contributing factor in lung cancer and other respiratory diseases. Death rates for lung cancer are higher in urban (more polluted) than in rural (less polluted) areas, and these differences cannot be entirely accounted for by the differences in smoking habits. In South Africa, New Zealand, and the United States, immigrants from England have a higher rate of lung cancer than native-born men with comparable smoking habits, and there is a strong presumption that air pollution in England may be the factor that leads to an increased incidence of the disease among emigrants from England. Similarly, other observations support the idea that air pollution plays a significant role in the disease, but at all levels of air pollution cigarette smokers suffer a much higher risk than nonsmokers, and heavy smokers develop lung cancer at a rate 15-20 times that of nonsmokers. Smoking is an obvious factor in lung cancer, but we must not conclude that it is the only relevant factor.

The relationship between smoking and lung cancer inferred from population sudies has received considerable support from clinical and autopsy studies. In an extensive and controlled blind study of the tracheobronchial tree of 402 male patients, Auerbach and his colleagues found that several kinds of change of the epithelium were much more common in the trachea and bronchi of cigarette smokers and subjects with lung cancer than in those of nonsmokers and of patients without lung cancer. The epithelial changes observed were: (1) loss of cilia; (2) more than two layers of basal cells; and (3) presence of atypical cells. The atypical cells and their arrangement were frequently disorderly. The degree of each of these changes increases in general with the number of cigarettes smoked. Extensive atypical changes were observed in men who smoked two or more packs a day. The American report concludes that some of the advanced epithelial hyperplastic lesions with many atypical cells seen in the bronchi of some cigarette smokers are probably premalignant (750). Other cytological and autopsy studies have also found epithelial changes in the respiratory tract, believed to be precursors of cancer, more frequently in smokers than in nonsmokers (709).

In noting the specific relevance of smoking to lung cancer, we should not fail to note the association between smoking and mortality in general, as well as the association between smoking and other diseases. Indeed, the most influential effect of smoking in respect to the numbers of people who die or become disabled results from the link between smoking and the development of premature coronary heart disease (711). Smokers have much higher risks of dying from many different diseases as compared with nonsmokers: bronchitis and emphysema (six to one), cancer of the larynx (five to one), oral cancer (four to one), and so on. Moreover, smoking has been found to affect such diverse bodily responses as the birth weight of babies and the development of genitourinary cancer. There is also growing indication that nonsmokers exposed to cigarette smoke in enclosed areas may be subject to some risks (see 711, pp. 87–108). Smoking is clearly one of the most significant risk factors in modern society affecting mortality, disability, and discomfort.

Case Two: Schizophrenia

The term "schizophrenia" has appeared at several previous points, although I have left the term undefined. It refers to a group of psychotic reactions involving disturbances in reality relationships and concept formation, and a variety of intellectual, affective, and behavioral disturbances varying in kind and degree. McGhie and Chapman (467) note that schizophrenia often involves disturbances in processes of attention and perception (including changes in sensory quality and the perception of speech and movement), changes in motility and bodily awareness, and changes in thinking and affective processes. Schizophrenic patients often give the impression that they are "retreating from reality," and appear to be suffering from unpredictable disturbances in their stream of thought. Although psychiatrists vary in the factors to which they give primary emphasis in making a diagnosis of schizophrenia, there seems to be substantial agreement in a descriptive sense as to the importance of particular kinds of thought disturbance in these conditions (769).

Like heart disease and cancer, schizophrenia is presumed to be a collection of many conditions having outwardly similar manifestations, and the advocates of particular etiological hypotheses span the range from biological to social determinism. In recent years the advocates of a social theory of schizophrenia have seized on some studies that indicate a relationship between social class and the occurrence of schizophrenia. Such findings are presumed to reflect the importance of sociocultural forces that are said to influence the risks of disease occurrence, and the inadequacies of personal resources that allow the individual to deal with stress. No attempt will be made here to consider the conflicting evidence concerning the etiological forces in schizophrenia. Our main concern will involve the factual issue under debate, whether social class is related to the occurrence of schizophrenia.

The epidemiology of schizophrenia is beset with a variety of complex conceptual and methodological difficulties, and as Mishler and Scotch have noted in their review of sociocultural factors in schizophrenia, trying to derive basic generalizations from the epidemiological literature on this topic is like "talking with the relatives of the deceased after returning from a funeral. Other than some platitudes, there is little that can be suggested that would remedy, alleviate, or eliminate the trouble" (519, p. 340). We have already noted the substantial difficulties of case finding in the study of mental disorders. To restate our earlier conclusion, it is possible to achieve a reasonable level of reliability in the diagnosis of schizophrenia under carefully standardized conditions in which the evaluators are trained to use the same criteria and share similar concepts. In situations where efforts are not made to standardize the diagnostic situation, reliability may be extremely poor. When the investigator depends on case records from hospitals and clinics, agreement by two independent evaluators on which cases should be included in the series for investigation may vary between 65 and 90 percent, whereas random assignment would achieve agreement varying between one-third and one-half. In short, even under careful conditions of assessment the diagnosis of schizophrenia is frequently difficult; when such diagnoses are made under hurried conditions by different doctors varying widely in their training and competence and using different definitions and criteria, diagnostic adequacy may become dubious indeed.

The study of the incidence of schizophrenia from the social point of view is still in a state of infancy. The investigations are not numerous, techniques are frequently crude, and the reliability of case finding is frequently unstated or undetermined. In reviewing some of the studies on social factors and schizophrenia, Mishler and Scotch have noted that:

> It has been particularly discouraging to the authors as social scientists to have to recognize the simplistic quality both of the social variables used in epidemiological studies and the forms of analyses into which they have been incorporated. Whereas in the investigation of almost every other problem, a relationship with social class would be the beginning of intensive analysis through a series of control and test variables, in the investigation of the epidemiology of schizophrenia it often stands for the complete analysis. In examining the social correlates of any other piece of complex behavior, the ecological and cultural characteristics of the groups in which the individuals are members would become an explicit part of the analysis through designs permitting such cross-comparisons, but in the study of schizophrenia it takes contradictions in findings to force such factors into researchers' awareness [519, pp. 342–43].

Among the most interesting problems in the epidemiology of schizophrenia is the relationship between socioeconomic status and occurrence of schizophrenia. One of the earliest studies, by Faris and Dunham (211) in Chicago, revealed that census areas having the highest hospital admission rates for schizophrenia were lowest on socioeconomic indicators. Similar studies were repeated in several places throughout the world with comparable results, although the magnitude of the relationship was not always as clear as it was in Chicago. One of the great difficulties in ecological studies such as these was in interpreting the result. To what extent did the socioeconomic aspects of an area have relevance to the occurrence of schizophrenia, and to what extent could these results be explained by the fact that schizophrenic patients do poorly in work and interpersonal relations and tend to drift into residence areas characterized by low socioeconomic status?

Most studies of the incidence of schizophrenia have been investigations of "treated incidence" or of "first admission to hospital," and not necessarily true incidence. It is difficult to evaluate the impact of the loss of cases (and therefore the problem of selection), since most epidemiological studies that have been undertaken with total populations relevant to schizophrenia have been of relatively isolated rural communities hardly comparable to large urban complexes. While some studies of incidence are limited to first admissions to hospitals, others, like the Hollingshead-Redlich study (330) and Jaco's study in Texas

(358), included patients being seen in outpatient psychiatric clinics and by private psychiatrists. There is no study of the relationship of incidence of schizophrenia to social class in an urban area that includes patients seen by general practitioners, private psychologists, faith healers, clergymen, and chiropractors. The total population studies that have been undertaken, although useful for other purposes, are too restricted in scope and the range of population included to serve us in illuminating the relationship between social background and occurrence of schizophrenia.

In reviewing nine studies relating incidence of schizophrenia to social characteristics, Mishler and Scotch note a somewhat consistent trend in findings concerning social class, although the studies themselves differ widely in methodologies used and populations involved:

> The most consistent finding, which emerges in eight of the nine studies, is that the highest incidence is associated with the lowest social-class groupings used in each study. In six studies it is the unskilled or laborers category, in a seventh it is the unemployed, and in the eighth it is the lowest of four social classes—defined by an index of occupation, education, and residence—that produces the highest rate [519, p. 326].

Unfortunately, perhaps the most sophisticated study in the group—the one by Clausen and Kohn in Hagerstown, Maryland—did not show any significant relationship between social class and incidence of schizophrenia. As Scotch and Mishler note, however, because of the small number of cases involved, the investigators used a crude socioeconomic dichotomy that may conceal a real difference between the lowest social segment and all others.

A substantial difficulty with most of the studies cited by Mishler and Scotch is the inadequate manner in which social class or socioeconomic factors have been measured. Often such information comes from records of dubious reliability but, even more important, such studies rely on the patient's occupational status, which may be influenced profoundly by his illness experience. Although studies of social mobility among the mentally ill do not consistently support the contention that the mentally ill are downwardly mobile (330), it is a commonplace among psychiatrists that schizophrenic patients tend to hold occupational statuses well below their educational and intellectual levels, and they are frequently unemployed. This appears to be particularly true of patients who have a long history of difficulties. A simple hypothesis to account for the relationship between social status and occurrence of schizophrenia appears to be more consistent with the facts; i.e., schizophrenics tend to have low socioeconomic status, in part as a consequence of their schizophrenic condition. In a British study by Goldberg and Morrison (271; 527), for example, in which father's occupation at the birth of the patient was the index of socioeconomic status, social class was not associated with incidence of schizophrenia. Consistent with this interpretation, Hare (313) found that the distribution of schizophrenic cases in family settings did not depart significantly from a random distribution, but that schizophrenic cases out of family settings departed from random to a significant degree, with a great excess of cases evident in the area of the city with many single-dwelling units (Bristol, England). Hare's results thus suggest that schizophrenics who move out of family contexts do so largely because of their personality disorders. In short, Hare's findings support the idea—as does the work of Goldberg and Morrison—that the relationship between schizophrenia and socioeconomic status has no etiological significance.

In a further analysis, Turner and Wagenfeld (706) examined the relationship between social class and schizophrenia and found, when using patients' occupation, a substantial overrepresentation of schizophrenics in the lowest occupational category. However, they also found that the fathers of schizophrenics were disproportionately of lower status, although to a lesser extent. The disproportionate number of schizophrenics of lower status seemed attributable more to failure to achieve expected status level, given their class origins and the changing occupational structure, than to a downward drift in the occupational status system, although both forces were obviously at work. This study provides considerable support for the idea that the relationship between social class and schizophrenia is a result of a social selection process, although the possibility of some social causative factors is left open (see 394 for an excellent review of the evidence).

Building on this possibility, Melvin Kohn (395) has suggested that schizophrenia is an outcome of genetic vulnerability interacting with environmental stress and impaired ability to deal with it due to socially learned conformity orientations. He infers the existence of these orientations from values such as obedience, good manners, and cleanliness, and suggests that underlying these is a rigidly conservative view of man, fearfulness, distrust, and fatalism. Such orientations that make it difficult to adapt resourcefully, he believes, are linked with lower social-class position and account for the frequently observed relationship between schizophrenia and social class. Kohn offers little evidence in support of his hypothesized association, and his argument presents other inconsistencies with existing data (494). Although it would be premature to dismiss such hypotheses arguing for the causative significance of social class, the data available to support these notions are really quite weak. As Clausen has noted: "The lack of consistency in findings relating to social class, social mobility, and migration, assessed for particular communities or populations, suggests that these dimensions of sociological analysis are not themselves crucially linked with schizophrenia" (119, p. 301; also see 190; 523; 706). Indeed, there is no clear-cut evidence indicating a causal link between social status and schizophrenia, although an inverse relationship between social class and psychological disorders has been commonly observed. The significance of social etiological factors appears more promising in other psychiatric conditions than in schizophrenia (171).

When one moves to the study of prevalence of schizophrenia and mental disorder generally, the picture changes somewhat. Although social class has no soundly demonstrated etiological significance in schizophrenia, the components of life implicated by this variable appear to have considerable significance in the course illness takes and the care patients receive. In their study initiated approximately in 1950, Hollingshead and Redlich (330) found that although 3 percent of New Haven residents could be characterized as Social Class I, this class contributed only 1 percent of all psychiatric patients treated by hospitals, clinics, and private psychiatrists. The lowest social stratum, which accounted for 18.4 percent of the New Haven population, contributed 38.2 percent of all treated psychiatric illnesses. The same trend characterized schizophrenic patients; the prevalence rate in the lowest social class was 795, while the prevalence rate in the two highest social classes was 111.

The data from Hollingshead and Redlich are most impressive in demonstrating the relationship of the social background of the patient and the kinds of psychiatric care he received. Ninety-eight percent of neurotics in the two highest social classes received some form of psychotherapy, while all higher-status neurotics received some form of treatment. Among the lowest social class only 67 percent of those diagnosed as neurotic received some form of psychotherapy, and 23 percent of the patients received only custodial care. In the case of schizophrenics, 24 percent of those in the two highest social strata received only custodial care, while the corresponding figure in the lowest social grouping was 57 percent. A similar analysis was carried out within the confines of a clinic where care presumably was to be provided irrespective of income, but even within this context socioeconomic differences in treatment received were clear and substantial (531). A follow-up study ten years later of patients in treatment in 1950 also demonstrated the persistence of socioeconomic differentials between 1950 and 1960 (49).

The size of prevalence differences described by Hollingshead and Redlich may be inflated to some extent by the manner in which these investigators measured social class. They used a three-factor index based on the patient's occupation, education, and residence. All of these factors could presumably be affected by the development of the patient's condition, Thus it is possible that Hollingshead and Redlich tended to underestimate the social background of mental patients, especially those in the hospital. The fact that the class differences in this investigation are so persistent and large, and similarly occur when comparisons among different categories of patients are undertaken, supports the authenticity of the findings. Differences in the incidence of schizophrenia by social class observed by Hollingshead and Redlich are much smaller than their prevalence differences, although they did note some variations. The numbers of cases on which incidence figures for schizophrenia were developed were too small, however, to be reliable.

The data presented by Hollingshead and Redlich concerning the outcome of patients in treatment help explain the large differential between the highest and lowest social segments in the prevalence of schizophrenia and mental disorders generally. It is apparent from the data that patients from the lowest social segment, many of whom were receiving no treatment at all, were "piling up" in hospitals, thus substantially multiplying the prevalence rate in this segment. Studies in both America and Britain suggest that after a particular period of time hospital staffs made little effort to try to get chronic patients out of the hospital, even when their symptomatology had diminished greatly. Instead, efforts were devoted to patients who had arrived more recently. As a result, chronic patients—particularly lower-class chronic patients—accumulated in hospitals (89; 615).

The differentials in treatment by social class are understandable—even if they are not excusable—in terms of the structure of psychiatric practice at the time the New Haven study was undertaken. This was prior to the mass introduction of new drugs and change in psychiatric and administrative outlooks. Psychotherapy, which is primarily a talking therapy, was believed to require a verbal orientation lacked by many uneducated lower-class patients. Similarly, psychotherapy was not consistent with the expectations of lower-class patients concerning the doctor's role and the meaning of treatment, and thus such therapy was frequently rejected by such patients even when it was available to them. Therefore, the failure of lower-class persons to receive psychotherapeutic care was due to a mutual rejection. Psychiatrists preferred to work with patients who were similar to themselves in social and cultural status and orientations, and lower-class persons frequently found it difficult to accommodate themselves to this unfamiliar kind of "doctor." We do not mean to imply that psychotherapy necessarily works (see, for example, 209). But those who received psychotherapy received interest, attention, and probably a sense of hope not available to other patients. These factors themselves can make a great deal of difference in returning to an ordinary way of life.

In recent years various changes have taken place in psychiatric care and in attitudes among hospital administrators. Almost without exception all patients receive some kind of treatment (drugs), which was not the case in 1950. With the aid of various new drug therapies and supporting community facilities, many patients who would have accumulated in the hospital in 1950 are returned to the community or are not hospitalized at all. Despite efforts to avoid chronicity among mental patients a new group of such chronic patients is evident, although many of them live in sheltered care and other residential situations in the community rather than in hospitals (629). This population is largely unemployed, of lower socioeconomic status, and maintained mostly on public-assistance grants. Schizophrenia continues to be a highly debilitating condition conducive to poor work performance and low economic status. While the context of care has changed a great deal in the last decade or two, many of the problems of care remain. These will be considered in chapter 17.

Chapter 8

STRESS, CRISIS, AND DISEASE

The term "stress" has come to sociology and psychology by way of the physical and biological sciences, and in a general sense it has been applied to disruptions in personal, social, and cultural processes that have some relationship to health and disease. Although use of the term has not always achieved great clarity, it serves to bring together various research findings frequently encompassed under more specific concepts such as fear, anxiety, and negative reinforcement. In uniting the work of many different disciplines and points of view, the study of stress has helped illuminate our understanding of human adaptation.

Study of stress events involves consideration of a stimulus, the characteristics of the person involved, and his response. In natural field situations it is frequently difficult to separate these components and the part they play in stress events. Within the experimental laboratory, however, it is sometimes possible to have sufficient control over the situation so that the stimulus, the subject's appraisal of it, and the response can be manipulated or measured separately. This can be illustrated by the work of Richard Lazarus and his colleagues.

Lazarus and his colleagues show experimental subjects a threat film dealing with primitive circumcision rituals (416; 417; 418; 419; 659; 660). This film shows several surgical circumcision operations in which the penis and scrotum of male adolescents are cut deeply with a sharpened piece of stone. All experimental subjects watch the same film; however, there are a variety of soundtracks or introductory comments that attempt to introduce varied attitudes of appraisal in the subjects. In one case the soundtrack emphasizes the threat-producing features of the film (the trauma soundtrack). In another the events in the film are presented from the point of view of a scientific, detached observer (the intellectualization soundtrack). In still another experimental variation the pain experienced by those being circumcised and the harmful aspects of the surgical operation are denied (denial sound-

track). Through manipulation of the soundtrack and introductory comments it is possible to control to some extent the way the subjects will
appraise the stimulus film.

Responses to the film are measured by continuous physiological
readings of the heart rate and skin conductance of those watching. Although the results are too complicated to report in detail here, in general they show that when defensive appraisal attitudes are available (for
example, the denial soundtrack), subjects experience a lower intensity
of physiological arousal as they watch the film. In short, the appraisal
of the film influences the amount of physiological stress experienced.
Less physiological stress is observed when defensive soundtracks accompany the film and when a defensive attitude is developed by the introductory comments. Lazarus and his co-workers also attempt to
measure various personality characteristics of those who respond to the
stress stimulus in various ways. Although much more work in this area
is necessary, it is clear that different kinds of people respond to stress
in various ways, are likely to appraise the threat stimulus from different
points of view, and benefit more from some kinds of defense than
others.

This valuable work adds importantly to our understanding of the
stress process. Such experimental studies of stress, however, strive to
investigate comparatively simple and controlled situations so that the
influence of particular variables can be studied unambiguously. Although much is learned in the process, some of the richness of natural
stress situations that involve long-term responses is lost, and therefore
it is necessary to supplement such studies with investigations of natural stress situations. The experimental situations help clarify views of
natural stress events, and the study of natural situations brings out new
variables requiring more detailed and controlled investigation.

The definition and investigation of stress are difficult. In physics
and biology, where the stress concept was first used, its meaning has
been fairly consistent. But it has been employed by behavioral scientists to refer interchangeably to emotional arousal, anxiety, depression,
life difficulty, physical exertion, and many other phenomena as well.
Moreover, behavioral scientists appear to disagree as to whether stress
must involve a negative or unfavorable appraisal of a stimulus or can
result from any situation of more than usual stimulation, even when
the stimulus is viewed as pleasant and attractive (e.g., is too much
pleasant stimulation stressful?). It should be clear that the scope of the
stress concept is wide and that its applicability has remained elusive.

In the biological field, Hans Selye, a noted student of stress mechanisms, has defined stress as "the state manifested by a specific
syndrome which consists of all the nonspecifically induced changes
within a biologic system" (633, p. 54). Thus to Selye "stress" is the re-

sponse common to many different agents acting on the organism. Various investigators have attempted to build a bridge between the biological stress discussed by Selye and social and psychological stress. Others have criticized the attempt to relate sociocultural stresses to biological stresses, and some have argued that physiological stress does not refer to a phenomenon similar to these other kinds of stress (see the discussion in 363, pp. 11–13). Regardless of one's position on this matter—and we will discuss contending positions later—it is generally recognized that serious methodological difficulties exist in building a sound bridge linking the concepts of biological, psychological, and social stress. Psychophysiologists have made a considerable effort to study the physiological reactions to particular experimental stimuli of emotional import. As Lacey has so lucidly shown, the relationships among various measures of stress differ widely among people and among the responses considered (405; 406).

Many investigators are troubled by the difficulties in defining stress clearly and the uncertainties in linking social, psychological, and physiological phenomena. When investigators move out of the laboratory and into natural field situations they tend to concentrate on one of two possible ways of defining stress operationally. Either they tend to study stress stimuli (or stress situations) or they focus on stress as a response. We shall briefly review each of these perspectives.

Stress Situations

The term "stress" has been used to refer to a situation that causes people to react as though they had been threatened. It has characterized physical, social, and cultural conditions likely to be discomforting for most people living within a specified group. Stress situations might include battle conditions, impending surgery, rapid cultural change, intense competition, life crises (such as the loss of a loved one or job demotion), natural disasters (floods, tornadoes, and earthquakes), acute illness or injury, frustration and failure, and isolation (14; 48; 193; 299; 362; 363; 479; 778). In other words, designation of certain circumstances as stress situations is based on an assumption: The investigator intuitively selects various aspects of the physical, social, and cultural environments that he assumes are likely to lead to experiences of discomfort for most people living within some designated group, the discomfort being reflected by both social and psychological responses.

The assumption that a stress situation will in all likelihood elicit specified changes in behavior requires examination. As Basowitz and his associates write, stimuli can be designated as stress regardless of the responses they evoke. They are called stress "because of their assumed or potential effect, although we well know that in any given case the organism's adaptive capacity, threshold, or previous learning may preclude any disturbance of behavior" (48, p. 7). That a stress situation will bring about specified changes in behavior or physiology serves as a plausible but unverified assumption. In any particular case it would be important to be able to differentiate stress situations by their power to induce these changes. But what criterion should one choose as defining what is stressful for *most* people? Should one regard a situation as stress if 50 percent of the population behave in ways specified? Or should one accept the level of 25 percent or 75 percent as more appropriate? Also, how intense a response must a situation evoke before we may legitimately call it stressful and distinguish it from other life events? Stress situations—those causing changes in behavior or physiology of a discomforting character—should be distinguished from all other possible sources of change.

Despite considerable interest in the role of stress events, research in this area was retarded for a long time because of the unavailability of instruments that could be used in epidemiological investigations of large populations. In recent years a great deal of research has been stimulated as a result of the development of the Social Readjustment Rating Scale (334), a list of life-change events weighted by scores indicating the relative level of expected adjustment required by each event. Whatever the limitations of the method, it has contributed to rekindling an interest in research in stress and to bringing this topic to the attention of investigators and practicing physicians. The Social Readjustment Rating Scale does have some limitations that ought to be corrected as research efforts in the area of stress and disease proceed.

The scale is unique in its emphasis on events requiring adjustments irrespective of whether positive or unpleasant feelings are associated with the events. As Holmes and Masuda explain:

> There was identified, however, one theme common to all these life events. The occurrence of each event usually evoked, or was associated with, some adaptive or coping behavior on the part of the involved individual. Thus, each item was constructed to contain life events whose advent is either indicative of, or requires a significant change in, the ongoing life pattern of the individual. The emphasis is on change from the existing steady state and not on psychological meaning, emotion, or social desirability [335, p. 46].

The innovative feature of the Social Readjustment Rating Scale, other than its obvious practicality, is that it emphasizes the measurement of life change and readjustment rather than the individual's perceptions of events that are noxious to him. Thus the scale includes changes that "are socially desirable and consonant with the American values of achievement, success, materialism, practicality, efficiency, future orientation, conformism, and self-reliance" (335, p. 46), such as marriage, outstanding personal achievements, pregnancy, gaining a new family member, change of residence, and having a vacation. Although findings using the scale often are interpreted as showing that life changes and readjustments, regardless of whether they are favorable or unfavorable, contribute to the occurrence of illness, the fact is that the scale cannot possibly demonstrate this contention since it is an assumption implicit in the way the scale has been constructed. Thus data based on the scale cannot resolve the theoretical issue of whether life changes in general or primarily adverse life changes affect the occurrence of illness.

Let us examine more specifically why the scale cannot be used to address the theoretical issue of what types of change affect the occurrence of illness. Discounting for the moment ambiguities in the description of events, it is apparent that the scale is composed of three types of items: those describing events that most people would be inclined to view positively, such as marriage, outstanding personal achievements, pregnancy, marital reconciliation with mate, vacation, and Christmas (6 items); those designating events that most people would view as adverse, such as troubles with the boss, death of a spouse, and sexual difficulties (13 items); and a variety of items that might describe either positive or adverse events depending on individual circumstances, such as major change in eating habits, major change in the health or behavior of a family member, major change in financial state, change to a different line of work, major change in living conditions, and change in residence (24 items).

The problems of interpreting responses in reference to the theoretical issue raised above should be evident. In the case of the mixed items, the investigator does not know whether the change being reported is positive or adverse—i.e., whether the person is reporting a promotion or a demotion, a large gain or a loss on the stock market, a move to a pleasant suburban area or to a slum. It is possible that respondents are more likely to respond to these mixed items in terms of adverse experiences than in terms of positive changes, but the investigator *does not know*. Further, there are more than twice as many adverse events in the scale than positive changes, and these adverse events are in general linked with higher readjustment scores. Thus scores on the scale are disproportionately weighted by items measuring adverse events, and it is not apparent that the rank-ordering of respondents on this scale would be very different from a rank-ordering using scales based exclusively on the measurement of adverse life events.

The relevance to illness of change in general as compared with adverse life changes cannot be assumed but must be empirically demonstrated. Although life-event research has been performed under a common rubric, it embodies diverse theoretical conceptions. One possible conception of the relationship of life events to varying physical conditions is that significant life changes call forth more than ordinary adaptive requirements, causing a cumulative wear-and-tear on the body and thus increased vulnerability to disease (633). The particular manifestations of disease may depend on genetic vulnerabilities or other risk factors. Within such a conception, large readjustments, even when they appear to be to the person's material and status advantage, require efforts that are physiologically costly and that have a cumulative effect on the functioning of the organism. While people may seek change and require challenges for continued growth, large and recurring change in living routines and life styles may have a long-term negative impact on health status. An alternative conception views changes in terms of their more negative features that threaten the physical capacity, status, security, and significant associations of the affected person (416). The construction of the scale does not allow us to differentiate which of these perspectives fits the facts better.

The problems are confounded when we consider the use of this scale in the study of different dependent variables. The scale has been used to study illness rates in general and specific morbidity conditions. The existing literature on stress and illness suggests a different picture depending on the condition being considered. Some problems, such as depression, appear to be associated primarily with loss events (556). In contrast, it has been suggested that changes in general may be risk factors in schizophrenia (96) or in coronary heart disease (335, p. 57). A scale that does not differentiate scores based on adjustments to adverse events from more positive changes results in general correlations that are not particularly helpful in understanding the roles that different types of life change may play in varying disease conditions. Unfortunately, much of the work based on the undifferentiated scale has a monotonous similarity, with little indication that our understanding is being advanced. It seems clear that the scale should be revised so as to facilitate separate scoring of readjustment to positive and negative changes, as well as to other qualitative differences among events.

In attempting to differentiate the items in the scale, it becomes clear how ambiguity of wording and varying levels of abstraction of different items cause difficulties in evaluation (92). At the simplest level it makes a great deal of difference, for example, in reference to the item "change in health of family member," which family member was involved, how close the respondent is to him, the extent and implications of the change in health, and what new burdens the illness placed on the respondent. Or in the case of a "son or daughter leaving home," it makes a great deal of difference if the child leaves home to marry or attend college, as compared with leaving home as a rebellious act or as a result of family disputes.

These problems, of course, can be corrected by further clarity in wording and greater specification of relevant events. But a more troublesome conceptual issue is involved in classifying events that appear to be socially desirable. Events commonly regarded as desirable, such as marriage and promotion, may, from another perspective, pose a variety of new coping problems to the individual affected and hence may result in adverse experiences. A new job may offer a person more status and remuneration, but it also may leave him insecure, anxious, and overloaded relative to his abilities. These new insecurities may overbalance the socially defined positive value of the promotion. Similarly, marriage, the arrival of a child, and moving into a new residence, however socially regarded, may involve major demands for readjustment and many new problems. Or the new role may take so much time and effort as to be physically exhausting or may distract the person from the protective or anticipatory coping that allows an insecure individual to maintain a reasonable adjustment to his life situation. Further developments of life-readjustment scales must include further specification of the degree to which events differentially tax persons.

Although use of the Social Readjustment Rating Scale has resulted in many findings supporting the hypothesis that readjustment is related to the occurrence of disease, most of these studies are open to serious methodological criticisms for the reasons already indicated as well as some others we will deal with later. Most of the studies are based on retrospective data, thereby making it difficult to ascertain to what extent the occurrence of illness affects people's perceptions of the life events to which they have been exposed. Moreover, many of the studies depend on measure of illness behavior in contrast to more objective measures of illness, making it uncertain to what extent social changes lead to modifications in the ways people react to illness and to what extent they affect the objective state of the person's health status. It is to the credit of Holmes and some of his co-workers that they have carried out some of their studies using a prospective design that minimizes the problems in interpreting the direction of causality (see, for example, 80). But even these studies involve confounding of independent and dependent variables, which makes it difficult to interpret the significance of the findings of a link between readjustment scores and illness. George Brown (92) has done a sophisticated analysis of some of the problems of interpreting results using the Social Readjustment Rating Scale. Repeating this analysis here would take us too far afield, but readers who are particularly interested in this area should consult his discussion.

In summary, one approach to stress is to focus on significant environmental changes regardless of how they may be defined by the people affected. But study of significant life changes or social situations that tax the ordinary person's coping capacities must concentrate on events that can be specified more clearly and that are less ambiguous in the demands they make. In contrast to simply knowing that a person experienced a job change, it would be more useful to know the demands of the new job and whether it overloaded or failed to challenge the individual's capacities. Ideally, we should like to define the demands of the job independent of the person's capacity to do it. While subjective reactions and reports may give us a richer sense of what is going on, using them makes it difficult to separate the definition of the objective event from the person's reactions to it. Emphasis on objective, independent measures of events obviously results in the loss of information that cannot be easily obtained in this way. As every clinician appreciates, there is a richness to human experience that is not readily captured by objective items. The best resolution is to work at several levels of analysis concurrently, being careful that we do not confuse the measures of objective events with people's reactions to them. Given this caveat, we now turn to the second major focus in stress research—the study of stress as a response.

Stress as a Response

The term "stress" has been used to refer to emotional tensions—anxiety, fear, depression, general discomfort—either reported or observed, from which it is inferred that the individual is exposed to some stress situation. At times the inferred stimulus is called stress; on other occasions the behavioral symptoms (anxiety, fear, and so on) are called stress, or sometimes strain. For the sake of clarity it is important that we specify and differentiate the environmental stimulus and the responses. Basowitz and his associates have indicated that allegedly "stressful situations" do not always produce discomforting responses in individuals:

> The training program affected individuals in a variety of ways and to different degrees, and it disturbed the entire experimental group, composed of men of varying strengths and weaknesses, in a limited manner. In addition, those who were disturbed often reacted idiosyncratically with respect to the system, function, or behavior affected, the degree and direction of the disequilibrium, and the type and amount of anxiety. Since a strictly scheduled exposure to danger and possible failure evoked such a wide variety of responses, it was apparent that stress does not conform to an a priori value judgment of what *should* happen, but can only be determined by observations of what does happen. In future research, therefore, we should not consider stress as *imposed* upon the organism, but as its *response* to in-

ternal or external processes which reach those threshold levels that strain its physiological and psychological integrative capacities close to or beyond their limits [48, pp. 288–89].

Unfortunately, the definition of what constitutes a stress response poses some difficult issues. On the physiological level it appears that different autonomic measures such as heart rate and skin conductance, which presumably measure the same inner state, yield low correlations (405; 406; 416). Although both of these indices rise under stress, one might obtain different results depending on the measure used, since they appear to be differentially affected by variation in subjects' biological constitutions. Even more troubling is the fact that subjective reports of stress are not highly correlated with various physiological indices. Since all of these kinds of responses may differ, it is not clear what it is that constitutes the most appropriate measure of stress.

These problems exist in part because stress is probably not a single response but one involving many dimensions. Also, the lack of correlation between psychic responses and autonomic responses is attributable in part to problems in measurement. While autonomic measures are taken continuously or at specific intervals, most subjective psychological measures are summary reports of total experience. It is not surprising, therefore, that the correlations between the measures are not very high. As measurement of psychological factors becomes more sophisticated, it is probable that correlation between psychological and physiological measures will increase somewhat.

In any case, it should be clear that the concept of stress response, like the concept of stress stimuli, is frequently difficult to specify in an unambiguous manner. As there is no central stress theory, and because the term binds together many varied conceptions and approaches, it is important to emphasize that the social conception of stress presented here is only one of many possible ways of approaching this area.

Elements of Crisis

Although the concept of stress has been used to refer to a great variety of social, psychological, and physical influences impinging on the individual, as well as to both adverse and positive events, the concept of crisis has been used by sociologists to describe broader and more large-scale challenges to individuals or social groups, such as the family or community. "Crisis" usually connotes an *unanticipated, adverse change* that disrupts ordinary patterns of adaptation and requires new adaptive routines. Davis, for example, used the term to describe "a relatively sudden and unanticipated disruption, of extensive and protracted significance, in the everyday activities, understandings, and expectations of a social unit" (160, p. 17).

The key feature of a "crisis" or "stress," as I use these terms, is a discrepancy between the demands of a situation and the capacity of the individual or group to deal with it comfortably. Such imbalances may exist in perceptions of the situation, in the objective facts, or both. This conception is similar to Lazarus's conclusion that "when the balance of power favors the harm-producing stimulus, threat is increased. As the balance of power tends to favor the counterharm resources, threat is reduced" (416, p. 119). The magnitude of crisis depends on the degree of perceived and/or actual imbalance and on the importance of the situation, either as perceived or in terms of objective consequences. If the situation is unimportant, it matters little how well or ineffectively the person or group responds.

The types of adaptive resources called for in everyday life are within the capacities of most people. Crises occur when there are major perceived changes in the adaptive requirements of the situation, and thus uncertainty as to the likely outcomes. One of the reasons for the focus on life-change events in the stress literature is that such events are likely to require adaptive techniques that are so different from the commonplace that individuals must reassess themselves in relation to the demands of their environment, and perhaps must also alter significant expectations, understandings, and meanings of everyday activities.

Crises may be viewed as a process through time or may be studied cross-sectionally in terms of their differential impact or the variations in response among persons affected. All crises of importance extend over a long period of time and require prospective investigation if their manifold dimensions are to be understood. Cross-sectional and retrospective studies fail to capture the complex processes through which people assign meaning to crisis events, seek actively to resolve them, explore alternatives, and adapt to their adverse features. In addition, adaptive response requires changes in perceptions, expectations, and imputed meanings, and retrospective reports may reflect the momentary needs of the person to reconsturct the past more than they reflect any objective reality. In studying crises through time it is frequently useful to divide the situation in stages, with the full realization that these stages are arbitrary delineations that frequently overlap or blend into one another.

Davis (160), in studying the adaptations of polio victims and their families, divides the process into four stages: prelude, warning, impact, and inventory. Although he does not define these stages formally, their character is reasonably clear. The prelude is the period of sensing a change, the possibility that something is wrong, This stage tends to be anticipatory and unstructured. The warning stage is defined by a perception that the situation may be serious. How such a perception develops depends on cues, in terms of both their source and their timing. During this period a serious search goes on to ascertain the nature of the difficulty and to sort out alternative possibilities. Davis reserves the concept of impact for the realization that the problem is serious. Impact can refer to a definitive diagnosis of a serious illness, a wife's indicating to her husband that she is divorcing him, or a student's being informed that he has flunked an important examination. In the inventory stage the people in crisis attempt to assess what has happened, to explain the event, to assess its meaning, and to make attributions of responsibility. Perhaps another stage ought to be added, termed "aftermath" or "reconstruction," in which people attempt to rebuild their lives in light of the preceding events, working out new forms of coping, resolving psychological issues, and building social networks consistent with new needs brought about by the crisis (760).

The nature of a crisis depends on a wide range of variables that define its magnitude (47). Among these are the *intensity* of the threatened or actual loss, its *extent through important dimensions* of the person's or group's life space, the *speed* with which it occurs, the degree to which the person is *prepared to cope* with the crisis or be overwhelmed by it, and its *duration or recurrent* nature. It also depends on the *reversibility* of the situation (479). In some crises, such as the loss of a loved one, only working through one's grief is possible; nothing the person can do can reverse the loss. Other crises, such as an important examination or a long rehabilitative process, provide continuing opportunities for the person affected to participate actively in mastering the situation.

Designation of stages in crisis may be a difficult and subtle process. Much of what happens in crises, particularly those of long duration, is anticipatory. The warnings, searches for understanding and meaning, and coping devices used may develop over long periods of time. Death of a loved one following a chronic illness, divorce and separation, and failure to attain a coveted and hard-sought educational degree or job may represent not the impact of a crisis but rather its culmination. In each case there may have been years of struggle, of attempts to cope, of challenge and failure. Thus the defining event, such as the formalized divorce or the death—although it may bring its own special grief—may be followed by a period of relief and relaxation. The process of "giving up" may occur well before any final resolution of the crisis.

Approaches to Psychosomatic Medicine

The area of psychosomatic medicine is characterized by many theories and research efforts based on different theoretical orientations (287).

However different these theories are, they share one common assumption: that discomforting life situations (i.e., stress) play a role in causing or contributing to the occurrence of illness. I have pointed out how particular social and community conditions can increase the extent to which people experience events as discomforting. There is therefore an indirect but clear link hypothesized between the conditions prevailing in a society and the occurrence of illness.

The importance of stress in illness is an issue still characterized by considerable uncertainty and disagreement. Research efforts in psychosomatic medicine vary widely in their designs and general adequacy, and in most diseases there are contradictory findings concerning the role of stress as an etiological agent. Until recently most psychosomatic ideas were based on casual clinical observations involving small groups of selected patients. Often the studies had inadequate control groups or no control groups at all. Concepts frequently were poorly specified, reasoning was often tautological, and claims were made that could not be supported by any substantial body of empirical findings. Despite these problems, which have characterized psychosomatic medicine to a greater extent than some other fields, this area constitutes one of the most provocative and challenging fields within medicine.

The psychosomatic field is enormously complicated and considerable theoretical and methodological clarification is necessary (see 287). All that can be done here is to present some of the major views concerning psychosomatic medicine, appraise them briefly, and suggest some of the more promising directions in psychosomatic research. The reader is urged to consult the sources cited for further appreciation of what psychosomatics involve.

Work in the psychosomatic area is based on the awareness that all psychological and social experience is associated with changing states of people's physiology. Although we are aware that our feelings are associated with bodily changes, it is quite another thing to demonstrate that these feelings produce bodily dysfunctions or increase susceptibility to a variety of diseases. Some investigators believe that disease is basically an exaggeration of normal physiological processes and that most normal adaptations that are easy to observe are characteristic of more pronounced reactions that are recognized as diseases (289). For example, it is well recognized that induced stress in some subjects increases the acidity of the stomach. Increased acidity of the stomach is not a disease, but when the acids in the stomach erode its walls, producing an ulcer, we do have a definite disease entity. Many investigators believe that demonstrating that stress increases the acidity of the stomach has important implications for understanding the role of stress in the development of ulcers. But there may be other factors involved as well, such as the susceptibility of the stomach walls to acid erosion. We must be cautious, therefore, in making the theoretical leap from observations concerning the role of psychic factors in normal physiological changes to those involving the role of psychic factors in disease, although studies of both kinds will be discussed.

Psychoanalytic Approach

The interest in psychosomatic disease in the United States has occurred largely within the context of the psychoanalytic approach. One of the leading theoreticians of the psychoanalytic school—Franz Alexander (10)—believed that emotional and somatic factors interact to produce many diseases and that psychic factors play a role in hysterical conversion symptoms, vegetative neurosis, and organic disease. The conversion symptom is viewed as an attempt to relieve an emotional tension that can find no adequate symbolic expression. In his later work he gave more attention to the *vegetative neurosis*, which he looked upon as a psychologically induced dysfunction of an organ concomitant with the emotional tension. Alexander believed that specific psychological dynamic constellations lead to specific bodily dysfunctions. For example, he believed that peptic ulcer was related to unconscious repressed desires for help and love that are unconsciously associated with the longing for food (which to Alexander is the most primitive form of love). The repressed desires lead to stomach secretion that if continued plays an important part in ulcer formation. Similar psychological constellations and patterns are seen as playing a part in other disease states.

The basic assumption of the psychoanalytic approach is that stress can manifest itself in a number of linked open systems. Stress that occurs in one system may be transferred to others so that several systems may play a part in the adaptive process. Roy Grinker (298), another proponent of the psychoanalytic school, believes that generalized infantile anxiety can become conditioned to certain fragmentary visceral patterns. In early life these may be functionally adaptive to specific stressors as the physiological expression of homeostatic disturbance, but in later life anxiety becomes intensified for various reasons and the old pattern reappears. Excessive occurrence of this infantile pattern, while it may be adaptive, can result in disease.

Grinker has posited a transactional view of five systems: the enzymatic system, including the hormones, the organ system, the nervous system, the psychological system, and the sociocultural system. When a given system is strained in handling a particular stressor, the minor preparatory changes in a related system become intensified and apparent as another response to the initial stimulus. Grinker sees this integration of systems as inherent in both the preparatory activity and the more intense reaction to "stress stimuli" impinging on any single system. Integration within any system is dependent on its capacity to act alone without strain before action in another system is initiated. When anxiety becomes too intense, disruptive effects ensue, bringing forth emergency substitutive mechanisms of defense (the intervention of other systems). Grinker rejects the belief held by Alexander that particular personality traits are associated with specific bodily changes and argues that each adult has his own way of responding to stress.

There are much data and opinion that challenge the idea that particular personality constellations are associated with specific bodily functions. Although Alexander was not concerned with personality traits as they are usually measured when he discussed "dynamic constellations," work linking particular personality traits to disease has produced inconsistent and inconclusive findings. The most important criticism of the psychoanalytic approach is that the theory itself is too abstract and poorly specified, and as it does not usually depend on controlled scientific investigation, the theory is frequently used to explain whatever observations are made. In short, the theory as it is used by analytic investigators has not allowed for disconfirmation of its hypotheses, which is a requirement of any scientific theory. We might note the comments of some recent critics who have reviewed the psychosomatic literature:

> The most obvious difficulty is that in spite of the repeated claims made that there exists a specific type of personality for each particular psychosomatic disorder, in fact, the descriptions of the different types are monotonously alike. Given any one description, it is almost impossible to say offhand which disorder it applies to .... It is the "dynamic approach" of psychoanalysis and the other "depth psychologies," which attempts to describe personality as a process of development. Unfortunately the results cannot be described as other than disappointing. Empirically, we find that the dynamics are always the same, and the interaction of libido, aggression, dependence, and so on, are much alike from one condition to another. Such differences as are found, depend much more on the differences between schools of thought or between different therapists, than between different disorders. The theoretical deficiency of this approach is that insufficient account is taken of non-individual and social factors [312, pp. 205–10].

> In the psychosomatic field, too, there have been successive theoretical models, each usually an advance on the old, and each occasioned by growing experience and continuing observation. And yet it is beginning to appear that there has too long existed among psychosomatic writers an attitude that more closely resembles the devout believer's than the skeptical scientist's.... This uncritical and indeed unscientific attitude has reflected seriously upon the reputation of psychiatric writers among their medical colleagues....

> One is impressed by the scale of the conceptualizations which these

authors [including Alexander and Grinker] have attempted. Each one has boldly sketched a design which is offered as a blueprint for the under-standing of very complex psychosomatic phenomena. However, the man-ner of the execution of their task is open to serious reservations . . . . Disin-terested presentation of all the evidence available is not always to be found in the papers on physiological regression. Instead, random isolated supporting evidence is sometimes quoted, while the solid mass of experi-mental and clinical data that contravenes the thesis is ignored [507, pp. 363, 367–68].

Life-Situation Approach

In some respects the life-situation approach is similar to the psycho-analytic, but it has a different emphasis. The approach has been reflected in the writings and research of Harold Wolff and his as-sociates, who have provided examples showing that noxious sub-stances applied to the body will call forth offensive and defensive reac-tions in the organism. They have also demonstrated clinically that such reactions can be generalized from *physically* threatening life situations, to *socially* threatening ones, such as loss of status, loss of security, or unsatisfactory interpersonal relations (780; 781). It is Wolff's conten-tion that when such conditioned responses occur frequently—in a vari-ety of situations perceived to be socially and personally defeating—symptom formation and tissue damage can result.

To illustrate Wolff's notion we can use an example from a laboratory demonstration by Graham, which Wolff cites in his book *Stress and Disease* (780). In this demonstration the tone of the small vessels of the subject's skin on both arms was assayed to determine the vessels' ca-pacity to hold the contents of the blood. After measurements were made, the left arm was struck forcefully and a red area appeared, as-sociated with a fall in capillary tone. Although the other arm was not struck, similar capillary changes took place. The experiment was then repeated, except that now a mock blow was delivered without actually touching the subject. This anticipated threat led to capillary changes similar to those obtained when the subject was forcefully struck. When the experiment was repeated again, this time with the subject being in-formed that a mock blow was about to descend, no change in capillary tone was observed.

Graham then used a subject who had a history of "hives," again measuring the capacity of the skin capillaries to hold their contents. Graham discussed a painful family situation with the patient. In this situation the capillaries of the forearm responded in a fashion similar to the pattern observed when the arm was struck. Wolff argues, as his basic theoretical assumption, that the bodily protective response pattern to a physical blow has been generalized to symbolic blows. It is his contention that when such response patterns occur with great frequency in response to threats to status and other forms of stress, they result in symptom formation and tissue damage.

Wolff and his co-workers have gathered considerable clinical and observational evidence over the years involving a variety of physiological responses, body systems, and disease conditions. Wolf and Wolff (778), for example, studying a gastric fistula patient, observed gastric hyperactivity during periods when the patient faced ordinary life situations that either frustrated him or evoked his anger and hostility. Similarly, in population studies Hinkle and Wolff (325; 326) reported that illness was associated with occupational and social conditions that frustrated the needs and aspirations of the individuals under study. Co-workers of Wolff, Thomas Holmes and his colleagues (315; 331; 332; 333), have found that life crises tend to accumulate in the two years preceding the onset or relapse of tuberculosis. These are just a few of the many examples of observations and population studies undertaken by Wolff and his colleagues. Wolff believed that:

> The stress accruing from a situation is based in large part on the way the affected subject perceives it; perception depends upon a multiplicity of factors including the genetic equipment, basic individual needs and longings, earlier conditioning influences, and a host of life experiences and cultural pressures. No one of these can be singled out for exclusive emphasis. The common denominator of stress disorders is reaction to circumstances of threatening significance to the organism [780, p. 10].

The principal advantage of Wolff's approach is that his conceptual ideas are relatively simple and not esoteric, and his operational research procedures are closely related to his ideas. Thus his theory has served as a useful general perspective for careful clinical observation, population studies, and various experimental investigations. In short, Wolff's approach has generated considerable research activity and a rich array of empirical findings.

It would be premature, however, to suppose that Wolff's theory is substantiated. Much of the evidence is fragmentary and illustrative, while other support is based on studies of questionable methodology and inadequate controls. Wolff is no doubt correct that physiological adaptive responses can be generalized to symbolic threats, but the true extent of this process and its role in a wide variety of disease states are unknown. Illustrating the "hives" reaction to symbolic threats among subjects predisposed to hives is different from demonstrating that this response is a universal one. As research on life situations and illness has proceeded, the enormous complexity of the processes of causation has become more evident. A fair conclusion concerning the possible factors that may contribute to such associations is summarized by Hinkle, a co-worker of Wolff, who has devoted his career to the study of these processes:

> Changes in significant social or interpersonal relationships are very often accompanied by changes in habits, changes in patterns of activity, changes in the intake of food and medication, and changes in exposure to potential sources of infection or trauma. They are also frequently associated with changes in mood, and with physiological changes directly mediated by the central nervous system. Any or all of these might affect the frequency or severity of illness [324, p. 40].

Although the work of Wolff and his co-workers and students has been extremely useful, theoretical conceptions relating life change and subjective response to illness are still not sufficiently specified. We must be able to indicate what types of event influence what illnesses under what conditions and through what processes. The field of psychosomatic research continues to be characterized by reports of gross correlations without the degree of specification necessary to push research, clinical applications, and basic understanding forward. Yet the area is an exciting one, worthy of our best efforts. Both the potentialities and the difficulties of developments in this field can be illustrated through a brief discussion of stress, Type A personality, and coronary heart disease.

Stress, Type A Personality, and Coronary Heart Disease

The previous chapter reviewed various risk factors associated with coronary heart disease, such as smoking, diet, and hypertension. These factors combined, however, still fail to account for much of the variance in disease occurrence. In recent decades a great deal of evidence has accumulated that supports the notion that psychosocial factors may play an important role. This view is hardly new; Sir William Osler in 1892 described the coronary-prone individual as a "keen and ambitious man, the indicator of whose engines are set at full speed ahead" (quoted in 430). While a variety of psychosocial factors appear to be implicated in coronary heart disease, the literature is inconsistent and some factors seem to be related to disease occurrence more consistently than others. There is difficulty in knowing how properly to conceptualize the factors that are most important or to identify the specific components that are causally related to coronary heart disease. In general, there is fairly consistent evidence that such factors as anxiety, depression, and sleep disturbance may play some role but relatively weak evidence to support the importance of such factors as social mobility, social incongruity, stressful life events, and dissatisfactions (366). Perhaps the most consistent and impressive evidence is found in relation to the role of the Type A coronary-prone behavior pattern (367).

Friedman and Rosenman (248), the first to attempt to measure the Type A behavior pattern, describe it as an

> action-emotion complex that can be observed in any person who is *aggressively* involved in a *chronic, incessant* struggle to achieve more and more in less and less time, and if required to do so, against the opposing efforts of other things or other persons .... Persons possessing this pattern also are quite prone to exhibit a free-floating but extraordinarily well-rationalized hostility [248, p. 67].

The key elements of this pattern are described as an

> intense striving for achievement; competitiveness; easily provoked impatience; time urgency; abruptness of gesture and speech; overcommitment to vocation or profession; and excesses of drive and hostility [367, p. 1034].

While Friedman and Rosenman refer to the behavior pattern as a "form of conflict" (248, p. 67), Jenkins sees it as a "deeply ingrained, enduring trait" (367, p. 1034).

The behavior pattern has been measured in two basic ways. Friedman and Rosenman developed an interview concerning such matters as the subject's ambition, drive, and competitiveness. The interviewers, however, are trained to focus less on the content of the answers than on such behavioral responses as rapidity of speech, movement of face muscles, body gestures, and degree of restlessness. Trained interviewers achieve reasonable degrees of reliability in typing individuals, and such typing has been more successfully correlated with coronary heart disease than have alternative ways of measuring the behavior pattern. An alternative to the interview is the Jenkins Activity Survey, in which respondents are asked such questions as "Do you ever have trouble finding time to get your hair cut or styled?" or "Has your spouse or some friend ever told you you eat too fast?" The activity survey is based on 54 questions and was validated using Type A and Type B respondents as assessed by the interview method. Factor analyses of the activity survey suggest that it has three independent components: hard-driving, job involvement, and speed and impatience.

An excellent example of the use of the activity survey is found in a prospective study of coronary heart disease by Jenkins, Rosenman, and Zyzanski (365). Data on the coronary-prone pattern were obtained prior to the four-year period in which disease occurrence was studied; a double-blind method was used so that those who evaluated the patients were unaware of the behavior pattern and those who administered and scored the activity survey had no involvement in patient evaluation. The investigators found that while the third of the sample with the lowest Type A scores had an annual rate of 8 cases of coronary heart disease per 100 men, the group with the highest scores had a rate of 14.3 per 100 men. Men who developed coronary disease after testing scored significantly higher on the Type A behavior pattern than those who did not. While, on the whole, the differences are not very large, the careful design of the study requires that we take them seriously. None of the individual subscales of the activity survey successfully differentiated cases from controls in this prospective study.

The studies of Type A reveal something important about behavioral traits implicated in coronary heart disease, but the conceptions of the nature of the type, its most important components, and its relationship to biological processes remain vague. Speaking of the hypothesized components of the Type A pattern, Leventhal has noted:

> It is not known how these behavioral components or attributes relate to one another, whether they necessarily occur together, or whether they are differentially related to risk. Furthermore, it is not known what external situational demands and internal dispositions are important in eliciting Type A behaviors, nor is it known if the variables eliciting the Type A behavior are the variables which directly affect the physiological precursors that contribute to CHD [430, p. 8].

While Jenkins maintains that this behavior pattern is not a stressful situation or a disturbed response, and Friedman and Rosenman argue that it is "not a complex of worries or fears or phobias or obsessions," its exact nature remains unclear. Jenkins speaks of "a style of behavior with which some persons habitually respond to circumstances that arouse them" and "a deeply ingrained, enduring trait," but these notations fail to depict a concept of personality or social development that accounts for the behavior or to indicate how they relate to biological processes. Although this constitutes a promising area for concentrated and valuable study, calls for major intervention programs based on current understanding appear to be premature and misguided (see 248).

Attitude Specificity

A major issue that has concerned psychosomatic investigators for several decades is whether particular personalities or psychological traits are associated with increased risks of specific diseases. The study of attitude specificity brings greater strength to this view. The notion underlying this work is that specific attitudes are correlated with particular physiological changes of a disease-like nature. In a paper in 1952, Grace and Graham (286) described several attitudes that they believed were associated with physiological responses characterizing a series of diseases. These impressions were derived from intensive interviews of patients with particular conditions. For example, they had the impression that hypertension was associated with an attitude of needing to be prepared to meet all threats, and that urticaria (hives) was associated with an attitude of feeling mistreated, and so on. In further observations and clinical studies by Graham and others, various attitudes appeared to be associated with particular patterns of physiological response, and the investigators were able to elicit such physiological responses among patients prone to particular conditions in interviews that dealt with their life situations (780). More recently Graham (288) has used an experimental situation in which hypnotic suggestions are given to normal subjects who are used as their own controls, and physiological measures are obtained that are relevant to the expected effects of the induced attitudes. To give the reader some idea of how these attitudes are induced experimentally, the instructions for the urticaria and hypertension attitudes are reproduced here:

> (Urticaria) You feel mistreated, unfairly treated, wrongly treated. There is nothing you can do about it, nothing you even want to do about it. You are thinking only of what happened to you. You just have to take it. You are the helpless, innocent victim of unfair, unjust treatment. Nobody should do a thing like that to you. That is the way you're feeling; that feeling gets stronger and stronger . . . .

> (Hypertension) We're going to do something to you; you have to be ready, on guard, prepared for whatever it is. It might be a burn, an electric shock, a needle stick. It's going to come; you just have to sit there and wait and try to be ready for whatever it is. You feel that you may be attacked and hurt at any instant; it may be painful, it may be dangerous. You feel that you are in danger. You're threatened every instant, you have to watch out [288, pp. 160–61].

Graham and his colleagues have obtained the physiological responses predicted from earlier observations when attitudes associated with Raynaud's disease, hives, and essential hypertension are suggested.

The study of attitude specificity and related experimental findings is a promising development in psychosomatic efforts. The differences observed under experimental conditions, however, do not prove a link between attitudes and risks of disease, although attitudes appear to be related to disease-like physiological reactions. Graham believes that these attitudes as induced in experiments are present in only mild forms and only for a short time; in real situations the attitudes may become powerful and persist for long periods of time. Graham believes his experiments capture in mild form a picture of how attitudes relate to disease states.

This development, although not new in its conceptions, involves a significant methodological advance. Graham's basic assumptions and theoretical dispositions are similar to those advanced by Alexander.

Graham however, has been able to describe "attitudes" or "dynamic personality configurations" so that they can be put into operation in experimental investigations. He believes that earlier investigations on personality specificity yielded ambiguous results because the "personality characteristics" or "attitudes" were not properly characterized or described. He would contend that we often lack adequate descriptive words to portray the most important attitudes from the perspective of psychosomatic investigations (see 287).

Although Graham has shown some links between specific attitudinal states and particular physiological responses, these attitudes may not be exclusively responsible for producing the physiological responses with which he has been concerned. It is possible that one of many attitudes may be associated with the same physiological response, and as one moves to the more difficult area of disease states there will be many persons who have the condition but do not appear to hold the relevant attitude. In any case Graham and his co-workers have opened a worthwhile area for investigation.

We must note that there are contradictions among promising approaches to psychosomatics. Earlier we discussed the interesting work of Stanley Schachter and Jerome Singer (611) and noted that it supports the idea that the same physiological arousal may lead to different emotional responses. On the face of it the work of Schachter and Singer seems to conflict with Graham's findings on attitude specificity. If the same arousal may lead to different emotions, how can each physiological pattern have a particular attitude associated with it? Graham would argue that when Schachter gave his subjects different degrees of information and put them in different experimental conditions, he brought about changes in both the psychological and physiological responses of the subjects. If one takes this point of view, the two lines of research become more compatible. The issues in psychosomatics are far from closed; there are many more questions than findings, and work is just beginning to clarify some of the problems in this complicated and difficult area within medical research.

The specificity approach to stress and illness suggests that we move toward greater refinements in both independent and dependent variables and attempt to understand the particular types of stress or other factors that are relevant for each specific disease. However, broad social and environmental factors may increase susceptibility to a wide variety of diseases and failures in functioning, and although attempts at greater specificity are important, they should be supplemented by a more general approach that examines how major environmental factors may be important in a variety of ways. As we noted in the previous chapter, smoking not only increases mortality and morbidity from lung and heart disease but also has much broader effects on biological functioning.

John Cassel (108) has noted serious difficulties with the traditional approach and suggests an alternative perspective:

> Logically, then, the problem can be formulated as two interrelated, but from a research point of view separate, questions. First, would be the identification of situations that are likely to evoke inappropriate adaptive responses. Populations exposed to such situations would be expected to manifest a wide spectrum of disease consequences which may or may not "fit" the existing clinical classificatory schemes. The nature or form of these manifestations would be the second type of question. Answers to this will not come from the identification of the processes involved in the situation alone, but must take into account the determinants of the particular adaptive devices utilized by various segments of the population. . . .Such a formulation, by allowing for multiple alternative options to any particular situation and by indicating the need to identify situations likely to evoke inappropriate adaptive responses, can provide leads as to what it is that needs to be quantified and what sorts of relationships would be acceptable as evidence of importance of these situations [108, pp. 203–204].

Although events causing maladaptive response may contribute to traditional disease entities, Cassel urges that we take a broader view than those suggested by existing classifications. Such an effort appears worthwhile, particularly since the conditions of living have been changing rapidly and will continue to change in dramatic ways. There is reason to anticipate that people will find social change difficult and that adaptations harmful to health will take many forms.

In recent years there has been a marked shift in the study of human adaptation from concern with intrapsychic defense mechanisms to much greater emphasis on the skills and supports required to meet typical life challenges. Associated with this shift is a growing realization that the medical model as a mode of studying adaptations is limited, and an increasing interest in exploring alternative educational and transactional models of human behavior (203). The challenge is to define those variables on both an individual and community level that are identifiable and measurable and that can be linked to health behavior and health levels in populations.

Illness Behavior and Psychosomatics

One feature complicating psychosomatic analysis involves the difficulty of separating the role of psychological factors in producing disease from their effect on the patient's attitude and response to his symptoms. Mechanic (482) has shown how the effect of illness behavior patterns on use of medical facilities may lead the medical investigator to observe that particular disease groups are characterized by considerable stress. Although psychosomatic investigators frequently conclude that such stress is causally related to the patient's condition, it is likely that many such conclusions are an artifact of the fact that persons with a particular condition are more likely to come into care when they are under stress than when they are not. The researcher must be cognizant of such patient response tendencies. For example, studies in industry that show a large proportion of sickness absence as being contributed year after year by a small proportion of employees may really be uncovering response tendencies of workers to their life situations. The fact that "sick workers" had more of all types of illness as well as the usual psychosomatic symptoms suggests that sickness absence may be a way of avoiding an intolerable job environment (there is evidence that these workers are dissatisfied with their jobs) (326). Perhaps the notion that workers are escaping from stress, using illness as an excuse, is a more reasonable explanation for the data available than the one more frequently posed—that stress produces illness of all kinds and involves all body systems (also see 379).

In a fascinating paper, Imboden and his colleagues (351) provide an illustration of a situation in which psychological symptoms unrelated to a condition may become merged with the illness, resulting in a constellation of chronic disability that is largely a product of the psychological condition. Imboden and his associates studied three groups of patients who had brucellosis, a relatively rare infection usually resulting from contact with Brucella in laboratory work. One group of patients had this acute infection but recovered on the average in about two months. In a second group the patient's disability became somewhat chronic, but these patients later recovered after being ill, on the average, for a year and a half. A third group of patients developed chronic disabilities and did not recover; this third group had an average illness duration of four years and five months. There was no differentiation among these groups on objective medical grounds that could account for the varying periods of disability characterized by fatigue, headache, nervousness, depression, backache, and generalized aches and pains.

On the basis of independent psychiatric and psychological evaluations the investigators found evidence of gross trauma characterizing the early life of the chronic patients, many of whom also had troubled life situations at about the time of their acute illness as compared with those who recovered quickly. The authors conclude that there are psychologically vulnerable patients. If stress reactions and acute infection occur at about the same time in such vulnerable patients, they may become intermingled in a larger chronic syndrome. The association in time between life troubles and the infection allows the patient to attribute all his feelings and difficulties to his condition, which he sees basically as physical. The chronic syndrome of brucellosis becomes an alternative to the recognition of psychological difficulties. Imboden and his colleagues have also studied delayed convalescence after Asian influenza (352), and they find a similar tendency for chronicity to be related to psychological difficulties existing at the time of infection.

In short, we find that psychosomatic work is complicated by the elaborations in disease that develop when a disease condition interacts with various aspects of the person and his environment. The psychosomaticist, like other investigators, benefits from a perspective that attempts to differentiate the illness, the patient's illness behavior, and the complicated interplay among these aspects and a wide variety of environmental influences.

In seeking to explain an observed relationship between the occurrence of discomforting life events and a particular disorder such as infectious disease, several interpretations are possible. These include: (1) stress contributes in some fashion to the incidence of infection (512); (2) the condition itself is a significant source of distress and weakens the person's incentive; (3) the condition serves as an excuse for avoiding distressful obligations and makes nonperformance of responsibilities acceptable (217); (4) the condition allows the person to justify to himself his failure to meet social responsibilities (137); or (5) the effect of the condition becomes confused with other feelings of distress so that the individual cannot clearly differentiate the source and attributes causality solely to the condition (352). Some of these possibilities imply varying processes of occurrence. Thus stress may affect the reported incidence of infection by lowering bodily resistance; or it may affect the person's behavioral patterns, including exposure to infection, eating, and sleeping; or it may affect the person's threshold to recognize discomfort, or his reactions to it.

In summary, there is much reason to believe that discomforting psychological states play an important role in at least some kinds of disease and may possibly have some role in all disease processes. At this point the empirical support for the influence of stress in disease processes is less than clear-cut and hardly adequate to merit dogmatic assertions about its relative role in relation to other etiological factors. There is no known disease outside the psychiatric disorders in which stress is clearly a necessary condition for occurrence, and even in the psychiatric area some investigators have their doubts about the importance of the stress factor. In contrast, it is fairly clear from many studies that stress is often a contributory factor in disease. Stress appears to play a more important role in some diseases than in others, but even in the infectious diseases there is reason to believe that stress can have a contributing role. We have already discussed some of the work on tuberculosis, streptococcal infections, brucellosis, and influenza. Consistent with this work is the finding that fever blisters or cold sores are due to a virus usually acquired in early life and continually present in the body of an infected person, but a morbid condition seems to occur only when various conditions (including emotional stress) upset the chemical balance in the body (185).

We must be willing to give proper recognition to the influence of stress in disease processes. But in our enthusiasm we must be careful not to impute greater significance to the concept than empirical results dictate. If the concept of psychosomatics is to play an important part in medicine, it must be based on a sound empirical foundation.

Part 4

**REACTIONS TO HEALTH
AND ILLNESS**

Chapter 9

ILLNESS BEHAVIOR

The term "illness" is used in two ways by analysts who study issues concerning health and illness. It can refer to a limited scientific concept (already discussed in our analysis of medical disease models) or to any condition that causes or might usefully cause an individual to concern himself with his symptoms and to seek help. The term "illness behavior" refers to any behavior relevant to the second, more general, interpretation. If we are to understand the process of illness, it becomes necessary to consider what goes on even before a person sees a doctor or some other health worker. Thus the study of the patient's perspective is an indispensable aspect of the analysis of health and disease.

Symptoms are differentially perceived, evaluated, and acted upon (or not acted upon) by different kinds of people and in different social situations. Whether because of earlier experiences with illness, differential training in respect to symptoms, or different biological sensitivities, some persons make light of symptoms and avoid seeking medical care. Others will respond to little pain and discomfort by readily seeking care, releasing themselves from work and other obligations, and becoming dependent on others (476). Thus the study of illness behavior involves the study of attentiveness to pain and symptomatology, examination of processes affecting the way pain and symptoms are defined, accorded significance, and socially labeled, and consideration of the extent to which help is sought, change in life regimen affected, and claims made on others. Although this chapter deals with illness behavior in general, the discussion elaborates only on help-seeking behavior, which is but one of many facets within the larger topic. The purpose of the chapter is thus to provide a general perspective in contrast to a comprehensive review of the voluminous literature that has developed in the area.

The study of illness behavior by its very nature requires study not only of those who seek care but also of those in the population who do not. Because illness behavior affects the utilization of medical care, choice of paths to possible advisors, and responses to illness in general, the selection of patients who seek help from general practitioners, clinics, or even hospitals is usually biased. Groups of patients with a particular disease selected from such populations will usually be biased compared with those in the general population with the same disease but untreated; this is particularly true for illnesses of high prevalence that are easily recognized by the public and known to have a benign course (482; 503).

Sociological Considerations

The study of help seeking falls into an aspect of sociological theory that might be referred to as the study of social selection. Social selection is one of the most pervasive processes characteristic of human communities, and its study concerns the identification of underlying principles of sorting and re-sorting that go on continuously among social groups. Subareas of the study of social selection include assortative mating, geographic migration, selection related to education, life careers, and achievement, and numerous other topics. Social-selection ideas have become increasingly important in theoretical conceptions of deviance in which attention is directed to the social processes through which particular persons are identified, processed, isolated, and confronted with restricted opportunity structures (427; 463; 618).

In making sense of processes of social selection, whatever the subarea of concern, attention is given to the characteristics of the individuals and groups involved that make them different in one way or another from others in the community. Attention is also given to the processes by which they interact with others in exchanging information about their social characteristics, skills and disabilities, and personal inclinations. Efforts must also be made to understand the underlying opportunity structure that makes differential choice possible and that either facilitates or retards certain possibilities. In short, selection problems have personal, interactional, and structural dimensions.

Although social selection is one of the central processes of social activity, much sociological investigation views it more as an irritation than as an object of inquiry. Because social selection is such a powerful process sociologists cannot ignore it, but in order to maintain credibility they must discount it. Students of complex organization, comparing varying types of social structures or management styles, must make a

credible case that it is the structural arrangements that are really important in contrast to the types of persons drawn to varying organizations.
Investigators of hospital programs or any other social program must, in
order to be taken seriously, convince us that the effects they observe are
related to a specific intervention in contrast to the types of clients
drawn to varying kinds of programs. Indeed, some social scientists,
recognizing the power of selection, take the position that serious study
without the randomization of selection effects is futile. Despite such
widespread recognition of social selection as a powerful and pervasive
social process, few sociologists take selection itself as the object of their
theory and inquiry.

It is possible to formulate varying hypotheses about selection that
have important implications for the way we construe social processes
more generally and what policy implications we derive from such understanding. Take, for example, the simple instance of a patient seeking
the assistance of a physician. One hypothesis about selection is that it
reflects the magnitude, quality, and seriousness of symptoms. This "rational" concept of medical utilization would lead one to anticipate that
characteristics of illness are the primary determinant of use of
physician services, and that exceptions flow from ignorance, misper-
ception, or poor communication; this is the way many physicians view
the utilization process. A contrasting hypothesis would maintain that
many of the problems brought to a physician resemble similar
problems of considerable prevalence that only occasionally lead to
care; thus knowledge of symptoms is not sufficient to make sense of
the use of physicians. What may differentiate those who seek care
from those who do not is a desire for social support, secondary gain as
reflected in release from work or from other obligations, or some other
social process unrelated to the illness or symptoms.

The perspective taken on a problem seemingly as simple as medical
utilization may have important implications for the types of questions
asked as well as a variety of practical concerns. To the extent that the
discrepancy between the character and magnitude of illness and
utilization is seen as little more than the result of distortions that
require correction, then there are few issues of intellectual concern.
The inquiry, however, may also attempt to probe somewhat deeper to
examine why people with similar symptoms behave differently, why
assistance is sought during some stages in illness rather than others,
and why the patient at a particular point in time comes to emphasize a
given set of symptoms. The most frequent reason given for seeing a doctor is the common cold. However, most people with colds do not consult doctors, and people who consult doctors because of colds on one
occasion may not do so on another. An adequate theory must do more
than explain a certain proportion of the variance in the dependent vari-

able; it must provide some way of accounting for the diversity of response not only among individuals and groups but within the life history of individuals. It is conceivable, for example, that the common cold is merely an excuse for visiting a physician with the desire to relieve the stress of a hated job or an unhappy family situation often constituting the primary motivation. The implication of such a hypothesis, in contrast to the rational theory referred to above, is that eliminating the prevalence of colds in the population is likely to have a less dramatic impact on utilization than might be expected. If the common cold as a justification became less viable, people would find other excuses to seek release from obligations or support.

Methodological Considerations

It is often difficult to pose interesting questions so that they are answerable. Although there are extensive reports and discussions on the "hidden agenda" in medical consultations and numerous attempts to analyze people's deeper motivations for seeking care when they do so for psychological problems (42), it is difficult to investigate these issues in a rigorous and replicable manner. Generally speaking, there are four methodological approaches to understanding the way people respond to symptoms and choose pathways for care.

Care Seeking as a Dispositional Variable

One way of attempting to understand the reasons people seek care from psychiatrists or some other type of helper is to attempt to isolate a dispositional trait and examine its correlates and social development. Such dispositional attributes may be measured directly through verbal reports, as with a measure of the propensity to seek medical or psychiatric care, or indirectly through the fact that some individuals have sought care from a particular help source and others have not. The fact of having sought help from, for example, psychiatrists defines the disposition, and the investigator then attempts to reconstruct through depth interviews or statistical manipulation of survey or other data both the antecedents and concomitants of such dispositions. Most of the literature has not gone beyond simple sociodemographic correlates of particular help-seeking patterns, and almost no direct study has been undertaken of the social development of different dispositions.

A variety of interesting issues concerning the social development of help-seeking dispositions remain highly problematic. For example, as noted in my discussions of the occurrence of illness, there are abundant studies indicating that women report various symptoms more frequently than men and use medical and psychiatric facilities more commonly (28; 177; 285; 304; 662). Many reasons are given by investigators to explain such differences: real differences in the prevalence of psychological disorder; characteristics of the measures used and judgments made of disorders that contain sex biases; women's lower threshold to perceive symptoms; differences between men and women in willingness to acknowledge the presence of symptoms; and psychobiological differences between men and women. Although each of these explanations is given from time to time, few investigators attempt to devise studies that allow competing hypotheses to be tested. Mechanic (483) found in a study of the socialization of attitudes toward illness that sex differences in reporting reactions to illness and pain were already apparent in children by the fourth grade, and increased as children became older. Aggregate data on sex and utilization of medical care suggest that women have higher levels of utilization at all ages except during childhood, when it is usually the mother who makes decisions for both boys and girls. However, Lewis (437) has shown that sex differences in using a school health service exist even among young children in an experimental child-initiated help-seeking system. A better understanding of the way differences by sex, as well as other important personal characteristics, emerge requires developmental inquiry. It will become clearer, however, that defining help-seeking predispositions is no easy matter and involves the same types of difficulty inherent in other predispositional investigation in developmental psychology, such as in the study of honesty or independence.

Interaction of Independent Variables

One of the most common approaches to studying help seeking is to carry out an epidemiological survey and to identify in the survey population those who have sought a particular type of care. Other data from the survey are then used to examine the ways the characteristics of those who seek care differ from those who do not. Such analysis allows the exploration of interactive effects and more complex models of help seeking. Mechanic and Volkart (502), for example, in a study of freshman students, found that both tendency to adopt the sick role and stress were related to the use of student health services. Stress was more influential, however, among those students with a higher propensity to use medical services, in affecting the actual rate of medical utilization. Thus it appeared that students had differential predispositions to cope by using health services; stress appeared to be the trigger that activated the disposition among those who were high on this variable. Stress probably led to other types of coping behavior among those who had lower dispositions to use medical services. Gurin and his associates (304), in a national survey of definitions and reactions to personal problems, suggested that different types of factors influence varying aspects of the help-seeking process, such as identification of the problem, decision to seek care, and particular type of practitioner consulted.

Structure of the Health-Delivery System

A third approach to studying utilization is to examine the help-giving organizations and the extent to which they either encourage care among certain groups or impose barriers to such care (469). Barriers may result from the location of sites of care, economic or other impediments to access, bureaucratic harassment, social distance between client and professional, stigma associated with seeking care, or the way in which agencies and professionals define their work and organize their efforts. Beginning with the early study of Myers and Schaffer (531) showing the varying accessibility of a psychiatric clinic to clients of different social statuses, many studies have illustrated the extent to which agencies express preferences for certain types of clients and the way social dissimilarity between clients and professionals results in difficulties in communication and disruption of service.

Processes of Illness Attribution

An illuminating approach to the study of the identification of and response to symptoms is investigation of the attribution process itself, and the ways people come to make sense and give significance to their experiences. One of the most consistent findings in the illness-behavior literature is that persons are more likely to take action for symptoms that in some fashion disrupt usual functioning, and that concepts of health are affected as much by total functioning as by the nature of the symptoms experienced (317). Persons experiencing changes in usual physical functioning and feeling states engage in various attempts to make sense of their experience, and they test various hypotheses about the seriousness and possible causes of their symptoms (495). The manner in which attributions are made affects the significance given to symptoms and the types of action pursued.

One of the most interesting dimensions of such attribution processes relevant to mental disorders is the way people come to attribute causality to their experiences, and more specifically the locus of causality. Under what conditions, for example, do people come to view their feelings or behavior as a consequence of a moral failure or of an illness for which they are not responsible? Particularly when definitions of mental disorder are imposed on individuals by other members of their social group, decisions must be made as to the extent to which the behavior or attitude of the patient reflects "badness" in contrast to "sickness," and these attributions are very much affected by the sociocultural context.

Attributions of causality have considerable implications for the care provided and for the course of disorder, and they may even dramatically affect programs of rehabilitation. For example, during World War II soldiers who experienced "breakdown" in combat were evacuated to the back lines, and their disorganized behavior was viewed as rooted in their early childhood socialization. The soldier, wishing to avoid further combat, readily accepted the attribution that the problem was rooted in his personality, and it was difficult to return these soldiers to active duty (266). The military later developed a psychiatric policy that defined stress reactions in combat as transient reactions. Although soldiers were given opportunities to rest, the definition of the situation was that this was a reaction in the normal range and that soldiers were expected to return to active duty. With this policy, many soldiers returned to effective functioning within their units. These policies have now been translated into community care of the mentally ill, and it is apparent that many patients suffering from psychological distress do extremely well with minimal intervention. At times, however, such policies are carried too far and it is assumed that community tenure by itself, without adequate supporting care, can allow disabled persons to function adequately. The basic point, however, should be clear: The manner in which the behavior is conceptualized has an important impact not only on the way the person affected sees himself and his efforts at continuing coping but also on the way he is perceived by the community in which he resides.

The study of the way people come to understand and conceptualize experiential change is perhaps the area most neglected in studies of reactions and help seeking. Although a variety of interview studies have attempted to reconstruct the attribution process, such retrospective reports may be closer to reconstructions of what took place in light of later experience than accurate descriptions of the attribution process itself. Although such studies as those of Clausen and Yarrow (122) provide a good intuitive sense of the processes of attribution and normalization, by focusing on patients we lose an understanding of those instances in which behavior was normalized and the person concerned did not become a patient. Moreover, retrospective reports may come to emphasize the more dramatic and unusual aspects of the process, neglecting those that are more mundane. Furthermore, to the extent that the individuals involved are coping with the problem effectively through attributions that normalize unusual feeling states, they may not experience consciously the extent to which their frames of reference are changing. Davis (160), in a study of adaptations to having a child with polio, followed families for several years and observed that although they changed significantly in confronting the crisis, they often failed to recognize the extent to which they had changed. Such lack of recognition may be part of the coping process. To the extent that adaptation is smooth and effective, one would anticipate that the actors themselves would not fully recognize the extent to which the situation required them to change.

As an initial formulation of the processes of illness attribution, it appears that persons tend to notice bodily sensations when they depart from more ordinary feelings. Each person tends to appraise new bodily perceptions against prior experience and his anticipations based on the experiences of others and on general knowledge. Many symptoms occur so commonly throughout life that they become part of ordinary expectations and are experienced as normal variations. Other experiences, such as a young girl's first menstruation, might be extremely frightening if prior social learning has not occurred, but would ordinarily be accepted as normal if it had. In analyzing responses to more unusual symptoms it is instructive to examine situations in which normal attribution processes become disrupted as a consequence of special kinds of learning; in this regard hypochondriasis among medical students is an interesting example.

Medical Students' Disease

It has frequently been observed that medical students experience symptom complexes that they ascribe to some pathologic process. This syndrome appears to have high prevalence—approximately 70 percent (347; 783). Factors contributing to the development of this syndrome usually include social stress and anxiety, bodily symptoms, and detailed but incomplete information on a disease involving symptoms similar to the bodily indications perceived by the student. Hunter, Lohrenz, and Schwartzman describe the process as follows:

> The following constellation of factors occurs regularly. The student is under internal or external stress, such as guilt, fear of examinations, and the like. He notices in himself some innocuous physiological or psychological dysfunction, e.g., extrasystoles, forgetfulness. He attaches to this an undeserved importance of a fearsome kind usually modeled after some patient he has seen, clinical anecdote he has heard, or member of his family who has been ill [347, p. 148].

It is not clear from such descriptions to what extent each of the components—stress, bodily symptoms, and external cues—is necessary to the process and what specific role each plays. Because both stress and bodily symptoms are common among students in general, and the phenomenon in question does not appear to occur so dramatically or with equal prevalence among them, it seems reasonable to suspect that the medical student's access to more detailed medical information contributes greatly to the attribution process.

Using the Schachter-Singer (611) formulation (discussed in Chapter 4), "medical students' disease" can be characterized as follows. Medical school exposes students to continuing stress resulting from the rapid pace, examinations, anxieties in dealing with new clinical experiences, and so on. Students are thus emotionally aroused with some frequency and, like others in the population, experience a high prevalence of transient symptoms. Exposure to specific knowledge about disease provides the student with a new framework for identifying and giving meaning to previously neglected bodily feelings. Diffuse and ambiguous symptoms regarded as normal in the past may be reconceptualized within the context of newly acquired knowledge. Existing social stress may heighten bodily sensations through autonomic activation, making the student more aware of his bodily state and motivating him to account for what he is experiencing. New information that the student may have about possible disease and similarity between the symptoms of a particular condition and his own symptoms establish a link that he would have more difficulty making if he were less informed. Moreover, the student—in the process of acquiring new medical information—may begin to pay greater attention to his own bodily experiences and may also attempt to imagine the way certain symptoms feel. This tendency may assist the development of the syndrome.

Woods, Natterson, and Silverman (783) found that, contrary to usual belief, "medical students' disease" was not an isolated experience linked to a particular aspect of medical training, but occurred with relatively equal frequency throughout the four years of medical school. Thus the syndrome's occurrence may depend on the coincidental existence of student arousal, the presence of particular bodily feelings, and cues acquired from new information about disease that seem relevant to existing symptoms. Hunter, Lohrenz, and Schwartzman (347), on the basis of their study, conclude that symptom choice is influenced by "a variety of accidental, historical and learning factors, in which the mechanism of identification plays a major role."

It is noteworthy that "medical students' disease" terminates readily and within a relatively short time. Woods and his colleagues (783) report that the syndrome sometimes disappears spontaneously, but more often through further study of the illness or by direct or covert consultation with an instructor or physician. They suggest that it is "reassurance" that limits the condition, but the term is exceedingly vague and has a variety of meanings. Most reports in the literature concerning more persistent hypochondria suggest that such patients are not easily reassured, and thus it would be useful to have more specific understanding of the mechanism by which "medical students' disease" is short-circuited.

One way in which the medical student discovers errors in attribution is through further understanding of diagnostics. As he learns more about the disease he may discover that the attribution he made does not really fit or that a great variety of symptoms may be characteristic of the clinical picture. Another possibility is that the stress in the student's life subsides with some relief in his anxiety, and his awareness of his symptoms may decline. The way the incorrect attribution comes to be corrected has never been studied, but possibly the student's growing knowledge of symptomatology sharpens his judgment about his own complaints. If clear knowledge is indeed necessary to disconfirm the attribution, the syndrome should be more persistent when knowledge is disputed and uncertain. In this light it is of interest that "medical students' disease" of a psychiatric character appears to be less transient and more chronic than such syndromes that develop around fears of physical illness. In the psychiatric area it is more difficult to separate the attribution from the entity to which the attribution is made.

Another issue concerns the origins of the initial attribution of illness. The conclusion reached by Hunter, Lohrenz, and Schwartzman (347) that identification plays a major part has already been noted, and is the most generally accepted psychiatric point of view. It appears however, that the concept of identification may be too diffuse and imprecise in encompassing such varied phenomena as the association between mother and child, audience and public figure, and the occurrence of a stomach pain and seeing a movie concerning a person with stomach cancer. An alternative perspective from which to analyze such influences would involve consideration of factors affecting the perception of personal vulnerability.

Although persons may vary widely in their sense of invulnerability—which appears to be linked with their levels of self-esteem—psychological survival generally depends on the ability of people to protect themselves from anxieties and fears involving low-risk occurrences to which all persons are exposed or dangers that they are powerless to prevent (362; 779). Feelings of invulnerability are threatened under circumstances of greatly increased risk such as combat and new and difficult experiences, but even under these conditions persons generally manage to maintain a relatively strong sense of invulnerability through various psychological defense processes and coping actions. However, a "near miss" can dramatically undermine one's sense of invulnerability and may lead to extreme anxiety and fear reactions. The death of a close friend or co-worker in combat (299), being involved in an automobile accident in which others are killed or suffer bodily injury, and learning that someone who is defined as having ability comparable to one's own has failed an important examination that one is intending to take (479) or serve to threaten the sense of security.

Basic to the undermining of a sense of invulnerability are social comparison processes. It is much less difficult to explain injury to people of unlike characteristics without threat to oneself in that one can attribute the injury to aspects of the person that are different from one's own. When such persons are more like oneself in terms of age, sex, life style, or routine, it is much more difficult not to perceive oneself at risk; personal intimacy and physical proximity similarly increase feelings of vulnerability.

Various studies suggest that self-esteem is an intervening variable between situation and response. Although the role of self-esteem is not fully clear, one possibility is that persons with high self-esteem see themselves as more capable of dealing with threatening situations and thus are less vulnerable (429). Awareness that one is able to cope and that one has had success in the past dealing with adversity insulates the person from anxiety (416). This concept of the self-esteem effect appears most reasonable in cases in which coping ability can affect the situation and realistically reduce threat; it is not so obvious that self-esteem reduces a sense of threat of impending illness. A sense of confidence may generalize to situations even when it is not particularly realistic, or may lead persons to focus less on bodily indications. This is clearly an area for more focused inquiry.

In sum, it has been maintained that most ordinarily occurring symptoms are considered normal or are explained in conventional frameworks, as when muscle aches are attributed to unaccustomed physical activity or indigestion to overeating. When such ordinary symptoms occur concomitantly with emotional arousal and when they are not easily explained within conventional and commonly available understandings, external cues become important in defining their character and importance. Such cues may be fortuitous or they may be the consequence of prior experience, cultural learning, or personal need for secondary gain.

The Historical Context

Reactions to illness are descriptive of the cultural and historical situation at a particular point in time. It is essential to distinguish between analytic generalizations, such as in the discussion of "medical students' disease," that may not be tied to any concrete historical context and generalizations that may be true at one point in time but not at some other. Much of the descriptive research on illness behavior linking social class, education, ethnicity, and other social factors to illness response and utilization of particular services may vary a great deal over time. For example, much of the literature of the past decade demonstrates certain continuities in the characteristics of individuals drawn to psychiatric care. Existing studies generally agree that such persons are more likely to be of higher educational and income levels, of urban or suburban residence, of Jewish identification or of low religious participation, and women (304; 374; 619). At a more analytic level it has been argued that persons inclined to seek psychiatric care are more likely to have developed vocabularies of distress (46), to have a cosmopolitan orientation (446), or to be part of a social circle of others who are friends and supporters of psychotherapy (374). In short, seeking care for psychiatric problems and remaining receptive to psychotherapy have been seen by a variety of students of the problem as indicative of being part of a subcultural milieu that is encouraging and supportive and that values the nature of the service given.

To complicate the issue, however, it is necessary to take into account that types of treatment are themselves linked to social movements, and have their own rise and decline over time as the appropriate fashion for a particular subgroup facing life problems or existential dilemmas. Psychoanalysis, for example, developed its roots in urban areas with many practitioners of urban, middle-class, Jewish origins. It is not surprising, therefore, that this form of therapy attracted persons with certain social characteristics and life inclinations. As the psychotherapeutic movement developed, it became more heterogeneous in its geographic location and the types of practitioners trained; as these characteristics changed, so did the clients drawn into treatment. Although there is no definitive study, there is every indication that both psychotherapists and their patients are becoming more like the general population than was true 20 or 30 years ago. Thus the social characteristics of clients drawn to such therapies are likely to change over time, becoming less distinctive. The kinds of result researchers are likely to obtain on the descriptive aspects of the selection of patients depend in part on the point in time at which they take a cross section of a continuing process.

Strategies for Studying Illness Response

At any single point in time, several interrelated issues exist in understanding the significance of sociocultural differences among patients who seek particular types of treatment (296). First, it is necessary to distinguish the extent to which social characteristics are related to seeking treatment because these are also related to the prevalence of certain problems requiring treatment. It is not clear to what extent these social characteristics are related to the occurrence of problems or to the care-seeking process. Second, it is necessary to distinguish the extent to which certain sociocultural processes are related to the inclination to seek care (or dependency on helping sources) as compared with their effect on the use of a particular source of care. It is obvious that Jewish identification, although related in many studies to the use of psychotherapy, does not increase the propensity to use Catholic counselors. Most studies in the literature confuse the issue of generalized sociocultural selection in seeking assistance for mental disorder with the issue of selection of specific forms of help (296).

Different patterns of illness behavior may be viewed from at least two general perspectives that are supplementary to one another. Such patterns of behavior may be seen as a product of social and cultural conditioning, because they may be experienced and enacted naturally in the social contexts within which they appear relevant. Or they may be seen as part of a larger coping process in which illness behavior is only one aspect of a coping repertory, an attempt to make an unstable, challenging situation more manageable for the person who is encountering difficulty.

Sociocultural Differences in Illness Behavior

Cultures are so recognizably different that variations in illness behavior in different societies hardly need demonstration. The idea implicit in much anthropological work is that primitive conceptions of illness are part of a learned cultural complex and are functionally associated with other aspects of cultural response to environmental threat. Some earlier investigations of illness behavior in America were based on the same idea—that different patterns of response to illness are culturally conditioned and functionally relevant. Thus Koos (399) observed that upper-class persons were more likely than lower-class persons to view themselves as ill when they had particular symptoms; when they were questioned about specific symptoms, they reported more frequently than lower-class persons that they would seek the doctor's advice. Koos's book provides many examples of circumstances in which decisions about health were weighed in relation to family and work needs, as well as in terms of family finances and other social needs competing with health care. Illness responses were thus described as part of a constellation of needs making different demands on a person's efforts, concerns, and finances. Saunders (609) described in some detail the differences between "Anglos" and Spanish-speaking persons in the American Southwest in attitudes and responses toward illness and in the use of medical facilities. Whereas the Anglos preferred modern medical science and hospitalization for many illnesses, the Spanish-speaking people were more likely to rely on folk medicine and family care and support that were more consistent with their cultural conceptions. Similarly, Clark (116) has described how Mexican Americans view various life situations and symptoms as health problems, in contrast to physicians who do not view these conditions with similar seriousness and alarm. Other problems among these people that are ignored and undefined are seen by physicians as serious health problems. Similar observations have been made concerning various American Indian groups and in a variety of other cultural contexts (424; 473; 553).

The role of cultural differences in illness behavior was nicely described by Zborowski (793) who, in a study of ethnic reactions to pain in a New York City hospital, observed that while Jewish and Italian patients responded to pain in an emotional fashion, tending to exaggerate pain experiences, "Old Americans" tended to be more stoical and "objective," and Irish more frequently denied pain. Zborowski also noted a difference in the attitude underlying Italian and Jewish concern about pain. While the Italian subjects primarily sought relief from pain and were relatively satisfied when such relief was obtained, the Jewish subjects were mainly concerned with the meaning and significance of their pain and the consequences of pain for their future welfare and health. In trying to explain these cultural differences, Zborowski reports that Jewish and Italian patients related that their mothers showed overprotective and overconcerned attitudes about the child's health and participation in sports, and that they were constantly warned of the advisability of avoiding colds, fights, and other threatening situations. Zborowski reports that

> crying in complaint is responded to by parents with sympathy, concern and help. By their over-protective and worried attitude they foster complaining and tears. The child learns to pay attention to each painful experience and to look for help and sympathy which are readily given to him. In Jewish families, where not only a slight sensation of pain but also each deviation from the child's normal behavior is looked upon as a sign of illness, the child is prone to acquire anxieties with regard to the meaning and significance of these manifestations [793, p. 28].

Although Zborowski presents something of a caricature, it is clear that he views the etiology of these behavioral patterns and attitudes as inherent in the familial response to the child's health and illnesses.

Suchman (681; 682), in a study of 5,340 persons in different ethnic groups in New York City, found that the more ethnocentric and socially cohesive groups included more persons who knew little about disease, were skeptical toward professional medical care, and reported a dependent pattern when ill. A more recent study of a Mormon population in Utah (261) suggests that Suchman's conclusions may have been subtantially influenced by the specific ethnic groups he studied. An ethnocentric and socially cohesive group that supports the use of modern medicine may encourage high acceptance and use of medical services.

The existing literature on illness behavior suggests considerable consistency in ethnic variations in illness behavior. Although such trends are clear in general, it is essential to note that the variation within groups is much greater than it is between groups, and thus such correlations among ethnic groups are not very useful for individual predictions. In any case, trends in illness behavior patterns differ in various groups and these patterns can have both healthy and unhealthy consequences. For example, the traditional concern about health among Jewish persons—especially the health of children—can under some circumstances lead to overconcern and encourage doubts and anxiety. Such concern and attention can also encourage a high standard of infant rearing and caring, as suggested by an early study of infant mortality among immigrants to America, which showed that although the Jewish group was foreign born, had just as many children, and had an income much lower than that of native-born whites, this group had the lowest rate of infant mortality of all of the groups studied, including the native-born white population (22).

Various studies reflect the importance of cultural and developmental experiences in determining reactions to threatening circumstances. Schachter (610), in a set of impressive experimental studies, showed that first-born and only children were more likely than other adults to desire to be in the presence of another person when threatened in adult life. Schachter believes that the attention given to the first child and the inexperience of parents are likely to instill a greater dependence on others in first-born and only children as compared with later-born children. Although birth order has not been studied directly in illness-behavior studies, several other investigations support the idea that past experience, habits, and social values help define—consciously and unconsciously—the manner in which complaints are made and the alternatives that will be utilized in challenging circumstances. These may vary by size of family and by birth order.

Under conditions of manageable difficulties, persons have a tendency to normalize or ignore symptoms that do not become too severe. For example, in a study by Mechanic and Volkart discussed earlier, it was found that when illness is of a kind that is common and familiar and when the course of the illness is predictable, presentation of the illness for medical scrutiny is substantially related to an index of inclination to use medical services (503). As symptoms become more atypical, less familiar, and less predictable in their course, the role of social and situational factors in prompting a person toward medical attention becomes less important. Cultural and social conditioning thus plays a major though not an exclusive role in patterns of illness behavior. Ethnic membership, family composition, peer pressures, and age-sex role learning to some extent influence attitudes toward risks, the significance of common threats, and receptivity to medical services, but the nature and quality of symptoms are also important.

Vocabularies of Distress

It is apparent that social learning will affect the vocabularies persons use to define their complaints and their orientations to seeking various kinds of care. It is reasonable to expect that persons from origins in which the expression of symptoms and seeking help is permissible and encouraged will be more likely to do so, particularly under stressful circumstances. In contrast, in cultural contexts in which complaining is discouraged, persons experiencing distress may seek a variety of alternative means for dealing with their difficulties. Zborowski (793), in describing the "Old American" family, stressed the tendency of the mother to teach the child to take pain "like a man," not to be a sissy, and not to cry. Such training, according to Zborowski, does not discourage use of the doctor, but it implies that such use will be based on physical needs rather than on emotional concerns. One might anticipate that persons with such backgrounds might be reluctant to express psychological distress directly, but might express such distress through the presentation of physical complaints. Kerckhoff and Back (382), in a study of the diffusion among female employees of a southern mill of a hysterical illness alleged to be caused by an unknown insect, found that the prevalence of the condition was high among women under strain who could not admit they had a problem and who did not know how to cope with it.

Pauline Bart (46), in comparing women who entered a neurology service but were discharged with psychiatric diagnoses with women entering a psychiatric service of the same hospital, found them to be less educated, more rural, of lower socioeconomic status, and less likely to be Jewish than those who came directly to psychiatric service. Bart suggests that these two groups of women were differentiated by their vocabularies of discomfort, which affected the manner in which they presented themselves. She also observed that 52 percent of the psychiatric patients on the neurology service had had a hysterectomy as compared with only 21 percent on the psychiatric service. The findings suggest that such patients may be expressing psychological distress through physical attributions, and thus exposing themselves to a variety of unnecessary medical procedures.

Reaction Pattern and Physiological Response

Observations from field studies concerning ethnic differences in the perception of pain have, in general, withstood not only repeated study but also more detailed scrutiny under laboratory conditions. Sternbach and Tursky (668), for example, brought Irish, Jewish, Italian, and "Yankee" housewives into a psychophysiological laboratory in which they administered pain by electric shock, recording skin potential responses. Their findings tended to support some of the observations made by Zborowski. They found, for example, that Italian women showed significantly lower tolerance for shock, and fewer of them would accept the full range of shock stimulation used in the experiment. The investigators believe that this response is consistent with the Italian tendency to focus on the immediacy of pain itself, as compared with the future orientation of the Jewish concern. Similarly, they believe that their finding that Yankee housewives had faster and more complete adaptation of the diphasic palmar skin potential has an attitudinal correlate to their "matter-of-fact" orientation to pain. As they note:

> This is illustrated by our Yankee subjects' modal attitude toward traumata, as they verbalized it in the interviews: "You take things in your stride." No such action-oriented, adapting phrase was used by the members of the other groups. The similarly undemonstrative Irish subjects may "keep a tight upper lip" but "fear the worst," a noxious stimulus being a burden to be endured and suffered in silence [668; p. 245].

We must be careful in generalizing conclusions from laboratory pain studies to pathological pain experiences. Henry Beecher (55), former anesthetist-in-chief at the Massachusetts General Hospital, reported on the failure of 15 different research groups to establish any dependable effects of even large doses of morphine on pain of experimental origin in man, although the effect of morphine on pathological pain is substantial. He found it necessary to distinguish between pain as an *original sensation* and pain as a *psychic reaction*. As Beecher notes, one of the difficulties with most forms of laboratory pain is that it minimizes the psychic reaction, which plays an essential role in pain associated with illness. For example, in a comparative study of pain he asked a group of wounded soldiers and a group of male civilian patients undergoing major surgery the same questions about their desire for pain medication. While only one-third of the soldiers wanted medication to relieve their pain, 80 percent of the civilians wanted such pain relief, although they were suffering from far less tissue trauma. He explains the variation in terms of differing definitions of pain in the two circumstances. The soldier's wound, Beecher explains, was an escape from the battlefield and the possibility of being killed; the civilian viewed surgical pain as a depressing, calamitous event. Beecher reports that the civilian group reported strikingly more frequent and severe pain, and he concludes that there is no simple, direct relationship between the wound per se and the pain experienced. He further concludes that morphine acts primarily on the reactive component of the pain experience, largely through a process of "mental clouding."

The reactive or definitional component in illness has long been recognized as a significant aspect not only in the definition of the condition but also in the patient's response to treatment. Physicians working with the severely ill are often impressed by the attitudinal component and its influence on the patient's condition. In its extreme form physicians have commented on the importance of the patient's "will to live," although it has been difficult to quantify this phenomenon or to present clear evidence in support of its importance. At best we have anecdotal reports of preparation for death and actual death following witchcraft, and we have already noted some physiological explanations that have been offered to explain the mechanisms involved in such impressive happenings (103; 229). If we are to integrate such events with our common conceptual schemes we require a better understanding of such phenomena as they occur in more subtle but also more readily observable forms.

The definitional components in response to difficult circumstances have been observed in natural situations in which physiological response also has been studied. Friedman and his colleagues (250; 251), in making observations of parents anticipating the death of their children who were suffering from neoplastic diseases, found that urinary 17-hydroxycorticosteroid levels in parents would vary from one parent to another and from one period in the child's illness to another. The period of highest distress as measured physiologically occurred for most parents well before the death of the child, the most common situation being when the child was put on the critical list for the first time. For some of the parents the death of the child seemed to be a relief, and it appears as if they had already worked through a substantial part of their grief prior to the death of the child. Other parents, who maintained hope despite evidence to the contrary and who showed little marked acceleration in 17-hydroxycorticosteroid levels at crucial points during the illness, seemed to experience a marked acceleration after the child died. The study illustrates both the tremendous variability in response to difficult circumstances and the probable link between coping reactions and physiological responses under stress (see also 658).

Illness Behavior as a Coping Response

The idea that illness is stressful and that it may engender further life difficulties requires no elaboration. What is interesting to the behavioral scientist, however, is the tremendous variability in response to what is presumably the same illness condition. While one person will hardly acknowledge a condition and refuse to allow it to alter his life, another with a milder form of the same condition will display profound social and psychological disabilities.

An emotional component has often been seen in the etiology or precipitation of illness (289; 326; 512; 591; 780). Often less appreciated is the importance of life difficulties in influencing illness behavior. Indeed, it appears from a careful scrutiny of psychosomatic evidence that distress is often more influential in its effects on seeking help and on the expression of illness than it is on the actual occurrence of the condition. What little evidence we have on this point suggests that a complaint of trivial illness may be one way of seeking reassurance and support through a recognized and socially acceptable relationship when it is difficult for the patient to present the underlying problem in an undisguised form without displaying weaknesses and vulnerabilities contrary to expected and learned behavior patterns.. In such circumstances the real problem may not even be consciously recognized. Various analysts of the medical consultation, such as Balint (42), note that the symptoms that the patient presents are frequently of no special consequence, but serve to establish a legitimate relation between patient and doctor. He maintains that the presentation of somatic complaints often masks an underlying emotional problem that is frequently the major reason the patient has sought help.

The response to bodily indications may also depend on the social acceptability of certain types of complaints, and even the nature and site of the complaint, according to Balint, are matters frequently negotiated between patient and physician. Harold Wolff (782) has also noted that minor pains in certain parts of the body may be more frequent because they are culturally more acceptable and because they bring greater sympathetic response. Hes (321), in a study of hypochondriac patients referred to a psychiatric outpatient clinic, noted the inhibition of emotional expression as a result of culturally determined taboos on complaining about one's fate and a culturally determined excessive use of bodily language.

Patients who express psychological distress through a physical language tend to be uneducated or to come from cultural groups in which the expression of emotional distress is inhibited. Such patients frequently face serious life difficulties and social stress, but the subculture within which they function does not allow legitimate expression of their suffering nor are others attentive to their pleas for support when they are made. Because of their experiences these patients frequently feel, sometimes consciously but more frequently on a level of less than full awareness, that expression of their difficulties is a sign of weakness and will be deprecated. They thus dwell on bodily complaints, some that are ever present and others that are concomitant with their experience of emotional distress. These patients are often elderly, lonely, and insecure, and they may be inactive enough to have time to dwell on their difficulties. When such patients seek out physicians they may use their physical symptoms and complaints as a plea for help.

Toward a General Theory of Help Seeking

If we are to make progress in the study of illness behavior, it becomes necessary to move beyond gross cultural and social differences in behavior patterns toward the development of a social-psychological model that gives a clearer conception of the processes involved when someone seeks help. In recent years there have been several attempts to do this (371; 379; 477; 597; 672; 795). Rosenstock (597) has suggested that health behavior relevant to a given problem is determined by the extent to which a person sees a problem as having both serious consequences and a high probability of occurrence. He further believes that behavior emerges from conflicting goals and motives and that action will follow those motives that are most salient and are perceived as most valuable. This perspective has been developed into a "health-belief model," and has been studied in some detail (54). Zola (795), approaching the problem from another perspective, has attempted to delineate five timing "triggers" in patients' decisions to seek medical care. The first pattern he calls "interpersonal crisis," in which the situation calls attention to the symptoms and causes the patient to dwell on them. The second trigger he calls "social interference"; in this situation the symptoms do not change but come to threaten a valued social activity. The third trigger—"the presence of sanctioning"—involves others telling him to seek care. Fourth, Zola discusses "perceived threat" and, finally, "nature and quality of the symptoms." The latter trigger involves similarity of symptoms to previous ones or to those of friends. Zola reports the impression that these triggers have different effects in various social strata and ethnic groups.

Ten Determinants

In the later sections of this chapter I shall present a more detailed model of help-seeking processes than is characteristic of earlier discussions. It is useful at this point, however, to list the types of variable affecting the response to illness that will characterize the analysis:

1. Visibility, recognizability, or perceptual salience of deviant signs and symptoms.
2. The extent to which the symptoms are perceived as serious (that is, the person's estimate of the present and future probabilities of danger).
3. The extent to which symptoms disrupt family, work, and other social activities.
4. The frequency of the appearance of the deviant signs or symptoms, their persistence, or their frequency of recurrence.

5. The tolerance threshold of those who are exposed to and evaluate the deviant signs and symptoms.
6. Available information, knowledge, and cultural assumptions
   and understandings of the evaluator.
7. Basic needs that lead to denial.
8. Needs competing with illness responses.
9. Competing possible interpretations that can be assigned to the
   symptoms once they are recognized.
10. Availability of treatment resources, physical proximity, and
    psychological and monetary costs of taking action (included are
    not only physical distance and costs of time, money, and effort,
    but also such costs as stigma, social distance, and feelings of hu-
    miliation).

There is considerable overlap among some of these variables, but consideration of each individual category provides us with clues that we
may otherwise neglect. When we inspect these ten groups of determinants, it becomes clear that what may appear salient to the definer
may not appear relevant to the physician. For example, recognizability
of symptoms is not necessarily correlated with medical views of their
seriousness. Similarly, some symptoms that are, for example, disfigur-
ing or disruptive or that bring about work disability may be self-limited
and medically trivial, while other symptoms (such as signs of cancer)
may have initially no disruptive effects at all. Yet one of the major cues
patients use in deciding to seek help is the disruption of their activities.
Illness behavior and the decision to seek medical advice frequently involve, from the patient's point of view, a rational attempt to make sense
of his problem and cope with it within the limits of his intelligence and
his social and cultural understandings, but this does not make it rational from a medical perspective.

Two Basic Questions

Whether we concern ourselves with the study of acute physical
disorders or with those more clearly characterized as chronic and behavioral problems, we face two distinct questions that are usually
mixed together in the data with which we commonly work. First, we
seek to understand the particular aspects of a person or his environment that lead to aberrant states of the person. Implicit in the statement
of this question is that we have some criterion for differentiating the
class of aberrants from the class of nonaberrants. Adequate case-finding
procedures that allow us reliably to differentiate cases from noncases
are not always available. Once a particular set of case-finding procedures is adopted, a variety of disciplines and approaches may be in-

volved in attempting to understand the reasons some people develop in particular aberrant ways while others do not. Questions of etiology are not the exclusive province of any one discipline and approach.

The second major issue implicated in the data involves the assumption that a certain degree of aberrance is given. The researcher attempts to ascertain the factors that lead to differential identification, definition, and treatment of aberrant persons. Here central concern is placed on the varied social processes involved in recognizing aberrance, labeling it, and dealing with it (50; 427). Also implicated are the various environmental factors we will discuss in chapter 16, which may lead to the exacerbation or the alleviation of symptom states. Stating what is logically correct in approaching a problem does not necessarily imply that it is possible to study such problems in a pure form unencumbered by other issues. The investigator who studies behavioral processes in the real world is frequently unable to isolate a group of persons with equal disease of a specified kind who can be studied in reference to etiological factors. At best he attempts to approximate these research conditions, and if he clearly understands the kinds of data that are desirable, he will find many opportunities to study etiological and other influences in a relatively rigorous way.

Unfortunately, a great deal of the literature concerned with illness and deviant behavior confuses the problem of which of the two questions specified is being attacked. Illness is rarely separated from illness behavior or from social and cultural patterns, even when it is possible to do so. This failure may result from adopting a traditional clinical perspective that assumes that aberrant persons come to the practitioner's attention because they are aberrant rather than as a consequence of an interaction between illness factors and personal and social processes. Studies that begin with known or treated cases of particular disorders risk confusing etiology with social and psychological processes leading to care unless the relationship between treated cases and untreated cases is clearly known. As already noted, such samples of known cases may be good approximations of all cases in particular illness areas, but this cannot be assumed and it is frequently untrue. At present we have insufficient information about the relationships between treated and untreated cases, particularly in the area of the behavioral disorders, to reach firm conclusions regarding the relationship between known and true total aberrance.

Examples of Help-Seeking Research

It is important to repeat that our knowledge about the processes that take persons along various paths to helping practitioners is limited. At most one can sketch the range of such processes and the length they can go in various cultural contexts and among various social groups. We know very little about the ways people use their friends and acquaintances in attempting to cope with distress, and not much more about the use of a great variety of nonmedical practitioners such as clergymen and lawyers, semimedical persons such as druggists, and marginal practitioners such as chiropractors and faith healers. Obviously such factors as cultural and group organization, kinship and friendship patterns, and medical orientations are important, but the help-seeking processes themselves need much illumination.

As Freidson (234; 235) has pointed out, patient behavior may vary widely, involving differing attempts to deal with the condition. The person may first try some remedies; he may discuss his troubles with neighbors, friends, and fellow workers in a casual way and explore various alternative explanations for the way he is feeling. He may ask the advice of others as to whether he should seek the care of a physician and which one; he may go to the doctor on a trial visit, comparing the diagnosis with his own conceptions and diagnoses made by friends and acquaintances. In short, as Freidson has pointed out, professional help seeking may occur through a lay referral system. In contrast, lay referral systems may have a very small influence on the person's behavior, or they may not exist at all. Freidson has discussed lay referral systems in the following way:

> Indeed, the whole process of seeking help involves a network of potential consultants, from the intimate and informal confines of the nuclear family through successively more select, distant, and authoritative laymen, until the "professional" is reached. This network of consultants, which is part of the structure of the local lay community and which imposes form on the seeking of help, might be called the "lay referral structure." Taken together with the cultural understandings involved in the process, we may speak of it as the "lay referral system." . . .
>
> Insofar as the idea of diagnostic authority is based on assumpted hereditary or divine "gift" or intrinsically personal knowledge of one's "own" health, necessary for effective treatment, professional authority is unlikely to be recognized at all. And, insofar as the cultural definitions of illness contradict those of professional culture, the referral process will not often lead to the professional practitioner. In turn, with an extended lay referral structure, lay definitions are supported by a variety of lay consultants, when the sick man looks about for help. Obviously, here the folk practitioner will be used by most, the professional practitioner being called for minor illnesses only, or, in illness considered critical, called only by the socially isolated deviate, and by the sick man desperately snatching at straws.
>
> The opposite extreme of the indigenous extended system is found when the lay culture and the professional culture are much alike and when the lay referral system is truncated or there is none at all. Here, the prospective client is pretty much on his own, guided more or less by cultural understandings and

his own experience, with few lay consultants to support or discourage his search for help. Since his knowledge and understandings are much like the physician's, he may take a great deal of time trying to treat himself, but nonetheless will go directly from self-treatment to a physician [234, pp. 377–78].

It would be oversimplification to assume, once we have isolated a pattern of care seeking and use of "lay referral systems," that a similar pattern will apply in different kinds of illness situations. The meanings attributed to illness vary widely, and with changing meanings variations in help-seeking patterns may occur. In some cases, for example, relatives and friends may encourage treatment, while in others they may deny the presence of symptoms and be reluctant to define the condition, as frequently happens with mental disorders. Various investigators have found that the patient and his family were reluctant to recognize the patient's difficulty as a psychiatric illness (120; 122; 608; 623; 790; 791). Often the problem was viewed as a physical condition, fatigue, or a reflection of the patient's personality or character. When the husband's symptoms were accompanied by physical indications, the wife frequently urged him to seek the help of a doctor. However, when the patient's difficult behavior was seen as a reflection of his personality, his meanness, or his lack of consideration, the problem was often thought of within a moral framework, and it frequently involved family conflicts.

A National Institute of Mental Health (NIMH) study group has described five trends that characterize the process through which wives attempt to cope with their husbands' increasingly difficult behavior (790):

1. The wife's first recognition of a problem depends on the accumulation of behavior that is not readily understandable or acceptable to her.
2. This forces her to examine the situation and adjust her expectations for herself and her husband in such a way as to account for his deviant response.
3. The wife's interpretation of the problem shifts back and forth from seeing the situation as normal on one occasion to abnormal on another.
4. She tends to make continuous adaptations to the typical behavior of her spouse, waiting for additional cues that will either confirm her definition or lead to a new one. She mobilizes strong defenses against her husband's deviant behavior.
5. Finally a point is reached at which the wife can no longer sustain a definition of normality and cope with her husband's behavior.

As Yarrow observes:

> The most obvious form of defense in the wife's response is the tendency to *normalize* the husband's neurotic and psychotic symptoms. His behavior is explained, justified or made acceptable by seeing it also in herself or by assuring herself that the particular behavior occurs again and again among persons who are not ill. . . . When behavior cannot be normalized, it can be made to seem less severe or less important in a total picture than an outsider might see it. By finding some grounds for the behavior or something explainable about it, the wife achieves at least momentary *attenuation* of the seriousness of it. By *balancing* acceptable with unacceptable behavior or "strange" with "normal" behavior, some wives can conclude that the husband is not seriously disturbed. Defense sometimes amounts to a thoroughgoing denial. This takes the form of denying that the behavior perceived can be interpreted in an emotional or psychiatric framework [790, pp. 22-23].

The results of the NIMH study, and those of many other investigators as well, support the observation that there is a stronger inclination to normalize or rationalize the symptoms of emotional disturbance than those of physical illness. There are various reasons to explain this tendency, including the cultural conceptions held by various groups concerning mental illness, the stigma attached to such conditions, and the difficulty—experienced even by experts—in differentiating between unusual personality traits and mental disorders. At the same time that we recognize this general tendency toward normalization of symptoms, we must also recognize the large range of variation in definitions of the same condition. Even within the area of mental illness, one finds many patients with no extraordinary symptoms who define themselves as sick or whose families view them as sick. The problem of definition is further complicated in that emotional and behavioral difficulties are often presented to the physician within the context of physical disease. Thus a frequent complaint among psychiatric patients is "nerves" or symptoms associated with psychiatric disturbance, such as inability to sleep, poor appetite, and tenseness. Although such patients and their families may be willing to see their problems within a physical perspective and seek help, they may resist redefinition of their problem as an emotional one.

Self-defined and Other-defined Illness

Now that we have developed some general approaches to the problem of help-seeking, the remainder of this chapter will be devoted to describing the processes through which symptoms are recognized and help seeking initiated. In developing this descriptive model of the identification of and response to deviant signs and symptoms, the same procedure will be followed in dealing with each relevant point. First I shall show the way this point affects our understanding of other-defined conditions, that is, those that refer to situations in which the patient resists the definitions of illness that others attempt to impose upon him. Most of the points will also be discussed in relation to self-defined illness. It will become evident that reactions to physical and psychological changes are part of the same general attribution process, and that many of the same factors are operative whether it is the person himself who is interpreting his feeling states or such attributions are made by others. In the context of help-seeking theory, mental disorder is different from physical disorder only in that the nature of the problem may lead to somewhat different scores on varying dimensions of importance. Thus any set of symptoms may be evaluated by the extent to which they disrupt normal functioning, their visibility to others, their perceived seriousness, the extent to which they elicit embarrassment, the extent to which treatment is perceived as effective, and so on. Analytically, consideration of the way a particular condition falls on relevant dimensions is more helpful than the gross distinction between psychiatric and nonpsychiatric conditions. Similarly, the underlying dimensions of the attribution process are not likely to be very different in a situation in which the person is defining his own problem in contrast to one in which interpretations of the problem are imposed by others, although in some circumstances self-attribution is more likely to involve attributions to external factors.

When I speak of self-defined illness, I do not wish to imply that lay referral systems and family pressures on the deviant may not play some part in seeking care. The major difference that should be noted between self- and other-defined conditions is that in the latter the person tends to resist the definition that others are attempting to impose upon him, and it may be necessary to bring him into treatment under great pressure and perhaps even involuntarily. Since psychotic conditions are most frequently other-defined, I shall give most attention to such conditions in discussing this category of complaints. It is important to remember, however, that under some circumstances nonpsychiatric conditions are other-defined. Other-definitions pertain frequently to the illnesses of children, and there are even occasions when great pressure is placed on adults to seek treatment for physical ailments when they deny illness or a need for care. In most situations of serious illness the sick person consults some other people before seeking care. Suchman (683) found, for example, that three-quarters of his respondents reported that they discussed their symptoms with some other person (usually a relative) before seeking care. It is Suchman's belief that such discussions result in "provisional validation" for the sick person to release himself from responsibilities and to seek medical care.

When other–defined conditions are considered, various complications occur. As noted in chapter 1, frames of reference in evaluating deviant behavior differ from one context to another, and such evaluations therefore frequently lack comparability. Also, because the evaluators may be located at different focuses of interaction with the person being defined, the behavior they see may differ significantly from the behavior seen by other evaluators. The patient's behavior at home may depart greatly from his behavior at work, and thus the view of family members and work associates need not necessarily coincide. Similarly, the behavior defined as symptomatic of mental illness may be related to an enduring stress in one aspect of the person's life rather than being indicative of a generalized response to most life situations.

Mental illness, as well as other forms of deviant response, becomes visible to others when they recognize the deviant's inability or reluctance to make expected responses in dealing with various social demands. Whether a particular behavior is viewed as a sign of physical or mental illness or as some deviant response such as selfishness or eccentricity will be contingent on the criteria used by evaluators. These criteria will depend on the evaluators' information, knowledge, values, orientations, and sometimes even on their own psychological needs. Thus such criteria may vary from person to person and from situation to situation.

The evaluator attempts to comprehend the deviant's behavior within the framework of his understanding and to assess the patient's motivation in relation to his actions. In a sense, the evaluator attempts to empathize with the patient (or in Mead's terms to take the role of the patient). If he feels he understands the motivation and there appears to be a rational link between normal motivation and the behavior, he is likely to see the behavior within the framework of badness (369). However, if the empathy process yields uncertainty and confusion as to what motives may have contributed to the response, the behavior is more likely to be labeled as odd, strange, or sick. As the population becomes more sophisticated in psychological thinking and in their understanding of psychodynamic ideas, it becomes possible for them to "understand" behavior psychologically and yet regard it as a reflection of sickness.

There are many behaviors, however, for which it is extremely difficult to make a decision as to whether the response is bad or sick, and much disagreement may result even among experts, depending on their frames of reference and their notions of responsibility. Many psychiatric symptoms are exaggerations of commonly occurring behavioral characteristics, and although the evaluator may find the person concerned difficult or selfish, he may tend to accept the behavior as part of the person's social character until it becomes too unbearable to tolerate ("the last straw"). There are other occasions when the deviant gives indications of appearing sick and bad at the same time, as when an understandable crime is committed, but is accompanied by bizarre patterns of behavior that are not of benefit to a rational criminal's welfare. It thus may become difficult to decide whether the deviant is a criminal, a potential mental patient, or both. These problems result in part because of the ambiguity of the concept of mental illness. In general, the concept of mental illness is frequently used as a social rather than as a disease label, and thus in practice the concept serves as a residual category for deviant behavior having no other clearly specified social label.

Variables in Illness Response

In reviewing the importance of social definitions in response to illness and help seeking, it is essential to remember the character of the symptoms themselves. Much of the behavior of sick persons is a direct product of the specific symptoms they experience: their intensity, the quality of discomfort they cause, their persistence, and so on. Many symptoms leave the person little alternative but to recognize that he has a medical condition and that medical care is essential. It is unlikely that a person experiencing a temperature of 105° will find definitions alternative to the idea that he is sick. And no matter how stoical a person is or how extreme his attitudes toward symptoms may be, a fractured leg, a broken back, a severe heart attack, an extreme psychosis, or any of a variety of other conditions is likely to bring him into care.

Suchman (683) has provided some evidence involving the influence of disturbing symptoms. He selected 137 cases from his larger survey of 5,340 persons in the Washington Heights community of New York City. This subsample included adults who during the two months previous to the interview had a specific illness episode that required three or more visits to the physician and incapacitated the person for five or more consecutive days or required hospitalization for a day or more. Thus these data pertain to a sample of relatively serious episodes of illness. Suchman found that pain was clearly the most important initial sign that something was wrong, and was mentioned by two-thirds of the respondents. Considerably less important were fever and chills (17 percent) and shortness of breath (10 percent). These symptoms were "usually severe, continuous, incapacitating, and unalleviated" and approximately three-quarters of the respondents reported that they immediately saw the symptoms as indicative of an illness. Although we do not know from this study how symptoms were perceived by those who did not seek medical care, this investigation does confirm that many of those who took action were motivated by the manner in which their symptoms developed and became evident.

A similar situation appears to exist in the area of psychiatric illness. Although there are vast differences in willingness to tolerate bizarre and difficult behavior, few relatives appear willing to house a patient who is suicidal, homicidal, incontinent, hallucinatory, delusional, or disoriented (168; 423). In short, if a person's behavior is sufficiently bizarre and disruptive, the probability is high that he will come into care. Social definitions of illness are relevant because many important and serious illness conditions develop in such a way that they are not particularly striking in their impact. It is this ambiguity surrounding the occurrence and severity of illness that makes the sociological concern useful. We must not forget, however, that the nature of the symptoms often are themselves the most powerful variables explaining why definitions of sickness are made and why care is sought (296).

Salience of Symptoms

Other-defined. Intervention in a situation of "assumed mental illness" by family, friends, and others in the community is dependent on the visibility or recognizability of symptoms. Lemert (426) has pointed out that when an "ill" person deviates from social expectations, his social visibility increases and others are constrained to respond accordingly to his behavior. In cases of violence and disorderly conduct, police action is often taken. When the behavior is neither violent nor clearly bizarre—such as with moderate depression, restlessness, extreme shyness—any action taken is likely to be initiated by the person himself or by family or friends. If a person suffers from hallucinations or delusions, but manages to keep them hidden, he is much less likely to be recognized and defined than if he openly discusses them. In any case, persons who are most visible may not be those who require treatment most. This is particularly striking when a seemingly normal person, without apparent warning, commits a brutal and senseless crime such as shooting several strangers or setting fires.

Self-defined. Whether a person recognizes a symptom of illness depends on how it presents itself and how recognizable it is to him. Many symptoms present themselves in a striking fashion, such as a sharp abdominal pain, an intense headache, or a high fever. Other symptoms have such little visibility (as in the early stages of cancer, tuberculosis, or hypertension) that they require special checkups to be detected in their early stages. Thus individual symptoms may vary from those that can be detected only indirectly to those that develop in an evident and unequivocal fashion.

There is one major finding in the literature that appears to be inconsistent with the notion that more visible symptoms are more readily defined. Ruth Goldsen (274), in a study of persons who delayed in seeking diagnosis for cancer symptoms, found a strong inverse relationship between noticeability of symptoms and delay. More than two-fifths of those who had a symptom that was noticeable to others delayed in seeking diagnosis; in contrast, only 27 percent delayed in the group who reported that their symptoms were not apparent to others. Of course, visibility is only one of many factors affecting the definition of a symptom. Although it is a necessary condition for defining a symptom and doing something about, it is not sufficient in and of itself for such a definition to take place. Such other factors as the perceived seriousness of the condition and incapacitation may be more powerful variables in motivating some action. Goldsen's results, as well as those of an earlier study by Leach and Robbins to which she refers, fail to control for the likelihood that signs of cancer that are noticeable to others, as in the case of skin cancer, present themselves differently from those that are not noticeable, as in the case of lung cancer or gastric cancer. The most common forms of observable cancer do not usually appear in a painful, alarming, or incapacitating fashion. Thus the observed relationship may well be the product of various uncontrolled conditions (related to the manner in which symptoms appear) that have profound effects on the way people respond to their symptoms.

Perceived Seriousness

Other-defined.   Whether a visible deviation will be identified and defined depends on how serious the deviation appears to others. By "perceived seriousness," I refer to estimates of present and future probabilities of danger. Many visible deviations go undefined because they appear harmless or even amusing. Such visible deviations may have some idiosyncratic function for the group, as is often the case with the "comic" or the natural "clown." Or perhaps the deviant may be thought of as eccentric or strange, but not sufficiently so to require any special notice of the person. However, should the behavior yield signs of danger in that it appears that it may be damaging to the individual concerned, his family, the community, or all of these, then the behavior may be defined as sickness and the person brought for treatment. There are so many possible indications of danger that there is little point in attempting to review them. Frequently the patient may do or say things that suggest threats to his life (for example, the collection of a stock of pills may suggest possible suicide) or to his reputation (he may begin to say things publicly that are harmful to his standing and the reputation of his family). Or his behavior may suggest threat for others, as in the case of the paranoid who believes that others are doing harmful things to him and who indicates that he intends to take revenge. The research literature suggests that bizarre behavior is most frightening to relatives and the community, and such behavior is thus seen as extremely serious (123; 157; 169; 170; 231; 423; 477).

Self-defined.   The perceived seriousness of a symptom will affect the likelihood that a person will respond to it. If the symptom is familiar and the person understands why he has the symptom and its probable course, he is less likely to seek care than if the symptom is unusual, strange, threatening, and unpredictable. As one of Koos's respondents remarked, "If I had a bad backache for two weeks, like that list says, I *think* I'd go to the doctor, but I can't say for sure. If I knew how I did it—say from lifting a bucket of coal—I might not go as quick as if I didn't know where it came from" (399, p. 34). Suchman (683) found that symptoms perceived as more serious brought about a greater degree of concern, were more likely to be viewed as indicative of illness, and were more likely to bring about contact with a physician. Levine (432), in a survey of almost 3,000 people concerning anxiety about illness, found that persons who perceived an imminent threat were more anxious than those who did not. Older persons did not find diseases that occur primarily among the young as frightening as serious diseases that had a high prevalence in their age group.

Extent of Disruption of Activities

Other-defined.   In the case of other-defined conditions, perceived seriousness and disruption of activities are highly correlated. Symptoms that are disruptive of social contexts are much more likely to be defined than those that do not have detrimental effects on social activities. The heavy drinker, for example, who drinks at home and does not make a nuisance of himself is of much less concern to others than the man who is visible and whose drunken behavior disrupts or interferes with the activities of other people. It is the latter type of alcoholic who primarily gets arrested and committed to mental institutions for alcoholism. Similarly, we have greater tolerance for a friendly drunk than an aggressive one. Angrist and her colleagues (29) found little tolerance for the mental patient who could not control her toilet habits. Such symptoms are not necessarily serious ones, but they create considerable inconvenience and embarrassment. Aged persons are hospitalized or placed in nursing homes frequently not so much because they have serious symptoms that can be helped through institutionalization but because their presence in the household is disruptive and inconvenient.

Self-defined.   Symptoms that are disruptive and that cause inconvenience, social difficulties, pain, and annoyance are more likely to be defined and responded to than those that do not, other factors remaining constant. People are more likely to become concerned and seek help if their symptoms interfere with their work and social activities and if they are bothersome. The girl anticipating her Saturday night date may become especially concerned about her acne. An athlete preparing for a game may be more concerned with slight pains in his knee than he would on some other occasion. Thus trivial symptoms of no medical importance can be bothersome and disturbing (as, for example, skin rashes that make it difficult for the housewife to wash dishes) while serious symptoms from a medical perspective (like cancer indications) may cause no disruption at all, at least for a time. Suchman (683) found that the degree of incapacitation caused by a symptom affected its interpretation and what the person did about it. Dorian Apple (33), in a study of the way laymen define illness, found that interference with usual activities was one of the major criteria used by laymen to define illness.

Frequency and Persistence of Symptoms

Other-defined. The probability of a definition of illness also depends on the frequency and persistence of the symptoms (427). Given a particular level of seriousness of behavior, the more frequently the behavior occurs, the more likely it is to be defined. A man who gets drunk occasionally is less likely to be defined as an alcoholic than one who is persistently in this condition. Obviously, if the deviant act is very serious, only one occurrence is sufficient for a definition to be formulated, as with the person who commits a homicide or one who attempts to take his own life.

Self-defined. Whether a person will define himself as requiring care will depend on the amount and persistence of his symptoms. The more persistently ill a person feels, other factors remaining constant, the more likely he is to seek help; frequent or persistent symptoms are more likely to influence a person to seek help than occasional recurring symptoms. Conditions usually viewed as requiring care tend to be severe, continuous, and unalleviated (683).

Tolerance Thresholds

Other-defined. The extent to which family members differ in their tolerance for deviant behavior is remarkable. Some families will note slight indications of aberrance and seek assistance quickly; others will delay defining a condition and seeking assistance in the face of evident and blatant symptomatology. There are clear cultural differences in respect to tolerance of deviation and the manner in which groups deal with the deviant. Eaton and Weil (194) investigated the Hutterite populations living in the northwestern part of the United States and in adjacent areas in Canada. They were interested in this group because it appeared that the prevalence of mental illness was considerably lower among the Hutterites than among comparable non-Hutterite populations, and Hutterites were rarely found in mental hospitals. These investigators concluded that the true prevalence of mental disorders was in fact no lower among the Hutterites than among the other groups studied, but appeared so because the Hutterites dealt with mental illness differently than did the surrounding community. Although Eaton and Weil's prevalence figures are suspect because of the case-finding methods they used, their description is interesting because it illustrates how differently the Hutterites cope with the mentally ill as compared with our traditional methods of care. They point out that the Hutterite members of the community were particularly solicitous and sympathetic to the Hutterite patient and that they continued to treat him as an important member of the community. The patient was relieved of responsibilities he could not handle, but was allowed to continue to function at the level at which he could cope. Thus patients were not removed from the community, rejected by their kin, and isolated from community life. Eaton and Weil believe that the nonaggressive course of mental illness among the Hutterites could be explained in part by the sympathetic mode of handling aberrance and caring for the mentally ill patient. The nonaggressive content of Hutterite culture, however, may be the primary reason for the nonaggressive course of mental illness among these people.

It is difficult to specify with complete clarity those factors that lead to differential tolerance. In general, attitudes of tolerance toward deviant behavior are related to general expectation levels of others when deviance is not involved. In the society at large, expectations of married people and those with dependent children are higher in some respects than expectations of nonattached persons. Middle-class people tend to hold higher performance expectations of family members than do members of the working class, and spouses tend to have higher standards of performance of their marital partners than parents have of their children. Various studies of tolerance of the performance of mental patients show that tolerance levels are higher among parents than spouses, higher in the working class as compared with the middle class, and higher in respect to the unattached than with those who are married (29; 88; 219; 231; 422).

The way families and individuals respond to particular deviant symptoms and whether they tolerate them or not depend on personal inclinations, attitudes toward the deviant person and a sense of loyalty to him, and knowledge and attitudes toward the possible alternatives for dealing with the symptoms. As was suggested earlier, however, there are limits to what most people are willing to tolerate in the way of bizarre symptoms. Symptoms that appear uncontrollable, unpredictable, and frightening have a high probability of being defined and acted upon.

Self-defined. An individual's tolerance for pain and discomfort and his values concerning stoicism and independence may also affect the way he responds to symptoms and what he does about them. Persons vary a great deal in the amount of discomfort they are willing to tolerate and the attention they give to bodily troubles. Earlier in the chapter we discussed how the meaning attributed to symptoms affected the ways they were viewed, as in the case of the differing attitudes of Jews and Italians to pain relief. Lambert and his colleagues (408) report on an interesting experiment that helps illuminate this matter. Volunteer subjects were subjected to pain produced by a modified blood pressure cuff fitted with hard rubber projections that pressed into the subject's arm when inflated. Half of the subjects were Christians and half Jews. In each case they were informed between sessions that the study was an attempt to check some research that showed that their particular group (Christians or Jews) could not tolerate as much pain as the other group. On the second trial both Jewish and Christian subjects tolerated significantly more pain than they had before they were aware of the fictitious hypothesis. It is clear that the amount of pain people are willing to tolerate will depend upon the significance and meaning they attribute to the painful event.

The amount of pain a person is willing to tolerate depends to some extent on what he has become accustomed to. Only a small proportion of human ills are ever seen and treated by a physician. Most people have some physical complaints almost all of the time, although they may notice them only occasionally and may regard them as trivial. Following World War II, a "healthy" population studied at the Peckham Health Center in London included only 9 percent who did not have some physiological or bodily disorder (557). This study took place, however, during a period when medical services were inadequate and when other needs were much more pressing. A more recent study of multiphasic screenings carried out in 10,709 apparently healthy subjects showed that 92 percent had some disease or clinical disorder (620). In short, being ill is not an unusual state of being, and much illness is ignored and tolerated.

Bases of Appraisal

Other-defined. The stage at which symptoms will be perceived as psychiatric will depend on the information, knowledge, and cultural assumptions of the evaluator. Depending on their information, persons

appraise and respond to psychiatric symptoms differently. Hollingshead and Redlich (330), for example, found that persons within the
higher-status groups came into treatment largely through referrals of
private physicians, family, friends, and self-referral. Persons in the
lowest-class group, who constituted a majority of hospitalized patients,
came into treatment involuntarily, largely through police, courts, and
other social agencies. None of the psychotic patients in the two highest-
status groups was referred through such routes, while 72 percent of
those diagnosed as psychotic in the lowest social stratum were referred
in this way. (Among schizophrenics entering treatment for the first
time the comparable figures were 0 and 76 percent.) Although there are
a variety of ways to interpret the Hollingshead and Redlich findings, it
seems reasonable to believe that there were at least two processes at
work. First, it is likely that upper- and middle-class persons are more
inclined than working-class persons to perceive particular indications
as symptoms of psychiatric disorder and thus to seek help more readily
before a crisis occurs. Second, it is probable that, once having defined
the need for treatment, patients in the various class groups have different information and knowledge concerning the way to arrange psychiatric intervention. While middle-class persons are more likely to
call in the doctor when difficulties develop, working-class persons are
probably more likely to call the police in handling the behavior of the
disruptive psychotic patient.

Self-defined.   The sophistication of patients about medical matters
varies from those who are aware of the latest therapeutic developments
even before their doctor to those who cannot identify the basic body
organs and have naive notions of bodily functioning. Such differences
in medical knowledge and understanding have considerable influence
on the ways people recognize, define, and respond to symptoms. Koos
(399), in his early study of symptoms, found great variations between
the highest and lowest social class in the recognition that such symptoms as lumps in the breast or abdomen, chest pain, fainting spells, and
blood in stools and urine required medical attention. Similarly, cancer
delay and other failures to seek assistance are associated with lack of
knowledge (404). Levine (432) found that those who were most fearful
of such diseases as arthritis, cancer, and birth defects tended to know
more about them. Such persons may have had more personal experience with others having such illnesses. Various studies show that attitudes and beliefs of individuals affect their willingness to take voluntary health actions such as obtaining immunizations and chest X-rays
(598). Preventive health response also depends on knowledge of the
safety and effectiveness of the health procedure. Willingness to conform to medical regimen similarly depends on the patient's understanding of the doctor's suggestions and the way in which such

suggestions fit his cultural notions (163). A frequent problem faced by the physician in providing care is the failure of the patient to conform to medical advice; this occurs most when the patient fails to take his drugs or return for follow-up because, subjectively, he feels well. From the patient's commonsense perspective, to stop medication or cancel a follow-up visit when he is feeling well is logical.

Needs for Denial

Other-defined. I have already discussed the strong tendency for the spouse of the mental patient to normalize and deny that he is suffering from a psychiatric disturbance. Such denial tendencies are motivated in part by the psychological need to maintain the situation under control. Psychiatric illness is terribly disruptive, not only in terms of its direct consequences for family life but also in terms of its meaning for the various members of the family: the stigma associated with psychiatric illness, the implicit guilt feeling of the spouse that she may be to blame in part for the psychiatric condition of other members of the family, and so on. At times such denial processes help maintain the coping efforts of various members of the family; on other occasions they lead to long delays in seeking help.

Various studies of parents of children who were disabled from polio or were dying from neoplastic disease show strong tendencies for relatives to deny the medical prognosis. Some parents of disabled children refused to recognize their handicap (160), while parents of dying children sometimes persisted in denying the prognosis in the face of discomfiting evidence. Instead they insisted that a cure would be found and maintained hope to the very end (250). It is extremely difficult to evaluate the functional value or problems to which such denial processes may lead. If there are treatment means available and the denial process keeps the person from seeking proper care, then it is clearly a liability in dealing with the situation. There are various occasions, however, characterized by uncertainty and a lack of viable alternatives where denial processes may serve to alleviate discomfort and facilitate "going on."

Self-defined. It is not at all clear to what extent anxiety and fear influence the failure to recognize symptoms and to seek care. The relationship is probably complex. For example, some anxiety about illness is correlated with knowledge about cancer, which, in turn, is correlated to some extent with shorter delay in seeking care. A high level of fear, in contrast, may lead to denial of symptoms and reluctance to seek care. There are obviously patients who are so fearful of particular diagnoses and medical procedures they associate with them (such as surgical intervention) that they significantly delay having them medically evaluated.

Competing Needs

As Rosenstock (597) has noted, behavior takes place within a context in which motives are frequently competing or in conflict. Health motives are not always the most central ones, especially to persons who are basically healthy. As one of Koos's respondents put it: "I wish I could get it fixed up, but we've just got some other things that are more important first. Our car's a wreck, and we're going to get another one. We need a radio, too, and some other things. . . . But it's got to wait for now—there's always something more important" (399, p. 37). Another one of his respondents remarked: "I wish I really knew what you mean about being sick. Sometimes I've felt so bad I could curl up and die, but had to go on because the kids had to be taken care of, and besides, we didn't have the money to spend for the doctor—how could I be sick?" (399, p. 30).

Alternative Interpretations

Other-defined. We have already seen that there is a strong tendency for relatives to normalize or explain away psychiatric symptoms. Such symptoms are frequently explained in terms of acceptable frames of reference, such as "he has been working very hard lately" or "everyone behaves this way, sometimes." In one sense normal frames of reference must be broken down by disconfirming evidence that sharply challenges and contradicts them. If the challenge is not sufficiently strong, the individual will frequently make the new information or observations consistent with his present frame of reference. The maintenance of normal frames of reference is possible because many symptoms characteristic of psychiatric patients occur commonly among persons in the community who are not psychiatrically ill. In the study of mental patient rehabilitation by Dinitz and his colleagues (29; 168; 169; 170; 422; 423), a control group of nonpatients was obtained to see how they compared with the patient group studied. Each urban patient in the study was matched with a neighbor who lived ten house numbers away. Each of these persons, as well as another significant person in the household, was interviewed for comparison purposes. Many symptoms occurred fairly commonly in the control-group population: "moving around restlessly" (50 percent), "always seems worn out or tired" (61 percent), "gets grouchy or bad-tempered" (57 percent), "acts tense or nervous" (62 percent), "gets depressed suddenly" (28 percent), "does not want to see people" (28 percent), "has trouble going to sleep" (26 percent), and so on (168). In fact, there were no significant differences between the two groups in the occurrence of many symptom items; included among such items were "makes no sense when talking," "walks, sits, or stands awkwardly," "moves around restlessly," "does not want to see people," and "gets grouchy or bad-tempered." Such symptoms as restlessness, anxiety, depression, and lack of interest in social activities, which are known to occur widely, are usually susceptible to a wide range of commonplace explanations and interpretations. In contrast, such symptoms as trying to hit or hurt someone, hearing voices, and making attempts to take one's life are more difficult to integrate within normal perceptual frames of reference.

Self-defined. The meanings persons give to symptoms are the product in some measure of their life situation. People who work long hours expect to be tired and are therefore less likely to see tiredness as indicative of an illness. Persons who do heavy physical work are more likely to attribute such symptoms as backache to the nature of their lives and work rather than to an illness condition. A wide variety of symptoms are possible to rationalize within frames of reference other than sickness. In contrast, such symptoms as severe fever do not readily fit a nonillness framework.

Accessibility of Treatment

Other-defined. The use of help facilities and the choice among possible alternative facilities depend on the relative accessibility of the facility to the person. The greater the barriers to a particular facility, the more likely that some other source of help will be chosen or some competing definition of the situation be applied. Barriers to care include economic costs, time, effort, and embarrassment. The lack of ease the patient may experience, as well as the stigma and humiliation resulting from his condition, may constitute significant costs or barriers to care. Stigma and humiliation may be intrinsic to his perception of his problem or they may be a consequence of his anticipation of the way the doctor will treat him.

The physical proximity of a mental hospital may have a considerable influence on rates of hospitalization from various communities. Some analysts believe that persons who live in close proximity to a mental hospital are more likely to have a relative hospitalized than those living farther away, because they can maintain contact with the patient without too much difficulty (427). Similarly, the availability of a hospital facility increases the likelihood that social agencies in the community will deal with particular problems that arise in the community by having the patient taken to the hospital (70). As mental-health and medical facilities in any area increase, they tend to have no difficulty locating clients. In one sense these observations suggest that there was an unfilled need in the community for such facilities. But such tendencies to absorb clients quickly are also probably the product of changes in accessibility of such increased facilities. Frequently costs are lower, waiting lists shorter, and appointments closer to the time they are requested.

Self-defined.   The costs of treatment clearly affect the use of medical facilities, as our discussion has already implied. Public health studies on immunization and preventive health practices indicate that convenience is a factor affecting whether people seek vaccination. Such factors as the necessary distance to travel, periods of day in which services are provided, and acceptability of the facilities from which such services are distributed affect receptivity to them (598). Similarly, embarrassment or shame resulting from not taking action, such as is implied by social pressure to participate, also influences personal action. In general, the factors affecting acceptance of health action are similar to those influencing voting, participation in various community affairs, and so on.

The use of a particular kind of help practitioner also depends on his cultural and social accessibility. Accessibility refers to whether or not the practitioner is perceived as responding to the person and his illness within a framework consistent with the patient's cultural expectations, the degree of stigma or social threat implied in using his services, anticipation of humiliation resulting from the treatment or from the manner in which the practitioner handles the patient, as well as other factors describing the kind of relationship that develops between practitioner and patient. Charles Kadushin (372) has shown that the choice of practitioner depends on the social distance between client and professional. Similarly, Lieberson (443) has shown that ethnic doctors in Chicago tend to concentrate their practices in areas where members of similar ethnic groups reside. Although Lieberson's data are not specifically directed to our point of concern, they suggest that ethnic doctors can practice most effectively with patients who share similar cultural perspectives.

Relationships among Help-Seeking Variables

Although I have described help-seeking influences individually, in real situations they interact together. Some of these variables tend to be associated to a substantial extent with one another, while others are relatively independent. Although I shall not attempt to illustrate in any detail the nature of such interdependence, a few examples will illustrate the point. Suppose that deviant behavior that has been present in a particular group context becomes more *frequent* and *persistent*; for example, consider the case of a person who had become inebriated from time to time in the past, but who now gets drunk several times a week. We would hypothesize that as the frequency of drunkenness increases, the fact of the person's situation would *become more evident* to friends, neighbors, relatives, and workmates. Because the drunken behavior occurs more frequently, it is more likely to be seen as indicative of some basic disturbance, i.e., the *perceived seriousness* of the situation increases. Also, more frequent drunkenness is likely to have a *disruptive influence* on family life, work performance, and other social activities. The family members who may have been *tolerant* of occasional binges in the past may now find the new pattern of behavior more difficult to tolerate. In seeking a solution for the problem that now is more salient, family members may seek *information* about alcoholism and treatment facilities. Although they previously may not have been willing to discuss the drinking problem of a family member with others outside the family, the *perceived seriousness* of the problem may now overcome the *perceived stigma*, and the family may seek alternatives more openly for dealing with the problem. They may discuss the difficulty with friends and neighbors and perhaps seek the assistance of their clergyman, their doctor, or even the police in handling the behavior of the deviant family member.

In contrast, consider the person who experiences an occasional stomach pain. He may notice it but attribute it to something he ate or to missing a meal, or he may just pay no attention to it. If the pain persists or occurs more frequently, he is more likely to become attentive to it. The more frequently the pain bothers him, the more likely it is that it will be *perceived as serious* and will *disrupt* his plans and activities. He becomes less *tolerant* of the symptom now that it bothers him more often, and finds that such alternative definitions as having eaten a meal that does not agree with him are no longer tenable as an interpretation of the symptom. He may thus see the symptom as a medical one and, if it is sufficiently severe, seek medical attention.

In reviewing factors affecting help-seeking, I have not dealt with every possible variable that may become implicated in such definitions. For example, the position and power of the person being defined affect the definitional process if there is disagreement between the person and those who are making the evaluation. Persons of power and influence have considerable control over their fate, and it is extremely difficult to force action upon them if they resist. For example, it would be difficult to define the president of the United States as disabled and unable to meet his responsibilities because of illness if he himself resisted this definition. Similarly, it is more difficult to take involuntary action in respect to high-status persons in the community as compared with persons of lower status.

It should be clear from this discussion that, in general, the factors influencing other- and self-defined conditions and those affecting definitions of physical and mental disorders are strikingly similar. Mental and physical disorders differ in many of their characteristics, but analysts frequently tend to exaggerate the analytic differences between these two phenomena. Moreover, it is possible to encompass both sets of processes within the same general model. There are several advantages in approaching care-seeking variables from a broad perspective. Such variables can be used to unify discussions of social factors in illness but, even more important, they facilitate the study of definitional processes in social and cultural systems other than our own. If our studies and understandings are to generalize to other contexts, we must develop ways of viewing social processes that are equally applicable to a variety of social and cultural systems.

Chapter 10

STRESS, CRISIS, AND SOCIAL ADAPTATION

In recent years the study of social adaptation has shifted from a primary concern with intrapsychic processes to a focus on social learning and psychosocial processes. Earlier formulations—derived from psychoanalytic theory and research—emphasized thought processes, particularly those associated with psychological pain and the mental mechanisms through which people accommodated psychologically to distressful life events. Learning theory, in contrast, sought to identify the sources of distress and disturbing behavior by specifying the types of reinforcement experiences that resulted in these outcomes and suggesting how learning principles could be used to modify the situation (43). Work focusing on psychosocial factors examines the active processes through which people define problems, struggle with them, and attempt to achieve an accommodation or mastery.

The psychoanalytic formulation of social adaptation, based on the verbalizations of patients in therapy, portrayed ego-defense manipulations as pathological processes. Since the perspective was oriented toward explaining disturbed functioning, only a single residual category—the concept of sublimation—remained to account for the more healthy forms of working through stressful situations in a socially useful fashion. Many of the neoanalytic writers were not as orthodox in their formulations and expanded the concepts of ego defense to characterize more ordinary aspects of everyday functioning, but much of their thinking remained constrained by their almost exclusive focus on intrapsychic processes in contrast to more active approaches among populations to solving problems in living.

The tide of research and analysis of social adaptation has now turned to a more comprehensive concern with the way people come to terms with the demands of living, particularly those that threaten distress and disruption (133). Not only is more attention focused on the sociocultural and psychosocial aspects of adaptation, but approaches to treatment also increasingly reflect an interest in teaching adaptive skills and in helping persons construct more effective social networks that assist them in managing their difficulties and insulating themselves against potential strains (664). The emphasis has turned from ego defense to coping in a social context and from a medical model of rehabilitation and prevention to one that can more aptly be described as educational.

Despite these gains, the study of coping remains handicapped by the absence of an adequate vocabulary to describe and teach the maneuvers through which persons successfully manage other people and events. In describing such maneuvers we inevitably lapse into psychological vocabulary because of the insufficiency of the concepts that describe the processes that concern us. There is a long tradition of conceptualizing problems of adaptation in psychological terms, and both scientific literature and commonplace language provide literally hundreds of terms that allow us to express what we feel or think. In contrast, attempts to describe interpersonal transactions and more complex social attachments are confronted with a poverty of concepts.

The problem of developing a suitable language to depict more complex coping maneuvers is not an easy one. If such a vocabulary is too concrete, the range of human actions and reactions it must encompass is so great as to make it impractical and inefficient. Social adaptation may include any and all human behavior, and if the net is too broad it is unlikely to capture much of general relevance. What is needed is a set of concepts at a more abstract level of analysis akin to such concepts as denial or projection within the theory of ego defense. Such concepts would direct our attention to important aspects of human adaptation, but would be more than descriptions of the concrete behavior being performed in a specified social situation. In this chapter I suggest a framework within which it might be possible to derive a useful set of concepts that are better attuned than existing language to the types of analysis needed.

Levels of Analysis

In the usual study of an illness or forms of deviant behavior, the entity of concern constitutes the dependent variable and attempts are made to identify causal factors that differentiate between those who do and do not display the pattern under consideration. While useful, such an approach tells us little about the broader effects of important clusters of independent variables. Such clusters, as was noted in chapter 8, may have more global effects than those measured through a particular dependent variable or, alternatively, individuals may react in varying ways depending on their own biological and social characteristics. The investigator of lung cancer, for example, may observe the relationship between smoking and pathological processes in the lung. By beginning with a study of diseases of the lung, however, it is unlikely that the association between smoking and coronary heart disease, low birth weight of newborns, and overall mortality will also be identified. The approach taken here is not only to examine particular reactions but also to focus on events of social significance as independent variables to consider their broader effects on human adaptation. We will explore the ways individuals come to terms with these events. One method of approach is no better than the other; they are directed to different, although complementary, issues in understanding patterns of health and disease in populations.

The major emphasis in this chapter, however, is on intervening variables—those forces that account for variations in adaptations among persons exposed to similar or comparable environmental events. These intervening variables are often difficult to study because we frequently lack adequate measures to depict the extraordinary complexity of adaptive response or to assess their role in ameliorating or short circuiting threat. Despite this difficulty there is appreciation that these intervening variables are of extraordinary importance, and that even the most extreme situations call forth a variety of responses and varying levels of harm in populations exposed to them. Any adequate understanding of the role of crisis in illness, illness behavior, or breakdown in behavioral functioning must come to terms with these intervening variables and the way they either protect the person from assault or speed the dissolution of effective behavior.

A Stress-Adaptation Perspective

It is useful to conceive of stress as characterizing a discrepancy between the demands impinging on a person—whether these demands be external or internal, whether challenges or goals—and the individual's potential or actual responses to these demands. Generally, when discrepancies develop or are anticipated they are associated with physiological changes, feelings of discomfort, and concern. The extent of physiological change and feelings of discomfort will depend on the importance of the situation or the extent of motivation, on the degree of discrepancy or failure anticipated or experienced, and on genetic and physiological factors. It should, therefore, be clear that there are many elements involved in a stress response.

The view presented stems in part from W. I. Thomas's concept of crisis (751). As long as social life runs smoothly, he believed, and as long as habits are adjustive, *situations* (in our terms, stress) do not exist. There is nothing to define circumstances when people have anticipated ways of responding. However, when habits become disrupted, new stimuli demand attention, and, when the usual situation is altered, we then have the roots of a crisis. Thomas believed that the difference between crisis and progress was dependent on the preparation of the individual to meet events, and that adjustment and control resulted from the individual's ability to compare a present situation with similar ones in the past and to revise judgments and actions in light of past experience:

> The explanation of any particular act of personal behavior must be sought on the ground of the experience of the behaving individual which the observer has indirectly to reconstruct by way of conclusions from what is directly given to him. We cannot neglect the meanings, the suggestions which objects have for the conscious individual, because it is these meanings which determine the individual's behavior; and we cannot explain these meanings as mere abbreviations of the individual's past acts of biological adaptation to his material environment—as manifestations of organic memory—because the meanings to which he reacts are not only those which material things have assumed for him as a result of his own past organic activities, but also those which these things have acquired long ago in society and which the individual is taught to understand during his whole education as [a] conscious member of a social group [751, p. 156].

Thomas's concept of crisis is important because it emphasizes that crises lie not in situations but in interactions between a situation and a person's capacities to meet it. Thomas saw crisis and progress as two sides of the same coin; stress situations offered the possibility of both. The outcome depended on the way the person came to terms with his situation. Thomas made another observation that has been too long neglected in the study of stress. He emphasized the importance of "education as a conscious member of a social group." In short, the preparation of an individual to deal with events is linked to social and cultural preparation, and these in turn are related to the functional adaptability of social systems (i.e., the extent to which their teachings fit the challenges people must face). There are at least five types of intervening variable that are crucial in understanding the perception of and response to crises.

Material Resources

Although the relationship between poverty and physical or social breakdown is certainly not direct, lack of material resources contributes to problems of adaptation among vulnerable persons and increases the probability of disorganized behavior. Inadequate nutrition, in particular, has been linked to a general vulnerability to disease resulting in increased mortality, and malnutrition affects both social and intellectual development. More generally, material resources lighten the person's load, eliminate tangential stresses because of the ability to purchase services, and create a more comfortable environment for dealing with the primary crisis. Material resources also open alternatives for coping that otherwise might not be available.

Appropriate Skills

The adequacy of any social group or of individuals depends on the effectiveness of cultural preparation and the availability of problem-solving tools necessary to deal with the typical problems presented by the environment. What may be an ordinary situation to those with skills or otherwise adequate cultural preparation is a crisis for those who lack them. Many if not most skills are socially learned in the developmental process in an informal way and are not recognized explicitly as skills by either teacher or learner. These skills include such subtle processes as formation of relationships, effective communication, empathy, and sensitivity, as well as the more tangible skills associated with dealing with particular tasks of a physical or conceptual nature. Many of the skills on which we depend are embedded in our uses of language, social rules, and ordinary social expectations, and we take them for granted. When the satisfactory enactment of these skills is blocked during social crises, we recognize their content more readily.

For example, a growing body of evidence suggests that the movement from one environment to another, such as from rural to industrial life and from country to city, is associated with a higher prevalence of disease of various kinds. Although these studies are complex and hardly definitive, they suggest that more recent migrants lack in some fashion the coping repertoires necessary to adapt to industrial conditions without physical and social strain. Although the specific components of such repertoires are yet to be isolated, they probably encompass a variety of attitudes, values, and daily routines that make it easier to cope with new environmental demands (109).

It seems to be of some advantage to separate conceptually cognitive defense processes from the more active problem-solving aspects of human adaptation. For this purpose a distinction between the concepts of coping and defense seems reasonable, despite the fact that it is sometimes difficult to separate these two concepts in practice. "Coping," as I use the term, refers to the instrumental behavior and problem-solving capacities of persons in meeting life demands and goals. It involves the application of skills, techniques, and knowledge that a person has acquired. The extent to which a person experiences discomfort is often the product of the inadequacy of such skill repertoires. In contrast to coping, the concept of defense (as I am using the term) refers to the manner in which a person manages his emotional and affective states when discomfort is aroused or anticipated. Thus defense involves in large part the inner techniques through which persons deal with their feelings of anxiety, discomfort, or threat. Most psychological discussions deal primarily with the study of defense and not with coping processes.

Perhaps I can make the coping perspective clearer by providing an example that illustrates the way this viewpoint differs from the more traditional one. A number of years ago I participated in a study of doctors who had applied for a coveted psychiatric residency at a major training institution. As part of the assessment procedure candidates were interviewed by the faculty of the institution in what the applicants regarded as a stressful group interview. One way of attempting to understand how candidates dealt with this stressful situation is through the traditional psychological stress approach. Understanding the personality, motivation, and past experiences of each candidate might clarify why he perceived the situation as he did, why he became aroused or did not become aroused, and why he did what he did when faced with the situation. Thus the emphasis within this approach would be to inquire as to what kind of personality the candidate had and what kinds of event in his past history influenced the ways he perceived and handled the stress situation.

The coping view, in contrast, takes what might be called a cross-sectional picture of the situation, as compared with the developmental-historical picture described above. Rather than attempting to explain the behavior of the candidate in terms of past events in his life, emphasis is given to appraising carefully the ways he approached the stress situation and the aspects of his approach that were effective or ineffective in dealing with the challenge. Thus one would attempt to assess how the candidate sized up the situation, how he prepared for it, and the efforts and skills he mobilized in the situation. Prime emphasis would be given to evaluating the effectiveness of varying modes of approach to the situation.

It was clear from the study that the candidates varied widely in the manner in which they attempted to come to terms with the stressful group interview. They differed in such aspects as how they sought information about the situation, the extent of anticipation of the areas that would come up during the interview, the extent of anticipatory rehearsal of answers, and preparatory problem-solving activity. Although the data from the study were not definitive, it was apparent that candidates who anticipated the situation to some extent and who made relevant inquiries from others who had previously experienced the same situation dealt with it in a more competent fashion. Thus the manner in which the candidate sought information affected the extent to which he anticipated what questions he would be asked and the extent of preparatory activity he could engage in before actually facing the situation himself.

In emphasizing the value of the cross-sectional approach, I do not wish to disparage the value of a historical-developmental emphasis. Indeed, we might have considerable interest in why some candidates made the effort to seek out information about the interview while others did not, and this may bear some relationship to their personalities and past developmental history. The point I wish to emphasize is that almost exclusive attention has been given in the past to the historical-developmental approach, to the serious neglect of the cross-sectional one.

The conceptual difference between coping and defense will become clear with some illustrations. The magnitude of distress one is likely to experience if he falls off a boat into ten feet of water depends on whether or not he can swim, and rather little on his psychological defensive capacities. Most life situations are not experienced as threatening because they do not tax people's capacities. Given adequate preparatory activity, a situation that under other circumstances may be highly threatening causes little concern; the reactions are so routine that the complexity of the response usually goes unrecognized. Indeed, these coping responses become so habituated that we often can do things more effectively than we can describe them, as, for example, driving a car.

Consider another example with which most people have had some experience. Upon entering a large city for the first time, the primary experience one has is a feeling of confusion and bewilderment. The city is so vast and complicated that it seems impossible to find one's way around it without assistance. Yet we know that with some exposure and experience it is relatively simple to learn the major pathways of a large city so that one feels at home there. Through practice— familiarity, if you like—what appeared (and is) an enormously complex task can be mastered relatively quickly. I contend that the central process in adaptation to stress involves practice, experience, and familiarity with modes of dealing with a situation.

In studies of combat situations it has become clear that preparation and experience play an important part in combat effectiveness. It is fairly obvious, for example, that the success of astronauts in space experiments is dependent on a long and technically complicated training experience during which plans are made for varying possibilities and contingencies, and the astronauts themselves are prepared to deal with these problems well before they are encountered (604). General combat training is less complicated and complete, and thus the soldiers' training and experience must take place in part under actual combat conditions. Studies have shown that when new recruits enter combat, there is an initial period in which coping skills must be acquired if the soldier is to function effectively. He must learn to distinguish between friendly and enemy battle noises, he must learn to judge the caliber and closeness of artillery projectiles, he must be able to spot snipers, to conceal himself effectively, and so on (383). These are not matters of psychological defense; they involve the learning of specific skills. The absence of such skills is related to unnecessary fear and anxiety. For example, when soldiers first enter combat they are frequently scared by noises of enemy fire, even though it is too far away to constitute any threat. As they learn to distinguish the meaning of battle noises, their stress responses to enemy fire that actually threatens them become more specific.

In a study of stress response among graduate students involved in Ph.D. preliminary examinations, the author analyzed the ways in which students met this challenge and the factors associated with different responses to the same threat (479). First it became clear that the way students viewed these important examinations was related to their location in the communication network. What they thought and what information they had were linked to their patterns of association with other students and the physical location of their offices. In this study it was quite simple to separate the students' instrumental attempts to deal with the examinations (coping) from their psychological defense processes. The students developed strategies for preparing for the examinations that were not consistent with ideals concerning how a scholar or researcher should prepare for his professional role. Instead, they cultivated a variety of shortcuts that they felt would increase their capacity to do well on the examinations. Becker and his colleagues (52), in a study of medical students, similarly found that the students respond to the need to "get through" and gear their strategies of preparation to this end, rather than in terms of the ideals held by their professors. In short, successful adaptation depends on developing skills, techniques, and solutions that allow a person to meet the pressures he faces.

The study of Ph.D. students, and many other studies as well, shows that when people feel unprepared to meet a situation they experience strong feelings of discomfort and disruption in mood. Such feelings of inadequacy may result from lack of appropriate knowledge and skills, the uncertainty and ambiguity involved in the situation, or particular traits of the person, such as low self-confidence. In general, persons who have strong skills and preparation are much more likely to feel confident than those who do not, but this is not always true. Although people may have adequate skills, they frequently have not had the opportunity to demonstrate them, and thus feel uncertain. Successful practice in coping with challenges is therefore a crucial component in successful adaptation.

Adequate Defenses

The ability to engage in effective behavior depends not only on constitution and past preparation but also on psychological capacities to deal with signals of danger and hopelessness that hamper continued coping efforts. Cultural and personal devices must be available to the person to contain and control feelings that impede long-term adaptations and to facilitate continued attention to ordinary activities rather than to flight or destructive forms of denial.

Building stronger personal defenses directly, through such processes as psychotherapy, is perhaps the most difficult aspect of improving adaptation, yet this is the area where traditional psychiatry and psychoanalysis have devoted their greatest emphasis. Despite several decades of concerted effort, we have yet to achieve impressive evidence that we can alter these intrapsychic processes, which form their roots very early in life, even prior to the sophisticated acquisition of language. A more indirect but effective route may be in enhancing efficacy through social supports.

Social Supports

A person's sense of efficacy, as well as tangible and symbolic assistance, depends on the extent and strength of his social networks. Strengthening such networks as a matter of social policy may be a far more powerful technique than an individual therapeutic approach. In this regard, an analogy from the accident field is instructive. Health-education programs have thus far found it relatively futile to attempt to alter significantly the incidence of automobile accidents through modifications of driving behavior. But we know that technological and legal aspects—such as seat belts, highway design, auto construction, and speed limits—have significant effects on the occurrence of injuries and fatalities.

It is a truism that people are interdependent, and that successful functioning depends on the material assistance and emotional support we receive from our fellows. The absence of such supports makes people vulnerable to interpersonal and environmental assaults and to a variety of other adversities. Often merely the knowledge that help is accessible gives people the confidence to cope. But during times of difficulty we depend heavily on the assistance and moral support of others. Threat increases a feeling of dependency and a need to affiliate (610), and adversity is often a stimulus to strengthened social cohesion.

Social supports are important in a wide variety of ways, particularly when people are under threat. Affiliation, the need to be in the presence of others, fulfills either a basic biological need or one acquired early in life. While the extent of such need varies depending on people's social development, the need for attachment is universal. At a broader social level, social networks are a source of resources, information, assistance, and encouragement. When levels of support are sufficiently strong they may provide the central meaning of a person's life and diminish the perceived impact of adversity. Some types of intimate relationships, for example, insulate women experiencing stressful life events from depression (97). When people feel secure that they are valued for who they are, the rough edges of competition, disappointment, and even failure are less consequential. In modern life the sense of comfort that people obtain from community is increasingly eroded, raising the stakes of competition and material success.

Sustained Motivation

Successful social adaptation depends on a continuing willingness to remain engaged and an ongoing commitment to social activities. While withdrawal is a natural and often an effective means of temporarily reducing a sense of threat, it becomes highly maladaptive in a social sense if it persists as a continuing pattern. As people deal with problems by withdrawing, their skills and social contacts tend to erode, and eventually they develop a sense of hopelessness. Continuing involvement in tasks and people is a significant aspect of maintaining psychological identity and social roles.

References, however, to hopefulness, involvement, and motivation beg the question of why some people have difficulty in maintaining their involvements. While in its ultimate sense this question involves such issues as the meaning of life and other metaphysical topics, from an analytic standpoint it is sufficient to analyze the social conditions under which a sense of loss of identity and willfulness occurs. At times such loss involves a personal existential crisis; more often it follows a significant break in the person's social network and sense of self brought about by a significant loss of a love object or of self-esteem.

Aspects of Adaptation

Several other concepts should be discussed in order to provide a more rounded view of the total picture of the processes of appraisal and social adaptation. These include *search for meaning, social attribution, social comparison*, and *dependence and power*.

Search for Meaning

In any crisis the people involved attempt to assess what is happening, to discover the meaning of it all. Meaning is a prerequisite for devising a coping strategy since it is only through some conception of what is going on that any reasonable response can be formulated. Many life situations are sufficiently clear-cut and common so that social definitions indicate, however ambiguously, how they are to be evaluated. Responses to such events as the death of a loved one, loss of a job, or failure on an important examination are in part socially structured, even though individuals experiencing these situations may feel varying degrees of inner turmoil. Other events are more personal and unique, more a product of one's total life situation than of a specific definable "stressor"; individuals experiencing them may have much more difficulty in arriving at a definition of the experience, its implications, and how to respond.

In the case of potential disasters some attempt is made to short-circuit individual response through social programming. Thus children in schools are drilled for the eventuality of a fire, and police, fire, and emergency personnel practice in mock drills to establish appropriate roles, definitions of responsibility, and coordination among varying efforts. At the individual level people are programmed through the mass media or through informal learning to substitute "packaged responses" for the usual search to understand what might be occurring. In health education, for example, people are urged to seek medical attention immediately if they have one of the signs of cancer. The intention of such educational efforts is to substitute a definite response—going immediately to a doctor—for the more usual attributional process through which an individual attempts to ascertain the significance and seriousness of a particular symptom.

The less a particular crisis is shared by others, the more uncertain and problematic the response. Becker (51) has described the social history of such drugs as LSD and marijuana in a way that assists us in understanding both the search for meaning and the way social expectations may affect the outcomes of potential crises. He points out that in the early history of use of both drugs frequent psychotic episodes were reported among users, but that such reports diminished as social experience with the drugs developed. When a drug user who was not part of a group of experienced users had a "bad trip," he experienced cognitions and feelings that he could not explain. The user thus felt panic and interpreted his experience as "going crazy." Such patients were seen in emergency rooms of hospitals by personnel who had little experience with such drug use and who conceptualized the user's panic as a psychotic episode. In contrast, users who experienced "bad trips" in the company of more experienced drug takers were given a less alarming interpretation of their experiences and were less likely to panic. Moreover, as hospital personnel became more familiar with the "bad trip" phenomenon they were less likely to conceptualize it as a psychosis and more likely to provide support for a definition of the agitation as an understandable response to a certain type of drug experience.

Persons going through a variety of life crises—alcoholism, coping with a retarded child, marital separation—are often surprised when they join self-help groups at finding how typical their experiences are. They come to appreciate that feelings and behavior that they thought unique are commonly shared by others in comparable situations, and that their reactions are less a product of their own failures and weaknesses than they are of a certain type of social situation. The process through which crises may alternatively be defined as "personal" or as a result of "social problems" is particularly important, since the latter definition helps maintain the person's self-esteem and provides many new opportunities to cope with distress more actively.

Attribution

People in the process of seeking meaning attempt to ascertain the cause of the events being experienced as well as the locus of responsibility. The attributions that are formulated give meaning its shape and may open or close options for dealing actively with the situation or the feelings it evokes. One of the most important dimensions of attribution concerns the way individuals determine the relative role of external or internal causes in shaping the event and feelings about it. Although the internality-externality dimension has been studied extensively, most of these studies are based on a simple questionnaire measure that fails to capture the true complexity of the variable.

Internality is a particularly useful personal attribute to the extent that it implies a sense of efficacy and an ability to shape one's life situation. Individuals having a sense of their own power and skills in a social situation can more readily direct the situation for their own advantage in contrast to persons who see life as determined by fate or forces outside their control. To sense oneself as powerless relative to the flow of events is an uncomfortable feeling and a poor position from which to cope actively and effectively with challenges requiring response.

To the extent, however, that individuals fail in an important way to achieve their goals and aspirations, externality—that is, attributing the cause of the failure to outside influences in contrast to one's own capabilities, skills, and performance—may do a great deal to mitigate distress. Internal attribution following failure is a form of self-blame, of feeling worthless and incompetent, and inevitably results in a deflated mood. Personal pain can often be alleviated by shifting the attributed cause from oneself to social or structural conditions. Some examples will illustrate this point.

Although most causes of death are more prevalent among those of lower socioeconomic status, suicide is an interesting exception. Since the classic study by Durkheim in 1897 (192), it has been observed frequently that persons of lower rank—whether in society at large or in smaller subsystems such as the armed forces—have a lower rate of suicide than those more advantaged (318). One interpretation of such rates is that the less advantaged, particularly minority groups faced with blocked opportunities or those on the lower rungs of a hierarchical organization, can explain their troubles more easily by external causes, while those with greater opportunity and advantage are more likely to blame themselves. Thus it is postulated that less advantaged persons engage in less self-blame and less self-aggression.

The ease of making attributions to external causes to explain one's problems depends on the availability of consensual validation. To make such attributions when others find them implausible is likely to be seen as inappropriate behavior or evidence of paranoia. However, when subgroups exist who validate external attributions and support the individual in arriving at such "meanings," they are much more frequent. The women's movement represents an interesting example of rapid historical change in the way in which many women explain their sense of discomfort. While prior to the movement many housewives felt a sense of malaise and unfulfillment, most could not explain their feelings in any terms other than their own inadequacies or failures as women, wives, and mothers. The women's movement has provided such women with a new set of interpretations of their personal feelings—explanations of distress in terms of existing inequalities, blocked opportunities, and exploitative role arrangements. As women's consciousness groups become more common, unhappy women have often found other women supporting their attributions of distress to social arrangements in the family and the community rather than to their own inadequacies.

Similar attributional tendencies are occurring among many other groups that are disadvantaged or stigmatized. There is some fragmentary indication, for example, that aged persons who explain their troubles as a result of the way society treats them in contrast to their own deterioration, and who have consensual support for such views, may have higher self-esteem than those who accept more traditional views of their plight. The development of self-pride movements among minority groups such as blacks also served to shift perception of the locus of cause for troubles from personal failings to discrimination and exploitation.

In sum, external attributions are most valuable for dealing with failure, but only when they do not interfere with taking an active stance toward one's problems. To the extent that external attribution stimulates a sense of powerlessness to change one's situation, it can be a major liability. Moreover, the process of external attribution must be consistent with reality and must be supported by some consensus or external validation. If such attributions are too bizarre or too inconsistent with social definitions of reality, they are likely to be stigmatized and may create more difficulties for the person than those they were intended to protect against.

Social Comparison

Individuals evaluate their skills and abilities, as well as the way to respond in an uncertain situation, through a process of social comparison. In such comparisons they tend to focus on individuals like themselves as a means of obtaining cues as to the meaning of events and the way to respond. Schachter and Singer (611), in a study described earlier, illustrate how individuals who have experiences they cannot account for are more susceptible to social influence. Emotional states, they argue, are a product of emotional arousal and social cues that provide cognitive understanding of the experience.

During life crises people face many uncertainties and insecurities. Because of the lack of objective standards to evaluate their feelings, moods, and coping responses, they look to others facing comparable problems as a guide. Students studying for important examinations compare studying strategies and their scope of knowledge with others also taking such examinations; parents facing the problem of coping with rebellious adolescents often measure their modes of response by others in their social circle; young women increasingly define their goals in terms of the career orientations and ambitions of their significant associates. Social comparison is thus a source of values, a means to evaluate one's adaptive responses, and a mode of measuring progress.

How a person comes to assess himself depends on those within his or her social context with whom comparisons are made. In many situations feelings and self-esteem depend not on the objective coping capacities of the individual but on the favorability and unfavorability of such comparisons. Black children, for example, in segregated schools maintain a higher level of self-esteem than black children in integrated schools (595). These differences reflect the types of comparison that seem appropriate in the two contexts more than individual academic and social skills.

Dependence and Power

The degree to which a crisis brings with it a sense of loss or powerlessness is contingent on the alternatives available to the person or groups involved. The magnitude and persistence of distress—in the case of loss of a loved one through death, separation, or divorce, in a failure to achieve aspirations or goals, or in the loss of cherished possessions—depend on the available alternatives or substitutes. Loss of a loved one in Western culture is such a tragic event because we view individuals as unique and irreplaceable, and by definition no alternative can substitute for the loss (752). There are suggestions from other cultures that where the emphasis is more on role reciprocity and less on the unique qualities of the role partner, the death of close relatives is seen as less traumatic. Similarly, the loss of a job or a friend or the failure to attain some objective is more or less of a crisis depending on what options remain.

In interpersonal relationships individuals are dependent on others who can mediate rewards for them. For example, a young woman may enjoy the company of a man who is fun to be with, appreciative of her, and an interesting conversationalist. Her dependence on him may be great if he is the only man available to her, and she may have considerably less leverage in the relationship than if she had a variety of attractive alternatives. When no alternatives are available, she has more to lose and may feel greater insecurity in resisting demands she prefers not to meet. When equally attractive alternative opportunities are available, she has greater bargaining power in her transactions.

All alternatives are not equal, of course. Power in relationships depends on having alternatives comparable in attractiveness to the relationship at stake. Thus an employee who has good job options can be more demanding; if his alternatives are considerably less attractive than the status quo, they have relatively little value in enhancing his relative power.

Persons require some sense of power relative to their interpersonal relationships and social situation. Without it they develop a strong sense of insecurity and are highly threatened by changes in their social environment. Such power is often accrued by developing skills and competence, taking an active stance toward living, and having a high level of social participation. Similarly, an effective form of anticipatory coping with many life situations is to develop options and alternatives to protect oneself against the capriciousness of situational contingencies.

Social-System Analysis in Stress Research

The extent to which individuals experience emotional distress and feelings of danger or inadequacy is dependent on the kind of society they live in, the kinds of challenge to which they are exposed, the goals to which they aspire, and the types of preparation they have to deal with these conditions and changing circumstances. In recent years there has been increasing concern and interest among behavioral scientists in discontinuities in social systems resulting in stress response. Merton (509), for example, has argued that social structures exert definite pressures upon certain people or subgroups, which influence them in the direction of particular deviant adaptations. He believes that when an incongruency develops between the cultural norms and goals and peoples' capacities to behave in accord with them, a state of anomie exists. Individuals who learn cultural goals and values but who fail to acquire the means to fulfill these, either because of their location in society or for some other reason, adapt to these anomic conditions in a variety of ways, some of which are more socially destructive than others. Cohen (134) has argued that delinquent subcultures result in part from structurally induced failure, made more humiliating by the American belief that "man should make something of himself."

In viewing stress from the social point of view, it becomes essential to consider not only personal strivings, strengths, and inadequacies, but also the manner in which these are shaped by the social structure of a community (376). Each of the central components defining stress from an individual point of view can be viewed in relation to the social structure and its effect in shaping the component. From the point of view of individual response there are at least three components that must be included in an analysis of adaptation: the person's skills and instrumental abilities (coping), his emotional state and ability to control it (defense), and his motivation or involvement in the situation. Thus in analyzing any situation we must consider not only whether an individual is prepared to meet a particular challenge but also whether he wants to. Each of the three dimensions described above has a societal complement that I shall call: (1) preparatory institutions; (2) incentive systems; and (3) evaluative systems. By "preparatory institutions" I refer to the various organizations and practices designed to develop skills and competence among persons in dealing with societal needs, demands, and challenges. This includes not only schools and formal apprenticeships but also informal opportunities for developing preparatory skills. By "incentive systems" I refer to the values and systems of reward and punishment within organizations and communities that influence activities in particular directions. By "evaluative institutions," I refer to the approval and support or disapproval and disparagement resulting from following particular courses of activity.

These dimensions on a personal and societal level are interrelated in various ways. The level of skills and competence in any population, for example, is dependent on preparatory systems; motivation is correlated in various ways with incentive systems; and social support and favorable evaluation facilitates psychological comfort and defensive processes. Less apparent, perhaps, are the likely relationships among the various subdimensions. For example, the stronger a person's coping skills, the less likely it is that when faced with a challenge he will suffer lack of confidence and discomfort. In short, inadequacy of preparation is one of the major determinants of the experience of stress. What people in different groups experience as challenges varies largely because such groups have differing preparatory and incentive systems.

Within particular social systems there is, of course, considerable variability in performance among people who share similar instrumental skills. It appears that when motivation is high, the task difficult, and performance uncertain, a high level of discomfort may be aroused. Thus the person's socioemotional defenses become important in dealing with the situation. A high level of discomfort interferes with the application of instrumental skills requiring effort and ability. To the extent that the person can control his emotional state, the coping process is facilitated; how well he performs will depend on the techniques and intrapsychic mechanisms by which he contains his emotional state. Whether his defenses restrict, distort, or falsify reality has no important meaning in and of itself. The relative usefulness and adequacy of defensive processes depend on the way defense affects coping. The primary function of psychological defense is to facilitate coping processes.

There are boundaries, of course, within which psychological defense must function if it is to be effective. First, defense processes cannot be so out of line with social definitions of reality that they lead to negative social evaluation and withdrawal of social support. Also, from the point of view of long-range adaptation, defense processes cannot be so restrictive that they lead the person to avoid taking advantage of preparatory opportunities. Defense is not an end in itself; defense processes divorced from coping or those that hinder the coping process are usually viewed as emotional disturbances.

I can illustrate this point with the study referred to earlier of Ph.D. students taking examinations. Some students who found the examinations anxiety provoking attempted to deal with their discomfort by avoiding other students and department affairs generally. Although such avoidance processes relieved their anxiety, it also prevented access to information important to their preparation, and thus they were handicapped in various ways. The most effective way of dealing with such anxiety appeared to involve selective exposure to the department and other students, with temporary avoidance during periods of intense anxiety and discomfort.

The adequacy of individual adaptation is closely linked to societal characteristics. Preparatory systems in a particular community may be more or less congruent with characteristic difficulties that people in this society are likely to face, and they impart more or less competence to deal with these difficulties. In formal educational areas this relationship is obvious; educational institutions are always revising their curricula toward greater compatibility with the state of knowledge in particular areas. This does not necessarily insure that formal education will be geared to societal needs and challenges, but at least this matter is open to a reasonable assessment. The adequacy of preparatory institutions in less formal areas is much more difficult to assess, and the discrepancies more difficult to correct. Are our preparatory institutions sufficient for allowing people to adjust satisfactorily to a rapidly changing, mobile, and heterogeneous community? Are people being adequately prepared to cope with a greater amount of leisure time? Are workers prepared adequately for early retirement without ultimate feelings of uselessness and despair? Obviously, improving preparatory institutions in these areas is much more difficult than bringing formal training in mathematics or social studies up to date.

Because typical difficulties and challenges in social life differ from one culture to another and change over time, the accommodation of preparatory institutions to these changes must be an ongoing process. Similarly, societal incentives and evaluative systems structure and channel motivation and adaptive processes. They affect not only what the person wants to do but, perhaps even more important, the means he can use in dealing with particular challenges.

In any social system it is likely that incentive and preparatory systems are highly related. Skills are provided for doing the things that are valued, but frequently the things that are valued are not necessarily those that pose the greatest challenges to human adaptive capacities and health maintenance. In any case, as the preparatory institutions of a society become discrepant with the challenges people must face in their daily life, problems of disruption and deviant behavior become evident. Many investigators believe that the problem of sickness is greatly exacerbated in such social systems.

Many crises are inevitable consequences of the organization of social life and are amenable to social amelioration. Some of these issues can be strikingly illustrated through a brief examination of the social position of the aged in the United States and many other advanced industrial societies.

The Social Position of the Aged

Growing old would be difficult in any society that values youth, work, and material success as much as Americans do. Prestige derives more from what people do than from "what they are," and as the old leave the work force they lose much of their identity. But, more significant, the old tend to have meager material resources and to suffer serious decrements in their health. Because of the cultural value of men marrying younger women and the significant female advantage in longevity, a large proportion of the aged suffer from long periods of widowhood and isolation.

Throughout most of human history aging occurred in the context of an extended family network, and there were enough useful tasks to be performed to keep the elderly occupied and involved to the extent of their physical ability. With industrialization, the emergence of the small nuclear family, and the shift of work from the home to the factory, there was diminishing need for the elderly and less tolerance for the frailties of old age. Families took less responsibility for maintaining the old in the household, and old persons were more likely to live by themselves or, when they were sufficiently frail, in mental hospitals and nursing homes. With occupational, geographic, and social mobility, the old not only live outside the households of their offspring but also are often geographically and psychologically isolated from them. Aging is inevitably accompanied by the death of one's closest relatives and friends, and the aged have little social support in dealing with these frequent personal losses. In short, aging can be an isolating and agonizing experience in American society, and the plight of the aged a tragic affair.

While aging is experienced as a personal crisis, it is largely socially caused. Since it is unlikely that we have the capacity or will to set back social trends, remedies must lie in developing group solutions that build the resources, coping capacities, supports, and involvement of the aged. While the United States invests vast resources in the medical care of the aged, these are devoted almost exclusively to staving off the infirmities and disabilities of old age or to long-term institutional care. Only meager resources are invested to maintain the social integration of the aged, to protect them from loneliness and inactivity, to insure their adequate nutrition, or to assist them in retaining a respectable identity. Quality of life of the aged could be enhanced if some of the resources now wasted on relatively pointless technological efforts were invested in programs to repair old social networks among the aged or to devise entirely new ones. The population of retired people have enormous resources of their own that would be valuable assets once such a program were initiated. What is needed is the construction of a basic model; the aged themselves could then do the rest.

Toward a Technology of Caring

The example of the aged is just one of many possibilities for improving health and the quality of life that are ripe for implementation. While medical care has become an enormous industry, it has focused primarily on illness and its cure and has given short shrift to a broad promotive and rehabilitative approach. The increased sophistication and capacity of technological medicine has probably done a great deal of good, although not without creating dilemmas of its own, but it is clear that marginal investments of further billions in more care of the same kind will not repay its cost. Medical technology, however sophisticated, must be practiced within the context of larger goals, and not as an end in itself. Many of the problems seen in physicians' offices stem at least in part from a lack of self-worth, social isolation, and a sense of hopelessness. These states not only cause distress on their own terms but also are related to the onset and course of disease, and to illness response. Thus the quality of caring in medical practice affects the individual and his health directly, and may do a great deal to diminish the progression of disease and disability.

It is unfortunately common for many physicians to conceive of the caring functions of medical care as simply the expression of kindness and acceptance of the patient. While this is no trivial aspect, "caring"—as I shall use the term in this book—constitutes a much wider range of techniques based not only on human feeling, or even on the techniques usually associated with the practice of psychotherapy, but on scientific knowledge of how to provide human support. Such support may be given directly to the person affected, to the person's most intimate others who must also adapt to the problem, or to larger social entities who devise alternative possibilities for dealing with varying types of life problems. Briefly, caring has both its personal and organizational aspects.

In short, caring is a technology the dimensions of which can be concretely identified, studied, manipulated, and transmitted to practitioners who apply the technology in concrete situations. Caring is thus much more than a communication of feeling; it finds expression in cultural values, social structure, patterns of social interaction, and socialization. Medical care, of course, is largely remedial. However dedicated or effective the health professional, therapy can never compensate for the absence or erosion of caring in the ordinary and mundane affairs of everyday life. Since health professionals have major responsibilities for dealing with problems that are often a product of the absence or erosion of caring, they must examine the range of options available, given their awareness that they have only limited control over the life circumstances of those whom they assist.

While many aspects of stress-related diseases are uncertain—as are the technologies available to deal with them—risk factors associated with life crises and dysfunctional behavioral response are often far more influential in explaining disease than many biological factors on which physicians focus. While physicians may devote great efforts to identifying the nature of a problem, sparing no cost in the application of expensive diagnostic technology, they often seem indifferent as to whether patients understand or pursue their recommended regimen. The discrepancy between efforts made to diagnose a problem and those made to secure compliance is very great. Also, particularly in dealing with stress-related disease, health-care personnel are often frustrated because they lack control over the environments of their patients, because their exhortations to reduce one's pace and change one's life style seem futile, and because they appreciate that patterns of living and behavior conducive to poor health are frequently associated with considerable social and cultural advantages as well as disadvantages. The concept and specification of a technology of caring is in itself a useful coping model for the health practitioner in achieving a sense of mastery over a domain associated with feelings of futility and lack of mastery. Much can be achieved by increasing the practitioner's sense of confidence that his intervention can make a difference.

It is a major thesis of this book that the technology of caring, however, is more than the practitioner's belief in his professional efficacy. The strategic position of the helping professional in identifying persons who are isolated or otherwise under stress may serve as an excellent opportunity to help organize and make use of the natural supportive networks already existing in the community. Clinics, for example, can organize or coordinate their efforts with groups of individuals who share certain common problems and who can help each other cope: the parents of disabled children, the isolated aged person, the alcoholic, the patient undergoing a particularly stressful medical experience, or the newly separated, divorced, or widowed. Even the solo practitioner can become more familiar with the resources available in the community and can help bring patients into contact with them. The strategic position of physicians and other helping professionals allows them to act as a powerful catalyst that helps the patient overcome initial reticence in becoming part of such a group, or at least in making contact with others who have successfully overcome a similar problem.

The effectiveness of self-help groups or groups of common interest—either as social supports or in enhancing coping capacities—is dependent on a variety of factors, many of which still remain uncertain. But it is clearly prudent for the health practitioner interested in dealing with risk factors associated with crisis to recognize clients' needs for social support and to use the means available in the community for providing it. With initiative, health personnel may even contribute to the development of such groups or serve as a professional resource for them. While prudence requires action, we should at the same time be giving greater effort to understanding more precisely the nature of these risk factors, the way they can be more effectively conceptualized, and the most effective possible interventions. It is my hope that this book will contribute something to each of these goals.

Part 5

THE MACRO SYSTEM OF HEALTH CARE

Chapter 11

MEDICAL-CARE SYSTEMS

Despite significant differences in ideology, values, and social organization, most Western developed countries—and probably most countries in the world—face common problems of financing, organizing, and providing health-care services. As populations demand more medical care, there is growing concern among nations to provide a minimal level of service to all and to decrease obvious inequalities. To use available technology and knowledge efficiently and effectively, certain organizational options are most desirable. Thus there is a tendency throughout the world to link existing services to defined population groups, to develop new and more economic ways to provide primary services to the population without too great an emphasis on technological efforts, to integrate services increasingly fragmented by specialization or a more elaborate division of labor, and to seek ways to improve the output of the delivery system with fixed inputs. Although all of these concerns characterize national planning in underdeveloped countries to some extent, they are particularly descriptive of tendencies among developed countries as they attempt to control the enormous costs of available technologies. Throughout the world there is increasing movement away from medicine as a solitary entrepreneurial activity and more emphasis on the effective development of health-delivery systems.

The goal of any medical system is to organize for the provision and distribution of health services to those who need them, and to use the resources, knowledge, and technologies available to prevent and alleviate disease, disability, and suffering to the extent possible under prevailing conditions. There are alternative ways by which these goals may be pursued, and the form health institutions take is related to the form of other societal institutions and to the economic, organizational, and value context of the society of which they are a part. Thus it becomes necessary to consider not only "ideal patterns" of health organization but also those most desirable, given the economic limitations and value context within which medical decisions must be framed. There is no single ideal pattern of health organization. Each pattern of health care that exists involves both advantages and costs, and although it is possible to discuss the consequences resulting from varying forms of organization, any total judgment favoring one system of medical organization over another must involve particular value choices.

Historical Background

Forms of medical institutions, as is the case with other social institutions, have not been organized to fit a particular rational plan of action. Medical institutions in various countries have developed over a considerable time in response to changes in technology, varying societal needs, and the pressures of a variety of interest groups. Medicine has really developed primarily in the past 100 years. Before that time medical practice consisted for the most part of trial-and-error attempts by self-appointed practitioners to deal with the ills of people. Although hospitals can be traced back as far as the pre-Christian era (592), it was not until late in the nineteenth century that hospitals cared for any large number of patients. As late as 1851 in England there were only 7,619 hospital patients enumerated in the census (1).

The roots of American medicine must be traced to England and the Continent. Among the practitioners who came to the early settlements were a few physicians holding university degrees, but for the most part they were ships' surgeons and others who became doctors through apprentice training (642). The elite of the British doctors were members of the Royal College of Physicians, who were drawn mostly from among the graduates of Oxford and Cambridge; as late as 1834 one could gain membership in the college for a payment of 50 guineas after completing three examinations lasting about 20 minutes each. Lower in status were the members of the College of Surgeons, who could perform surgery, mostly in the patient's home, but could not give medicines internally. The third group of practitioners, the apothecaries, were tradesmen who learned their job during apprenticeship; these men, drawn from a lower social background, could charge for their medicine but not for their advice (1). Finally, there were abundant quacks who greatly outnumbered those qualified practitioners and who sold their wares for what they could get.

The first American doctors soon took on their own apprentices, and doctors in America generally learned their trade through observation and practice rather than any formal course of education. In the middle of the nineteenth century any man with an elementary education could become a doctor by taking a course for a winter or two and passing an examination, and even as late as 1900 there were many medical students who could not have gained entrance to a good liberal arts college (643). The beginnings and early development of medicine in the United States were not in any sense glorious, and it was not until Osler and Welsh formed their group at Johns Hopkins in the 1890s that we had any development in America of which foreigners took note. American research and scientific inquiry in medicine in the nineteenth century contributed little of lasting importance (643).

The first American hospital was established in Philadelphia in 1751. It was for the sick poor, to provide lodgings for patients who came to Philadelphia for medical care, and for the purposes of medical education. The hospital was set up under voluntary auspices and was governed privately. Unlike its British counterpart, which we will review shortly, it allowed attending doctors to admit patients and charge fees, although it catered primarily to the sick poor who could not pay for their own care (643). Doctors appointed to the Pennsylvania Hospital served without payment and therefore depended on private patients for their income. The pattern of organization of this hospital typifies the dominant pattern that developed in America (78; 195). The typical doctor in a voluntary hospital continues to be a part-time man who uses the hospital for his private patients. Unlike most European countries, America has not evolved a special class of hospital-based doctors who are separate and distinct from the community practitioner, although some hospitals have such doctors.

Except for the distinction noted above, American medical practice usually followed European developments, and the elite group of early American doctors sought their training in Europe. Most American hospitals were founded on the English pattern, and in both countries hospitals developed initially, at least in the eighteenth and early nineteenth centuries, on a voluntary basis. During this period, given the conditions in hospitals, it was better to receive medical care in the home; the hospital was meant primarily for the poor whose home conditions were deprived and inadequate. In England the sick poor went either to a voluntary hospital or an almshouse; patients with chronic, incurable, terminal, and frequently infectious conditions were usually not acceptable to the voluntary hospitals, which were increasingly concerned with medical education and medical research, thus seeking out the most interesting cases for their purposes. Ultimately the workhouses were also to be transformed into hospitals.

The growth of hospitals in the nineteenth century in England was greatly encouraged by doctors who wanted hospitals for teaching and research. While in the eighteenth century hospitals had been established to help the sick poor, in the following century they developed to serve the teacher and his student (1). Whereas in the early days doctors accepted honorary posts in voluntary hospitals largely for charitable purposes, later hospital appointments brought the doctor rewards in fees for teaching as well as professional prestige. Hospital appointments were attractive but limited, and within each of the major teaching hospitals one could find young, ambitious doctors who were frustrated in their aspirations for higher position and who coveted a hospital appointment with its associated rewards, They were further frustrated by the difficulties of developing their special interests, which required facilities and equipment that their elders were not readily willing to grant. In a situation of scarce facilities, advances in new areas would necessarily involve costs for those already established. The ambitious and aspiring specialists were therefore blocked by the "old guard," who were protective of their status and generalists in their approach. Abel-Smith notes the advantages of such specialization: "The young doctor with a meagre practice had little hope of demonstrating to the influential patient that his total skill was greater than that of his senior. It was, however, easier to cultivate a reputation for special skill in treating one particular condition. Specialization was a form of self-advertisement" (1, p. 22). It was these men who went off and established special hospitals, and thus caused the proliferation of such institutions in London and the provinces.

By the second half of the nineteenth century medicine had become a competitive enterprise, and the general practitioner without a hospital position looked with envy upon his more prestigious competitors. In addition to the monetary rewards available from such positions, the prestige that had come to be associated with them gave the hospital doctor a competitive advantage in finding wealthy private clients. Moreover, as medicine developed as a healing art, more patients who could afford private fees came seeking medical care from the prestigious voluntary hospitals that provided free care, and from the point of view of the disenfranchised doctor, the hospital did not distinguish those who could afford to pay for their medical care from those who could not. Thus the hospital doctors were continually barraged with criticism for dispensing too many free services to those who could pay. The community doctors also opposed hospital charges of any kind, since this would mean competition for them. From their point of view it was most advantageous that all hospital care be free, so that those who could pay for medical services would be excluded. One of the forces contributing to the present split between the general practitioner and the consultant in England was the continued efforts of nonhospital doctors to limit the more general activities in community practice that hospital doctors were willing to undertake.

It is important to recognize, as Professor Brian Abel-Smith illustrates in his book *The Hospitals*, from which most of this discussion is taken, that the nationalized British Health Service was a stage in the evolution of British social services and that it "expressed values and embodied traditions both of long duration" (1, p. 502). By the second half of the nineteenth century the poor had gained the right to institutionalized care when they were sick. In the Metropolitan Poor Act of 1867 it was explicitly acknowledged that it was the obligation of the state to provide hospitals for the poor. Free care for the poor was supported by the medical profession, for the general community practitioners felt that their competitive position was more secure if hospital care was free and there was a rigid division between those who paid the entire cost of their treatment and those who paid nothing at all.

The organization of medical care in England became more chaotic in the late nineteenth century and the first decade of the twentieth century. Conditions in the hospitals and infirmaries had improved during the preceding period and more patients, even middle-class ones, were demanding hospital care. The heavy demand for the better hospital facilities required selection and generally the hospitals were most receptive to the acutely ill. Because facilities were limited, acute patients were cared for in the public infirmaries established by the 1867 Poor Law, while those with chronic problems were sent to the workhouse. The consequence was to replace some of the destitute sick for whom these infirmaries were intended with acutely ill persons who could afford to pay for their own care. In contrast to the better infirmaries, the workhouses offered a low standard of nursing services. As late as 1905 many patients were still being nursed by old and feeble-minded paupers in facilities poorly suited for their care. The situation was complicated by the fact that when those better off replaced the poor in the more adequate public infirmaries, the poor in many areas were denied care by the public services outside the workhouses. These problems associated with other difficulties and sources of dissatisfaction ultimately led to the establishment of the National Insurance Act of 1911.

The National Insurance Act provided wage earners, but not their families, with a general practitioner service, partially paid for through insurance payments. General practitioners were not unattracted to this scheme since it provided the panel doctor (who provided services under the National Insurance Act) with a secure source of income. The scheme thus provided the working man with care outside the hospital and encouraged development of the trend for hospitals to be used for consultation in contrast to providing general medical services. The actual organization of general practice was not altered to any large extent, as general practitioners were treated as individual contractors operating from their own premises. They were paid a flat sum for each patient for whom they undertook to provide care. As Abel-Smith notes, this form of organization reversed previous incentives in that services provided by the outpatient departments of the hospitals for panel patients no longer detracted from the financial status of the general practitioner, since he received a fixed capitation payment for each of his patients. Indeed, now the incentive existed for the general practitioner to turn his most complex and troubling patients over to the hospital, and it is likely that this led doctors to refer patients to hospitals more readily. This pattern has persisted in Great Britain for the most part to this very day. This change had important consequences, as Abel-Smith notes:

> General practice had always been divorced from the urban hospitals. This was not a problem while hospitals and general practitioners catered for different segments of the population. Continuity of care was not disturbed. The general practitioner, aided occasionally by a consultant, supervised all the treatment in the patient's home. The hospital in its turn provided all the treatment for some poor persons—both general practitioner and specialist services. The juniors examined the outpatients and referred the cases requiring further care to their seniors and then continued to look after these cases in the wards under the consultant's supervision. Thus though medical care was provided without knowledge of the patient's home circumstances, continuity of care could be provided during any one illness. When the "poor" obtained general practitioners under the Act, continuity of care was disturbed: the notes which passed between the general practitioner and the hospital were a weak link in the lengthened chain of medical care. On the other hand, many patients who had previously "shopped around" obtained the services of one general practitioner. And it was now more difficult to go "gadding round" the outpatient departments [1, pp. 247–48].

Following World War I the voluntary hospitals were in poor financial shape and patients were asked to pay what they could for their care. This once again revived the animosity of the general practitioners, as there was little guarantee that hospitals would not accept on a paying basis patients who would ordinarily receive their care from general practitioners. "Thus the historic conflict between the general practitioners and the voluntary hospitals, after a temporary lull following the 1911 Insurance Act, was revived" (1, pp. 334–35). At the same time, patients who were contributing toward their care in voluntary hospitals were more critical and demanding. Treatment came to be seen more as a right than as a charity.

Between the two world wars medical care was in ferment. With the development of medical science, hospital and medical care had become more important to the population. Practitioners themselves had encouraged the proliferation of small, poorly located hospitals that for the most part were the context for the provision of poor medical care. Many of the voluntary hospitals also deteriorated because of financial difficulties, and the hospital system on the whole was unplanned, poorly organized, and inefficient. World War II made the difficulties of hospital care, finance, and organization even more evident; the increased solidarity brought about by the war in this highly class-conscious society provided further impetus for the demands that a truly national scheme be developed. The birth of the National Health Service in 1948 organized the nation's hospitals into 14 regional boards that had responsibility for all of the hospitals, both voluntary and public, with the exclusion of the teaching hospitals associated with medical schools.

As already noted, the National Health Service was a creature of the past; its creation combined many of the irrationalities and organizational absurdities that existed prior to the nationalized service. Essentially the service had three parts. The hospital system was organized on a regional basis in a more rational fashion, improving to some extent the distribution of beds and facilities. Almost all of the hospital-based doctors benefited in one way or another from the nationalization of health services. Doctors at the voluntary hospitals retained their freedom but were to be paid for services previously rendered free. The staffs of hospitals previously belonging to the local authorities—that is, the old public infirmaries—were to be paid more and subjected to less supervision. Because the creation of a true national health service depended on its acceptance by the consultants, the government was not unwilling to "bribe" them. The lower-status local authorities and general practitioner service did not fare so well. Having lost their hospitals, the local authorities were left with the responsibility for a variety of peripheral functions they had taken on through time. The general practitioners were perhaps the greatest losers in the bargain. They were now more completely disenfranchised from hospital work, as previously some general practitioners took on work in small hospitals that could not support a consultant. Under the new regional organization of hospitals, this work would be undertaken by salaried consultants. Although the general practitioners retained the right to control some beds in the smaller cottage hospitals for obstetrical cases, for the most part general practitioners were to be excluded from hospital work. Moreover, the salaried consultants were no longer in any sense dependent on private referrals from general practitioners, and this has perhaps led to an attitude that more readily indicates the status distinction between the general practitioner and the consultant. Although it was anticipated that the conditions of general practice would be improved through the establishment of general practice centers supplied with ample diagnostic facilities and ancillary help, neither the practitioners themselves nor the successive governments were enthusiastic about the idea. The doctors coveted their independence, distrusted both government and local authorities, and were wary about operating under the gaze of their medical colleagues. The government, preoccupied with other problems of great magnitude following World War II, was reluctant to expend the substantial sums necessary to improve the conditions of general practice. In recent years new efforts have been made to improve the organization and quality of care provided by general practitioners, but the general practice service is still the weakest component of the National Health Service.

The development of medical care in the United States is more varied, more recent, and much more difficult to describe in any systematic fashion because a study comparable to Abel-Smith's does not exist for the United States. Some important differences between the two countries should be noted, however. By the nineteenth century Great Britain was a highly urbanized country. London, the center for medical education, specialization, and the growth of voluntary hospitals, already had a long urban history and tradition. In contrast, America was frontier country and largely rural. Distinctions among the apothecary, the physician, and the surgeon, so important in the development of English medicine, were inappropriate in the American context with its population scattered over a vast land area. Doctors did everything, and the typical European distinctions did not develop (667). Moreover, as already noted, American medicine in the nineteenth century was full of quackery, medical education was inferior, physicians were frequently ignorant, licensing standards were low, and medical research was to a great degree worthless (642; 667). Although hospitals began to play an important role in medical practice by the end of the nineteenth century, it was not until after World War I that the pattern of medical care changed significantly (667).

Hospitals developed slowly in the United States. In 1873 there were only about 100 hospitals in the country that did not deal with mental disorders. By 1935 the number was approaching 6,800 (592). In the late nineteenth century there was an acceleration in the development of new hospitals, and the motives were not too different from those in England. The newly developing specialties could not easily be accommodated into the existing structure of voluntary hospitals because of the lack of facilities and economic resources. Physicians thus encouraged the development of special hospitals that catered to their specialty (592). But for the most part medical practice was general, and most doctors viewed themselves as engaged in general practice. In 1928, 74 percent of American doctors reported themselves as general practitioners; by 1942 only 49 percent so identified themselves; and today the man who views himself as a generalist is increasingly less common.

With the twentieth century have come tremendous developments in clinical medicine, cellular physiology, medical bacteriology, endocrinology, and surgical intervention. Accompanying improvements in medical knowledge and understanding are a variety of instruments, technologies, and laboratory aids useful in diagnosis and treatment. With the development of medical knowledge, medical care has become more specialized and has involved a large number of new professions and medical ancillaries. All of these facilities and personnel have been gathered together in one context, the hospital, that serves as an educational institution, a center for medical research, and the center for a variety of treatment and preventive endeavors (770). The health industries have become one of the largest sectors of our economy, and hospitals have become one of our largest employers. In recent decades hospital costs and problems have multiplied at a stultifying rate, and medical care has become one of our most complex social institutions.

Modern Organizational Problems

As the preceding historical discussion has suggested, medical care is a vast and complex industry. Any brief attempt to describe problems must involve superficialities and oversimplifications, and such a discussion is unlikely to take into account the fantastic diversity typical of the towns and municipalities and the state and federal agencies that provide and finance medical-care institutions. When one assumes a comparative perspective, which attempts to compare social systems with different histories and social institutions, the problem becomes even more complex and difficult, and it is no easy task to evaluate the consequences of differing systems for organizing care. First of all, it is impossible to ascertain what might have happened had some other pattern of medical care been provided at some point in the past. Comparisons across countries are confounded by the tremendous cultural, social, and economic differences between social systems. All we can do here is to note some of the significant problems and interesting points of comparison. In the future we shall have more experimental ventures that attempt to evaluate the consequences of differing forms of providing medical services under conditions that are more effectively controlled.

One of the basic problems faced by all modern medical systems is the enormous cost of providing medical care (657). Modern medical technology is expensive; health workers must undertake long periods of training, and demand salaries commensurate with their educational investments; and treating each serious illness may involve the participation of a very large health team, a wide range of services, expensive tests, the use of costly equipment, and the occupancy of space. Individuals use an increasing number of health services per capita, and hospital administrations have grown remarkably over the years. Most people are born and die in hospitals, and are likely to make several other visits there during their lifetime. Also, with the increasing number of aged persons in the population there is a higher rate of use of services, as older people require more medical and hospital services than younger people.

In comparing countries varying in their economic status and wealth, it becomes particularly difficult to distinguish clearly what consequences flow from the form of medical organization, as compared with those that flow from economic investments in health and available capital for such expenditures. It is one thing to ask which country provides the most and the best health care; it is quite another matter to investigate the relative value received for the investment made in health care. In any planned allocation of resources—and even in economic systems such as the United States, where medical planning is highly decentralized—the value of increased provision of health care is weighed in relation to other social needs and to political contingencies. Governments—like people—have limited resources, and they must make decisions about how to distribute these resources in dealing with competing demands. Whether to increase expenditures in the area of health as opposed to housing, education, or highways, involves the development of a system of priorities that may be difficult to determine to everyone's satisfaction, and persons of good will may vigorously disagree with one another.

In comparing various nations, it is important to note that decisions concerning health investments occur on a different basis. In Great Britain, for example, most expenditures for medical and dental care are public and result from decisions of the central government. The United States—which has a mixed medical system—makes both large-scale private and public investments in health through individual consumer expenditure, government programs, and private philanthropy. Although government may vary its contribution to health from one period to another, and although its agencies may be able to stimulate private expenditures for health through cost-sharing programs and various tax mechanisms, investments come from many sources. As we will note later, one of the greatest problems in Great Britain in the past decade— contrary to the usual stereotype—was the failure to invest sufficient funds in health care to fulfill the stated ideals of the British Health Service, even in a modest way. Some experts believe that mixed systems of medical investment, such as that in the United States, have advantages over those supported through a single source (23; 25). It is argued that mixed investment stimulates improvement and experimentation, while a single source of finance tends to perpetuate the system that exists. Although this general hypothesis may be correct, it is difficult to substantiate it on the basis of simple comparisons. The economic problems of these two countries are vastly different, and the development of the National Health Service took place within a context of many pressing problems resulting from World War II and a difficult economic situation (196). Because the United States has had more free capital for investment in health than has Britain, one must be cautious in attributing limited health investment in Britain to its form of medical organization rather than to other factors. Moreover, as we shall indicate later in this chapter, the open-ended nature of financing of medical care in the United States has resulted in an inability to control escalating medical-care costs.

It is extremely difficult to specify what is a proper level of investment in health as compared with other spheres of human activity. It is not difficult to absorb substantial increases in health expenditure; as people become more affluent their rate of utilization of medical resources rises. In an economy of scarcity, however, it is extremely important to attempt to distinguish what degree of expenditure will make a significant difference in respect to mortality and morbidity, and what proportion of the investment provides a convenient service but has no great consequence for the health of people. Under conditions of scarcity, funds may more reasonably and productively be invested in education or public transportation than in some facets of health care.

From the perspective of community health there are two major considerations in designing the organization of medical services. First, it is important that services be available to people who need them and who can most benefit from them. Second, it is essential that the qualtity of these services be maintained and developed. To achieve the distribution goal it is necessary to: recruit and train sufficient health personnel; provide adequate facilities for rendering needed services to the population; and insure access to these services among persons in various geographic areas and in different social strata. Quality of services depends on caliber of manpower (their training in terms of skills and orientations to patients), effectiveness with which care is organized and provided, availability of resources, and incentives for high-quality care and continued innovation.

At present there is no well-formulated theoretical approach to an overall understanding of health-care systems. As was observed in the historical discussion, the evolution of health-care delivery systems is shaped by the historical and social context in which these systems are embedded. Such factors as economic organization, ideological forces, available technology, and preexisting professional organization affect the availability of resources, access to medical care, distribution of health-care services, and ultimately the quality of health care. The Soviet health service, for example, began under Lenin and developed during Stalin's regime. The structure that developed reflected Leninist-Stalinist ideology as to the nature of the Soviet state and the role of medicine in promoting the health of the state (218). Abundant physician and other resources were made available to improve health, and medicine intruded into the affairs of the citizen to a degree we would find exceptional in our own society (26; 217). But as part of their philosophy the Soviets gave great emphasis to industrial and environmental health and preventive medicine, particularly to preserve the essential working force and to insure productivity. Similarly, developments in Chinese medicine were profoundly influenced by Maoist ideology, particularly in relationship to its rural emphasis, its reliance on ancillary medical personnel, and its attempts to avoid excessive professionalization and bureaucratization and to stress self-reliance. But Chinese medicine still reflects ancient patterns and traditional patient-practitioner healing relationships (339; 572; 644).

Medical sociologists are currently struggling to develop theoretical perspectives that are helpful in examining varying medical-care systems on a broad basis. This effort is useful because a disproportionate emphasis in the field thus far has been given to microsociological studies (12). A number of young medical sociologists are attempting to use the theories of society of Karl Marx as an organizing perspective for examining processes of medical care. These efforts are new and not yet particularly productive, but attempts to look at medicine, as well as at other social institutions, from diverse points of view contribute to a richer discussion. It is hoped that this discussion will be more than competing rhetoric and will lead to varying predictions from different theoretical frameworks that are empirically open to verification or refutation. One attempt to suggest a Marxist perspective is found in Waitzkin and Waterman (754). The flavor of their argument and approach is suggested by the following quote:

> It is by no means clear that a humane health care system is possible in a capitalist society. The institution of medicine is intimately tied to the broad sociopolitical framework of a society. Under capitalism, the right of individual citizens to decent health care remains an ambiguous principle. Despite widespread concern about the costliness, maldistribution, and poor quality of services, the medical profession and large American corporations continue to exploit illness for profit. In this sociopolitical context, it is probably naive to presume that a responsive and effective health system can emerge through incremental reforms—without basic (and perhaps revolutionary) transformation of the social order [754, pp. 15–16].

Although Waitzkin and Waterman suggest many provocative ideas, their book suffers from a lack of specification of criteria by which capitalist and socialist systems might be compared, or a clear definition of such terms as "humane," "decent health care," "quality," "effective," and "responsive." Without specific criteria and clear definitions, the quoted statement remains vague and ideological.

The framework I shall use to examine the macro issues, in contrast, concerns the means used by varying nations having different economic and social ideologies to determine allocations for medical care, to choose varying allocations within the health sector, and to contain overall expenditures. Such means are closely related to how the system functions as a whole and to the adaptations made by doctors and patients. In short, the organizing principle of this discussion is the concept of rationing. This framework is suggested in a tentative way, with the full realization that it is incomplete and requires a great deal of further elaboration and empirical study. I hope that the readers of the book will find this approach sufficiently engaging to participate in carrying out studies that contribute to its elaboration and refinement.

Rationing Medical Care

Medicine throughout the world has undergone an enormous development in specialized knowledge and technology in recent decades. While these advances have brought considerable progress in treating some diseases, most of the major diseases affecting mortality and morbidity—from heart disease and the cancers to the psychoses and substance abuse—are poorly understood, and existing efforts, while they ameliorate suffering and sometimes extend life, are not able to cure or prevent the incidence of most of these conditions. The technologies that do exist are often extraordinarily expensive, require intensive professional manpower, and must be applied repeatedly during the long course of a chronic condition. To take an example in which success has been quite impressive, such as in hemodialysis and transplantation in end-stage kidney disease, intensive and expensive efforts, which on a per capita basis consume a high level of expenditure, must be made over a long period to sustain life and functioning (227). As these halfway technologies have developed—intensive-care units, radiation therapy for cancers, coronary bypass surgery—the aggregate costs of medical care continue to move upward, with medical services consuming a larger proportion of national income. In the United States, for example—where in 1940 the costs of health care were $4 billion and 4 percent of the gross national product—present costs are approaching $140 billion and 9 percent of the gross national product and are estimated to be well over 200 billion by the 1980s. While the proportional increase is not as large in nations having a centralized prospective budgeting process, as in England, the trend is the same and continues to be a source of concern among all thoughtful people.

Since illness and *dis-ease* are common conditions of mankind and their prevalence is extremely high in varied populations, as has been demonstrated by morbidity surveys (765), there is almost unlimited possibility for the continued escalation of medical demand and medical expenditures. As people have acquired higher and more unrealistic expectations of medicine, demands for care for a wide variety of both major and minor conditions have accelerated. No nation that follows a sane public policy would facilitate the fulfillment of all perceptions of need that the public might have. As in every other area of life, resources must be rationed. The uncontrolled escalation of costs in developed countries is in part a result of techniques of rationing being in a process of transition, and most countries have yet to reach a reasonable end point in this transitional process, whether for political or other reasons. The process is one of movement from *rationing by fee* through a stage of *implicit rationing* through resource allocation to a final stage of *explicit rationing*. In this process the role of physician shifts from entrepreneur to bureaucratic official, and medical practice from a market-oriented system to a rationalized bureaucracy. These shifts, in turn, have an important bearing on the psychological meaning of the doctor-patient relationship and on the flexibility of medicine as an institution to meet patient expectations.

Types of Rationing

In the traditional practice of medicine and in much of the world today, the availability of medical care has been dependent on the ability to purchase it. Those with means could obtain whatever level of medical care was available, while those without means were dependent on whatever services were made available by government, philanthropists, the church, or physicians themselves. Since affluence was limited and medical technology and knowledge offered only modest gains, the marketplace was a natural device for rationing services. Indeed, it worked so well that physicians were often supporters of government intervention and direct payments for care since such support increased their opportunities for remuneration.

Fee-for-service as an effective system of rationing broke down due to a variety of factors. First, medical technology and knowledge expanded rapidly, greatly increasing the costs of a serious medical episode and imposing on the ill a financial burden that was large and unpredictable. Associated with this was a growing demand on the part of populations for means of sharing such risks through benevolent societies and insurance plans and, as costs mounted, for government to assume a growing proportion of these expenditures. Because of the traditions of medical practice, however, and the political monopoly that physicians had gained over the marketplace, the rise of third-party payment was not associated with careful controls over the work of the physician and the way he generated costs. While third-party payment increased access to services, the orientations of increasingly scientific and technologically inclined physicians resulted in a large acceleration in the use of diagnostic and treatment techniques. The consequence has been an escalation of costs that we now view as almost inevitable. Physicians have been trained to pursue the "technological imperative"—that is, the tendency to use any intervention regardless of cost if there is any possibility of benefit for the patient (255). This contrasts with a cost-benefit calculation in which there is consideration of the relative costs and benefits of pursuing a particular course of action. The "technological imperative," when carried to its extreme, incurs fantastic expense for relatively small and at times counterproductive outcomes.

Many developed nations shifted quite early from fee-for-service rationing to what I have referred to as *implicit rationing*. Under health-insurance plans in various European countries, rationing was imposed either by the centralized prospective budgeting procedures of the government, as in England, or through the limited resources available to "sickness societies" that contracted with physicians and hospitals for services for their members. For example, in England under the National Health Insurance Act of 1911, and later through the establishment of the National Health Service in 1946, the central government budgeted fixed amounts for providing community medical services on a capitation basis; hospital services were provided for as of 1948 on an established budget. Similarly, sickness societies in other countries had to enter contractual agreements with physicians within the means available, thus limiting the extent of services that could be rendered.

In European countries that adopted national health insurance through an indirect method, such as mandated employer-employee contributions, governments increasingly assumed a larger proportion of the costs of physician services and institutional care. Since government had little control over the way costs were generated by physicians and hospitals, there was continuing pressure for increased expenditures by both patients and physicians. Governments took on the obligation in making up deficits between costs generated by health professionals and the funds available from employer-employee contributions. They did so either by raising the social security tax rates or by making larger contributions each year from general revenues. In England, where the government had direct budgetary control, costs were more successfully contained, but there were constant pressures from professionals for increased expenditure. Despite direct control the proportion of national income allocated to health care escalated, but at a lesser rate than in many other countries with more open-ended budgeting systems.

Implicit rationing depends on the relationship between available services and demands for their use. Limited resources, facilities, and manpower are made available, and the health-care system adapts to demand by establishing noneconomic barriers (500, pp. 87–97). Health professionals, having their own styles of work and professional norms, accommodate as many patients as they can, making judgments as to priorities and need. Access to services may be limited by long appointment or referral waiting periods, limited sites of care (and therefore longer barriers of distance and inconvenience), longer waiting times, bureaucratic barriers, and so on. Rationing may also occur through the control exercised over the extent of elaboration of services—laboratory tests ordered, diagnostic techniques used, rate of hospitalization, number of surgical interventions, and time devoted to each patient. Capitation or salary as forms of professional payment tend to limit the extent of these modalities; fee-for-service increases the rate of discrete technical services for which a fee is paid (265; 589).

Implicit rationing has the effect of limiting expenditures, but not necessarily in a rational way. Such rationing is based on the assumption that the professional is sufficiently programmed by his socialization as a health practitioner to make scientifically valid judgments as to what constitutes need, what treatment modalities are most likely to be effective, and which cases deserve priority. It is supposed that the exercise of clinical judgment will result in rational decision making. But as Eliot Freidson (242, pp. 136–37) has noted, evaluation of medical judgment by professional peers is so permissive that only "blatant acts of ignorance or inattention" are clearly recognized as mistakes. Moreover, it is the more knowledgeable, aggressive, and demanding individuals who get more service, and these patients are usually more educated, more sophisticated, but less needy (322). In short, under implicit rationing the assumption is that physicians exercise agreed-upon standards for care and that services are equitably provided in light of these standards. The fact is that these standards are murky if they exist at all, and even the most obvious ones have little relationship to any existing knowledge on the implications of varying patterns of care for patient outcome. Under these conditions the most effective and vocal consumers may get more than their share of whatever care is available. Moreover, given the ambiguities of practice, physicians and other health professionals may play out their own personal agendas, cultural preferences, and professional biases. Being remunerated on salary, they may work at a comfortable and leisurely pace; they may choose to emphasize work they find most interesting, neglecting important needs of patients, such as those for empathy and support, the fulfillment of which may be perceived as professionally less satisfying.

There is considerable evidence that systems of implicit rationing provide care at lower cost because of the limited budget available and the containment in provision of resources and manpower, but there is little evidence to support the contention that the result is a fairer allocation of social resources. Under implicit rationing large disparities continue in the availability of facilities, allocation of manpower and resources per capita (and in relation to known rates of morbidity in the population), and access to services (147; 322; 451). Affluent areas tend to retain more facilities, manpower, and other resources, and relatively little redistribution takes place. There are large variations from area to area and institution to institution in the procedures performed, workload, ancillary assistance available, and level of technology.

Governments are seeking means to move from implicit to explicit forms of rationing. The idea of explicit rationing is not only to set limits on total expenditures for care but also to develop mechanisms for arriving at more rational decisions as to relative investments in different areas of care, varying types of facilities and manpower, new technological initiatives, and the establishment of certain minimal uniform standards. The difficulty with establishing such priorities and standards is the overall lack of definitive evidence as to which health-care practices really make a difference in illness outcomes. While standards for processes of care are readily formulated, it is difficult to demonstrate for most facets of care that such process norms have any clear relationship to outcomes that really matter. Indeed, randomized trials tend to show that routine use of such expensive innovations as coronary intensive care or longer hospitalizations for a variety of diseases seems to make little difference in measurable outcomes (130).

The difficulty of imposing explicit rationing, however, is more political than scientific. While there is always danger in establishing general guidelines that the overall formulation will not fit a specific case, medical practice offers many instances in which intelligent restrictions on practices of physicians are likely to lead to both improved and more economical practice. The fact is that physicians resist such guidelines as intrusions on their professional judgment and autonomy, and tend to do whatever they can to subvert them. Even with a certain amount of slack, intelligent guidelines sensitive to the realities of medical practice and human behavior can be an important contribution toward more effective rationing than usually exists under the implicit system.

A variety of techniques are used under many insurance systems to restrict the options of health practitioners (265). The most straightforward is the simple exclusion or restriction of certain types of services that may involve large costs but dubious benefits—for example, psychoanalysis, orthodontia, rest cures, and plastic surgery for cosmetic purposes. In the case of essential components of treatment, the program may set maximal numbers of procedures that will be paid for or establish required time intervals between procedures that can be repeated and remain eligible for coverage. These limitations have the function of restricting the physician's discretion to a modest degree, although in theory they can be extended. Another technique is to limit the cost of a treatment by requiring the physician to provide justification if he wishes to exercise a more expensive option. Since physicians tend to dislike additional paperwork, reasonable guidelines are likely to be effective.

Some countries require prereview by government physicians for specified expensive procedures. If prereview is used too extensively it becomes a costly and inefficient technique but, if used sparingly to control expensive work of dubious effectiveness and possible danger as well, it can have effects both as a deterrent and as a means of controlling irresponsible practitioners. Particularly in the area of surgical intervention and perhaps also in the use of dangerous classes of drugs, prereview functions both to reduce costs and to encourage a higher quality of care. In short, both government itself and nongovernmental insurance programs are becoming more bold in intruding on areas that physicians regard within their discretion. We have every reason to anticipate that this trend will continue.

Doctor-Patient Interaction

Each of the types of rationing described tends to be associated with a particular mode of physician-patient interaction, although there is great variation within each type dependent on the personalities of the actors involved, the workload and work flow, and the incentives operative in any particular situation. Eliot Freidson (235; 239; 242) has written extensively on these types of relationships, and in this section I draw heavily on his work. It is my contention that as rationing varies from fee-for-service to implicit to explicit, the influence shifts from client control to colleague control to bureaucratic control and the nuances in the physician's role shift from entrepreneur to expert to official.

Freidson has illustrated convincingly how the shift from fee-for-service practice to prepaid group practice is accompanied by less flexibility and responsiveness by the physician. When retention of the patient is no longer an economic issue, there is no need to "humor the patient" or to bend to the patient's wishes when they are contrary to the physician's best judgment. Freidson argues that in the prepaid situation colleagues are a more important reference group, and while the physician may be more inflexible he may practice a higher standard of medical care. The extent of differences between fee-for-service and prepaid practice depends greatly on the competition for patients in any practice area. As competition increases, physicians may be more willing to provide greater amenities to patients and to be flexible in responding to their requests in order to retain their patronage. When the physician has more patients than he requires, there may be little client control even in the fee-for-service situation. As the physician becomes less dependent on the patient—either because he is only one of a large number of physicians servicing an enrolled population or because he is in a favorable competitive situation—he can more easily play the role of the neutral expert whose decisions are isolated from any personal financial stake.

In theory, implicit rationing encourages the physician to play the role of expert, but in actuality the difficulty lies in the ambiguity of his expertise. Since the physician by the very nature of his work is required to come to many social decisions unrelated to his technical expertise, and since physicians differ radically in these social judgments, there is no clear basis for these decisions. For example, consider the frequent issue of whether a hospitalized mother should be sent home or retained for a few more days because the physician anticipates that her family will expect her to resume usual duties or that she may be inclined to reassume responsibilities too quickly. In theory, when the patient must incur part of the fee, such potential cost will influence the decision. However, when third parties assume the cost, neither the physician nor the patient has any incentive to choose the more parsimonious decision. If the physician acts as an expert, his bias is to use resources if he sees any potential benefit to the patient. Incentives to do otherwise come only when he is faced with a limitation of resources. A global budget without further guidelines—although it may restrict the physician's actions to some extent—does not insure rational decision making and may encourage highly preferential behavior depending on the physician's perceptions of and attitudes toward the patient.

Most existing prepaid group practices seem to conserve resources more by controlling inputs—numbers of primary-care physicians, beds, and specialists—than by affecting directly the manner in which physicians make decisions in allocating resources. While it has been alleged that the incentives for physicians to avoid unnecessary work may be an important factor, there is no impressive evidence that such incentives substantially affect decision making itself (500). Most of the rationing that takes place seems to be at the administrative planning level, with physicians adjusting to whatever the resources available. Thus in most prepaid group practices or in health centers or polyclinics physicians still retain the role of expert.

As health-care plan administrators or government officials attempt to tighten expenditures by moving toward a system of explicit rationing, physicians are pushed into the role of bureaucratic official. The case of the Soviet physicians, described by Field (217), who were limited in the number of sickness certifications they could issue provides an extreme example of how bureaucratic regulation can limit the options available for physician decision making. While no explicit rationing system in the world has gone this far in any systematic way, there is a discernible tendency toward greater administrative control. In such circumstances the physician must determine explicitly which patients are more in need of a particular service and develop ways to discourage or influence other patients who insist on such service. Increasingly, for example, the physician will require prereview of certain decisions by other physicians or have some decisions reviewed after the fact. The intrusion of such requirements for review can have a significant effect on decision making, particularly on the "technological imperative."

Everywhere in the world physicians have retained considerable autonomy; even in such highly bureaucratized contexts as military medicine, industrial medicine, and the health services of Communist countries physicians have persisted in their roles more as experts than as bureaucratic functionaries. The shift is more nuance than drama, and while such tendencies will grow, rationing is more likely to be imposed on the total framework of services and less on the decisions of the individual physician treating a particular patient. Yet it is clear that the types of rationing adopted will have an important influence on the form taken by medical services and on the types of relationships that evolve between health professionals and patients. I shall discuss such relationships in greater detail in chapters 14 and 15. In chapters 12 and 13, however, we turn to an examination of why new forms of administering health-care services are necessary, and why the medical marketplace fails to distribute services fitted more closely to patient's needs and expectations.

Chapter 12

THE FAILURE OF THE MEDICAL MARKETPLACE

Medical-care resources are limited in every society, and no society can respond to all of the perceived needs and demands people may make. Some assessment must be made concerning the amount of a society's resources that should be devoted to health care relative to other endeavors and the way these resources should be distributed. There are two basic ways of making such determinations: through the marketplace and through planning. The marketplace model is based on the premise that the consumer is in the best position to determine the value he places on a particular product or service and the relative value of spending his dollars for one thing rather than another. From this point of view the marketplace is seen as the best means of determining the amount of health care people want relative to other commodities and services and the manner in which resources spent on health care should be distributed. In response to the argument that some people have too little money to buy health care, advocates for the marketplace argue that they should be given money to spend in terms of their own priorities and preferences rather than have outsiders determine what they need.

The planning model is based on different premises. The purpose of health-care services, advocates of this model would argue, is to provide care to the population relative to the needs for services and the likelihood that people can benefit from them. Although people are unlikely to know their own needs, experts should determine the basic elements of service necessary and plan the provision and distribution of services in light of these judgments. The planning model is premised in part on the assumption that people do not necessarily know, or are unable to anticipate, their own interests, and thus the intervention of third parties is necessary to insure that the needs of the people are met.

These descriptions of both models are vast simplifications. Even advocates of the marketplace recognize that there are common goods shared by all citizens (such as defense) that are in their interests but that the private marketplace would not provide for because the stake of any individual citizen is not sufficiently large for him to invest in defense relative to other things. Moreover, if other persons make such investments, the noninvestor benefits as much as they do (542). In such situations the market does not work properly, and outside intervention is believed to be merited. Furthermore, economists advocating market approaches recognize that markets are always imperfect, but believe that the overall solution produced by the marketplace is better than that brought about by administrative trial and error. In examining the way markets work, economists usually focus on whether or not the market is distributing products and services in relation to the true preferences of the consumer (what economists call "allocative efficiency"). They also give attention to whether the distribution of products and services is in accord with the population's concept of fairness, which is handled under the notion of equity (759).

From the point of view of many medical-care experts—and I share this point of view—the medical marketplace, particularly as it exists in the United States, does not distribute medical services in a fair or cost-effective manner. An organization approach can be said to be cost effective when the structure relative to alternative forms of organization yields greater benefits as reflected in various measures that are valued: prevention of disease, improved health status, decreased disability, and greater security and satisfaction. Although providing basic medical services to subgroups of the population that have not had adequate care may have an important impact on their health, offering more and more services to those already well provided for is less likely to contribute to better health. Yet medical resources tend to be disproportionately available to the more affluent despite the fact that those who are poor have greater objectively determined medical-care needs (6).

While the issue is sometimes raised as to why medical care should be any different from other services or commodities in the way it should be distributed, there is a widely shared national consensus that every American ought to have access to necessary medical care that meets minimal standards of quality. As Klarman has noted:

> The right of all sick persons to receive health and medical care according to need represents the expressed consensus of all segments of American society and every shade of political opinion. Although a person's income and assets are known to influence the volume of health and medical services he receives and perhaps also their quality (certainly the amenities), we like to believe that nobody goes without the adequate minimum merely because he cannot pay [393, p. 13].

This consensus has become even more solidified in recent years, as evidenced by the growing acceptance that medical care is a "right," by the embodiment of this concept in legislation passed by the Congress, and by the opinions of the population measured in polls (677). Even Victor Fuchs, an economist skeptical of the value of medical care in affecting objective outcomes such as better health or decreased disability, has argued for a universal health program because "it could have a considerable symbolic value as one step in an effort to forge a link between classes, regions, races, and age groups" (257, p. 150). It is not insignificant that a conservative president—hardly known for his liberal views on social welfare legislation—said the following in his 1971 health message:

> Just as our National Government has moved to provide equal opportunity in areas such as education, employment and voting, so we must now work to expand the opportunity for all citizens to obtain a decent standard of medical care. We must do all we can to remove any racial, economic, social or geographic barriers that now prevent any of our citizens from obtaining adequate health protection. For without good health, no man can fully utilize his other opportunities [538].

At the very least, the availability of services to the poor increases their sense of security and gives them a feeling of more equity relative to others in the population.

The medical marketplace, as it exists in the United States and many other countries, is a complex mixture of private and public investment, social regulation, and professional governance. Although the medical market is not unique in having imperfections, the fact that medical care involves so many exceptions to traditional economic assumptions makes application of the marketplace model very dubious. Such thoughtful economists as Arrow (36) and Klarman (393) have noted these extreme deviations. As Klarman notes:

> For any single characteristic of health services that is presumably distinctive it may be possible to find an analogue in the behavior of some other good or service. What is rare or unlikely, however, is another good that shares all of these characteristics or so many [393, p. 11].

In the pages that follow I review ten dimensions on which medical care departs significantly from usual economic models of the marketplace. Although I have borrowed heavily from Arrow (36) in defining many of these dimensions, the discussion emphasizes considerations that are often overlooked or underemphasized by economists. The first three characteristics to be discussed—problems of information, product uncertainty, and the extent to which social and professional norms dictate treatment processes—are closely related.

Problems of Information

A great deal has been written about the special problems the consumer faces in assessing the value of medical care. Most of this discussion, however, has focused on the inaccessibility of information because of controls over advertising, and has not come to terms with the special complexity of consumer judgments of the medical product. As Arrow notes:

> The demand for information is difficult to discuss in the rational terms usually employed. The value of information is frequently not known in any meaningful sense to the buyer; if, indeed, he knew enough to measure the value of information, he would know the information itself. But information, in the form of skilled care, is precisely what is being bought from most physicians, and, indeed, from most professionals. The elusive character of information as a commodity suggests that it departs considerably from the usual marketability assumptions about commodities [36, p. 946].

Arrow emphasizes, although he does not draw out its full implications, that "medical care belongs to the category of commodities for which the product and the activity of production are identical. In all such cases, the customer cannot test the product before consuming it, and there is an element of trust in the relation" (36, p. 949). The consumer has difficulty appraising the medical product in part because of its complex nature, but also because of its ambiguous and intangible character. Although the contact between patient and physician sometimes results in the prevention and cure of definable illness or the alleviation of pain and disability, much medical care serves to comfort and sustain, to relieve anxiety, and to provide a sense of security to persons who believe that they may have a serious illness. Also, as was emphasized earlier, medical care frequently serves as a means by which individuals seek release from other social obligations or find legitimate reasons to explain personal failure (137; 549). In short, medical care is not only a set of technical operations designed to intervene in the occurrence of morbidity but is also a complex social institution that is intimately related to other aspects of social functioning.

As we noted in our discussion of illness behavior, the decision to seek medical care is a highly complex social and psychological process. Although some patients visit physicians with concepts of a clearly defined need, many present only vague feelings of malaise, worry, and discomfort. The patient responds in terms of general well-being as well as in terms of specific symptoms, and may have no clear idea of the nature of his problem or be entirely unwilling to confront it. Many life problems are masked by diffuse physical symptoms because patients are unprepared psychologically to deal with them or because expectations in their relevant social groups inhibit certain forms of expression. The role of the physician is thus in many respects a socially sustaining one requiring a considerable level of trust and acceptance by the patient. In one sense it is accurate to say that many patients really do not know what they want when they purchase medical services, because motivating needs are often not at a level of general awareness; trust in the physician frequently becomes a central aspect of the relationship (42).

The ongoing relationship between patient and physician serves as a source of information for the patient about the necessity of varying degrees of assessment and treatment. At least two problems make the transfer of information to the patient exceedingly difficult. First, a significant number of patients who are anxious and worried have serious psychological barriers to receiving and processing information about their medical condition and needed medical care (440). A variety of studies indicate the difficulties even conscientious physicians have in attempting to help patients understand their illness, the character and uncertainties of required treatment, and the need to conform to a specific medical regimen. Second, a conscientious attempt by the physician to maximize the patient's understanding and facilitate the patient's participation in treatment decisions would be a time-consuming process. Given the physicians' patient load and the cost of their time, such participation on more than a nominal level would be very expensive. The typical patient has been socialized to put his faith in a physician and to trust him to take the necessary actions; such expectations and the real constraints and practicalities of the medical context mean that few physicians lack control over decision making once the patient has initiated the contact.

Although economic discussions have exaggerated the importance of advertising as a means of increasing consumer information about medical commodities, the availability of such information does have relevance for pricing practices. This is true particularly of discrete aspects of treatment such as the costs of drugs or surgical fees. In conjunction with performance data that, I believe, can be made available in understandable form, pricing information would at least provide certain choices that are presently not available or exceedingly difficult to make, given the existing marketplace. This applies particularly to insurance for medical care, in which policies currently available in the private market are so complex and lacking in uniformity as to leave a strong suspicion that the complexity is designed to minimize comparison (322).

Product Uncertainty

Related to the problem of the consumer's lack of information—but in some ways beyond it—is the uncertainty of the medical product. As Arrow notes:

> Uncertainty as to the quality of the product is perhaps more intense here than in any other important commodity. Recovery from disease is as unpredictable as is its incidence. In most commodities, the possibility of

learning from one's own experience or that of others is strong because there is an adequate number of trials. In the case of severe illness, that is, in general, not true; the uncertainty due to inexperience is added to the intrinsic difficulty of prediction. Further, the amount of uncertainty, measured in terms of utility variability, is certainly much greater for medical care in severe cases than for, say, houses or automobiles, even though these are also expenditures sufficiently infrequent so that there may be considerable residual uncertainty [36, p. 951].

In recent years the problem of uncertainty has been made more intense by brilliant technical achievements in medical care that extend life in individual cases (e.g., kidney transplants and hemodialysis) and also by growing evidence that increased investments in medical care do not appear to improve substantially trends in longevity and measured levels of health (2; 567). Given the uncertainty, even the medically sophisticated patient is usually left with little opportunity to make his own evaluation of what he is getting; he must accept this on trust. The judgment is even more difficult in the case of serious illness because the technologies available to the physician are not only uncertain but often dangerous as well. Thus the physician must follow a complex cost-benefit calculus that considers not only the potentiality of a given procedure in contributing to the patient's health but also possible risks in terms of the patient's age, general health, and other circumstances. The difficulties of such decisions are not easily remedied by introducing advertising or competition.

The consequence of such uncertainty and the social and professional norms that relate to it is that the physician controls the definition of utility in the medical relationship. There is, of course, some role for the operation of consumer perceptions and tastes. Certainly the initial contact with a physician, the purchase of dental or preventive services, the willingness to return to the physician as requested, and cooperation in treatment are under the patient's control. But even in these matters the uncertainty of medical care often results in the docile patient behavior that physicians expect. Aspects of medical care under the control of consumers are relatively few in contrast to components of demand either exclusively or predominantly controlled by providers, such as hospitalization, length of hospital stay, diagnostic procedures used, specific treatments prescribed, and consultations or referrals with other physicians (393, p. 15). In short, once the patient has put himself in the hands of the physician, he has relatively little to say about the character of his workup or treatment, although he is free to go to another doctor or to refuse treatment. I do not wish to suggest that patients are always docile and cooperative, never challenge the physician's judgment, or do not demand specific tests and treatments; they obviously do take challenging stances, and this is viewed by physicians as a serious management problem (241). Once the patient has entered the relationship, however, there is an implicit understanding that most judgments will be the task of the physician.

One of the dangers implicit in the relationship from an economic point of view is that physicians tend to be active and generally believe "that treatment is dictated by the objective needs of the case and not limited by financial considerations" (36, p. 950). Thus, despite the uncertainties of medical intervention, physicians tend frequently to take actions without weighing medical benefits against social and personal costs. There is little question that the expansion of third-party insurance decreases the salience of costs for both patients and physicians and contributes to the promotion of the technological imperative (555).

Norms of Treatment

As noted above, one of the significant aspects of medical care in contrast to most other services is that its most expensive components are almost exclusively under the control of physician decision making in contrast to consumer choice. Further, the provision of treatment is often made without serious determination of the patient's ability or willingness to pay. This does not imply that hospitals and physicians do not take measures to insure that they will be paid for their services. It is significant, however, that providers must be sensitive to public scandals resulting from refusal of services to a needy person because of inability to pay. It is this necessary sensitivity that makes medical care so different from many other products.

Certainly there are distinctions to be made between routine and discretionary services and those of a more acute and demanding character. Although many providers will refuse discretionary services without evidence of ability to pay, emergency services—no matter how expensive—will ordinarily be provided without economic determinations. When the patient is comatose or otherwise unable to make an informed decision, institutions will even obtain court judgments to carry out procedures defined as lifesaving against the wishes of close relatives. While this discussion goes far afield into the arena of ethical norms, I contend that this active stance toward treatment in a less obvious form characterizes medicine more generally and governs the way in which medical care is practiced at least in hospital contexts.

Professional dictation over the character of necessary medical work has important consequences for understanding the difficulty in achieving an effective distribution of physician resources relative to the population. Because physicians have great control over the amount of demand generated, the input of additional physicians has only a marginal effect on location patterns. The physician exercises control over the amount of time he spends with the patient, the number and type of diagnostic procedures used, the degree of follow-up, and the performance of discretionary treatment. Although patients theoretically can refuse to agree to physician decisions, they usually have no basis for such decisions nor do they feel comfortable in challenging a physician whom they may need at some future time (291). Therefore they depend on the physician to define the necessary services, and it is this control that facilitates the absorption of considerable physician resources in individual communities without affecting price or relocation of practice. Recall that physicians are trained to be active and to take the view that one ought to take whatever steps one can without weighing the economic costs and benefits (255). When the patient is complaining of discomfort, the possibilities for medical activity are almost unlimited. Given more time, the physician can pursue almost any problem more vigorously and intensively.

Because medical work is under the control of the physician to such a large extent, the work actually done tends to reflect his particular training, abilities, and interests. Thus there is a tendency for the specialty inclinations of the physician to shape the way he manages a problem, just as the nature of the patient's complaint shapes what he does. Because of the discretionary and intangible nature of much of medical work, imbalances among different types of physicians do not adjust easily to characteristic demand in the population. One consequence of overspecialization is thus the production of more elaborate and expensive procedures than many medical-care experts deem necessary. The above argument does not depend on the assumption that physicians cynically and purposely generate work they wish to do, although this undoubtedly happens. The range of discretionary activity is facilitated by the ambiguities and uncertainties of medical practice itself, its uncertain impact on health status, the important subjective component in the patient's response, and the lack of clear and agreed-upon guidelines as to what constitutes a desirable or optimal pattern of care under varying circumstances (178). The result is that physicians with similar training—and even working in the same organizational settings with similar patients—develop different styles of work and use of diagnostic procedures and laboratory aids (297). Moreover, as Freidson (242) has observed in his intensive study of one large group practice, physicians tend to reject the legitimacy of norms concerning appropriate use of many medical procedures and of the laboratory. The concept of medical judgment covers a wide area indeed!

Uninsurable Risks

Arrow notes that

> a great many risks are not covered, and indeed the markets for the services of risk-coverage are poorly developed or nonexistent. . . . Briefly, it is impossible to draw up insurance policies which will sufficiently distinguish among risks, particularly since observation of the results will be incapable of distinguishing between avoidable and unavoidable risks, so that incentives to avoid losses are diluted [36, p. 945].

Given the character of the medical insurance market, many persons with even ordinary needs for insurance are unable to purchase adequate coverage. Commercial plans attempt to capture low-risk consumers, and their nonprofit competitors have been weary of accumulating high-risk persons. Prior to Medicare, for example, aged persons—because of high risks of illness and disability—were in many instances unable to purchase insurance; persons with high-risk indications still find such purchase difficult if they are not covered by group plans. Individuals with histories of chronic illness who, of course, have high needs for medical care often cannot obtain insurance. This is particularly true of areas such as psychiatric care in which insurance companies are uncertain as to the way to estimate aggregate risks.

Erratic Demand

From a behavioral point of view, medical-care costs are somewhat akin to taxes—people dislike paying them. Unlike most commodities in which people trade money for some positive utility, medical-care costs are often perceived as unexpected losses of utility. This attitude, I believe, stems from the fact that people expect to remain healthy, and the need for medical care is often perceived as a chance event or "bad luck" that not only brings discomfort but also deprives one of needed funds.

The irregular and unexpected character of medical demand has important implications for the way consumers make their needs known for certain required services. At any point in time most people are reasonably healthy and medical care is not particularly important to them. Although people are generally aware of potential risks of illness, most maintain their sanity through a sense of invulnerability and the assumption that unpleasant events happen to other people. Having no special need or opportunity to test the marketplace for services that are categorically specific, most people generally assume that the medical sector could respond effectively to almost any eventuality. Thus the existing production of medical services is constructed on the basis of professional concepts in contrast to the force of demand generated by groups who anticipate certain needs.

Although diseases occurring frequently in the population, or those of special interest to physicians, usually are provided with ample facilities for treatment, others are neglected. It is not necessarily the rare medical problem that tends to be neglected, since it is often of special interest to physicians and medical researchers. Conditions that tend to be neglected are reasonably common, occur most frequently among groups with relatively less social status and influence, and are viewed with less interest by physicians perhaps because they do not feel particularly effective in dealing with them. Such problems include mental illness and mental retardation, the chronic diseases of old age, and the sociomedical problems of deviants and the poor. The ability to organize in order to make needs known in categorical disease areas may relate to the distribution of that disease by socioeconomic status (648).

Because of the complexity of disease patterns and the difficulties and costs of obtaining information on services that one has only a low probability of ever needing, there is little awareness of the problems others face in obtaining care for an autistic child, for a child with special orthopedic problems, or for a spouse with multiple sclerosis or schizophrenia. If the anguish of those who need such services could be widely known and appreciated, there would no doubt be strong consensus that the services ought to be available. Organizational efforts are necessary to bring these needs to the public consciousness. Some "disease groups" are better organized and can more easily dramatize their needs, and some include persons with more status, power, and organizational skills.

Externalities

Economists use the concept of externalities to refer to benefits or costs that accrue to others because of one's own behavior. In explaining the concept they usually cite the example of communicable diseases in which failure to obtain immunizations poses risks to others. Such examples tend to neglect the fact that in a partial welfare state, in which there is some public obligation for the disabled and indigent, there are major financial externalities in providing medical care. This is particularly true when such medical care prevents serious and chronic illness that would result in high maintenance and support costs for taxpayers in general. One difficulty here concerns a lack of clarity about the components of medical care that truly limit later morbidity, chronicity, and disability. Certainly some components of care meet this definition: adequate birth control, prenatal and postnatal care, immunization, nutritional services, and correction of defects and disabilities that limit learning and development. It is reasonable to maintain that to the extent that medical care serves to enhance health, there are major incentives in seeing that the care is provided.

Another type of externality stems from the fact that the ordinary person, whether for psychological, ethical, social, or esthetic reasons, prefers in his daily activities not to confront others who are sickly, disabled, and pathetic. To the extent that ordinary medical care reduces evident human misery and the confrontation of the well with the ill, one could anticipate that benefits would be perceived by the well. The social system has dealt with many such problems through the social control functions of the state, which keep such unfortunates out of sight in special institutions. Although the conditions that prevail within many of these institutions would repel the person with average sensibilities, the lack of visibility of conditions holds back a larger societal demand for improved care. In the examples above, the actual benefits to any individual are relatively small as compared with the costs of organizing for change. Moreover, if others take the initiative we gain from their efforts as much as from our own, thus providing little incentive for personal action (542).

Research in medicine involves large intergenerational externalities because future beneficiaries perhaps gain most. Although there is evidence that patients treated in teaching and research institutions receive higher-quality care than those treated elsewhere (281), many of the benefits of research accrue to people other than the subjects, while those who are subjects assume most of the risks. Without explicit public intervention, therefore, there is likely to be considerable underinvestment in research (256, p. 109). The externalities involved should supply incentives for financing the more expensive care of teaching institutions, which is intimately tied to both patient care and education.

Lack of Overt Price Competition

Traditional price discrimination practiced in medicine—that is, the physician's adjustment of his fee in terms of the patient's ability to pay—was clearly incompatible with the competitive model (36; 384; 385). With substantial increases in third-party payment for the poor, however, it is not evident that such price discrimination remains a prevalent pattern. Given the ethical barriers to price competition and advertising, prices are not greatly responsive to changing demand.

Perhaps the most evident example of price maintenance is the high cost of general surgery despite an excess of general surgeons operating well below their capacities (342). Patients apparently do little if any comparative pricing of surgeon's fees (assuming this is possible), and whatever inclination might have existed to do so has been diminished further by surgical insurance.

Restricted Entry

Since publication of the analysis by Friedman and Kuznets (249) arguing a link between physician income and restriction of entry into the profession, it has become commonplace to argue that a dominant aspect of the medical-care marketplace is the control physicians exert over the entry of other providers of medical service (385). This issue has been exaggerated in that variations in entry, barring a large surplus of providers, would not be a major threat to physicians within the market as presently constructed. Indeed, there is considerable evidence that physicians have been quite willing to have their number increased substantially in recent years, and the barriers to practice among foreign-trained physicians are less than rigorous. Between 1960–1961 and 1975–1976 the number of first-year medical students in the United States increased from 8,298 to 15,295. During this period the number of graduates increased by approximately two-thirds. In addition, there has been a steady flow of foreign-trained physicians into the United States.

None of this suggests that there has been no intention to restrict the number of physicians, and certainly the number of students seeking to enter medical education far exceeds the places available. Among the arguments for limiting the number of physicians are: (1) too many physicians generate excessive, costly, and dangerous procedures: (2) open entry would result in lower-quality doctors using powerful technologies with great potential for harm; and (3) quality medical education is exceedingly expensive and must be publicly subsidized to attract a sufficiently large, capable, and diverse group of students; non-subsidized education would attract the wrong student mix, suggesting that because physician education probably should be subsidized, we should educate only as many physicians as we really require.

A recent study by the Institute of Medicine (356), prepared for the Congress, attempted to separate educational costs for medical students from other costs with no direct relationship to instruction. It was estimated that educational costs in the medical schools varied from $6,900 to $18,650 per student a year, with an average of $12,650. Almost $8,000 of this figure was allocated to instructional activities, the remainder to that component of patient care and research essential to education. Adjusting this figure for offsetting research and patient-care revenues yields a net educational average cost per student per year of $9,700. Only a small component of this cost is covered by tuition, and federal funds now account for at least half of medical-school revenues in the United States (357).

At present there is a strong demand for medical-school places. Studies of students who have been rejected by medical schools report firm persistence in their desires and attempts to obtain entry (431), and it is clear that the average qualifications of accepted students have increased substantially in recent years (183). Medicine is perceived as a profession that is secure, that provides high income and status, and is personally rewarding. Given these factors, it seems apparent that present subsidies are excessive unless they are tied to important social goals that cannot be achieved by the existing market for medical services, such as redistribution of physicians by geographic area and activity and increased enrollment of the poor, minority groups, and women. (Present subsidies are tied to such social goals, but only to a limited extent.) In all likelihood open entry to medical education would increase the quantity of physician services and result in some reduction in medical-care prices. There are, however, some dangerous implications for open entry from the standpoint of quality and total cost.

Professional Dominance

A far more serious problem concerns the dominance of medicine over other health occupations (240) and the political and legal barriers to transferring certain aspects of medical work to physician substitutes, except under conditions acceptable to physicians. As Arrow has noted:

> There is a second aspect of entry in which the contrast with competitive behavior is, in many respects, even sharper. It is the exclusion of many imperfect substitutes for physicians. The licensing laws, though they do not effectively limit the number of physicians, do exclude all others from engaging in any one of the activities known as medical practice. As a result, costly physician time may be employed at specific tasks for which only a small fraction of their training is needed, and which could be performed by others less well trained and therefore less expensive [36, p. 956].

There is reluctance on the part of physicians to grant a quasi-independent status to other manpower in the performance of any traditional medical function, even when physicians are unprepared to perform the function themselves. The argument against the autonomy of other health professionals, as in the case of open entry to medical education, is that the public is in no position to make complex judgments of quality, and therefore standards of care would fall. Although this argument does have some merit, particularly in the context of hospital or more complex medical work, it seems reasonably clear that such middle-level professionals as nurse-practitioners can be trained to assume many primary-care functions in a responsible and effective way (436).

Another aspect of monopoly results from the scale necessary to support many secondary and tertiary medical facilities (256, pp. 102–3). Most American communities cannot support more than one hospital or more than one or a limited number of specialists or subspecialty services. Because a relatively large scale and overhead are necessary to achieve efficient practice, competition among providers is often disastrous in terms of total cost and amount of waste involved. The characteristic solution is the nonprofit hospital that has a monopoly status in many American communities. It is generally noted, however, that physicians dominate hospital structures and manipulate them in their own interest, and that the lack of economic incentives and cost-reimbursement schemes results in waste, inefficiencies, and unnecessary duplication.

Misallocated Supply

Another unique aspect of medicine concerns the possible dangers implicit in oversupply of certain types of services. A variety of studies show that a significant proportion of serious illnesses are iatrogenic, that is, they result directly from physician action or the treatment process. Every major medical diagnostic procedure and treatment carries both potential benefits and risks. Part of the judgment required of physicians is that they make judicious choices that maximize benefits while minimizing undesired consequences of diagnostic procedures or treatments. In many cases of serious illness this involves a tricky calculus, because the therapeutic modalities of greatest potential often carry grave risks. To the extent that dangerous procedures are performed when not required, risk to health mounts unnecessarily. In the fee-for-service system of medical care in which physicians are remunerated for each component of service provided, there are strong incentives to generate marginal medical work that increases total risks to the population and is expensive as well (589). This tendency is exacerbated when excess resources are concentrated in particular geographic areas (101; 762). Although greater competition among providers might lead to reductions in price for any given service, competition may also result in excessive production of medical work, greater overall cost, and excessive risk of iatrogenic conditions. Moreover, the abundance of specialists and subspecialists tends to encourage the application of a highly technological and expensive approach to many ordinary problems.

Because of these many imperfections, the medical-care market fails to achieve a reasonable balance between needs in the population and the provision and distribution of resources. The result is large medical-care costs that then lead government or insurance programs to seek to contain them in one fashion or another. The breakdown of the fee-for-service system as a rationing device then leads to attempts to impose implicit or explicit rationing, making use of various planning principles. Planning the delivery of complex services is no simple matter; it depends not only on a sound set of service delivery principles but also on a good understanding of the way patients and health practitioners respond to varying types of incentives. In the next chapter we turn to a consideration of the elements of medical care and their interrelationships.

Chapter 13

PRIMARY, SECONDARY, AND TERTIARY MEDICAL CARE

In planning the provision of health care, it is necessary to distinguish among primary-, secondary-, and tertiary-care services. "Primary care" generally refers to the ordinary outpatient care provided by office-based or clinic-based practitioners who are a point for first contact and appraisal and who provide less complex and continuing care to patients. The discussion will make clear, however, that there are varying ways of conceptualizing primary care. Secondary and tertiary care, usually more specialized and expensive, constitute later links in a referral process from primary-care contexts. "Secondary care" most often refers to office-based specialty services such as those provided by a cardiologist or nephrologist, or to much of hospital services. "Tertiary care," in contrast, refers to more complex services and procedures that are found only in more specialized hospitals that have greater technical expertise. Such services might include hemodialysis and transplantation, complex open-heart surgery, perinatal monitoring, highly specialized diagnostic techniques, and radiation therapy.

Within a planned health service the primary-care sector provides accessibility to care for the population, necessary appraisal, and continuing treatment and supportive services. The primary service can also arrange access and referral to more specialized services when appropriate (438). To achieve this effectively, primary services must be well integrated and coordinated with other components of the system and must have the resources necessary to insure that the patient with special needs can reach more specialized and appropriate levels of care. Although it is easy to talk about the logical connections and appropriate coordination between varying levels of service, effective integration and cooperation are difficult to achieve whether the system is planned or constitutes a competitive marketplace. In both types of systems the actors may behave quite differently from the expected

350

rational pattern, and one of the jobs of medical sociologists is to understand the factors that lead to distortions in the expected pattern. With these thoughts in mind we turn to a consideration of the basic components of the medical-care system.

Elements of Primary Care

In recent years a great deal of confusion has been generated around the term "primary care." Everyone seems to understand what the term means but, unfortunately, their concepts are very different, with varying implications for the appropriate organization of health-care facilities. Nations everywhere are struggling with ways to constrain the forces of specialization and subspecialization and integrate the fragmented components of service in an effective, responsive, and economical fashion. Models abound: general and family practitioners, nurse practitioners, the general internist, the physician's assistant, the prepaid practice, the multispecialty group, the medical foundation, consumer health cooperatives, free clinics, hospital-based group practices, and many more. On what basis, then, can choices among them be made?

Many discussions of primary medical care confuse the organizational, service, and manpower dimensions. The most typical view of primary care in the United States is that it is the care given by physician generalists: general practitioners, family practitioners, and general internists and pediatricians. It is assumed that the training received by such practitioners prepares them to provide the initial instances of care and to take continuing responsibilities for the needs of the patient. Unfortunately, existing evidence indicates that such physicians often carry out highly complex medical and surgical procedures that are more appropriately performed by physicians who are more conversant with such techniques and who perform them frequently enough to do them well. While a significant proportion of general practitioners in the United States still perform major surgery (491), this is hardly an appropriate primary-care function under modern circumstances. Conversely, many specialists—obstetricians, surgeons, and the like—insist that they devote significant amounts of their time to primary care, and thus the shortage of primary-care physicians is exaggerated. The issue, however, is not only what they do but also how they go about doing it, and this relates to the medical-care system as a whole.

Some commentators on primary care suggest that the way to resolve the issue is simply to allocate various functions on the basis of experience to primary, secondary, and tertiary care. This approach misses the key point that the practice of medicine is a conceptual and intellectual endeavor in which physicians with varying training and orientations perceive, evaluate, classify, and manage comparable patients differently. In many instances the management of patients demands more than following established formulas. Good medical management results from listening to the patient, getting to know the person, and developing a clinical context in which the patient is truly willing to confront his or her problems. Well-trained primary-care physicians should be different from specialists not only in what they do but also in the way they do it. Many patients first contacting a physician are in a stage in which their perceptions of their own problems are somewhat vague and ambiguous. This is, as I have already described, not only because the patient lacks medical knowledge but also because a wide variety of life problems motivate people to seek the assistance of the physician, and often the patient has not fully sorted out these problems. Moreover, unlike most patients seen in hospital practice, many patients in primary care are not "sick" in the conventional sense of the term. Thus what the physician defines as important, what he inquires about, and the way he evaluates the patient's symptoms and illness behaviors must be directed by his personal knowledge of the patient; the physician's appraisal often affects the way the patient comes to view his problem. Physicians trained in varying ways tend to focus on different aspects of the problem, emphasizing their own particular interests and knowledge. What is needed in primary care is a physician with a broad orientation.

Primary care involves more than the training of an individual type of practitioner; it is part of an organizational system of services. For example, in most planned medical-care systems there are designated primary-care physicians who have responsibility for the initial contacts with a sick patient, for assuming continued responsibility for a fixed number of patients, and for dealing with the more common problems of this population on a continuing basis. These systems are usually established in such a way that patients are required to seek more specialized services through the referral of their primary doctor. Similarly, secondary- and tertiary-care facilities are organized in relation to the system as a whole, and efforts are made to coordinate the varying levels of care. Although the particular type of practitioner employed at varying levels of care is not an unimportant issue, the major focus shifts to defining responsibilities for care functions at each level. There are a variety of alternatives for organizing different types of personnel to carry out the necessary functions: physicians, nurse-practitioners, physician assistants, nurse-specialists, and so on. In this sense primary care is a set of functions, not a particular type of practitioner. Once we conceive of primary care as an array of services provided by teams of specially trained personnel, not only do we have more options but, more important, we can design the primary-care service to deal with the special problems of particular population areas. Needs and patterns of illness vary by subculture, socioeconomic status, and geographic location. We need different models of primary care for urban ghettos, rural communities, and suburbia.

In designing medical care for any population it is essential to achieve an appropriate balance among the varying levels of care, and there seems to be no doubt that in the United States we have lost our sense of balance. It is instructive to hear the views of Dr. Paul Beeson, formerly chairman of the Department of Medicine at Yale University, professor of medicine at Oxford University, and now in the role of distinguished physician in the Veterans Administration:

> There are 22,000 in family practice in the United Kingdom and 70,000 in family practice in the United States. There are 8,000 in specialist practice in the United Kingdom and 280,000 in specialist practice in the United States. . . . The striking difference is economy in the use of specialists. To me this is the most obvious reason why America has a badly distributed, excessively costly system. If we could begin to shift our ratio of specialists to primary physicians toward that of Britain, I think we would cease to hear about the need for more doctors or for training para-medical assistants. I have no doubt at all that a good family doctor can deal with the great majority of medical episodes quickly and competently. A specialist, on the other hand, feels that he must be thorough, not only because of his training but also because he has a reputation to protect. He, therefore, spends more time with each patient and orders more laboratory work. The result is waste of doctors' time and patients' money. This not only inflates the national health bill but also creates an illusion of doctor shortage when the only real need is to have the existing doctors doing the right things [57, p. 48].

The development of an effective primary-care approach must give attention to those who actually seek services and to the larger community as well. This may involve the mobilization not only of doctors, nurses, technicians, and physician assistants, but also nurse-practitioners, health educators, and social workers. To the extent that the population is sufficiently large, it becomes more economical than in smaller practices to provide supporting services to facilitate comprehensive care and care more attuned to patients with less common needs, such as the parents of retarded children, the bereaved, or spouses of the chronically ill.

Primary care, if it is to be effective, must be accessible to the populations it serves. Accessibility includes financial access as well as the ability to reach the facility, to schedule a prompt appointment, and to be protected from unnecessary bureaucratic hassles. Services must be accessible not only to the aggressive, motivated, and sophisticated patient but also to those who are more timid, frightened, and suspicious. When persons are worried and feel a need for evaluation, there should be a source of care readily available that has the capacity to assess the problem. It is pointless to ration care at the primary-care level since anxious patients are not in a position to evaluate their needs for care. Economy must be achieved through a proper balance of primary as compared with more specialized services, and through more careful consideration by physicians as to whether the additional procedures and tests they order are likely to bring benefits commensurate with their costs. In assessing the problem, the primary-care source must have the ability to deal with it promptly within reasonable limits. If this capacity is insufficient it must be linked with other services so as to ensure that appropriate management will occur.

Effective Primary Care

In the United States, as well as many other countries, attempts are now being made to correct a pattern of medical education in which physicians have been poorly prepared to practice good primary care. The models of diagnostic assessment and treatment provided in the teaching hospital have been ill-fitted to many types of problem faced by primary-care physicians, but other models or experience have not been an important part of the educational process. Physicians have been taught to be disease oriented rather than to be concerned with problems of health and functioning. Moreover, they have left their training knowing almost nothing about the behavioral or psychiatric aspects of disease; they have had little experience in working cooperatively with other primary-care personnel; they have had little familiarity with community problems or social services; and they have been poorly equipped to deal with many of the more common chronic problems seen in ambulatory medical care. While they focused on the search for disease in its narrow sense, they probably saw the less common conditions so infrequently that it is doubtful that they could provide optimal medical management for such conditions.

The problem of providing effective primary medical care is not only an American problem but is endemic to medical-care systems throughout the world. Almost everywhere there is growing emphasis on the establishment of health centers and polyclinics that aggregate physicians so that they can provide patient care in a comprehensive way, utilizing the gains in medical technology and diagnostic aids with the support of a variety of other health workers. Medical schools in the United States are developing models for primary care and are teaching students how to work more appropriately in such contexts.

There are, of course, a variety of models emerging and no unanimity on the optimal approach. Given the range of practice contexts in the United States, there is no single best model, and it is probably useful to retain a healthy diversity. The approach growing most rapidly is the training of family practitioners, and while I think this is a constructive trend, I am concerned that the definition of such efforts is as much political in character as it is based on careful intellectual and scientific conceptions of the place of family practice in the total medical-care arena. Family practice is too focused on the idea that primary care consists of the skills embodied in an individual practitioner, and gives too little attention to the effective organization of the various members of the team who must be responsible for providing primary-care services to a defined population.

In recent years we have heard a great deal about how the family practitioner takes care of the entire family but very little careful specification of what this really means. Usually the concept of family medicine refers to little more than the fact that the practitioner is trained to assume a wider scope of responsibility than the usual specialist, including responsibilities in general medicine, obstetrics, pediatrics, and psychiatry. While medical care under some circumstances may be enhanced by the same practitioners looking after all the members of a single family, this is not always true, and it is frequently impractical. First, family members are often geographically separated and may, in any case, have varying preferences in regard to medical care. Second, some family members, such as adolescents, may find it more difficult to relate to a physician who is also close to his or her parents. Third, if physicians function as agents of individual patients—and I believe firmly that they should—the physician may feel conflicting loyalties when family members are in conflict with one another, and may have difficulty in performing his role.

A more reasonable use of the concept of family medicine in ambulatory medical care is as a guide to the informational process. The family is the most intimate group in modern society, and the individual's genetic, psychological, and social proclivities are linked to family history and family process. Moreover, many of the stresses and strains that affect people's lives and many of the supports that they depend on are found within the family structure. Thus effective medical care, whether carried out by a physician who calls himself a family practitioner or by any other kind of doctor, must consider the family context and interaction patterns among its members. This requires not that the physician treat the entire family but rather that he understand the manner in which family difficulties and family supports affect the patient's health and the implementation of his medical care.

Elements of Secondary Care

Secondary care involves medical services that require either more specialized facilities than those available in the office of the primary-care practitioner or more specialized technical knowledge than he is likely to have. As we noted in the discussion of primary care, some countries clearly separate the office-based first-contact care from hospital care, and each type of care is provided by a different type of practitioner. In the United States, however, most office-based physicians divide their time between primary-care and secondary-care functions because they take responsibility for much hospital care in addition to their office-based practices.

As the medical sciences have developed and doctors have increased their technical and scientific ability to affect the course of disease and impairment, the hospital has become the main work place for the care of the sick patient. It has also become the primary context for training doctors and nurses and for medical research. A good hospital makes available the equipment and laboratories necessary for the diagnosis and treatment of disease, trained nursing staff and other health ancillaries to look after patients and their needs, specialists in various fields who can be consulted concerning the care of the patient, and technical apparatus and rehabilitation facilities. Complicated surgery and medical care are no longer the result of the efforts of one or a few physicians but rather a product of a large coordinated team. The hospital is also an efficient care unit in that it brings the doctor's patients together in one work place, allowing careful surveillance of their progress and conserving the physician's time and efforts.

The major problem that any health system must deal with is the organization of the hospital and its coordination with care provided in the doctor's office, in other health agencies, and in the home. In addition to the many economic problems that hospitals face, there are three basic sets of organizational issues that must be dealt with:

1. Hospitals must be organized, distributed, and coordinated on a geographic basis so as to ensure efficient utilization and accessibility to those in the population who require hospital services. Also, hospitals must be located in areas where they can effectively recruit physicians, nurses, and other health personnel.

2. Hospitals must be organized so as to ensure sufficient services to different kinds of patients who require services. If such services are to be provided at a reasonable cost, it is necessary that the hospital be prepared to deal efficiently with widely varying problems. Decisions must be made concerning relative resources to be devoted to the care of acute and chronic cases. Similarly, decisions must be made on the relative emphasis and resources to be devoted to outpatient versus inpatient services and to intensive-care versus minimal-care units. Much waste in hospitals has resulted from the failure to diversify services and to have flexible alternatives for dealing with patients who require differing facilities and varying levels of care.

3. Decisions must be made on the organization, management, supervision, and coordination of staff who represent different professional and other work groups, each with their own ideologies and perceptions of work roles.

These three general sets of issues by no means exhaust the questions of interest. There are innumerable other concerns of importance, such as the role of hospitals as training institutions, the problems of finance, maintenance, and capital investment, the growing militancy and unionization of nurses and other hospital workers, and the role of research.

In the United States there are several kinds of general hospitals, in addition to specialized hospitals such as psychiatric institutions and others dealing with specific illness conditions. Most typical is the general voluntary hospital dealing with short-term cases; such hospitals account for the majority of nonpsychiatric beds. Less important, but common, are municipal hospitals, which are run and financed by a government unit such as a city or county. Proprietary hospitals are those organized for the purpose of earning a profit; these hospitals tend to be small and inefficient and, in general, provide a lower standard of medical care than nonprofit voluntary hospitals. Most important in research and training are the various university hospital complexes, which take on a variety of functions in addition to providing medical care. Then there are several other kinds of hospitals to deal with special populations, such as those operated by the Veterans Administration. This short description hardly captures the diversity of hospitals; they vary by the types of service they provide, by the way in which they are managed and controlled, by their physical size and financial support, by type and extent of facilities, composition of staff, and overall quality (see 232).

Because of the considerable government subsidy for hospital building in the United States, providing an adequate number of hospital beds for the population has not been a problem in contrast to unequal distribution of beds in different areas, rapidly increasing costs of hospital care, recruitment of qualified medical and nursing staff, duplication of resources, inefficiencies, and problems of maintaining a high standard of medical care. Indeed, it is now recognized that too many hospital beds provide an incentive for unnecessary use and push up the costs of medical care.

The most substantial problem faced by American communities is maintaining costs of quality medical care at a reasonable level. This can be accomplished through coordinated planning and greater cooperation among hospitals, avoidance of needless duplication of expensive resources within the same community, sharing of scarce personnel, and more efficient practices generally. Since hospitals and health-care personnel tend to be concentrated in urban areas, future pressures will be toward regionalization of hospitals so as to serve surrounding rural localities and thus limit the proliferation of small, inefficient, and poorly staffed hospitals in small communities. While some kinds of facilities are better organized on a local level, other very expensive and less frequently used services are better organized on some regional basis (471). Although regional planning is developing in the United States, it is likely to increase significantly in the future.

A major problem hospitals face involves the organization of services within the hospital. It is well recognized that hospitals have devoted their attention disproportionately to short-term acute illness and have relatively neglected the care of the chronically ill. In recent years there has been an interest in developing more adequate services for such patients, and although these trends require further encouragement, the course of events will inevitably lead to greater attention to the needs of chronic patients (468). Similarly, as the hospital has been recognized as an efficient work place, more and more outpatient services attached to hospitals have developed. While aged persons are increasingly cared for in nursing homes, which have grown into an enormous industry, these institutions suffer from a lack of professionalism, low-quality care, and an excessive concern for profit making. As improvements develop in nursing homes and other paramedical institutions, the hospital will be used for the purpose for which it is organized and not as a substitute for far less expensive facilities that are not presently available in many communities. Although abundant money will continue to flow into the health sector, administrators must inevitably give greater attention to costs and must institute checks to insure that expensive hospital care is not undertaken unnecessarily. Finally, as hospitals develop more flexible alternatives for providing less concentrated care for patients who can meet some of their own needs, the costs of providing care for particular groups of patients will be further controlled. Hospitals will be able to concentrate their scarce nursing personnel where they are most needed. All of these changes create difficult problems of coordination, communication, and planning. Because hospitals are relatively conservative institutions and their staffs are jealous of their professional traditions and prerogatives, it is not surprising that some of the anticipated problems of change appear insurmountable to many administrators. These problems of organizing hospital services follow in large part from the nature of medical-care activity (262), and they are fairly common in hospitals the world over.

Although the problems of providing hospital care are similar in different countries, the means adopted to deal with these problems vary substantially. As already illustrated, professional staffing in hospitals varies considerably when one compares North American countries with European ones. Hospital physicians in America are usually not employed directly by the hospital, although the hospital is their work place. The typical doctor usually establishes a practice in the community by opening a private office or joining a group of other doctors in a clinic, and at the same time he acquires privileges to practice in one or more of the hospitals in his community. He thus establishes a private link with his patients but can bring them into the hospital when it is necessary. The same doctor cares for both hospitalized and nonhospitalized patients and, therefore, he may look after very sick patients and those with relatively less serious problems at the same time. Although he may seek the consultation and help of other doctors in the care of his patients, the responsibility for the patient is his. In contrast, British hospitals maintain their own staff of consultants who assume complete responsibility for the care of the patient when he enters the hospital. The general practitioner in Britain usually does not have a role in hospital care except in the obstetrics area, and when the patient enters the hospital the general practitioner no longer retains any significant voice in his treatment.

The advantages and disadvantages of separating the care of the patient in the hospital from that within the community have been argued many times; both systems offer advantages and disadvantages. The American system allows the doctor to assume continuous care for his patient and provides the patient with some security in knowing that his doctor is looking after him and his interests. Moreover, the general practitioner, given considerable latitude in the care of his patient, is encouraged to maintain and develop his skills; because his work is more varied, it is also more interesting. In contrast, the most important advantage of the British system is that it insures, to a greater extent than in America, that the very sick patient and the more complex case will be looked after by a specialist who is more competent by training and experience to deal with such problems. While an American doctor may see a particular serious disorder a few times a year and may not be acquainted with the latest information in caring for patients with particular uncommon illnesses, the British consultant, in specializing in such serious cases, sees many more of them and is better prepared to cope with them. There is no doubt that concentrated work on more uncommon diseases gives the doctor greater experience and proficiency in treating those afflicted with these diseases. In short, both systems of care have significant advantages and costs. The best way to maximize the advantages of both systems is a question worthy of some consideration.

Nursing and the Hospital

Although physicians dominate the division of labor involving medical and medically related tasks, the quality of nursing care is a central feature of high-quality care in the hospital. Indeed, the quality of nursing care may be the single most important factor affecting successful patient care in the hospital context and in patient outcome (262). Nursing as a profession is in a state of ferment reflecting not only the changing nature of health tasks and the focuses of work but also larger changes in the society, including the women's movement, modifications in sex roles, and a new professional militancy in the nursing profession itself. Nursing is seeking new outlets for its professional commitments, striving for a certain level of autonomy in relationship to physicians and other health workers, and seeking recognition for its unique role in patient care. Although the outcome of this ferment is still somewhat unclear, new trends are emerging in nursing that are likely to continue for many decades and will significantly affect staff relationships in hospitals.

In seeking roles of greater prestige and autonomy, nurses who have felt some dissatisfaction with more traditional nursing tasks have moved into three more specialized aspects. First, there has been a strong trend, particularly among nurses with baccalaureates, to pursue more administrative aspects of nursing work. Such tasks take the nurse away from direct patient care and give her a role in supervising wards, directing the work of aides and licensed practical nurses, record keeping, and continuing education activities. The tendency for the best-trained nurses to move into administrative positions is a matter of concern to many observers of nursing because the major benefit of nursing comes from the direct contact between an effective nurse and the patient. Unfortunately, an increasing proportion of the actual nursing care given to patients is provided not by the most highly trained nurses but rather by nursing aides and practical nurses. Second, nurses have pursued a more autonomous role and greater responsibility through more specialized nursing functions in the hospital. The growth of new technologies has opened opportunities for nurses to develop unique competence in certain technical phases of medical work. Such functions include those of the intensive-care nurse, who has a major role in monitoring the patient's progress through the critical phase of illness, and those of the dialysis nurse, who develops specialized talents in dealing with equipment and patient problems characteristic of that endeavor. Similar opportunities exist in specialized burn units, newly developing trauma centers, and open-heart surgery. Many of these nurses with more specialized technical competence have received training as clinical nurse specialists.

A third route that has opened in recent years for nurses who aspire to a more independent role is that of the nurse-practitioner. Such nurse-practitioners are increasingly used in the care of the chronic patient who requires chronic ambulatory surveillance, in the care of children in ambulatory medical settings, and in the monitoring of health status in health maintenance-type programs. Unlike most nursing roles that are based in the hospital, the nurse-practitioner has increasing opportunities in the ambulatory-care sector. Although in theory nurse-practitioners are fully capable of performing a great many of the ordinary primary-care functions usually assigned to physicians, the acceptability of such practitioners in competition with physicians raises political issues that set limits on their use and on the rapidity with which this role will develop. Although physicians seem to be receptive to nurse-practitioners as part of a clinical team in which the nurse is under the physician's supervision, there is much greater resistance to nurse-practitioners as independent practitioners in competition with the physician.

Good nursing care requires judgment and sensitivity and also demands that the nurse make a variety of decisions concerning the patient's needs, the presence or absence of an emergency, the meaning of the patient's communication and concerns and the appropriate response, and many other matters that are important in the course of a patient's illness. The authority system of care in the hospital, however, is designed to make it appear that the nurses' responses are reactive to physician judgments and orders. Thus while nurses frequently exercise important powers of decision, they must do so subtly, avoiding the appearance of being in command. Because nurses are in much closer contact with patients than are physicians, they often have information that would argue against certain physician assessments and decisions. If the nurse is to "get on" in the system she must learn to express her opinion unobtrusively, to suggest alternatives rather than contest physicians' views, and to show deference to doctors' expertness and authority (605). Although many nurses learn to work quite successfully within this system in a fashion that makes excellent use of their judgment and knowledge of the patients, others became almost immobilized and lose confidence in their ability to act independently (328).

The training characteristic of the three-year diploma schools developed out of the need of hospitals for nursing services. Such training was based strongly on a service philosophy and tended to reinforce the deference of the nurse to physician authority. In contrast, the baccalaureate nurses, who were recruited from higher-status families and who were more likely to be educated by staffs with stronger professional orientations, were made to feel more conscious of their lack of status and power. They were therefore more likely to seek tasks that gave them supervision over others and greater autonomy, but such tasks also removed them from direct patient care. Other nurses reacted to the dilemma characteristic of their role by viewing nursing as an occupation secondary to their primary role as wife and mother, often leaving the labor force following marriage and during the childbearing period. These nurses, having a utilitarian orientation toward their work, tended to see it as a means of supplementing their family income (305). They had relatively little identification with nursing as a profession, felt little sense of solidarity with other nurses, and probably constitute the group of nurses hardest to enlist in any type of collective action.

Although the number of nurses in the nation has been large in the past a significant proportion were not in the active labor force. The tendency to leave the labor force was often attributed to the fact that nursing is a female occupation and a large number of nurses leave employment to marry and to rear their children. A variety of other factors, however, contributed to this tendency. First, developing out of a service orientation and with work roles based largely in hospitals, nursing salaries were relatively low considering the number of skills required and the demands of work. As nursing salaries increased and attitudes toward working women changed in recent years, a larger proportion of nurses remain in or return to the work force. Second, many nurses are married and have family responsibilities, but the positions available to them frequently involve hours that are difficult to coordinate with child-rearing and family responsibilities. Third, hospitals have been quite inflexible in providing occupational opportunities for part-time nurses or for those who required other than routine scheduling in order to make their work and family responsibilities compatible. In short, the failure to retain nurses in the work force reflected an imperfect marketplace in which employers had not made the adaptations necessary to retain personnel. As these conditions have changed the proportion of nurses employed has increased substantially. The alleged nursing shortage is thus somewhat of a mirage; indeed, we may soon be facing an oversupply (15).

There is clear indication that the recruitment of nurses has been changing in recent years as nursing education has come within the confines of formal university education, either on the community-college or the baccalaureate level. The core of the pool of students attracted to community-college nursing programs, a two-year program of training that constitutes the largest source of new nurses, are from middle-income families, are older, and are more frequently married and with families (520). These programs also attract more men than previously. In contrast, the baccalaureate programs, which have been increasing rapidly, attract students from upper-middle-class families with a relatively high level of academic achievement in high school. Indeed, the social composition of nursing students in baccalaureate programs is very much like that of college students in general. While these facts have little significance in and of themselves, understanding the changing auspices of nursing education and shifts in recruitment into nursing gives us a better sense of the difficulties that are likely to arise as these new nurses come face to face with physician authority and control. These relationships are clearly in ferment and arouse considerable emotions among practitioners in both groups. To the extent that we understand these strains we can comprehend the conditions and structures that might lead to more harmonious and effective patient care.

A major problem in the organization of nursing is the failure to be clear as to what the rubric really includes and what should be the lines of task organization and specialization. Although medical care has witnessed an elaborate stratification of physicians into specialties and subspecialties as knowledge and technology have expanded, the assumption in hospitals is still that nurses are interchangeable and can readily be rotated among tasks and types of units. Changes in science and technology should affect the organization of nursing as well as medicine, but it has been organizationally convenient for administrators and physicians to assume that nurses can be shifted from one service or task to another as bed occupancy changes or work pressures vary. This may be convenient administration but it is not necessarily a sound pattern for patient care.

As Hans Mauksch has noted, the history of nursing is closely interwoven with the history of women (464). Physicians and administrators, who are primarily male, tend to view the nurse as having the attributes of wife and mother, doing whatever home and family require, responding largely to others' definitions of her tasks. Some of the conflicts emerging between doctors and nurses reflect the growing attack by women in the society at large on these assumptions implicit in the cultural history of the sexes. This point in our cultural history thus gives us an opportunity to meditate as to what the organizational domain of nursing should ideally be if it were stripped of its sexist context. Simply from a patient-care perspective, what would be the optimal organization of the responsibilities and tasks of the nurse?

Nursing roles consist of both technical and socioemotional components. Nurses are responsible for the continuing care of the patient, for implementing the physician's decisions concerning the patient, for making the patient comfortable and secure, and for being responsive to the patient in a way that shows compassion and understanding of the problems the illness creates not only for physical functioning but also for self-concept and social adjustment. The nurse must negotiate among her roles as a technician, counselor, and educator.

The proper conditions for performing this role are a good grasp of the technical aspects of the illnesses being dealt with and their relationship to social factors, a keen knowledge of the patient and modes of responding to stress and discomfort, and an understanding of the types of adjustment problem patients are likely to face in the short run and long term and of how the patient might work toward overcoming them. To fulfill these conditions nurses would have to specialize in more limited spheres, just as doctors do, in order to achieve adequate command over their work and to maintain a continuity of contact with the patient.

A key question in the care of the hospital patient is the assignment of responsibility of overall care. Although in theory this responsibility is assigned to the physician, he is poorly located from a situational standpoint to exercise it effectively. The private physician, who spends most time and effort outside the hospital, does not have the continuity of contact necessary to monitor the patients successfully, to perceive and respond to their emotional upheavals, or to coordinate among all the personnel involved in the care of the patient. Residents and interns also have many defined responsibilities and face considerable work pressures, and because of their training and orientations give greater attention to technical medical tasks than to communication and coordination or to patients' rehabilitative needs. It has been suggested that the situational location of the nurse is ideal for overall coordination of patient care and responsibility. If the nurse did specialize in certain areas of patient care and had a more specific definition of her responsibilities, she would be in a good position to carry out the coordination function more effectively than it is carried out at present.

While nursing functions require more specific definitions within such a system, the responsibility of the nurse would have to be enlarged. Coordination of care is a 24-hour effort, and if nurses play this role they must assume continuing responsibility for patients assigned to them. In such a system some nurses would no longer be employed on a shift basis but would have to be available when needed. While such a role may place burdens on the nurse, it would also make her work more meaningful and provide a more authentic basis for professionalization. The physician would serve as a consultant to the team in such a system of care, but he would give up some of the autonomy and control that he cannot successfully exercise in any case.

The above discussion is not to imply that such an organizational scheme is on the horizon or even that it is appropriate for most nursing functions. It would be appropriate to experiment in this area to devise a form of organization that is better attuned to the management of the broad problems patients face and to the growing complexity of the medical-care effort itself. Change does not come easily, particularly when it challenges traditional cultural assumptions and vested interests. However, as we look ahead at changes both in the society at large and in patterns of medical care, it seems clear that there will be opportunities to rethink nursing functions and the relationship of nursing to medicine in a fashion better fitted to advances in medical and behavioral knowledge and technology.

The Sociology of the Hospital

Most of my discussion thus far has been based on the economic and administrative literature. Although the hospital literature is vast, it is only in recent years that sociologists have made hospitals a major area of study, and for the most part their concern has been concentrated on the study of mental hospitals rather than general ones. I am still inclined to agree with Perrow's assessment (559) that the sociological literature on general hospitals is by and large trivial. There are many studies of attendants and nurses, but far fewer studies of doctors and other decision makers. Much of the literature concerns simple interaction patterns that have no great theoretical or practical import, and such research is frequently the product of the fact that such interactions are easy to observe and the participants are not difficult to interview. Unfortunately, as Perrow remarks, medical sociology in this area can be characterized as technology (questionnaires) without goals. In this section only those directions that seem more promising will be reviewed (for a collection of some of the better studies on hospitals, see 238).

One of the aspects of the hospital most fascinating to organizational theorists is its rapidly changing technology. In just a few decades the hospital has become one of the most complex of all social organizations. It is characterized by considerable technical specialization, multiple tasks and lines of authority, complicated community relationships, changing social roles, and well-developed professional groups and systems of stratification. Thus it serves as a context for studying interactions among goals, technology, specialization, authority, and decision making. From a theoretical point of view, sociologists have been most interested in the fact that the hospital does not conform to the typical bureaucratic model first formulated by Max Weber. Instead it is characterized by many lines of authority, various sources of power, and complicated lines of communication. One of the most interesting studies in this context was the investigation by Goss (280) in which she argues that the Weberian conception of a rationally organized hierarchical line of authority and an impersonal division of labor on the basis of specialized competence does not fit the situation of the hospital. She observes that the hospital is characterized by an advisory bureaucratic model that is based on administrative authority within the administrative realm, but in which doctors retain the power to make decisions regarding matters within their professional expertise. In the medical realm the doctor, Goss argues, regards administrative directives as advice that need not be heeded if, in his opinion, it would be detrimental to the well-being of his patient.

Because the hospital brings together so many diverse types of professional specialists and ancillary workers, it is not surprising that organizational sociologists have been intrigued by the social roles in hospitals, the ways they interlink with one another, and their changing character. Similarly, there has been concern with the changing relationships among the various decision-making groups within the hospital, such as the board of trustees, the medical group, and the hospital administrative staff. Much of the literature has focused on the conflicts in jurisdiction that develop and on the manner in which these groups resolve their varying points of view. Considerable emphasis has also been devoted to the hospital as a complex bureaucracy and the difficulties of integrating and coordinating its various elements. Finally, increasing attention is being given to the intraorganizational environment of the hospital and the ways it relates to other organizations.

The sociological literature on general hospitals has three major faults:

1. Most studies are descriptive of one or two hospitals and fail to capture the diversity in size, organization, and complexity that characterize such institutions. Few studies include any significant sample of hospitals, although there is at least one major attempt to study organizational problems in a sample of general community hospitals (262; see also 323 for a more macro approach).

2. Organizational theorists have for the most part failed to come to any consensus as to the most important independent and dependent variables worthy of study. As a consequence, the hospital literature is superficially joined together by the fact that all of these studies took place in the context of hospitals but range over a wide variety of variables and provide little accumulated systematic knowledge.

3. One of the most important concerns in the study of most organizations involves the relationship between the organization's goals and performance. We are concerned with what business firms produce and the profits they earn, and similarly we should be concerned with what hospitals try to do and how well they succeed. However, students of the general hospital concern themselves only rarely with the performance variables (that is, the kind and quality of medical care), although it is probably the most crucial dimension of the hospital's function and existence. Goss (281) provides an excellent review indicating the way characteristics of hospitals such as type of ownership relate to performance variables. Much more such work is necessary.

A good example of work relating social structure to performance is the study of social stratification and hospital care by Melvin Seeman and John Evans (626; 627). It is the kind of research that sociologists must do if they are to contribute in a significant way to understanding the hospital context. Seeman and Evans studied a 600-bed university-affiliated general hospital. They measured ward stratification through interviews with nurses who described the status behavior of the attending physician who was in charge of a given ward. Each nurse was asked to describe the attending physician's behavior in terms of ten items (for example, "Requires that the nurses follow the medical hierarchy in reporting any marked change in the patient's condition," or "Keeps a certain professional distance between himself and the other ward personnel"). Wards in which the physician in charge tended to maximize status differentials were regarded as highly stratified. Each of the 14 wards studied received a stratification score, and among the highly stratified wards five were surgical and two medical, while among those characterized as having low stratification three were surgical and four medical.

The investigators also used three kinds of data to characterize performance: (1) objective data based on medical records; (2) reputational data based on superiors' ratings of the intern; and (3) subjective reports of the interns on their own behavior. The objective data were based for the most part on the medical records of 3,783 patients during a four-month period, and the performance measures derived from them were based on the conception the investigators developed of seven hospital functions: selection (measured by length of patient stay), supply (measured by personnel turnover), service (measured by medication errors), communication (measured by frequency of consultations), control (measured by frequency of deviations from routine performance), discovery (measured by autopsy rates), and teaching (measured by the intern's rating of teaching quality). Seeman and Evans provide evidence that ward stratification is related to patient's length of stay, job mobility of personnel, attending physician's use of psychiatric and social services, occurrence of medication errors, and teaching quality of the various wards. Similarly, ward stratification is related to the interns' reports of what goes on and the ratings made by superiors of the interns. Thus there is correspondence among the various measures of performance used by the investigators. As Seeman and Evans note:

> The gist of the matter is that the highly stratified units are characterized by a significantly different kind of performance: for example, the internes say that these units are poorer in their communication to and about the patient, and that they are likewise poorer in their performance of the teaching function; the medical records indicate that the highly stratified units use the consultation process less heavily (especially psychiatric and social service

consults), and that the turnover among nursing staff is relatively high; and finally, the interne's superior (at least his "independent" superior) rates the quality of interne performance lower on these highly stratified units [627, p. 203].

Although the size of the relationships that Seeman and Evans demonstrate is modest, their consistency makes a strong case for their validity. Further study along these lines is obviously called for.

Revans (583) has also found that performance in hospitals is related to organizational characteristics, and he believes that staff communication is particularly important. Although innumerable articles argue for improvement in communication in hospitals and medical care, studies demonstrating that improving communication makes a difference in medical care are relatively rare. We need more experimental studies such as an investigation (199) that selected a random group of patients undergoing surgery and gave them simple information, encouragement, and instruction concerning their impending surgery and means of alleviating postoperative pain. The researchers, however, were not involved in the medical care of the patients studied, and they did not participate in decisions concerning them. An independent evaluation of the postoperative period and the length of stay of patients in the experimental and control groups showed that the communication and simple instruction made a real difference.

In another study, reported by Skipper and Leonard (652), children admitted to a hospital for tonsillectomy were randomly divided into experimental and control groups. Patients in the control group received the usual care, whereas in the experimental situation mothers were admitted to the hospital by a specially trained nurse who tried to facilitate communication and to maximize the mothers' opportunities to express their anxiety and to ask questions. An attempt was made to give mothers an accurate picture of the realities, including what routine events to expect and when they were likely to occur. Mothers in the experimental group experienced less stress. Their children experienced smaller changes in blood pressure, temperature, and other physiological measures; they were less likely to suffer from posthospital emesis and made a better adaptation to the hospital. These children made a more rapid recovery following hospitalization, displaying less fear, less crying, and less disturbed sleep than children in the control group. In considering this study we note that tonsillectomy is one of the most frequent surgical procedures performed in the United States, and the main cause of hospitalization of children (723). Controlled studies have demonstrated tonsillectomy to be a dubious surgical procedure in the great majority of cases, and psychological problems have been found to be a major adverse effect of the procedure, especially in young children. Thus the importance of alleviating the distress of mother and child when the procedure is performed should not be minimized.

Although sociological studies relating organizational factors to patient outcomes are rare, there is some further information from medical audit studies relating organizational characteristics of hospitals to the quality of medical care. For example, the frequently cited Trussell study (142) found large variations in the quality of medical care, and poor medical care was more frequently found in particular kinds of hospitals than in others. Board-certified specialists provided much better care than general practitioners, and the proportion of board-certified physicians is related to other characteristics of the hospital. In general, the more likely the hospital was to be involved in medical education, the better the quality of care, and board-certified doctors practiced better medicine in hospitals with training programs than those without them. In studies such as the Trussell investigation it is extremely difficult to separate the effect attributable to hospital organization from that produced by the fact that better hospitals attract more dedicated and better qualified staff. Even if one controls for the proportion of board-certified physicians, variations within this group are as great as within the group of those who are not certified. Thus the finding that board-certified physicians in university hospitals practiced better medicine than those in other kinds of hospitals may be the product either of the organization of university hospitals or of the fact that university hospitals draw the best people in the board-certified group. Given the quality of medical educational institutions in New York, the latter interpretation is probably at least partly correct, although organizational factors may also be important.

In a survey of directors of medical education in community hospitals, Hage (307) found that they report more controls exercised on the work of medical staff if they also report that half or more of the active staff doctors are board certified. This study suggests that hospitals characterized by a large proportion of certified specialists also have a tighter form of organization. Roemer and Friedman (590) found that highly structured medical-staff organization, including the use of full-time salaried physicians, seems to improve patient care. One inference that may be drawn from these various studies is that tighter staff organization may improve direction of the organization and quality control of medical work. If such control becomes too rigid or authoritarian, however, communication breaks down and care suffers. Future studies will have to investigate more specifically the manner in which different forms of organization in comparable hospitals affect the quality and kinds of medical care provided.

It is pointless to attempt to describe the wide range of variables that have characterized hospital studies (see 559). Our historical discussion makes clear that modern practices are in part an outgrowth of earlier patterns that changed to meet new challenges and needs as well as new developments in technology. Perrow, approaching the medical-care field from the organizational frame of reference, has come to the same conclusion as the one this book attempts to present:

> Organizations are, of course, made up of people, and people interact in meaningful ways so that informal, stable patterns of behavior and perspectives emerge which have organizational consequences. People also bring a variety of personal characteristics to bear upon their performance and seek a variety of personal goals and satisfactions. These "nonformal" aspects of formal organizations are part of the distinctive province of sociologists ... [328, p. 966].

One of the strongest points in the emerging literature is the growing interest in studying hospitals not as separate organizations but in relation to the social, political, and economic environments in which they function. Such studies would thus emphasize the ways the hospital as a social entity adapts to such changes as national health insurance, new federal regulations, and changing modes of reimbursement.

Coordination of Services

In both the United States and Great Britain it is generally recognized that it is valuable to coordinate various aspects of medical services with other social services. Because a wide range of life difficulties becomes obvious to the doctor, he is in a particularly good position to send patients to agencies that can help them and to be of value in providing a coordinated plan for dealing with the problems that arise (364). In the United States the private physician is frequently poorly informed about the services available for his patients, and many important services are not effectively utilized. Hospitals more frequently have social-work or social-service staff who know something about the community helping agencies and thus are better able to put patients in contact with such services as child-care clinics, housekeeping help, vocational rehabilitation, and mental-health centers. In particular disease areas voluntary organizations make efforts to seek out persons needing help, but in general coordination of services is frequently haphazard, and quite often persons in need of particular services are unaware of their availability. As medical practice in the United States grows into a more organized pattern through the development of larger group practices and more community and regional organization, further efforts will be made to deal with such problems of coordination more effectively.

In Great Britain the problems of coordination are somewhat different, as medical and social services are mainly provided by various government units. Thus the basic problem involves the organization and coordination of government services. One of the most difficult problems the National Health Service faces is coordinating the services provided by the various components of the health system: the hospitals, the general practitioner, and various local authority workers. Since I have already discussed the hospital and the general practitioner, I shall say a few words about the local authorities.

The local authorities have been prominent in providing antenatal care and home midwifery since 1918. The child and welfare clinics run by the local authorities give advice on child rearing to mothers, distribute food for babies and routinely examine them, provide immunizations, and so on. In schools the health authorities provide free milk, meals, routine health inspections, and free clinics, and do some of the work with children such as immunizations. In aftercare and community care the local authorities may provide sheltered workshops, living hostels, and other facilities.

Although all of the services provided are important and necessary, often the fact that these responsibilities are shared by various aspects of the health service leads to confusion, and it sometimes becomes unclear as to who is to assume the central responsibility and authority in the care of the patient. Perhaps more distressing is that the lack of coordination leads to an inferior pattern of distribution of services, and much is lost that could be achieved by coordination and cooperation. In the maternity and child-care area, for example, antenatal care and immunizations can be obtained from both the health authority and the general practitioner. Similarly, home obstetrics—which still occurs quite commonly in England—involves responsibility shared between a local midwife and a general practitioner. If a mother has her baby in a hospital, she may receive various kinds of care and treatment from a general practitioner, the hospital's obstetrics staff, and several local or regional welfare authorities. Because responsibility may be ambiguously defined and communication faulty, patient care can easily become confusing, if not chaotic. Problems of coordination become even more complex when the welfare services provided by the Ministry of Labour become involved. The British have attempted to remedy problems of coordination through a managerial reorganization of the National Health Service, thus mandating greater communication among representatives of each level of care in each practice area. It remains to be seen to what extent such a managerial approach can realistically improve traditional difficulties in communication at the level of the individual practitioner.

Utilization Patterns

It should be apparent from what I have already said that although all modern medical systems have both hospital and general practitioner services, these are not necessarily used in the same way. The manner in which medical services are provided reflects ideological concepts of medical care and, perhaps more important, the significant pressures that medical systems face in coping with illness.

Analysts have been puzzled by the rather large variation in utilization patterns in modern Western medical systems, such as those found in the United States, Great Britain, and Sweden (23). In the United States and Sweden the admission rate to hospitals is higher than in Great Britain, but the average American patient spends a shorter time in the hospital than the average patient in England and Sweden. On the other hand, America and Great Britain have comparable average rates of utilization of outpatient services, while the Swedish figure has been considerably lower. How does one make sense of these confusing trends?

Let us first note that international comparisons concerning utilization are tricky, and such gross comparisons as we have indicated above are probably the cumulation of many subtle differences, including differences in measurements of utilization. Thus our interpretation must be tentative. One possibility is that these different rates reflect true differences in rates of illness; as all three countries have a similar mortality experience, we must probably seek an interpretation elsewhere. The difference in rates of hospitalization and length of stay in the hospital between the United States and Britain probably reflects several factors associated with the organization of medical care. First, I have already noted that the British situation is characterized by a shortage of beds and an emphasis on the care of the patient in his home. It is likely, therefore, that patients are less readily hospitalized and, when they are, have more severe illnesses and require longer care. I noted the lack of continuity between general medical practice and hospital care in England. In the United States the same doctor usually looks after the patient in the hospital and outside, and thus when he hospitalizes a patient he is already familiar with the case and can expedite the patient's care. When a patient is hospitalized in Great Britain it probably takes somewhat longer for the consultant to familiarize himself with the patient's problem, and thus care would be slower. It is interesting that in situations in America in which the British pattern is followed, as in Veterans Administration hospitals and other hospitals dealing with referral of welfare cases, periods of hospitalization are closer to the British pattern. Furthermore, differences in rate of referral to hospital and length of stay are complicated by such categories as maternity cases; most babies are born in hospitals in the United States, while in Great Britain and in Sweden confinements at home are more common. More complicated confinements are brought into the hospital in Great Britain and Sweden, and here we might reasonably expect a longer length of stay.

Then there are other complicating factors, such as differences in staff available to deal with the patients, shortage of equipment and resulting delays in diagnostic work, requirements concerning patient stay relating to the training of particular professional groups (such as midwives in England), differences in medical opinions concerning desirable length of stay, and bureaucratic procedures generally. If this does not complicate matters enough, there are still further relevant factors. For example, decisions on the necessary length of hospitalization may depend on the facilities available to the patient after he leaves the hospital and the adequacy of care he is likely to receive when he returns home. Because the organization of paramedical care facilities varies from one country to another, and because the economic status and related adequacy of housing also varies, different decisions about length of hospital care in these countries may be desirable.

Perhaps most important, we must not fail to realize that there are vast differences in rates of hospitalization and length of hospitalization within each of these countries, and these differences are probably more worthy of analysis. Averages are frequently not illuminating statistics, as they tend to combine in one figure widely divergent experiences. Revans (583), for example, in his studies of British hospitals, has shown vastly different lengths of stay for similar medical conditions. He has observed that long stays are associated with high staff turnover and dissatisfaction among nursing staff. It is not clear from this study whether long stays result directly from staff dissatisfaction or from the resultant shortage of nursing staff. In any case his study illustrates the importance of looking at variations among hospitals within the same medical system.

When we view differing patterns of use of outpatient facilities, the analysis is further complicated by varying illness behavior patterns among different groups and the contingencies leading to help seeking. Since these factors have been thoroughly reviewed in earlier chapters, I shall not repeat the discussion here.

Elements of Tertiary Care

Tertiary care is differentiated from secondary care by a further level of complexity and expense. It often involves highly trained teams of physicians, nurses, and other health professionals who provide care to the patient over a fairly extended period of time. It is also typically accompanied by the use of expensive technologies such as heart-lung machines, artificial kidneys, and hyperbaric chambers. Such procedures may involve long and continuing efforts with the patient over many years, as in the continuing monitoring of the transplant patient or the extended care of the seriously burned patient, but more often they represent episodic contacts between the medical system and a patient to deal with a single rare condition during its acute phase.

Although there is no precise definition of the boundary between secondary and tertiary care, tertiary refers to the types of service usually found in teaching hospitals or large medical centers, but not in the typical community voluntary hospital. As in our earlier discussion of primary care, however, there is conceptual confusion in this way of characterizing the issue. Effective tertiary care is part of a system of services that is planned and coordinated in relation to the organization of primary- and secondary-care facilities in a region. In an unplanned system there is a tendency for tertiary-care facilities to proliferate so that they are in excess supply relative to the objective need for them in the community. Each hospital attempts to develop the full spectrum of facilities and services, thus resulting in the duplication of facilities for treating rare and complex diseases. This is not only very expensive, but some of these units have so few cases of the relevant conditions that physicians working in the area do not really maintain their skills in providing optimal care. For example, open-heart surgical units have proliferated in hospitals, but many of them have only a very small volume of cases per year.

Parker (546) has suggested five criteria to define the character of tertiary care: superspecialization and a narrow focus, a high level of technology and skills, concern with rare and complex conditions, discontinuous service, and service to a large population. Because the types of condition appropriate for tertiary care are only a small fraction of the illnesses that occur in populations, tertiary-care facilities must serve larger population groups by acting as recipients of referrals from secondary and primary sources of care. While primary medical care must be readily accessible to the population it serves in a geographic sense, it is uneconomical for tertiary care to be organized in this way because of the expensive technical facilities and personnel needed and the fact that it is inefficient to decentralize such facilities because of the lesser demand for these types of service. Thus effective planning and integration of the components of service are essential, and greater efforts are being made to organize tertiary-care facilities in relation to specific regions for which they are responsible.

Because of the lack of a planned system in the United States, with proper allocation of functions among primary, secondary, and tertiary sectors, there is considerable confusion about the role of the tertiary-care institution. Some 1,500 hospitals are designated as "teaching" hospitals, and approximately 900 are associated with medical schools (257, p. 89). These hospitals tend to specialize in the care of more complex and difficult conditions, but they also cover the gamut of more ordinary hospital services and specialized outpatient care. The ethos of institutions associated with medical schools favors the more complex case and a specialized and technological approach to problems. While appropriate for the complex case, such orientations are frequently excessive for the more ordinary secondary functions. Moreover, the types of management characteristic of care in teaching hospitals—and thus in the training of medical students and house staff—are not particularly appropriate to the vast number of patients who come seeking primary medical care, but these are the patients for whom most doctors in training will eventually have to care. The teaching hospital encourages an excessive dependence on the laboratory, on more esoteric diagnostic procedures, and on the newest techniques. While these may be appropriate for the very sick patient or the difficult and puzzling case, when used routinely they consume enormous resources with little benefit for patients.

As the technologies for tertiary care have developed, they provide increasing opportunities to extend life for the hopeless patient as well as for those with greater potential. These technologies not only pose problems of cost and allocation of resources but also involve enormous legal, ethical, and social issues. We shall return to these types of problem later in the book, but now turn to examine medical care from the point of view of the various actors involved: physicians, nurses, other health personnel, and patients.

Part 6

THE MICRO SYSTEM OF HEALTH CARE

Chapter 14

PHYSICIANS

While physicians constitute only a small fraction of all health-care personnel, their social and political influence extends far beyond what their numbers would suggest. Physicians not only have vast control over the organization and provision of all medical services and the work settings of most other health professionals, but also have disproportionate influence on health and social policies through their high social status and their elaborate organization of interest groups for political as well as professional purposes.

A Social Profile

The role of the physician has exceedingly high prestige in American society and in most societies of the world (327; 581). In the United States it ranks with such lofty occupations as Supreme Court justice and governor of a state and has higher status than any other professional group. Medicine is thus attractive to recruits who value status and income, seek a challenging and interesting occupation, enjoy exercising judgment, and wish to do good. Because of the preparation necessary for admission to medical school and the long training and high costs of medical education, students from higher-status families are disproportionately selected into the profession. Although more recent efforts have been made to select minority-group members, more women, and students from rural areas, medicine will remain disproportionately urban, white, male, and upper-middle-class in its recruitment for a long time to come.

In 1975 there were 114 medical schools in the United States, with ten more in the process of development. The total entering freshman medical class in 1975–1976 was 15,295, 24 percent of whom were women (278). Entry into medical school has become extremely competitive; there are approximately nine applicants for every available position, and the students admitted tend to have high aptitude and excellent grades. Although the competition for medical school has varied with the perceived attractiveness of other occupations over time, the aspiration to be a physician has been persistently strong. Administrators at elite universities are alarmed at the large proportion of undergraduate students expressing a desire to go to medical school and at the alleged vicious competition among them for grades.

Selection in Medical Education

A great deal has been written about the attitudes and personality characteristics of students selected into medicine, but it is clear that there is tremendous diversity in this population and that the profile changes with modified social definitions over time (258). Studies have found that medical students are high on endurance and need for achievement but lower on needs for change and succorance (282). Some medical educators worry that the emphasis on hard scientific performance among medical admissions committees results in the selection of students whose interpersonal skills and human concerns are not as well developed as their scientific abilities. Others worry that medicine tends to attract students who may be more committed to economic incentives than to social concerns. While all of these tendencies may exist on a statistical basis relative to students choosing other fields, medical students still constitute a heterogeneous group. Greater personality and social selection probably occurs when the student decides on a specialty interest.

Socialization

The process of medical education is demanding. Over a period of four years the student acquires not only massive amounts of information and a great variety of skills but also many attitudes and values that are shaped by the demands of medical work, a sense of confidence in his ability to take care of practical problems, and a repertoire of behavior shaped by clinical experience and responsibility (52). The applied character of clinical medical work, as Eliot Freidson (239, p. 78) has noted, "gives rise to a special frame of mind oriented toward action for its own sake, action based on a radical pragmatism."

A large number of students come to medical school with the intention of becoming primary-care physicians. Given the uncertainties of the role of the medical student during training, however, the student is influenced by the context and values dominant in the training situation. When students begin medical school they have only a limited understanding of the nature of medical work or of the possible choices they will have. Medical school and even the internship and early residency years confront them with a more complex reality to which they have to make a continuing series of personal, social, and academic adjustments (52; 518). As reality tends to diminish their naive idealism and makes them aware of the complexity and uncertainty of clinical problems, they begin to take on a more professional and limited perspective. Mastering the broad scope of medicine with a sense of competence and confidence is a difficult task in the light of modern developments. A physician who concentrates his efforts on a specialty has a much greater sense of mastery over the relevant material and can feel more secure that he knows what he is doing. Thus the young physician aspiring to reduce anxiety about his own competence is intuitively drawn to a more limited sphere of activity that gives him or her a greater sense of self-confidence. Medical-school values strongly reinforce this process.

Specialty Choice

The process by which a physician enters a specialty is a mixture of social selection, personal interest, accident, and opportunity, and is also dependent on the cast of characters who teach in the various specialities at a particular medical school. A student's interest in psychiatry, for example, might develop in a school where the department is strong and has high standing, but not in one where the psychiatrists are weak and poorly regarded. Similarly, the relative social standings of specialties change over time with changing definitions and advances in science and technology. Thus it is difficult to speak in broad generalities about the selection process. Many students make definitive choices prior to medical school, while others may drift for several years of postgraduate education before choosing. Many students with defined preferences change them as they become aware of new fields and opportunities. Despite the idiosyncratic aspects of the process, both general impressions and empirical studies suggest that there are substantial differences among recruits to various specialties in terms of social background, personality, and values (135). Such differences probably reflect both social selection and the influence of certain types of work on doctors' values, self-images, and presentations of self.

It might be useful to suggest some of the selective tendencies believed to be characteristic of varying specialties despite the changing character of the specialties over time. Some specialties, for example, tend to be almost exclusively male (surgery, radiology, urology) while others have much higher representation of women (pediatrics, anesthesiology, dermatology, psychiatry). Jews tend to be drawn disproportionately to psychiatry and more politically liberal students to psychiatry and pediatrics. The image of the internist is that of the intellectual problem solver, while the surgeon is seen as more aggressive and active. The family practitioner, in contrast, tends to be less conceptual and more gregarious than the internist. Psychiatry is seen to draw recruits who are abstract and playful about ideas, while surgeons tend to be more concrete and moralistic. Psychiatrists tend to be high on Machiavellianism, while surgeons tend to be low (113, pp. 346–47). Within-specialty variation may exceed the differences between specialties, and while these gross generalizations are suggestive, they have no great practical significance. Certain types of medical activities, much as any other tasks, require certain skills and orientations. A physician who does not enjoy people, who is exceedingly exacting, and who has little tolerance for ambiguity would in all probability do better in pathology than in family medicine. When physicians choose specialties incompatible with their personal needs, some re-sorting goes on throughout their careers.

We know relatively little about the factors that influence the types of practice physicians enter following their residency training. Practice location is affected by personal preferences, economic opportunities, and the location of the institution in which the student received his residency training (666; 792). Residents trained in a particular area become acquainted with it and with the medical community, and often find a practice niche in an area nearby (529). Students trained in an area or institution in which they have had experience in a multi-specialty group practice are more likely to enter such a practice (570). The probability that a resident will perform primary care, establish a rural practice, or work in a health center is likely to depend on his or her having had a good experience as a resident in such a practice setting. To the extent that residency programs provide good models for such practices, there is increased likelihood that young doctors will see these as viable opportunities. Also, while general practitioners tend to be distributed more widely, specialists are more likely to locate in urban and suburban centers close to hospitals and other physicians.

The Context of Medical Practice

Thus far the discussion of physicians and their development has proceeded from the perspective of the individual medical recruit. The behavior of physicians is determined not only by their social and personality characteristics and by the influence of the training environment of the medical school and residency program but also by the context of medical practice. The three major dimensions defining this context include specialization, degree of group organization, and the system of remuneration.

Specialization

The most salient aspect of medical organization is the extent to which physicians have divided into specialties and subspecialties. There are 22 approved medical specialty boards in the United States (104), organizations that voluntarily certify in specialties physicians who attain a certain level of training and who pass specified examinations. Such board certification, which has no official legal status, often brings higher remuneration in salaried positions and may be a criterion for higher payment under various public and private insurance programs. The largest boards are internal medicine, surgery, pediatrics, obstetrics and gynecology, radiology, psychiatry and neurology, and pathology. Family practice, the newest board, established in 1969, is growing rapidly. The large boards such as internal medicine and surgery include many subspecialties, with opportunities to receive certification in a subspecialty such as nephrology or cardiology. Other recognized subspecialties within internal medicine include allergy, gastroenterology, and pulmonary disease.

The establishment of boards and subspecialties is as much a political process through which physicians come to dominate a specified domain and restrict competition as it is a reaction to the mandates of an increasingly sophisticated technology (670). While the traditional concept of the specialist was as a consultant physician who assisted the generalist with problems that were puzzling or of greater complexity than he could handle, existing specialization is organized around population groups (pediatrics, adult medicine, geriatrics), types of technology (radiology, radiation therapy, anesthesiology), organ systems (nephrology, cardiology, dermatology), etiologies (infectious disease), and specific disease categories (pulmonary disease, psychiatry). The most recent distortion of the concept of the consulting physician was the development of the American Board of Family Practice, which in effect defines the generalist as another kind of specialist.

Many countries attempt to maintain a balance between the doctors of first contact (general practitioners, family physicians, general internists, and general pediatricians) and those who are more limited in their scope of work. While no country has completely retained the traditional concept of the consulting specialist, those that organize medicine through the public service tend to restrict the number of specialist positions available. In European countries where there is a division between general practitioners and hospital physicians, generalists constitute a larger proportion of all doctors. Physicians cannot establish themselves as specialists unless hospital positions are available, and thus there are limits on the proliferation of specialists who are expensive and not essential.

Although there are many contentious issues among the numerous specialties, from a public-policy viewpoint the major distinction is between physicians who engage in primary medical care and those who perform other medical tasks, such as providing specialty care on referral or providing more complex services in hospitals. As noted in discussing primary care, differences between primary and specialist practitioners are not simply a matter of what they do but also a matter of the way they do it. One important aspect of primary care is the attitude of the physician, his assumptions and storage of information about the particular patient, and the way he goes about evaluating the patient's complaint. What the physician sees as important, what he inquires about, and the way he evaluates the patient are all dependent on his training and orientations (57). In understanding the ways varying types of general and subspecialty training affect medical practice, it is necessary to have better data on the ways patients with comparable presenting complaints are evaluated and managed differently by physicians with varying types of training and by physicians who have continuing relationships with these patients, as compared with those who see such patients only on an irregular basis and do not take continuing responsibility for their care. Are there differences, for example, among a family physician, a general internist, and a cardiologist in the ways they go about evaluating and managing varying types of chest pain? The focus here is on the strategies of evaluation used by different physicians and their implications for effective outcome, cost, and patient satisfaction.

Degree of Group Organization

The second crucial element defining the physician's work is the extent to which he operates as an independent practitioner in contrast to being part of a larger group organization. Although physicians have traditionally worked as independent practitioners out of their own offices or in people's homes, physicians' work is now more commonly based in clinics, health centers, or hospitals. In the United States, while most physicians still operate as individual entrepreneurs, selling their services on a fee-for-service basis, there has been a persistent trend toward group practice (63; 470), particularly among more recent graduates. The vast majority of physicians are also highly dependent on their hospital privileges. Approximately 60 percent of American physicians are in office-based practice, while another 25 percent are primarily in hospital-based practice (a majority residents and interns) (104). A study by the American Medical Association in 1975 found almost 70,000 physicians in groups (63). Most groups tend to be small (three or four physicians), and a majority of doctors are in multispecialty in contrast to single-specialty or general-practice groups (63; 470). While groups are prevalent in the Pacific Northwest and in the East North Central states, the nongroup, office-based physician still constitutes the national mode in the United States.

Group practice also appears to be growing elsewhere in the world, stimulated by a willingness among young doctors to enter such practice and by the advantages of group organization for sharing responsibilities and providing greater opportunities for control over one's schedule. The major impediment is a need to adjust one's style of work to the style of others and to give up some autonomy. For the most part physicians adjust by developing small groups in which informal agreements prevail in contrast to formal rules. Thus, for example, in England, where there have been economic incentives for group organization in recent years, many such groups have emerged, but they tend to be small (493). Greatest group organization is found in countries that provide ambulatory care through health centers and polyclinics, developed either by the state or by large insurance funds. The 1975 American Medical Association study found only 101 groups with 50 or more physicians in the United States. The larger groups are more likely than the smaller groups to be organized on a prepaid basis, but the vast majority of groups of any size are largely engaged in fee-for-service practice (63).

Most of the advantages of group structure come from having a sufficient patient load to justify the acquisition of expensive facilities and equipment and the use of a variety of middle-level health practitioners who increase the physician's productivity and scope of practice. Large groups facilitate the development of preventive programs, opportunities for continuing education, and control over one's schedule of work. But the larger the group, the greater the pressure for the physician to adjust his practice style to others; disputes develop over such issues as equitable remuneration, productivity, and administrative rules (570). Many physicians not in groups adapt to the need for economy of scale by developing independent arrangements with other physicians to share facilities and personnel, and even to cover for one another, without incurring the perceived disadvantages of accommodating to a formal organizational arrangement. Some of the new comprehensive medical foundations are a communitywide response of physicians to meet competition of prepaid group practices by offering consumers insurance for medical care on a prepaid basis, but without requiring the physician to alter his pattern of practice (200).

Studies of physicians practicing in large prepaid group practices suggest that, despite differences in organization, doctors do not fun-

damentally practice differently from those in the traditional mode
(707). Certainly mode of clinic organization, patient load, and types of
remuneration have some impact on patterns of practice in a way to be
reviewed later in the chapter, but the amount of variance in practice behavior among doctors having the same roles in the same organizations
is substantial (297). Thus it is clear that the physician's prior socialization and values have an important impact on style of practice independent of organizational factors; such differences are supported by the
widely shared norms of "medical responsibility" and "clinical experience" (242).

Systems of Remuneration

The effort and commitment the physician gives to his work depend
on the rewards he receives. Such rewards include his income, status
and esteem, appreciation of patients, and the satisfaction that comes
from the knowledge of doing one's job well. Because of the lack of visibility of the office-based physician's work to the general public or even
to other doctors, the income earned by the physician tends to become
an important symbol of his success. Thoughtful physicians worry about
the lack of a system of rewarding the physician in office-based patient
care through means other than income, because this allows economics
to have too large an effect on performance. Physicians often tend to
carry out procedures that are remunerative, neglecting those for which
payments are not made through insurance (such as patient education or
listening to the patient). It would be difficult to change the system and
substitute other types of rewards for income because the physician's office work is not easily observable to anyone but patients, and patients
are not usually a reference group for the physician because their judgments tend to be based primarily on the physician's manner rather than
on technical criteria.

Because of the symbolic importance of income as an affirmation of
the doctor's worth, physicians tend to be extraordinarily sensitive to
how they are paid; few other issues seem to arouse comparable emotion.
The mode most doctors favor in the United States is the fee for service,
which rewards them on a piecework basis in proportion to the work
they do. Various studies indicate that doctors in office-based practice
work longer hours and see more patients when they are paid on a fee-
for-service basis than when they are on salary or on capitation (receiving a fixed sum per patient per year) (491).

There are a remarkable number of variations in the ways physicians
are remunerated from one country to another and under varying insurance mechanisms (265). In general, physicians tend to favor the system

of remuneration to which they are most accustomed, assuming that remuneration is adequate, and they resist changes in it in the fear that structural changes will erode their economic position. Moreover, the evidence suggests that physicians adapt their behavior to whatever system of remuneration exists (265, p. 289), performing those procedures that are most likely to be rewarded by the scheme within which they work.

There are basically four major ways to remunerate physicians, with infinite variations and combinations. The first is the fee for service in which physicians receive an established amount for every specific procedure performed. Some fee schedules are highly specified; the relative value studies of the California Medical Association include thousands of procedures, although some 600 entries account for most payments made to physicians (153). The second mode of paying doctors is on a salary—a fixed amount for specified hours or sessions. Third, doctors may be paid on capitation, a fixed amount per unit of time for each patient or family for whom the doctor takes responsibility. The amount of capitation can be adjusted by the characteristics of the patient, the attributes of the doctor, or the characteristics of the practice setting. Thus the amount of capitation per person may be higher if the patient is 65 or over, if the doctor has special training, or if the practice is located in a rural area. Finally, doctors may be paid on a case-payment method, fixed sums for giving patients all necessary care. Obstetricians often provide prenatal and delivery services to mothers on such a basis.

Another important distinction is the way the patient pays for care as compared with the way the physician is paid. Patients, for example, may purchase a prepaid plan, but the physicians rendering services may be paid on a salary, a capitation basis, or on a fee for service. Moreover, patients may purchase insurance on a service or indemnity basis. When the insurance is on a service basis, the physicians may have to negotiate the fee schedule with the health plan. In the indemnity situation the patient usually pays the doctor and is reimbursed at some level by his insurance. Thus there is no direct relationship between physician and insurance plan. Some doctors refuse to accept patients on a service benefit plan or insist on charging the patient more for the service than the fee schedule established by the insurance plan.

Each form of payment tends to have distinct advantages and disadvantages, and it is difficult to achieve an effective balance among the competing payment mechanisms (265; 589). Fee for service encourages the physician's hard work and commitment to the patient, and fee-for-service physicians tend to show greater responsiveness to and interest in their patients (500, pp. 99–118). Studies in this area, however, refer to the patient's direct payment to the physician, and we know very little about the consequences of fee for service when it is paid indirectly, as in a comprehensive foundation plan. The major disadvantage of fee for service is that it creates an incentive for unnecessary and sometimes dangerous procedures, particularly discretionary surgical interventions (589). It also tends to encourage the performance of technical procedures in contrast to communication, listening, and explanation.

Salary and capitation are seen as the payment methods most likely to direct the physician's attention to necessary medical tasks rather than to implicit economic incentives. Their advantage allegedly is that the revenue for care is known in advance and expenditures can be controlled, and that they require the physician to establish priorities in the use of his time and effort on the basis of need rather than on the patient's ability to pay. Fixed payment, however, provides little incentive for the physician to work long or irregular hours. Physicians on salary or capitation are more likely to decide on what they regard as a reasonable work week for the remuneration received, and they are more likely to devote time to leisure and other personal activities. While the fee-for-service physician may be reluctant to make necessary referrals for fear of losing patients to competitors, it is alleged that capitation and salaried physicians refer too readily, placing an excessive burden on their colleagues and on specialists (225; 242). Salary and capitation, in the absence of other incentives, provide no encouragement for thorough care. Patients are more likely to feel that physicians on salaries or capitation are less responsive, less interested in them, and more inflexible (235; 500). As Freidson (239, pp. 98–108) has noted, there is less client control in the encounter when the physician is less dependent on the patient's fee. Similarly, while case payment makes costs predictable for the patient or insurance plan, without careful monitoring there is no assurance that physicians will not provide less service than patients require.

A major problem in formulating an adequate remuneration system is the lack of clear standards regarding the amount of care that is truly necessary. Much of medical care is discretionary and not easily demonstrated to have discernible influence on outcomes. With the lack of clear objective standards, political considerations determine the method of payment. In the United States physicians have been wedded traditionally to the fee-for-service method. Doctors know that this method is financially advantageous for them, amenable to their control, and most difficult for government to manipulate. Health-care plans and financing sources, however, dislike the open-ended nature of the fee-for-service system and the lack of control over expenditures for physicians' services. Fixed payments allow them to predict and control costs more easily, although the actual cost depends on the size of salaries or capitation values. Because fixed-payment systems allow third parties greater potential control over amount of future remuneration, physicians are wary of them. They believe that such control would be used in fiscal crises.

Physicians, on the whole, work long hours and have great responsibility. Moreover, their work confronts them with difficult social and moral dilemmas and a high degree of personal stress (152; 226). A majority of doctors believe strongly that they should be rewarded in proportion to investments of their time and effort, and that the fee-for-service method is the fairest system for relating remuneration to effort. Increasing numbers of doctors, however, will accept a fixed-payment system as long as the salaries are consistent with their aspirations. The tendency to favor fee for service apparent in the United States is not universal, since its advantage depends on an affluent population willing and able to expend funds for physician services. In much of the world where the population's income is too low to afford much private service, public subsidy of medical care through capitation or physician's salaries tends to increase physicians' total earnings, because they are frequently paid for many services that they previously provided free. Even public programs in the United States, such as Medicare, have had this effect. Indeed, most systems of national health insurance, when first enacted, increase physicians' incomes unless stringent controls are put on types and amount of payment. Such controls are usually not adopted at first, however, because proponents wish to gain physicians' cooperation in enactment and implementation of new programs. Controls are usually added after the fact, an aspect that makes physicians particularly fearful of government control over the means of remuneration.

The Work of the Doctor

The physician's style of work depends on his specialty, the organization of his practice, his workload, his professional socialization, and his personality and particular preferences (500, pp. 107–12). Different tasks require varying organizational arrangements and call for diverse types of scheduling. Some medical tasks are easily scheduled in a regularized way, such as psychiatric outpatient therapy, dermatological consultation, or anesthesiology. Other roles such as delivering babies or family practice are more subject to scheduling uncertainties. Since most available data on the physician's workday refer to primary-care physicians, the discussion that follows will pertain primarily to physicians in office-based practice—general and family physicians, internists, pediatricians, and obstetrician-gynecologists.

The Workday

Most office-based physicians in the United States, as already noted, are in single-handed fee-for-service practice. Such doctors, on the average, report spending the bulk of their working time seeing patients in their offices, with part of the day devoted to seeing their patients in the hospital and talking on the phone. While the average doctor in prepaid practice reports spending fewer than 40 hours a week seeing patients, fee-for-service practitioners report approximately 25 percent more time on such activities (499). It appears from existing data that physicians in prepaid group practice have their time more rigidly scheduled, with the group adapting to patient demand by establishing an appointment queue. In contrast, fee-for-service practitioners appear to exercise greater flexibility in scheduling, often "working in" patients who wish to see them.

While many patients, particularly mothers and the elderly, prefer physicians who are willing to make house calls, the American doctor for all practical purposes no longer does so. While doctors may make some visits to the elderly who are restricted to bed or to other patients on occasion, very few physicians in the United States spend any significant amount of their time on this function. The average British general practitioner may still spend several hours a day visiting patients in the home (491). In contrast, the American primary-care physician, who has hospital responsibilities, spends time in the hospital and much more time with patients on the phone.

British general practitioners see many more patients a day, on the average, than do American doctors. General practitioners in the United States tend to see more patients than primary-care physicians in the specialties of internal medicine, pediatrics, and obstetrics. American doctors, in contrast to British general practitioners, use more diagnostic procedures and laboratory tests. American general practitioners use fewer diagnostic procedures than do internists, but are more likely to undertake without referral such minor procedures as taping sprains, excising simple cysts, opening abscesses, and suturing lacerations (491). Of course, each specialty adopts procedures that are consistent with its emphasis and the particular population groups with which it works. Thus pediatricians, obstetricians, and internists use a somewhat different array of procedures.

Although variations in types of practice between nongroup and group practitioners are not large, there are significant differences in the manner in which doctors practice in large prepaid groups and in fee-for-service practice. Physicians in many of these prepaid groups work on a contractual schedule and, because of the salaried system of payment, have little economic incentive to expand their hours of work. Prepaid group practices tend to schedule additional patients for primary-care physicians when demand is large, putting greater pressure on physicians to process patients more quickly. Prepaid group practitioners are more likely to complain than solo fee-for-service doctors that they do not have sufficient time for each patient, although they work shorter hours and report more time for leisure (499).

Social Role and Orientations to Patients

As biomedical science and the specialization associated with medical advance have developed, physicians have come to view their work more narrowly. The flow of patients into medical care, however, reflects not only serious physical illness but social and psychological need, the desire to legitimate failure or diminished functioning, and search for secondary advantages through the certification of illness or disability.

The divergence in viewpoint between the technically oriented physician and the patient has contributed to the current dissatisfaction with the organization of medical care (500). Physicians generally prefer to deal with conditions that pose a diagnostic challenge and that they feel they can do something about. In contrast, they often feel uncomfortable with psychological or psychosocial problems, not only because they have no great efficacy in treating them but also because they have never been trained to feel comfortable in evaluating these problems and providing supportive care. Moreover, care for such problems—unlike the application of discrete technical procedures—is time consuming and often increases the uncertainties of the physician's day. Thus for the typical physician they constitute bottlenecks that increase the difficulties of handling one's practice. In recent years family-practice residency training programs have been training the physician to handle such problems with greater confidence and responsiveness. It is too early to evaluate the impact of these programs.

One manifestation of the physician's intolerance for psychosocial problems is the tendency to characterize such patients as "trivial" or "crocks." The patients defined as trivial are those who have ordinary and common complaints such as upper-respiratory infections, insomnia, and fatigue. From the physician's perspective many of these patients have either self-limited conditions or problems the physician can do nothing about, and thus consultation is unjustified. The crock, in contrast, tends to be a persistent complainer who has been evaluated repeatedly but with no observable organic basis for the complaint. Such attributions tell us more about the way physicians define their work than about the needs of patients for assistance. There is little question that from a technical organic point of view most of these patients do not require sophisticated technical care. However, such patients are often fascinating from a psychosocial perspective. Exploration of their problems beyond the initial complaint frequently suggests that the initial presentation of symptoms is a means of justifying the consultation, and that the patient has a "hidden agenda" of problems really troubling him or her (495).

Physicians, of course, vary in their personalities, the organization of their practices, and the way they respond to patients. In a variety of studies of physicians in the United States and England, I have found that attributions of triviality were related to the physician's concept of the appropriate range of medical complaints, to the method of payment, and to the intensity of patient demand (500). British general practitioners, for example, who are paid on a capitation basis, appear to schedule their office hours in terms of some concept of what is reasonable given their fixed level of renumeration. They then attempt to accommodate the patients who wish to consult them within these hours. When physicians have a heavy patient load, they must keep their minds not only on the individual patient but also on keeping the queue moving. Patients with vague complaints or psychosomatic or psychosocial problems require considerable time to assess their real problems or to have an opportunity to talk. The doctor who knows that many patients are waiting to see him feels pressure to move the patient along and often treats the symptom rather than the "whole patient." The doctor often deals with his feelings of frustration and his knowledge that he really did not give the patient sufficient time by attributing triviality to the patient.

One solution to the pressure of patient load is to work longer hours, allocating more time to each patient. A physician on a fixed salary or a capitation system, however, has no economic incentive to do so, although he may follow such a procedure because he is conscientious. The system of remuneration is an important factor affecting the style of practice. American fee-for-service physicians tend to increase their hours of patient care with increased demand and are less likely to attribute triviality to their patients. Unlike their British counterparts, fee-for-service primary-care physicians are reinforced for every additional consultation and thus are less likely to feel frustrated by the commitment of time. Doctors in large prepaid group practices who are paid on a salaried basis react more like the British general practitioners than like their counterparts in fee-for-service practice (499).

Although the structure of practice and the system of remuneration have an important influence, the doctor's attitudes and training also affect styles of practice. In a study of British general practitioners, I (490) classified doctors into four groups based on their levels of use of diagnostic facilities and on the extent to which they were tolerant of broader functions such as dealing with birth control, marital difficulties, excessive drinking, and anxieties about child care. Doctors who had a broad view and a high use of technical facilities were called "moderns" and those low on both dimensions were called "withdrawers." Those high only on diagnostic use were characterized as "technicians," and those who were high solely on perceived scope of practice were called "counselors." Moderns were less likely to characterize their patients as trivial, were more likely to do psychotherapy, and included a high proportion of members of the Royal College of General Practice. Moderns also seemed more intellectually active in other ways, as evidenced by a higher tendency to read *The Lancet,* a sophisticated medical journal. The withdrawers were most likely to attribute triviality to their patients, were the least likely to acknowledge responsibility for psychiatric patients or to do psychotherapy, gave the least time to their practices, were least satisfied, had least contact with other doctors, had least training in social aspects of medicine, and did the least reading of professional journals.

There were some major differences between the counselors and the technicians. Counselors were older doctors, were more likely to be in solo practice, were less likely to rely on an appointment system, and gave somewhat less effort on the average to their practices. Technicians, in contrast, reported greater professional contact and less satisfaction and were more likely to attribute triviality to patients. In general, the technicians included more of the younger doctors who had been trained to be reliant on diagnostic technology and who also were more intolerant of nonmedical problems and supportive aspects of the physician's role. The counselors were more likely to be old-timers who depended on talking and supportive therapies and clinical judgment more than on the laboratory. The moderns, who seemed to combine the best of both groups, were not particularly distinct from other doctors by age or practice organization. However, they appeared to be much more committed to continuing education.

Another way of viewing the practice style of the physician is described by Freidson (242, pp. 44–48) in his depiction of physicians in fee-for-service and prepaid practice as the merchant, the expert, and the bureaucratic official. The merchant is the traditional entrepreneurial physician who sells his services in a market on a fee-for-service basis. Depending on the competitiveness of the marketplace, patients may have some control in these circumstances, demanding a certain flexibility and responsiveness from the doctor and threatening to go elsewhere if the doctor is rigid or unresponsive. In the expert-layman relationship the client puts himself in the hands of the doctor on the assumption that the doctor knows best and implicitly agrees to comply with the doctor's advice. "Analytically, expertise gains its authority by its persuasive demonstration of special knowledge and skill relevant to particular problems requiring solution. It is the antithesis of the authority of office" (242, pp. 46–47). The third style, characterized by many physicians in large bureaucratic organizations, is the official who controls access to services and client abuse. Patients have a contract entitling them to specified services that they may claim. The physician, however, is the official gatekeeper who is expected to ration the use of scarce services in terms of patient need, itself an intangible concept. In this context the patient may demand services on the basis of his contractual rights, thus forcing the physician to play the role of the bureaucratic official. As Freidson notes, such patients—however uncommon they may be—may infuriate the physician because their claims challenge the physician's assumptions about his role, which are based largely on the view of the physician as expert. In any case, as patients in all medical settings grow more educated and sophisticated and become more aware of consumerism as an issue, physicians are frequently faced with demands for a different type of relationship (314; 579).

As medical settings become better organized and as financing on a prepaid, prospective, or global budget is more commonly instituted, physicians face increasing conflicts between their roles as agents of patients and as officials of health-insurance plans (500, pp. 49–57). In order to achieve controls over costs, organizational devices are developed to create tension between the physician's economic interests and provision of care to patients. This pattern exists, for example, in certain health maintenance organizations in which physicians are penalized for excessive costs in caring for a defined population. Although it is unlikely that physicians would consciously deny effective service to those who need it, much of medical care is discretionary and uncertain, and such incentives can have a considerable effect on practice. In many respects this situation is the obverse of the fee-for-service situation in which it is in the physician's economic interest to use any procedure, even unnecessary and possibly dangerous ones, however small the gain. In all cases appropriate monitoring and controls are necessary to insure that economic incentives do not produce pathological practice tendencies.

Physicians respond not only to the economic and organizational contexts of their practices and to their own personality needs but also to the characteristics and behavior of patients. Doctors can identify more easily with patients who share their cultural orientations and life styles, and they tend to find such patients more attractive. They respond as well, however, to the interesting medical challenge, the nonroutine, the appreciative patient, and the patient who gives them proper deference. Like others in the society, physicians have concepts of more or less worthy patients and may give varying effort to different patients, including such matters as resuscitation (684; for a somewhat contrasting view see 152, pp. 52–61).

Satisfactions and Dissatisfactions

The overwhelming majority of physicians appear to be extremely satisfied not only in general but also in relation to most dimensions of their occupational role. This is not surprising in that a number of studies have shown that job satisfaction is related to perceived status, although the appropriate reference group may vary from one study to another (270). Physicians in the United States have been encouraged for the most part to organize and practice as they wish, with extraordinary autonomy and control over their conditions of work. Moreover, the existing health-care system has been sufficiently flexible to allow physicians with varying personalities, interests, and personal goals to seek out specialized functions and practice settings consistent with their desires and without serious economic disadvantage; thus it should be no surprise that the average physician is relatively content with things as they are.

The literature on job satisfaction suggests that, although perceived adequate remuneration is an important condition for satisfaction, once a certain level of remuneration is reached, attention focuses on nonremunerative aspects of work satisfaction such as conditions of work, perceived autonomy, and opportunities for self-improvement and self-actualization (210). Assessments of remuneration also tend to be relative to remuneration of other colleagues in varying work settings and to the past history of remuneration (505). Any changes that threaten the relative standing of the profession are vigorously resisted. Colombotos (139; 140), for example, found that prior to Medicare physicians were opposed to the program, but supported it overwhelmingly following its implementation. The key to this observation is that the Medicare program basically maintained the existing payment system and became a tremendous economic asset for physicians. In contrast, the Medicaid program—a federal-state matching program that in some states seriously attempts to regulate physicians' fees and conditions of reimbursement—has had more difficulty in achieving physician cooperation.

Physicians in the United States earn extremely high incomes; the average net estimated income for 1973 was more than $50,000 (739, p. 91). Although physicians feel threatened by impending national health insurance, the rise of malpractice insurance rates, the growing controls of governmental agencies over their activities, the development of consumerism in medical care, and criticisms in the mass media, the threat has yet to affect their earnings significantly. Indeed, most government programs that increase the insurance coverage of the population result in increases in physicians' incomes. Yet many physicians are worried about the future and feel that the conditions of their work are being threatened by new government regulations and social changes. It is clear that medicine is in a process of transition and that physicians, while maintaining a great deal of autonomy, will no longer exercise the authority and control that they took for granted in the past.

Data on satisfaction of physicians by practice settings are relatively sparse, but even the data available have limited utility in that social-selection factors influencing choice of work settings cannot be differentiated from the effects of the settings themselves. We can, of course, supplement such data by comparing those who leave particular work settings with those who stay, but even here the dynamics are hazy and only limited information is available. Given the fact that doctors are likely to vary in their personal needs and aspirations, it is not surprising that some sorting goes on within cohorts over time. Physicians may try one or another form of practice, find it incongruent with their needs and desires, and shift to another form of practice. Because group practice has been growing in recent years relative to other forms of practice, it is evident that more doctors are going into this form of practice than leaving it, and data on multispecialty groups show relatively low turnover and consistent growth (470). Although only a minority of doctors are in group practice, there is no evidence of any major differences in satisfaction between doctors in such settings and those in other forms of practice (491).

In studying a dispute between the government and British general practitioners, Faich and I (505) illustrate how a sense of dissatisfaction can develop as a result of perceived inequities and relative deprivation despite the fact that the actual levels of remuneration do not support these perceptions. In addition, status insecurities and other problems were expressed through conflicts over remuneration because payment issues were the regularized means for dealing with doctors' grievances. I have (489) also found that the most important factor related to the general practitioner's frustration and dissatisfaction was heavy patient load. Doctors who had too many patients took various shortcuts that violated their professional standards. These doctors did not feel they were being remunerated adequately relative to the effort their practices demanded.

Data on American doctors were collected from national samples of 1,458 physicians and an additional 262 general practitioners and pediatricians in large prepaid practices (491; 499). Ninety-five percent of the doctors surveyed reported being very or fairly satisfied, although rates of satisfaction were somewhat but not substantially lower among physicians in the large prepaid group practices. There were no major differences between group and nongroup physicians in overall satisfaction. As with the British general practitioners, most dissatisfaction was expressed relative to time pressures. Only small minorities of American physicians expressed dissatisfaction with professional contacts, income, incentives, office facilities, hospital privileges, or status and esteem. Among American group practitioners there is a positive relationship between number of doctors in the group and satisfaction with professional contacts. Among nongroup practitioners type of practice organization was not related to satisfaction.

Attitudes, Values, and Ideologies

Although physicians occupy positions on the entire political spectrum, a majority describe themselves as politically conservative and identify with the Republican party. Office-based, nongroup physicians tend to be more conservative than physicians in groups or in hospital-based practice; doctors in prepaid practice and academic medicine are most likely to hold liberal attitudes (141; 497, pp. 69–87). General practitioners have more conservative attitudes than internists or pediatricians. These general descriptions do not control for varying ages among physicians in the different subgroups or for differences in social background. While interesting, none of these facts is particularly crucial. What is especially important is the fact that physicians' political views are highly correlated with the way they view the organization and delivery of medical care.

In my study of receptivity to health-care delivery among a national sample of primary physicians (497, pp. 69–87), I found that conservative doctors and those describing themselves as Republicans were more likely to oppose government financing, changes in organization—such as prepaid practice, remuneration by salary, and neighborhood health centers—peer review, and the use of physician extenders. Using multiple regression techniques, I found that physicians' political-philosophical orientation was the most consistent and substantial predictor of attitudes toward changes in the delivery system. It was the only predictor among 38 different variables that consistently achieved substantial correlations with varying measures of organizational change and between group and nongroup practitioners. Goldman (273), studying a sample of graduates from the Yale University School of Medicine between 1930 and 1976, also found that political philosophy was the strongest predictor of attitudes toward medical care. Colombotos and colleagues (141), in studying a national sample of physicians, interns, residents, and medical students, have made similar observations. These studies suggest that the debates over medical care, often represented as technical issues for which medical training and expertise are especially relevant, are in fact predominantly political in nature.

Doctors who are liberal are more likely to be Jewish, to come from larger communities, and to be from the northeastern part of the United

States (497). They are also more likely to be in group practice, particularly in larger groups and in groups on non-fee-for-service arrangements. Doctors in group practice who were more liberal also saw fewer patients, had a more limited scope of practice, had lower incomes, and were less likely to be members of their local medical societies. They were more likely to believe that physicians have responsibility to advise and care for the psychological problems of patients and that it is proper for government officials to evaluate the care patients receive.

The most extensive study of physicians' views on national health insurance is a national survey in 1973 of 2,713 senior physicians, 1,303 interns and residents, and 3,419 medical students carried out by Colombotos and his colleagues (141). They found that 56 percent of physicians were in favor of national health insurance, and 83 percent believed it to be inevitable. Since increases in insurance without strict regulation tend to enhance the income of physicians, it is more revealing to examine physicians' attitudes toward varying features of a health-insurance program. Physicians overwhelmingly prefer a plan administered by existing private and nonprofit third parties as compared with a federal agency like the Department of Health, Education, and Welfare. Moreover, a majority prefer a plan based on private health insurance to one based on the social security concept. Three-fifths of physicians oppose a plan supporting prepaid group practice, and the vast majority oppose payment by annual salary or capitation. Three-quarters of the physicians favor a plan in which they would be paid a customary fee for each service. Colombotos and his associates found that national health insurance is more favored by women doctors, blacks, doctors in the Northeast, those under age 44, hospital-based practitioners, and teachers, researchers, and administrators. While psychiatrists and pediatricians were most favorable, surgeons and general practitioners were least favorable, and primary-care doctors were less positive than physicians in referral work. The higher the physician's income, the more unfavorable his attitudes; those who received no income through salary of any kind were most negative. Finally, doctors in training (medical students, interns, and residents) were much more positive than physicians in practice.

In my surveys of primary-care physicians in varying types of practice (491), physicians' attitudes were found to be most unfavorable toward federal financing of health care, renumeration by salary, peer review of office-based practice, peer review by physicians from outside one's own community, and prepaid practice. They strongly support peer review in hospitals (also see 141), multiphasic health testing, and new practitioners. In each case, however, degree of support was a function of the extent to which these innovations would be under the physician's control. On most dimensions general practitioners were least favorable and pediatricians most favorable, and in each specialty area group practitioners were more favorable than nongroup practitioners. Prepaid practitioners are more favorable than nonprepaid practitioners to all of these innovations except multiphasic screening as part of the doctor's practice. In all probability this is because of the large amount of time prepaid doctors must devote to annual examinations that are part of many prepayment contracts.

The ideology of physicians depends on background characteristics, the nature of their work, and their self-interest. In general, physicians who tend to support social reform are those who appear to have the least to lose from it, although we must take into account that physicians have in part preselected themselves into different types of work and practice settings on the basis of their social orientations.

Although the data are sparse, there is some evidence that social orientations affect the types of medical task to which different physicians are drawn. In a study in New Haven, for example, Hollingshead and Redlich (330, pp. 161–65) compared the social background of psychiatrists drawn to analytic-psychological orientations (A-P) as compared with those who were more directive and organic (D-O). The A-P psychiatrists were much more likely to be first- and second-generation Americans, were more likely to come from Jewish backgrounds, tended not to identify with organized religion, were upwardly mobile, and were more likely to be intermarried. D-O psychiatrists, in contrast, had a higher representation of "old Americans," were more likely to be Protestant, were less upwardly mobile, and were more integrated in the social life of the New Haven community. Many of these observations have been supported by a study of psychoanalysts, psychiatrists, clinical psychologists, and psychiatric social workers. Psychoanalysts were found to be closer in political orientation—as well as on many other dimensions—to clinical psychologists and social workers than they were to psychiatrists (319). These data suggest that the character of the work performed is more closely related to social orientations than it is to the actual educational degree achieved (M.D., Ph.D., or M.S.W.). In all probability, this is more a result of social selection than the effect of work contexts, although both processes may contribute to similarities and differences among varying types of practitioners.

The medical practitioner, whose social origins are largely of the bourgeoisie, has a strong commitment to independence, social and economic individualism, and class status (239, pp. 172–73). A variety of studies over the years have indicated that medical students have strong economic motivations, although they also value working with people and being of service. In a 1970 survey of 21,000 college seniors, future medical students stood high relative to others on such values as "service to others," "working with people," "working independently," and "interest in work activities," but reported little interest in free time or travel. They were highest of any group on the value of security (39). Also, as Freidson has illustrated, medicine—being an applied activity involving emphasis on the individual case in contrast to more global concepts such as mankind or the social good—results in a "special frame of mind, oriented toward action for its own sake. . . . Such action relies on firsthand experience and is supported by both a will to believe in the value of one's actions and a belief in the inadequacy of general knowledge for dealing with individual cases" (239, p. 178). These values manifest themselves in what Fuchs (255) has called the "technologic imperative" and have enormous consequences for the costs of medical care as well as other matters.

The Politics of the Profession

As medical work has undergone continued stratification by specialty and types of work setting, the common interests shared by all doctors have been somewhat diluted. Physicians criticize one another in public, are more willing to testify in malpractice litigation, and show greater or less loyalty to maintaining a common front. While physicians in varying contexts have more conflicts based on their own interests, they still share in common the needs of public acceptance of their claims to special expertise and maintenance of their special privileges and monopoly as supported by licensing and state authority. In the sense that the physician's status and power are dependent on political organization, they have a strong incentive to exercise collective influence.

The American Medical Association (AMA) constitutes the single largest medical professional organization and generally has the support of the rank-and-file physician, despite the feelings of a significant minority that the AMA does not represent their views. Four-fifths of the physicians studied by Colombotos and associates (141, p. 382) felt that doctors disagreeing with the policies of the AMA should work within the organization to change it rather than organize in other ways. Relatively small groups of doctors on the extreme right and on the extreme left have organized new groups, but they are relatively unimportant compared with the AMA. Greater competing power lies with various specialty associations and the Association of American Medical Colleges (AAMC), which represents academic medicine. As physicians become more specialized, they see their welfare as being more dependent on the fate of their fellow specialists than on physicians in the aggregate. As medical policy and the economics of care have become more complicated, specialty groups and the AMA clash more frequently, or one specialty group comes into conflict with others over the definition of a common domain. Many of the specialty groups have sufficient resources to maintain good communication with their members, lobby for favorable legislation, initiate litigation, and generally support the interests of their members.

The stand of any group of doctors on a particular issue depends on a variety of factors. Most important is their stake in a particular controversy. The technical guidelines for the administration of the federal program for patients with chronic uremia may be emotional issues for transplant surgeons and nephrologists, but may be totally irrelevant for most other doctors. The method of remunerating hospital radiologists or anesthesiologists may be crucial for them but of little concern to the office-based pediatrician. Federal financing for staffing of mental-health centers may be an important economic issue for many psychiatrists but may be opposed on purely philosophical grounds by other physicians who have no stake in the matter. In general, each medical subgroup pursues the issues of greatest importance for itself with the tacit support of uninvolved doctors. Disputes become bitter when different groups of doctors have sharply conflicting interests, as occurred on such issues as the support of regional medical programs, federal subsidy for medical students, and differential fee schedules for generalists and specialists. The AMA finds it increasingly difficult to mediate among all the conflicting groups it encompasses, and in recent years the AMA itself has become less monolithic, less united, and less powerful.

The AMA is a national organization with affiliated state and county associations. Membership in the national organization is achieved only through membership at the local level, although local membership may or may not require membership in the national organization. Much of the recent attrition of AMA membership came through changes in the requirement for such membership as a condition for local society membership. Many physicians prefer local membership without national affiliation. Although local societies are highly autonomous and although election to state and AMA offices occurs through local and state election procedures, the types of physician elected to the AMA House of Delegates tend to be "medical politicians" with a long involvement in local medicopolitical affairs. They tend to be exceedingly conservative and much involved with preserving the economic and political status of the medical profession. Although physicians dislike the designation of a "trade union," the AMA has served these purposes admirably.

The AMA is also a professional organization, however, and provides an enormous range of publications dealing with general medicine, scientific matters in various specialties, and health economics, as well as a widely distributed periodical dealing with health issues for the general public. Much of the budget and efforts of both national and local organizations are devoted to matters of medical-care standards, professional education, and medical ethics. Unlike many other professional organizations, however, its unique influence comes through quasi-official functions such as approving medical schools, which it does jointly with the AAMC and which is the criterion then used by state licensing boards in granting medical licenses. Similarly, the AMA jointly with the American Hospital Association (AHA) approves hospitals for postgraduate physician education. Since federal programs frequently use as criteria for reimbursement or federal support certification or approval by such organizations as the AMA, the AAMC, and the AHA, the standards promulgated by these interest groups have effects beyond the simple functions performed.

The AMA and local medical associations used their influence and power to penalize physicians who were innovators or who held viewpoints contradictory to organizational policy (349; 530). Because membership in good standing was a prerequisite for such functions as hospital privileges, becoming eligible for specialty boards, and obtaining a medical license in a new locality, physicians had to be wary of alienating their medical society colleagues. At times the medical societies used their powers quite viciously to threaten or penalize prepaid group practice physicians. For the most part such powers have now been greatly eroded, and medical society membership is much less important for establishing a practice or being professionally successful. This erosion results from changes in attitudes, the fragmentation of the profession, and changes in the legal context of medical practice. To the extent, however, that local medical societies come to control professional standards review organizations (structures developed to review medical work in institutions receiving funds under federal programs)—and the legislation was written to give medical societies the initial opportunity—they may be able to regain some of the influence that has eroded. It would be ironic but not unusual, given past experience, if legislation opposed by much of the medical profession resulted in a consolidation of their position and influence.

The state and local medical societies are highly autonomous and pursue issues of greatest concern at the grass roots level. In addition, they often take on major responsibilities in sponsoring insurance plans and, more recently, medical-foundation plans. Local societies in some states become competitors with one another in selling insurance programs, and at times such competition has become acrimonious. Medical societies may differ a great deal in their programs, philosophy, and leadership, and it is naive to view the profession as a monolith without internal competing interests. Physician service programs are often organized jointly with Blue Cross plans, and relationships between these organizations may have great significance. There are no major sociological studies as yet of such relationships (for a definition of some of the issues see 414).

It has been argued that the center of power of the medical profession has shifted from the office-based practitioner to "professional monopolists" and "corporate rationalizers." Professional monopolists are mainly physicians in medical schools or large medical centers who "exploit organizational resources for their personal or professional interests," while corporate rationalizers are "hospital administrators, medical school directors, public health officials, directors of city health agencies, heads of quasi-public insurance (Blue Cross), state and federal health officials" who seek "to expand the powers of their home institutions" (11, pp. 141, 143). Alford has argued, with very little evidence, that problems in health care result from competition and conflict between these two groups. Each manipulates the system to serve its own purposes, resulting in failure to meet basic needs, empire building, excessive expenditures, and waste. Although there is little doubt that the influence of large medical organizations in medical affairs has grown substantially in recent decades—particularly in large urban areas with many medical centers such as New York and Boston—power in much of the country still resides with the local practitioners. Although they may have little direct influence on federal policy or the development of new programs, the care they give depends essentially on their definition of their work and on their medical and social orientations. Not all important decisions emanate from Washington, and the individual physician still has tremendous influence with the consumer.

Perhaps the single most neglected aspect of the physician's influence comes from his intimate knowledge of and relationship to patients who occupy important policy-making positions. However critical patients may be of physicians in general, most patients trust their personal doctors and respect their judgments. Legislators and government administrators, who may have no great stake in particular policy issues concerning medical care and no intimate knowledge of them, may be influenced by the viewpoints of their own physicians. During major policy confrontations, organized medicine has urged doctors to talk to their patients about the issues and to bring to their attention the physician's viewpoint.

Although it cannot be easily documented, there is considerable anecdotal indication that physicians in individual localities develop considerable political influence through their access to policy makers. All the physician need do is make himself accessible to the policy maker whenever illness develops in his family and be conscientious and dedicated. Patients who receive responsive care during times of personal crisis are highly appreciative and feel indebted to the doctor. Moreover, when they receive such responsive care they have a perception of the physician as a person of integrity and public commitment and thus put high value on the doctor's views on matters relating to medicine. It is difficult to find a person more grateful than one whose family has been guided through a critical illness by a physician who demonstrated interest, compassion, and competence. Gratitude and dependence are major sources of power.

Professional Standards

There are many studies suggesting that the quality of medical practice departs significantly from the standards taught in medical schools, and even studies of performance in teaching hospitals suggest that these efforts leave much to be desired. There is abundant evidence of excessive and inappropriate surgery, inappropriate use of antibiotics and other drugs, failure of follow-up, and lack of coordination in care with duplication of service or conflicting therapies. The most pervasive view among doctors is that the remedy to these problems is in peer review and continuing education, and the professional standards review organization legislation is an attempt to make such review a more widespread process.

More than any other sociologist, Eliot Freidson (242) has directed his attention to the processes of professional self-regulation, and although his excessive pessimism may be in part a product of his focus on ambulatory as compared with in-hospital care, he has been a keen observer of the difficulties. In essence, Freidson argues that effective peer review is extraordinarily difficult because of the acceptance among physicians of the values of autonomy and clinical judgment as a major aspect of dealing with the individual case, the limited observability of the actual performance of physicians, and the commonly shared notions that the individual physician ought to be trusted and that mistakes are an inevitable consequence deriving from medical work. Moreover, since all physicians are vulnerable to criticism, a rule of etiquette prevails that protects one's colleagues. Freidson observes that physicians distinguish between mistakes that are normalized and those that are seen as more deviant. In many situations physicians make judgments that in retrospect appear not to have been optimal; normalization is seen as justifiable in that the decision appeared to be reasonable when it was made. Freidson notes:

> The ambiguity introduced into the idea of error or mistake by the idea of judgment is such that the possibility of utilizing consistent technical rules

for evaluating and controlling mistakes seems to be very much reduced, if not precluded for all practical purposes. . . . With the rules removed, the criteria for evaluating one's own and one's colleagues' work become so permissive as to allow extremely wide variation in performance. Only gross or blatant acts of ignorance and inattention which all physicians would be united in recognizing and condemning remained securely in the category of deviant mistakes [242, pp. 136–37].

The practical task of even establishing standards for hospital care to be used as part of a peer-review process is formidable. The development of professional standards review organizations was motivated by goals that may be contradictory—improving the quality of care and reducing the costs of care. Standards have the effect of reducing variance in behavior; if the standard is higher than the statistical norm, it results in increased procedures and more care, which may frustrate the goal of controlling costs. Medical care is largely a matter of judgment, and most of the standards that presently exist are rules of process (rules about the way the doctor should proceed, what tests he should order, and so on) and not decisions based on outcome experience. It is conceivable that standards established on the basis of medical judgments of reasonable process may increase costs substantially without materially affecting the welfare of patients.

The idea of peer review of hospital and medical work through agreed-upon process standards is also likely to reinforce a mode of decision making based on individual patients rather than on the needs of populations. In deciding on the allocation of limited resources—and medical resources, despite their abundance, are limited—it is necessary to consider not only the care received by those who find their way into treatment but also those not in treatment who should be. The focus of peer review is on the hospitalized patients and not on others who may need such care but were not hospitalized. Only a monitoring approach based on the study of populations can rectify such errors of omission.

The potentialities and possible dangers of mandated peer review through professional standards review organizations depend on a variety of issues: the way norms are formulated and the amount of local discretion allowed; who controls the review organizations and the way they use their influence; the ability to depersonalize the process of evaluation so that strong rules of etiquette that protect colleagues (on the principle that "there but for the grace of God go I") are substantially weakened; and the development of graded sanctions so that the peer group is not faced with imposing such large sanctions on an offending physician that the magnitude of the penalty is a disincentive to taking action. The politics surrounding the development and control of professional standards review organizations and the procedures to be followed are fierce, and it is too early to evaluate the effort. The review organizations are not without potentialities, but there are great dangers of cooptation and subversion.

The Future

The profession of medicine is in a state of active transition stimulated by the growth of science and technology, changing public expectations, increased government financing and regulation, and the dilemmas inherent in its existing forms of organization. Each year it becomes more difficult for the profession to maintain traditional organizational forms in face of the onslaught of new developments, new regulations, and changing public demands. As patients become more sophisticated and as the consumer self-help movement develops, patients will demand greater equality and sharing of information in their relationships with physicians. Moreover, physicians are confronted with increasingly difficult social and ethical choices involving great uncertainty and requiring some effort on their part to balance competing medical, economic, and social interests. The profession has shown extraordinary adaptive capacities to organizational change, as in the development of shared arrangements among independent practitioners, the growth of physician-run insurance plans, and, more recently, the organization of medical foundations. Physicians now must demonstrate adaptability to a new type of relationship with patients. These accommodations will slowly change the basic character of medical organization and transfer the locus of control from the individual physician to physician administrators, medical-society committees, planning groups, and consumer boards.

With social change, organized practice will look more appealing to many medical graduates. Such practice will relieve their continuing responsibilities, provide time for leisure and continuing education, support their practice efforts with more sophisticated facilities, nurse-practitioners, and other health workers, and minimize the growing sense of threat from malpractice litigation. As the images of medicine change, younger physicians may see organized practice as more rewarding and less frustrating. In addition, medical organizations will develop new ways of coping with the frustrations of bureaucracy and new types of patient relationships. Transitions are usually slow and difficult and leave many who are committed to older ways frustrated and angry. The fact is, however, that medical science and technology have gone too far to accommodate the physician as an individual entrepreneur. Like an old soldier, he is unlikely to die, but he will slowly fade away.

Chapter 15

PRACTITIONER AND PATIENT

When patients come to a professional helper, the structure of the helping situation is more limited than it is in informal contacts in which help may be provided by friends, neighbors, and relatives. The helper, being a member of a particular professional group and practicing within the context of a particular organizational form, will have an organized and formalized perspective and limited options. What can and cannot be done may be limited not only by law but also by professional ethics, interprofessional politics, time, and the organization of practice.

When the patient visits a physician he comes with an image of the physician's role and the way it should be performed. This image reflects the societal definition of the physician's role and subcultural expectations as well as the conceptions formed by the patient from prior experience or from hearing about experiences of other people. It is within this frame of reference that the patient attempts to evaluate the professional qualifications and capabilities of the doctor. The extent to which the doctor can meet these expectations may play an important part in the patient's conformity to his prescribed treatment (163), the likelihood of return visits, and even the therapeutic effect gained through the influence of the physician's authority (72). The cues patients use to estimate the doctor's competence, however, may not reflect his technical abilities and knowledge, as most patients cannot assess these qualities. Instead, the cues usually reflect the doctor's apparent interest in the patient, willingness to give time to hear the patient's complaint, and similar indications of concern that are important to the patient. The doctor's willingness to socialize with the patient may be seen as an index of his interest; his confidence and authority may be perceived as indications of his expertise; and a rapid diagnosis and treatment plan may be viewed as evidence of his competence. One cannot simply summarize the kinds of trait that make patients feel confident; patients vary widely in their sophistication, their medical knowledge, and the traits they find pleasing in a doctor. The compatibility of patient expectations and physician's performance, however, has important implications for the success of the relationship.

It is often illuminating to seek out disruptions in patient-practitioner relationships because they may tell us something about the frames of reference of the participants and where they may or may not be consistent. Patients' complaints about a physician may or may not reflect on his competence, but they usually indicate a failure to fulfill expectations in some important way. Whether the patient expects the physician to take a hand in his problem and tell him how to live or insists that the doctor give him a prescription, failure to conform to expectations is likely to raise doubts as to the doctor's adequacy and helpfulness. Goffman (268), in his discussion of the presentation of self, emphasizes contradictions between what an actor does and the impression the audience may obtain from his performance. He points out that for all performers certain aspects of the performance must be planned so that the actor can control the definition of the situation. Unless the doctor plans his behavior in light of the patient's orientations and perspectives, the full therapeutic possibilities may not be exploited.

Physicians and patients often operate within different assumptive worlds and frequently lack awareness of the extent to which their assumptions are different. Various studies show that the amount of medical information patients have is different from what most physicians believe it to be (568; 607), and that physicians often fail to appreciate the real reasons patients are seeking their help. Medical practice inevitably requires changing patients' stereotypes and expectations as well as treating their symptoms. The success of the doctor-patient relationship is in large part based on the extent to which doctor and patient share common frames of reference.

One of the most frequently studied aspects of practitioner-patient communication involves the factors affecting conformity with medical advice. Research indicates that even in the case of relatively simple therapies, such as the prescription of a course of antibiotics, high levels of nonadherence occur (66). When patients are taking several drugs simultaneously—each with different instructions concerning amount, frequency, and persistence, and each with the possibility of a variety of unpleasant side effects—failures of treatment are to be anticipated unless there is great trust in the relationship and unless physicians communicate the need and the procedures to be followed. Many patients adhere to those aspects of medical advice that are least difficult and least disruptive of personal habits. Regimens that require greater patient judgment and are more complex often result in nonadherence. Compliance can be facilitated by encouragement and support, by effective instruction, and by fitting the regimen into ordinary life routines (346; 397).

Milton Davis (163), in an intensive study of continuing doctor-patient interactions in a general medical clinic of a large teaching hospital, attempted to isolate factors intrinsic to the interaction that would explain compliance with medical regimens. Although Davis notes that the literature shows the proportion of noncompliant patients to vary from 15 to 93 percent of all patients, he feels his finding that approximately one-third of the total group of patients disregards the doctor's advice is a reasonable minimal estimate. Davis found that failure to adhere to medical regimens was related to deviant communication between doctor and patient, difficulties in communication, and attempts by doctors and patients to control each other. Revisits between an authoritative patient and a doctor who accepted such participation passively helped promote patient noncompliance. When tension occurred and did not find release within the relationship, noncompliance was also more likely. Finally, when doctors sought information without giving patients feedback, the patients were unlikely to respond to the doctors' advice.

Although a large number of studies have sought to identify the individual characteristics of cooperative and uncooperative patients, the findings tend to be unimpressive and inconsistent; moreover, the indications are that patients do not behave consistently across varying situations (691). Although research carried out on the basis of the health-belief model (54) and on modes of interaction between patient and practitioner is more promising, this work is also plagued by inconsistencies in findings among studies. A major problem with these approaches, as has already been suggested in my discussion of expectations, is that patients and practitioners enter such relationships with varying perspectives, expectations, and information; the interaction that follows is not static but rather is a result of the particular fit that evolves between patient and therapist.

Svarstad (691) has made an important contribution to this literature by focusing on the instruction process itself. She directs her attention to the way the physician transmits his expectations and his modes of motivating the patient. In developing her conceptions she observed eight physicians in their relationships with 153 adult patients, and subsequently interviewed the patients concerning their understanding of the instructional process. In her conceptualization the instructional process affects the patient's perception of the expectations of the physician, the patient's evaluation of the treatment plan, and the degree of adherence with advice. She provides impressive evidence that physicians must recognize and respond to patient feedback, which serves to clarify misunderstanding or ambiguities, and that they must take account of patient complaints about the treatment plan, adverse side effects, and past behavior in response to previous advice given by the physician. Svarstad's approach is particularly valuable, relative to more traditional studies, because it identifies trouble spots in the communication process that are correctable with improved training or feedback to physicians on their own behavior. Although it is impossible to change the social characteristics of "uncooperative patients," assuming that such exist, it is possible to improve the techniques for communication and feedback in practitioner-patient relationships (see 690).

The Community Context of Medical Practice

The medical contract—and medical practice in general—can be defined within a narrow technical-scientific frame of reference, and many physicians trained in traditional medical schools would prefer to define their work in this limited way. Yet the practice of medicine is as much a social activity as a medical one, and disease concepts are frequently used as social as well as medical designations. The social importance of medical practice is attested to by the many studies of the utilization of medical services that illustrate the wide variety of problems presented to doctors. It seems apparent that the physician occupies a sustaining role within Western society in that the problems and difficulties presented by patients go well beyond what the doctor himself may regard as within his limited technical-scientific expertise. Why patients insist on bringing nonmedical problems to physicians is an issue that has received a variety of interpretations.

In recent years Western countries have experienced a tremendous increase in the utilization of medical resources and a substantial growth of the health industries (428). This development is in part a consequence of general affluence, increased consumer purchasing power, and the growing provision of medical resources with new medical and governmental developments. There are many analysts, however, who believe that the utilization pressures placed on medical resources are also in part a consequence of the bureaucratization of societal institutions and associated changes in ways of living. It is contended that as opportunities for close personal contacts diminish and as populations become increasingly geographically mobile, problems that have been previously handled in familial, social, and religious contexts are transferred to formal sustaining professionals (doctors, lawyers, social workers). Although a wide variety of professionals deal with problems that in previous decades were dealt with by informal sources of help, it is generally believed that physicians have experienced the most substantial part of this additional consumer demand. Because the formal structure of the doctor-patient relationship provides a legitimate way for expressing intimacy and requesting help, it is only natural that various psychosocial problems and other problems in living be brought to the physician. The more general and central sociological problem—which has been of vital concern to social theorists for generations—involves the whole range of consequences of change from social relationships based on primary contacts to ones more dependent on secondary (or bureaucratic) organization.

Even in societies that place a high value on bureaucratic forms of organization, it is generally recognized that personal growth requires a certain degree of intimacy, and that various social roles—if they are to be fully effective—must be organized to insure the opportunity for the expression of intimate feelings and attitudes and for the provision of close personal supports. Yet at the same time that societies become more bureaucratic, so do the sustaining professions, and there are many pressures toward formalization of socializing and sustaining professional relationships. These pressures are the consequence of the need for more efficient and economical organization and distribution of services to meet growing demands for such services and of the need for insuring minimum standards of care as such programs are extended to new groups in the population through insurance and government programs. It is not clear, however, to what extent such relationships can be bureaucratized without seriously damaging the emotional sustenance functions of the helping professions. Because there is a limited pool of professional persons, some degree of efficient organization is essential. However, there may be a point at which the degree of achieved organization begins to subvert some of the basic functions and values of professional service.

When we think of providing bureaucratic controls in medical practice, we usually conceive of medicine in its narrow perspective—that is, as an applied science rather than as a sustaining profession. As more clear-cut technical skills have become available to doctors, they have become more inclined to see medicine in its restricted medical aspects, and doctors who have been trained in modern hospital-based medical schools and in the various specialties and subspecialties resent providing some of the services that were seen as part of the role of the traditional general practitioner. In addition, the technical-scientific orientation of the physician is more easily organized within a bureaucratic format than are many of the caring functions that are more difficult to program and that require a great deal of attention to the unique characteristics of the patient. Good bureaucratic organization of the technical aspects of medicine allows medical services to reach more people and thus may facilitate a more economical and equal distribution of care. It may also, however, encourage impersonality, disinterest, and lack of humane care on the part of both medical and nonmedical personnel. As the efficiency and rationality of medical care increase in an organizational and scientific sense, the structures developed may limit the possibilities for responding sensitively to the more subtle personal problems of patients.

The social process I have been describing is not unique to medical practice. We know, for example, that large schools and universities with increasing bureaucratization often have better facilities and higher-level staff, and they accommodate larger numbers of students. Such general institutions of learning can offer excellent technological and vocational training as well as good training in languages and other well-defined subject areas. These educational institutions seem to suffer, however, in the communication of more intimate, personal, and professional values and viewpoints, which usually cannot be dispensed in an impersonal fashion but must be learned in the process of informal association with scholars and scientists (115). In short, such structured institutions may be better in communicating the content of knowledge than in influencing attitudes and orientations toward inquiry.

Many forces within medicine encourage the increased bureaucratization and rationalization of the technical components of medical care, but some countervailing efforts are being made. As costs have increased with the development of technology and the growth of social insurance providing greater access to care, the most frequent demands call for efficiency and improved management. While one cannot quarrel with these concepts, those advocating them too frequently show a noticeable lack of concern with the humane aspects of medical care and its ethical underpinnings. We must remain attuned to the fact that, as we strive to bring medical care to more people at some fixed cost, inevitably we increase the workload of health personnel and develop organizational forms to expedite their tasks. The difficulty of meeting some problems, however, brings on others, because it is the harassed and busy health worker who is most likely to pay attention to the specific technical task and not to the person. Also, as we seek to reap the benefits of increased knowledge we create a highly elaborate and specialized division of labor in which specialists attend to their particular roles while continuity of care and coordination frequently suffer.

The issue is not simply a matter of not caring to do better. The problem is that, as we choose to emphasize certain priorities, difficulties develop in other areas. Certainly medicine is more humane when physicians and other health professionals take more time with the patient, but in doing so they may exclude others from the opportunity to be cared for at all. Under conditions of work pressure, physicians and nurses give more attention to the technical and measurable aspects of their defined role and less to the intangibles that may have great meaning for patients. As one eminent physician, quoting Willie Sutton, put it in addressing this issue: "I rob banks because that's where the money is" (353). But as I have attempted to demonstrate throughout, physicians are inclined to overestimate the relative importance of the technical procedures they perform in contrast to the caring services such as social support, reassurance, and reeducation. The fact is that medicine has been deficient in dealing adequately with many patients who require these types of care.

Given the dimensions of medical demand, the availability of medical resources, and the growing bureaucratization of medical organization, it is likely that these problems of impersonal care will become even more pronounced, although there are new attempts to develop medical and nursing personnel who are more responsive to the broader conceptions of these helping roles. We have already noted the growth of residency training in family practice and primary care, areas in which greater emphasis is being given to new roles and responsibilities of physicians in ambulatory care. Recent years have also seen considerable development of nurse-practitioners, and there is evidence that such practitioners can provide many basic primary-care functions as well as physicians and often are more successful in providing caring services to the patients for whom they are responsible. In hospital care there is more emphasis than has been traditional on team efforts that give more responsibility to nurses, social workers, and pharmacists. Teamwork involves a variety of problems, and frequently the costs of maintaining effective care teams make it difficult to sustain these efforts at a level of excellence, to say nothing about the kinds of problem that arise in teams made up of varying professionals who are competitive and may develop resentments, hostilities, and impedances to communication.

Because physicians are trained to deal primarily with the diagnosis and treatment of disease and not with many subtle interpersonal and reeducation strategies, and given the fantastic complexity of even the more narrow medical functions, one might reasonably argue that the technical-scientific aspects of medicine ought to be separated from sustaining and caring aspects of patient care. At least in theory, these functions can be assigned to varying types of personnel who are differently trained and who perform varying facets of the patient-care role. Such notions, while they can be implemented to some extent in well-organized clinics and medical services, break down if the physician does not also remain attentive to the broader aspects of patient care and the personal needs of the patient. Theory must confront certain realities:

1. Patients often expect physicians to perform specific functions; if they do not, communication and cooperation break down.
2. Many patients, because of their particular patterns of illness response and behavior, present emotional and psychosocial problems in the context of physical complaints, and adequate assessment and treatment require a sensitivity to this fact.
3. The course of the patient's condition, his attitude, and his cooperation are all likely to depend on the extent to which the physician, as well as other personnel, communicates an interest in and understanding of him as a person as well as someone suffering from a particular disease.
4. Behavioral and interpersonal factors are implicated in the cause and course of disease, and physicians cannot responsibly ignore these.
5. Physicians require patient rapport and receptiveness to providing information to perform adequately even their more narrow technical functions. Neglecting the interpersonal aspects of care leads to barriers to communication and information acquisition and frequently results in poor management of the patient and poor patient outcomes (189).

In short, from the patient's perspective disease is seen in terms of functioning as a whole, and a physician can neglect the broader aspects of his role only at great risk to the quality of care.

Medicine represents a classic example of the traditional sociological observation concerning the advantages and costs of bureaucracy (509; 510). Bureaucracy allows a more efficient and effective standard of medical practice and facilitates the distribution of medical services to more people. However, bureaucracies also develop certain rigidities and inflexibilities in dealing with specific unique problems in that there is a tendency toward standardization of modes of professional practice. The dilemma we face is that the bureaucratic form most appropriate for the efficient organization of scientific medical work is not the best form to deal with the emotional sustenance aspects of medicine, nor does it encourage the flexibility and variation that are so useful in dealing with social and emotional problems. We should be careful in defining and viewing bureaucracy as the villain. Although bureaucracy involves costs, its advantages often heavily outweigh the disadvantages. There are obviously varying bureaucratic forms, and it is likely that different functions in medical practice require different kinds of bureaucratic organization. It is not difficult, for example, to conceive of a bureaucracy that defines its main goal as the social and emotional sustenance of patients and that gears its activities and rules so that this goal is given the highest priority. The difficulty in modern medicine is that although medical bureaucracies often give lip service to the social and emotional needs of patients, the bureaucratic organization continues to reflect the priority given to technical-scientific aspects of the medical role.

Let us consider briefly the kinds of bureaucratic organization that best promote technical-scientific goals and those that are most consistent with social-emotional goals. Within the technical-scientific organization chief consideration is given to the means to achieve most efficiently a high level of diagnostic work. In this setting medical assessment is highly specialized, on the assumption that experts in particular fields are more knowledgeable than a general doctor. Moreover, time units are developed that allow adequate evaluation to take place without sacrificing the efficiency of the doctor's output. Although a high level of diagnostic work may be maintained, much work is carried out by different departments located in different places in the medical context. The patient thus becomes a unit that is moved from department to department, each department viewing the patient in terms of its specialized function and giving highest priority to its particular task. It should be clear that such forms of organization provide many examples of failure to meet patient needs in a wider sense.

One can conceive of a bureaucratic organization that prescribes that high priority be given to the patient's education and to his social and emotional needs. Thus the organization may assign the patient to a general doctor. This doctor is expected to evaluate the patient and assess his diagnostic needs and to accompany the patient to the various specialized departments while explaining the procedures and offering sustenance. All specialized evaluation and care are given in the presence of the patient's general doctor, and he is expected to provide continuity in medical care, visit the home when the patient requests it, and serve as a medical advisor and teacher. Obviously such a system of medical bureaucracy would be inefficient and costly, and it probably would be difficult to recruit doctors to work within such a bureaucratic setup, given present professional values. I am not arguing that this would be the most desirable mode of structuring medical care; I am suggesting, however, that it is hypothetically possible to structure bureaucracies (leaving out economic considerations) that provide every citizen with care and attention similar to that received by the president of the United States from the White House physician.

In stating extreme possibilities, we should note that there have been frequent attempts to provide medical care in a fashion that offers some compromise between the two forms of bureaucratic organization described. In general, however, given the technical complexity of medical care and the associated costs, most medical bureaucracies place the greatest emphasis on the scientific-technical components of medicine. If present trends in medical care continue, it is unlikely that the situation will improve substantially in coming years; indeed, it may get a great deal worse.

Although bureaucratic forms vary for different purposes, thus fulfilling needs differently, bureaucracy itself, regardless of the form it takes, poses problems in dealing with emotional and social difficulties. It encourages specialized activity, routinized procedures and modes of operation, and standardized modes of training and evaluating personnel, and there is a strong tendency for bureaucracies to try to limit client control. Professionals in this context are more likely to orient themselves to organizational rewards and the opinions of their colleagues than they are to the special needs and demands of their patients. Thus there is a tendency for barriers to develop between doctor and patient, as relationships tend to become stereotyped and flexibility is limited by organizational needs and values. This is not to imply that more desirable relationships have existed outside of bureaucratic forms, because we know that private solo medical practice has often been equally impersonal. It does appear, however, that bureaucracy presents additional barriers to improvisation and the development of unique solutions.

Bureaucratic organization of medical practice may provide further barriers to the development of a close relationship between doctor and patient. As clinics become larger and more impersonal, patients find it more difficult to contact their doctor without first dealing with a variety of intermediaries. They may find that doctors are rotated in such a fashion that they do not see the doctor they wished to see and, moreover, they may have difficulty in ascertaining who is responsible for dealing with their cases. Of course these problems can be avoided, but they are much more likely to exist and persist within bureaucracies than in traditional forms of medical practice.

In noting some of the difficulties that develop in the bureaucratization of medical services, we must not fail to appreciate the tremendous advantages gained from such forms of organization, both for the doctor and for the general population. Thus the alternative to bureaucratic organization is not a return to traditional forms of practice. What is necessary is a greater degree of flexibility and choice within medical bureaucracies; with a greater consciousness of the problems bureaucracy brings, it is possible to devise organizational procedures that guarantee special attention in overcoming these deficiencies.

The Sick Role Revisited

When the patient's definition of his illness becomes crystallized and he seeks professional help for his problem, it can be said that he is entering the "sick role." The concept of the sick role is an ideal type in the sense that it is a theoretical model that attempts to depict the patient's behavioral orientations when he seeks medical care, but is not itself a description of empirical reality. It thus constitutes a perspective for viewing patient behavior, although it does not necessarily describe accurately what the patient's behavior will be. There is a great tradition in sociology for the use of such ideal types, although sociologists disagree about the value of such concepts. Note the following criticism by Blau and Scott:

> To exploit Weber's insightful theoretical analysis, it is necessary, in our opinion, to discard his misleading concepts of the ideal type and to distinguish explicitly between the conceptual scheme and the hypotheses. The latter can then be tested and refined rather than left as mere impressionistic assertions [71, p. 34].

Although I tend to agree with Blau and Scott and feel that the concept of the sick role has frequently been carried to absurd extremes, it is important to recognize the value of some of Parsons's insights concerning the position of the sick.

Parsons (549) argues that being sick is a role as well as a condition in that there are institutionalized expectations of the sick, and associated with them are particular sentiments and sanctions. He believes that there are four aspects to these institutionalized expectations as they affect the sick:

1. The sick are allowed *exemption from social-role responsibilities,* and this requires that others accept the idea that they are suffering from an illness condition. Parsons notes that the physician serves as a "court of appeal" in legitimizing sickness. He further suggests that exemption from normal responsibilities is not only a right but also an obligation in that others may insist that a person withdraw from his usual social roles because of sickness.
2. The sick person is also exempted from *responsibility* for his condition in that he is not usually expected to be able to get well by his own decision or will. Thus it is assumed that he needs help, and this assumption serves, in Parsons's words, "as a bridge to the acceptance of 'help.' "
3. The patient is *expected to want to get well.*
4. He is expected to *seek technically competent help,* and to *cooperate* with the helper in trying to get well. Parsons suggests that

once a patient has called in a physician, he assumes the obligation to cooperate with him in getting well.

Parsons does not imply that these steps always go together or that
they do not vary. Indeed, he is alert to various contingencies that may
affect conformity to institutionalized expectations, such as the severity
of the patient's condition. Some of the popularizers of the sick role
have applied the concept too glibly without an awareness of the many
nuances that affect the behavior of the patient. There is good reason to
believe that patients recognize to some extent these expectations that
Parsons posits. For example, in one study we asked mothers of young
children to describe a good patient. Seventy-nine percent of the
mothers said that good patients are those who do what the doctor tells
them. Other items they mentioned included not bothering the doctor
with minor symptoms, describing fully and accurately, being considerate of the doctor's time and schedule, and having confidence in his
judgment. It is clear that mothers accept the idea that the patient should
be *dependent* on the doctor's authority. Similarly, Suchman (683) in
his medical-care study in New York City found that 90 percent of his
respondents agreed that they were willing to do absolutely everything
the doctor advises, although they also expressed a strong desire to be
informed by the doctor as to what was going to happen. Consistent with
these observations, we might note that patients who tell the doctor
what they expect him to do, such as insisting that he order a particular
test or prescribe a particular medication, tend to make the physician
angry because he feels the patient is not accepting his authority.

Motivations for Seeking Medical Care

People visit the physician because they have a problem; most frequently they come because they believe they are ill. In one sense, at
least, all persons seeking advice from a physician and presenting a
symptom are "diseased." There is something in their life condition that
impels them to seek help. Aside from clear emergencies and acute
stages of serious illness that scarcely permit alternatives, any visit to a
physician represents a conscious choice on the part of the patient. It
signifies a preference for this course of action as compared with other
possible alternatives such as prayer or self-treatment, and in this sense
it is a clear-cut decision. Although physicians are usually visited for
the benefit of their technical skills and knowledge, at times other considerations prevail. Various observations suggest that patients seek
from the physician not only adequate medical care but sympathetic
emotional support as well (127). A medical consultation thus may rep-

resent more than a desire for "scientific medicine" and its emphasis on physical diagnosis and medication (126).

Such patient visits are not purely individual and idiosyncratic. To be sure, the individual patient may have an exaggerated pattern of illness behavior or particular eccentricities. Yet the fact that the patient seeks out the physician more frequently than other professionals suggests that the role of the physician, as opposed to other roles, has achieved a certain stereotyped significance in our society. Not only is the physician widely regarded as a man of knowledge and science, capable of ferreting out the meaning of puzzling symptoms, but he is also frequently pictured as a kindly, thoughtful, warm person, deeply interested in and committed to the welfare of the individual patient. Certain stereotyped and structural features of the physician's role in contemporary Western society make him an attractive ally in times of difficulty or stress (344).

Despite the trust placed in the doctor as a general advisor and helper, the patient may find himself greatly disappointed with the service he receives. Many doctors resist the patient who does not present a clear physical difficulty. As medicine has become more scientific, the physician, better trained than ever before and surer in his skills for treating various physical disorders, hesitates in the face of demands of patients who seek skills and services he feels uncertain of and often unqualified to provide. Moreover, heavy patient loads and limited time encourage the physician to emphasize clear physical symptomatology and the acute conditions for which he feels he can apply his knowledge and skills and in which he visualizes himself as performing a tangible service. The patient who presents physical complaints without clear evidence of organic problems is someone with whom the physician has difficulty in coping, and such conditions frequently cannot be dealt with effectively within the context of the physician's organized routines.

The failure of the doctor to deal successfully with the variety of problems brought to him is attested to by the persistence of competing systems of healing with little scientific basis. Despite the attacks of the American Medical Association designed to eliminate and regulate such competitors, nonscientific systems of healing have persisted and continue to be recognized and used, in part because the physician has frequently failed to use effectively his role in treating the whole man. The chiropractor, the spiritual healer, the Christian Science practitioner, and many other nonscientific helpers are frequently more attuned than physicians to the psychological needs of their clients, and often the theories of disease they advocate are culturally and psychologically consonant with the views and hopes of their clients (127). In contrast, scientific medicine frequently clashes with patients' cultural beliefs and viewpoints and with their psychological needs, and thus scientific medicine does not always take full advantage of the treatment context for bringing about patient improvement through encouragement, support, and suggestion.

Let us consider this point in more detail. Data about illness that the physician uses in assessing the patient contain two kinds of information: one on the state of the patient (for example, a description of symptoms or dysfunctions), and the other on the patient's reactions to his condition, i.e., his complaints. The physician's diagnosis is influenced by each of these kinds of information. Within the traditional medical model, the patient lodges a complaint and the physician attempts to account for, explain, or find justification for it through his investigation. Logically, if not empirically, the diagnostic situation involves two sets of facts: historical data and symptoms reported by the patient or other informants about his condition, and data obtained by the physician through a systematic examination for abnormal signs and through laboratory investigation. Thus it is logically possible for physicians to hypothesize that some patients are not medically ill if they note substantial discrepancies between the patient's complaints and other findings elicited through an independent investigation of the complaints.

Although this logical mode of procedure may be useful from a limited perspective based on a disease model, it may be highly inappropriate to the fulfillment of the doctor's social role. Consider, for example, the case of an anxious woman with many social difficulties who suffers from frequent feelings of unhappiness and a variety of diffuse aches and pains. She may go to a doctor and outline her physical maladies, but on examination he finds no physical illnesses of significance. Being busy and not oriented to providing support or encouraging the patient to talk about her problems in any detail, he informs the patient that there is nothing medically wrong with her and that there is no further need for medical evaluation or treatment. He may further inform the patient that her complaints are a manifestation of her unhappiness and not a result of any disease. Although the patient continues to suffer from her complaints and may feel dissatisfied with the attention she received, it would be incorrect to say that the doctor did not fulfill his *scientific-medical* role, assuming that his assessment of the situation is correct.

A friend then advises the patient to visit a local chiropractor. Although our patient is relatively well educated and sophisticated and has a suspicion that chiropractors are quacks, she may, like many other patients, visit one feeling that she has nothing to lose because she has received no real help from the physicians she has consulted. The chiropractor responds to the patient in a welcoming fashion; he explains to her, perhaps, that her aches and pains result from a subluxation of her spinal column, or he may provide some other explanation and suggest a course of treatment. Although the patient may be skeptical about the doctor's explanation, she may still consent to try the treatment suggested. During the treatment the chiropractor manipulates her body physically so that she feels that something is being done to her. At the same time he talks with her, allowing her to ventilate her problems and dissatisfactions. Our hypothetical patient may soon find that she feels better, and she may attribute this to the treatment she has received. In this example it is clear that the limited scientific-medical approach to the patient is not consistent with her emotional needs and desires. Although she may regard some of the interpretations offered by the chiropractor as unlikely, the healer is responding to the patient in a manner that meets her needs.

Patients visit nonmedical healers for many reasons. It is significant, however, that many of these people have visited physicians prior to using quasi-medical healers (127; 756) and have found this relationship unfulfilling. Often these are patients to whom physicians offer no hope or relief. Although physicians may be correct in their information that there are no effective remedies or palliatives for a particular condition, such scientifically correct information may be inconsistent with the needs of the patient, who may then seek to fulfill his hopes elsewhere. Incompatibilities between the doctor's scientific perspective and patient needs may exist on a cultural as well as on a psychological level. Patients tend to hold views concerning their illnesses, and they have expectations about the way the doctor should deal with them. These expectations may come from family and friends or they may be a consequence of particular subcultural learning. If the doctor fails to understand these expectations and cultural stereotypes, much of his ability to affect the patient's behavior may be undermined. In short, the fact that an approach to the patient's condition is scientifically correct does not necessarily mean that it is effective or consistent with lay expectations.

The fact that the patient presents physical symptoms to the physician may or may not be significant. There are few "well" people who could not find physical symptoms to present to a physician to justify a medical visit. Indeed, the physician's expectation is that the patient will describe some physical complaints, and the typical patient will cope with the situation by presenting some symptoms to the doctor, even if these are not the complaints motivating the visit. We all have aches and pains—a variety of symptoms occur very commonly. Thus, Balint argues, the patient presents symptoms to the physician during unorganized phases of "illness"; then, through a negotiation of doctor and patient, the patient settles down to a more organized illness phase (42).

Some patient visits represent attempts to reverse adaptive failures that the patient experiences. In the course of routine living many persons experience interpersonal difficulties in the form of shattered or unrequited love or friendship, or fail in being "accepted." Seeking support and assurance, but often reluctant to admit the source of his concern, the patient may *recognize* new organic symptoms or *redefine old ones* as worthy of medical care and thus seek the gains of the doctor-patient relationship. As Balint has observed:

> One of the commonest conflicts of man is caused by the discrepancy between his need of affection and the amount and quality of affection that his environment is able and willing to grant him. Some people fall ill to secure the attention and concern they need, and the illness is a claim to, a justification of, and simultaneously the expiation for, the extra amount of affection demanded [42, p. 276].

Strategies in Medical Decision Making

We have noted earlier that the doctor's approach to the patient is one that has developed through medical training and experience. The application of disease models is one useful routine through which the doctor attempts to assess the patient's problem. Most doctors, however, do not practice in the fashion in which they have been trained. The pressures of time, patients, and competition lead the doctor to adopt a variety of shortcuts and other useful strategies that may detract from the quality of the care he renders but allow him to function more effectively within the contexts and settings within which he works. These adaptations are at times so discrepant from the standards taught in medical school that medical educators ask themselves why they have failed so badly in teaching their students to practice a high standard of medical care.

The development of adaptive strategies for evaluating and caring for the patient is important in all medical contexts; in general community practice, however, it is even more essential because assessment and decision making are usually arrived at on the basis of limited evaluation and exploration of the patient's difficulty. The problem of uncertainty is a basic component of many medical decisions, and every physician must learn to live with this. Scheff (614) has noted that medical decision making in circumstances of uncertainty is not vastly different in its basic logic from legal or statistical decision making tasks. When the physician searches for illness to justify a complaint but has no positive findings, he must choose between further assessment and evaluation or no further exploration. The choice of sustained exploration involves a variety of risks and costs: (1) it takes time and costs money; (2) the diagnostic procedures themselves involve risks to the patient's health; and (3) the continued search may be upsetting to the patient and under some circumstances may induce the patient to see himself as more ill than his condition warrants. On the other hand, if the physician stops his search too soon he may fail to detect a serious condition that requires early evaluation and treatment. Thus the doctor must balance the costs of making each of these types of error. He can, of course, decide that it is more desirable to make one kind of error than another, and most clinicians believe that it is safer to explore too much than too little. Medical training emphasizes the importance of investigating the rare but dangerous possibilities so that such conditions can be reversed before it is too late (see 58). Because many mild and self-limited conditions present themselves in a fashion similar to some serious ones, the doctor must develop a strategy for dealing with such uncertain situations.

Not all doctors develop the same strategies, nor do they opt to take the same kinds of risk. Some physicians attempt to reduce uncertainty by developing habits of thorough examination, sustained exploration, and a tendency to check out as many possibilities as feasible. If the process is carried too far the doctor may depend too much on extensive tests, even when the diagnostic techniques may entail greater risks than the diagnosis the physician is attempting to confirm. In contrast are doctors who develop a probability strategy; they assume that most common symptoms will turn out to be clinically trivial and are willing to risk a serious error on the assumption that too thorough investigation does most people more harm than good, and that those who are really sick will eventually be "picked up" anyway. Such physicians use "psychosomatic" labels too readily and frequently do not give sufficient attention to excluding other possibilities that may have contributed to the patient's symptoms.

Perhaps the most useful strategy in such situations of common symptomatology is one that attempts to minimize the risks of both types of error in conformity with the maxim, "above all else, do no harm." Doctors employing such a strategy will undertake investigatory work to a moderate degree in an attempt to make a limited but thorough evaluation of the patient's complaint. In each case the doctor weighs the relative value of undertaking further work against the costs of further work. Once he feels reasonably confident that he has not missed something obvious he assumes a "wait and see" attitude. Such a strategy involves following the patient and observing the course his symptoms take. In most cases the symptoms will be self-limited, but if they are not the doctor has not lost contact with the patient and can follow up on necessary diagnostic work. This discussion is based on impressionistic observations. There is no study of risk-taking calculations and strategies of doctors, making this an area ripe for an ardent investigator.

Although the above description depicts extreme types (and doctors may not be as far apart as the description suggests), there is considerable disagreement among doctors as to the best diagnostic strategies. Hospitals, for example, vary enormously in the percentage of normal appendixes that are removed. Some surgeons cut too readily, as reflected by the fact that more than half of the appendixes removed are normal; in other hospitals the number of normal appendixes removed is so low as to suggest that decisions concerning surgical intervention may be too conservative and that willingness to assume the risk of ruptured appendixes is perhaps too high. To take another example, doctors frequently prescribe antibacterials for prophylactic use, that is, as a protective measure in anticipation of a possible infection that would pose a serious threat to the patient's condition. On the other hand, antibacterial drugs can be dangerous, and they involve a certain element of risk for the patient. Thus good medical strategy is to use antibacterials for prophylactic purposes only when the risk of infection is high. Myers (532), in a study of 24 community hospitals, found that the use of antibacterials in hernia surgery varied from 9.2 percent to 100 percent of all cases. Whether the use of antibacterials is indicated should depend on the nature of the patient's condition. Myers argues that it is well known that uncomplicated inguinal hernias should not be complicated by infection after surgery if high standards of selection and preparation of patients and surgical asepsis are maintained. Use of dangerous drugs for prophylactic reasons in such surgery, he argues, is an indication of poor-quality care. In contrast, complicated herniorrhaphy involves higher risks of infection and therefore use of antibacterials is more justified. The findings in this investigation, however, are troubling. Antibacterials were used in 38.2 percent of all simple cases, but not used in 47.8 percent of all complicated cases. Myers further reports that 84 percent of the patients with simple hernias who received antibacterials received them specifically for prophylactic use; particularly surprising is that the percentage receiving antibacterials for prophylactic use in complicated hernia ("in which the possibility of infection is greater") was almost identical to the percentage receiving such drugs in simple hernia situations.

In part the situation described above illustrates the variable quality of medical care, but it also probably reflects the vast differences in the strategies of doctors in different hospitals. Some doctors take the position that the gains from prophylactic antibacterials justify their use even when the risks of infection are only moderate. Others take the position that such dangerous drugs should be used only when the risks are high. It is obvious from Myers's data that in some hospitals the policy was to use prophylactic antibacterials in all cases; other hospitals were extremely conservative in their use—perhaps too conservative!

A similar situation persists in general practice. Penicillin and other antibacterials are extremely useful if the patient has a bacterial infection but are of no use if he has a viral condition. The physician cannot make his decision based only on inspection. For example, if the patient presents a sore throat, the infection may be of either a bacterial or a viral source. If the patient does have a strep throat, a bacterial condition that may have serious consequences if not treated promptly, a course of antibacterials is indicated. On the other hand, if the physician prescribes a course of antibacterials when the source of the infection is a virus, he is taking needless risks because these drugs can be dangerous. What strategy should the doctor use? In each instance this should depend on the relative danger of following one course rather than another and on the relative probabilities that these risks will materialize. Thus the following considerations are relevant:

1. What are the dangers of damage if the condition is not treated or treatment is delayed?
2. What is the probability that the use of antibacterials will eventuate in harm?
3. What is the probability that this patient's condition is bacterial?

Most sore throats are not strep throats, and thus the medical student is usually told to test for a bacterial infection before beginning a course of antibacterial treatment. The conservative medical position is that the risks of delay in treatment are less than the risks of unnecessary treatment because the probability will be high that most patients will not have a bacterial infection. In contrast, some doctors in argument, and many more in practice, take the position that prophylactic antibacterial treatment is merited. They argue that frequently they can differentiate with fairly good predictive power which sore throats are bacterial (although this remains to be demonstrated!) and thus can insure that early treatment is begun, increasing the comfort of the patient and limiting the possible risks resulting from an untreated condition. Between these two positions are those who would use prophylactic antibacterial treatment in some cases and not in others depending on the patient's age, other disease conditions he may have, and so on. It is not my purpose to suggest the medical strategies that should or should not be adopted, but rather to emphasize the relevance of strategies in dealing with uncertainty in medical decision making.

In situations of uncertainty, the nature of the doctor's adaptive strategies will frequently be influenced by the pressures on him and the contingencies of his practice. It is not surprising that general practitioners in the community frequently choose to treat rather than to wait, because they know that the patient expects to be treated and that they will be held culpable by the patient for a failure to treat. In contrast, physicians at university medical schools or in large group practices who are independent of client control are more likely to be attuned to the standards of their medical colleagues and thus are more likely to opt in the direction of prevailing medical opinion on such treatment practices. Other factors also affect the strategies adopted. Fashions are adopted in different cases, or the economics of medical care may affect the strategy. For example, European doctors depend much less on laboratory investigation than do their American counterparts. Let me emphasize once again the importance of such contextual variables, because too frequently the cause of such discrepancies is sought by attempting to locate deficiencies in medical education rather than in attempting to understand the social factors influencing medical practice (138).

The patient with a high inclination to use medical care poses a special source of difficulty for the physician in his attempt to develop a reasonable strategy for dealing with the patient. When a patient comes to a general physician complaining of physical distress, as many do, the doctor may come to the conclusion that this patient does not suffer from a significant disease condition and may make the decision to search no longer for a physical basis. There is no end to the depth of exploration that is theoretically possible, and the doctor knows that he must live with the fact that he can never really prove that there is no underlying physical basis; at best he can assure himself that the probability of such a "cause" is small. At some point he must begin to consider the risks of continued exploration: the dangers of the various diagnostic procedures, the economic costs of continued searching, and the probability that continued searching may reinforce the attitude of the patient that he is indeed physically sick. To add to these costs are those suffered by the doctor, such as the expenditure of time with no results. Many physicians in these circumstances feel frustrated because they lack perspectives and strategies for coping with the patient who is not clearly ill. Thus the relationship is frequently terminated with no attempt to seek the origin of the patient's trouble on a nonphysical basis, and the patient is informed that there is nothing really wrong with him. The problem with this strategy is that although it may get the patient "off the doctor's back," he will probably move on to some other doctor and begin the entire searching process again, with its various associated risks. Since so many patients conform to this general portrait, one of the greatest challenges medicine faces is to develop better strategies for approaching them.

The Doctor's Influence on the Patient's Condition

When we think of the influence of the doctor we are usually attuned to the efficacy of his treatment techniques, but much of the influence of the doctor on the patient is nonspecific and emanates from his position of authority, suggestive powers, and influence strategies (55; 163; 337; 338; 441; 638). In recent years the study of such influences has been designated as the study of the placebo effect. The word "placebo" comes from the Latin verb "to please" and has been defined by Shapiro as the "psychological, physiological or psychophysiological effect of any medication or procedure given with therapeutic intent, which is independent of or minimally related to the pharmacologic effects of the medication or to the specific effects of the procedure, and which operates through a psychological mechanism" (637, p. 299). The history of medication in medicine, as Shapiro points out, is incredible; it includes such substances as dung from crocodiles, geese, and sheep; blood from bats, frogs, and turtles; and oils from ants, wolves, spiders, and earthworms. After reviewing the matter in detail, Shapiro concludes that "we are led to the inescapable conclusion that the history of medical treatment for the most part until relatively recently is the history of the placebo effect, since almost all medications until recently were placebos" (637, p. 301). So much for the past.

In recent years there has been a vast outpouring of papers documenting the significance of placebo effect in almost every area of medical activity. One can demonstrate such effects in the treatment of almost every disease, and there are occasions when the impact of suggestion is to affect not only the reported feeling state of the patient but also his general physiological and disease responses (also see 777 on this point). Interestingly, placebos lead not only to patient improvement, but frequently to undesirable side effects as well (337). Common side effects reported after the administration of placebos include drowsiness, headaches, and nervousness. Also reported with some frequency are nausea, constipation, vertigo, dry mouth, and gastrointestinal distress. Less frequently reported symptoms include unsteady gait, mental confusion, motor retardation, and stumbling and falling. Thus we can perhaps observe a modern medical corollary to anthropologists' observations of voodoo death.

Beecher (55) has collected considerable data to show that the effectiveness of a placebo is much greater when the patient is distressed than when he is not. Placebos, for example, have very little effect on relieving pain inflicted in the laboratory but are impressive in relieving pain following surgery. Beecher has accumulated data from several laboratories that show placebos have a significant effect in relieving pain of angina pectoris, seasickness, headache, and cough. In reviewing fifteen studies totalling 1,082 patients he found an average of 35.2 (plus or minus 2.2) percent relieved significantly by placebo. In contrast, Beecher calculates the effectiveness of placebos in relieving experimentally contrived pain as 3.2 percent; thus the placebo is ten times as effective in relieving pain of pathological origin (where distress is an important factor) than it is in relieving pain that has been experimentally contrived.

Studies in social psychology have shown that under situations that are difficult, usual habits and problem-solving patterns may be disrupted and behavior may become disorganized. Under these conditions the directions that coping attempts take depend on the one hand on external influences and stimuli that serve to define the circumstances and their meaning, and on the other on past experience and preparation. We will discuss each of these in turn.

Schachter and Singer (611) have shown the way external cues influence behavior and feeling states under conditions of altered physiology. They demonstrated that whether subjects experienced anger or euphoria when injected with epinephrine was dependent on whether they had: (1) an *appropriate explanation* for their altered physiological state and (2) *directive external cues*. When the individual had an appropriate explanation for his feelings he had little need for evaluating himself in terms of environmental stimuli and was not very much affected by them. However, when individuals had no immediate explanation for their altered feelings, external cues became important and, in the experimental situation, determined the emotional state. The same type of altered physiological experience was variously interpreted as happiness or anger depending on cues determined by confederates of the experimenter who were playing the roles of subjects. Thus we see that when persons lose their bearings, environmental cues play an important part in helping them make sense of their subjective states. Placebos may serve as cues in a similar way during illness among persons who are in a state of distress.

The importance of suggestive powers has long been recognized among physicians, and they are impressive in faith and religious healing, psychotherapy, and in the work of a variety of marginal "nonscientifically" oriented healers such as chiropractors and Christian Science practitioners. Jerome Frank has presented an interesting case in support of the idea that influence processes in psychotherapy are similar in many respects to those influences operating in thought reform and faith healing. Frank argues that faith or placebo effect plays an important part in healing processes and is essential to psychotherapy:

> But placebos can have deep and enduring effects. An instructive example of the power of the placebo is the lowly wart. Warts have been shown by sev-

eral dermatologists to respond to suggestion as well as to any other form of treatment. One of the most careful studies is that of Bloch. He was able to follow 136 cases of common warts and 43 cases of flat warts over a period of two and one-half years. Of the former group 44 percent, of the latter 88 percent were healed by painting them with an inert dye. About half of the cures occurred after one treatment, while less than 3 percent required more than three sessions. Bloch found that cases which had previously been treated unsuccessfully by the usual means responded just as well as untreated cases, and he adequately ruled out the possibility that his cure rates might represent the percentage that would have healed without any treatment. Since warts are a definite tissue change caused by an identifiable virus, this cure by placebo may serve as a prototype of an organic disease cured by faith. In this case the faith seems to operate to change the physiology of the skin so that the virus can no longer thrive on it.

Placebos can also heal more serious tissue damage, if it is directly related to the patient's emotional state. In a recently reported study two groups of patients with bleeding peptic ulcer in a municipal hospital in Budapest were compared. The placebo group received an injection of sterile water from the doctor, who told them it was a new medicine which would produce relief. The control group received the same injection from nurses who told them it was an experimental medicine of undetermined effectiveness. The placebo group had remissions which were "excellent in 70 percent of the cases lasting over a period of one year." The control group showed only a 25 percent remission rate. The cure of warts and peptic ulcers by suggestion is not as spectacular as religious miracle cures, but qualitatively the processes involved seem very similar [228, pp. 35–36].

Work thus far on placebo effect has amply documented its persistence and importance, but these investigations have been much less consistent in delimiting the specific contexts that most influence such effects and the particular kinds of personalities who show the greatest proneness to them. Several studies claim to have isolated the particular kinds of personality who are generalized placebo reactors (55; 220; 370; 413; 528). Some of these studies have such significant methodological deficiencies that they must be discounted; others reporting a placebo reactor do not agree on his characteristics, and some of the observations are diametrically opposed. Several studies fail to substantiate the hypothesis of the existence of generalized placebo reactors. In one study, for example, Liberman (442) investigated 52 obstetric patients under three different conditions of pain: labor pain, postpartum pain, and experimental (ischemic muscle) pain.* Using control groups to evaluate placebo effect, Liberman found that his results did not confirm the presence of consistent placebo reactors. The obstetrical patients responded to each placebo situation independently, and there was no sig-

---

* This appears to be the one kind of experimental pain that can be affected by placebo.

nificant tendency toward a consistent response in the three situations. Although the presence of a placebo reactor is a phenomenon yet to be confirmed, there is little question that the context of the situation in which the patient is treated and the attitude of those performing the treatment play some part in the magnitude and direction of the placebo effect. The studies available are, however, not sufficiently definitive to lead to any unambiguous generalizations concerning the contexts and treatment variables that magnify the placebo response. It appears that placebo effects are generally largest when those who administer inert drugs do so with a confident sense of hope and when those who receive them are emotionally aroused.

Illness Behavior and Medical Care

In chapter 9 I discussed the concept of illness behavior in some detail. If this concept is truly as important as was suggested, it should have some implications for medical care. The value of illness-behavior considerations can be illustrated by a study at the Massachusetts General Hospital (794). The hypothesis was that the patient's cultural background would influence the way the patient presented his symptoms and thus the way the doctor evaluated them. The analysis was undertaken because the investigator had the impression that more Italian than Irish or Anglo-Saxon patients were being labeled as psychiatric problems, although there was no objective difference in the extent to which members of these groups reported psychosocial problems. Zola selected a group of 29 patients who presented themselves at the medical and ear, nose, and throat clinics, but for whom no medical disease was found. There was good reason to believe that these groups of patients did not differ in the extent of their life difficulties, but it was clear that their mode of cultural expression was very different. Italians are more emotional in the presentation of symptoms and give more attention and expression to pain. Zola found that psychogenesis was implied in the medical reports of 11 of the 12 Italian cases, and in only 4 of the 13 remaining cases. Although this was not a well-controlled study, the results suggest that the patient's cultural mode of expression affected the way the doctor viewed him and the way he was medically evaluated.

The place of illness behavior is particularly important in disorders that are diagnosed largely through behavioral manifestations and the patient's social history, for it is particularly difficult to separate symptoms from subcultural patterns of expression and affect, and from different behavioral patterns among the various social strata. Similarly, it is in such disorders that symptoms and etiological factors are more frequently confused with factors that may lead differentially to social intervention and the seeking of care.

The provision of care depends to a considerable extent on the social and cultural processes that lead particular people to define themselves as requiring care or that lead others to define them as targets for community action. Many factors unrelated to the severity of illness and incapacity may assist in the selection of patients for care, while other persons requiring attention to a greater extent go unnoticed.

We all recognize that there are many persons in the general population who require care and treatment and who can benefit by it, but who do not come to the attention of care facilities. Conversely, there are some who have developed an overdependence on the physician, psychiatrist, or social agency who can be adversely affected by particular kinds of intensive care and attention. Although psychiatrists, especially those more dynamically oriented, often work under the assumption that all persons can benefit from therapy—or at least that it will not harm them—and although the plea for help is usually taken on pragmatic grounds as proof of the need for psychiatric assistance, it is important to consider the counterproposition that certain kinds of assistance, however well meaning, can be detrimental for certain patients. There are those, for example, for whom excessive focus on symptoms and life difficulties may reinforce an already hypochondriacal pattern, induce or encourage further displays of illness behavior, and bring about reduced coping effectiveness. As we have already noted, illness is one of the few widely recognized and acceptable reasons for failing to meet social responsibilities and obligations, and thus the sick role often carries advantages for those who wish to escape the difficulties of meeting social expectations without incurring disapproval. Improper use of the sick role and willingness to encourage persons to assume the role of patient without careful consideration of its implications involve serious dangers. The improper use of the sick role under some circumstances can reinforce "immature" and "irresponsible" patterns of behavior. Military psychiatrists have learned—and this is consistent with the observations of Beecher discussed earlier—that under military conditions in which persons often wish to evade responsibilities and dangers, the sick role may offer clear advantages. This is one of the reasons military organizations often make it so difficult to be sick, and why totalitarian governments have done so during periods of labor shortage.

The issue is not, of course, whether we should adopt a permissive approach to illness or subjugate health organizations to other social institutions. From the perspective of a free medical system (that is, one in which the doctor acts primarily as the patient's agent and on his behalf), the doctor-patient relationship is frequently based on substantial trust, and the doctor has considerable influence in affecting the patient's feeling state and behavior. As we have noted, patients often seek care when they are distressed, and there is extensive evidence that distressed persons are highly suggestible and open to influence (229). Thus the doctor's attitudes toward the patient and his illness are important forces that can be used to support coping efforts or to encourage disability.

Part 7

MENTAL DISORDER AND MENTAL HEALTH

Chapter 16

SOCIAL AND PSYCHOLOGICAL ISSUES

The referral of a patient for care and treatment can be characterized in terms of the inner disturbance shown by the patient, the degree of social disability evident in his response to his environment, or even the referral process itself (the patterns of illness behavior and societal reaction that bring the patient under the scrutiny of a variety of social agencies). These characterizations often cover common ground and are frequently constructed on the basis of similar information concerning the patient, yet each orients us to somewhat different issues and concerns relevant to illness, and each suggests different possible alternatives for therapeutic intervention and the provision of care.

The study of the mentally ill continues to be typified by considerable uncertainty and profound disagreements. Experts differ among themselves in their appraisals of the nature and character of mental disorder: its nosology, its etiologies, the efficacy of various forms of intervention, and many other important issues.

While considerable progress has been made in the care of psychiatric patients in the past two decades, it has been due more to changing social definitions and practices than to new understanding of disordered behavior. We have also had an opportunity to learn—and I hope we have learned the lesson well—that there are no easy solutions; progress in the care of the mentally ill, particularly the psychotic patient, requires basic knowledge that still eludes us and sustained approaches to management of patients that are difficult and costly. Much of the thinking of the 1960s—however useful in mobilizing public opinion and widespread support for mental-health efforts—was simpleminded and excessively optimistic. The danger now is that we may be entering one of the historically recurrent cycles in which naive optimism is followed by pessimism and by the dangerous myth that without biological breakthroughs progress is impossible.

Psychiatric treatment is characterized by a vast variety of phar-

435

macological, psychological, psychodynamic, and social approaches. They vary from traditional forms of psychotherapy to a wide variety of group experiences—from patient government to sensitivity training, from operant conditioning to models of coping education, from transcendental meditation to reevaluation counseling. Indeed, one gets the impression that almost everything goes, with little critical awareness of which techniques are effective with which patients under which conditions. No matter how far out or untested the technique, if performed by a health professional it tends to be called "treatment." Psychiatry continues to have a poorly developed research foundation, and departments of psychiatry still do too little investigation.

Nevertheless, despite the confusions and ideological ferment of the past two decades, we have achieved some useful advances in our frames of reference for viewing disordered behavior and its more effective management. Awareness that psychotic disorders are not simply a more serious manifestation of commonly occurring distress and impairment but rather appear to have distinctive natural histories and epidemiological pictures is a major condition for further progress. We are moving from the vague conception that a standard therapy fits all psychiatric problems to a more careful description, and we are now searching for more targeted interventions. As we have gone—as a matter of public policy—from dependence on hospital settings to a variety of community-care situations, we have been confronted by the bitter realization that administrative policies, however well intentioned, are no substitute for adequate knowledge of the cause or progression of disorder and the conditions most likely to contain or alleviate it. While informed and humane administrative policies are a prerequisite for a sound approach to mental illness, such an approach must depend on better understanding of the etiology of specific disorders and their outcomes in varying environments and treatment settings.

It is useful to review some of the valuable results of the ideological ferment of the past twenty years. First, it led to the realization that whatever genetic and neurobiological factors are involved in the causation of the psychoses, they interact in complex ways with social and cultural factors; mental illnesses are a product of these interactions. Second, whatever these predispositions, they may be exacerbated or contained by the manner in which psychotic patients are defined and managed and by the nature of the social environment in which they live. Third, the ideological debate on the nature of mental health so debased the use of psychiatric concepts that there is now a new awareness of the need to avoid both a glib disease perspective and a crude social labeling approach; efforts are being made to define concepts more carefully and to improve the classification of psychiatric phenomena. As long as the concept of schizophrenia, for example, was used to refer to everything, it meant nothing. Both the collaborative American-British study (146) and the cross-national World Health Organization study (786) illustrate the value of being more careful in describing disorder. Better description is a prerequisite for more adequate understanding and control in the future.

From the perspective of the administration of mental-health care, the turmoil of the 1960s has given us all a renewed appreciation of the civil rights of the mentally ill and the dangers of the self-fulfilling prophecy. With the shift to community care we have again come to appreciate the disservice professionals can do to patients under the guise of treatment when they engage in excessive restrictions and thereby foster dependency. It is now more difficult than before to confuse custodialism for the purpose of community comfort with effective treatment efforts. We are also learning that changing our concepts, and even our administrative practices, is inadequate for the real demands of managing psychotic patients effectively. Community care without sustained programs of follow-up and support is an invitation to a new type of erosion of human potential, except now it occurs in a community and not in a custodial institution. The realities of community care are forcing a reconsideration of the appropriate role of mental-hospital care in the entire spectrum of services, a rethinking of the concept of dangerousness and the ways we can make better predictions about who must be involuntarily detained, and a more realistic view of both the benefits and the costs of alternative means of managing psychotic patients.

The difficulty in organizing professionals for providing long-term care to chronic patients should not be underestimated. Developing programs for such patients is almost always difficult and frustrating, and involves activities that are not particularly likely to bring prestige or recognition. Professionals often lack the skills necessary for political implementation or for dealing with numerous problems of community resistance and funding. It is too easy and too enticing to retreat to familiar professional routines and comfortable patterns of work rather than to persist in the face of recalcitrant communities and patients who seem to have intractable disorders. While we can talk about the need for changes in psychiatric education, changing the status and rewards of different kinds of professional work, and the challenge of caring for chronic psychiatric illness, we delude ourselves if we think this is any more than reformist rhetoric. Major changes in the professional stances of the relevant professions will depend either on a major advance that can be applied without too much disruption in ongoing organization or on fundamental changes in the way services for mental disorders are paid for and choice of those who will be eligible for payment.

One of the adverse consequences of the expansion of mental-health concepts in the 1960s was the redirection of attention from the needs of the psychotic patient. If large proportions of the population were mentally impaired, as some studies suggested (see, for example, 174)—and if such impairments were only a precursor of more severe pathology—then it seemed less compelling to devote large resources to the relative few who suffered from chronic psychiatric illness. Instead, it seemed sensible to devote attention to moderate disabilities before they became severe (105). Community mental-health centers had diffuse missions and found it easier—and perhaps professionally more rewarding—to focus on assistance for those with less severe disorders. The major difficulty was that the theory of preventive psychiatry was more rhetoric than substance.

As we move toward national health insurance in the coming years, the manner in which psychiatric benefits are defined within this program is likely to have an important effect on how psychiatric personnel spend their time and what attention will be devoted to psychotic patients. It is already apparent that various interest groups are active in seeking to influence the definition of those benefits. Although a discussion here of psychiatric benefits under national health insurance would take me too far afield, I should note that maintenance of parallel systems of medical and mental-health services, as they are now organized, will reinforce a tendency to neglect the problems of the less attractive and more chronic patients. In my view, general mental-health services for more ordinary problems of living ought not to be categorically organized or financed. There is, however, a need for categorical services in the mental-health sector, and such financing should be targeted specifically for the care of chronic psychotic patients and others with similarly severe conditions.

Development of better programs of intervention depends on continuing research programs. Not only must we understand the genetic, biochemical, and environmental factors contributing to psychoses, but we must also develop a more adequate grasp of the intervening variables that help explain why, for example, only some people with genetic predispositions actually develop psychoses while others do not; why some children of two mentally ill parents do so badly while others not only achieve adequate adjustment but appear to cope admirably; why some children with particular symptoms at an early age appear to have self-limited conditions while others enter on a trajectory of one disaster after another. Some of the studies by Lee Robins (see, for example, 587) and others have documented the devastating and discouraging course of behavior disorder problems in childhood; it is one of the great challenges of epidemiological study to understand the process of such disorders and the ways we might more successfully intervene.

The foregoing general assessment of the social status of psychiatric and social care of mental patients leads us now to a more structured discussion of the conceptions and evolution of psychiatric treatment. The reader may wish at this point to review the earlier discussion on the relationships between illness and deviance and on general theoretical frameworks for viewing such issues. The purpose of this chapter is to consider sociological conceptions of the origins of mental disorder and the approach of treatment facilities to mental patients. A more general and interdisciplinary introduction to the field of mental health, and perspectives of causes and treatment, can be found in my book, *Mental Health and Social Policy* (488).

Implications of Models of Treatment

Each approach to treatment and care implies a model of the relationship of doctor and patients, the expectations they have of one another, and the responsibilities they are expected to assume. Within the traditional concept of the medical model, the patient having put himself in the hands of the physician accepts his dependence upon him and yields readily to his authority and expert knowledge. The physician, having assumed responsibility, diagnoses the patient's difficulty and decides on treatment. Implicit in the relationship is that the patient need do no more than obey the doctor's directives, although the physician is in a position to maximize therapeutic potential by the attitude and encouragement he communicates to the patient. This conceptualization is oversimplified, and in practice there are many deviations from this model, yet the basic structure of the relationship is fairly clear. It is apparent that the use of physical methods in psychiatry falls within this tradition.

In contrast, the psychodynamic psychiatrist uses a semimedical model. Although the condition of the patient is still viewed as an illness, considerably more responsibility is vested in the patient for his own cure. Explicit in the relationship is the idea that no directive procedure itself will produce a cure. Only through the effort and continued motivation of the patient can effective treatment be evolved. Thus within this approach the authority of the physician as a healing agent is undermined to some extent, and the therapist is unwilling to assume the more traditional stance of authority and responsibility. Indeed, such a stance is frequently viewed as detrimental to effective care.

Typically the psychiatrist focuses on the patient's problem as one involving psychological impairment that is a result of an interaction between a particular inherited constitution and a particular psychological-developmental history. The psychotherapist thus seeks the nature and origin of the problem through an exploration of the intrapsychic history of the patient. The therapist works under the assumption that through psychodynamic exploration and analysis the condition of the patient can be alleviated. In contrast, the psychiatrist who is more concerned with physical methods, although he may recognize the importance of psychosocial development, works under the assumption that the patient's condition can be alleviated without necessarily probing the past or the patient's conception of it. Although there is some degree of psychological impairment in all mental disorders, it is not necessarily obvious that manipulation of the patient's intrapsychic conceptions is necessary for alleviation of his distress or impairment. This indeed is the basic assumption underlying the use of nonpsychological methods in psychiatry, and once this assumption is clearly understood a large range of possibilities based on the same assumption follows. The basic idea I wish to convey in this discussion of forms of intervention in psychiatric disorders is that an overemphasis on psychological aspects of problems in living may be quite costly and relatively ineffective when considered in light of other possibilities and considerations in rehabilitating the mentally ill.

Perhaps my argument can be made most clearly if we begin by considering the psychodynamic tradition. The psychodynamic position is a deterministic one that views mental disorders as aberrations of individual intrapsychic development. Thus emphasis is given to the history of the personality rather than to situational focuses such as confused communication systems, distorted roles, extraordinary social demands, social stress, or any of a variety of other contextual variables. Although such situational problems often are intensified by inadequate and distorted psychological response, it does not necessarily follow that the psychological responses are the most dominant and important aspects of the total pattern, nor is it clear that the best way of dealing with such situations involves the reorganization of individual personalities, even assuming we had the capacity and knowledge to do this effectively. Furthermore, the psychodynamist tends to view ineffective social performance largely as an attribute of inadequate psychological functioning. Thus such important factors as cultural preparation, task and interpersonal skills in work and interpersonal relations, and organizational factors affecting behavior are viewed as less important than the "basic condition."

The basic logic of alternative nonpsychological approaches to psychiatric intervention is not necessarily inconsistent with the psychological model. For example, the distinction in rehabilitation between illness and disability is consistent with traditional psychodynamic theory. It is generally recognized that persons with intrapsychic difficulties may make better or lesser adjustments to the social demands they face depending on their socially learned capacities and on the adequacy of the fit between their "abnormal psychic needs" and social demands. Indeed, it follows directly from the psychodynamic view that certain pathological intrapsychic conditions may lead to socially constructive behavior that is supported and rewarded in particular social settings. Thus persons suffering from psychological impairments in a psychiatric sense may not only find satisfying social roles that contain their pathology but may even have extraordinary and effective social identities that are energized by their "psychic impairments" independently assessed.

Without entangling ourselves in a discussion of the relative merits of viewing social interaction in terms of the personal history of actors or in terms of the interaction of situational aspects, we might note that both views leave ample room for the construction of therapeutic interventions on a social level. It is evident that given various states of psychological aberration, it is possible to contain them. The degree of containment depends on the social context within which such aberrations become evident and the degree to which they can be used, tolerated, and supported within the social setting. Thus, given a particular definition of a problem, it is important to consider the extent to which it is valuable to make a frontal attack on the psychological orientations and intrapsychic organization of the patient, or perhaps whether it is wiser to prepare the patient to accommodate to his situation and help him minimize the distress he experiences from his problem. This might be accomplished by changing some aspects of the patient, changing some aspect of his living situation by working with the family to improve communication and understanding, or by helping him to find a better fit between his psychological and social capacities and the social context within which he functions.

We must be careful to distinguish to what degree a patient's social impairment is a derivative of his condition and to what extent the disability he suffers is in part a product of his own definitions of his situation and a harmful environmental context. In recent years there has been a growing awareness that much of the disability suffered by patients is not necessarily the result of the natural history of illness itself, but is often the consequence of the way that the patient has been dealt with by associates, treatment personnel, and the community (771). The recent and impressive shift in the course of hospital careers gives credence to the importance of the distinction between primary and secondary aspects of a condition. There is now impressive evidence that modes of handling patients have a considerable effect on the extent and character of disabilities (93; 774). There is substantial reason to justify concern with the varying environments under which secondary handicaps can be minimized and primary conditions interfere with social adjustment to a minimal extent. The fact that social variables have proved relevant in such disorders as schizophrenia suggests their greater relevance for the many conditions that produce substantially less innate disability.

Labeling Theory

One approach to chronic illness developed by sociologists is the so-called labeling perspective. While this conception views chronic mental illness as a consequence of certain social processes, these notions have not been tested very fully; when they have been tested, often they have not withstood rigorous scrutiny (see, for example, 284). The conception, however, has been very provocative and has stimulated interesting studies that have added to our understanding. One of the major difficulties with the labeling approach is that it is not a coherent theory, and there are a variety of views as to the main elements of the theory, to what phenomena they apply, and under what conditions (622). Crude and general statements of the theory—for example, the contention that labeling causes mental illness—are obviously overstated and clearly inconsistent with much of the available evidence. However, labeling theory has much greater relevance in understanding the development of secondary disabilities and the processes that contribute to them. The purpose of this discussion is not to adjudicate among the varying conceptions and disagreements concerning the scope and relevance of the labeling approach; there is already a large and growing literature attempting to do this. Our purpose is to draw from this body of work in order to understand better the processes that contribute to variations in chronicity among patients who suffer from some primary impairment such as schizophrenia or alcoholism.

In discussing the contributions of labeling theory we must continue to keep in mind that the etiologies of the various psychiatric disorders are not well understood and that conceptions of them cover a wide range including physiological defect, genetic disposition, distortions of early psychological development, and severe social stress. There is no sign that we shall discover "essential causes" in the near future, and it is evident that the conditions called "mental illnesses" involve complex interactions among constitutional states, psychological development, and social experience. Knowledge proceeds in two ways. One approach is to engage in interdisciplinary studies in which geneticists, psychiatrists, and social scientists carry out complex collaborative investigations in which they seek to identify the relevant interactions among biological, psychological, and social factors. Another approach is to attempt to expand knowledge by pushing a particular framework as far as it can possibly go, with full appreciation that it is hardly the entire story. Some biological scientists, for example, attempt to account for all illness manifestations through biological models. In their enthusiasm they sometimes confuse the process of acquiring knowledge with the reality of the phenomena themselves, which are almost always multidimensional and caused by complex interactions. Thus they may exaggerate the importance of biological or genetic factors and not give sufficient weight to other types of factor. Similarly, social scientists—particularly those associated with the labeling perspective—have found it a useful research strategy to approach the mental-health field with a tendency to exaggerate sociological influences. While some of the early theorists, such as Scheff, were fully conscious of what they were doing in pushing a theoretical perspective beyond what the empirical world warranted (427, pp. 26–27), others less creative and less thoughtful became proponents of a vulgar form of labeling theory that they confused with empirical reality. Let us now examine some of the basic ideas of labeling theory and how it developed. I emphasize the earlier work because some of the earlier theorists, such as Lemert and Scheff, were more careful and thoughtful than many others who later joined the labeling bandwagon.

Edwin Lemert (427) is one of the social theorists who has attempted to address himself in a systematic fashion to the distinction between individual aberrance and the development of a deviant social career. His argument begins with the recognition that known or defined deviation is only a small proportion of the total number of instances of deviant behavior in the community. Much deviant behavior does not become visible to other people because it is hidden or enacted in private; it is frequently situational, transitory, or sporadic, and usually constitutes an unimportant aspect of the individual's development, significant role enactments, and total identity. Thus he believes that it is extremely important to separate the occasional deviant behavior of large numbers of "normal" or "usual" persons from deviant behavior that is organized as a central part of a person's social identity, as with the chronic mental patient, the professional criminal, and the exclusive homosexual. As Kinsey (389) so clearly demonstrated, for example, the prevalence of single homosexual experiences is relatively high among males, and such experiences may occur naturally in normal development or in particular social contexts such as in boys' schools, camps, and other segregated institutions. Certainly it is important to distinguish people with transitory homosexual experience from the exclusive homosexual whose entire social identity for long periods of time may be organized around his deviant sexual pattern. Only a small proportion of boys who may have engaged in homosexual experience at some point in their lives become "homosexuals."

Lemert designates sporadic, situational, and unorganized deviance as primary, and deviant behavior organized as part of a deviant identity as secondary. Primary deviation, in Lemert's terms, may stem from a large number of different biological, psychological, and social factors; such deviation may result from genetic and physical defects, from conventional subcultural learning not accepted by the larger community, or from particular psychosocial forms of development. Thus, he argues, primary deviation of any particular type—whether it be mental illness, crime, or delinquency—has no unitary aspect. Secondary (or systematic or career) deviation—that is, deviant behavior that is central to a person's identity and behavior—presents the sociologist with a distinctive sociological question in answer to which he can provide a unique perspective: What are the social forces that lead from occasional or sporadic deviant behavior that is not central to a person's identity to the development of a deviant career and a deviant self-image?

The probability, for example, that a primary homosexual will become a career homosexual depends on a variety of contingencies according to Lemert's theory. These contingencies include the frequency with which the primary pattern occurs, its visibility, whether it is recognized and, if so, what the reaction is, general tolerance for this kind of deviant, and the extent to which recognition excludes the person so defined from normal channels of community participation and status. This process can be illustrated by elaborating on a simple example suggested by Kinsey (389). Visualize two small-town high school boys both of whom have some homosexual experience. The first boy has a few experiences but is not detected; his casual experiences do not persist for one reason or another, or they occur occasionally but are not discovered or defined. The second boy, perhaps, is discovered during his first experience. He may be harshly reprimanded, and others in the school and the community generally become aware of the incident. This may lead to derisive behavior on the part of others, and the boy may be excluded from various social groups. It would not be inconceivable that many mothers would be reluctant to allow their daughters to date this boy, and it is not unlikely that other boys would ostracize him. This process may push him into association with other boys, similarly defined as deviant, who are also excluded for a variety of reasons from ordinary social participation. These experiences and restrictions on opportunities for further interaction have an impact on the boy's self-image, and he, too, may begin to doubt his "normalcy." According to Lemert, this process can become a vicious circle creating great pressures toward further deviant behavior. Although the argument has been oversimplified, societal reaction theories view the chronic deviant career as developing through a sequential pattern, and it is implied that the further the process proceeds the greater is the probability that the person will become a career deviant.

Lemert's contribution is important in that he points so clearly to the fact that the development of career deviation may be dependent on a variety of social influences in addition to those that bring about the primary deviant pattern. Thus, given the same degree of primary deviance, subsequent social experience may alter substantially the course this pattern takes and may determine whether deviance is transitory or whether it becomes organized as part of the social identity of the person. Moreover, unlike later investigators, Lemert does not exclude the possibility that the primary source of deviance (such as the nature and quality of the problem) can be one of the possible major influences resulting in secondary deviance. For example, the primary factors contributing to schizophrenia may be so severe and disabling that they account for a chronic pattern of behavior independent of other factors.

Lemert's theoretical approach is not without significant difficulties, and it remains to be seen to what extent his formulation will receive empirical support. One of Lemert's basic propositions is that the amount and degree of deviation figure importantly in who becomes subject to social definitional processes. It is through such social definitions that opportunities for primary deviants become restricted, producing changes in self-conception and thus further enactments of deviant behavior, and so on, in a vicious circle. Although we note vast differences in the way people respond to the same objective disability or situation, the amount and degree of deviant behavior may still be the most significant factor leading to social definitions. The extent to which social influences play a part in such social processes as Lemert describes may be limited to a particular range of behavior and adaptation, and these social processes may be less important in cases in which the physiological disability or physical liabilities become too great. In any case, Lemert has attuned us to some major issues, and the fact that social influences are found to be prominent in such disabling patterns as schizophrenia suggests that the range within which social influences play a part in the development of deviant careers can be rather large.

Thomas Scheff (616; 618) has restated many of Lemert's ideas in hypothesis form to suggest what areas must be investigated in order to clarify and attempt to verify some of the basic ideas relevant to Lemert's explanation. Scheff argues that mental disorders are residual deviant behavior and arise from fundamentally diverse sources. He presents evidence to show that the rate of unrecorded and unrecognized residual deviance is extremely high relative to the rate of treated mental illness, and that much of such behavior is denied or is not explicitly recognized and is transitory with changing circumstances. Scheff believes that many aspects of mental illness are a combination of conscious and unconscious role playing that may occur when particular social forces are present. Although deviants do not explicitly learn the role of the mentally ill, Scheff hypothesizes that persons are able to assume such roles because they learned the stereotyped imagery of mental disorder from early childhood, and this imagery is inadvertently but continuously supported and supplemented through the movies, TV, radio, newspapers, and magazine stories. Scheff believes that deviants who are labeled as mentally ill may receive a variety of rewards and secondary gains by assuming and enacting the role. When such persons attempt to return to normal, conventional roles, opportunities are often restricted; they may be punished through the stigma associated with their past situation, difficulties in obtaining adequate employment, or difficulties in interpersonal affairs resulting from the fact that they have occupied the role of the mentally ill. Frequently, for example, protests by mental patients who deny that they are sick or who believe they have improved sufficiently to return to their normal life situation are taken as further evidence that they are not really well. Similarly, previous deviant status makes a person suspicious in the eyes of others. Finally, Scheff believes that the transition from primary to secondary mental disorder often occurs during social and personal crises when the individual concerned is very upset. When the person is labeled as mentally ill, he is in a state of considerable arousal and is highly suggestible. Under such circumstances he may willingly accept the definition of illness placed upon him.

Scheff recognizes that his theory is to some extent an overstatement that neglects the tremendous constitutional and personality differences among persons that make them more or less susceptible to the processes he describes. His purpose is to draw the social implications of the theory so explicitly that it is clear where research efforts from a sociological perspective are most needed. This perspective, when viewed as a theoretical thrust, is extremely valuable and contributes in a meaningful way to our understanding of chronicity. The theory has been taken too literally, however, and many sociologists fail to give sufficient attention and respect to various outcomes resulting from differences in personality and biological traits.

There have been several attempts to examine the extent to which varying labeling ideas either fit or contradict the empirical evidence. For the most part, however, the critics and defenders of labeling theory have talked past one another, failing to engage the crucial issues and the ways they might best be approached. Labeling theory, as I have suggested in discussing the work of Scheff and Lemert, is a theory of process in varying social contexts. A successful appraisal of labeling theory requires specification of the way these processes of labeling and self-identity change under varying conditions and of when these factors are more or less important. Instead, much of the debate is posed in oversimplified terms; the argument is whether labeling theory is right or wrong rather than under *what conditions* it contributes to our understanding of specific phenomena. Moreover, much of the cross-sectional data purporting to test labeling hypotheses are so crude, as are the hypotheses themselves, that the argument about the value of the perspective tends to generate more heat than light.

In discussing the appropriateness of labeling theory for understanding alcoholism, Lee Robins (588) has posed, in my view, the most sophisticated challenge to its proponents. Since her critique is highly constructive and important, I shall present it in some detail. First, Robins notes that predictors of deviance tend to be similar for both labeled and unlabeled deviants if the severity of the deviant behavior is taken into account. The severity control is necessary because persons who engage in more severe and frequent deviant behavior, as Lemert recognized, are more likely to be labeled. Second, she notes that all of the common forms of deviance decrease with age, although the cumulation of labeling associated with deviance must obviously increase over a person's life span. Third, she notes that although labeling theorists tend to believe that a person labeled as a thief or as mentally ill will tend to develop these types of behavior pattern, generally it is found that specific types of deviance in early life are associated with later deviance, but not necessarily of the same type. For example, young girls caught stealing are more likely in later life to be suicide attempters, sexually promiscuous, and alcoholic than they are to be thieves. Fourth, a variety of studies indicate that parents' deviance is predictive of the child's deviance in respect to schizophrenia, alcoholism, and crime even when the child is separated from the parents and does not know the parents' identification, as in the case of infant adoptees. Summarizing her conclusions specifically in relation to alcoholism, Robins notes:

> The process of labeling in alcoholism is rather different from that imagined by the labeling hypothesis. The alcoholic is likely to be first labeled by a member of his own social circle, not by some official. And even that label occurs only after many years of showing behavior that warrants the label of alcoholism, thus suggesting that labeling is seldom premature. In fact, the alcoholic's liability to premature labeling seems rather less than the likelihood that his identity as an alcoholic will be denied long after evidence for problem behavior is clearly available. His deviant behavior appears to be self-sustaining over many years, even when unlabeled, in part because it produces physical dependence. While we do not know for certain whether labeling improves or decreases the chances of recovery, evidence would

seem to indicate that internalization of the label may actually help to improve the chances rather than lowering them. At any rate, there certainly is no evidence that being labeled an alcoholic encourages excessive drinking. Nor is there evidence that the label of alcoholic is irreversible when improvement in drinking behavior does take place, as it frequently does in middle age [588, p. 29].

Unlike many of the labeling theorists who seem satisfied with gross generalities concerning the effects of labeling, Robins considers the conditions under which labeling processes may be more or less important in affecting the course of deviant behavior. She suggests that perhaps labeling effects are less important in cases of behavior such as drinking, in which the behavior "is not disjunctive with normative behavior, but is only an exaggeration of that behavior" (588, p. 30). In contrast, behaviors such as homosexuality, which are more disjunctive with normal patterns, may be much more influenced by processes of social labeling.

Even Robins's critique, excellent as it is, does not speak directly to the more subtle processual conceptions of the labeling process in chronic deviant careers. For example, take her observation concerning the relationship between age and deviance. Examination of the labeling process in terms of its social-psychological aspects involves investigation of the dynamics among behavior, feedback, and interpretation of the feedback as it evolves over time with particular others. Thus, in our earlier example of the high school student involved in a homosexual incident, the issue is not whether he is discovered but the nature and intensity of the reaction, the way information about the incident is relayed to others, the extent to which the youth is ridiculed and actually excluded from certain social opportunities, and the extent to which he has allies who are sympathetic to his plight. A simple assertion that older deviants have been labeled as deviant more often than younger deviants, and therefore should have higher rates of deviance, does not really speak to the more subtle conceptions of labeling theory. If Robins misjudges the testable issues, however, the fault lies primarily with the labeling theorists themselves. They have been vague and inconsistent in their formulations and often have substituted rhetoric about labeling for more precise statements of the hypotheses that are crucial to their conceptions.

In summary, it seems fairly clear that processes of labeling, exclusion, and self-identity formation are important in deviant careers. But the concept of labeling is too vague to describe the more subtle factors that may influence whether an alcoholic, schizophrenic, or homosexual manages to make a more or less adequate adjustment to his situation. Much as the concept of stress described earlier, the concept of labeling defines an area of research activity rather than a precise referent. What is needed is a specification of the types of reaction, support, and interpersonal environment that either exacerbate or retard the development of chronic deviant careers. Moreover, the hypotheses must be specific to varying types of deviance because we cannot reasonably expect that the same factors conducive to functioning for an impaired schizophrenic are relevant to short-circuiting a delinquent career. Robins may or may not be correct about the types of deviance to which the labeling perspective applies, but she is right in indicating the need to specify the problem in a way that reformulates the question to one that seeks to define the conditions under which deviant careers are encouraged or limited.

Psychiatric Hospitalization and Community Care

The future of the mental hospital as an appropriate means of treating psychiatric patients is very much in doubt. The last two decades have witnessed an enormous shift from the mental hospital to psychiatric treatment in community hospitals and in community-care programs. Despite these shifts, there continue to be significant numbers of chronic patients, particularly schizophrenics, who will suffer handicaps throughout their lives and who will require continuing services. Although some psychiatrists and mental-health professionals believe that there is absolutely no need for mental hospitals and that those remaining should be phased out or closed, others continue to support the mental hospital as an important component of the total service pattern, particularly for psychotic patients. (For a debate on this issue see 746.)

The state of our mental hospitals today and the provisions for mental patients are not a result of a consistent developmental trend. Many of the changes in care have occurred in cycles, and the systems of care developed have often retrogressed (166). Perrow describes the situation nicely with the caption "Mental Hospitals: From Milieu Treatment to Milieu Treatment in One Century" (559). Indeed, many of the more modern views of mental patient care are strikingly similar to "moral treatment," which existed in Europe and America in the nineteenth century. Moral treatment assumed that psychiatric illness could be self-limited if the patient was treated in a considerate and friendly fashion, if he had an opportunity to discuss his troubles, and if his interest was stimulated and he was kept actively involved in life. Deutsch quotes a statement concerning the philosophy of moral treatment from the writings of a doctor in New York State in 1911. Moral treatment, he explains,

> consists in removing patients from their residence to some proper asylum; and for this purpose a calm retreat in the country is to be preferred: for it is

found that continuance at home aggravates the disease, as the improper association of ideas cannot be destroyed . . . have humane attendants, who shall act as servants to them; never threaten but execute; offer no indignities to them, as they have a high sense of honour . . . let their fears and resentments be soothed without unnecessary opposition; adopt a system of regularity; make them rise, take exercise and food at stated times. The diet ought to be light, and easy of digestion, but never too low. When convalescing, allow limited liberty; introduce entertaining books and conversation. . . [quoted in 166, pp. 91—92].

The idea of moral treatment is attributed to Philippe Pinel, a French doctor appointed as director of the Bicêtre, a "notorious hell-hole," following the French Revolution. Pinel is credited with "striking the chains from these miserable creatures" and inaugurating a program based on kindness and sympathy. A large proportion of those released from their chains proved to be harmless, and a new social movement was under way. Pinel's program was based on his belief that psychological factors were important causes in emotional disturbances, as were social forces and an inadequate "education." Treatment of the insane, he believed, was only a form of education, and intelligent understanding coupled with a minimum of mechanical restraint would bring good results (4).

Innovation, however, moves slowly, and although moral treatment was established in some institutions in America in the mid—nineteenth century, most patients received no better treatment than in the past. The history of the treatment of the mentally ill in America, as in the rest of the world, is hardly encouraging. In early colonial America patients were either cared for in their own homes or incarcerated in jails. Frequently chained and mistreated, they existed in abject misery. During the witchcraft period the mentally ill were hanged, tortured, and generally persecuted.

Regarded as sub-human beings, they were chained in specially devised kennels and cages like wild beasts, and thrown into prisons, bridewells and jails like criminals. They were incarcerated in workhouse dungeons, or made to slave as able-bodied paupers, unclassified from the rest. They were left to wander about stark naked, driven from place to place like mad dogs, subjected to whippings as vagrants and rogues [166; p. 53].

The history of responsibility for the care of the mentally ill is equally bleak. Since local settlements were responsible for caring for their dependents, destitute and distracted persons were driven from the community, and in some areas would be publicly whipped if they returned. Inhabitants were forbidden to lodge strangers, and outsiders who looked as if they might become public charges were "warned out of the community." Indeed, it was a frequent practice for communities to "spirit away mentally ill paupers under the cover of night, and to place them in a distant town or neighboring county in the hope of thus ridding themselves of the burden of supporting them" (166, p. 45). Eight special institutions were established for the mentally ill in the first quarter of the nineteenth century. Six of these were formed by incorporated groups on a semipublic basis, and two were state institutions. These institutions, however, could deal with only a small proportion of the mentally ill, and the insane poor were neglected for the most part; those who were violent were treated as criminals, while those more harmless were not distinguished from other paupers.

Whatever germ of moral treatment that existed in the United States and in other parts of the world had a limited development. The crusade of Dorothea Dix for better treatment for the mentally ill was primarily a reaction to the conditions existing among those mentally ill paupers who were dealt with as if they were hardened criminals or worse. Her cry before the Massachusetts Legislature in 1843, which was typical of her approach was as follows: "I proceed, Gentlemen, briefly to call your attention to the state of Insane Persons confined within this Commonwealth, in *cages, closets, cellars, stalls, pens: Chained, naked, beaten with rods*, and lashed into obedience!" (quoted in 166, p. 165). By the time she had finished her crusade 20 states had either established new mental hospitals or enlarged old ones. This humanitarian and noble thrust was ironically to provide the background for the development of systems of large custodial institutions in the United States and elsewhere that set the tone for the care of the mentally ill until very recently.

By 1860, 28 of the 33 states had established insane asylums. In the preceding period there was considerable optimism about treatment, with claims of substantial levels of cure. A prominent psychiatrist later helped undermine the sense of optimism by showing that institutions were counting the same patient as cured each time the patient was released from the institution. Retrospective analysis of the original data and the critique suggests that the criticisms were excessive and that there was some basis in the claims (77), but the critique had its impact nevertheless. It is, of course, difficult to assess the true effects of these institutions; in any case, there was sufficient diversity among them to preclude generalizations. Yet it is reasonable to suspect that the effect of the institutions and the moral treatment provided by some proved helpful to many patients. Bockoven's analysis of the available statistics certainly supports such a conclusion (77). As Rothman observes: "Medical superintendents designed their institutions with eighteenth-century virtues in mind. They would teach discipline, a sense of limits, and a satisfaction with one's position, and in this way enable patients to withstand the tension and the fluidity of Jacksonian society" (600, p. 154).

There is reason to believe that in the better institutions moral treatment and the organizational regimens associated with it were modestly effective. The basic ideology, whatever its emphasis on discipline, was humane, and in its early stages staffing was reasonable. The relationships reported between patients and staff were sympathetic, and the cause of mental illness was seen as a product of the environment rather than as a consequence of the worthlessness of the patient. However, all this changed rapidly with growing industrialization and urbanism in the last half of the nineteenth and early part of the twentieth centuries. With changes in the social structure, tolerance for chronic patients and alien foreigners (who were heavily represented among them) decreased significantly. Institutionalization was now a convenient way to cope with deviants of all sorts who were difficult to deal with in a rapidly growing and dynamic community (300). Although legislators provided for asylums, they could not keep up with the new demands for incarceration. With overcrowding and change in the social characteristics of the clientele, an era of custodianship began to emerge. Abuses in these institutions became more prevalent, the social characteristics of persons sent to them were increasingly seen as less desirable, and persons who had options began to avoid these settings. The asylums thus became warehouses for the hopeless, the impoverished, and persons with little power and discredited social status.

The development of custodianship accompanied growing skepticism concerning the rehabilitative effects of asylums. Yet the institutions continued to be subsidized and built because they performed needed functions for an increasingly industrialized society that was less able than before to tolerate deviance. With a growing sense that mental disorders were intractable, diminished attention was given to the environmental conditions of care. This was justified by a feeling that mental disorders were organic and unresponsive to environmental treatment, reinforced by the increasing number of chronic patients sent to asylums from other types of institutions (600). Thus institutions developed techniques for managing masses of patients with limited personnel and facilities and at minimum cost.

The outcome of these forces was a sense of hopelessness and a need for regimentation and control over patients. How else could a small staff deal with hordes of patients destined to a hopeless future? Legislatures faced other needs, and the clients of the asylums, like inmates in prisons today, were hardly a group to influence political decisions. The reformers who played an important part in the earlier history of the asylum were pushed out by the growing professionalization of the psychiatric profession (300). The irony was that the new professionals had so little to offer in their stead.

Mental Hospitals

Until the 1960s the typical mental patient was still being treated in state mental hospitals characterized by large size, bureaucratic organization, and limited staff. Beginning in the middle 1950s there was a significant decrease in the number of resident patients in mental hospitals, although rates of admission actually increased (118). A strong trend emerged, however, moving care away from the mental hospital to mental-health centers and other outpatient facilities, special treatment programs, community-care programs, sheltered care, and general voluntary hospitals. Many states began a policy of closing their large mental hospitals or reducing resident populations, but such institutions continue to exist—often inadequately financed, impersonal in the care they provide, and inadequately staffed. In such institutions patients often remain inactive, uninterested, and unmotivated to attempt to cope with their circumstances. In Goffman's terms, the mental hospital is a total institution. He notes that the key fact of the total institution is "the handling of many human needs by the bureaucratic organization of whole blocks of people" (269, p. 6), whether or not this is a necessary or effective means of social organization for the circumstances. The central features of total institutions are the bringing together of groups of coparticipants who live their lives in one place—thus breaking down the barriers usually separating different spheres of life—and under one authority that organizes the different features of life within an overall plan. Goffman describes some of the details as follows:

> First, all aspects of life are conducted in the same place and under the same single authority. Second, each phase of the member's daily activity is carried on in the immediate company of a large batch of others, all of whom are treated alike and required to do the same things together. Third, all phases of the day's activities are tightly scheduled, with one activity leading at a prearranged time into the next, the whole sequence of activities being imposed from above by a system of explicit formal rulings and a body of officials. Finally, the various enforced activities are brought together into a single rational plan purportedly designed to fulfill the official aims of the institution [269, p. 6].

Total institutions need not have deleterious effects. They are organizations for the purpose of changing people and their identities; in sociological parlance, they are resocializing institutions. To the extent that individuals share the goals and aspirations of the institutional administrators and the institution successfully changes them in a desired direction, one might argue that such institutions are worthwhile and desirable. Universities, for example, are total institutions, and they fit most of Goffman's criteria, as do most mental hospitals. General hospitals, which people enter voluntarily and frequently leave with gratitude, also meet Goffman's criteria on many counts. The attractiveness or unattractiveness of a total institution depends on its goals and the extent to which its participants are committed to these values. Mental hospitals have been unattractive institutions in that patients frequently were incarcerated involuntarily, ostensibly for their own welfare, but once in the hospital very little of a constructive nature was done for them. Moreover, the hospital had many destructive consequences. It often removed the patient from his community context and did little to maintain his relationships with family, friends, and community. It stigmatized him, often intimidated him, and in forcing adaptations to hospital life did little to maintain personal skills that would allow later readjustment to the community (59; 269). Because it was assumed that the course of mental illness was independent of the hospital environment (as in earlier centuries it was assumed that mentally ill persons did not require heat and furniture, as they were impervious to their environment), patients were left without work and other activities to stimulate their interest in living and the maintenance of life skills (767). In short, they were "institutionalized."

Institutionalism

John Wing (771) has argued that institutionalism is influenced by three general factors: (1) the actual social pressures to which an individual is exposed after admission to an institution; (2) the pattern of susceptibility or resistance to various types of institutional pressures that the individual possesses when he is first admitted; and (3) the length of time that the patient is exposed to these institutional pressures. Wing found that as length of hospital stay of schizophrenics increased (degree of impairment remaining constant) there is a progressive increase in the proportion of patients who appear apathetic about life outside the hospital. In contrast, very little relationship could be shown between length of stay and symptoms of schizophrenia measured by a clinical evaluation or behavior during a week of observations made by a senior ward nurse. In short, although marked symptom change did not occur with the increasing passage of time, hopefulness and willingness to attempt to cope with life stress deteriorated.

Wing (773) more recently has maintained that the components of the institutional syndrome are difficult to separate. Patients who become long-term residents tend to be selected not only on the basis of their illnesses, but also on the basis of their social characteristics. They often do not have strong ties with the community, family, or work; and are vulnerable because of their age, poverty, and lack of social interests and ties; also, these patients often are not concerned with the problems of personal liberties and restrictions and may find the hospital environment preferable to community residence because this environment meets their needs and makes minimal demands on them. Ludwig and Farrelly (452) point to the same phenomenon and maintain that the problem of getting hard-core schizophrenic patients out of the hospital results in part from the patients' chronicity or their desire to remain there. Ludwig and Farrelly's argument is well described by the statement of a schizophrenic patient who told them, "You can't railroad me out of here."

In a study of long-stay female schizophrenic patients in three British mental hospitals, Brown and Wing (93; 774) observed large social differences in the manner with which patients were dealt. For example, three times as many long-stay patients left the ward some time during the day at one hospital as compared with another, and there were similar differences among hospitals in the numbers possessing a toothbrush or such articles as rings and watches, in the provision of reasonable clothes, and in the amount of locker space. When differences in age, length of stay, and social class composition were taken into account, the hospital characterized by the greatest social deprivation contained significantly more patients who showed muteness or severe poverty of speech and fewer patients who were moderately ill. Brown and Wing considered the possibility that differences in the selective flow of patients into these three hospitals could account for the course that illness followed and the regime imposed on the patients. They found, however, that there was little support for the selection hypothesis and some evidence against it.

Although a hopeful attitude does not necessarily insure that rehabilitation can be achieved, a poor attitude among patients makes rehabilitation impossible. Institutional environments greatly influence the attitudes of patients. Mechanic (475), in studying two facilities for alcoholic patients, observed substantial differences in patient attitudes depending on whether they entered the facility voluntarily or involuntarily. While only 9 percent of the voluntary patients reported that they expected to drink again when leaving the facility, 37 percent of the involuntary patients reported an intention to drink again. The facility in which most of the involuntary patients were hospitalized also had a much smaller group of voluntary patients on the same ward. Although these voluntary patients did not appear to differ from voluntary patients at the other center, 53 percent reported an intention to drink after leaving the hospital. The differences between these two voluntary groups of patients were accounted for by the differing group environments within which they lived.

Although it is generally believed that the introduction of new drugs was the main factor in reversing the trend of long stays in mental hospitals, evidence from individual hospitals shows that this reversal began to occur before the changes in chemotherapy were inaugurated (95). For most of the large mental hospitals, however, the introduction of drugs provided the impetus in that it gave staff a new optimism and helped undermine the attitude of hopelessness and resignation that had become so common. Drug effects also appear to have made it more possible to handle patients without restraints and have made relatives more tolerant of the patient and more receptive to his return to the community (551).

In a classic experiment Pasamanick and his colleagues (551) randomized 152 schizophrenic patients referred to a state hospital into three groups: (1) a drug home-care group; (2) a placebo home-care group; and (3) a hospital control group. Patients treated at home were visited regularly by public-health nurses and were seen less frequently by other staff mental-health professionals. Patients were involved in the study for periods of from six to thirty months. The investigators found that 77 percent of the drug home-care patients remained continuously at home in contrast to 34 percent of those receiving placebos. They estimated, using the hospital control group as a base, that the 57 home patients receiving drugs saved over 4,800 days of hospitalization and that the 41 patients in the placebo group saved over 1,150 inpatient days. They also observed that members of the control group treated in the hospital required rehospitalization more frequently after they returned to the community than did the patients who were treated at home on drugs from the very start. A five-year follow-up of the patients in the original study (159), however, suggests the difficulty of maintaining a reasonable level of functioning without aggressive community care. Five years later the favorable differences in the drug home group were no longer evident; the investigators attribute this to the expiration of the experimental program.

The attitudes of relatives play an important role in release from mental hospitals or in avoidance of hospitalization in the first place (295). Studies have shown that hospitals often failed to return chronic patients to the community because of problems of resettlement even though their symptoms had diminished or disappeared. Such patients frequently continued to live in hospitals, with little effort made to return them to the community unless there was a relative willing to receive the patient (89; 615). Brown has demonstrated that whether the patient was visited during the first two months of his hospital stay provided a clear distinction between patients staying less than and more than two years in the hospital (89). Prior to the changes in Britain in hospital policies concerning retention, Brown found that 75 percent of patients who were visited were released in less than two years; among patients who were not visited, 83 percent stayed in the hospital more than two years. Brown repeated the analysis using data on admissions after hospital policies had changed, hypothesizing that the relationship between visiting and length of retention would be diminished substantially. This hypothesis was confirmed; under new hospital policies, efforts were being made to relocate patients who were not visited and who probably had few relatives or friends who could support them in an attempt to readjust to the community. It has become easier to relocate such persons with the development of community care in Britain.

The changes that took place with the introduction of tranquilizers in the mid-1950s also appear to have diminished social background differences in release rates. Previously, the rate of release was substantially related to the patient's education or occupation, but this difference decreased significantly in the later period. Linn (445), in a study of Saint Elizabeth's Hospital in Washington, D.C, found that in 1953–1954, before tranquilizers were used, only 28 percent of the psychotic patients with grade-school education were released within a year as compared with 46 percent of those with higher educational status. After the introduction of tranquilizers two years later, the comparable release figures were 62 percent and 73 percent.

Moving to a social-psychological level of analysis, many investigators have noted the manner by which expectation systems affect the behavior and attitudes of mental patients. The patient who finds himself in the hospital or in a therapeutic relationship is expected to conform in a general way to a range of expectations relevant to patients (206; 269; 477). Within many of the models available for dealing with psychiatric patients, treatment can take place only if the patient is willing to recognize that he suffers from an emotional difficulty and is ready to invest some effort in helping the staff help him. Patients who deviate from these expectations—who deny that they have problems or who attempt to place their problems within a perspective inconsistent with psychiatric practice—are disruptive to the hospital and disturbing to staff and other patients. Patients who attempt to deny that they are sick—although such denials may constitute efforts to "save face"—may find their denials viewed by staff as further manifestations of illness, and not infrequently staff will confront patients with evidence of bizarre behavior engaged in at some previous time. Such confrontations are often ways of pressuring the patient to adopt the expected role of the patient and to recognize that he is sick. In short, there are many pressures on the patient from staff and other patients to organize his behavior within the context of a patient role. Indeed, failure to do this is likely to create a variety of problems for the patient in accommodating to hospital life.

From all indications, the introduction of psychoactive drugs made it possible for hospital staff to control certain kinds of symptoms that they found very troublesome and that created considerable difficulty for the patient within the context of the hospital. Since patients' aggressive and agitated behavior could be moderated, staff members had diminished need for restraints and more confidence in their ability to control the patients' behavior. Thus, indirectly, the introduction of drugs probably served to make patients more susceptible to influence and suggestion, and ward personnel developed greater confidence in influencing patient behavior through means other than coercion. Whether the change in hospital careers resulted directly or indirectly from the new drugs is for the most part an academic question. There is no doubt, however, that this new technology had a pervasive influence on social change.

Alternatives to Hospitalization

The development of new ideologies in mental-health care in the 1960s signaled a trend toward a variety of types of community care. Patients who had formerly been housed in mental hospitals now lived in the community with families, in their own rooms and apartments, in sheltered situations such as halfway houses, in board and care facilities, and in nursing homes. Some of the impetus for community care derived from economic problems in supporting increased and improved mental-hospital care; when the shift came to community care, administrative processes of release moved much more rapidly than the development of effective community-care services. Frequently patients were returned to situations in the community in which they were isolated, unemployed, and received little care, and in some instances were worse off than they had been in the hospital. It soon became apparent that disabilities associated with institutionalism could develop as readily in community contexts and nursing homes as in the traditional mental hospital. Social isolation, lack of participation, and an apathy syndrome were common characteristics of the chronic mental patient who was now residing in the community.

As hospital policies shift toward returning and retaining patients in the community, new mechanisms and supports are required not only to help the inadequate patient maintain himself but also to help the families and living groups who interact with the patient to cope with social crises. "Community care," like "human relations" and "mental hygiene," is an ideological movement concerning the care of the mentally ill, and proponents are sometimes carried away in their enthusiasm. For the most part, however, community-care technologies are still undeveloped, and in returning impaired patients to the community we do not eliminate illness or the social problems that illness may cause. Rather we shift some of the responsibilities and burdens of care from the hospital to the community (95). Communities are willing to tolerate such increased burdens because they, too, come to accept the ideologies implied in new policies toward caring for the mentally ill. Since mental illness does cause community and family difficulties, changes in retention and release policies on the part of mental hospitals must be accompanied by the willingness to provide services to the community that help people to cope with the crises that inevitably occur (551). Although it is not clear as yet what services are most valuable to the community, it seems plain that shifting the burden of care of the mentally ill from hospital to community must be accompanied by continued efforts to provide the best possible system of services to aid families with a mentally ill member.

There have been a variety of demonstrations and experiments concerning alternatives to mental hospitals (341). Among the more exciting examples is the "Training in Community Living" program, a rigorous experiment to compare an educational-coping approach to patients in the community with a progressive hospital-care unit (664). An unselected group of patients seeking admission to a mental hospital were randomly assigned to experimental and control groups. Subsequent analysis showed that these randomized groups did not differ on any significant variable. While the control group was given in-hospital treatment linked with community aftercare services, the experimental group was assisted in developing an independent living situation in the community, given social support, and taught simple living skills. Patients in both groups were evaluated by independent researchers at intervals of four, eight, and twelve months. The experience indicated that it was possible for patients who were quite impaired to be cared for almost exclusively in the community. Moreover, compared with control patients, patients in the experimental group made a more adequate community adjustment as evidenced by higher earnings from work, involvement in more social activities, more contact with friends, and more satisfaction with their life situation. At each follow-up the experimental patients had less symptomatology than the controls. In short, assuming that a logical and aggressive community program is developed, it is possible to treat even very impaired patients effectively in a community context. Thus far, however, the development of such services has been very slow.

One trend particularly characteristic of California, which has been closing its mental hospitals, is to depend on local board and care facilities as an alternative to mental hospitals. It is difficult to characterize such facilities in general because they vary so much in size, program, and quality. Some are excellent supportive facilities that improve the quality of the patient's life, while others provide physical and social care inferior to even the poorest mental hospitals (629). A similar situation exists in nursing homes, where there is great variability and where many patients, once admitted, lead an inactive, uninvolved life with little program to minimize their disabilities and improve the quality of their lives (674). It is obvious that all of these institutions require more careful appraisal and monitoring and more social regulation to protect the interests of the dependent patients for whom they assume responsibility.

Other Contextual Influences

Investigators who have studied mental hospitals have emphasized the manner in which unfavorable hospital environments can produce disability above and beyond the expected pattern resulting from the natural course of the patient's condition. If the problem is broadened, then investigators must be concerned with the more general issue of the way different environmental contexts may affect the outcome of the patient's condition. The study of environmental contexts must include, therefore, both hospital and nonhospital influences. In the long run it may be more important to understand the influence of family and work contexts on the course of illness in contrast to the literature's emphasis on hospitals. Once we recognize that the course of illness cannot be separated from the context within which it occurs, we will be in a better position to understand how mentally ill people can be supported and maintained.

We have a great deal to learn about environmental and psychological influences on illness in general and the ways they may act to modify the course of a particular condition. The range of such influences is suggested by Querido and his colleagues (571), who studied 1,630 patients suffering from a variety of medical conditions in a general hospital in Amsterdam. They found a significant difference in the chance of recovery between patients who had to cope with problems apart from their physical illness and those who did not. Querido concludes:

> Our investigation has shown that a favourable clinical prognosis was made in 1,128 of 1,630 cases. This means that medical science offered the possibility of recovery to over 69 per cent, but our follow-up showed that only 660 of the 1,128 favourable prognoses were realized. Even if this phenomenon of "distress" is regarded merely as a plodding and worrying attitude to

life or as a psychological peculiarity of the patient, it is plain that such a mental attitude on the part of the patient reduces the efficiency of the hospital by almost half [571, p. 46].

Although one may wish to attribute Querido's results to other than environmental factors, the influence of environmental factors on illness becomes evident in such studies as the one by Brown, Monck, Carstairs, and Wing (94). These investigators followed for one year 128 schizophrenic men released from the hospital. The severity of symptoms suffered by these patients was assessed just before discharge, and 101 of the patients were seen at home with their relatives two weeks after discharge. During this home interview the amount of "expressed emotion" in the family was measured. The investigators found that patients returning to a relative who showed "high emotional involvement" (based on measures of "expressed emotion," hostility, and dominance) deteriorated more frequently than patients returning to a relative who showed "low emotional involvement." Although it is not perfectly clear whether emotional involvement in general or the particular kind measured accounts for the deterioration, this study shows clearly the way the family environment is associated with the patient's ability to function. Obviously a great deal more work is required in this area before the precise factors that affect deterioration in positive and negative ways are isolated (91).

Unfortunately, most of what we know about contextual influences on illness states comes from studies of the hospital rather than from other contexts. Basically, the literature is concerned with two types of factors: deprivational and human relations. Many of the studies of large mental hospitals emphasized deprivational features and noted that such deficiencies as lack of staff, facilities, personal possessions, and personal freedoms had a demoralizing effect on patients and adversely affected their conditions. Three types of effect are implied in the discussion of deprivations. First, deprivation of adequate diet, exercise, and amenities led to poor health. Second, it is suggested that lack of facilities and personal possessions and liberties was demoralizing in that it led patients to feel a lack of dignity and worth. Third, it is argued that the scarcity of resources required greater adaptations on the part of staff members to maintain control and get the most pressing work accomplished, and this led to rigidity, regimentation, use of patients as workers, and threats and punishments directed toward uncooperative patients (59; 269; 559; 613).

The human-relations advocates see disturbances of human relations and communication as a central problem within mental hospitals (110; 111; 559; 663). For the most part, however, these investigators have studied small hospitals rich in staff and resources. Stanton and Schwartz, for example, provide abundant examples of the way staff conflicts are related to patient disturbances, and they argue strongly that administrative matters directly affect patient behavior (663).

Educational Coping Models

In my earlier discussion of coping and adaptation (chapter 10) I emphasized that successful performance depended not only on psychological state but also on coping skills, preparation and practice, and networks of social support. I have also indicated that new programs of community care, such as "Training in Community Living," have built on an educational coping model in order to improve social functioning and the quality of life of patients in the community. Most clinicians who work with the mentally ill, however, still focus primarily on a developmental-historical approach. They emphasize psychological barriers and techniques and give relatively little attention to the strategies or techniques through which persons deal with tasks and other people. This failure is implicit in the psychological bias and in the entire orientation to the patient. Instead of exploring the nature of the patient's life difficulties that lead him to seek care or lead others to insist that he be removed from his social situation, emphasis is given to early child development and relationships. Instead of attempting to assess the patient's techniques of dealing with work and other people through independent interviews with reliable informants, often reliance is placed exclusively on the perceptions, views, and perspectives of the patient. Moreover, therapy designed to change the patient often is undertaken without giving careful consideration to the situation and problems to which he must return, the skills he will require, and the attitudes and feelings about his disabilities among significant persons in his environment. Obviously all of these aspects may be undertaken to some extent on one occasion or another, but I suggest that the manner in which these areas are investigated and the relative attention they receive in the formulation of care implies that they are too frequently viewed as secondary in the care of the patient.

It would be foolish to feel confident that the educational perspective will make a revolutionary difference in the provision of care. Skills are difficult to teach and resources for teaching skills are limited. Nor has it been conclusively proven that the learning of such skills would make an essential difference to patient rehabilitation. Comparatively speaking, however, the coping approach sets a more modest task for the therapist than the rather nebulous notions of "psychic reorganization" and "reintegration" that often are viewed as the outcome of extensive psychotherapy. It is reasonable to believe that we can improve patients' coping effectiveness either by changing or modifying their level of instrumental efforts or by attempting to alter the social conditions under which they live so that their skills are more adequate and their disabilities less obvious. We must recognize, of course, that often a person's ability to accomplish difficult tasks or to deal with the social environment depends on aspects of his development and status over which we have little control: intelligence, health and physical stamina, past psychological preparation and education, and material wealth. But frequently patients have psychological and social potentialities that could be mobilized with adequate instruction, preparation and environmental supports.

One advantage of this approach is that it focuses attention and emphasis on the patient's current level of social functioning and encourages a much more detailed and careful assessment of how the patient functions in a variety of nonhospital settings. Thus the mental-health professional is in a better position to appreciate those areas in which the patient's functioning is grossly deficient, as well as those that are more easily remediable. This view focuses the therapist's attention more directly by specifying what is and is not worthy of emphasis and by keeping the attention of the patient on his present condition and future needs.

A person's ability to achieve mastery in any situation depends on his ability to mobilize effort when effort is necessary, on the manner in which efforts are organized and applied, on his psychological and instrumental abilities and skills, and on the extent to which he has social and environmental supports. The mobilization of effort, assuming some level of motivation, may be facilitated by developing personal and external controls that make it easier to adopt good work habits. Apparently a frequent technique used by persons undertaking a large variety of tasks involves breaking the task into a number of smaller units that can be completed within a relatively short time so that the felt accomplishment motivates the attack on the following units. Such "spacing techniques" are used by writers, long-distance runners, drivers, and persons engaged in repetitive tasks (207). It is likely that persons who suffer from a problem of mobilizing their intended efforts at work can benefit from a routinized, structured job, because such fluctuations in work perseverance are likely to be minimized if the flow of work continues with a limited number of decisions required of the worker. In general, from a rehabilitation viewpoint persons who suffer from difficulties in mobilizing efforts probably do not prosper in work involving little structure. From the viewpoint of retraining patients with perseverance problems, carefully scheduled work often might be an advantage in the development of work habits and functional attitudes.

The problem of the organization of effort involves the manner in which persons anticipate situations, the ways they seek information about them, the extent of planning, preparation, and rehearsal in a psychological and social sense, the testing of problem solutions, the consideration and preparation of alternative courses of action should the situation require it, and the allocation of time and efforts. When one begins to look at this problem with mental patients, it is astonishing how poorly their efforts are organized (649). In general psychiatric practice the ineffectual organization of effort often is seen as a byproduct of the patient's condition and not a basic component of it. From the viewpoint of intervention, however, attack on some of these problems of organization may produce valuable results for the patient's self-confidence and mental state generally. We sometimes fail to give due emphasis to the obvious fact that successful performance results in large part from the way people learn to approach problems and learn from their past experience and training and from the experience of others (702). If patients seem unable to learn from experience, it seems reasonable to help the patient assess his situation better and to increase his own skills in doing this.

Patients frequently lack simple information, skills, and abilities; because such patients often come from an impoverished family and social environment, it is really not so incredible that they lack simple preparatory approaches to life. Many of these skills can be taught as an aspect of rehabilitation, and the acquisition of new skills can inspire confidence and further involvement in other aspects of the treatment process. Similarly, there is no reason why attempts to improve more complex instrumental skills should not be undertaken. Success in community life depends largely on the skills persons have in dealing effectively with others. Differences in the development and application of such skills may vary substantially by social class, and rehabilitation may involve overcoming handicaps of social position as well as those of psychological impairment. Through experience and practice persons learn to deal with a variety of problems in diverse ways. Persons who have had more opportunities for varied interpersonal experiences are more likely to develop effective social repertories. This is an important area, especially in the rehabilitation of the culturally impoverished.

Interpersonal skills are difficult to communicate and teach because they are often subtle and frequently are not overtly commented upon or even recognized. This applies particularly to the presentation of self (268) and the various forms of interpersonal negotiation that make up such a large part of our social contact with others. A partial list of such techniques or modes of relevant behavior may make the point somewhat clearer: initiating new relationships; developing alternative social relationships; distributing interpersonal investments as a preparation against the threat of loss; interpersonal influence techniques; techniques of ingratiation; handling hostility and aggression through humor; interpersonal trading and compromise; learning to keep interpersonal channels open and yet protect oneself simultaneously (interpersonal allocation and pacing techniques); learning how to withdraw interpersonally in a graceful fashion and learning how to allow others to escape embarrassment; participation, helpfulness, and developing social currency (making others like you). We are not used to thinking about behavior in this way, and it is difficult to do so without either voicing platitudes or reverting to a vocabulary of personality traits. A great deal of work is required to describe more adequately these subtle but important interpersonal skills.

Finally, we cannot overestimate the importance of social support and stimulation, but we must recognize that social networks not only provide support but also can be extremely detrimental in adaptation by encouraging excessive dependence, by stimulating excitement, anxiety, and competition, and by interfering with coping efforts (94). The effective use of social support involves planning if one is to take advantage of family and group resources and at the same time avoid typical difficulties. There are many dimensions to the problems of providing an adequate social context for psychiatric rehabilitation. Both living accommodations and work vary widely in variety and intensity of social stimulation. Work-mates and family members are likely to have definite attitudes toward the manifestations of the patient's disabilities, and particular attitudes and living conditions can have damaging effects on rehabilitation. Thus adequate preparation of the patient's family may be as important in the long run as preparation of the patient himself. Such considerations involving social stimulation apply similarly to the hospital environment and to the training and preparation of staff engaged in rehabilitation efforts.

Other social features may complicate the rehabilitation problem. Matters of traveling, housing conditions, proximity to the homes of relatives, help with chores during particularly stressful periods, difficulties with the law, and financial problems all become pertinent and require some assessment and consideration in resettlement decisions. All of these matters are considered in any good psychiatric center, but casual consideration is no substitute for a careful, direct assessment depending not only on the patient for information but also on a number of others to whom he has important social bonds.

One of the major difficulties in attempts to improve coping skills of patients is the problem of assessment of patient needs. Since it is impossible to observe the patient in a wide variety of life circumstances and relationships, appraisals must be based on information provided by informants. It is not clear that we know how to ask the questions that will elicit the most relevant facts. Until we have an adequate social history-taking device, such coping approaches will be handicapped. Such assessments must concentrate on the manner in which the patient copes with work, family, and a variety of interpersonal situations. Patients usually are unable to make these assessments themselves. However, it is possible through careful interviewing and systematic attempts to observe behavior of the patients in a variety of settings to get a much more adequate picture of patients' skills and capacities in dealing with interpersonal and task settings. By focusing attention on how the patient gets on with various significant persons in his life (his family, siblings, employers, workmates, and relatives) and the manner in which he organizes his efforts to deal with tasks and work, one can get a good idea of coping skills. This is especially true if careful investigation of the patient is linked with efforts to question various relatives and friends in identical areas. It is similarly important to gain some appreciation of how the patient lives his life: the ways he spends his leisure and meets his responsibilities, the difficulties he has had, and the expectations and aspirations he holds. Only after such assessments are made does it really become possible to appreciate the areas in which it is feasible to attempt to produce change and the areas that are relatively less responsive to change. Particularly important is some appreciation of the ways the patient appears to others at work and in his home context as well as in the hospital, because changing superficial traits that threaten others or make the patient noticeable can often ease the patient's adjustment to a new situation. Finally, one must have a good conception of the extent to which the patient's disability is a product of forces over which he has little control, such as a poor housing environment, relatives who have an intolerant view of his condition, and inability to find suitable work.

Looking at present-day psychiatric services, one of the major problems is the inactivity of patients and the loss of time orientations. Failure to remedy these problems produces serious disabilities for living in a modern industrial society. The activities provided within the context of rehabilitation programs are often of the "play" variety, and patients frequently have difficulty finding meaning in the various new "social therapies" that may appear to them as group "griping." Often the hospital personnel are themselves vague as to the role and function of these group aspects of care in the rehabilitation of the patient. The introduction of ideas about the therapeutic community certainly has been important to the extent that these ideas implied a humanistic attitude about care, but the functions of group processes in rehabilitation never have been clearly worked out.

Work for mental patients has been a useful innovation in that it implies a healthy attitude about rehabilitation, involves patients in activities relevant for rehabilitation, plays some part in preventing institutionalism, and often helps buttress the patient's low confidence in himself. Thus work often plays a role in avoiding one of the most deleterious experiences in maintaining coping skills and efforts—the expenditure of large periods of time doing little of personal and social significance, and resultant deterioration.

Yet work presents many difficult problems in rehabilitation programs. Often the variety of work and level of skill required are not compatible with the patient's needs and abilities, and it is conceivable that the wrong kinds of work for particular patients can be harmful experiences in that they dampen motivation and demonstrate the extent to which the patient has fallen in the hierarchy of skills and competence in the view of the community. The ability to bring into treatment settings the variety and levels of work necessary for good rehabilitation programs depends largely on external conditions involving community attitudes and the employment market. In the final analysis, if work in rehabilitation is training for life, high levels of work are required for many patients, and it is usually advantageous to have patients employed in ordinary community jobs.

An appropriate model for rehabilitation requires considerable flexibility. In many cases an educational model seems more applicable than a medical model to what is often attempted and visualized in good rehabilitation programs. In one sense the ideal program might be viewed as a school in which the educational program, like a good tutorial, takes into account the social, educational, and psychological needs of the student. In the final analysis, mental patients suffer from inadequate and improper socialization. They have failed to acquire the psychological and coping skills necessary for reasonable social adjustment. Such failures may be the product of inherited incapacities, brain damage, impoverished childhood circumstances, inadequate training for dealing with stress, or a variety of other reasons. The source of the difficulty is not the most important factor from the educational perspective; the question as to whether the remedy can be effected by some form of educational program is the more salient issue.

The idea of mental-health programs as educational programs is not necessarily an extension of the various gimmicks and pseudotherapies that have been instituted from time to time without clear conceptions of their role and function. The clear function of the school model would be to direct attention to the need of patients to improve or develop new task and interpersonal skills that would enhance their chances of making a successful adjustment to community life. Such an approach, of course, is not exclusive of physical therapies and other psychiatric procedures that play an important role in preparing patients for and supporting them during their educational training. But rehabilitation is seen within a perspective of patient retraining to the extent that it is possible.

There are many advantages in an educational model as compared with a medical one. Successful adaptation requires some ability to act as one's own agent, and one of the disadvantages of the medical models is the tremendous dependence the patient develops on physicians, nurses, and other ancillaries who encourage and reward dependency. An educational approach would encourage higher expectations concerning personal responsibility and initiative. Moreover, the educational model is a common one in our society. Although esteem for education may not be shared equally by members of all social strata, the didactic model is familiar to persons from all social segments and one with which they all have had considerable experience. Such a model may be far more acceptable to patients, especially lower-class patients, who find most psychiatric methods difficult to understand and who have greater familiarity with the educational approach than with modern psychodynamics. Moreover, because patients share to a greater extent in the educational process and are more likely to understand the goals toward which they are moving, it becomes considerably more likely that they can play a meaningful, active role in their own rehabilitation—the development of new skills. In this sense active striving toward self-improvement may also be useful in bolstering a patient's feelings of self-confidence and competence.

From the viewpoint of the care of the mentally ill, the educational model can be particularly useful in that it makes the difficulty of the patient appear more reasonable to the uninformed and minimizes the stigma attached to the patient's difficulty. Because this approach places such emphasis on the normal potentialities of the mental patient, it may decrease social distance between treatment personnel and patients and between hospital and community. There is evidence that others find mental patients more acceptable when their problems are posed in interpersonal terms (as problems of living) in contrast to "illness of the mind." The proper organization of an educationally oriented rehabilitation program would depend on the attitude and training of staff. If staff were imbued with old concepts of catering to patient dependency, such attitudes would do much to interfere with the development of such a program. Thus the successful implementation of the idea depends on staff preparation and the training and development of new staff perspectives.

Finally, when we think of hospitals as educational institutions we must be clear as to what kind of educational model is advocated. The educational model is not a cheap and easy way out of the problem of caring for the mentally ill. In many cases the time and efforts of a first-rate tutorial system will be required, but the tutors need not be psychiatrists, psychologists, or social workers. The teaching of different skills will require different types and levels of staff, and no single professional group could provide the many necessary services. Because patients often lack self-confidence and basic learning approaches, the educational program should be tailored to the needs and levels of skill of patients. One does not teach the student calculus until he has learned some algebra, and it is a devastating experience for a person to find himself in a context in which he is expected to learn techniques for which he lacks basic preparation. Thus such a program must allow for the scheduling and reinforcing of mastery experiences, because one of the greatest stimuli for future striving is the experience of mastery and accomplishment.

If such an enterprise is to be successful, it cannot be a careless venture. It involves careful planning and elaborate assessments of patient assets and needs, as well as an assessment of community opportunities. In many areas an individualized approach will be required. Thus it is not an easy or even an inexpensive solution. I emphasize this because one can easily pervert the educational model in the care of the mentally ill to promote nonrehabilitation perspectives and stances. The major component of the approach just described is a change in viewing the care of the mentally ill from an effort for reforming psyches to one of changing skills.

I cannot end this discussion without returning explicitly to the question of values. All approaches to care imply particular values. A coping approach obviously assumes that patients should develop skills that allow their reabsorption into the social fabric. There will be those who find such an implication obnoxious. Indeed, one of the appealing aspects of psychodynamic therapies is that they imply no such specific adjustment philosophies, and the educational model if applied involuntarily can be wasteful and damaging. In any case, the educational model is not incongruous with personal choice. If used with a democratic perspective, it offers patients opportunities to redress basic inadequacies and deficiencies. Patients who prefer to reject these attempts to readjust them to their social context are obviously difficult to integrate into such a program. In any case, the problem of values is an aspect of all rehabilitation approaches, and the extent to which respect for human dignity and freedom is shown in any program depends largely on the way the program is administered.

Whether we can teach coping skills to mental patients in any significant sense is a matter for careful assessment and evaluation. What is perhaps more important than the particular techniques suggested and advocated is the willingness to think about and to reconsider alternative methods for organizing and providing care. Once one breaks away from the medical model in its various forms, it becomes apparent that there are many alternative perspectives for developing care resources (121). We need to know a good deal more about the ways such alternatives may be implemented and the effects they may have in practice.

Chapter 17

FERMENT AND CHANGE

One of the major difficulties in organizing community environments for the care of the mentally ill is the lack of predictability of the social and political climate. Part of the problem also resides in the fact that we have not yet learned how to balance successfully, or even measure, the social costs for the community against the advantages and ideologies of community care. Despite much rhetoric, there is continuing difficulty in maintaining a supportive network of mental-health services, in part because of funding problems and the lack of stability in funding patterns; in part because of the difficulty in continuing a sense of innovation and momentum in the care of chronic patients, which is a frustrating task; in part because of the difficulties resulting from the reactions and pressures of communities that accept the idea of community care, but in other people's communities; and in part because knowledge essential for effective treatment is lacking.

There is a large gap between the enunciation and the implementation of goals. It is one thing to assert a right to treatment; it is quite another to get legislatures to appropriate the funds or build the network of services required to implement the right. We can talk about less restrictive alternatives and spin legal theories, but it is to no avail if we lack choices in levels or patterns of care. We can theorize about the constructive role of appropriate work in the rehabilitation of mental patients and its contribution to the sense of dignity and self-esteem of the patient, but we have an uphill battle when 10 percent of the labor force is unemployed and employers face a buyer's market.

As we have moved a larger proportion of patients into community-care contexts, we have come face to face with massive resistance from politicians, communities, and neighborhoods. No one has adequate information to assess the extent to which the problems that received considerable publicity in New York and California are characteristic of the nation as a whole, but it is evident that in most areas of the country there has been inadequate development of networks of appropriate services consistent with the prevalent rhetoric. A recent inquiry in California, examining the social functioning of patients in board-and-care facilities throughout the state, found that the best predictor of their levels of integration was the degree of community acceptance of the facility (629). Mental-health officials, instead of making efforts to develop an appropriate community climate, often follow the line of least resistance, and locate patients in areas that already suffer from disorganization and anomie. Moreover, there is ample indication that a growing number of patients previously managed within the mental-health system are being processed through the criminal-justice system, charged with minor and vague violations to justify their removal from the community.

In implementing social policy relevant to the desegregation of schools and busing, we have learned how difficult it is to translate social goals into action. Mental health officials must give attention to the concentration of mental patients being relocated in the community, if for no other reason than obvious political desire to avoid a community backlash. While the courts have not sustained the right of a community to pass ordinances restricting the residence of mental patients, it is hard to believe that a community that wishes to do so can be a healthy place for carrying out programs of community integration. Even the most cursory review of the history of mental-health law, I believe, would support the proposition that no matter how wise the courts or how passionate the beliefs of public-interest lawyers who have come to the defense of the mentally ill, the development of effective and just solutions depends on the larger context of care and the quality of program alternatives. No legal theory or social ideology, no matter how forceful, can substitute for the willingness of the community to provide the resources for adequate care or for the availability of knowledgeable and committed personnel who are willing to struggle with the frustrating problems involved in providing continuing care on a long-term basis for chronic patients.

In recent years major changes have taken place in the provision of mental-health care, in part because of the development of new technologies such as drugs and new administrative attitudes and in part because of the momentum of new ideologies, changing social values, and the growth of a vigorous movement in support of the civil liberties of the mentally ill. In understanding where we are, it is helpful to examine where we have been in the past two decades.

Two Decades of Constructive Chaos

The hospital pattern of care for the mentally ill in the United States evolved over a long period, and the conditions to which the mentally ill were exposed were brutal and deprived. In the first part of the twentieth century the major humanizing influence on mental-patient care in the United States was the mental hygiene movement. Clifford Beers, a former mental patient who exposed the dehumanizing aspects of mental-patient care, began a new humanistic ideology encompassed in the organization of the National Association for Mental Health. Although the mental hygiene movement stimulated improvement in hospital conditions and concern for the mentally ill, it did little to retard the pattern of providing for the mentally ill in large custodial institutions.

The pattern of psychiatric care that existed in 1955 and still exists to some extent today, but in less pronounced form, was less than encouraging. Psychiatry had become an important specialty, yet the best-trained practitioners, unlike their European counterparts, usually practiced on a private basis and dealt primarily with middle-class neurotic patients. The more disturbed psychotic patients, who were committed to mental hospitals, had little intensive contact with professionally trained helpers. In 1950 approximately 85 percent of the psychiatric specialists were engaged outside the public mental hospitals, although such hospitals had approximately 85 percent of all resident mental patients in the United States (559). Similarly, in 1950 only about one-fifth of the trained psychiatric social workers and a very small number of psychologists and graduate nurses worked in mental hospitals. The mental hospital was run for the most part by untrained attendants.

In recent years there has been a substantial improvement in the staffing of mental hospitals, but the bulk of the services of the psychiatrist continue to be distributed on a private fee-for-service basis, and too little attention of American psychiatrists is devoted to the problems of lower-status psychotic patients. This is in sharp contrast to the British pattern of psychiatric care, where the best-trained psychiatric practitioners are concentrated in public programs. It is evident in the United States that many of the most severely impaired patients have been neglected or provided with limited and unimaginative programs, and that much that could be accomplished toward their rehabilitation with a proper orientation and motivation has been left undone (82; 368).

Many European psychiatrists see American psychiatric practice as an aberrant activity molded by motivations for economic gain obtainable through private practice. Although economic factors are relevant, the reasons for the course of American psychiatric practice are more complex than an economic interpretation would suggest. American psychiatrists have been influenced more by psychoanalytic ideas and less by traditional medical ideas than their European counterparts; this professional stance gives them little confidence in treating severely disordered patients who are not particularly sophisticated or receptive to psychiatry. The well-trained, psychologically oriented psychiatrist who chooses to work in hospital settings or in community-care programs for impaired patients, thus sacrificing professional status, money, and psychological comfort, quickly becomes frustrated when he realizes the inappropriateness of his training and skills in dealing with large groups of disordered patients. Psychotherapy is not a feasible solution, yet that is what the American psychiatrist has been trained to do. In addition, it is frequently difficult to obtain involvement and cooperation from attendants and nurses because such staff often wish to maintain their own power and position. They must control and supervise the activities of patients, and they tend to resist changes that make this already difficult task more arduous (478; 480; 613). It is not surprising, therefore, that the typical American psychiatrist enters private practice, which is consistent with his training and theoretical frame of reference and financially and psychologically more comfortable. This trend is further aided by the psychiatric status system in the United States, which places the highest value on psychotherapy and a very low value on mental-hospital practice or rehabilitation.

The extent to which the distribution of psychiatric services is seen as a problem will depend on the frame of reference used in viewing the situation. If one assumes that psychiatric specialists, like other medical specialists, should tackle the most difficult and serious problems of morbidity, then the distribution of psychiatric services seems somewhat misdirected. In contrast, if one assumes that psychiatrists should do what they know best how to do—and many psychiatrists are most proficient in psychotherapy skills—then it is logical that psychiatrists be located in office-based practice. The latter view implies that psychiatry is radically different from other specialties in the medical world. Moreover, there is little evidence that psychiatrists perform psychotherapy more expertly than do many other types of health professionals. One can reasonably argue that the proper work of the psychiatrist should be focused on traditional mental illness and not on more ordinary problems of living.

Psychiatrists are not a homogeneous group; they differ in their orientations, interests, and skills. Unfortunately, we do not have any thorough studies of the social structure of the psychiatric profession, but some smaller investigations provide some indications of the profession's organization. Hollingshead and Redlich (330), in describing New Haven psychiatrists, suggest that there are two basic types who differ in their method of therapy and training for therapy. The first group have an analytic and psychological orientation (the A-P psychiatrist), and they treat the patient by analyzing his behavior, relationships, and motivation according to various psychoanalytic and psychological theories. Those who are less orthodox practice a variety of forms of "insight therapy," but for the most part their procedures are nondirective. Such psychiatrists tend not to work in mental hospitals, and in New Haven the dominant university psychiatrists were of the A-P variety. In contrast, the directive and organic psychiatrists (the D-O group) attempt to change the patient through directive and supportive methods such as assertion, suggestion, manipulation, and reassurance. The D-O psychiatrist is more likely to rely on drugs, physical methods, and other medical procedures. It is not surprising, then, that the D-O psychiatrist is more willing to work in the mental-hospital context than his A-P counterpart.

With the success of various drugs in psychiatric treatment, the development of new programs and approaches, and a diminution of orthodoxy in psychiatric training in America, these two types have become merged to a greater extent than they were in 1950. However, there is no question that the A-P psychiatrist dominates American psychiatry to a much greater extent than in most other countries. Although there is a strong group of A-P psychiatrists in Britain, for the most part British psychiatry is strongly organized around the D-O perspective.

Szasz and Nemiroff (697) have taken exception to Hollingshead and Redlich's classification of psychiatrists and, in a factor analytic study of the opinions of psychoanalysts, argue that there is little support for the assumption that psychiatric practitioners can be divided into two discrete groups. Because Szasz and Nemiroff's study was devoted exclusively to psychoanalysts, their data cannot possibly test the validity of the Hollingshead-Redlich classification. However, they did find that A-P psychiatrists do use drugs and a variety of directive and organic methods. Although the Hollingshead-Redlich portraits are not exact representations of reality, they suggest the varying orientations that characterize different psychiatrists.

The Mental Health Study Act

Although there were some advances in the United States in manpower development and mental-health research following World War II, they had little impact on mental-hospital practice; federal aid to the states for mental-health services actually decreased during the Korean War. The states were faced with a fiscal crisis, and were seeking ways to reduce mental health costs (625). Although the tranquilizers were being introduced—thus providing new opportunities—most states had inadequate facilities, personnel, and financial resources for implementing new ideas about care. The Hoover commission, studying government reorganization, criticized the abrupt reduction in federal support for state mental-health services, and the states themselves were fully aware of their limitations.

Congressional action in 1955 was a response to the crises in individual states characterized by severe shortages of personnel and facilities and the inability, with the resources available, to break the harmful custodial pattern. In 1961 the Joint Commission on Mental Illness and Health, established by the Congress, published its well-known report, *Action for Mental Health* (368). This report was sweeping in its conclusions and bold in its demands for change in mental-health care. It argued strongly for an increased program of services and more funds for basic long-term mental-health research. It recommended that expenditures in the mental-health field be doubled in five years and tripled in ten years. It argued for new and better recruitment and training programs for mental-health workers. It suggested the expansion of treatment programs for acutely ill patients in all forms of facilities including community mental-health clinics, general hospitals, and mental hospitals. It argued for the establishment of community mental-health clinics, suggesting that one would be appropriate for every 50,000 persons in the population. It attacked the large state mental hospitals and suggested that these be converted to smaller regional intensive treatment centers with no more than 1,000 beds. It recommended new programs of care for chronic patients as well as for aftercare and other rehabilitation services. In short, these were wide-ranging and ambitious demands, and they fell on receptive ears in Washington. Many of these recommendations resulted in federal programs. Perhaps the most far-reaching legislation was the program for building and later staffing community mental-health clinics.

The new direction of mental-health policies in the United States, however, did not flow directly from the report of the joint commission. *Action for Mental Health* (368) was largely an ideological document, sufficiently ambiguous to allow various interest groups to read into it what they wished. It is therefore not surprising that a vigorous political battle resulted at the federal level between those psychiatrists with a public-health viewpoint, who wished to develop completely new precedents for mental patient care, and those psychiatrists more wedded to the traditional medical model, who felt that considerable federal assistance should be invested in improving the quality of mental hospitals. Those who favored a more radical break with the past system of providing mental-health services through state and federal hospitals were more influential with President Kennedy, and the final decision was to give independent mental-health centers first priority. This was a crucial decision and one that implicitly endorsed the viewpoint of the public-health psychiatrists that serious mental illness was not inherently different from the larger range of psychological difficulties common in the community.

Implementation of many of the recommendations of the joint commission was considered within a favorable social climate. First, the American economy was then in a strong position, and abundant funds were available for meeting domestic needs. Second, the president himself was committed to the program in mental health and mental retardation, and the mental-health professional community presented a united front. Third, psychiatric drugs had changed the climate of mental-health care as well as administrative attitudes, and the public was favorable to improved mental-health programs. Finally, the harmful consequences of the custodial hospital environment had been effectively illustrated, and the public had become aware of the unequal access to psychiatric services of the poor as compared with the rich. The success of the joint commission was due less to its insightful analysis than to the receptive climate in the country at the time it produced its report. Probably any reasonable set of recommendations would have been acceptable, given the timing and the national mood.

The 1960s were characterized by large investments in mental health professional training, mental-health services, and construction and staffing of new facilities. It was also a period of great turmoil in which many mental-health professionals, in their excessive optimism, made claims of expertise and effectiveness that had little basis in reality. As more treatment became available in community mental-health centers the boundaries of mental-health concepts seemed to broaden, and many of the centers concentrated their efforts on ordinary problems of living rather than dealing with the difficulties of hard-core mental illness (496). Although with new administrative policies chronic patients were increasingly returned to the community, often only very limited and unimaginative services were available to them.

The 1960s also witnessed considerable confusion between concepts of mental health and mental illness. Mental-health professionals with a broad social view of behavior became activists on the assumption that many of the causes of mental illness were rooted in the social structure and that early efforts could prevent more serious pathology. The difficulty was that they lacked sound theories or data on which to proceed, and much of social psychiatry as it came to be practiced was highly politicized. Because no clear distinction was made between the ordinary problems of living that many mental-health professionals dealt with and more traditional mental illnesses, confusion about the boundaries of mental-health services was compounded. Moreover, the 1960s were characterized by vigorous attacks on the concept of mental illness itself, and one could find reputable psychiatrists and mental-health professionals on every side of every issue. One result was a tendency to neglect the needs of many impaired psychiatric patients who were mentally ill in the more traditional sense of the concept.

Although the number of mental-health centers, community programs, and mental-health personnel that were envisioned in the 1960s never fully materialized, the mental-health sector grew enormously during this period. The numbers of psychiatrists, social workers, psychiatric nurses, psychologists, and mental-health aides vastly increased, and availability of funds for buildings, staffing, and service programs led to significant increases in the availability and accessibility of ambulatory psychiatric services throughout much of the United States. The Vietnam War and its aftermath, however, and disillusion with the programs of the "Great Society" resulted in the curtailment of funds for mental-health programs. After many years of continuing growth, public subsidy of the mental-health sector decreased in real dollars. The Nixon administration was hostile to mental-health programs and thus phased out support for community mental-health centers on the contention that they had been unsuccessful and, when challenged, on the contention that they had been so successful that further federal subsidy was no longer necessary. Similarly, subsidy of psychiatric and other mental-health professional training was significantly curtailed. It was clear by 1975 that the climate in which the joint commission's recommendations had flourished had changed radically. It was time for consolidation and reassessment. With the new Carter administration, a presidential commission has been appointed to assess future policy directions.

The rapid growth of mental-health efforts in the 1960s brought many constructive changes, but it was also characterized by much confusion. When community mental-health centers, for example, were originally envisioned, there were three basic aims: (1) to treat acute mental illness; (2) to care for incompletely recovered mental patients either short of admission to a hospital or after discharge from the hospital; and (3) to be a center for mental-health education. Many experts viewed the second function as the most important. In practice, however, these functions were neglected in favor of dealing with "easier" and "more pleasant" clients. There has been considerable reaction to this failure, and federally funded centers are now required to give greater programmatic attention to the chronic mental patient who may have more permanent impairments. But the expectations of these centers are so broad that it is not clear that they will perform any function well.

Provision of Services

While it is important to understand the social and cultural characteristics that lead patients and their families either to accept or to resist definitions of disorder and treatment efforts, it is even more crucial for psychiatric services to be aware of the ways their own patterns of organization may hinder accessibility and effective use of assistance, particularly for the chronic patient. It is necessary to establish that the treatment program itself is one that a reasonable man or woman would wish to take advantage of. Unfortunately, much of the care available for patients with mental impairments could not pass this rather simple test, and one of the contributions of community-care innovations is that they offered alternatives to the rather dreary care available in most mental hospitals.

At a more conceptual level, we have learned that health-delivery systems, even when they involve no financial barriers to care, erect a variety of other social and psychological barriers that keep certain patients out of their systems or induce a lack of continued participation and cooperation. There are many ways services come to be rationed: by the limitation of resources provided to deal with a given patient load; by the location of sites of care and the difficulties involved for patients and their families in reaching such locations; by creating social distance between providers and patients due to overprofessionalization and other barriers to communication; by excessive waiting time to obtain services and other noneconomic costs that can divert those who are ambivalent about using services to begin with; and by the stigmatization of patients and their families.

The organization of effective community care in contrast to hospital programs requires a major shift from traditional bureaucratic perspectives to more organic organizational concepts. Although even the most traditional and hierarchical mental-hospital organization had to be attuned to some extent to its larger social and political environment, its programs were relatively insulated and separated from community visibility and pressures; such organizations maintained their own bureaucratic cultures. There has been considerable innovation in staff roles in many of these institutions in recent years, but the fact is that such hospitals continue to retain relatively rigid professional role structures, and each of the relevant professional groups has staked out its own territory and professional routines. The rather marked shift to treatment of psychiatric patients in community voluntary hospitals has also followed this bureaucratic emphasis. Indeed, these hospitals are so wedded to the traditional medical model that the psychiatric units tend in their organization to resemble the typical medical service in which different psychiatrists, responsible for varying patients, pass through during the day to make rounds but take little responsibility for the milieu or for dealing with patients' secondary disabilities.

In contrast, effective community care must be exceedingly sensitive to its environment and give attention to such varied concerns as community acceptance, the employment market, the integrity of the welfare and social services system, housing availability, and relationships with police and other social agencies. Professionals involved in the administration of such programs must be on the scene, away from the usual insulation, security, and lack of realism of the professional office. Putting it somewhat differently, the professional in the community-care context is a facilitator, coordinator, and integrator. He must become tolerant of more fluid roles and relationships and be able to work on a more equal basis with a wide range of other mental-health professionals as well as with community participants. In this context he is no longer afforded the protection of his medical status or mystique.

In the lingo of the organizational theorist, there is a variety of reasons explaining why classical models of organizational functioning cannot fit the provision of human services at the community level: The goals are too many and varied and often intangible; the technologies available are not clearly specified and often uncertain; the environment in which programs must operate is unpredictable and changing; the requirements for action in any particular case cannot be unconditionally specified; and the professionals themselves tend to be cosmopolitans with value systems that lead them to reject, subvert, and manipulate traditional bureaucratic rules and structures. In contrast, an organic model of organizational functioning is more attuned to the realities of community care. The name of the game is coordination, and individuals must engage in definition and redefinition of tasks as they relate to others also involved in programming. Responsibilities are fluid and somewhat open-ended, and the task requires commitment that goes beyond the application of any particular technical function. Professionals in this context become brokers who must negotiate among varying interests and agencies, and effectiveness resides in the ability to get things done and not in a traditional authority structure, special degrees, or the mask of medical competence.

The most difficult tasks in any community treatment program are instilling and maintaining a sense of commitment and momentum among program personnel. Treating chronic mental patients is difficult, and their problems are often intractable; thus they require effective and aggressive services over the long range. In the early stages of any new program there is a sense of excitement and innovation. Both personnel and patients feel that something new is being attempted and accomplished. The energy that comes from such involvement is a powerful treatment force, but it is difficult to maintain indefinitely. People get tired; they seek to regularize their work patterns; they desire to control the uncertainties and unpredictabilities in their environment. Thus they tend to push toward the bureaucratization of roles and the clear-cut definition of responsibilities and turfs. They become smug, less sensitive to clients, and less committed to the jobs to be done.

No organizational system seems to have been able to deal effectively with the problem. The Chinese experiment involves collective mobilization, social disruption, and professional reeducation as a means of dealing with natural tendencies toward bureaucratization, but of course we would like to find somewhat less profound methods of maintaining commitment to social goals. There are some techniques that are available for encouraging commitment, some less disruptive than others. Perhaps the most typical way in our own society is by recruitment and turnover of personnel. This brings to the organization people who are fresh and enthusiastic and who have new concepts. In the health-services area, however, continuity is essential, and the costs of professional turnover beyond some point may well exceed the benefits. The most viable alternative, in my view, is to maintain a sense of participatory democracy among program personnel. Personnel must be allowed to modify programs from time to time, not so much because the changes themselves will be a technical improvement but because participants will feel more enthusiastic about and more committed to programs that they helped formulate and in which they have a stake.

Community care for chronic mental patients without sustained efforts of follow-up and support is an invitation to a new type of erosion of human potential, except now it occurs in a community and not in a custodial institution. With the shift to community care we have also learned the extent to which professionals can be a disservice to patients under the guise of treatment when they engage in excessive restrictions and foster dependency. We must remain vigilant to the fact that care that encourages dependency rather than incentives to cope can be exceedingly detrimental. Similarly, focusing on life difficulties and symptoms in contrast to potential assets and strengths may reinforce an illness behavior pattern, thus reducing coping effectiveness. Mental-health professionals must never forget that chronicity of illness is one of the few widely recognized reasons for failing to meet social responsibilities. While mental patients obviously have major handicaps that require persistent and sympathetic professional efforts, the mental-health professional must be alert to the possibility that he may be reinforcing ineffective behavior.

The language of social behavior, of course, has moral as well as scientific import. Our language implies a vocabulary of motives, and the way we characterize the problems of patients has an impact on their future motives and efforts. One of the major advances of community care has been an increasing tendency to move away from deterministic models of social functioning and to encourage patients to utilize their potential capacities. We must continue to move in this direction but with empathy and avoidance of a crass and cynical behaviorism. The ability to do this depends in large part on forces beyond the control of mental-health professionals. It depends on the social and political context of community care.

Involuntary Hospitalization

The 1960s were a period of emphasis on the extension of civil liberties and civil rights (516); activist lawyers—drawing on the work of critics of the mental-health system—legally confronted such issues as the ways in which people were committed to mental hospitals, the manner in which they were cared for, and the arbitrary loss of many of their rights (see, for example, 204).There were few areas in public affairs in which the rhetoric of state protection and the realities were as discrepant as in the treatment of the involuntary mental patient. The mental-hospital system—using the instrument of involuntary commitment statutes —served the community by detaining persons defined as mentally ill who were perceived as disruptive, dangerous, or bizarre, and whom the community wished to exclude. While the conditions in these institutions were very poor, as has already been described, the rationale for detention was usually described as "care and treatment" in the interests of the detained rather than of those who wished to detain them. As the community mental-health movement developed, the educated public became conscious of the abuses of commitment processes, the terrible conditions that often prevailed in institutions for the mentally ill and mentally retarded, and the debilitating effects of prolonged hospitalization and custodial care on patients' capacities for social functioning. The civil-rights movement for the mentally ill fought its battle on two major related areas: processes of civil commitment and the patient's right to treatment. A review of each of these areas and the ways they developed will provide some sense of the revolution that has been taking place in the rights of the mental patient.

The Dilemma of Civil Commitment

Civil commitment allegedly has four functions: (1) protecting the community against the dangerous acts of the mentally ill; (2) providing treatment and care to those who need it; (3) protecting from their own acts persons believed to be irresponsible; and (4) removing from the family and community people who are not dangerous but bizarre and bothersome (673). For the most part, however, civil commitment has served better as a means of social control of deviance than as a resource for the mentally ill. The situation is changing, and voluntary commitments now outnumber involuntary hospitalizations, but progress remains uneven, and grave problems continue to exist in fitting the alleged goals of civil-commitment processes with the realities. Although the state of Virginia had a commitment law as early as 1806, for the most part the incarceration of the mentally ill in the United States was informally administered until the middle of the nineteenth century. At this point considerable concern had developed about unjustified commitment of sane people to mental institutions, and as early as 1845 Chief Justice Shaw of the Massachusetts Supreme Court laid down the precedent that individuals could be restrained only if dangerous to themselves or others and if restraint was conducive to restoration (166). This basic principle has served as the foundation of many state statutes concerning the involuntary commitment of the mentally ill. Although these statutes were originally developed to protect the rights of individuals who were not "insane," they became the mechanisms that facilitated increasing commitments to mental hospitals.

The concept of mental illness, as we have noted in earlier chapters, is particularly slippery, and the concept of danger is almost never clearly defined. Consequently, many mentally ill people were committed involuntarily to mental hospitals, although they literally were not a dangerous to themselves or others (485), nor was there any good reason to believe that they could benefit from the care provided, which was custodial and frequently dehumanizing (see 179). Although many states have what seems to be reasonable legislation concerning commitment, the formal requirements for legal commitment are frequently not followed or are manipulated in a variety of ways (see 617). Moreover, judgments of what constitutes sufficient "danger" vary from one psychiatrist to another, although there is probably agreement on extreme cases. For example, Dr. C. Hardin Branch (81), a well-known psychiatrist and former president of the American Psychiatric Association, suggested that psychiatrists should be allowed to intervene in cases without legal impediments if a person can be "considered injurious to himself or others." Examples of what he might consider injurious are cases in which "the lack of judgment caused by [a person's] mental illness leads him into business enterprises so bizarre that they bankrupt him and his family," or when a professional person "behaved in such a peculiar way that he irrevocably damaged his reputation for continued professional activity" (81; p. 137). The question is not simple, for how is one to establish criteria of poor judgment in business enterprise or peculiar professional behavior? The history of business and professional life is abundant with examples of business risk-taking ventures and professional behavior, regarded as bizarre by others, that led to ultimate success. Who is to be the final arbiter?

The psychiatrist and the person being defined may have views of the situation that vary widely, and if such definitions are to lead to involuntary commitment they may involve conflicts between liberty and psychiatry if legal safeguards are not maintained (617; 695). As confirmed psychiatric disease theories do not exist for the most part, expert determinations enforced involuntarily upon a person often reflect the use of psychiatry for the purposes of social control. Psychiatrists frequently urge involuntary commitment to insure that the patient is treated, and they openly concede that danger is not the "real" issue. In making these decisions it is not always clear that psychiatrists weigh the risks involved in such involuntary action for the patient in comparison to the risks of failing to take any action at all (614; 616; 617). Too often such decisions are expedients to deal with difficult situations that could be handled more adequately if the community took its responsibility toward the mentally ill more seriously.

It should be clear that I am not alluding to obvious cases of danger such as serious threats of suicide, where most psychiatrists would agree that some form of detention was warranted. I refer primarily to those cases in which the patient is detained involuntarily because his actions in the eyes of psychiatrists or others are injurious to the patient's or his family's social standing, reputation, or financial solvency. This is not to deny that mental illnesses exist and that they cause difficulties for families and the community nor that such conditions may have definite genetic or psychological etiologies and that they may be susceptible to effective intervention. The central issue here is whether enforced hospitalization is an adequate mode of coping with such problems when they arise and whether such an approach is consistent with the patient's long-range welfare.

The concepts of injury and danger, as used in evaluating persons with presumed mental disorders, have some curious social implications. The psychiatrist may come to the conclusion that a person is not acting in his self-interest and is injuring himself and others when he engages in bizarre and irresponsible behavior. When such persons become sufficiently disturbing to their families or others, the psychiatrist may be brought in by interested parties in order to change the definition of the situation sufficiently to reduce the strain on those who are coping with the problem. The psychiatrist, by asserting that the difficult behavior is a consequence of a "mental disorder," sets the stage for exercising alternatives for coping with the situation that would not be possible without his medical opinion. Without considering at this point whether the person is or is not ill, we must recognize that psychiatry performs a social role as well as a medical one in that a psychiatric opinion legitimizes courses of action in dealing with the patient that would be difficult without his support.

When the patient's behavior is dealt with within a psychiatric frame of reference it is treated in a manner somewhat different from usual forms of social control. In the usual situation (i.e., law enforcement) it is clear that action is taken first in the interests of the community and not in the interests of the deviant. Social control within the psychiatric frame of reference implies, in contrast, that action is taken primarily for the good of the patient as well as for the benefit of other parties, and it is presumed frequently that the patient is no longer in a position to appreciate the possible alternatives or to assume responsibility for his behavior.

The assessment as to whether a person is suffering from a serious mental disorder should be separate from the question of whether this person is dangerous or a fit subject for involuntary care. In practice, however, these distinctions are frequently not made, and the psychiatric assessment itself is used as a sufficient basis for taking involuntary action. Thus it should be obvious that often the questions as to whether danger is imminent or whether injury is likely to result are not the real issues, although these may be the terms used to justify the course of action taken. The threat of injurious and dangerous behavior is treated quite differently in contexts in which the behavior is not alien to usual social standards and practices. We do not generally interfere with persons who wish to damage themselves as long as they do so through culturally acceptable means. The point I wish to emphasize is that it is important to consider the functions that psychiatry performs as a social institution and as a representative of various social agencies in the community. It is quite clear what the psychiatrist does when he is an agent of an individual patient who seeks his care voluntarily. However, the extent to which psychiatry constitutes a system of social control when dispensed through social and legal agencies and private organizations has received attention only more recently as a result of legal intervention.

The psychiatrist who must make decisions about mental health and danger finds himself in many respects in an impossible situation. Unlike the objective and impartial scientist, the psychiatrist usually is an agent of a particular person or social unit, and it is the psychiatrist's obligation to consider the interests of the person he represents. In social life, however, persons often have *conflicting* and *incompatible* interests, and thus the way the psychiatrist will see the situation inevitably depends on whose interests he identifies himself with (310). One need look no further than the typical court case involving "legal insanity" to realize that the psychiatrist's view of a case will depend on whether he represents the prosecution or the defense. In short, such decisions inevitably involve social dilemmas; from the perspective of the patient's mental health, it may be best that he remain in the community and not be involuntarily detained. As we all know, however, this may not always be in the interests of the spouse's or neighbor's mental health.

It is important to realize the extent to which the psychiatrist may see himself as playing a mediating role between people whose interests may be opposed. The course of action that may benefit the patient most may be one that also places an excessive burden on his family and the community. Mental patients frequently create extremely difficult problems for others, especially those with whom they live and work. Although from a legal perspective they may not be violating the law, they may by their behavior threaten and frighten others and produce a state of familial and emotional turmoil (95). Such persons are particularly upsetting to their spouses and children, and frequently a psychiatrist has been called in because the family's resources in coping with the problem have been exhausted and the consequences of the patient's behavior are seriously disruptive. Thus removal of the patient to the hospital, even when it is against his will and desire, may constitute from the point of view of the psychiatrist and the community a humanitarian gesture motivated by the consideration of the best interests of all concerned.

Although involuntary hospitalization for a time may appear reasonable in light of the tremendous familial and social problems resulting from the disruptive and bizarre behavior of some mentally ill persons, there are many issues that complicate this matter. Involuntary hospitalization perhaps could be justified if it were used as a last resort in coping with the difficult problems that some mentally ill persons bring about. Unfortunately, involuntary commitment is frequently merely a convenient way of coping with the problem of the mentally ill before other less radical alternatives have been exhausted (617). Given the shortage of professional personnel and the tremendous work burden of most courts, judges and psychiatrists have not always been as patient or persistent as they should be in attempting to find other solutions or to convince the patient that he should enter care voluntarily. Frequently the patient has been involuntarily committed to the hospital without having the issue discussed with him and his views and feelings considered. Thus the involuntarily hospitalized patient often has felt betrayed and taken advantage of, and it is well recognized that this is not an effective way to initiate a therapeutic situation.

The issue of involuntary hospitalization is further complicated by our values concerning civil liberties. Regardless of what difficulties the mental patient may cause for others, he as an individual is protected by particular constitutional guarantees against involuntary hospitalization unless it is clear that he is a threat to others or himself (695). Although many states have clearly protected the rights of the mental patient in statutes concerning the procedures for involuntary commitment, all too often under the hurried workload of the courts these guarantees are honored more in their breach than in their observance. Involuntary hospitalization is necessary under some conditions (such as when the patient threatens bodily harm to others), but these procedures are used far too frequently when other alternatives for dealing with the problem are possible. It is important that involuntary hospitalization be seen not as a usual procedure but as a rare alternative that is exercised with proper safeguards consistent with our civil libertarian ideals. We should note that although the misuse of involuntary hospitalization is still prevalent, efforts are being made to provide care for the mental patient under more desirable voluntary procedures, and the development of new community programs makes this more possible.

Lawyers working in the field of mental patients' rights have pursued primarily procedural issues, giving mental patients who are facing commitments many of the same rights available to criminal defendants. In a landmark case in Wisconsin (*Lessard v. Schmidt*) stimulated by the new legal activism, the court found that mental patients threatened with civil commitment have rights to timely notice of the charges, notice of right to a jury trial, aid of counsel, protection against self-incrimination, and proof that they are mentally ill and dangerous "beyond a reasonable doubt." Although some judges now try to work within these procedural guidelines, others ignore them. Serious application of these rights in concrete cases can be enormously difficult and depends on professional assistance that is frequently unavailable. Thus with even the best of legal intentions there remains a great discrepancy between legal theories and realities. Real progress, however, has been made in making commitment processes more rigorous in many jurisdictions and in shortening, without apparent harm, the length of time that patients spend in hospitals under civil commitment statutes. Effective procedures nonetheless require more than procedural rules; they require real community alternatives for dealing with the human problems that bizarre and mentally ill patients pose for their families and the community.

There are no simple and obvious solutions for dealing with mentally ill persons who disrupt community life. Psychiatrists and judges are called on to deal with difficult and uncertain situations. Often they must operate with incomplete information, insufficient time, and inadequate resources for making a careful investigation of the problem and the circumstances surrounding the case. Moreover, they are under strong pressures to remove the patient from the community to alleviate the strain on others who have been faced with the problem. When resources and time are limited and when inadequate treatment alternatives exist in the community, it is not surprising that involuntary hospitalization is used. It is a procedure that serves the community that wishes to have the mentally ill patient removed. Frequently it is assumed that hospitalization will have some benefit for the patient, but it is much less often recognized that the hospital could do the patient harm. In any case, the pressures of the social circumstances surrounding decision making in this area encourage behavior that favors involuntary hopitalization in circumstances of uncertainty. But legal agitation has had its impact. As Stone notes, "Psychiatrists who once committed people because it was the easiest thing to do are increasingly diffident. Courts are apt to be more scrupulous in reaching their decisions; lawyers are more frequently involved in preventing confinement; and hospitals are more fastidious about their own role" (673, p. 43).

The debate concerning the appropriate role of civil commitment continues to rage between activist lawyers and many mental-health professionals. State reforms in commitment procedures, as in California's Lanterman-Petris-Short law, lead some psychiatrists to argue that their powers to protect the community against dangerous mentally ill patients are too limited, while others believe that commitment procedures make it too easy to deprive people of their freedom in an area where prediction is very uncertain. The community faces certain dilemmas in cases of some mental patients who frighten, threaten, or in other ways disrupt social activities. If it becomes impossible to deal with these persons through civil commitment, we have every reason to believe that alternatives will be found—some, such as imprisonment, that may be less desirable for the patients involved. The goal is to achieve better alternatives to either prisons or mental hospitals, and this depends on the willingness of the community to provide the necessary resources to develop appropriate programs. It is still unclear how to balance properly the civil liberties of mental patients in relation to the needs of the community to avoid certain types of disruption and possible danger.

Stone (673) has suggested a five-step procedure through which assessments might be made as to the appropriateness of civil commitment: (1) reliable diagnosis of a severe mental illness; (2) assessment as to whether the person's immediate prognosis involves major distress; (3) availability of treatment; (4) the possibility that the illness impaired the person's ability to make a decision as to whether he or she was willing to accept treatment; and (5) assessment as to whether a reasonable man would accept or reject such treatment. Stone's conception is that when there is convincing evidence of a serious illness causing suffering for which treatment is available and the patient's refusal of treatment is irrational, then civil commitment is merited. He calls this the "thank you" theory on the assumption that the patient in a rational state of mind would seek to receive the available services. Stone notes:

> This is the Thank You Theory of Civil Commitment: it asks the psychiatrist to focus his inquiry on illness and treatment, and it asks the law to guarantee that treatment before it intervenes in the name of parens patriae. It is radical in the sense that it insists that society fulfill its promise of benefit when it trenches on human freedom. It is also radical in that it divests civil commitment of a police function; dangerous behavior is returned to the province of criminal law. Only someone who is irrational, treatable, and incidentally dangerous would be confined in the mental health system [673, p. 70].

The "thank you" theory is a reasonable solution only to the extent that one has sufficient trust in the integrity and reliability of psychiatric practice in its everyday sense. Many people do not have this trust, and psychiatric practice is enormously variable. To such persons it would be wrong to trade off the patient's civil liberties for unwanted treatment on the basis of psychiatric assessments. Moreover, in the busy pace of everyday practice such judgments may be much more unreliable than the theoretical possibility allows. A more stringent test for commitment might be a requirement to present evidence that all less restrictive alternatives have been exhausted and that the community has indeed made efforts to provide less restrictive alternatives, but they do not fit the specific case.

As I have emphasized throughout, problems in civil commitment are but symptoms of more basic problems in the organization and delivery of mental-health services. Until we develop better patterns of service and make them more widely available, disputes will continue on civil commitment procedures no matter how many procedural guarantees the courts provide. A related aspect of this problem is involved in another area of litigation: the "right to treatment."

Right to Treatment

"Right-to-treatment" litigation relates to civil commitment procedures. If civil commitment were used more sparingly and only as a final alternative, many fewer involuntary patients would be hospitalized and existing facilities and staff could better meet their needs. Mental hospitals, however, still serve as warehouses for the chronically ill, the aged, the retarded, and a variety of other unfortunates who have been kept there only because there was no place else to send them. Care is often custodial in contrast to active treatment or rehabilitation. Although there were some early precedents in right-to-treatment decisions, the breakthrough came in *Wyatt* v. *Stickney* in which the court held that involuntarily committed patients "unquestionably have a constitutional right to receive such individual treatment as will give each of them a realistic opportunity to be cured or to improve his or her mental condition" (see 498, p. 233). The court found that the defendant's treatment program was deficient because it failed to provide a humane psychological and physical environment and a qualified staff in sufficient number to administer adequate treatment and individualized treatment plans. The court proposed detailed standards, which it defined as "medical and constitutional minimums."

Right-to-treatment decisions reveal the hypocrisy of detaining individuals involuntarily for care and treatment without providing it. The court held that "To deprive any citizen of his or her liberty upon the altruistic theory that the confinement is for humane therapeutic reasons and then fail to provide adequate treatment violates the very fundamentals of due process" (498, p. 233).

There are as yet no definitive data on the full consequences of the right-to-treatment decisions even in Alabama, where the decision applied. There is evidence, however, that large numbers of patients were released from Alabama hospitals following the decision, more than would have been expected on the basis of existing trends or patterns in adjacent states. Similarly, there is considerable evidence that right-to-treatment legislation assisted, if it did not affect directly, efforts to increase Alabama's mental-health budget and the staffing patterns in its psychiatric institutions (421). In short, it is difficult to come to any conclusion other than that *Wyatt* v. *Stickney* contributed to a climate· that brought greater support and investment for mental-health facilities and programs in Alabama. While we know little about the fate of the patients who were released either to the community or to nursing homes, indications are that they had varying experiences, some not very conducive to a high quality of social functioning. Many remain institutionalized in the community or in nursing homes but, on balance, the result seems favorable (420).

On the urging of litigants, the Alabama court established a large number of standards mandating changes in staffing, physical resources, and treatment processes. In the sense that implementation of such standards has alleviated the horrible conditions that were documented as prevalent, they obviously contribute to humanitarian goals. It is not at all clear, however, that the standards promulgated were optimal for achieving the best outcomes that would be possible relative to cost if such resources were to be used as part of an overall mental-health strategy including both inpatient and community care of the mentally ill. The nature of the litigation process required an approach that focused on the involuntary hospital patient because the "handle" was the argument that the deprivation of liberty for humane therapeutic reasons without the provision of treatment was a violation of due process of law. This need for a "handle" forced the litigants to view the mental-health system narrowly and to focus their attention on only one aspect of care, allowing the possibility of displacement of the problem to other parts of the mental-health system not attacked so easily by litigation.

The hospital standards promulgated had a variety of limitations. They tended to reinforce a medical model of treatment and highly stratified roles among health professionals at the same time that health experts are becoming aware of the limitations of professional dominance and rigidly enforced roles. They encouraged allocation of resources to hospital care in contrast to a network of community facilities more appropriate to the management of mental-health problems in the community. They demanded that expensive and scarce medical resources be devoted to the parts of the mental-health system where they may be most ineffective in affecting treatment outcomes and thus yield a low cost-benefit outcome. Perhaps most dangerous of all is that such court decisions can encourage a practice of indiscriminate dumping of patients in the community without providing an adequate network of community care that facilitates their social functioning and alleviates the social costs for families and community of having highly disabled persons resident in the community.

The middle-class bias of the litigants made it almost inconceivable to them that the patients released could be better off in the hospitals, given their obvious shortcomings. Study of the situation of some chronic mental patients, however, suggests that lower-status and highly disabled patients often find it more comforting to reside in institutions than in the community (452). Once the patients are released to the community they are no longer protected by the right-to-treatment decision and are at the mercy of prevailing conditions and resources, which are often minimal and less adequate than those available even in substandard hospitals.

Although there is evidence of the benefits of right-to-treatment litigation for patients in Alabama (420), we also have some indication of possible dangers of too rapid deinstitutionalization by considering what has occurred in more progressive areas of the nation. While communities have been relatively quick to alter administrative policies so as to avoid hospitalization and to release hospitalized patients as rapidly as possible, an adequate framework of community services to assist the mentally ill and their families has been exceedingly slow to develop. As economic pressures have mounted for federal and state governments, as well as for localities, there has been less willingness to invest the resources to meet even minimally the needs of patients in the community, and community mental-health centers have frequently avoided the most impaired patients (114). Various agencies—each attempting to protect its budget—shift the responsibilities to others, leaving many needy patients unattended, living under appalling conditions, and frequently victimized (537).

There is growing indication that large numbers of greatly impaired patients have been dumped in some communities without adequate financial, social, or treatment resources. In large cities many live with other deviants in "welfare hotels" in disorganized areas or frequently find themselves in substandard facilities run for profit by operators who provide few treatment resources. Given the poor conditions to which they are exposed, these patients frequently experience an exacerbation of symptoms and insecurities and, given their limited coping capacities, they face horrendous life problems.

In view of these considerations, it is difficult to be too confident in estimating the benefits of the right-to-treatment litigation. Certainly we can applaud the motives of those who brought such litigation and the ideals of decency and justice that the approach implied. But administrative systems are highly complex and adaptable entities, and pressures on one part of the system may just make problems more intense in other parts. A major limitation of the litigation approach is the difficulty of viewing the system as a whole in contrast to seeking particular constitutional remedies.

Under an adequate system of entitlement to medical care, with medical care economically and geographically accessible, the mechanisms to provide community mental-health care would be more readily available. A just and effective rehabilitation system must exist within a larger framework of medical care, and this issue depends on fundamental decisions made through legislative processes. Certainly right-to-treatment litigation may arouse the conscience of the legislature, and it may promote equity by making citizens aware that the care provided is far less adequate than political rhetoric has suggested.

In sum, we have been living through a period in mental-health care that can be characterized as one of constructive chaos. Much is happening in this area and there is a great receptivity to new ideas and programs. But the area is also characterized by unsubstantiated claims and extreme ideologies. If we are to obtain the potential benefit that can be derived from the existing ferment, it is essential that we approach current developments with a critical eye and a skeptical perspective. Models of care for national support must be rigorously scrutinized and the effects of such programs compared with alternative models. A sound mental-health policy must rest ultimately on a strong empirical base.

Part 8

PROSPECTS BEFORE US

Chapter 18

HEALTH CARE AND SOCIAL POLICY

In recent years medicine has undergone enormous changes. Not only has there been a remarkable development of the science of medicine and its technology, but the institutional forms for providing care are in the process of revolution as well. Within the traditional medical model the contract was between patient and practitioner; the ethical responsibility of the physician was clear even if the reality departed from the norm. However, the technology and economics of medicine increasingly require new forms of organization, and the physician's primary responsibility to the patient may come into conflict with the physician's responsibility to the institution, the medical group, the community, and even the future development of medical science and medical education (500). Medicine now consumes a larger proportion of the gross national product and greater governmental expenditures than in the past, and government—as well as a variety of other third parties—has elaborated the complexity of the relationship between the patient and the helping institutions, and has a stake in the way medicine is practiced. Greater complexity of medicine is inevitable, but this makes it even more important that we devote attention to the policy aspects of health care and to some of the important social, ethical, and legal issues.

To review the great variety of issues that are important in policy would require many volumes, and yet too superficial a view would fail to communicate the complex interplay among medical practice, government, social attitudes and values, and the legal system. Thus this chapter emphasizes a few examples to illustrate the complexity of social policy considerations and the larger context in which they are embedded. It is hoped that the reader will be stimulated to examine my other books on social policy issues in health care (488; 492; 497; 500), as well as those of others, and to begin a more intensive study of the policy choices that will help determine the future of medical care in the United States and elsewhere.

495

Medicare and Medicaid

In the middle 1960s the federal government instituted two new programs for the provision of medical care that are of extensive magnitude and that account for vast expenditures. Medicare is a federally financed program providing uniform medical benefits to elderly people covered by the social security retirement program. The program includes two parts: (1) a hospital insurance plan for recipients over 65 and (2) a voluntary supplementary medical insurance plan covering physicians' services and other benefits in which the federal government shares the cost with recipients. Both parts of the program are subject to certain coinsurance and deductible provisions that have been modified from time to time with new legislation.

Title 19 of the Social Security Act (better known as Medicaid) is a program of federal subsidies to states that provide care to medically indigent persons according to certain guidelines established by the federal government. These programs, however, unlike Medicare, are under the control of the individual states. Eligibility and provisions for care vary a great deal from one area to another, and recipients are subject to means tests to determine their eligibility. While Medicare consists basically of a program of national health insurance for persons 65 and over, Medicaid is conceived as and administered very much in the tradition of welfare medicine (669).

While in theory Medicare benefits are equally available to all persons in the population over 65, in reality there are vast inequalities in their provision. Karen Davis (162) has shown that wide differences exist in the use of services and in the receipt of benefits by income, race, and geographic location. Under the program the populations with the poorest health have had lower rates of utilization of care than the more affluent groups. Persons with incomes over $15,000 a year, for example, received twice the amounts for physician services as compared with those with incomes of less than $5,000. Whites had 30 percent more payments for inpatient hospital care per person and 60 percent more payments for physician services than blacks. Whites also received more than twice the payments received by blacks for extended-care facility services. Davis also found large variations among geographic areas.

There are a variety of reasons for these disparities among groups in a program that was intended to redistribute social benefits to the most needy, and the result is not different from many other social programs. First, the necessary requirements for coinsurance and deductibles put a greater burden on the relatively poor recipient and discourage use of medical care. Although the additional payments of the poorest elderly are subsidized by the Medicaid program, it is the near-poor group who are not eligible for Medicaid who receive the fewest services under Medicare (162). Second, both the amount and quality of medical facilities and resources are distributed so as to favor the more affluent elderly. In the areas with more and better resources, the elderly come to use services more and to have access to more specialized types of services. Third, in some areas discrimination against the poor and members of minority groups continues to exist and serves as a barrier to needed care. Fourth, patterns of utilization behavior formed among poverty groups prior to Medicare and Medicaid may continue to inhibit some poor persons from obtaining necessary services that are consumed routinely by those more affluent.

Medicaid is a more difficult program to study or even describe because it varies so greatly from one locality to another depending on eligibility, traditions in welfare adminstration, and the response of the medical community. Unlike Medicare, Medicaid continues a long tradition of welfare medicine, and its administration at both the federal and state levels builds on prior programs, procedures, and personnel associated with earlier welfare legislation providing medical assistance to specified indigent populations (669). Although in theory patients in the Medicaid program can obtain services from any eligible physician, many continue to obtain care from emergency rooms, hospital outpatient departments, and other sources of care that have traditionally provided medical service to poverty populations. Frequently Medicaid patients do not have easy access to physicians' offices and clinics, and some providers refuse to participate in the Medicaid program because of fee schedules and other limitations placed on physicians by the programs. In part to meet the access gap, "Medicaid mills" have developed that frequently provide a poor level of service to indigent populations and have prospered from this pattern.

There is a great deal of abuse of the Medicaid program by unscrupulous practitioners, but such abuse is not unique, as exposes of Medicaid would suggest. The private practice of medicine and the existence of private insurance to cover medical care bills on a fee-for-service basis are open to a great deal of manipulation and chicanery by practitioners who desire to maximize their incomes. Physicians have been sufficiently powerful to make them relatively immune to monitoring or review, and both government and other third parties who pay the bulk of medical-care bills have been quite timid in questioning the manner in which practitioners and institutions charge for their services and justify their operating procedures. Failure to come to grips with the payment issues in American medicine constitutes a major aspect of the irrationality of service patterns and contributes to an uneven distribution of practitioners and facilities and to barriers to access to medical care among varying population groups. One of the more promising developments has been experimentation on the part of both Medicare and Medicaid with contracts with prepaid groups to provide comprehensive services to populations covered by these legislative programs. While some of these experiments have been subject to abuse, as in the provision of services to medically indigent patients in California by profit-health maintenance organizations, such ventures are necessary in developing the experience within the medical organizational pattern in the United States to administer effective means of guaranteeing necessary services to those covered by government programs.

As the statistics presented earlier in this volume indicate, implementation of Medicare and Medicaid has contributed to vast improvements in the care of the most impoverished sections of our population and has helped immeasurably in dealing with the illness burden suffered by the aged. Without minimizing these benefits, we must also note that these gains have been accomplished only at an enormous financial cost and without fundamental alteration of the existing system of health services in the United States. The consequence is that these programs have helped to reinforce the absurdities of the organization and provision of medical services in the United States rather than to alter them. The problems characteristic of Medicare and Medicaid are simply a reflection of the problems of the medical-care system as a whole. Although some Medicare recipients cannot receive needed service because requirements for coinsurance and deductibles pose significant barriers for them, many other Americans face similar barriers because of the limited provisions of their private insurance policies. Just as many Medicaid recipients are limited in seeking care by the practitioners available and willing to serve them, so are many other Americans limited in achieving necessary access. Just as these programs may encourage unnecessary and wasteful procedures of care, so does the entire insurance structure and the modes we use for financing care and paying practitioners and facilities. In short, the problem is not Medicare and Medicaid; the problem is the way we organize and finance the provision of medical services. In addressing this question we turn to a brief consideration of the criteria for the development of national health insurance in the United States.

Criteria for National Health Insurance

A great deal has been written about national health insurance, and the details of the various plans being advocated change too quickly to be usefully described in a book of this type. All systems of national health insurance arise from the structures already existing in a country, with the details worked out in the processes of political bargaining and compromise. For our purposes here it is more useful to look at some general considerations in examining different proposals for national health insurance than it would be to compare details of the many alternative plans being discussed.

A basic issue underlying various health-insurance proposals involves political philosophy. Is medical care a right, and to what extent is it the role of government to insure medical care for everyone in contrast to those who are particularly needy? To what extent should people be held responsible for their own medical costs and be required to share part of such costs through out-of-pocket payments or private insurance? Should scarce medical resources be rationed on the basis of the willingness of people to pay for them, or should they be planned in an attempt to distribute the existing resources according to need as assessed by professionals and health planners? Proposals for national health insurance cover the entire spectrum from those that advocate no more than a federal subsidy for purchase of private insurance among those with low incomes to other proposals that guarantee the entire population comprehensive medical-care services financed directly by the federal government (see 712).

The manner in which national health insurance is financed has important implications for redistribution of income. If the available services are shared more equally among Americans through government intervention and financed to a greater extent through progressive taxes, such as the income tax, then the effect is a redistribution of resources to the poorer segments of the population. In contrast, if the financing is largely through payroll taxes then the less affluent must contribute a larger proportion of their incomes than those with higher incomes. Depending on how the payroll taxes are structured, the financial burden placed on groups with lower incomes may vary. In any case, the method of financing national health insurance will have a great influence on who bears the cost and indirectly on distribution of income.

Much of the infighting concerning national health insurance involves questions of what populations will be covered, what types of care will be covered, and the extent to which the plan works with the existing health-care structure or attempts to develop mechanisms to change it. It is in respect to these matters that much controversy exists. There are those who support increased federal subsidy and involvement but want no interference with the existing structure of services. They believe that the federal government should support the existing efforts of the private sector to meet medical-care needs. Others point to the irrationalities of the existing system of health-care services and maintain that government involvement without restructuring of health services will consume vast amounts of public funds and yet fail to correct the inequities of the medical-care system that have plagued us for decades. Moreover, they argue, there must be a limit to total expenditures for medical care, and such a limit can be instated only by firmer government involvement and regulation of the health sector, and particularly by instituting a global prospective budget. Similarly, concepts of what should be covered vary from a total comprehensive-care package to only catastrophic costs, and from elimination of all economic barriers to service to complex schedules of deductibles and coinsurance. Later in this discussion I shall specify my personal value preferences in relation to national health insurance criteria, suggesting the direction in which our efforts should go. I should emphasize that this statement represents my own views and does not attempt to review the advantages and disadvantages of the many alternative proposals that have been advocated.

Although those who support the existing structure of health services—particularly the fee for service private sector—talk frequently as if resources are unlimited, consideration of national health insurance must take into account the likely available resources, competing social goals, and needs for efficiency. An important national goal is to achieve an adequate level of service for all citizens at reasonable cost, one that does not unnecessarily take resources that are needed to meet other social priorities. Whereas it is possible to debate the amount of resources that should reasonably go into medical care relative to other social needs, it is clear that we are approaching—if we have not already exceeded—a reasonable limit. When more than 8 percent of the gross national product is consumed by the health sector, without indication of the trend leveling off, there is reason to feel concerned. Thus the key issue is not whether we should or should not ration services but rather the means by which we do so and the resulting consequences for dignified care, equity, and efficiency.

Various persons in the health-policy field have advocated that patients be given vouchers to buy health insurance or health services up to a certain amount, and that the patients themselves finance any further needs or desires for service beyond this subsidized minimum. Although there is a deceptively intriguing aspect to such proposals, they fail to take account of the unpredictable and uneven need for medical services in the population and the fact that the burden of illness falls heavily on relatively small proportions of the population whose needs cannot be predicted beforehand. Distributing entitlements to care as only first-dollar coverage leaves those who are particularly needy in unfortunate straits. A major goal for national health insurance would be to share risks, not to concentrate them. Some of the shortcomings of providing a fixed number of dollars can in part be remedied by the way these dollars are distributed, as, for example, in Martin Feldstein's proposal (215) that establishes the patient's liability on the basis of income and limits the total amount that any patient would pay to some proportion of his income. Such a proposal deals with the regressive nature of giving each individual a fixed number of dollars, but not with other defects of such a voucher system.

More basic defects of a voucher approach are its failure to establish any means of control over the spiraling costs of medical care, the absence of any incentives to insure that access to care will be available, and the lack of any mechanism to increase the efficiency, effectiveness, and appropriateness of the present system of health-care services. The consequences of such a policy would be to solidify, and possibly to exaggerate, the irrationalities in provision of services that now exist. We should have learned this lesson well from our experience with Medicare and Medicaid. Although these programs brought assistance to many people, they contributed to an exaggeration of the structural problems of providing effective care rather than correcting them. A voucher system will not correct problems in the provision of care. Indeed, it may lead to more unnecessary surgery and more use of unproven and perhaps dangerous procedures because it provides more dollars for care without any controls. Thus it may reinforce the existing physician bias toward more expensive treatments and the technologic imperative.

Proposals for catastrophic health-care insurance suffer from many of the same problems. Such proposals do not come to terms with the imbalances between primary care and more specialized services, lack of equity, limited access to care, and a tendency toward the most costly types of service. The very nature of catastrophic insurance encourages more expensive hospital and surgical care once the catastrophic level has been reached, because at that point there is no incentive for patient or physician to ration carefully and to conserve medical resources (257). Although some pressures to ration can be brought about by cost-sharing features, instituting coinsurance at the catastrophic level tends to defeat much of the purpose of such insurance—to keep patients' medical costs below a certain proportion of their income and to eliminate barriers to needed care.

One intriguing aspect of voucher systems is the suggestion that they give consumers greater choice to obtain their medical services wherever and on whatever terms they wish. It is difficult to disagree with the proposition that greater choice for consumers among delivery systems is a desirable goal, not so much because it will control physicians' decisions but rather because it adds to patients' satisfaction. Though economic competition may reduce the price of some individual components of care, it is likely to increase total costs by encouraging unnecessary care required to sustain the viability of competitive facilities. The price of individual services is less of an issue for the nation than are total costs of medical care, and the production of unnecessary services in a competitive system is not only wasteful but also conducive to iatrogenic disease through excessive use of risky procedures. In short, the core of the issue is not the competitiveness of the marketplace, as advocates of the voucher approach would have it, but rather which of the alternative means for rationing services is most likely to be equitable and efficient and least likely to encourage a pathological service pattern.

Certainly there are significant and unreasonable restrictions concerning new personnel and types of care in the medical marketplace. This is an area in which major remedies are available, particularly if health-care delivery systems are organized and paid for in a way that provides incentives for substituting less expensive personnel for some physician services. The dominance of physicians over decision making dictates an emphasis on high technology when simpler approaches are sometimes more useful. Moreover, the existing imbalance between generalists and specialists, as well as between physicians and other health professionals, exaggerates the reliance on high technology. Incentives for professionals to establish priorities through prospective budgeting procedures offer the most viable hope for controlling the perversions of the technologic imperative. This is not to suggest that prospective budgeting does not have its own problems, as indicated in chapter 11, or that high technology does not contribute importantly to good-quality medicine. What we need is a better balance between technologies appropriately used and the epidemiology of illness in the population (438). We must also take steps to insure that services are available to geographic and social groups that will have a guaranteed entitlement to them. Perhaps the ultimate expression of the value of the entitlement to health care, as Victor Fuchs (257) has suggested, is that a national health-insurance plan "could have considerable symbolic value as one step in an effort to forge a link between classes, regions, races, and age groups."

Charles Fried (247), a lawyer at Harvard, has objected to the implications of prospective budgeting on the basis of ethical theory. In his view it is monstrous for the physician to do less than what is possible because of economic calculations. If this is so, medicine has always been a monstrous endeavor. There have always been limits to the scope of medical care that physicians could provide because of patients' inabilities to pay, competing demands on the physician's time, and personal judgments in making decisions as to which patients were more worthy of attention. Thus the alternative is not to introduce rationing where it does not already exist but to make the rationing process more equitable, more explicit, and under greater control of general guidelines than under the control of the purse.

In sum, the right to health care means that government will assure each person a reasonable level of health services and will take steps to insure that the entitlement can be exchanged for services in the medical marketplace. It means further that when rationing processes are imposed, as inevitably they will have to be, the rules for rationing will be applied fairly on the basis of reasonable categorization and be neither frivolous nor discriminatory. This does not imply that everyone has the exact right to the same services, just as public education does not imply that children who differ in their capabilities and needs must be given identical attention in every instance. The actual scope of entitlement at any given point must be an issue for public discussion and political consideration, not a matter solely for the professional community.

The right to health care, as I have defined it, does not restrict the individual from buying additional or substitute services if he wishes, just as the right to public education does not forbid the purchase of private educational services. But I believe that the nation has a responsibility to insure the viability of health care for all its citizens, and thus those who wish elite services should not be able to purchase them at the cost of undermining the interests of all. I would no more provide tax incentives for those who wish to opt out of the national health system, whatever that might be, than I would for those who prefer private schools for their children. I would hope that we would have sufficient choice in any system we design so that this would not become a pressing issue.

There are no panaceas, and the path between conception and implementation is not an easy one (569). It is dangerous to expect too much or to focus on facile theories far removed from the detailed processes of designing and delivering services for a wide variety of problems and for people with different needs, tastes, and expectations. Nor can we underestimate the barriers that special interests are likely to impose. The present system exists in part because it serves the interests of particular powerful groups who will not yield their power and control easily. But we have the resources, the knowledge, and the potentialities for offering every American a decent standard of medical care, probably within the range of cost we are already investing. Only the future will tell if we had the will and wisdom to proceed.

The Medical Malpractice Dilemma

Many of the important legal and ethical issues in health care reflect the complexity of medical technology and changing social forces. Medicine is just one of many social institutions, and it is affected not only by its own internal development but also by changes in other sectors. Understanding medicine therefore requires understanding trends in the

504   Prospects before Us

society at large—trends in values, social resources, public attitudes, and the social structure in general. Rather than say a little about each of many social and ethical dilemmas, I have chosen one to illustrate the complex relationship between medicine and other social forces. The problem of medical malpractice is thought of by many people simply as a technical issue; it is vastly more complex than that.

Current medical malpractice problems are symptomatic of deeper issues in the practice of medicine, in our system of social insurance, and in the fabric of our society. The noisy manifestations of the malpractice debate—complaints about staggering increases in the insurance premiums physicians pay in certain vulnerable specialties (540, pp. 41–42) or about contingent fees of attorneys (708, p. 18)—are perhaps some of the least important aspects. As is true of many other problems, the symptoms are more easily treated than the basic malady, but symptomatic treatment at best buys time to reflect and to consider more basic long-term approaches.

A great deal has been written about malpractice, but pertinent data to answer many obvious questions are not readily available. Thus it becomes difficult to distinguish the speculative but plausible hypothesis from the true state of affairs. This discussion can do little to remedy this basic shortcoming because we have no new data to clarify issues where they have become obfuscated. My objectives, however, are to define the basic issues underlying the malpractice dilemma, to clarify some common concepts that are amenable to research, and to suggest certain hypotheses that deserve examination.

Medical malpractice litigation is said to perform two important functions: (1) to deter physicians from lax, careless, or negligent behavior (98, p. 242; 540, pp. 42–44) and (2) to compensate patients injured as a consequence of the negligence of the hospital, physician, or ancillary health-care personnel. As to the first function, it is assumed that the threat of possible malpractice litigation encourages prudent behavior beyond that which is learned in the training of the health professional. Particularly in the case of the hospital, such a threat is believed to result in greater attention to risks with low probability (such as those due to inadequate safety precautions, unavailability of specialized equipment that is needed infrequently, or inadequate supervision of personnel). It is not clear what proportion of malpractice claims or dollars awarded is related to such problems (708, pp. 5–12), but it is assumed that since hospitals are rated by risk, there is an incentive operating to avoid malpractice claims (708, pp. 41–42).

Although physicians are not usually rated by risk beyond the nature of their specialized fields, it is assumed that the stigma associated with a malpractice judgment is a significant deterrent to carelessness. It is not obvious, however, that physicians perceive malpractice claims as stigmatizing, and it appears that some feel merely harassed and persecuted by the claims. Some fragmentary and inadequate data suggest that physicians may have sympathy for a colleague who is sued and may refer patients to such a colleague to insure that he does not suffer financially from malpractice litigation (624, pp. 138–39). Perhaps the most troublesome aspect of having a malpractice claim made against a physician is the anxiety, lost time, and uncertainty that may be involved. Even when such claims are rejected and physicians vindicated, being sued is an unpleasant and disruptive experience. Thus the costs to the physician must be weighed not only in terms of the awards actually made but in terms of the total costs of becoming entangled in such an incident. A claim made against a conscientious physician may cause him considerable suffering and may distract him from his best efforts.

The second generally accepted function of the malpractice mechanism is to compensate persons who suffer injury as a result of errors in treatment. But medical malpractice suits are at best a capricious and inequitable means of compensation. While some claimants obtain large awards, others suffering from equally serious injuries receive no compensation at all. If our social insurance system were more satisfactory and provided ample compensation for necessary medical costs and for disability resulting in dependence, the malpractice issue would be a less important concern for us. Although there would still be a need to deal with compensation for pain and suffering resulting from negligence, this is probably the aspect of malpractice having the least social significance. Because we do not have an adequate system of health-care insurance and because assistance for the disabled and dependent is modest, the manner in which the medical malpractice mechanism compensates victims of negligence looms more significant.

The Growth of Litigation

In recent decades medical science and technology have experienced dramatic growth accompanied by increasing specialization and subspecialization of medical care and a larger and more heterogeneous mix of health-care manpower (294). Public expectations concerning the performance of the medical sector have also grown, stimulated by the mass media's treatment of impressive developments in medical technology and knowledge. All of these changes—as I shall attempt to illustrate—contribute both to the probability that errors will occur and that patients, becoming cognizant of errors, will make claims against physicians.

Physicians have available an increasingly powerful technology for evaluating and treating disease that can cause havoc when incorrectly applied. The traditional practitioner with his little black bag was able to affect disease in only a modest way, but his possibilities of doing harm were also more limited than at present. Given the complex technology that physicians now command, human error having important adverse consequences is inevitable even when physicians are fully qualified, careful, and prudent. Even a small lapse in judgment or attention in the application of a complex and risky treatment or diagnostic procedure may have major consequences for the patient in terms of pain experienced or resultant disability. While we all might agree that a certain probability of adverse events is to be expected in the use of high-risk procedures (such as heart catheterization or particular types of biopsies), the physician has no assurance that a malpractice claim will not be made against him when such adverse consequences occur, nor that a finding of fault will not result.

The uncertainty experienced by the physician results in part from the ambiguity of medical standards and the unknown criteria for a finding of malpractice. The occurrence of adverse events varies a great deal among physicians and hospitals and depends both on the quality of the professionals and on the types of cases involved; it has been demonstrated repeatedly that teaching hospitals in general provide higher-quality care than proprietary hospitals (281). The fact that variations in performance exist does not imply that those with poorer performance are guilty of malpractice, yet it remains unclear what standard of medical practice will be perceived by judge or jury as below the acceptable minimum. The determination is arrived at through the process of an adversary proceeding in which claimant and defendant marshal evidence to sustain their positions. Given the nature of this process, it is quite possible that adverse effects, which may be reasonably anticipated in at least some cases in which complex diseases are treated with dangerous medical techniques, may be seen by juries as instances of malpractice.

The problem is made especially difficult in that the existence of a given probability of adverse events does not mean that the occurrence of such events is not a result of error. For example, we can predict quite reliably the approximate deaths and injuries due to automobile accidents in the coming month. We know, given our system of highways, the construction of automobiles, human error in driving, and variable weather conditions, that in the aggregate a certain rate of accidents is inevitable. This does not mean that in any particular accident we cannot specify that the proximate cause of the injury was the error of one of the parties involved. Similarly, while statistically it may be inevitable that a gastroenterologist, in inserting gastroscopes in thousands of patients' stomachs, will pierce the wall of an individual's stomach, any instance in which the stomach is injured may be due to momentary negligence or an error of judgment on the part of the physician. While we recognize that there are errors in all human activities and thus it is unjust to stigmatize the physician in such cases, it still may be fair to compensate the injured patient.

An element in the apparent increase in malpractice awards is the unwillingness of hospitals, physicians, and insurers to contest small claims, even when their merits are dubious, because of the costs of prolonged litigation (30; but see 380). There is a tendency to agree to small settlements to avoid the harassments of litigation. It has been alleged that awareness of this among lawyers encourages litigation that would not have been pursued had defensive efforts been more persistent. In conjunction with certain other incentives for litigation, including the contingent fee and the absence of a requirement to pay costs in an unsuccessful suit, it is not surprising that malpractice litigation occurs more commonly in the United States than in other countries in which these incentives do not exist (7; 761). Depending on one's perspective, the American system may be thought superior in providing poor litigants a fair opportunity to seek redress under circumstances in which they feel they have been injured. The inhibition of such litigation in many countries may reflect too strong a bias in favor of the authority of the medical profession.

The emerging medical organization that has accompanied growing medical knowledge and technology has also probably contributed to increased litigation. As a larger number of people are involved in a patient's care, the risks of error in communication and follow-up treatment are very much increased. Similarly, the fragmentation of care leads to an erosion of the relationships between doctors and patients and of the quality of communication and trust (500). Thus misunderstandings between doctor and patient are more likely to occur and patients are less likely to develop loyalty and commitment to a physician. When things go wrong they are more likely to feel that he is blameworthy and are more likely to consider litigation.

Evidence for this point of view is at best fragmentary. One study in California found that patients who sued doctors reported that the doctors had been unresponsive and had insisted on large payments despite adverse results (73; 74). Some additional support comes from a study of consumer attitudes conducted by the Temple University Institute of Survey Research (560). In this national study involving 1,017 interviews the surveyors found that while respondents had favorable attitudes toward the technical competence of physicians, most people felt that relationships with doctors had deteriorated over the last 20 years (560). A subgroup of respondents reported that either they or members of their families had suffered a negative medical-care experience. Persons reporting such negative experiences were more likely to report also that today's doctors maintained poor doctor-patient relationships (560, p. 678). Major reasons given for the view that physicians have become less dedicated were that they are too interested in money, less accommodating and more difficult to reach, and more impersonal or inconsiderate (560, p. 678). Although it is impossible to infer causal relationships from correlational findings, these data are at least consistent with the hypothesis that deteriorating and impersonal doctor-patient relationships contribute to the malpractice problem.

Still another factor in the rise of litigation is the changing character of both the medical and legal communities. Until relatively recently it was difficult to litigate a malpractice case successfully because of the unavailability of medical testimony (37, pp. 9–10). As American medicine has become more fragmented, medical testimony is more accessible to patients and their attorneys (708, pp. 36–37). Physicians now more commonly concede that they have a responsibility to testify for a patient they believe has been wronged. Similarly, it appears that lawyers are more willing to accept malpractice work, and firms have emerged that specialize in this area (see, for example, 757; see generally 230). It has been alleged that receptivity among lawyers to malpractice litigation increased following the implementation of no-fault automobile insurance. Any serious test of that allegation would require a comparison of data obtained over time from states with and without no-fault automobile insurance. It seems more likely that growing litigation in the medical area is a result of a variety of factors, including the increased availability of medical testimony. Lawyers tend not to accept malpractice work unless medical corroboration is available (167, p. 99). Finally, all of these changes are concurrent with growing sophistication among consumers, increasing acceptance of consumer rights, and greater accessibility to legal services.

There is little question that the growth of medical technology and its dramatic achievements have done a great deal to increase popular expectations of the possibilities of medical treatment. People often expect miracles but are less tolerant of the dangers associated with the use of new techniques. Evidence from other areas of medical-care research suggests that when patients have unrealistic expectations about their medical treatment they feel more angry and dissatisfied with their care and pose more difficult problems of medical management and social adjustment (see 199; 363). It seems reasonable to extrapolate from such studies the principle that public expectations—to the extent they are unrealistic—contribute to growing disappointment in experience and to greater expressions of dissatisfaction, thus contributing to malpractice litigation.

Perhaps most basic—but also more vague—is a growing sense of distrust in contemporary American society. Trust is the glue that cements human relationships, that allows us to proceed—though inadequately informed—with some confidence that the claims made by

others are reliable. We live in a period in which all claims are scrutinized and it has become common to see the motives and sincerity of
people challenged. With the increasing complexity of technology and
social organization there is an enormous proliferation of rules, regulations, and contracts that help to define rights and obligations. Yet even
in the most bureaucratic context written rules are but a small fraction of
the understandings required to carry out activities. Flexibility and
discretion are necessary for effective performance, and these must
depend to some extent on trust. As trust becomes more unstable, efforts
are made to formulate more and more rules to govern behavior, but the
proliferation of rules and the difficulty of writing them in a way that
will achieve the desired ends result in inefficiencies and tendencies
toward manipulation. In short, when the level of distrust becomes too
high social institutions are threatened, and an attempt to impose further rules and regulations will prove an inadequate remedy.

It is difficult to assess to what extent current malpractice difficulties
reflect growing distrust of physicians. Available evidence continues to
support the assertion that physicians are highly regarded by the public
and continue to occupy a privileged status among American occupations (581). But the medical profession in recent years has been subjected to a barrage of criticisms, both from outside and from within, that
has contributed to some loss of trust and confidence. With unfavorable
mortality and morbidity statistics, misuse of human subjects in experimentation, dominance and control in the profession's self-interest, and
profiteering and chicanery on the part of a few physicians in public
programs, the public has been given considerable basis for insecurity.
And this has occurred at the same time that the public has become in
some sense more dependent on medical care for general social sustenance due to the erosion of other social institutions such as the church,
the kinship group, the neighborhood, and the family. The public seems
to share a strange ambivalence about medical care, characterized by
high and often unreasonable expectations, a strong sense of dependency, and a critical attitude. It is precisely when people expect too
much that they are most likely to suffer disappointment.

None of the foregoing should be taken to mean that medicine and
the way it is practiced has made no contribution to the growing sense of
dissatisfaction. Certainly there have been abuses, and the thrust of
medical organization has not been toward the preservation of close
doctor-patient relationships, educational dialogues between practitioners and patients, or the humanization of medical services. While
physicians are often kind and helpful, their priority has been the absorption and efficient application of new technologies, and not medical
practice as a broader social endeavor. But even if their priorities had
been different, it is not clear that the problems we now face could have

been avoided. The malpractice crisis reflects the larger society of which it is a part, and it may be that there is only a limited amount that physicians can do to alleviate it.

The Epidemiology of Litigation

Although it is difficult to locate current data on the occurrence of malpractice claims, the estimates from the National Commission on Medical Malpractice will serve our purposes. Patients tend to be naive about the possibilities and dangers of medical treatment, and to lack any clear standard by which to decide whether the physician behaved negligently. Thus patients may use a variety of standards such as bad outcome, apparent irregularities in the physician's behavior, or advice of friends or relatives as clues to the possibility that they have suffered a wrong. Desire to take some action against a physician may result as much from superficial clues that the patient associates with a bad outcome as from any objective medical circumstance. Or conceivably the motivation for a complaint may result as much from a desire for retribution for what the patient feels is callous and inhumane behavior on the part of the physician as from any serious negative outcome. We know too little about the way medical encounters that are eventually litigated compare with ordinary medical encounters.

Once a patient has come to believe that negligent behavior has occurred he is likely to make inquiries, discussing his experiences with relatives and friends. If he is to make a claim he must find a lawyer willing to pursue the case, and this too will depend on whether he finds an appropriate legal pathway. He may be discouraged by his initial contact with a lawyer who is uninterested in such a case or views the grievance as either inappropriate or unprofitable to pursue. The ability to make successful contact with a suitable lawyer probably depends both on the patient's sophistication and social network and on the characteristics of the bar in the region in which he lives.

On the basis of data from 26 of the largest malpractice insurance carriers, the staff of the Commission on Medical Malpractice estimated that a malpractice incident was reported or alleged by physician or patient for one of every 158,000 patient visits (708, p. 12; see 603). A claim was made for one of every 226,000 visits (708, p. 12). Only one in ten claims ever reached trial, and one-half of the payments made in response to claims in 1970 were for less than $2,000 (603, p. 21). Although the number of cases initiated and the dollar amounts have escalated somewhat in the past few years, the above description remains accurate (158).

A contentious issue is whether too many malpractice suits are being filed. Many physicians feel that litigation is often mischievous and unduly encouraged by a variety of incentives that are not present in other countries (540). Among the procedures often discouraged elsewhere are the contingent fee, the doctrine of *res ipsa loquitur*, the use of juries, and the absence of the requirement that the loser pay the winner's litigation costs (7, p. 860; 761, pp. 851-53). It is important to recognize, however, that the United States differs in fundamental ways from some of the other countries with which it is compared. American culture encourages an attitude less acceptant of authority and more willing to challenge it than almost any other country in the world. We also have a heterogeneous population, a wide variety of alternative value systems and life styles, and extremely effective national systems of communication. The population is highly mobile geographically, and people's ties with neighborhoods and communities are weak. Moreover, American medicine is more complex, heterogeneous, technologically developed, and uneven in quality than that of most comparably developed nations. Americans are also more likely to have high expectations of their medical care, and probably have better access to lawyers. Thus, regardless of incentives for litigation inherent in the legal system, the conditions exist, particularly in urbanized areas, for a demanding and aggressive stance toward the medical-care system. In England, and perhaps in other countries, patients are more docile and accepting of whatever care they are given (487).

If we had an adequate definition of "fault" we could determine through investigation those cases in which injury resulted from negligence and compare them with malpractice claims filed and awards actually made. In the absence of such data some indirect indication of whether too many claims are being made can be obtained through surveys of lawyers and patients. The national malpractice commission surveyed lawyers who reported that they accepted approximately one in eight claims among clients alleging malpractice (167, pp. 99–101). About half of the claims rejected by the lawyers were attributed to a lack of liability. Before lawyers accepted a malpractice case they usually required evidence that there was a reasonable possibility of malpractice, corroborated by a physician's opinion. Attorneys reported that malpractice claims took more time to litigate than other negligence work and felt that they were turning down worthy claims because the stakes were too small in relation to the required work.

The Temple University survey referred to earlier provides some data from a consumer perspective. About two-fifths of the 1,017 respondents reported that they, their spouses, or their dependents had suffered a negative medical-care experience within the past ten years (560, pp. 668–75). Such reports, of course, reflect only the perceptions of the respondents and provide no indication of the degree of malpractice involved. But it is interesting that only 37 respondents, or 8 percent of respondents reporting adverse experiences, indicated that legal advice was considered (560, pp. 674–75). Only 14 respondents took the matter up with a legal adviser, and six made a claim of malpractice. Of these, two later withdrew the claim without settlement, two settled before trial, and two claims were still in process at the time of the study (560, p. 675). Thus it appears that very few of the grievances experienced lead to claims of negligence.

These two studies provide some indirect indication that the number of claims made against physicians is not excessive, given the extent to which patients perceive grievances and the extent to which lawyers feel that claims of negligence have some merit. Moreover, physicians working in the area of quality assurance have reported that serious errors occur frequently and that a large proportion of hospital records show major errors of omission or commission (708, p. 10). While only some of these errors may result in serious adverse consequences for the patient, any of them potentially can become an issue in a malpractice suit. Lawyers apparently feel that too much work is involved in pursuing small claims, and in any case the costs of initiating litigation would leave litigants with very little compensation. Indeed, one of the major problems with the existing malpractice mechanism is the high administrative cost and the modest compensation left for the litigant (708, p. 34; 466, p. 17). A countervailing tendency, as suggested earlier, may be the willingness of defendants to settle small suits quickly to avoid their nuisance value, thus encouraging such claims. But it is likely that the deterrent against small claims is the more powerful influence.

The Problem of Defensive Medicine

One of the most confused areas involved in the malpractice discussion concerns the allegations of defensive medicine. Physicians have been vocal in their claims that the current malpractice situation encourages them to engage in protective maneuvers that are expensive but have relatively little value (164, p. 942; 584; 708, p. 14). Some state that the growing litigation induces them to use expensive and sometimes risky diagnostic procedures to provide a record protecting them against liability, should their behavior be at issue. To the extent that this occurs, it unnecessarily inflates the costs of medical care. Other physicians claim that the threat of litigation forces them into a defensive posture when performing certain procedures or treating certain types of injuries associated with high rates of litigation. In neither case is there much hard evidence that defensive medicine significantly distorts the process of medical care.

Hershey (320) has tried to narrow the issue by defining defensive medicine as a "deviation from what the physician believes is sound practice and which is generally so regarded, induced by a threat of liability" (320, p. 72). The key phrase here is "generally so regarded," the content of which is difficult to define. The core of the difficulty in making sense of defensive medicine is the looseness and ambiguity of medical standards. Defensive medicine occurs presumably because physicians feel that they are vulnerable to charges of negligence when they fail to perform certain "unnecessary" tests or procedures such as a skull X ray following head trauma. Physicians would be vulnerable if they did not use such procedures because other physicians, competent in their specialty, may testify in malpractice cases that the performance of such procedures is essential for an appropriate assessment of the patient's injury. Since physicians find it difficult to agree about many aspects of diagnosis and treatment, the physician who wishes to follow a less elaborate course of evaluation and treatment may feel that he becomes vulnerable in the event of a claim against him. It is alleged that this leads to the use of unnecessary procedures.

The purpose of standards is to bring the practice of each physician to a minimal norm of acceptable practice. To the extent that a standard is established when there is considerable disagreement, the standard induces persons to practice differently from the way they would in its absence. For those who agree with the standard, it is seen as a definition of appropriate care; for those who see the standard as unrealistically high, conformity constitutes defensive medicine. In short, arguments about defensive medicine inevitably reflect disagreements and confusion about the practice of medicine itself.

If defensive medicine were as great a problem as many physicians allege, one might expect certain regional variations in practice. For example, one would suppose that in states or localities with high rates of litigation physicians in particular specialties would be much more likely to use certain procedures in dealing with problematic cases than would comparable physicians in low-litigation areas. Although there are no large-scale studies of the question, one attempt to examine this hypothesis found little evidence in its support and suggested that varying patterns of physician behavior are more likely to reflect local norms and professional customs than the threat of litigation (164, pp. 959–60). Although it is no doubt true that some physicians order tests and procedures that they feel are unnecessary due to their fear that a lack of such testing may lead to liability, the fact may be that these tests and procedures should be done. The real issue is one of standards, and in this area medicine is in a muddle. As a result, there are some crucial issues of defensive medicine, but they are different from the examples physicians usually cite.

Most of what is regarded as acceptable community practice is based on judgments of medical process, not of outcome. These judgments are made without serious consideration of their cost-effectiveness. Thus certain practices that are based entirely on process judgments have become normative, even in some cases in which outcome studies raise serious questions about the value of the procedure. Such norms defining customary practice make it difficult for a physician to act solely on the basis of the research literature when this literature is not consistent with custom.

Take, for example, the proliferation of intensive coronary-care units. While many physicians believe such units to be of value in saving lives, controlled trials fail to support this belief, at least for many common cardiac incidents (130; 462). But given the climate of physician opinion and customary practice, a medical group would feel extremely vulnerable to malpractice claims if it departed from the use of coronary intensive care despite a belief that such care is unnecessary and expensive. When there is division in the medical community concerning the value of a given procedure, a prudent physician is likely to lean toward doing too much, since physicians involved in a malpractice trial might be able to make a more convincing case to a jury that the procedure should have been undertaken. Since the outcome of a contest between adversaries is in doubt when the medical situation is unclear, the uncertainty is likely to reinforce the technologic imperative.

From a purely economic point of view, an important question about the existing malpractice mechanism is the extent to which it increases the total aggregate costs of medical practice by reinforcing conservative decisions. As resources for medical care become more limited relative to the increasing technological possibilities, medical planners will have to develop means to establish priorities and to determine which procedures truly enhance outcome. Whether they will do so through government-promulgated standards, through local standards developed by professional standards review organizations or peer review groups, through consumer participation and input, or some combination of all three, is not clear. What is required is a mechanism for legitimizing the standards adopted so that professionals who conform to them can feel relatively safe from negligence claims. Such standards should also reflect cost-effective practice so that they do not further reinforce the technologic imperative and the trend of increased medical-care costs.

Distributive Effects of Litigation

The existing malpractice mechanism is an inequitable way of compensating persons who suffer adverse consequences as a result of negligence. It is inequitable because the awareness of medical error, the process of making a claim, and the amount of compensation paid are not congruent with the adversities suffered by patients because of negligence. Compensation tends to be much influenced by a variety of social, psychological, and personal factors. Moreover, the true costs involved in bringing and contesting claims are substantial, and only a modest proportion of the money awarded constitutes actual compensation to the litigant. While no-fault insurance has been advocated for the medical-care area, such a proposal leaves unsolved the problem of distinguishing adverse outcomes resulting from negligence from those that are the product of natural development of the patient's condition or that result unavoidably from high-risk therapy. Many medical measures are dangerous but are used to forestall even greater adverse consequences related to an illness. Under the existing tort system the adversary process reaches the necessary decisions as to which incidents can be said to flow from physician error as opposed to other causes. Under a no-fault system other fact-finding and decision-making techniques would be necessary.

The key point is that the malpractice problem is but a symptom of more basic problems in the organization and provision of health care and social services. An effective substitute for the existing system must be sensitive to the changing balance of power between patients and physicians and must contain adequate channels for patients who feel wronged or harmed to state their grievances and to receive fair consideration. The development of such an alternative system will require our long-term efforts (see 16 and 316).

Chapter 19

THE FUTURE OF MEDICAL SOCIOLOGY

In closing, I would like to raise briefly some issues concerning the development and direction of the field of medical sociology as a scholarly enterprise and as an area of applied research (also see 486). As noted in the introduction, medical sociology consists of efforts to develop sociological ideas within the contexts of medical systems and to study important applied issues concerning disease processes and patient care.

A large proportion of the sociological effort is devoted to applied concerns. In this capacity the sociologist performs a role structurally similar to that of the clinical psychologist, the market researcher, and the biostatistician. A number of years ago Robert Straus (675) suggested that medical sociology be logically divided into two categories— sociology *of* medicine and sociology *in* medicine. The former, he argued, was concerned with studying such factors as organizational structure, role relationships, and the functions of medicine as a system of behavior; the latter, as he described it, concerned collaborative research or teaching and the integration of concepts and techniques. Straus observed that these two types of medical sociology appeared to be incompatible, and he indicated that he felt that the sociology of medicine could be carried out best by persons outside the formal medical setting who do not become too closely identified with medical teaching or clinical research.

The sociologist who is interested in the medical field finds himself in somewhat of a dilemma. If he keeps his distance from the doctor and the medical setting, he often loses the opportunity to become immersed in the medical context and to become familiar with the problems and difficulties that characterize medical care. If he becomes too immersed in the medical context, in contrast, he frequently loses his unique perspective and the opportunity to make a distinctive contribution. The sociologist as a sociologist brings to the medical context a perspective and tradition that are quite different from those that prevail there. As a student of social processes he usually seeks to attack a general rather than a specific problem and a theoretical issue rather than an applied need (although these need not be incompatible). Thus he must formulate the sociological aspects of his problem, which may involve analyzing the assumptions underlying medical organization and behavior and the ideologies and values his medical colleagues hold. In doing this he must often take an attitude more skeptical than theirs, and this may produce particular strains in his relationships with his medical associates. Being a dissenter among a group of prestigious persons, the sociologist often wishes to avoid conflict and to represent his discipline favorably. Thus the pressure is great to allow his medical colleagues to define the problem and the nature of the sociologist's contribution to it; perhaps too often the sociologist, in trying to gain acceptance in this context, yields more of his perspective than he realizes. Whatever merit such "team perspectives" may have, something may be lost from the point of view of sociology and medicine, for the sociologist is no longer prepared to provide a unique point of view.

Perspectives open to the sociologist should not be limited, and it is precisely for this reason that it is important that sociologists do not confine their investigations in reference to the limited perspectives of particular professional groups. One can look at medical contexts simultaneously from a variety of perspectives—from the point of view of the physician who wishes to provide good medical care, facilitate his work, retain his independence, and resist intervention in his relationships with his clients; from the perspective of the patient who similarly may wish the medical context to be designed so that every wish and psychological urge is supported with nurture and care; from the point of view of the hospital administrator who may want good medical care but also wishes to prevent waste and inefficiency; and from the point of view of the medical faculty who, unhampered by the competition and pressures of primary care, find it difficult to understand why practitioners are not practicing better medicine. We must not forget that human perspectives are greatly influenced by the situations in which people find themselves; the problems people see often depend on the pressures, discomforts, and conflicts they themselves experience. In this sense medicine as a social institution is not very different from industry or education. The perspectives that medical people adopt tell us something about their jobs and problems as they see them. The sociological perspective, however, is more than a view of one or another participant in the human situation. It is an attempt to represent the interaction of perspectives and actions (345).

In recognizing the dangers of becoming too immersed in the medical context, it is equally important to note the dangers of being too distant from it. Sociologists who have only casual contact with physicians and medical organizations sometimes jump to injudicious conclusions that could not be maintained if they had any appreciation of the complexities and difficulties intrinsic to the medical decision-making role. No doubt doctors, like other professionals, are concerned with their self-interest. But not every aberration in medical practice is explainable on the basis of such interpretations. Although we must be careful that we do not raise medical ideology to sociological gospel, we must also guard against the opposite error that fails to attribute any integrity or dignity to the motives of medical men.

The importance of social science to medicine is not dependent on demonstrating "social causation" of disease. There is a long tradition in social and physical rehabilitation that is premised upon the idea of controlling disability associated with a condition rather than reversing the condition itself. Many conditions are irreversible, given the current state of knowledge and technology. Thus attempts are made to provide devices for the person, or techniques for changing his living situation, so that his condition, injury, or defect results in the least possible disability. This can be achieved by changing some aspects of the person and providing him with new skills, as in the provision of artificial hands or seeing-eye dogs and the development of artificial talking devices for those who have had cancer of the larynx and can no longer engage in conventional speech. In each of these cases individuals are provided with new tools that help them overcome the disability resulting from the basic condition and a period of training that allows them to accommodate to their use. Disability can also be contained, as in the physical rehabilitation field, by controlling the environment in various ways. Thus housewives who have disabling conditions may continue to meet role expectations with the help of special kitchen equipment. In short, the operating principle of such rehabilitation attempts is to change the skills and environment of a person so that his condition results in the least possible disability and disruption of life patterns, and sociologists can contribute significantly in this endeavor.

As the sociology of medicine has developed, sociologists increasingly find employment outside the university in health agencies, government, foundations, consulting firms, and a variety of other contexts. As we move into the 1980s, employment opportunities in academic institutions are likely to be limited, and many more medical sociologists will develop careers outside sociology departments. They will become engaged in health-planning efforts, evaluation research, demonstration projects, policy research, and a variety of other activities for which disciplinary training has not fully prepared them (165). In all likelihood training programs will change to accommodate to a new type of job market, but if past experience is any guide, they will change slowly and over a relatively long period of time. Thus the student of medical sociology will often have to take the initiative in familiarizing himself with subjects and skills that are not routinely taught in sociology departments.

The student embarking on a career in medical sociology outside a sociology department will confront different values, assumptions, and norms of behavior from those he or she is most used to. First, the student will find that the accepted value of study of a problem for its own sake—because the student is curious or wants to understand—is not as widely accepted outside the university. The student will more frequently have to justify his interest in a project in terms of possible applications or policy significance. Although the sociology department may give great emphasis to theoretical perspectives, methodological niceties, and qualified conclusions, those outside will be more impatient, expecting the investigator to report what he or she has learned that will be useful in some fashion in relation to some pressing need. The practical matter of the job at hand will take on supreme importance, and the concerns of the discipline will receive little priority. The medical sociologist who cannot remove himself from the traditional concerns of the discipline will soon give the impression of being impractical and inflexible.

Although the medical sociologist is taught to seek understanding of social phenomena with the realization that it may not be possible to change conditions in the short run, he will frequently confront government officials, legislators, and public-health workers who care less about explanations and understanding and more about those variables that can be manipulated through public policies. Thus the emphasis is on what can be done rather than on understanding the larger forces affecting health, disease, or nonutilization of health-care facilities. Although the restriction of studies and policy analysis to variables that can be manipulated through public policy may seem one-dimensional to the student, he can console himself with the fact that the concerns of Adam Smith, Karl Marx, Charles Darwin, and Sigmund Freud may have seemed equally academic, but their ideas changed the world. Most projects outside of academic institutions are designed to deal with practical issues, and the medical sociologists who work in such contexts must accommodate to this fact.

The nature of social-medical research requires much more complex inquiries than have been traditional in sociology, and many problems require interdisciplinary endeavors. The effective medical sociologist must know not only his own area but must familiarize himself with the problems he is working on, the relevant activities of related disciplines, and the ways his own work and the work of those from other disciplines might interrelate. The sociologist interested in schizophrenia must remain aware of the developments in psychiatric diagnosis and in population genetics as well as in his own interests in coping theory, social class, and stressful life events. Similarly, the student interested in the social epidemiology of coronary heart disease must know a great deal about the condition he is studying, nonsocial risk factors, and many other matters. Interdisciplinary study is often difficult. Persons from different disciplines and traditions must learn to understand each other's perspectives and to communicate effectively. This is not always easy, and it takes a great deal of time, but the medical sociologist who fails to develop such skills will find his opportunities restricted.

As medical sociologists come to work in a variety of agencies, with roles that relate to policy, they find that political considerations govern their activities to a much greater extent than in the university. They discover that decisions are made more frequently in the process of political bargaining than in response to what the existing data might suggest. If the sociologist expects his research to lead directly to policy implementation, he is likely to be bitterly disappointed. If he has a long-range perspective and recognizes that his research helps create a climate of opinion and opens new considerations in policy formulation, then he is more likely to find gratification in his role.

It is clear that social approaches and the work carried out by medical sociologists and health-services researchers play a more important role in the medical-care system than ever before. Medical sociologists are being called upon to participate in the development and expansion of innovations in treatment and in the delivery of health-care services through their roles both in design of interventions and in evaluation. Medical care is presently in flux, providing an opportunity for new interventions and also an opportunity to evaluate them in order to assess their impact. It is not unusual for programs developed for one purpose to meet different needs, and it is essential to describe very carefully the development of new programs and their impact on varying groups. Such evaluations have often been promised but rarely performed, both because of the technical and practical difficulties of carrying them out and because evaluation research is often a serious threat.

In moving into a variety of new roles that will become possible as a result of the further development of health planning, professional standards review organizations, behavioral science in medical schools, and contract and evaluation research, the medical sociologist would do well to remember people's tremendous abilities to mold the environment for their own purposes and needs and would benefit from directing attention beyond the formulation of new social ideas in health to the manner in which they become implemented and the purposes for which they are used. Such scrutiny has considerable potential for enhancing both effective action and the sociological enterprise.

BIBLIOGRAPHY

General Sources

In addition to the references listed below, which can be used to pursue various particular interests, Litman (450) has prepared an extensive bibliography by subject in the area, and a fairly detailed bibliography is also available in *Handbook of Medical Sociology* (232). It might be useful to note as well those journals that publish articles on medicine and medical care most commonly of sociological interest. Students can learn a great deal by scanning these journals from time to time or by pursuing in greater detail issues of particular interest to them.

Although articles of interest to medical sociology occasionally appear in the *American Journal of Sociology*, the *American Sociological Review*, and *Social Forces*, the most relevant articles appear in the *Journal of Health and Social Behavior*, a specialized medical-sociology journal published by the American Sociological Association. Some of the best articles on health-care research appear in the *New England Journal of Medicine*, a high-quality journal directed toward the general physician, and *The Lancet*, a British medical journal, also often carries articles of high quality dealing with social implications. Occasional articles appear as well in the *Journal of the American Medical Association*. Research on medical care is more commonly reported in *Medical Care*, *Inquiry*, and the *Journal of Health Services*. While *Medical Care* is the most general source for the reporting of research results from health-services research, the *Journal of Health Services* maintains a strong operations research emphasis. *Inquiry*, a journal published by the Blue Cross Association, tends to carry articles dealing mainly with the economics of care; more theoretical papers on the economics of health can be found occasionally in the *American Economic Review* and the *Journal of Human Resources*. Discussions involving a comparative national perspective are found most often in the *International Journal of Health Services*.

523

Another journal giving emphasis to social science in contrast to medical care is *Social Science and Medicine*. General articles on public health, as well as some epidemiological studies, are found in the *American Journal of Public Health* and the *Milbank Memorial Fund Quarterly* (now entitled *Health and Society*). Other general sources for social-epidemiological study include the *Journal of Chronic Diseases* and the *British Journal of Preventive and Social Medicine*. Every disease, of course, has its own epidemiology, and important epidemiological studies are reported in a vast number of specialty journals.

There are many journals dealing with psychiatry and its various facets. For the report of empirical investigations I have found the *Archives of General Psychiatry* and the *British Journal of Psychiatry* most useful. The *American Journal of Orthopsychiatry* is more socially oriented than the above journals, but it also tends to be more ideological and less empirical. Other relevant journals carrying articles dealing with social psychiatry and community care include *Mental Hygiene*, the *Journal of Nervous and Mental Disease*, the *American Journal of Psychiatry*, *Social Psychiatry*, and the *Journal of Community Mental Health*. *Psychiatry*, a journal started by Harry Stack Sullivan, tends to maintain a strong social-science perspective but with a psychoanalytic orientation.

There are a vast number of medical journals dealing with specialized topics of interest to social scientists. Many of them, such as the *Journal of Medical Education*, commonly have articles by social and behavioral scientists. In recent years, with growing interest in the social aspects of medicine, there has been a proliferation of new journals dealing with social topics. Some new journals that would be of interest to behavioral science students include the *Journal of Human Stress*, the *Journal of Medicine and Philosophy*, and the *Journal of Health Politics, Policy and Law*. For keeping up on social and economic news dealing with medical care, both *Medical Economics* and *Medical World News* keep a close eye on current events and give some view of the issues that currently concern doctors. The *AMA News* is a rich source of current events, seen primarily from organized medicine's point of view.

There are several thousand medical journals in the world dealing with every conceivable topic, problem area, and subspecialty. Almost every health profession has its own journal, and the larger ones, such as nursing, have numerous journals. Students interested in a specific topic ought to consult the *Index Medicus*, which catalogs most of the world's medical literature and is a handy aid for pursuing any specific topic of medical interest. The National Library of Medicine has computerized this index (MEDLARS), which allows the student or researcher to obtain a computerized printout of references on almost any subject. The usefulness of the MEDLARS system, however, depends on one's ability to program rather specific reference requirements. If the designations are too general, the computerized printout of references includes too much junk. Most university medical libraries have facilities for using the MEDLARS system, and the services are often provided free or at modest cost to the student or researcher.

There are excellent sources reporting vital statistics, results of national health surveys, health-resources statistics, and data on health manpower. Particularly useful are the various research and discussion series published by the National Center for Health Statistics, and lists of their publications and research series are available from them. The World Health Organization of the United Nations provides valuable social-demographic and health information from most countries of the world. The National Center for Health Services Research and Development maintains a publication series on health-services research, and many of their publications are available through the National Technical Information Service in Springfield, Virginia. Excellent statistical reports on national health care are issued by the Social Security Administration, and numerous substantive reports on a great array of problems are published directly by the National Institutes of Health and the Alcohol, Drug Abuse, and Mental Health Administration. A continuing flow of reports are available from various congressional committees dealing with health-care legislation, and the American Medical Association in recent years has issued a monthly title source index, *Medical Socioeconomic Research Sources*.

One of the greatest problems for a new student of medical sociology and health-services research is the proliferation of publications dealing with health care. Much of it is worthless, and only a minority of the publications provide any new primary data and analysis. For the beginner I suggest concentrating on the more central and accessible sources: the *Journal of Health and Social Behavior*, *Medical Care*, the *New England Journal of Medicine*, *Health and Society*, the publications of the National Center for Health Statistics, and the two or three major publications in the student's particular area of interest or disciplinary concern. If the student is in sociology, it is valuable to scan routinely the *American Sociological Review*, the *American Journal of Sociology*, and *Social Science and Medicine*. If more interested in economics, it would be more appropriate for the student to focus on the *American Economic Review*, the *Journal of Human Resources*, and *Inquiry*. If in public health, the *American Journal of Public Health* would be a major source, and so on.

References

1. Abel-Smith, Brian. 1964. *The Hospitals, 1800—1948*. London: Heinemann.

2. Abel-Smith, Brian. 1967. An International Study of Health Expenditure and Its Relevance for Health Planning. Public Health Paper no. 32. Geneva: World Health Organization.

3. Abel-Smith, Brian, and K. Gales. 1964. British Doctors at Home and Abroad. Occasional Papers on Social Administration, no. 8. Hertfordshire: Codicote Press.

4. Ackerknecht, Erwin H. 1959. A Short History of Psychiatry. Translated by S. Wolff. New York: Hafner.

5. Aday, Lu Ann. 1972. The Utilization of Health Services: Indices and Correlates. National Center for Health Services Research and Development, DHEW Publication no. (HSM) 73-3003. Washington: Government Printing Office.

6. Aday, Lu Ann. 1975. "Economic and Noneconomic Barriers to the Use of Needed Medical Services." Medical Care 13 (June): 447–56.

7. Addison, Phillip H., and Peter Baylis. 1973. "The Malpractice Problem in Great Britain." In Report of the Secretary's Commission on Medical Malpractice, DHEW Publication no. (OS) 73-88 and 73-89, pp. 854-70. Washington: Government Printing Office.

8. Aiken, Linda H. 1976. "Chronic Illness and Responsive Ambulatory Care." In The Growth of Bureaucratic Medicine: An Inquiry into the Dynamics of Patient Behavior and the Organization of Medical Care, by David Mechanic, pp. 239-51. New York: Wiley-Interscience.

9. Alderman, Michael H. 1977. "High Blood Pressure: Do We Really Know Whom to Treat and How?" New England Journal of Medicine 296 (March 31): 753-55.

10. Alexander, Franz. 1950. Psychosomatic Medicine: Its Principles and Applications. New York: Norton.

11. Alford, Robert R. 1972. "The Political Economy of Health Care: Dynamics without Change." Politics and Society 2 (Winter): 127-64.

12. Alford, Robert R. 1975. Health Care Politics: Ideological and Interest Group Barriers to Reform. Chicago: University of Chicago Press.

13. Allport, F. 1934. "The J-Curve Hypothesis of Conforming Behavior." Journal of Social Psychology 5: 141-83.

14. Altman, Isidore, and W. W. Haythorn. 1965. "Interpersonal Exchange in Isolation." Sociometry 28: 411-26.

15. Altman, Stuart. 1971. Present and Future Supply of Registered Nurses. DHEW Publication no. 72-134. Washington: Government Printing Office.

16. American Arbitration Association. 1976. Statutory Provisions for Binding Arbitration of Medical Malpractice Claims. National Center for Health Services Research, DHEW Publication no. (HRA) 77-3165. Washington: Government Printing Office.

17. American Nurses' Association. 1976. Facts about Nursing, 74-75. Kansas City: American Nurses' Association.

18. Andersen, Ronald. 1968. A Behavioral Model of Families' Use of Health

Services. Research Series 25. Chicago: Center for Health Administration Studies.

19. Andersen, Ronald, Björn Smedby, and Odin W. Anderson. 1970. *Medical Care Use in Sweden and the United States: A Comparative Analysis of Systems and Behavior.* Research Series 27. Chicago: Center for Health Administration Studies.

20. Andersen, Ronald, and John F. Newman. 1973. "Societal and Individual Determinants of Medical Care Utilization in the United States." *Milbank Memorial Fund Quarterly* 51 (Winter): 95–124.

21. Andersen, Ronald, Joanna Kravits, Odin W. Anderson, and Joan Daley. 1973. *Expenditures for Personal Health Services: National Trends and Variations, 1953–1970.* U.S. Health Resources Administration, DHEW Publication no. (HRA) 74–3105. Washington: Government Printing Office.

22. Anderson, Odin W. 1958. "Infant Mortality and Social and Cultural Factors: Historical Trends and Current Patterns." In *Patients, Physicians and Illness: A Sourcebook in Behavioral Science and Health,* edited by E. Gartly Jaco, pp. 10–24. New York: Free Press.

23. Anderson, Odin W. 1963. "Health Services Systems in the United States and Other Countries: Critical Comparisons." *New England Journal of Medicine* 269: 839–43, 896–900.

24. Anderson, Odin W. 1963. "The Utilization of Health Services." In *Handbook of Medical Sociology,* edited by Howard E. Freeman, Sol Levine, and Leo G. Reeder, pp. 349–67. Englewood Cliffs, N.J.: Prentice-Hall.

25. Anderson, Odin W. 1972. *Health Care: Can There Be Equity? The United States, Sweden, and England.* New York: Wiley-Interscience.

26. Anderson, Odin W. 1973. "Health Services in the USSR." Selected Papers, no. 42. Chicago: Graduate School of Business, University of Chicago.

27. Anderson, Odin W., and J. Feldman, 1956. *Family Medical Costs and Voluntary Health Insurance: A Nationwide Survey.* New York: McGraw-Hill.

28. Anderson, Odin W., and Ronald Andersen. 1972. "Patterns of Use of Health Services." In *Handbook of Medical Sociology,* 2d ed., edited by Howard E. Freeman, Sol Levine, and Leo G. Reeder, pp. 386–406. Englewood Cliffs, N.J.: Prentice-Hall.

29. Angrist, S., et al. 1963. "Tolerance of Deviant Behavior, Posthospital Performance Levels, and Rehospitalization." In World Congress of Psychiatry, Third, Montreal, 1961, *Proceedings,* edited by R. A. Cleghorn, vol. 3, pp. 237–41. Toronto: University of Toronto Press.

30. Annas, George J. 1974. "Medical Malpractice: Are the Doctors Right?" *Trial* 10 (July/August): 59–63.

31. Antonovsky, Aaron. 1967. "Social Class, Life Expectancy and Overall Mortality." *Milbank Memorial Fund Quarterly* 45 (April): 31–73.

32. Antonovsky, Aaron. 1972. "A Model to Explain Visits to the Doctor: With Specific Reference to the Case of Israel." *Journal of Health and Social Behavior* 13 (December): 446–54.

33. Apple, Dorrian. 1960. "How Laymen Define Illness." *Journal of Health and Human Behavior* 1: 219–25.

34. Apple, Dorrian, ed. 1960. *Sociological Studies of Health and Sickness.* New York: McGraw-Hill.

35. Arens, Richard. 1974. *Insanity Defense.* New York: Philosophical Library.

36. Arrow, Kenneth J. 1963. "Uncertainty and the Welfare Economics of Medical Care." *American Economic Review* 53 (December): 941–73.

37. Averbach, Albert. 1960. *Handling Accident Cases.* Rochester, N.Y.: Lawyers Cooperative.

38. Back, Kurt W. 1972. *Beyond Words: The Story of Sensitivity Training and the Encounter Movement.* New York: Russell Sage Foundation.

39. Baird, Leonard L. 1975. "The Characteristics of Medical Students and Their Views of the First Year." *Journal of Medical Education* 50 (December): 1092–99.

40. Bakwin, H. 1945. "Pseudodoxia Pediatrica." *New England Journal of Medicine* 232: 691–97.

41. Bales, Robert F. 1944. "The 'Fixation Factor' in Alcohol Addiction: An Hypothesis Derived from a Comparative Study of Irish and Jewish Social Norms." Ph.D. dissertation, Harvard University.

42. Balint, Michael. 1957. *The Doctor, His Patient and the Illness.* New York: International Universities Press.

43. Bandura, Albert. 1969. *Principles of Behavior Modification.* New York: Holt.

44. Barber, Bernard, John J. Lally, Julia Loughlin Makarushka, and Daniel Sullivan. 1973. *Research on Human Subjects: Problems of Social Control in Medical Experimentation.* New York: Russell Sage Foundation.

45. Baric, L. 1969. "Recognition of the 'At-Risk' Role: A Means to Influence Health Behavior." *International Journal of Health Education* 12: 24–34.

46. Bart, Pauline B. 1968. "Social Structure and Vocabularies of Discomfort: What Happened to Female Hysteria?" *Journal of Health and Social Behavior* 9 (September): 188–93.

47. Barton, Allen H. 1969. *Communities in Disaster: A Sociological Analysis of Collective Stress Situations.* Garden City, N.Y.: Doubleday, Anchor.

48. Basowitz, H., et al. 1955. *Anxiety and Stress.* New York: McGraw-Hill.

49. Beam, L., et al. 1964. "Social Class and Schizophrenia: A Ten-Year Follow-Up." In *Blue-Collar World: Studies of the American Worker,* edited by Arthur Shostak and William Gomberg, pp. 381–91. Englewood Cliffs, N.J.: Prentice-Hall.

50. Becker, Howard S. 1963. *Outsiders: Studies in the Sociology of Deviance.* New York: Free Press.

51. Becker, Howard S. 1967. "History, Culture and Subjective Experience: An Exploration of the Social Bases of Drug-Induced Experiences." *Journal of Health and Social Behavior* 8 (September): 163–76.

52. Becker, Howard S., Blanche Geer, Everett C. Hughes, and Anselm L. Strauss.

1961. *Boys in White: Student Culture in Medical School*. Chicago: University of Chicago Press.

53. Becker, Howard S., Blanche Geer, and Everett C. Hughes. 1968. *Making the Grade: The Academic Side of College Life*. New York: Wiley.

54. Becker, Marshall H., ed. 1974. *The Health Belief Model and Personal Health Behavior*. Thorofare, N.J.: Slack.

55. Beecher, Henry K. 1959. *Measurement of Subjective Responses: Quantitative Effects of Drugs*. New York: Oxford University Press.

56. Beecher, Henry K. 1961. "Surgery as a Placebo." *Journal of the American Medical Association* 176: 1102–1107.

57. Beeson, Paul B. 1974. "Some Good Features of the British National Health Service." *Journal of Medical Education* 49 (January): 43–49.

58. Beeson, Paul B., and Walsh McDermott, eds. 1963. *Cecil-Loeb Textbook of Medicine*. 11th ed. Philadelphia: Saunders.

59. Belknap, Ivan. 1956. *Human Problems of a State Mental Hospital*. New York: McGraw-Hill.

60. Bem, Daryl J. 1965. "An Experimental Analysis of Self-Persuasion." *Journal of Experimental Social Psychology* 1 (August): 199–218.

61. Benjamin, Bernard. 1965. *Social and Economic Factors Affecting Mortality*. The Hague: Mouton.

62. Benjamin, Bernard. 1968. *Health and Vital Statistics*. London: Allen and Unwin.

63. Bennett, Edward H. III. 1976. "Medical Group Practice in the United States, 1975." In *Reference Data on Profile of Medical Practice, 1975–76*, edited by James R. Cantwell, pp. 9–21. Chicago: American Medical Association.

64. Benson, Herbert. 1975. *The Relaxation Response*. New York: Morrow.

65. Berg, Robert L., ed. 1973. *Health Status Indexes*. Chicago. Hospital Research and Educational Trust.

66. Bergman, Abraham B., and Richard J. Werner. 1963. "Failure of Children to Receive Penicillin by Mouth." *New England Journal of Medicine* 268 (June 13): 1334–38.

67. Bergner, Marilyn, Ruth A. Bobbitt, William E. Pollard, Diane P. Martin, and Betty S. Gilson. 1976. "The Sickness Impact Profile: Validation of a Health Status Measure." *Medical Care* 14 (January): 57–67.

68. Bice, Thomas W., et al. 1972. "International Comparisons of Medical Care: Behavioral Results." *Milbank Memorial Fund Quarterly* 50: 57–63.

69. Biddle, B.J., and E.J. Thomas. 1966. *Role Theory: Concepts and Research*. New York: Wiley.

70. Bille, M. 1963. "The Influence of Distance on Admissions to Mental Hospitals." *Acta Psychiatrica Scandinavica* 39: 226–33.

71. Blau, Peter M., and W.R. Scott. 1962. *Formal Organizations*. San Francisco: Chandler.

72. Bloom, Samuel W. 1963. *The Doctor and His Patient*. New York: Russell Sage Foundation.

73. Blum, Richard H. 1957. *The Psychology of Malpractice Suits.* San Francisco: California Medical Association.

74. Blum, Richard H. 1960. *The Management of the Doctor-Patient Relationship.* New York: McGraw-Hill.

75. Blum, Richard H. 1962. "Case Identification in Psychiatric Epidemiology: Methods and Problems." *Milbank Memorial Fund Quarterly* 40 (July): 253-88.

76. Bockoven, J. Sanbourne. 1957. "Some Relationships between Cultural Attitudes toward Individuality and Care of the Mentally Ill." In *The Patient and the Mental Hospital,* edited by Milton Greenblatt et al., pp. 517-26. New York: Free Press.

77. Bockoven, J. Sanbourne. 1972. *Moral Treatment in Community Mental Health.* New York: Springer.

78. Bonner, Thomas N. 1957. *Medicine in Chicago: 1850-1950.* Madison, Wisc.: American History Research Center.

79. Bradburn, Norman M. 1969. *The Structure of Psychological Well-Being.* Chicago: Aldine.

80. Bramwell, Steven T., Minoru Masuda, Nathaniel N. Wagner, and Thomas H. Holmes. 1975. "Psychosocial Factors in Athletic Injuries." *Journal of Human Stress* 1 (June): 6-20.

81. Branch, C.H. 1963. "Legal Problems Related to the Care of the Mentally Ill." *New England Journal of Medicine* 269: 137-42.

82. Branch, C.H. 1963. "Preparedness for Progress." *American Journal of Psychiatry* 120: 1-11.

83. Brenner, M. Harvey. 1976. *Estimating the Social Costs of National Economic Policy.* Fifth Report to the Congressional Research Service of the Library of Congress.

84. Breslow, Lester, and P. Buell. 1960. "Mortality from Coronary Heart Disease and Physical Activity of Work in California." *Journal of Chronic Disease* 11: 421-44.

85. Brim, Orville G., Jr. 1960. "Personality Development and Role Learning." In *Personality Development in Children,* edited by Ira Iscoe and Harold W. Stevenson. Austin: University of Texas Press.

86. Brooke, James W. 1970. "Medical Malpractice: A Socio-Economic Problem from a Doctor's View." *Willamette Law Journal* 6 (June): 225-33.

87. Brooks, Alexander D. 1974. *Law, Psychiatry and the Mental Health System.* Boston: Little, Brown.

88. Brown, George W. 1958. "Post-Hospital Adjustment of Chronic Mental Patients." *Lancet* 2: 685-89.

89. Brown, George W. 1959. "Social Factors Influencing Length of Hospital Stay of Schizophrenic Patients." *British Medical Journal* 2: 1300-1302.

90. Brown, George W. 1960. "Length of Hospital Stay and Schizophrenia: A Review of Statistical Studies." *Acta Psychiatrica et Neurologica Scandinavica* 35: 414-30.

91. Brown, George W. 1967. "The Family of the Schizophrenic Patient." In

Recent Developments in Schizophrenia: A Symposium, edited by Alec Coppen and Alexander Walk, pp. 43–59. Ashford, Kent: Headley.

92. Brown, George W. 1974. "Meaning, Measurement, and Stress of Life Events." In *Stressful Life Events: Their Nature and Effects*, edited by Barbara Snell Dohrenwend and Bruce P. Dohrenwend, pp. 217–43. New York: Wiley-Interscience.

93. Brown, George W., and J. K. Wing. 1962. "A Comprehensive Clinical and Social Survey of Three Mental Hospitals." In *Sociology and Medicine: Studies within the Framework of the British National Health Service*, edited by Paul Halmos. Sociological Review Monograph no. 5. New York: Humanities Press. Keele, Staffordshire: University of Keele.

94. Brown, George W., et al. 1962. "Influence of Family Life on the Course of Schizophrenic Illness." *British Journal of Preventive and Social Medicine* 16: 55–68.

95. Brown, George W., et al. 1966. *Schizophrenia and Social Care*. New York: Oxford University Press.

96. Brown, George W., and J. L. T. Birley. 1968. "Crises and Life Changes and the Onset of Schizophrenia." *Journal of Health and Social Behavior* 9 (September): 203–14.

97. Brown, George W., Máire Ní Bhrolcháin, and Tirril Harris. 1975. "Social Class and Psychiatric Disturbance among Women in an Urban Population." *Sociology* 9 (May): 225–54.

98. Brown, James M. 1970. "Social Resource Allocation through Medical Malpractice." *Willamette Law Journal* 6 (June): 235–52.

99. Bruce, Robert A. 1974. "The Benefits of Physical Training for Patients with Coronary Heart Disease." In *Controversy in Internal Medicine II* edited by Franz J. Ingelfinger, Richard V. Ebert, Maxwell Finland, and Arnold S. Relman, pp. 145–61. Philadelphia: Saunders.

100. Buell, P., and Lester Breslow. 1960. "Mortality from Coronary Heart Disease in California: Men Who Work Long Hours." *Journal of Chronic Disease* 11: 615–26.

101. Bunker, John P. 1970. "Surgical Manpower: A Comparison of Operations and Surgeons in the United States and in England and Wales." *New England Journal of Medicine* 282 (January 15): 135–44.

102. Bunney, William E. 1977. "The Psychobiology of Depression." In *Research on Disorders of the Mind: Progress and Prospects*, pp. 7–9. U.S. National Institute of Mental Health. Washington: Government Printing Office.

103. Cannon, W. G. 1942. "Voodoo Death." *American Anthropologist* 44: 169–81.

104. Cantwell, James R., ed. 1976. *Reference Data on Profile of Medical Practice*. Chicago: American Medical Association, Center for Health Services Research and Development.

105. Caplan, Gerald. 1964. *Principles of Preventive Psychiatry*. New York: Basic Books.

106. Cartwright, Ann. 1964. *Human Relations and Hospital Care*. London: Routledge & Kegan Paul.

107. Cartwright, Ann. 1967. *Patients and Their Doctors: A Study of General Practice*. London: Routledge & Kegan Paul.

108. Cassel, John. 1970. "Physical Illness in Response to Stress." In *Social Stress*, edited by Sol Levine and Norman A. Scotch, pp. 189–209. Chicago: Aldine.

109. Cassel, John, and Herman A. Tyroler. 1961. "Epidemiological Studies of Social Change: Health Status and Recency of Industrialization." *Archives of Environmental Health* 3 (July): 25–33.

110. Caudill, William A., et al. 1952. "Social Structure and Interaction Processes on a Psychiatric Ward." *American Journal of Orthopsychiatry* 22: 314–34.

111. Caudill, William A., and Edward Stainbrook. 1964. "Some Covert Effects of Communication Difficulties in a Psychiatric Hospital." *Psychiatry* 17: 27–40.

112. Chase, H. C. 1965. "White-Nonwhite Mortality Differentials in the United States." In *Health, Education, and Welfare Indicators*, June, pp. 27–38. Washington: Government Printing Office.

113. Christie, Richard, and Florence L. Geis. 1970. *Studies in Machiavellianism*. New York: Academic Press.

114. Chu, Franklin D., and Sharland Trotter. 1974. *The Madness Establishment*. New York: Grossman.

115. Clark, B. 1962. *Educating the Expert Society*, chap. 6. San Francisco: Chandler.

116. Clark, Margaret. 1959. *Health in the Mexican-American Culture*. Berkeley: University of California Press.

117. Clausen, John A. 1956. *Sociology and the Field of Mental Health*. New York: Russell Sage Foundation.

118. Clausen, John A. 1959. "The Sociology of Mental Illness." In *Sociology Today*, edited by Robert K. Merton, Leonard Broom, and Leonard S. Cottrell, Jr., pp. 485–508. New York: Basic Books.

119. Clausen, John A. 1965. "A Discussion of 'Sociocultural Factors in the Epidemiology of Schizophrenia.'" *International Journal of Psychiatry* 1: 301–303.

120. Clausen, John A. 1966. "Mental Disorders." In *Contemporary Social Problems*, 2d ed., edited by Robert K. Merton and Robert A. Nisbet. New York: Harcourt.

121. Clausen, John A., and M. Kohn. 1954. "The Ecological Approach in Social Psychiatry." *American Journal of Sociology* 60: 140–51.

122. Clausen, John A., and Marion Radke Yarrow. 1955. "Paths to the Mental Hospital." *Journal of Social Issues* 11: 25–32.

123. Clausen, John A., and Marion Radke Yarrow, eds. 1955. "The Impact of Mental Illness on the Family." *Journal of Social Issues* 11: entire issue.

124. Clausen, John A., and Robert Straus, eds. 1963. *Medicine and Society.* Philadelphia: American Academy of Political and Social Science.

125. Clute, K. L. 1963. *The General Practitioner: Study of Medical Education and Practice in Ontario and Nova Scotia.* Toronto: University of Toronto Press.

126. Clyne, Max B. 1961. *Night Calls: A Study in General Practice.* Philadelphia: Lippincott. London: Tavistock.

127. Cobb, Beatrix. 1958. "Why Do People Detour to Quacks?" In *Patients, Physicians and Illness: A Sourcebook in Behavioral Science and Health,* edited by E. Gartly Jaco, pp. 283–87. New York: Free Press.

128. Cobb, Beatrix, et al. 1954. "Patient-Responsible Delay of Treatment in Cancer." *Cancer* 7: 920–26.

129. Cobb, S., and J. Rosenbaum. 1956. "A Comparison of Specific Symptom Data Obtained by Nonmedical Interviewers and by Physicians." *Journal of Chronic Disease* 4: 245–52.

130. Cochrane, A. L. 1972. *Effectiveness and Efficiency: Random Reflections on Health Services.* London: Nuffield Provincial Hospitals Trust.

131. Commission on Chronic Illness. 1957. *Chronic Illness in a Large City: The Baltimore Study.* Cambridge: Harvard University Press.

132. Cochrane, A. L., et al. 1951. "Observers' Errors in Taking Medical Histories." *Lancet* 1: 1007–1009.

133. Coelho, George V., David A. Hamburg, and John E. Adams, eds. 1974. *Coping and Adaption.* New York: Basic Books.

134. Cohen, A. K. 1955. *Delinquent Boys: The Culture of the Gang.* New York: Free Press.

135. Coker, Robert E., Jr., et al. 1966. "Medical Careers in Public Health." *Milbank Memorial Fund Quarterly* 44 (April): pt. 1, entire issue.

136. Cole, Philip. 1974. "Morbidity in the United States." In *Mortality and Morbidity in the United States,* edited by Carl L. Erhardt and Joyce E. Berlin, pp. 65–104. Cambridge: Harvard University Press.

137. Cole, Stephen, and Robert Lejeune. 1972. "Illness and the Legitimation of Failure." *American Sociological Review* 37 (June): 347–56.

138. Coleman, James S., Elihu Katz, and Herbert Menzel. 1966. *Medical Innovation: A Diffusion Study.* Indianapolis: Bobbs-Merrill.

139. Colombotos, John. 1969. "Physicians and Medicare: A Before-After Study of the Effects of Legislation on Attitudes." *American Sociological Review* 34 (June): 318–34.

140. Colombotos, John. 1971. "Physicians' Responses to Changes in Health Care: Some Projections." *Inquiry* 8 (March): 20–26.

141. Colombotos, John, Corinne Kirchner, and Michael Millman. 1975. "Physicians View National Health Insurance: A National Study." *Medical Care* 13 (May): 369–96.

142. Columbia University School of Public Health and Administrative Medicine. 1960. *The Quantity, Quality, and Costs of Medical and Hospital Care.* New York: Columbia University Press.

142a Comfort, Alex J. 1964. *The Process of Ageing*. New York: Signet.

143. Committee of Government Operations, U.S. Senate. 1959. *Patterns of Incidence of Certain Diseases throughout the World*. Washington: Government Printing Office.

144. Cooley, Charles H. 1902. *Human Nature and the Social Order*. New York: Scribner. A paperback edition was issued by Schocken in 1964.

145. Cooley, Charles H. 1924. *Social Organization*. New York: Scribner. A paperback edition was issued by Schocken in 1962.

146. Cooper, J. E., R. E. Kendell, B. J. Gurland, L. Sharpe, J. R. M. Copeland, and R. Simon. 1972. *Psychiatric Diagnosis in New York and London: A Comparative Study of Mental Hospital Admissions*. Maudsley Monograph Series, no. 20. London: Oxford University Press.

147. Cooper, Michael H. 1975. *Rationing Health Care*. New York: Halsted.

148. Cooperstock, Ruth. 1971. "Sex Differences in the Use of Mood-Modifying Drugs: An Explanatory Model." *Journal of Health and Social Behavior* 12 (September): 238–44.

149. Cornish, M. J., et al. 1963. *Doctors and Family Planning*. Publication no. 19. New York: National Committee on Maternal Health.

150. Coutu, W. 1951. "Role-Playing vs. Role-Taking: An Appeal for Clarification." *American Sociological Review* 16: 180–87.

151. Crandell, Dewitt L., and Bruce P. Dohrenwend. 1967. "Some Relations among Psychiatric Symptoms, Organic Illness, and Social Class." *American Journal of Psychiatry* 123 (June): 1527–38.

152. Crane, Diana. 1975. *The Sanctity of Social Life: Physicians' Treatment of Critically Ill Patients*. New York: Russell Sage Foundation.

153. Crncich, John. 1976. "The Making of the California Relative Value Studies: The Ideology and Administration of Pricing Policy in the Fee-for-Service Medical Market." Program in Health Administration, University of Wisconsin, Madison.

154. Croog, S. H. 1961. "Ethnic Origins, Educational Level, and Responses to a Health Questionnaire." *Human Organization* 20: 65–69.

155. Crowne, Douglas P., and David Marlowe. 1964. *The Approval Motive: Studies in Evaluative Dependence*. New York: Wiley.

156. Cumming, Elaine, and John Cumming. 1956. "The Locus of Power in a Large Mental Hospital." *Psychiatry* 19: 361–70.

157. Cumming, Elaine, and John Cumming. 1957. *Closed Ranks: An Experiment in Mental Health Education*. Cambridge: Harvard University Press.

158. Curran, William J. 1976. *How Lawyers Handle Medical Malpractice Cases: An Analysis of an Important Medicolegal Study*. National Center for Health Services Research, DHEW Publication no. (HRA) 76-3152. Washington: Government Printing Office.

159. Davis, Ann E., Simon Dinitz, and Benjamin Pasamanick. 1972. "The Prevention of Hospitalization in Schizophrenia: Five Years after an Experimental Program." *American Journal of Orthopsychiatry* 42 (April): 375–88.

160. Davis, Fred. 1963. *Passage through Crisis.* Indianapolis: Bobbs-Merrill.

161. Davis, K. 1938. "Mental Hygiene and the Class Structure." *Psychiatry* 1: 55–65.

162. Davis, Karen. 1975. "Equal Treatment and Unequal Benefits: The Medicare Program." *Milbank Memorial Fund Quarterly (Health and Society)* 53 (Fall): 449–88.

163. Davis, Milton S. 1968. "Variations in Patients' Compliance with Doctors' Advice: An Empirical Analysis of Patterns of Communication." *American Journal of Public Health* 58 (February): 274–88.

164. Defensive Medicine Project. 1971. "The Medical Malpractice Threat: A Study of Defensive Medicine." *Duke Law Journal* 1971 (December): 939–93.

165. Demerath, N. J. III, Otto Larsen, and Karl F. Schuessler, eds. 1975. *Social Policy and Sociology.* New York: Academic Press.

166. Deutsch, Albert. 1949. *The Mentally Ill in America: A History of Their Care and Treatment from Colonial Times.* 2d ed. New York: Columbia University Press.

167. Dietz, Stephen K., C. Bruce Baird, and Lawrence Berul. 1973. "The Medical Malpractice Legal System." In *Report of the Secretary's Commission on Medical Malpractice,* DHEW Publication no. (OS) 73-88 and 73-89, pp. 87–167. Washington: Government Printing Office.

168. Dinitz, Simon, et al. 1961. "The Posthospital Psychological Functioning of Former Mental Hospital Patients." *Mental Hygiene* 45: 579–88.

169. Dinitz, Simon, et al. 1961. "Psychiatric and Social Attributes as Predictors of Case Outcome in Mental Hospitalization." *Social Problems* 8: 322–28.

170. Dinitz, Simon, et al. 1962. "Instrumental Role Expectations and Posthospital Performace of Female Mental Patients." *Social Forces* 40: 248–54.

171. Dohrenwend, Bruce P. 1966. "Social Status and Psychological Disorder: An Issue of Substance and an Issue of Method." *American Sociological Review* 31 (February): 14–34.

172. Dohrenwend, Bruce P. 1973. "Some Issues in the Definition and Measurement of Psychiatric Disorders in General Populations." In *National Meeting of the Public Health Conference on Records and Statistics, Fourteenth, U.S. National Center for Health Statistics, Proceedings,* pp. 480–89. Washington: Government Printing Office.

173. Dohrenwend, Bruce P., and Barbara Snell Dohrenwend. 1965. "The Problem of Validity in Field Studies of Psychological Disorder." *Journal of Abnormal Psychology* 70: 52–69.

174. Dohrenwend, Bruce P., and Barbara Snell Dohrenwend. 1969. *Social Status and Psychological Disorder: A Causal Inquiry.* New York: Wiley-Interscience.

175. Dohrenwend, Bruce P., Edwin T. Chin-Shong, Gladys Egri, Frederick S. Mendelsohn, and Janet Stokes. 1970. "Measures of Psychiatric Disorder in Contrasting Class and Ethnic Groups: A Preliminary Report of On-Going Research." In International Symposium, Aberdeen University, 1969, *Psy-*

chiatric Epidemiology: Proceedings, edited by E. H. Hare and J. K. Wing, pp. 159–202. London: Oxford University Press.

176. Dohrenwend, Bruce P., and Barbara Snell Dohrenwend. 1974. "Psychiatric Disorders in Urban Settings." In American Handbook of Psychiatry, 2d ed., edited by Silvano Arieti, vol.2, pp. 424–47. New York: Basic Books.

177. Dohrenwend, Bruce P., and Barbara Snell Dohrenwend. 1974. "Social and Cultural Influences on Psychopathology." In Annual Review of Psychology 25: 417–52. Palo Alto, Calif.: Annual Reviews.

178. Donabedian, Avedis. 1973. Aspects of Medical Care Administration: Specifying Requirements for Health Care. Cambridge: Harvard University Press.

179. Donaldson, Kenneth. 1976. Insanity Inside Out. New York: Crown.

180. Donnelly, Richard C., et al. 1962. Criminal Law: Problems for Decision in the Promulgation, Invocation and Administration of a Law of Crime. New York: Free Press.

181. Dorn, H. 1959. "Mortality." In The Study of Population, edited by Philip Hauser and Otis Dudley Duncan, pp. 437–71. Chicago: University of Chicago Press.

182. Douglas, Jack D. 1967. The Social Meanings of Suicide. Princeton: Princeton University Press.

183. Dube, W. F., Frank T. Stritter, and Bonnie C. Nelson. 1971. "Study of U.S. Medical School Applicants 1970–71." Journal of Medical Education 46 (October): 837–57.

184. Dublin, Louis I., et al. 1949. Length of Life: A Study of the Life Table. Rev. ed. New York: Ronald.

185. Dubos, René. 1953. "The Gold Headed Cane in the Laboratory." In National Institutes of Health, Annual Lectures, pp. 89–102. Washington: Government Printing Office.

186. Dubos, René. 1959. Mirage of Health: Utopias, Progress, and Biological Change. New York: Harper.

187. Dubos, René. 1965. Man Adapting. New Haven: Yale University Press.

188. Dubos, René, and Jean Dubos. 1952. The White Plague: Tuberculosis, Man, and Society. Boston: Little, Brown.

189. Duff, Raymond S., and August B. Hollingshead. 1968. Sickness and Society. New York: Harper.

190. Dunham, H. W., et al. 1966. "A Research Note on Diagnosed Mental Illness and Social Class." American Sociological Review 31:223–27.

191. Dunnell, Karen, and Ann Cartwright. 1972. Medicine Takers, Prescribers and Hoarders. London: Routledge & Kegan Paul.

192. Durkheim, Emile. 1951. Suicide: A Study in Sociology. Translated by John A. Spaulding and George Simpson. New York: Free Press.

193. Dyk, R., and A. Sutherland. 1956. "Adaptation of the Spouse and Other Family Members to the Colostomy Patient." Cancer 9: 123–38.

194. Eaton, J. W., and R. J. Weil. 1955. *Culture and Mental Disorders*. New York: Free Press.

195. Eaton, Leonard K. 1957. *New England Hospitals, 1790–1833*. Ann Arbor: University of Michigan Press.

196. Eckstein, Harry. 1958. *The English Health Service: Its Origins, Structure, and Achievements*. Cambridge: Harvard University Press.

197. Edwards, A. 1953. "The Relationship between the Judged Desirability of a Trait and the Probability that the Trait Will Be Endorsed." *Journal of Applied Psychology* 37: 90–115.

198. Edwards, A. 1964. "The Assessment of Human Motives by Means of Personality Scales." In *Nebraska Symposium on Motivation*, edited by David R. Levine. Lincoln: University of Nebraska Press.

199. Egbert, Lawrence D., George E. Battit, Claude E. Welch, and Marshall K. Bartlett. 1964. "Reduction of Postoperative Pain by Encouragement and Instruction of Patients." *New England Journal of Medicine* 270 (April 16): 825–27.

200. Egdahl, Richard H. 1973. "Foundations for Medical Care." *New England Journal of Medicine* 288 (March 8): 491–98.

201. Elinson, Jack. 1974. "Toward Sociomedical Health Indicators." *Social Indicators Research* 1 (May): 59–71.

202. Elinson, Jack, ed. 1976. "Sociomedical Health Indicators." *International Journal of Health Services* 6: entire issue.

203. Engel, George L. 1977. "The Need for a New Medical Model: A Challenge for Biomedicine." *Science* 196 (April 8): 129–36.

204. Ennis, Bruce J. 1972. *Prisoners of Psychiatry: Mental Patients, Psychiatrists, and the Law*. New York: Harcourt.

205. Erhardt, Carl L., and Joyce E. Berlin, eds. 1974. *Mortality and Morbidity in the United States*. Cambridge: Harvard University Press.

206. Erickson, K. T. 1959. "Patient Role and Social Uncertainty: A Dilemma of the Mentally Ill." In *Advances in Psychiatry*, edited by M. B. Cohen, pp. 102–23. New York: Norton.

207. Everett, H. 1966. "Inner Techniques for Performing Arduous Tasks." *Mental Hygiene* 50: 124–31.

208. Eyer, Joseph. 1975. "Hypertension as a Disease of Modern Society." *International Journal of Health Services* 5: 539–58.

209. Eysenck, H. J. 1965. "The Effects of Psychotherapy." *International Journal of Psychiatry* 1: 99–142; discussion of Eysenck, pp. 144–78; reply to discussants, pp. 328–35.

210. Faich, Ronald G. 1969. "Social and Structural Factors Affecting Work Satisfaction: A Case Study of General Practitioners in the English National Health Service." Ph.D. dissertation, University of Wisconsin, Madison.

211. Faris, Robert E. L., and H. W. Dunham. 1939. *Mental Disorders in Urban Areas*. Chicago: University of Chicago Press.

212. Fejfar, Zdenek. 1967. "Some Aspects of the Epidemiology of Arterial

Hypertension." In *The Epidemiology of Hypertension*, edited by Jeremiah Stamler, Rose Stamler, and Theodore N. Pullman, pp. 188–92. New York: Grune & Stratton.

213. Feldman, Jacob J. 1960. "The Household Interview Survey as a Technique for the Collection of Morbidity Data." *Journal of Chronic Disease* 11: 535–57.

214. Feldman, Jacob J. 1966. *The Dissemination of Health Information: A Case Study in Adult Learning.* Chicago: Aldine.

215. Feldstein, Martin S. 1971. "The Feldstein Plan." In Conference on National Health Insurance, *National Health Insurance: Proceedings,* edited by Robert D. Eilers and Sue S. Moyerman, pp. 223–26. Homewood, Ill.: Irwin.

216. Field, Mark G. 1953. "Structured Strain in the Role of the Soviet Physician." *American Journal of Sociology* 58: 493–502.

217. Field, Mark G. 1957. *Doctor and Patient in Soviet Russia.* Cambridge: Harvard University Press.

218. Field, Mark G. 1967. *Soviet Socialized Medicine: An Introduction.* New York: Free Press.

219. Fischer, G. J. 1965. "Socio-Economic Factors and Outcome of Released Mental Patients." *Journal of Health and Human Behavior* 6: 105–10.

220. Fisher, S., and S. Fisher. 1963. "Placebo Response and Acquiescence." *Psychopharmacologia* 4: 298–301.

221. Fletcher, C. M. 1952. "Diagnosis of Pulmonary Emphysema: An Experimental Study." Royal Society of Medicine, London, *Proceedings* 45: 577–84.

222. Fletcher, C. M., and P. D. Oldham. 1959. "Diagnosis in Group Research." In *Medical Surveys and Clinical Trials*, edited by L. J. Witts. London: Oxford University Press.

223. Fogarty, John E., International Center for Advanced Study in the Health Sciences. 1976. *Preventive Medicine, U.S.A.* New York: Prodist.

224. Foote, Nelson N. 1951. "Identification as the Basis for a Theory of Motivation." *American Sociological Review* 16: 14–21.

225. Forsyth, Gordon, and Robert F. L. Logan. 1968. *Gateway or Dividing Line? A Study of Hospital Out-Patients in the 1960s.* New York: Oxford University Press.

226. Fox, Renée C. 1959. *Experiment Perilous: Physicians and Patients Facing the Unknown.* New York: Free Press.

227. Fox, Renée C., and Judith P. Swazey. 1974. *The Courage to Fail: A Social View of Organ Transplants and Dialysis.* Chicago: University of Chicago Press.

228. Frank, Jerome D. 1959. "The Dynamics of a Psychotherapeutic Relationship." *Psychiatry* 22: 17–39.

229. Frank, Jerome D. 1961. *Persuasion and Healing: A Comparative Study of Psychotherapy.* Baltimore: John Hopkins Press.

230. Frankel, Kimberly C. 1970. "Medico-Legal Communication." *Willamette Law Journal* 6 (June): 193–223.

231. Freeman, Howard E., and Ozzie G. Simmons. 1963. *The Mental Patient Comes Home*. New York: Wiley.

232. Freeman, Howard E., Sol Levine, and Leo G. Reeder, eds. 1972. *Handbook of Medical Sociology*. 2d ed. Englewood Cliffs, N.J.: Prentice-Hall.

233. Friedson, Eliot. 1959. "Specialties without Roots: The Utilization of New Services." *Human Organization* 18: 112–16.

234. Freidson, Eliot. 1960. "Client Control and Medical Practice." *American Journal of Sociology* 65 (January): 374–82.

235. Freidson, Eliot. 1961. *Patient's Views of Medical Practice*. New York: Russell Sage Foundation.

236. Freidson, Eliot. 1961–62. "The Sociology of Medicine: A Trend Report and Bibliography." *Current Sociology* 10–11, no. 3.

237. Freidson, Eliot. 1963. "Medical Care and the Public: Case Study of a Medical Group." American Academy of Political and Social Science, *Annals* 346: 57–66.

238. Freidson, Eliot, ed. 1963. *The Hospital in Modern Society*. New York: Free Press.

239. Freidson, Eliot. 1970. *Profession of Medicine: A Study of the Sociology of Applied Knowledge*. New York: Dodd, Mead.

240. Freidson, Eliot. 1970. *Professional Dominance: The Social Structure of Medical Care*. New York: Atherton.

241. Freidson, Eliot, 1973. "Prepaid Group Practice and the New 'Demanding Patient.'" *Milbank Memorial Fund Quarterly (Health and Society)* 51 (Fall): 473–88.

242. Freidson, Eliot. 1975. *Doctoring Together: A Study of Professional Social Control*. New York: Elsevier.

243. Freidson, Eliot, and B. Rhea. 1962. "Processes of Control in a Company of Equals." *Social Problems* 11: 119–31.

244. Freidson, Eliot, and Judith Lorber, eds. 1972. *Medical Men and Their Work: A Sociological Reader*. New York: Aldine-Atherton.

245. Freud, Anna. 1937. *The Ego and the Mechanisms of Defence*. London: Hogarth.

246. Freud, Sigmund. 1914. *Psychopathology of Everyday Life*. London: Allen & Unwin.

247. Fried, Charles. 1976. "Equality and Rights in Medical Care." *Hastings Center Report* 6 (February): 29–34.

248. Friedman, Meyer, and Ray H. Rosenman. 1974. *Type A Behavior and Your Heart*. New York: Knopf.

249. Friedman, Milton, and Simon Kuznets. 1945. *Income from Independent Professional Practice*. New York: National Bureau of Economic Research.

250. Friedman, S. B., et al. 1963. "Behavioral Observations on Parents Anticipating the Death of a Child." *Pediatrics* 32: 610–25.

251. Friedman, S. B., et al. 1963. "Urinary 17-Hydroxycorticosteroid Levels in Parents of Children with Neoplastic Disease." *Psychosomatic Medicine* 25: 364–76.

252. Fromm, Erich. 1941. *Escape from Freedom*. New York: Holt.

253. Fromm, Erich. 1955. *The Sane Society*. New York: Holt.

254. Fry, John. 1966. *Profiles of Disease: A Study in the Natural History of Common Diseases*. Edinburgh: Livingstone.

255. Fuchs, Victor R. 1968. "The Growing Demand for Medical Care." *New England Journal of Medicine* 279 (July 25): 190–95.

256. Fuchs, Victor R. 1973. "Health Care and the United States Economic System: An Essay in Abnormal Physiology." In *Economic Aspects of Health Care*, edited by John B. McKinlay, pp. 95–121. New York: Prodist.

257. Fuchs, Victor R. 1974. *Who Shall Live? Health, Economics, and Social Choice*. New York: Basic Books.

258. Funkenstein, Daniel H. 1971. "Medical Students, Medical Schools, and Society during Three Eras." In *Psychosocial Aspects of Medical Training*, edited by Robert H. Coombs and Clark E. Vincent, pp. 229–81. Springfield, Ill.: Thomas.

259. Gardner, E. A., et al. 1964. "Patient Experience in Psychiatric Units of General and State Mental Hospitals." *Public Health Reports* 79: 755–67.

260. Garland, L. H. 1959. "Studies of the Accuracy of Diagnostic Procedures." *American Journal of Roentgenology* 82: 25–38.

261. Geertsen, Reed, Melville R. Klauber, Mark Rindflesh, Robert L. Kane, and Robert Gray. 1975. "A Re-Examination of Suchman's Views on Social Factors in Health Care Utilization." *Journal of Health and Social Behavior* 16 (June): 226–37.

262. Georgopoulos, Basil S., and Floyd C. Mann. 1962. *The Community General Hospital*. New York: Macmillan.

263. Ginzberg, E., et al. 1959. *The Ineffective Soldier: Lessons for Management and the Nation*. 3 vols. New York: Columbia University Press.

264. Glaser, William A. 1963. "American and Foreign Hospitals: Some Sociological Comparisons." In *The Hospital in Modern Society*, edited by Eliot Freidson, pp. 37–72. New York: Free Press.

265. Glaser, William A. 1970. *Paying the Doctor: Systems of Remuneration and Their Effects*. Baltimore: John Hopkins Press.

266. Glass, A. J. 1958. "Observations upon the Epidemiology of Mental Illness in Troops during Warfare." In Walter Reed Army Institute of Research, *Symposium on Preventive and Social Psychiatry*, pp. 185–206. Washington: Government Printing Office.

267. Glueck, Sheldon. 1963. *Law and Psychiatry*. London: Tavistock.

268. Goffman, Erving. 1959. *The Presentation of Self in Everyday Life*. Garden City, N.Y.: Doubleday, Anchor.

269. Goffman, Erving. 1961. *Asylums: Essays on the Social Situation of Mental Patients and Other Inmates*. Garden City, N. Y.: Doubleday, Anchor.

270. Goffman, Erving. 1961. "Role Distance." In *Encounters: Two Studies in the Sociology of Interaction*. Indianapolis: Bobbs-Merrill.

271. Goldberg, E. M., and S. L. Morrison. 1963. "Schizophrenia and Social Class." *British Journal of Psychiatry* 109: 785–802.

272. Goldberger, J. 1914. "The Cause and Prevention of Pellagra." *Public Health Reports* 29: 2354–57.

273. Goldman, Lee. 1974. "Factors Related to Physicians' Medical and Political Attitudes: A Documentation of Intraprofessional Variations." *Journal of Health and Social Behavior* 15 (September): 177–87.

274. Goldsen, R. 1957. "Some Factors Related to Patient Delay in Seeking Diagnosis for Cancer Symptoms." *Cancer* 10: 1–7.

275. Goldsen, R. 1963. "Patient Delay in Seeking Cancer Diagnosis: Behavioral Aspects." *Journal of Chronic Disease* 16: 427–36.

276. Gonda, T. A. 1962. "The Relation Between Complaints of Persistent Pain and Family Size." *Journal of Neurology, Neurosurgery and Psychiatry* 25: 277–81.

277. Goode, William J. 1960. "A Theory of Role Strain." *American Sociological Review* 25 (August): 483–96.

278. Gordon, Travis L., and W. F. Dubé. 1976. "Datagram: Medical Student Enrollment, 1971–72 through 1975–76." *Journal of Medical Education* 51 (February): 144–46.

279. Gortmaker, Steven L. 1977. "Stratification, Health Care, and Infant Mortality in the United States." Ph.D. dissertation, University of Wisconsin, Madison.

280. Goss, Mary E. W. 1963. "Patterns of Bureaucracy among Hospital Staff Physicians." In *The Hospital in Modern Society*, edited by Eliot Freidson, pp. 170–94. New York: Free Press.

281. Goss, Mary E. W. 1970. "Organizational Goals and Quality of Medical Care: Evidence from Comparative Research on Hospitals." *Journal of Health and Social Behavior* 11 (December): 255–68.

282. Gough, Harrison G. 1971. "The Recruitment and Selection of Medical Students." In *Psychosocial Aspects of Medical Training*, edited by Robert H. Coombs and Clark E. Vincent, pp. 5–43. Springfield, Ill.: Thomas.

283. Gove, Walter R. 1973. "Sex, Marital Status, and Mortality." *American Journal of Sociology* 79 (July): 45–67.

284. Gove, Walter R., ed. 1975. *The Labelling of Deviance: Evaluating a Perspective*. New York: Halsted.

285. Gove, Walter R., and Jeannette F. Tudor. 1973. "Adult Sex Roles and Mental Illness." *American Journal of Sociology* 78 (January): 812–35.

286. Grace, W. J., and D. T. Graham. 1952. "Relationship of Specific Attitudes and Emotions to Certain Bodily Diseases." *Psychosomatic Medicine* 14: 243–51.

287. Graham, David T. 1972. "Psychosomatic Medicine." In *Handbook of Psychophysiology*, edited by Norman S. Greenfield and Richard A. Sternbach, pp. 839–924. New York: Holt.

288. Graham, David T., et al. 1962. "Physiological Response to the Suggestion of Attitudes Specific for Hives and Hypertension." *Psychosomatic Medicine* 24: 159–69.

289. Graham, David T., and Ian Stevenson. 1963. "Disease as Response to Life

Stress: 1. The Nature of the Evidence." In *The Psychological Basis of Medical Practice*, edited by Harold I. Lief, Victor F. Lief, and Nina R. Lief, pp. 115–36. New York: Harper.

290. Graham, Saxon. 1958. "Socio-Economic Status, Illness, and the Use of Medical Services." In *Patients, Physicians and Illness: A Sourcebook in Behavioral Science and Health*, edited by E. Gartly Jaco, pp. 129–34. New York: Free Press.

291. Gray, Bradford H. 1975. *Human Subjects in Medical Experimentation: A Sociological Study of the Conduct and Regulation of Clinical Research*. New York: Wiley-Interscience.

292. Greenblatt, Milton, et al. 1955. *From Custodial to Therapeutic Patient Care in Mental Hospitals*. New York: Russell Sage Foundation.

293. Greenblatt, Milton, Daniel J. Levinson, and Richard H. Williams, eds. 1957. *The Patient and the Mental Hospital*. New York: Free Press.

294. Greenfield, Harry I. 1969. *Allied Health Manpower: Trends and Prospects*. New York: Columbia University Press.

295. Greenley, James R. 1972. "The Psychiatric Patient's Family and Length of Hospitalization." *Journal of Health and Social Behavior* 13 (March): 25–37.

296. Greenley, James R., and David Mechanic. 1976. "Social Selection in Seeking Help for Psychological Problems." *Journal of Health and Social Behavior* 17 (September): 249–62.

297. Greenlick, M., and D. Freeborn. 1971. "Determinants of Medical Care Utilization: On Choosing the Appropriate Measure of Utilization." Keynote address delivered at the Engineering Foundation Conference on Qualitative Decision Making for the Delivery of Ambulatory Care, Henniker, N.H.

298. Grinker, Roy R. 1953. *Psychosomatic Research*. New York: Norton.

299. Grinker, Roy R., and John P. Spiegel. 1945. *Men under Stress*. New York: McGraw-Hill.

300. Grob, Gerald N. 1966. *The State and the Mentally Ill: A History of Worcester State Hospital in Massachusetts, 1830–1920*. Chapel Hill: University of North Carolina Press.

301. Gross, Neal, et al. 1958. *Explorations in Role Analysis*. New York: Wiley.

302. Group for the Advancement of Psychiatry. 1960. *Preventive Psychiatry in the Armed Forces: With Some Implications for Civilian Use*. Report no. 47. Topeka.

303. Guerrin, R. F., and E. F. Borgatta. 1965. "Socio-Economic and Demographic Correlates of Tuberculosis Incidence." *Milbank Memorial Fund Quarterly* 43: 269–90.

303a Guillemin, Roger. 1977. "Endorphins, Brain Peptides That Act Like Opiates." *New England Journal of Medicine* 296 (January 27): 226–28.

304. Gurin, Gerald, Joseph Veroff, and Sheila Feld. 1960. *Americans View Their Mental Health*. New York: Basic Books.

305. Habenstein, Robert W., and Edwin A. Christ. 1963. *Professionalizer, Traditionalizer, and Utilizer.* 2d ed. Columbia: University of Missouri.

306. Haddon, William, Jr., Edward A. Suchman, and David Klein, eds. 1964. *Accident Research: Methods and Approaches.* New York: Harper.

307. Hage, Jerald. n.d. "The Consequences of Occupational Specialization: The Example of the Medical Profession." Department of Sociology, University of Wisconsin, Madison.

308. Hall, Calvin S., and Gardner Lindzey. 1957. *Theories of Personality.* New York: Wiley.

309. Hall, Jerome. 1960. *General Principles of Criminal Law.* 2d ed. Indianapolis: Bobbs-Merrill.

310. Halleck, Seymour, and M. Miller. 1963. "The Psychiatric Consultation: Questionable Social Precedents of Some Current Practices." *American Journal of Psychiatry* 120: 164–69.

311. Hamburg, D. A. 1957. "Therapeutic Hospital Environments." In Walter Reed Army Institute of Research, *Symposium on Preventive and Social Psychiatry,* pp. 479–91. Washington: Government Printing Office.

312. Hamilton, Max. 1955. *Psychosomatics.* New York: Wiley.

313. Hare, E. H. 1956. "Family Setting and the Urban Distribution of Schizophrenia." *Journal of Mental Science* 102: 753–60.

314. Haug, Marie R. 1976. "The Erosion of Professional Authority: A Cross-Cultural Inquiry in the Case of the Physician." *Milbank Memorial Fund Quarterly (Health and Society)* 54 (Winter): 83–106.

315. Hawkins, N. G., et al. 1957. "Evidence of Psychosocial Factors in the Development of Pulmonary Tuberculosis." *American Review of Tuberculosis and Pulmonary Disease* 75: 768–80.

316. Heintz, Duane H. 1977. *An Analysis of the Southern California Arbitration Project, January 1969–June 1975.* National Center for Health Services Research, DHEW Publication no. (HRA) 77-3159. Washington: Government Printing Office.

317. Hennes, James D. 1972. "The Measurement of Health." *Medical Care Review* 29 (December): 1268–88.

318. Henry, A. F., and J. F. Short, Jr. 1954. *Suicide and Homicide.* New York: Free Press.

319. Henry, William E., John H. Sims, and S. Lee Spray. 1971. *The Fifth Profession: Becoming a Psychotherapist.* San Francisco: Jossey-Bass.

320. Hershey, Nathan. 1972. "The Defensive Practice of Medicine: Myth or Reality." *Milbank Memorial Fund Quarterly* 50 (January): 69–98.

321. Hes, Jozef Ph. 1968. "Hypochondriacal Complaints in Jewish Psychiatric Patients." *Israel Annals of Psychiatry and Related Disciplines* 6 (December): 134–42.

322. Hetherington, Robert W., Carl E. Hopkins, and Milton I. Roemer. 1975. *Health Insurance Plans: Promise and Performance.* New York: Wiley-Interscience.

323. Heydebrand, Wolf V. 1973. *Hospital Bureaucracy: A Comparative Study of Organizations.* New York: Dunellen.

324. Hinkle, Lawrence E., Jr. 1974. "The Effect of Exposure to Culture Change, Social Change, and Changes in Interpersonal Relationships on Health." In *Stressful Life Events: Their Nature and Effects,* edited by Barbara Snell Dohrenwend and Bruce P. Dohrenwend, pp. 9–44. New York: Wiley-Interscience.

325. Hinkle, Lawrence E., Jr., and N. Plummer. 1952. "Life Stress and Industrial Absenteeism." *Industrial Medicine and Surgery* 21: 363–75.

326. Hinkle, Lawrence E., Jr., and H. G. Wolff. 1957. "Health and the Social Environment: Experimental Investigations." In *Explorations in Social Psychiatry,* edited by Alexander H. Leighton, John A. Clausen, and Robert N. Wilson, pp. 105–32. New York: Basic Books.

327. Hodge, Robert W., Paul M. Siegel, and Peter H. Rossi. 1964. "Occupational Prestige in the United States, 1925–63." *American Journal of Sociology* 70 (November): 286–302.

328. Hofling, Charles K., Eveline Brotzman, Sarah Dalrymple, Nancy Graves, and Chester M. Pierce. 1966. "An Experimental Study in Nurse-Physician Relationships." *Journal of Nervous and Mental Disease* 143 (August): 171–80.

329. Hollingshead, August B. 1961. "Some Issues in the Epidemiology of Schizophrenia." *American Sociological Review* 26: 5–13.

330. Hollingshead, August B., and Fredrick C. Redlich. 1958. *Social Class and Mental Illness: A Community Study.* New York: Wiley.

331. Holmes, Thomas H. 1962. "Psychosocial and Psychophysiological Studies of Tuberculosis." In *Physiological Correlates of Psychological Disorders,* edited by Robert Roessler and Norman S. Greenfield, pp. 239–55. Madison: University of Wisconsin Press.

332. Holmes, Thomas H., et al. 1957. "Psychosocial and Psychophysiologic Studies of Tuberculosis." *Psychosomatic Medicine* 19: 134–43.

333. Holmes, Thomas H., et al. 1961. "Experimental Study of Prognosis." *Journal of Psychosomatic Research* 5: 235–52.

334. Holmes, Thomas H., and Richard H. Rahe. 1967. "The Social Readjustment Rating Scale." *Journal of Psychosomatic Research* 11: 213–18.

335. Holmes, Thomas H., and Minoru Masuda. 1974. "Life Change and Illness Susceptibility." In *Stressful Life Events: Their Nature and Effects,* edited by Barbara Snell Dohrenwend and Bruce P. Dohrenwend, pp. 45–72. New York: Wiley-Interscience.

336. Homans, G. C. 1961. *Social Behavior: Its Elementary Forms.* New York: Harcourt.

337. Honigfeld, Gilbert. 1964. "Non-Specific Factors in Treatment: 1. Review of Placebo Reactions and Placebo Reactors." *Diseases of the Nervous System* 25: 145–56.

338. Honigfeld, Gilbert. 1964. "Non-Specific Factors in Treatment: 2. Review of Social-Psychological Factors." *Diseases of the Nervous System* 25: 225–39.

339. Horn, Joshua S. 1969. *Away with All Pests: An English Surgeon in People's China, 1954–1969.* New York: Monthly Review Press.

340. Horney, Karen. 1951. *Neurosis and Human Growth.* London: Routledge & Kegan Paul.

341. Huey, Karen. 1976. "Alternatives to Mental Hospital Treatment." *Hospital and Community Psychiatry* 27 (March): 186–92.

342. Hughes, Edward F. X., Victor R. Fuchs, John E. Jacoby, and Eugene M. Lewit. 1972. "Surgical Work Loads in a Community Practice." *Surgery* 71 (March): 315–27.

343. Hughes, Edward F. X., Eugene M. Lewit, Richard N. Watkins, and Richard Handschin. 1974. "Utilization of Surgical Manpower in a Prepaid Group Practice." *New England Journal of Medicine* 291 (October 10): 759–63.

344. Hughes, Everett C. 1958. *Men and Their Work.* New York: Free Press.

345. Hughes, Everett C. 1961. *Students' Culture and Perspectives: Lectures on Medical and General Education.* Lawrence: School of Law, University of Kansas.

346. Hulka, Barbara S., John C. Cassel, Lawrence L. Kupper, and James A. Burdette. 1976. "Communication, Compliance, and Concordance between Physicians and Patients with Prescribed Medications." *American Journal of Public Health* 66 (September): 847–53.

347. Hunter, R. C. A., J. G. Lohrenz, and A. E. Schwartzman. 1964. "Nosophobia and Hypochondriasis in Medical Students." *Journal of Nervous and Mental Disease* 139 (August): 147–52.

348. Huntley, Robert R. 1963. "Epidemiology of Family Practice." *Journal of the American Medical Association* 185 (July 20): 175–78.

349. Hyde, David R., et al. 1954. "The American Medical Association: Power, Purpose, and Politics in Organized Medicine." *Yale Law Journal* 63: 938–1022.

350. Illich, Ivan. 1976. *Medical Nemesis: The Expropriation of Health.* New York: Pantheon.

351. Imboden, J. B., et al. 1959. "Brucellosis: 3. Psychologic Aspects of Delayed Convalescence." *Archives of Internal Medicine* 103: 406–414.

352. Imboden, J. B., et al. 1961. "Symptomatic Recovery from Medical Disorders." *Journal of the American Medical Association* 178: 1182–84.

353. Ingelfinger, Franz J. 1968. "The Arch-Hospital: An Ailing Monopoly." *Harper's Magazine* 237 (July): 82–87.

354. Inkeles, Alex. 1963. "Sociology and Psychology." In *Psychology: A Study of a Science,* edited by Sigmund Koch, vol. 6, pp. 317–87. New York: McGraw-Hill.

355. Institute of Medicine. 1973. *Infant Death: An Analysis by Maternal Risk and Health Care.* Washington: National Academy of Sciences.

356. Institute of Medicine. 1974. *Costs of Education in the Health Professions.* Washington: National Academy of Sciences.

357. Institute of Medicine. 1974. *Newsletter* (July).

358. Jaco, E. Gartly. 1960. *The Social Epidemiology of Mental Disorders.* New York: Russell Sage Foundation.

359. Jaco, E. Gartly, ed. 1972. *Patients, Physicians and Illness: A Sourcebook in Behavioral Science and Health.* 2d ed. New York: Free Press.

360. Jahoda, Marie. 1958. *Current Concepts of Positive Mental Health.* New York: Basic Books.

361. Jahoda, Marie. 1963. "Some Notes on the Influence of Psychoanalytic Ideas on American Psychology." *Human Relations* 16: 111–29.

362. Janis, Irving L. 1951. *Air War and Emotional Stress: Psychological Studies of Bombing and Civilian Defense.* New York: McGraw-Hill.

363. Janis, Irving L. 1958. *Psychological Stress: Psychoanalytic and Behavioral Studies of Surgical Patients.* New York: Wiley.

364. Jefferys, Margot. 1965. *An Anatomy of Social Welfare Services.* London: Joseph.

365. Jenkins, C. David, Ray H. Rosenman, and Stephen J. Zyzanski. 1974. "Prediction of Clinical Coronary Heart Disease by a Test for Coronary-Prone Behavior Pattern." *New England Journal of Medicine* 290 (June 6): 1271–75.

366. Jenkins, C. David. 1976. "Recent Evidence Supporting Psychologic and Social Risk Factors for Coronary Disease," pt. 1. *New England Journal of Medicine* 294 (April 29): 987–94.

367. Jenkins, C. David. 1976. "Recent Evidence Supporting Psychologic and Social Risk Factors for Coronary Disease," pt. 2. *New England Journal of Medicine* 294 (May 6): 1033–38.

368. Joint Commission on Mental Illness and Health. 1961. *Action for Mental Health.* New York: Science Editions.

369. Jones, E.E., and Richard DeCharms. 1957. "Changes in Social Perception as a Function of the Personal Relevance of Behavior." *Sociometry* 20: 75–85.

370. Joyce, C. R. B. 1959. "Consistent Differences in Individual Reactions to Drugs and Dummies." *British Journal of Pharmacology* 14: 512–21.

371. Kadushin, Charles. 1958. "Individual Decisions to Undertake Psychotherapy." *Administrative Science Quarterly* 3: 379–411.

372. Kadushin, Charles. 1962. "Social Distance between Client and Professional." *American Journal of Sociology* 67: 517–31.

373. Kadushin, Charles. 1964. "Social Class and the Experience of Ill Health." *Sociological Inquiry* 34: 67–80.

374. Kadushin, Charles. 1969. *Why People Go to Psychiatrists.* New York: Atherton.

375. Kahl, J. 1957. *The American Class Structure.* New York: Holt.

376. Kahn, Robert L., et al. 1964. *Organizational Stress: Studies in Role Conflict and Ambiguity.* New York: Wiley.

377. Kaplan, Berton, John Cassel, and Susan Gore. 1977. "Social Support and Health." *Medical Care* 15 (May, suppl.): 47–58.

378. Kark, Sidney L. 1974. *Epidemiology and Community Medicine.* New York: Appleton.

379. Kasl, S.V., and S. Cobb. 1966. "Health Behavior, Illness Behavior and Sick-Role Behavior." *Archives of Environmental Health* 12:246–66, 531–41.

380. Keeton, Robert E. 1973. "Compensation for Medical Accidents." *University of Pennsylvania Law Review* 121 (January): 590–617.

381. Kendall, Patricia L. 1971. "Medical Specialization: Trends and Contributing Factors." In *Psychosocial Aspects of Medical Training,* edited by Robert H. Coombs and Clark E. Vincent, pp. 449–97. Springfield, Ill.: Thomas.

382. Kerckhoff, Alan C., and Kurt W. Back. 1968. *The June Bug: A Study of Hysterical Contagion.* New York: Appleton.

383. Kern, R. P. 1966. *A Conceptual Model of Behavior under Stress.* Technical Report 66-12. Washington: Human Resources Research Office, George Washington University.

384. Kessel, Reuben A. 1958. "Price Discrimination in Medicine." *Journal of Law and Economics* 1 (October): 20–53.

385. Kessel, Reuben A. 1970. "The A.M.A. and the Supply of Physicians." *Law and Contemporary Problems* 35 (Spring): 267–83.

386. Kety, Seymour S. 1977. "The Biological Substrates of Schizophrenia." In *Research on Disorders of the Mind: Progress and Prospects,* National Institute of Mental Health, pp. 2–6. Washington: Government Printing Office.

387. Kilpatrick, G.S. 1963. "Observer Error in Medicine." *Journal of Medical Education* 38: 38–43.

388. King, S. 1962. *Perceptions of Illness and Medical Practice,* pp. 91–159. New York: Russell Sage Foundation.

389. Kinsey, Alfred C., et al. 1948. *Sexual Behavior in the Human Male.* Philadelphia: Saunders.

390. Kitagawa, Evelyn M., and Philip M. Hauser. 1964. "Trends in Differential Fertility and Mortality in a Metropolis, Chicago." In *Contributions to Urban Sociology,* edited by E. Burgess and D. Bogue, pp. 59–85. Chicago: University of Chicago Press.

391. Kitagawa, Evelyn M., and Philip M. Hauser. 1973. *Differential Mortality in the United States: A Study in Socioeconomic Epidemiology.* Cambridge: Harvard University Press.

392. Kitsuse, John, and Aaron Cicourel. 1963. "A Note on the Use of Official Statistics." *Social Problems* 11: 131–39.

393. Klarman, Herbert E. 1965. *The Economics of Health.* New York: Columbia University Press.

394. Kohn, Melvin L. 1968. "Social Class and Schizophrenia: A Critical Review." In *The Transmission of Schizophrenia,* edited by David Rosenthal and Seymour S. Kety, pp. 155–73. New York: Pergamon.

395. Kohn, Melvin L. 1973. "Social Class and Schizophrenia: A Critical Review and a Reformulation." *Schizophrenia Bulletin* 7 (Winter): 60–79.

396. Kohn, Robert, and Kerr L. White, eds. 1976. *Health Care: An International Study.* Report of the World Health Organization, an International Collaborative Study of Medical Care Utilization. London: Oxford University Press.

397. Komaroff, Anthony L. 1976. "The Practitioner and the Compliant Patient." *American Journal of Public Health* 66 (September): 833–35.

398. Komarovsky, Mirra. 1940. *The Unemployed Man and His Family.* New York: Dryden.

399. Koos, E. 1954. *The Health of Regionsville: What the People Thought and Did about It.* New York: Columbia University Press.

400. Kramer, M. 1963. "Some Problems for International Research Suggested by Observations on Differences in First Admission Rates to Mental Hospitals of England and Wales and of the United States." In World Congress of Psychiatry, Third, Montreal, 1961, *Proceedings,* edited by R. A. Cleghorn, vol. 3. Toronto: University of Toronto Press.

401. Kreitman, Norman. 1961. "The Reliability of Psychiatric Diagnosis." *Journal of Mental Science* 107: 876–86.

402. Kreitman, Norman, et al. 1961. "The Reliability of Psychiatric Assessment: An Analysis." *Journal of Mental Science* 107: 887–908.

403. Kutner, Bernard, et al. 1958. "Delay in the Diagnosis and Treatment of Cancer: A Critical Analysis of the Literature." *Journal of Chronic Diseases* 7: 95–120.

404. Kutner, Bernard, and G. Gordon. 1961. "Seeking Care for Cancer." *Journal of Health and Human Behavior* 2: 171–78.

405. Lacey, J.I. 1959. "Psychophysiological Approaches to the Evaluation of Psychotherapeutic Process and Outcome." In *Research in Psychotherapy,* edited by E.A. Rubenstein and M.B. Parloff, pp. 160--208. Washington; American Psychological Association, Division of Clinical Psychology.

406. Lacey, J.I. 1967. "Somatic Response Patterning and Stress: Some Revisions of Activation Theory." In *Psychological Stress: Issues in Research,* edited by M.H. Appley and R. Trumbell. New York: Appleton.

407. Lalonde, Marc. 1974. *A New Perspective on the Health of Canadians: A Working Document.* Ottawa: Ministry of National Health and Welfare.

408. Lambert, W.E., et al. 1960. "The Effect of Increased Salience of a Membership Group on Pain Tolerance." *Journal of Personality* 28: 350–57.

409. Langner, Thomas S. 1962. "A Twenty-Two Item Screening Score of Psychiatric Symptoms Indicating Impairment." *Journal of Health and Human Behavior* 3 (Winter): 269–76.

410. Langner, Thomas S., et al. 1963. *Life Stress and Mental Health: The Midtown Manhattan Study.* New York: Free Press.   .

411. LaPiere, Richard. 1959. *The Freudian Ethic.* New York: Duell, Sloan & Pearce.

412. Lasagna, L. 1955. "The Controlled Clinical Trial: Theory and Practice." *Journal of Chronic Diseases* 1: 353–67.

413. Lasagna, L., et al. 1954. "A Study of the Placebo Response." *American Journal of Medicine* 16: 770–79.

414. Law, Sylvia A. 1974. *Blue Cross: What Went Wrong?* New Haven: Yale University Press.

415. Lawrence, P.S. 1948. "Chronic Illness and Socio-Economic Status." In *Patients, Physicians and Illness: A Sourcebook in Behavioral Science and Health*, edited by E. Gartly Jaco, pp. 37–49. New York: Free Press.

416. Lazarus, Richard S. 1966. *Psychological Stress and the Coping Process.* New York: McGraw-Hill.

417. Lazarus, Richard S. 1966. "The Study of Psychological Stress." In *Anxiety and Behavior*, edited by C.D. Spielberger. New York: Academic Press.

418. Lazarus, Richard S., et al. 1962. "A Laboratory Study of Psychological Stress Produced by a Motion Picture Film." *Psychological Monographs* 76, no. 553.

419. Lazarus, Richard S., and E. Alfert. 1964. "Short-Circuiting of Threat by Experimentally Altering Cognitive Appraisal." *Journal of Abnormal and Social Psychology* 69: 195–205.

420. Leaf, Philip J. 1977. "Legal Intervention into a Mental Health System: The Outcomes of *Wyatt* v. *Stickney*." Ph.D. dissertation, University of Wisconsin, Madison.

421. Leaf, Philip J. 1978. "The Medical Marketplace and Public Interest Law," pt. 2. In *Public Interest Law: An Economic and Institutional Analysis*, by Burton Weisbrod in collaboration with Joel F. Handler and Neil K. Komesar. Berkeley: University of California Press.

422. Lefton, Mark, et al. 1962. "Social Class, Expectations, and Performance of Mental Patients," *American Journal of Sociology* 68: 79–87.

423. Lefton, Mark, et al. 1966. "Former Mental Patients and Their Neighbors: A Comparison of Performance Levels." *Journal of Health and Human Behavior* 7:106–13.

424. Leighton, Alexander H., and Dorothea C. Leighton. 1945. *The Navaho Door.* Cambridge: Harvard University Press.

425. Leighton, Dorothea C., John S. Harding, David B. Macklin, Allister M. Macmillan, and Alexander H. Leighton. 1963. *The Character of Danger: Psychiatric Symptoms in Selected Communities.* New York: Basic Books.

426. Lemert, Edwin M. 1946. "Legal Commitment and Social Control." *Sociology and Social Research* 30: 370–78.

427. Lemert, Edwin M. 1951. *Social Pathology.* New York: McGraw-Hill.

428. Lerner, Monroe, and Odin W. Anderson. 1963. *Health Progress in the United States, 1900–1960.* Chicago: University of Chicago Press.

429. Leventhal, Howard. 1970. "Findings and Theory in the Study of Fear Communications." In *Advances in Experimental Social Psychology*, edited by Leonard Berkowitz, vol. 5, pp. 119–86. New York: Academic Press.

430. Leventhal, Howard. 1976. "Type A, Work Stress, and Coronary Heart Disease Risk." Research proposal, Department of Psychology, University of Wisconsin, Madison.

431. Levine, D., and C. Weisman. 1974. "Career Patterns of Unaccepted

Applicants to Medical School: A Case Study in Reactions to a Blocked Career Pathway." Paper presented at the Colloquium on the Career Development of Physicians, Association of American Medical Colleges.

432. Levine, G.N. 1962. "Anxiety about Illness: Psychological and Social Bases." *Journal of Health and Human Behavior* 3: 30–34.

433. Lewin, Kurt. 1952. "Group Decision and Social Change." In Readings in Social Psychology, edited by G.E. Swanson et al. New York: Holt.

434. Lewis, A. 1936. "Melancholia: Prognostic Study and Case Material." *Journal of Mental Science* 82: 488–558.

435. Lewis, A. 1953. "Health as a Social Concept." *British Journal of Sociology* 4: 109–24.

436. Lewis, Charles E., and Barbara A. Resnik. 1967. "Nurse Clinics and Progressive Ambulatory Patient Care." *New England Journal of Medicine* 277 (December 7): 1236–41.

437. Lewis, Charles E., Mary Ann Lewis, Ann Lorimer, and Beverly B. Palmer. 1975. "Child-Initiated Care: A Study of the Determinants of the Illness Behavior of Children." Center for Health Sciences, University of California, Los Angles.

438. Lewis, Charles E., Rashi Fein, and David Mechanic. 1976. *A Right to Health: The Problem of Access to Primary Medical Care.* New York: Wiley-Interscience.

439. Lewis, Lionel S., and Joseph Lopreato. 1962. "Arationality, Ignorance, and Perceived Danger in Medical Practices." *American Sociological Review* 27 (August): 508–14.

440. Ley, Philip, and M.S. Spelman. 1967. *Communicating with the Patient.* London: Staples.

441. Liberman, R. 1962. "An Analysis of the Placebo Phenomenon." *Journal of Chronic Diseases* 15: 761–83.

442. Liberman, R. 1964. "An Experimental Study of the Placebo Response under Three Different Situations of Pain." *Journal of Psychiatric Research* 2: 233–46.

443. Lieberson, Stanley. 1958. "Ethnic Groups and the Practice of Medicine." *American Sociological Review* 23: 542–49.

444. Lilienfeld, Abraham M. 1976. *Foundations of Epidemiology.* New York: Oxford University Press.

445. Linn, E. 1959. "Patients' Socioeconomic Characteristics and Release from a Mental Hospital." *American Journal of Sociology* 65: 280–86.

446. Linn, Lawrence S. 1967. "Social Characteristics and Social Interaction in the Utilization of a Psychiatric Outpatient Clinic." *Journal of Health and Social Behavior* 8 (March): 3–14.

447. Linn, Lawrence S., and Milton S. Davis. 1971. "The Use of Psychotherapeutic Drugs by Middle-Aged Women." *Journal of Health and Social Behavior* 12 (December): 331–40.

448. Linton, Ralph. 1936. *The Study of Man.* New York: Appleton.

449. Linton, Ralph. 1956. *Culture and Mental Disorders.* Springfield, Ill.: Thomas.

450. Litman, Theodor J. 1976. *The Sociology of Medicine and Health Care: A Research Bibliography*. San Francisco: Boyd & Fraser.

451. Logan, R.F.L. 1971. "National Health Planning: An Appraisal of the State of the Art." *International Journal of Health Services* 1 (February): 6–17.

452. Ludwig, Arnold M., and Frank Farrelly. 1966. "The Code of Chronicity." *Archives of General Psychiatry* 15 (December): 562–68.

453. MacBryde, C. M., ed. 1957. *Signs and Symptoms: Applied Pathologic Physiology and Clinical Interpretation*. 3d ed. Philadelphia: Lippincott.

454. Madigan, F. C. 1957. "Are Sex Mortality Differentials Biologically Caused?" *Milbank Memorial Fund Quarterly* 35: 202–23.

455. Manis, Jerome G., Milton J. Brawer, Chester L. Hunt, and Leonard C. Kercher. 1963. "Validating a Mental Health Scale." *American Sociological Review* 28 (February): 108–16.

456. Manis, Jerome G., Milton J. Brawer, Chester L. Hunt, and Leonard C. Kercher. 1964. "Estimating the Prevalence of Mental Illness." *American Sociological Review* 29 (February): 84–89.

457. Marks, Isaac M. 1969. *Fears and Phobias*. New York: Academic Press.

458. Marlowe, David, and Douglas P. Crowne. 1961. "Social Desirability and Response to Perceived Situational Demands." *Journal of Consulting Psychology* 25: 109–15.

459. Marmot, Michael G. 1975. "Migrants, Acculturation and Coronary Heart Disease." Report prepared for the National Heart and Lung Institute, Bethesda, Md.

460. Martin, Samuel P., Magruder C. Donaldson, C. David London, Osler L. Peterson, and Theodore Colton. 1974. "Inputs into Coronary Care during Thirty Years: A Cost Effectiveness Study." *Annals of Internal Medicine* 81 (September): 289–93.

461. Matarazzo, J. D. 1965. "The Interview." In *Handbook of Clinical Psychology*, edited by B. B. Wolman, pp. 403–50. New York: McGraw-Hill.

462. Mather, H. G., et al. 1971. "Acute Myocardial Infarction: Home and Hospital Treatment." *British Medical Journal* 3 (August 7): 334–38.

463. Matza, David. 1969. *Becoming Deviant*. Englewood Cliffs, N.J.: Prentice-Hall.

464. Mauksch, Hans O. 1972. "Nursing: Churning for Change?" In *Handbook of Medical Sociology*, 2d ed., edited by Howard E. Freeman, Sol Levine, and Leo G. Reeder, pp. 206–30. Englewood Cliffs, N.J.: Prentice-Hall.

465. Mayer, K. B. 1955. *Class and Society*. Garden City, N.Y.: Doubleday.

466. McDonald, Donald, ed. 1971. *Medical Malpractice: A Discussion of Alternative Compensation and Quality Control Systems*. Santa Barbara, Calif.: Center for the Study of Democratic Institutions.

467. McGhie, A., and J. Chapman. 1961. "Disorders of Attention and Perception in Early Schizophrenia." *British Journal of Medical Psychology* 34: 103–16.

468. McKeown, Thomas. 1965. *Medicine in Modern Society*. New York: Hafner. London: Allen & Unwin.

469. McKinlay, John B., and Diana B. Dutton. 1974. "Social-Psychological Fac-

tors Affecting Health Service Utilization." In *Consumer Incentives for Health Care*, edited by Selma J. Mushkin, pp. 251–303. New York: Prodist.

470. McNamara, Mary E., and Clifford Todd. 1970. "A Survey of Group Practice in the United States." *American Journal of Public Health* 60 (July): 1303–13.

471. McNerney, W. J., et al. 1962. *Hospital and Medical Economics: A Study of Population, Services, Costs, Methods of Payment, and Controls*. 2 vols. Chicago: Hospital Research and Educational Trust.

472. Mead, G. H. 1934. *Mind, Self, and Society*. Chicago: University of Chicago Press.

473. Mead, Margaret, ed. 1953. *Cultural Patterns and Technical Change*. New York: World Federation for Mental Health, UNESCO.

474. Mechanic, David. 1959. "Illness and Social Disability: Some Problems in Analysis." *Pacific Sociological Review* 2 (Spring): 37–41.

475. Mechanic, David. 1961. "Relevance of Group Atmosphere and Attitudes for the Rehabilitation of Alcoholics." *Quarterly Journal of Studies on Alcohol* 22 (December): 634–45.

476. Mechanic, David. 1962. "The Concept of Illness Behavior." *Journal of Chronic Diseases* 15 (February): 189–94.

477. Mechanic, David. 1962. "Some Factors in Identifying and Defining Mental Illness." *Mental Hygiene* 46 (January): 66–74.

478. Mechanic, David. 1962. "Sources of Power of Lower Participants in Complex Organizations." *Administrative Science Quarterly* 7 (December): 349–64.

479. Mechanic, David. 1962. *Students under Stress: A Study in the Social Psychology of Adaptation*. New York: Free Press.

480. Mechanic, David. 1963. "The Power to Resist Change among Low-Ranking Personnel." *Personnel Administration* 26 (July–August): 5–11.

481. Mechanic, David. 1963. "Religion, Religiosity, and Illness Behavior: The Special Case of the Jews." *Human Organization* 22 (Fall): 202–208.

482. Mechanic, David. 1963. "Some Implications of Illness Behavior for Medical Sampling." *New England Journal of Medicine* 269 (August 1): 244–47.

483. Mechanic, David. 1964. "The Influence of Mothers on Their Children's Health Attitudes and Behavior." *Pediatrics* 33 (March): 444–53.

484. Mechanic, David. 1965. "Perception of Parental Responses to Illness: A Research Note." *Journal of Health and Human Behavior* 6 (Winter): 253–57.

485. Mechanic, David. 1966. "Community Psychiatry: Some Sociological Perspectives and Implications." In *Community Psychiatry*, edited by Leigh M. Roberts, Seymour L. Halleck, and Martin Loeb, pp. 201–22. Madison: University of Wisconsin Press.

486. Mechanic, David. 1966. "The Sociology of Medicine: Viewpoints and Perspectives." *Journal of Health and Human Behavior* 7 (Winter): 237–48.

487. Mechanic, David. 1968. "General Medical Practice in England and Wales:

Its Organization and Future." *New England Journal of Medicine* 279 (September 26): 680–89.

488. Mechanic, David. 1969. *Mental Health and Social Policy.* Englewood Cliffs, N.J.: Prentice-Hall.

489. Mechanic, David. 1970. "Correlates of Frustration among British General Practitioners." *Journal of Health and Social Behavior* 11 (June): 87–104.

490. Mechanic, David. 1970. "Practice Orientations among General Medical Practitioners in England and Wales." *Medical Care* 8 (January–February): 15–25.

491. Mechanic, David. 1972. "General Medical Practice: Some Comparisons between the Work of Primary Care Physicians in the United States and England and Wales." *Medical Care* 10 (September–October): 402–20.

492. Mechanic, David. 1972. *Public Expectations and Health Care: Essays on the Changing Organization of Health Services.* New York: Wiley-Interscience.

493. Mechanic, David. 1972. "Rhetoric and Reality in Health Services Research." *Health Services Research* 7 (Spring): 61–65.

494. Mechanic, David. 1972. "Social Class and Schizophrenia: Some Requirements for a Plausible Theory of Social Influence." *Social Forces* 50 (March): 305–309.

495. Mechanic, David. 1972. "Social Psychologic Factors Affecting the Presentation of Bodily Complaints." *New England Journal of Medicine* 286 (May 25): 1132–39.

496. Mechanic, David. 1973. "The Sociology of Organizations." In *The Administration of Mental Health Services,* edited by Saul Feldman, pp. 138–66. Springfield, Ill.: Thomas.

497. Mechanic, David. 1974. *Politics, Medicine, and Social Science.* New York: Wiley-Interscience.

498. Mechanic, David. 1974. "The Right to Treatment: Judicial Action and Social Change." In *Politics, Medicine, and Social Science,* pp. 227–48. New York: Wiley-Interscience.

499. Mechanic, David. 1975. "The Organization of Medical Practice and Practice Orientations among Physicians in Prepaid and Nonprepaid Primary Care Settings." *Medical Care* 13 (March): 189–204.

500. Mechanic, David, 1976. *The Growth of Bureaucratic Medicine: An Inquiry into the Dynamics of Patient Behavior and the Organization of Medical Care.* New York: Wiley-Interscience.

501. Mechanic, David. 1976. "Stress, Illness, and Illness Behavior." *Journal of Human Stress* 2 (June): 2–6.

502. Mechanic, David, and Edmund H. Volkart. 1961. "Stress, Illness Behavior, and the Sick Role." *American Sociological Review* 26 (February): 51–58.

503. Mechanic, David, and Edmund H. Volkart. 1960. "Illness Behavior and Medical Diagnoses." *Journal of Health and Human Behavior* 1 (Summer): 86–94.

504. Mechanic, David, and Margaret Newton. 1965. "Some Problems in the Analysis of Morbidity Data." *Journal of Chronic Diseases* 18 (June): 569–80.

505. Mechanic, David, and Ronald G. Faich. 1970. "Doctors in Revolt: The Crisis in the English National Health Service." *Medical Care* 8 (November–December): 442–55.

506. Mellinger, G. D., et al. 1963. "A Comparison of the Personal and Social Characteristics of High and Low Accident Children." Paper delivered at the biennial meeting of the Society for Research in Child Development, Berkeley, Calif.

507. Mendelson, M., et al. 1956. "A Critical Examination of Some Recent Theoretical Models in Psychosomatic Medicine." *Psychosomatic Medicine* 18: 363–73.

508. Merton, Robert K. 1957. "The Role-Set." *British Journal of Sociology* 8: 106–20.

509. Merton, Robert K. 1957. *Social Theory and Social Structure*. Rev. ed. New York: Free Press.

510. Merton, Robert K. et al. 1952. *Reader in Bureaucracy*. New York: Free Press.

511. Merton, Robert K., George Reader, and Patricia L. Kendall, eds. 1957. *The Student-Physician: Introductory Studies in the Sociology of Medical Education*. Cambridge: Harvard University Press.

512. Meyer, R. J., and R. J. Haggerty. 1962. "Streptococcal Infections in Families." *Pediatrics* 29: 539–49.

513. Meyer, R. J., et al. 1963. "Accidental Injury to the Preschool Child." *Journal of Pediatrics* 63: 95–105.

514. Milbank Memorial Fund Commission. 1976. *Higher Education for Public Health*. New York: Prodist.

515. Miller, F. J. W., et al. 1960. *Growing up in Newcastle upon Tyne*. London: Oxford University Press.

516. Miller, Kent S. 1976. *Managing Madness: The Case against Civil Commitment*. New York: Free Press.

517. Miller, Neal E. 1975. "Applications of Learning and Biofeedback to Psychiatry and Medicine." In *Comprehensive Textbook of Psychiatry*, 2d ed., edited by Alfred M. Freedman, Harold I. Kaplan, and Benjamin J. Sadock, vol. 1, pp. 349–65. Baltimore: Williams & Wilkins.

518. Miller, Stephen J. 1970. *Prescription for Leadership: Training for the Medical Elite*. Chicago: Aldine.

519. Mishler, Elliot G., and Norman A. Scotch. 1963. "Sociocultural Factors in the Epidemiology of Schizophrenia." *Psychiatry* 26: 315–51.

520. Montag, Mildred L. 1972. *Evaluation of Graduates of Associate Degree Nursing Programs*. New York: Teachers College Press.

521. Mooney, H. W. 1962. *Methodology in Two California Health Surveys*. U.S. Public Health Service Monograph no. 70. Washington: Government Printing Office.

522. Moriyama, I. M., and L. Guralnick. 1956. "Occupational and Social Class

Differences in Mortality." In *Trends and Differentials in Mortality*, pp. 61–73. New York: Milbank Memorial Fund.

523. Morris, J. N. 1959. "Health and Social Class." *Lancet* 1 (February 7): 303–305.

524. Morris, J. N. 1964. *Uses of Epidemiology*. 2d ed. Baltimore: Williams & Wilkins. Edinburgh: Livingstone.

525. Morris, J. N., et al. 1953. "Coronary Heart Disease and Physical Activity of Work." *Lancet* 2: 1053–57, 1111–20.

526. Morris, J. N., and J. A. Heady. 1955. "Social and Biological Factors in Infant Mortality." *Lancet* 1 (February 12): 343–49.

527. Morrison, S. L. 1959. "Principles and Methods of Epidemiological Research and Their Application to Psychiatric Illness." *Journal of Mental Science* 105: 999–1011.

528. Muller, B. 1965. "Personality of Placebo Reactors and Non-Reactors." *Diseases of the Nervous System* 26: 58–61.

529. Mumford, Emily. 1970. *Interns: From Students to Physicians*. Cambridge: Harvard University Press.

530. Munts, Raymond. 1967. *Bargaining for Health: Labor Unions, Health Insurance, and Medical Care*. Madison: University of Wisconsin Press.

531. Myers, J., and L. Schaffer. 1954. "Social Stratification and Psychiatric Practice: A Study of an Out-Patient Clinic." *American Sociological Review* 19: 307–10.

532. Myers, R. S. 1961. "Quality of Patient Care: Measurable or Immeasurable." *Journal of Medical Education* 36: 776–84.

533. Nader, Ralph. 1965. *Unsafe at Any Speed: The Designed-In Dangers of the American Automobile*. New York: Grossman.

534. Nathanson, Constance A. 1975. "Illness and the Feminine Role: A Theoretical Review." *Social Science and Medicine* 9 (February): 57–62.

535. Nathanson, Constance A. 1975. "Sex, Illness, and Medical Care: A Review of Data, Theory, and Method." Department of Population Dynamics, Johns Hopkins University.

536. Newcomb, Theodore M. 1950. *Social Psychology*. New York: Dryden.

537. New York Times. 1974. "Mental Care Is Called 'Revolving Door.'" March 18, p. 1.

538. Nixon, Richard M. 1971. "Health Message of 1971." February 18. Washington: The White House.

539. Norris, Vera. 1959. *Mental Illness in London*. New York: Oxford University Press. London: Chapman & Hall.

540. O'Connell, Jeffrey. 1975. *Ending Insult to Injury: No Fault Insurance for Products and Services*. Urbana: University of Illinois Press.

541. Ødegård, Ø. 1965. "Discussion of 'Sociocultural Factors in the Epidemiology of Schizophrenia.'" *International Journal of Psychiatry* 1: 296–97.

542. Olson, Mancur, Jr. 1968. *The Logic of Collective Action: Public Goods and the Theory of Groups*. New York: Schocken.

543. Ortmeyer, Carl E. 1974. "Variations in Mortality, Morbidity, and Health

Care by Marital Status." In *Mortality and Morbidity in the United States*, edited by Carl L. Erhardt and Joyce E. Berlin, pp. 159–88. Cambridge: Harvard University Press.

544. Overholser, W. 1953. *The Psychiatrist and the Law*. New York: Harcourt.

545. Paffenbarger, Ralph S., and Wayne E. Hale. 1975. "Work Activity and Coronary Heart Mortality." *New England Journal of Medicine* 292 (March 13): 545–50.

546. Parker, Alberta W. 1974. "The Dimensions of Primary Care: Blueprints for Change." In *Primary Care: Where Medicine Fails*, edited by Spyros Andreopoulos, pp. 15–80. New York: Wiley.

547. Parkes, C. Murray. 1963. "Interhospital and Intrahospital Variations in the Diagnosis and Severity of Schizophrenia." *British Journal of Preventive and Social Medicine* 17 (April): 85–89.

548. Parkes, Colin Murray. 1972. *Bereavement: Studies of Grief in Adult Life*. London: Tavistock.

549. Parsons, Talcott. 1951. *The Social System*. New York: Free Press.

550. Parsons, Talcott. 1972. "Definitions of Health and Illness in the Light of American Values and Social Structure." In *Patients, Physicians and Illness: A Sourcebook in Behavioral Science and Health*, 2d ed., edited by E. Gartly Jaco, pp. 107–27. New York: Free Press.

551. Pasamanick, Benjamin, Frank R. Scarpitti, and Simon Dinitz. 1967. *Schizophrenics in the Community: An Experimental Study in the Prevention of Hospitalization*. New York: Appleton.

552. Patrick, D. L., J. W. Bush, and Milton M. Chen. 1973. "Toward an Operational Definition of Health." *Journal of Health and Social Behavior* 14 (March): 6–23.

553. Paul, Benjamin D., ed. 1955. *Health, Culture, and Community: Case Studies of Public Reactions to Health Programs*. New York: Russell Sage Foundation.

554. Paul, John R. 1958. *Clinical Epidemiology*. Chicago: University of Chicago Press.

555. Pauly, Mark V. 1974. "The Behavior of Nonprofit Hospital Monopolies: Alternative Models of the Hospital." In *Regulating Health Facilities Construction*, edited by Clark C. Havighurst, pp. 143–61. Washington: American Institute for Public Policy Research.

556. Paykel, E.S. 1974. "Life Stress and Psychiatric Disorder." In *Stressful Life Events: Their Nature and Effects*, edited by Barbara Snell Dohrenwend and Bruce P. Dohrenwend, pp. 135–49. New York: Wiley-Interscience.

557. Pearse, I.H., and L.H. Crocker. 1944. *The Peckham Experiment*. London: Allen & Unwin.

558. Pemberton, John, and H. Willard, eds. 1958. *Recent Studies in Epidemiology*. Oxford: Blackwell.

559. Perrow, Charles. 1965. "Hospitals: Technology, Structure, and Goals." In *Handbook of Organizations*, edited by J. March. Chicago: Rand McNally.

560. Peterson, James L. 1973. "Consumers' Knowledge of and Attitudes toward

Medical Malpractice." In *Report of the Secretary's Commission on Medical Malpractice*, DHEW Publication no. (OS) 73–88 and 73–89, pp. 658–757. Washington: Government Printing Office.

561. Peterson, O.L., et al. 1956. "Analytic Study of North Carolina General Practice." *Journal of Medical Education* 31 (pt. 2): 1–165.

562. Phillips, Derek L. 1965. "Self-Reliance and the Inclination to Adopt the Sick Role." *Social Forces* 43: 555–63.

563. Phillips, Derek L., and Bernard E. Segal. 1969. "Sexual Status and Psychiatric Symptoms." *American Sociological Review* 34 (February): 58–72.

564. Phillips, Derek L., and Kevin J. Clancy. 1970. "Response Biases in Field Studies of Mental Illness." *American Sociological Review* 35 (June): 503–15.

565. Polgar, S. 1962. "Health and Human Behavior: Areas of Interest Common to the Social and Medical Sciences." *Current Anthropology* 3: 159–205.

566. Pollard, William E., Ruth A. Bobbitt, Marilyn Bergner, Diane P. Martin, and Betty S. Gilson. 1976. "The Sickness Impact Profile: Reliability of a Health Status Measure." *Medical Care* 14 (February): 146–55.

567. Powles, John. 1973. "On the Limitations of Modern Medicine." *Science, Medicine and Man* 1 (April): 1–30.

568. Pratt, L., et al. 1957. "Physicians' Views on the Level of Medical Information among Patients." *American Journal of Public Health* 47: 1277–83.

569. Pressman, Jeffrey L., and Aaron Wildavsky. 1973. *Implementation: How Great Expectations in Washington Are Dashed in Oakland; or, Why It's Amazing that Federal Programs Work at All, This Being a Saga of the Economic Development Administration as Told by Two Sympathetic Observers Who Seek to Build Morals on a Foundation of Ruined Hopes.* Berkeley: University of California Press.

570. Prybil, Lawrence D. 1970. "Physicians in Large, Multi-Specialty Groups: An Investigation of Selected Characteristics, Career Patterns, and Opinions." Ph.D. dissertation, University of Iowa.

571. Querido, Arie. 1959. "An Investigation into the Clinical, Social, and Mental Factors Determining the Results of Hospital Treatment." *British Journal of Preventive and Social Medicine* 13: 33–49.

572. Quinn, Joseph R., ed. 1972. *Medicine and Public Health in the People's Republic of China.* Washington: John Fogarty International Center for Advanced Study in the Health Sciences.

573. Quinney, E.R. 1963. "Occupational Structure and Criminal Behavior: Prescription Violation by Retail Pharmacists." *Social Problems* 11: 179–85.

574. Rabkin, Judith G., and Elmer L. Struening. 1976. "Life Events, Stress, and Illness." *Science* 194 (December 3): 1013–20.

575. Raines, G. N., and J. H. Rohrer. 1955; 1960. "The Operational Matrix of Psychiatric Practice." *American Journal of Psychiatry* 111: 721–33; 117: 133–39.

576. Rainwater, Lee, and William L. Yancey. 1967. *The Moynihan Report and the Politics of Controversy.* Cambridge: M.I.T. Press.

577. Redlich, Fredrick C. 1953. "Definition of a Case for Purposes of Research in Social Psychiatry Discussion." In *Interrelations between the Social Environment and Psychiatric Disorders*, pp. 118–22. New York: Milbank Memorial Fund.

578. Redlich, Fredrick C. 1957. "The Concept of Health in Psychiatry." In *Explorations in Social Psychiatry*, edited by Alexander H. Leighton, John A. Clausen, and Robert N. Wilson, pp. 138–64. New York: Basic Books.

579. Reeder, Leo G. 1972. "The Patient-Client as a Consumer: Some Observations on the Changing Professional-Client Relationship." *Journal of Health and Social Behavior* 13 (December): 406–12.

580. Reif, Laura Jean. 1975. "Cardiacs and Normals: The Social Construction of a Disability." Ph.D. dissertation, University of California, San Francisco.

581. Reiss, Albert J., Jr. 1961. *Occupations and Social Status*. New York: Free Press.

582. Reissman, F. 1962. *The Culturally Deprived Child*. New York: Harper.

583. Revans, R.W. 1964. *Standards for Morale: Cause and Effect in Hospitals*. London: Oxford University Press.

584. Ribicoff, Abraham. 1970. "Medical Malpractice: The Patient vs. the Physician." *Trial* 6 (February/March): 10–13, 22.

585. Robertson, Leon S. 1975. "Factors Associated with Safety Belt Use in 1974 Starter-Interlock Equipped Cars." *Journal of Health and Social Behavior* 16 (June): 173–77.

586. Robertson, Leon S. 1976. "Estimates of Motor Vehicle Seat Belt Effectiveness and Use: Implications for Occupant Crash Protection." *American Journal of Public Health* 66 (September): 859–64.

587. Robins, Lee N. 1966. *Deviant Children Grown Up: A Sociological and Psychiatric Study of Sociopathic Personality*. Baltimore: Williams & Wilkins.

588. Robins, Lee N. 1975. "Alcoholism and Labelling Theory." In *The Labelling of Deviance: Evaluating a Perspective*, edited by Walter R. Gove, pp. 21–33. New York: Halsted.

589. Roemer, Milton I. 1962. "On Paying the Doctor and the Implications of Different Methods." *Journal of Health and Human Behavior* 3 (Spring): 4–14.

590. Roemer, Milton I., and Jay W. Friedman. 1971. *Doctors in Hospitals: Medical Staff Organization and Hospital Performance*. Baltimore: Johns Hopkins Press.

591. Roessler, Robert, and Norman S. Greenfield. 1962. *Physiological Correlates of Psychological Disorders*. Madison: University of Wisconsin Press.

592. Rosen, George. 1963. "The Hospital: Historical Sociology of a Community Institution." In *The Hospital in Modern Society*, edited by Eliot Freidson, pp. 1–36. New York: Free Press.

593. Rosenberg, Charles E. 1962. *The Cholera Years: The United States in 1832, 1849, and 1866*. Chicago: University of Chicago Press.

594. Rosenberg, Morris. 1965. *Society and the Adolescent Self-Image*. Princeton: Princeton University Press.

595. Rosenberg, Morris, and Roberta G. Simmons. 1971. *Black and White Self-Esteem: The Urban School Child.* Rose Monograph Series. Washington: American Sociological Association.

596. Rosenhan, D.L. 1973. "On Being Sane in Insane Places." *Science* 179 (January 19): 250–58.

597. Rosenstock, I.M. 1960. "What Research in Motivation Suggests for Public Health." *American Journal of Public Health* 50: 295–302.

598. Rosenstock, I.M., et al. 1959. "Why People Fail to Seek Poliomyelitis Vaccination." *Public Health Reports* 74: 98–103.

599. Roth, Julius A. 1963. *Timetables: Structuring the Passage of Time in Hospital Treatment and Other Careers.* Indianapolis: Bobbs-Merrill.

600. Rothman, David J. 1971. *The Discovery of the Asylum: Social Order and Disorder in the New Republic.* Boston: Little, Brown.

601. Royal College of Physicians. 1962. *Smoking and Health.* London: Pitman Medical.

602. Rubel, A.J. 1960. "Concepts of Disease in Mexican-American Culture." *American Anthropologist* 62: 795–814.

603. Rudov, Melvin H., Thomas I. Myers, and Angelo Mirabella. 1973. "Medical Malpractice Insurance Claims Files Closed in 1970." In *Report of the Secretary's Commission on Medical Malpractice,* DHEW Publication no. (OS) 73–88 and 73–89, pp. 1–25. Washington: Government Printing Office.

604. Ruff, G.E., and J. Korchin. 1964. "Psychological Responses of the Mercury Astronauts to Stress." In *The Threat of Impending Disaster,* edited by G. H. Grosser et al. Cambridge: M.I.T. Press.

605. Rushing, William A. 1962. "Social Influence and the Social-Psychological Function of Deference: A Study of Psychiatric Nursing." *Social Forces* 41 (December): 142–48.

606. Russek, H.I. 1959. "Role of Heredity, Diet, and Emotional Stress in Coronary Heart Disease." *Journal of the American Medical Association* 171: 503–508.

607. Samora, Julian, Lyle Saunders, and Richard F. Larson. 1961. "Medical Vocabulary Knowledge among Hospital Patients." *Journal of Health and Human Behavior* 2 (Summer): 83–92.

608. Sampson, H., et al. 1962. "Family Processes and Becoming a Mental Patient." *American Journal of Sociology* 68: 88–96.

609. Saunders, Lyle. 1954. *Cultural Differences and Medical Care: The Case of the Spanish-Speaking People of the Southwest.* New York: Russell Sage Foundation.

610. Schachter, Stanley. 1959. *The Psychology of Affiliation: Experimental Studies of the Sources of Gregariousness.* Stanford: Stanford University Press.

611. Schachter, Stanley, and J. Singer. 1962. "Cognitive, Social, and Physiological Determinants of Emotional State." *Psychological Review* 69: 379–99.

612. Schachter, Stanley, and L. Wheeler. 1962. "Epinephrine, Chlorproma-

zine, and Amusement." *Journal of Abnormal and Social Psychology* 45: 121–28.

613. Scheff, Thomas J. 1961. "Control over Policy by Attendants in a Mental Hospital." *Journal of Health and Human Behavior* 2 (Summer): 93–105.

614. Scheff, Thomas J. 1963. "Decision Rules, Types of Error, and Their Consequences in Medical Diagnosis." *Behavioral Science* 8: 97–107.

615. Scheff, Thomas J. 1963. "Legitimate, Transitional, and Illegitimate Patients in a Midwestern State." *American Journal of Psychiatry* 120: 267–69.

616. Scheff, Thomas J. 1963. "The Role of the Mentally Ill and the Dynamics of Mental Disorder." *Sociometry* 26: 436–53.

617. Scheff, Thomas J. 1964. "The Societal Reaction to Deviance: Ascriptive Elements in the Psychiatric Screening of Mental Patients in a Midwestern State." *Social Problems* 11: 401–13.

618. Scheff, Thomas J. 1966. *Being Mentally Ill: A Sociological Theory.* Chicago: Aldine.

619. Scheff, Thomas J. 1966. "Users and Non-Users of a Student Psychiatric Clinic." *Journal of Health and Human Behavior* 7: 114–21.

620. Schenthal, J.E. 1960. "Multiphasic Screening of the Well Patient." *Journal of the American Medical Association* 172: 1–4.

621. Schneider, D. 1947. "The Social Dynamics of Physical Disability in Army Basic Training." *Psychiatry* 10: 323–33.

622. Schur, Edwin M. 1971. *Labeling Deviant Behavior: Its Sociological Implications.* New York: Harper.

623. Schwartz, C. 1957. "Perspectives on Deviance: Wives' Definitions of Their Husbands' Mental Illness." *Psychiatry* 20: 275–91.

624. Schwartz, Richard D., and Jerome H. Skolnick. 1962. "Two Studies of Legal Stigma." *Social Problems* 10 (Fall): 133–42.

625. Scull, Andrew T. 1977. *Decarceration: Community Treatment and the Deviant.* Englewood Cliffs, N.J.: Prentice-Hall.

626. Seeman, Melvin, and John W. Evans. 1961. "Stratification and Hospital Care: 1. The Performance of the Medical Interne." *American Sociological Review* 26 (February): 67–80.

627. Seeman, Melvin, and John W. Evans. 1961. "Stratification and Hospital Care: 2. The Objective Criteria of Performance." *American Sociological Review* 26 (April): 193–204.

628. Segal, Bernard E., Robert J. Weiss, and Robert Sokol. 1965. "Emotional Adjustment, Social Organization and Psychiatric Treatment Rates." *American Sociological Review* 30 (August): 548–56.

629. Segal, Steven P., and Uri Aviram. 1977. *The Mentally Ill in Community-Based Sheltered Care: A Study of Community Care and Social Integration.* New York: Wiley-Interscience.

630. Seiler, Lauren H. 1973. "The 22-Item Scale Used in Field Studies of Mental Illness: A Question of Method, a Question of Substance, and a Question of Theory." *Journal of Health and Social Behavior* 14 (September): 252–64.

631. Seligman, Martin E.P. 1975. *Helplessness: On Depression, Development, and Death.* San Francisco: Freeman.

632. Sellin, J.T. 1938. *Culture, Conflict and Crime.* Bulletin 41. New York: Social Science Research Council.

633. Selye, Hans. 1956. *The Stress of Life.* New York: McGraw-Hill.

634. Selzer, Melvin L., Paul W. Gikas, and Donald F. Huelke, eds. 1967. *The Prevention of Highway Injury.* Ann Arbor: Highway Safety Research Institute, University of Michigan.

635. Sewell, William H., and Robert M. Hauser. 1975. *Education, Occupation, and Earnings: Achievement in the Early Career.* New York: Academic Press.

636. Shanas, Ethel, Peter Townsend, Dorothy Wedderburn, Henning Friis, Poul Milhøj, and Jan Stehouwer. 1968. *Old People in Three Industrial Societies.* New York: Atherton.

637. Shapiro, Arthur K. 1959. "The Placebo Effect in the History of Medical Treatment: Implications for Psychiatry." *American Journal of Psychiatry* 116 (October): 298–304.

638. Shapiro, Arthur K. 1960. "A Contribution to a History of the Placebo Effect." *Behavioral Science* 5: 109–35.

639. Shapiro, Sam, Edward R. Schlesinger, and Robert E.L. Nesbitt, Jr. 1968. *Infant, Perinatal, Maternal, and Childhood Mortality in the United States.* Cambridge: Harvard University Press.

640. Shepherd, Michael, A.N. Oppenheim, and Sheila Mitchell. 1966. "Childhood Behavior Disorders and the Child Guidance Clinic: An Epidemiological Study." *Journal of Child Psychology and Psychiatry* 7: 39–52.

641. Sheps, Cecil G., and Eugene E. Taylor. 1954. *Needed Research in Health and Medical Care: A Bio-Social Approach.* Chapel Hill: University of North Carolina Press.

642. Shryock, Richard Harrison. 1960. *Medicine and Society in America, 1660–1860.* New York: New York University Press.

643. Shryock, Richard Harrison. 1966. *Medicine in America: Historical Essays.* Baltimore: Johns Hopkins Press.

644. Sidel, Victor W., and Ruth Sidel. 1973. *Serve the People: Observations on Medicine in the People's Republic of China.* Boston: Josiah Macy, Jr., Foundation.

645. Sigerist, Henry E. 1951. *A History of Medicine.* New York: Oxford University Press.

646. Sigerist, Henry E. 1958. *The Great Doctors.* Garden City, N.Y.: Doubleday, Anchor.

647. Sigerist, Henry E. 1960. *On the Sociology of Medicine.* Edited by Milton I. Roemer. New York: MD Publications.

648. Simmons, Ozzie G. 1958. *Social Status and Public Health.* Social Science Research Council Pamphlet no. 13. New York: The Council.

649. Simmons, Ozzie G., and Helen M. Hughes. 1965. *Work and Mental Illness.* New York: Wiley.

650. Simmons, Roberta G., Susan D. Klein, and Richard L. Simmons. 1977.

Gift of Life: The Social and Psychological Impact of Organ Transplantation. New York: Wiley-Interscience.

651. Skinner, B.F. 1971. *Beyond Freedom and Dignity.* New York: Knopf.

652. Skipper, James K., Jr., and Robert C. Leonard. 1968. "Children, Stress, and Hospitalization: A Field Experiment." *Journal of Health and Social Behavior* 9 (December): 275–87.

653. Slesinger, Doris P. 1976. "The Utilization of Preventive Medical Services by Urban Black Mothers." In *The Growth of Bureacratic Medicine: An Inquiry into the Dynamics of Patient Behavior and the Organization of Medical Care,* by David Mechanic, pp. 197–219. New York: Wiley-Interscience.

654. Smith, M.B. 1959. "Research Strategies toward a Conception of Positive Mental Health." *American Psychologist* 14: 673–81.

655. Smith, M.B. 1961. "'Mental Health' Reconsidered: A Special Case of the Problem of Values in Psychology." *American Psychologist* 16: 299–306.

656. Snyder, Charles R. 1958. *Alcohol and the Jews: A Cultural Study of Drinking and Sobriety.* New York: Free Press.

657. Somers, Herman Miles, and Anne Ramsay Somers. 1961. *Doctors, Patients, and Health Insurance: The Organization and Financing of Medical Care.* Washington: Brookings.

658. Speisman, J.C. 1965. "Autonomic Monitoring of Ego Defense Process." In *Psychoanalysis and Current Biological Thought,* edited by Norman S. Greenfield and William C. Lewis, pp. 227–44. Madison: University of Wisconsin Press.

659. Speisman, J.C., et al. 1964. "Experimental Analysis of a Film Used as a Threatening Stimulus." *Journal of Consulting Psychology* 28: 23–33.

660. Speisman, J.C., et al. 1964. "Experimental Reduction of Stress Based on Ego-Defense Theory." *Journal of Abnormal and Social Psychology* 68: 367–80.

661. Spitzer, Robert L. 1976. "More on Pseudoscience in Science and the Case for Psychiatric Diagnosis." *Archives of General Psychiatry* 33 (April): 459–70.

662. Srole, Leo, Thomas S. Langner, Stanley T. Michael, Marvin K. Opler, and Thomas A.C. Rennie. 1962. *Mental Health in the Metropolis: The Midtown Manhattan Study.* New York: McGraw-Hill.

663. Stanton, Alfred H., and Morris S. Schwartz. 1954. *The Mental Hospital: A Study of Institutional Participation in Psychiatric Illness and Treatment.* New York: Basic Books.

664. Stein, Leonard I., Mary Ann Test, and Arnold J. Marx. 1975. "Alternative to the Hospital: A Controlled Study." *American Journal of Psychiatry* 132 (May): 517–22.

665. Stein, Leonard I., and Mary Ann Test. 1976. "Training in Community Living: One-Year Evaluation." *American Journal of Psychiatry* 133 (August): 917–18.

666. Steinwald, Bruce. 1974. "Physician Location: Behavior versus Attitudes." In *Reference Data on Socioeconomic Issues of Health,* edited by Barry S.

Eisenberg, pp. 34–41. Chicago: AMA Center for Health Services Research and Development.

667. Stern, B.J. 1945. *American Medical Practice*. New York: Commonwealth Fund.

668. Sternbach, Richard A. and B. Tursky. 1965. "Ethnic Differences among Housewives in Psychophysical and Skin Potential Responses to Electric Shock." *Psychophysiology* 1: 241–46.

669. Stevens, Robert, and Rosemary Stevens. 1974. *Welfare Medicine in America: A Case Study of Medicaid*. New York: Free Press.

670. Stevens, Rosemary. 1971. *American Medicine and the Public Interest*. New Haven: Yale University Press.

671. Stockwell, E.G. 1962. "Infant Mortality and Socio-Economic Status: A Changing Relationship." *Milbank Memorial Fund Quarterly* 40: 101–11.

672. Stoeckle, J., et al. 1963. "On Going to See the Doctor: The Contributions of the Patient to the Decision to Seek Medical Aid." *Journal of Chronic Diseases* 16: 975–89.

673. Stone, Alan A. 1975. *Mental Health and Law: A System in Transition*. Center for Studies of Crime and Delinquency, National Institute of Mental Health, DHEW Publication no. (ADM) 75–176. Washington: Government Printing Office.

674. Stotsky, Bernard A. 1970. *The Nursing Home and the Aged Psychiatric Patient*. New York: Appleton.

675. Straus, Robert. 1957. "The Nature and Status of Medical Sociology." *American Sociological Review* 22 (April): 200–204.

676. Straus, Robert, and Selden D. Bacon. 1953. *Drinking in College*. New Haven: Yale University Press.

677. Strickland, Stephen P. 1972. *U.S. Health Care: What's Wrong and What's Right*. New York: Universe.

678. Stunkard, Albert J. 1976. *The Pain of Obesity*. Palo Alto, Calif.: Bull.

679. Suchman, Edward A. 1960–1961. "A Conceptual Analysis of the Accident Phenomenon." *Social Problems* 8: 241–53.

680. Suchman, Edward A. 1963. *Sociology and the Field of Public Health*. New York: Russell Sage Foundation.

681. Suchman, Edward A. 1964. "Sociomedical Variations among Ethnic Groups." *American Journal of Sociology* 70 (November): 319–31.

682. Suchman, Edward A. 1965. "Social Patterns of Illness and Medical Care." *Journal of Health and Human Behavior* 6: 2–16.

683. Suchman, Edward A. 1965. "Stages of Illness and Medical Care." *Journal of Health and Human Behavior* 6: 114–28.

684. Sudnow, David. 1967. *Passing On: The Social Organization of Dying*. Englewood Cliffs, N.J.: Prentice-Hall.

685. Sullivan, Harry Stack. 1953. *The Interpersonal Theory of Psychiatry*. New York: Norton.

686. Susser, Mervyn. 1968. *Community Psychiatry: Epidemiologic and Social Themes*. New York: Random House.

687. Susser, Mervyn. 1973. *Causal Thinking in the Health Sciences: Concepts and Strategies in Epidemiology.* New York: Oxford University Press.

688. Susser, Mervyn, and W. Watson. 1971. *Sociology in Medicine.* 2d ed. New York: Oxford University Press.

689. Sutherland, Edwin H. 1961. *White Collar Crime.* New York: Holt.

690. Svarstad, Bonnie L. 1974. "The Doctor-Patient Encounter: An Observational Study of Communication and Outcome." Ph.D. dissertation, University of Wisconsin, Madison.

691. Svarstad, Bonnie L. 1976. "Physician-Patient Communication and Patient Conformity with Medical Advice." In *The Growth of Bureaucratic Medicine: An Inquiry into the Dynamics of Patient Behavior and the Organization of Medical Care,* by David Mechanic, pp. 220–38. New York: Wiley-Interscience.

692. Symposium on the Relative Progress of the American Negro since 1950. 1963. *Journal of Negro Education* 32 (Fall): entire issue.

693. Szasz, Thomas S. 1960. "The Myth of Mental Illness." *American Psychologist* 15: 113–18.

694. Szasz, Thomas S. 1962. "Bootlegging Humanistic Values through Psychiatry." *Antioch Review* 22: 341–49.

695. Szasz, Thomas S. 1963. *Law, Liberty, and Psychiatry: An Inquiry into the Social Uses of Mental Health Practices.* New York: Macmillan.

696. Szasz, Thomas S. 1965. *The Ethics of Psychoanalysis.* New York: Basic Books.

697. Szasz, Thomas S., and Robert A. Nemiroff. 1963. "A Questionnaire Study of Psychoanalytic Practices and Opinions." *Journal of Nervous and Mental Disease* 137 (September): 209–21.

698. Terris, Milton, ed. 1964. *Goldberger on Pellagra.* Baton Rouge: Louisiana State University Press.

699. Tessler, Richard, David Mechanic, and Margaret Dimond. 1976. "The Effect of Psychological Distress on Physician Utilization: A Prospective Study." *Journal of Health and Social Behavior* 17 (December): 353–64.

700. Thibaut, John W., and Harold H. Kelley. 1959. *The Social Psychology of Groups.* New York: Wiley.

701. Thomas, W. I., and F. Znaniecki. 1927. *The Polish Peasant in Europe and America.* 2 vols. New York: Knopf.

702. Torrance, E.P. 1965. *Constructive Behavior.* Belmont, Calif.: Wadsworth.

703. Tousignant, Michael, Guy Denis, and Rejean Lachapelle. 1974. "Some Considerations Concerning the Validity and Use of the Health Opinion Survey." *Journal of Health and Social Behavior* 15 (September): 241–52.

704. Trussell, Ray E., and Jack Elinson. 1959. *Chronic Illness in a Rural Area.* Commission on Chronic Illness, *Chronic Illness in the United States,* vol. 3, pp. 365–66. Cambridge: Harvard University Press.

705. Turner, R. 1956. "Role-Taking, Role Standpoint, and Reference-Group Behavior." *American Journal of Sociology* 61: 316–28.

706. Turner, R. Jay, and Morton O. Wagenfeld. 1967. "Occupational Mobility

and Schizophrenia: An Assessment of the Social Causation and Social Selection Hypotheses." *American Sociological Review* 32 (February): 104–13.

707. U.S. Department of Health, Education, and Welfare. 1967. *Report of the National Advisory Commission on Health Manpower.* Vol. 2. Washington: Government Printing Office.

708. U.S. Department of Health, Education, and Welfare. 1973. *Report of the Secretary's Commission on Medical Malpractice.* DHEW Publication no. (OS) 73–88 and 73–89. Washington: Government Printing Office.

709. U.S. Department of Health, Education, and Welfare, Health Services and Mental Health Administration. 1973. *The Health Consequences of Smoking.* DHEW Publication no. (HSM) 73–8704. Washington: Government Printing Office.

710. U.S. Department of Health, Education, and Welfare, Center for Disease Control. 1974. *The Health Consequences of Smoking.* DHEW Publication no. (CDC) 74–8704. Washington: Government Printing Office.

711. U.S. Department of Health, Education, and Welfare, Center for Disease Control. 1975. *The Health Consequences of Smoking.* DHEW Publication no. (CDC) 76–8704. Washington: Government Printing Office.

712. U.S. Department of Health, Education, and Welfare, Social Security Administration. 1976. *National Health Insurance Proposals: Provisions of Bills Introduced in the 94th Congress as of February 1976.* DHEW Publication no. (SSA) 76–11920. Washington: Government Printing Office.

713. U.S. National Center for Health Statistics. 1963. *Origin, Program, and Operation of the U.S. National Health Survey.* Series 1–1. Washington: Government Printing Office.

714. U.S. National Center for Health Statistics. 1964. *The Change in Mortality Trend in the United States.* Series 3–1. Washington: Government Printing Office.

715. U.S. National Center for Health Statistics. 1964. *Cycle I of the Health Examination Survey: Sample and Response, United States, 1960–1962.* Series 11–1. Washington: Government Printing Office.

716. U.S. National Center for Health Statistics. 1964. *Health Survey Procedure: Concepts, Questionnaire Development, and Definitions in the Health Interview Survey.* Series 1–2. Washington: Government Printing Office.

716a U.S. National Center for Health Statistics. 1964. *Vital Statistics of the United States, 1962.* Vol. 11, pt. A. Washington: Government Printing Office.

717. U.S. National Center for Health Statistics. 1965. *Infant and Perinatal Mortality in the United States.* Series 3–4. Washington: Government Printing Office.

718. U.S. National Center for Health Statistics. 1965. *Plan and Initial Program of the Health Examination Survey.* Series 1–4. Washington: Government Printing Office.

718a U.S. National Center for Health Statistics. 1965. *Vital Statistics of the*

United States, 1963. Vol. 11, pt. A. Washington: Government Printing Office.

718b U.S. National Center for Health Statistics. 1965. Vital Statistics of the United States, 1963. Vol. 11, pt. B. Washington: Government Printing Office.

719. U.S. National Center for Health Statistics. 1966. Report of the International Conference on the Perinatal and Infant Mortality Problems of the United States. Series 4–3. Washington: Government Printing Office.

720. U.S. National Center for Health Statistics. 1966. Vital Statistics of the United States, 1964. Vol. 11, pt. A. Washington: Government Prtinting Office.

721. U.S. National Center for Health Statistics. 1967. Three Views of Hypertension and Heart Disease. Public Health Service Publication no. 1000, Vital and Health Statistics Series 2, no. 22. Washington: Government Printing Office.

722. U.S. National Center for Health Statistics, Health Services and Mental Health Administration. 1971. Design and Methodology of the 1967 Master Facility Inventory Survey. Public Health Service Publication no. 1000, Vital Health Statistics Series 1, no. 9. Washington: Government Printing Office.

723. U.S. National Center for Health Statistics. 1971. Surgical Operations in Short-Stay Hospitals for Discharged Patients, United States, 1965. Public Health Service Series 13, no. 7. Washington: Government Printing Office.

724. U.S. National Center for Health Statistics, Health Services and Mental Health Administration. 1972. Uniform Hospital Abstract: Minimum Basic Data Set. DHEW Publication no. (HSM) 73-1451, Vital and Health Statistics Series 4, no. 14. Washington: Government Printing Office.

725. U.S. National Center for Health Statistics, Health Services and Mental Health Administration. 1973. Net Differences in Interview Data on Chronic Conditions and Information Derived From Medical Records. Vital and Health Statistics Series 2, no. 57. Washington: Government Printing Office.

726. U.S. National Center for Health Statistics, Health Resources Administration. 1974. Health Resources Statistics. DHEW Publication no. (HRA) 75–1509. Washington: Government Printing Office.

727. U.S. National Center for Health Statistics, Health Resources Administration. 1974. Limitation of Activity and Mobility Due to Chronic Conditions, United States, 1972. DHEW Publication no. (HRA) 75–1523, Vital and Health Statistics Series 10, no. 96. Washington: Government Printing Office.

728. U.S. National Center for Health Statistics, Health Resources Administration. 1974. Mortality Trends for Leading Causes of Death; United States, 1950–69. DHEW Publication no. (HRA) 74–1853, Vital and Health Statistics Series 20, no. 16. Washington: Government Printing Office.

729. U.S. National Center for Health Statistics, Health Resources Administration. 1974. National Ambulatory Medical Care Survey: Background and

Methodology; United States, 1967–72. DHEW Publication no. (HRA) 74–1335, Vital and Health Statistics Series 2, no. 61. Washington: Government Printing Office.

730. U. S. National Center for Health Statistics, Health Resources Administration. 1975. *Health Interview Survey Procedure, 1957–1974.* DHEW Publication no. (HRA) 75–1311. Vital and Health Statistics Series 1, no. 11. Washington: Government Printing Office.

731. U.S. National Center for Health Statistics, Health Resources Administration. 1975. *Physician Visits: Volume and Interval Since Last Visit; United States, 1971.* DHEW Publication no. (HRA) 75–1524, Vital and Health Statistics Series 10, number 97. Washington: Government Printing Office.

732. U. S. National Center for Health Statistics, Health Resources Administration. 1975. *Quality Control in the Hospital Discharge Survey.* DHEW Publication no. (HRA) 76–1342, Vital and Health Statistics Series 2, no. 68. Washington: Government Printing Office.

733. U.S. National Center for Health Statistics, Health Resources Administration. 1975. *Selected Operating Financial Characteristics of Nursing Homes, United States: The 1973–74 National Nursing Home Survey.* Washington: Government Printing Office.

734. U.S. National Center for Health Statistics, Health Resources Administration. 1975. *Vital Statistics of the United States, 1971.* Vol. 2, *Mortality,* pt. A. Washington: Government Printing Office.

735. U.S. National Center for Health Statistics, Health Resources Administration. 1975. *Vital Statistics of the United States, 1973.* Vol. 2, *Mortality,* sec. 5. Washington: Government Printing Office.

736. U.S. National Center for Health Statistics, Health Resources Administration. 1975. *Vital Statistics Report: Annual Summary for the United States, 1974.* Vol. 23, no. 13. Washington: Government Printing Office.

737. U.S. National Center for Health Statistics. 1976. "Advance Report: Final Mortality Statistics, 1974." *Monthly Vital Statistics Report* 24, no. 11, supplement (February 3). Washington: Government Printing Office.

738. U.S. National Center for Health Statistics, Health Resources Administration. 1976. *Development of the National Inventory of Family Planning Services.* DHEW Publication no. (HRA) 76-1312, Vital and Health Statistics Series 1, no. 12. Washington: Government Printing Office.

739. U.S. National Center for Health Statistics, Health Resources Administration. 1976. *Health: United States, 1975.* DHEW Publication no. (HRA) 76–1232. Washington: Government Printing Office.

740. U.S. National Center for Health Statistics. 1977. "Advance Report: Final Mortality Statistics, 1975." *Monthly Vital Statistics Report* 25, no. 11, supplement. Washington: Government Printing Office.

741. U.S. National Health Survey, Public Health Service. 1961. *Reporting of Hospitalization in the Health Interview Survey.* Series D, no. 4. Washington: Government Printing Office.

742. U.S. National Health Survey, Public Health Service. 1961. *Health Interview Responses Compared with Medical Records.* Series D, no. 5. Washington: Government Printing Office.

743. U.S. National Health Survey, Public Health Service. 1963. *Comparison of Hospitalization Reporting in Three Survey Procedures.* Series D, no. 8. Washington: Government Printing Office.

744. U.S. National Health Survey, Public Health Service. 1964. *Medical Care, Health Status, and Family Income; United States.* Series 10, no. 9. Washington: Government Printing Office.

745. U.S. National Institute of Mental Health, Health Services and Mental Health Administration, National Clearinghouse for Mental Health Information. 1970. *Lithium in the Treatment of Mood Disorders.* Publication no. 5033. Washington: Government Printing Office.

746. U.S. National Institute of Mental Health. 1974. "At Issue." *Schizophrenia Bulletin* 11 (Winter): 4–17. Washington: Government Printing Office.

747. U.S. President's Commission on Federal Statistics. 1971. *Federal Statistics: Report of the President's Commission.* 2 vols. Washington: Government Printing Office.

748. U.S. President's Science Advisory Committee, Executive Office of the President. 1972. *Improving Health Care through Research and Development: Report of the Panel on Health Services Research and Development.* Washington: Government Printing Office.

749. U.S. Public Health Service, National Vital Statistics Division. 1963. *Mortality by Occupation Level and Cause of Death among Men 20 to 64 Years of Age; United States, 1950.* Special Reports, vol. 53, no. 5. Washington: Government Printing Office.

750. U.S. Public Health Service. 1964. *Smoking and Health.* Publication no. 1103. Washington: Government Printing Office.

751. Volkart, Edmund H., ed. 1951. *Social Behavior and Personality.* New York: Social Science Research Council.

752. Volkart, Edmund H. 1957. "Bereavement and Mental Health." In *Explorations in Social Psychiatry,* edited by Alexander H. Leighton, John A. Clausen, and Robert N. Wilson, pp. 281–307. New York: Basic Books.

753. Volkart, Edmund H. 1960. "Man, Disease, and the Social Environment." *Stanford Medical Bulletin* 18: 29–33.

754. Waitzkin, Howard B., and Barbara Waterman. 1974. *The Exploitation of Illness in Capitalist Society.* Indianapolis: Bobbs-Merrill.

755. Waldron, Ingrid. 1976. "Why Do Women Live Longer Than Men?" pt. 1. *Journal of Human Stress* 2 (March): 2–13.

756. Wardwell, W. 1952. "A Marginal Professional Role: The Chiropractor." *Social Forces* 30: 339–48.

757. Waxman, Henry. 1975. "A Health Care Slide." *Trial* 11 (May/June): 23–24, 28.

758. Wechsler, Henry, Leonard Solomon, and Bernard M. Kramer, eds. 1970. *Social Psychology and Mental Health.* New York: Holt.

759. Weisbrod, Burton A., in collaboration with Joel F. Handler and Neil K. Komesar. 1978. *Public Interest Law: An Economic and Institutional Analysis.* Berkeley: University of California Press.

760. Weiss, Robert S. 1975. *Marital Separation*. New York: Basic Books.

761. Welch, Rebecca. 1973. "Medical Malpractice in Canada." In *Report of the Secretary's Commission on Medical Malpractice*, DHEW Publication no. (OS) 73–88 and 73–89, pp. 849–53. Washington: Government Printing Office.

762. Wennberg, John, and Alan Gittelsohn. 1973. "Small Area Variations in Health Care Delivery." *Science* 182 (December 14): 1102–1108.

763. White, Kerr L. 1970. "Evaluation of Medical Education and Health Care." In *Community Medicine: Teaching, Research, and Health Care*, edited by Willoughby Lathem and Anne Newbery, pp. 241–70. New York: Appleton.

764. White, Kerr L. 1975. "International Comparisons of Medical Care." *Scientific American* 233 (August): 17–25.

765. White, Kerr L., et al. 1961. "The Ecology of Medical Care." *New England Journal of Medicine* 265: 885–92.

766. White, Kerr L., and Maureen M. Henderson. 1976. *Epidemiology as a Fundamental Science: Its Uses in Health Services Planning, Administration, and Evaluation*. New York: Oxford University Press.

767. Williams, R.H., ed. 1962. *The Prevention of Disability in Mental Disorders*. DHEW Monograph 1, Public Health Service Publication no. 924. Washington: Government Printing Office.

768. Willie, Charles V. 1959. "A Research Note on the Changing Association between Infant Mortality and Socio-Economic Status." *Social Forces* 37 (March): 221–27.

769. Willis, J.H., and D. Bannister. 1965. "The Diagnosis and Treatment of Schizophrenia: A Questionnaire Study of Psychiatric Opinion." *British Journal of Psychiatry* 111: 1165–71.

770. Wilson, R.N. 1959. "The Physician's Changing Hospital Role." *Human Organization* 18: 177–83.

771. Wing, J.K. 1962. "Institutionalism in Mental Hospitals." *British Journal of Social and Clinical Psychology* 1 (February): 38–51.

772. Wing, J.K. 1966. "The Measurement of Psychiatric Diagnosis." Royal Society of Medicine, London, *Proceedings* 59: 1030–32.

773. Wing, J.K. 1967. "The Modern Management of Schizophrenia." In *New Aspects of the Mental Health Services*, edited by Hugh Freeman and James Farndale, pp. 3–28. New York: Pergamon.

774. Wing, J.K., and George W. Brown. 1961. "Social Treatment of Chronic Schizophrenia: A Comprehensive Survey of Three Mental Hospitals." *Journal of Mental Science* 107: 847–61.

775. Wing, J.K., J.E. Cooper, and N. Sartorius. 1974. *Measurement and Classification of Psychiatric Symptoms*. New York: Cambridge University Press.

776. Witts, L.J., ed. 1959. *Medical Surveys and Clinical Trials*. London: Oxford University Press.

777. Wolf, Stewart. 1959. "The Pharmacology of Placebos." *Pharmacological Reviews* 11 (December): 689–704.

778. Wolf, Stewart, and Harold G. Wolff. 1943. *Human Gastric Function: An Experimental Study of a Man and His Stomach*. New York: Oxford University Press.

779. Wolfenstein, Martha. 1957. *Disaster: A Psychological Essay*. New York: Free Press.

780. Wolff, Harold G. 1953. *Stress and Disease*. Springfield, Ill.: Thomas.

781. Wolff, Harold G. 1955. "Stress and Adaptive Patterns Resulting in Tissue Damage in Man." In *The Medical Clinics of North America*. Philadelphia: Saunders.

782. Wolff, Harold G. 1963. *Headache and Other Head Pain*. 2d ed. New York: Oxford University Press.

783. Woods, Sherwyn M., Joseph Natterson, and Jerome Silverman. 1966. "Medical Student's Disease: Hypochondriasis in Medical Education." *Journal of Medical Education* 41 (August): 785–90.

784. Woolsey, T. D. 1958. "The Concept of Illness in the Household Interview for the U.S. National Health Survey." *American Journal of Public Health* 48: 703–12.

785. Wootton, B. 1959. *Social Science and Social Pathology*. London: Allen & Unwin.

786. World Health Organization. 1973. *Report of the International Pilot Study of Schizophrenia*. Vol. 1. Geneva.

787. Wray, Joe. 1975. "Health Maintaining Behavior of Mothers in Traditional, Transitional and Modern Societies." Paper presented at meeting of the American Association for the Advancement of Science, New York City.

788. Wrong, Dennis H. 1961. "The Oversocialized Conception of Man in Modern Sociology." *American Sociological Review* 26: 183–93.

789. Yankauer, A., and N.C. Allaway. 1958. "The Relation of Indices of Fetal and Infant Loss to Residential Segregation: A Follow-Up Report." *American Sociological Review* 23: 573–78.

790. Yarrow, Marion Radke, Charlotte Green Schwartz, Harriet S. Murphy, and Leila Calhoun Deasy. 1955. "The Psychological Meaning of Mental Illness in the Family." *Journal of Social Issues* 11:12–24.

791. Yarrow, Marion Radke, et al. 1955. "The Social Meaning of Mental Illness." *Journal of Social Issues* 11: 33–48.

792. Yett, Donald E., and Frank A. Sloan. 1974. "Migration Patterns of Recent Medical School Graduates." *Inquiry* 11 (June): 125–42.

793. Zborowski, Mark. 1952. "Cultural Components in Responses to Pain," *Journal of Social Issues* 8: 16–30.

794. Zola, I., 1963. "Problems of Communication, Diagnosis, and Patient Care." *Journal of Medical Education* 38: 829–38.

795. Zola, I. 1964. "Illness Behavior of the Working Class." In *Blue-Collar World: Studies of the American Worker*, edited by Arthur Shostak and William Gomberg. Englewood Cliffs, N.J.: Prentice-Hall.

INDEXES

Index of Names

Index of Subjects

Defined populations, 315
Definition of the situation, 66, 408, 441, 484
Degenerative heart disease, 169
Deinstitutionalization, 491
Delay in seeking care, 32, 284, 425
Delinquency, 102, 163, 305, 444, 449
Delusions, 101, 277
Demand for care, 328, 345, 413
Demands of medical work, 380
Demographic studies, 157–80
Demography, 5
Denial, 72, 222, 223, 269, 284, 291, 298
Denmark, 139
Dental services, 9, 199, 340
Dependency, 188, 197, 235, 260, 262, 263, 299, 304–305, 404, 437, 465, 468, 481, 509
Depersonalization, 80, 103
Depression, 71, 101, 104–105, 109, 112–13, 179, 184, 206, 223, 227, 229, 238, 244, 277, 299
Deprivation, social, 171, 455
Deprivation syndrome, 174, 175, 461
"Depth psychologies," 235
Dermatologists, 429
Dermatology, 381, 383, 389
Desegregation of schools, 472
Desensitization, 79, 113
Determinism, 50
Developed countries, 61, 98, 159, 315, 328, 329
Development, intellectual, 294
Developmental-historical approach, 295, 462
Developmental process, 294
Deviant behavior, 25–52, 64, 78, 86, 99–102, 111, 250, 270, 272, 275, 276, 280, 287–88, 291, 305, 307, 442–49, 482
Deviant sexual pattern, 444
Deviant social career, 443, 444, 445, 448, 449
Deviants, sociomedical problems of, 344
Diabetes, 57, 114, 137, 158, 160, 161, 169, 170, 171, 182, 186, 209
Diagnosis, 28, 95–99, 140, 152, 153, 199; reliability in, 96, 105–11, 215, 488
Diagnostic: aids, 354; assessments, 106; authority, 271; facilities, 321; procedures, 330, 340, 342, 348, 390, 423, 426, 506; technology, 310, 393; work, 373, 415
Diarrhea, 120, 157
Diet, 57, 60, 134, 157, 162, 164, 176, 207, 461
Dignified care, 500
Dignity, 461, 471
Diploma schools, 361

Directive and organic orientations (D-O), 399
Disability, 4, 11–60, 65–67, 75, 78, 84, 85, 86, 120, 151, 168, 181, 182, 185, 194, 198, 199, 244, 250, 255, 266, 336, 338, 343, 344, 345, 391, 431, 435, 438, 440, 441, 442, 445, 458, 460, 462, 466, 505, 506, 518
Disasters, 64, 224, 300
Discharge from short-stay hospitals, 201
Discharge status, 152
Discretion, 332, 509
Discrimination, 192, 303, 497
Disease, 54, 130–40, 203; agents of, 209; causes of, 131; chronic, 137, 344 (*see also* Chronic illness); communicable, 344; concepts of, 25–27, 31, 51, 55, 88, 100, 113–15, 410; concept in psychiatry, 99–105, 111–13; control of, 157, 204; course of, 121, 136, 358; definition of, 27, 28, 478; distribution of, 3–4, 5; etiology of, 136; of heart, 171; ill-defined, 159; incidence of, 132; incurable, 122; infectious, 186, 208, 209, 246; metaphors, 114; model, 95–99, 420–22; occurrence of, 189, 191, 208; perspective, 105, 436; prevalence of, 294; prevention of, 336; social demography of, 184–85; susceptibility to, 233, 242; theories of, 419; transmission of, 204; vulnerability to, 227, 294; *see also* Illness
Disease, International Classification of, 153, 181
Disorderly conduct, 277
Disruptions in learning, 39
Dissatisfaction, 238–39
Distance, 287
Distorted roles, 440
Distress, 57, 61, 122, 181, 183, 185, 188, 197, 245, 255, 264, 266, 267, 271, 290, 305, 309, 427, 488; modes of expressing, 186, 188, 260, 264, 267
Distribution of health-care services, 9, 315, 325, 335, 336, 371, 411, 414
Distribution of physicians, 341
Distribution of products, 336
Distribution of psychiatric services, 474
Distribution of resources, 12, 349
District of Columbia, 173
Distrust, 509
Disturbed thinking, 101
Division of labor, 6, 7, 315, 359, 365, 412
Divorce, 100, 162, 180, 232, 304, 310
Dizziness, 187
Doctor: *see* Physician
Dominance, 461
Dominance of medicine, 14
Dopamine, 113

Freedom, 488
French Revolution, 450
Freudian view, 72−73
Friends, 271, 272, 277, 283, 288, 407, 421, 454, 457, 510
Functional physical capacity, 182
Functioning, 242, 254, 255, 338, 354, 456, 463, 490, 491; *see also* Coping, Adaptation
Funding, 437, 471
Future orientation, 59, 225, 265

Gall bladder diseases, 186
Gastric fistula, 237
Gastroenterologists, 506
Gastroenterology, 383
Gastrointestinal distress, 427
General practitioners, 22, 129, 154, 318, 319, 320, 321, 322, 351, 353, 355, 359, 369, 371, 382, 383, 384, 389, 390, 396, 397, 398, 411, 425; in England, 390, 392, 396; referrals from, 321; *see also* Primary care
Genetic disorders, 44
Genetic factors, 203, 212, 213, 218, 227, 292, 438, 442, 443
Geneticists, 442
Geographic conditions, 185, 325, 347−48, 353, 356, 496
Geographic mobility, 19, 410, 511
Georgia State Sanitarium, 133
Geriatrics, 383
Germ theory, 209
Gestation, 141
Gigantism, 46
"Giving up," 232
Global budget, 325, 327, 329, 330, 333, 394, 500, 502
Goals, 71, 164, 302, 304, 305, 347, 366, 370, 453, 480; conflicting, 268
"Goodness-badness" perspective, 49, 50
Government, 14, 19, 22, 48, 61, 63, 64, 68, 69, 85, 119, 300, 321, 324, 328, 331, 332, 333, 337, 349, 370, 388, 395, 403, 411, 495, 496, 497, 499, 503, 519; controls, 18, 125, 389, 370, 395, 514; financing, 389, 397, 473, 495; reorganization, 475; *see also* Federal government
Grades, competition for, 380
Graduate students, 21, 297
Grave's disease, 97
Great Britain: *see* England
"Great Society," 478
Grief, 162, 232, 266
Gross national product, 495, 500
Group commitment, 76
Group practices, 6, 342, 370, 384, 385, 396, 398, 426
Group solutions, 308
Growth, 44, 46; and development, 56

Guilt, 256, 284
Gynecology, 383

Habits, 164, 206, 238, 263, 408
Hagerstown, Maryland, 217
Halfway houses, 458
Halfway technologies, 327
Hallucinations, 101, 103, 109, 277
Happiness, 26, 183, 184
Hard driving, 239
Harm-producing stimulus, 231
Harvard University, 502
Harvard University Medical School, 21
Hawaii, 173
Head trauma, 513
Headaches, 187, 244, 277, 427, 428
Healing occupations, 6−7, 27−29
Health: behavior, 4, 10, 60, 61, 131, 189, 200, 268, 283, 287, 409, 477; -belief model, 268, 409; -care administration, 10, 195; -care innovations, receptivity to, 397; centers, 333, 354, 382, 384, 385; definitions of, 55; education, 10, 77, 298, 300, 353; -examination survey, 146, 187, 192; interview surveys, 182; knowledge of, 187, 195; levels of, 340; maintenance, 2, 307; maintenance organizations, 361, 394, 498 (*see also* Prepaid group practice); neglect of, 209; planners, 499; programs, participation in, 191; risks, 63; salience of, 187; -services research, 8, 10, 15, 128−30, 520; social responses to, 4; status, 25, 164, 168, 181, 182, 183, 197, 227, 228, 336, 342, 361; as a value, 34−35; value of, 67−69
Health, Education, and Welfare, Department of, 398
Health Insurance Plan of Greater New York, 150
Health Opinion Survey, 183
Health Services Research and Development, Panel on, 152
Heart, 122; catheterization, 506; disease, 5, 28, 57, 70, 158, 159, 160, 161, 182, 187, 203, 209, 327 (*see also* Coronary heart disease); functioning, 42; -lung machines, 373; patients, 114; rate, 223, 230
Height, 45
Help, plea for, 267
Help seeking, 9, 19, 20, 146, 411, 418−22; behavior, 249−89; processes, 18, 131; research, examples of, 270−73; theory, 268−73; variables, relationships among, 287−89
Helplessness, 71
Hemodialysis, 327, 340, 350
Hemoglobin, 96
Hemorrhoids, 186
Heredity, 207, 212
Hernia, 182, 186, 424